THE
UNION
CAVALRY
COMES OF AGE

THE UNION CAVALRY

COMES OF AGE

Hartwood Church
to Brandy Station, 1863

ERIC J. WITTENBERG

Foreword by Edward G. Longacre

BRASSEY'S, INC.
Washington, D.C.

Library of Congress Cataloging-in-Publication Data

Wittenberg, Eric J., 1961–
  The Union cavalry comes of age : Hartwood Church to Brandy Station, 1863 / Eric J. Wittenberg ; foreword by Edward G. Longacre.—1st ed.
    p. cm.
Includes bibliographical references and index.
  ISBN 1-57488-442-5 (hardcover : alk. paper)—
  1. United States. Army. Cavalry—History—Civil War, 1861–1865. 2. United States—History—Civil War, 1861–1865—Cavalry operations. I. Title.

  E492.5.W58 2003
  973.7'41—dc21

                                          2003001876

Hardcover ISBN 1-57488-442-5
(alk. paper)

Printed in the United States of America on acid-free paper that meets the American National Standards Institute Z39-48 Standard.

Brassey's, Inc.
22841 Quicksilver Drive
Dulles, Virginia 20166

First Edition

10 9 8 7 6 5 4 3 2 1

This book is respectfully dedicated to the memory of the brave men who followed the guidon of the Army of the Potomac's Cavalry Corps into battle, 1863–1865.

From this day to the ending of the world,
But we in it shall be remember'd
We few, we happy few, we band of brothers;
For he to-day that sheds his blood with me
Shall be my brother; be he ne'er so vile. . . .

—William Shakespeare,
Henry V, Act 4, Scene 3

"If you want to have some fun, jine the cav'ry"

—A popular song of the era,
of the same title, often
attributed to J. E. B. Stuart

⊶ CONTENTS ⊷

·⇒ LIST OF MAPS ⇐·

One of the more dramatic episodes of the Civil War is the evolution—or, as Eric Wittenberg puts it, the "coming of age"—of the Union cavalry in the eastern theater of operations. In large part it is a story of obstacles surmounted, limitations extended, and mistakes overcome. When the fighting began in the spring of 1861, the mounted branch of the Army of the Potomac was hampered by inexperienced troopers, embryonic support facilities, and leaders whose only claim to authority was seniority in the prewar Regulars. Not surprisingly, for two years the erstwhile store clerks and mechanics in the Union cavalry were out-performed, and often humiliated, by the riders of the Army of Northern Virginia, most of whom had been conversant with horsemanship and weaponry since early youth.

Things began to change early in 1863. Many factors combined to reverse the trend of Union defeat, including the ascension of Maj. Gen. Joseph Hooker to command the Army of the Potomac. Committed to upgrading the quality of every component of his army, "Fighting Joe" ensured that his horsemen received more modern weapons, more abundant ammunition and equipment, more rigorous training, and more talented, more energetic leaders. Not the least of his reforms was to group his mounted regiments—which previously had been scattered about the Virginia theater in small detachments—into a corps almost 10,000 strong. The power and cohesion that resulted raised the cavalry's morale to heights that soon produced victories in the field. For the remainder of the war, the confidence and ability of the army's horsemen continued to grow, until they gained a clear and consistent advantage over their once-invincible opponents.

The story of the Union cavalry in the East has been told before, but in almost every instance as part of a broad study of army or corps operations. Never before has the watershed period between Fredericksburg and Gettysburg received the detail and depth of coverage this study gives it. Wittenberg's scope and focus enable him to chronicle not only major clashes of arms but also skirmishes, raids, reconnaissances, and other small-scale operations. The story is told, as much as possible, in the words of the participants, a feat made possible by the author's use of a wealth of first-person sources, many never before cited. Furthermore, he gives due consideration to nonoperational subjects such as organization, administration, and leadership. In sum, *The Union Cavalry Comes of Age* fills a gap in the literature of one of the most important combat arms of the nineteenth-century American army.

—Edward G. Longacre
author of *Lincoln's Cavalrymen*

Traditionally, historians have focused on the 1863 Gettysburg Campaign as the turning point for the Army of the Potomac's Cavalry Corps, holding that the events of June and July 1863 marked the coming out party for the blueclad horsemen. From that moment forward, goes the conventional wisdom, the Federal mounted arm was on equal footing with its Southern counterpart. In fact, the conventional wisdom does not do justice to the travails of the Federal cavalry. It had its coming out party during Maj. Gen. John Pope's Second Bull Run Campaign during the hot summer of 1862, and began maturing in the aftermath of the Battle of Antietam in the fall of 1862.

This study will demonstrate that the Army of the Potomac's cavalry turned the corner and became a powerful and effective force during the winter and spring of 1863, beginning with Maj. Gen. Joseph Hooker's formation of the Cavalry Corps in February. Maj. Gen. George Stoneman, Jr., a member of the legendary West Point class of 1846, was the first commander of the Cavalry Corps. The dyspeptic career horse soldier cast a long shadow over the rest of the Civil War. The taxing regimen of drill and training that Stoneman initiated paid immediate dividends. It came to full fruition in the Shenandoah Valley Campaign of 1864, when the Union cavalry, by then the largest, best mounted, and best equipped force of horse soldiers the world had ever seen, played a decisive role in an entire campaign. Stoneman, a Democrat, has been largely unappreciated because of the ignominious end of his tenure in command of the Cavalry Corps.

Likewise, Brig. Gen. William Woods Averell, a West Pointer from New York, also a lifelong Democrat, brought professionalism and experience to the Cavalry

Corps. Known as one of the finest drillmasters in the entire Army of the Potomac, his troopers became one of the most well trained and best disciplined units in the army. He brought the same degree of professionalism to his duties as a division commander in the newly formed Cavalry Corps. Averell's men fought the first large-scale all-cavalry battle of the Civil War, acquitting themselves quite well in the Battle of Kelly's Ford. Like Stoneman, Averell was swept aside and relegated to the dustbin of history.

Both George Stoneman and William Averell deserved a better fate. Both men played major roles in the development of the powerful Union cavalry force, and both have been denied the recognition they rightly deserve for their contributions. Instead, they fell victim to Hooker's relentless campaign to find someone to blame for the debacle at Chancellorsville, to the detriment of their lives and professional careers. As a result, most historians have largely ignored or downplayed their roles in the evolution of the Army of the Potomac's Cavalry Corps. This book will, hopefully, right that wrong.

It will also examine the lives and careers of other men who emerged as forces to be reckoned with in the Union mounted arm, soldiers such as Brig. Gen. Alfred Pleasonton, Brig. Gen. John Buford, Brig. Gen. David McMurtrie Gregg, Col. Thomas C. Devin, Capt. Wesley Merritt, and Col. Judson Kilpatrick. It will evaluate other forgotten soldiers who played an important role in the early days of the Army of the Potomac's Cavalry Corps: Col. Alfred N. Duffié, a French expatriate hiding from an ugly secret, and Col. Luigi Palma di Cesnola, an Italian count who was victimized by Pleasonton's rabid xenophobia. It will pay tribute to fallen heroes like Col. Benjamin F. "Grimes" Davis, a Southerner who remained loyal to the Union and paid for his loyalty with his life. Finally, it will tell the stories of the common soldiers who bore the travails of the cavalry service in 1863. I have always believed that I cannot do a better job of telling the stories of these horse soldiers than they did. Accordingly, wherever possible, I prefer to allow them to tell their stories in their own words.

The men learned to fight as cohesive units, and they learned to operate in masses. They mastered new tactics and evolved into dragoons, men who could fight equally adroitly mounted or dismounted. Under the tutelage of seasoned professionals like Stoneman, Averell, Buford, and Gregg, these ungainly city boys became expert horsemen and mastered the art of scouting and screening. And they fought. At Kelly's Ford, during the Stoneman Raid, and at the great Battle of Brandy Station, they fought their grayclad counterparts saber-to-saber and stirrup-to-stirrup. For the first time in American history, horse soldiers fought in large, massed formations, adding punch to the Army of the Potomac's infantry.

Brig. Gen. Fitzhugh Lee's Hartwood Church Raid of February 1863 greatly embarrassed the Federal cavalry, and a taunting note left behind by Lee provided the impetus for what became the Battle of Kelly's Ford. The fight at Kelly's Ford on St. Patrick's Day 1863, in particular, was a milestone. It was the first time that a large force of Federal cavalry was the aggressor that came out spoiling for a fight against the Southern cavalry. Neither the Hartwood Church Raid nor the critical Battle of Kelly's Ford has ever had a detailed tactical treatment, and both have been long overdue for one. This book will provide that detailed analysis.

The following two passages, one by a Confederate and the other by a Federal, reflect the savage nature of the combat at Kelly's Ford. "A cavalry charge is a terrible thing. Almost before you can think, the shock of horse against horse, the clash of steel against steel, crack of pistols, yells of some poor lost one, as he lost his seat and went down under those iron shod hoofs that knew no mercy, or the shriek of some horse overturned and cut to pieces by his own kind," recalled Pvt. William Henry Ware of the 3d Virginia Cavalry. "It is Hell while it lasts, but when man meets his fellow man, face to face, foot to foot, knee to knee, and looks him in the eye, the rich red blood flows through his veins like liquid lightning. There is blood in his eye, Hell in his heart, and he is a different man from what he is in the time of peace."

"It was like the coming together of two mighty railroad trains at full speed. The yelling of men, the clashing of sabers, a few empty saddles, a few wounded and dying, and the charge is over. One side or the other is victorious, perhaps, only for a few minutes, and then the contest is renewed," observed Sgt. George Reeve of the 6th Ohio Cavalry. "A charge of this kind is over almost before one has time to think of the danger he is in."

Likewise, this book will address the Stoneman Raid of 1863, often cited by the men who participated in it as the turning point of the war for the Army of the Potomac's Cavalry Corps. It also examines the fight of the 6th New York Cavalry in Alsop's Field on April 30, 1863, as well as the futile and costly charge of the 8th Pennsylvania Cavalry at Chancellorsville two days later. The book concludes with the great Battle of Brandy Station, where the two mounted foes spent fourteen hours slugging it out on the plains of Culpeper County, Virginia, in what became the greatest cavalry battle ever seen on the North American continent. The lives of the men who fought and bled are documented here, as are the stories of the men who led them into battle. Without the trials and tribulations described in this book, the Army of the Potomac's Cavalry Corps never would have matured into the potent fighting force that it became during the second half of the Civil War.

As with every project of this nature, there are many people to whom I am deeply indebted. My friends Bryce A. Suderow and Steve L. Zerbe greatly assisted me in gathering the primary source material that makes up the bulk of this narrative. Tonia J. Smith of Pinehurst, North Carolina, also helped track down useful and important material, some of which has never been used in any accounts of these actions. Tonia also read early drafts of this manuscript and gave me useful feedback that made this a better book. Blair Graybill of Charlottesville, Virginia, also helped run down important primary source material for me, as did Ben Ramirez of Flint, Michigan. Jean-Claude Reuflet of Vincennes, France, a descendant of Alfred Duffié's, provided me with the fascinating story of the Frenchman's life and web of deceit. Thomas P. Nanzig of Ann Arbor, Michigan, the historian of the 3d Virginia Cavalry, provided me with the memoir of Robert T. Hubard and also read and commented upon my manuscript. David G. Douglas of Ridley Park, Pennsylvania, kindly shared the letters of his ancestor, Capt. Leonard Williams of the 2d South Carolina, providing insight into the fighting at Stevensburg on June 9, 1863. Sue Martin of Fairplay, New York, provided valuable primary source material on the April 30, 1863, fight in Alsop's Field. I am grateful to them for their help and support, and to the archivists at any number of institutions for their assistance in identifying and duplicating primary source materials for use in this project.

My good friend and favorite battlefield stomping companion, Col. Jerry F. Myers (U.S. Army, retired), spent hours on the ground with me and in reviewing my manuscript. I am, as always, deeply grateful to Jerry for his efforts and dedication to improving the quality of my work. Clark B. "Bud" Hall, the official historian of the Brandy Station Foundation, has spent several wonderful days showing me the Brandy Station and Kelly's Ford battlefields over the years, and I am grateful to Bud, not only for his time and effort, but also for his friendship, support, and guidance. Each time I visit the battlefield with him, I come away with a new appreciation, not only for the men who fought there, but also for Bud's dedication to saving that piece of our heritage. I also learn more and more from Bud about the battle itself, coming away with another useful suggestion of places to look for additional primary source material.

Ben Fordney of Harrisonburg, Virginia, is the authority on George Stoneman and his military career. Ben was kind enough to review my manuscript and comment upon it.

Likewise, J. David Petruzzi read the early drafts of this manuscript and provided valuable input and insight, as did Maj. Michael Nugent and Joel Brubaker. My friends and fellow cavalry historians Robert F. O'Neill, Jr., Andrew W. German, and Horace Mewborn also performed that valuable service for me. Greg Mertz, the gifted National Park Service historian, reviewed the manuscript and gave me quite a bit of useful feedback. Greg also showed me some of the more obscure portions of the Chancellorsville battlefield where some of the events described in this book took place.

Don Pfanz, also a gifted Park Service historian, assisted in tracking down additional primary source materials that helped to make this a better, more complete work. Prof. Daniel E. Sutherland of the University of Arkansas, who has studied both the Chancellorsville Campaign and the war in Culpeper County, Virginia, lent his unique perspective to a review of my work, and I appreciate his time and effort. Edward G. Longacre, the well-known cavalry historian, also reviewed the manuscript and wrote the foreword. Prof. Michael Lewis of Williams College in Williamstown, Massachusetts, helped me track down an elusive photograph of Jeb Stuart's able adjutant. Michael McAfee kindly granted me permission to use a photograph of Col. Luigi Palma di Cesnola. Likewise, Roger Hunt, who may have the largest collection of Civil War images going, provided me with a fine wartime photograph of Lt. Col. Hasbrouck Davis of the 12th Illinois Cavalry. I appreciate the effort, input, and suggestions each of these people gave me. Once again, Blake Magner's fine maps grace the pages of this book. I am grateful to Blake for drawing my maps and for his support and friendship over the years.

This is the fourth book that I have done with the good people at Brassey's. I appreciate their faith in my work, and I also appreciate their dedication. David Arthur, my editor, and Don McKeon, the publisher, have provided my work with a home, and I am grateful to them for that. Their faith in me is gratifying and I hope that I have not disappointed them. I value the relationship that has evolved, and I look forward to working with them again in the future.

I am deeply grateful to my parents, Joseph and Leah Wittenberg, for their support and encouragement over the years. They always inspired me to study and learn, and I hope that my efforts reflect that. Finally, I am most grateful to my wife and best friend, Susan Skilken Wittenberg, without whose unflinching love and support none of this would be possible.

FORMATION OF THE CAVALRY CORPS:
ARMY OF THE POTOMAC
FEBRUARY 1863

In September 1862, just before the Battle of Antietam, Brig. Gen. John Buford, a thirty-six-year-old West Pointer, received orders to report to the Army of the Potomac's headquarters at Rockville, Maryland. Buford and his weary brigade of horse soldiers had just completed an arduous season of scouting and fighting during the Second Bull Run Campaign, and Buford had received a painful knee wound on August 30, 1862, in the closing action of the Second Battle of Bull Run. Buford reported to headquarters, recounted his activities during the Second Manassas Campaign, and then received a surprise when Maj. Gen. George B. McClellan, the commander of the Army of the Potomac, appointed him the army's chief of cavalry.[1]

While technically the chief of all cavalry operations for the Army of the Potomac, this position did not carry field command of the mounted troops. Instead, it was a staff assignment devoid of authority to command troops in the field. When McClellan created the position of chief of cavalry of the Army of Potomac at the end of March 1862, the order stated, "The duties of the chiefs of artillery and cavalry are exclusively administrative, and these officers will be attached to the headquarters of the Army of the Potomac." The chief of cavalry inspected the troops as necessary, and made certain that they were properly armed and equipped. However, the chiefs of cavalry were not to "exercise field command of the troops or their arms unless specially ordered by the commanding general, but they will, when practicable, be selected to communicate the orders of the general to their respective corps." Regular supply requisitions and reports of the various elements of the cavalry flowed through the office of the chief of cavalry.[2] Brig. Gen. George

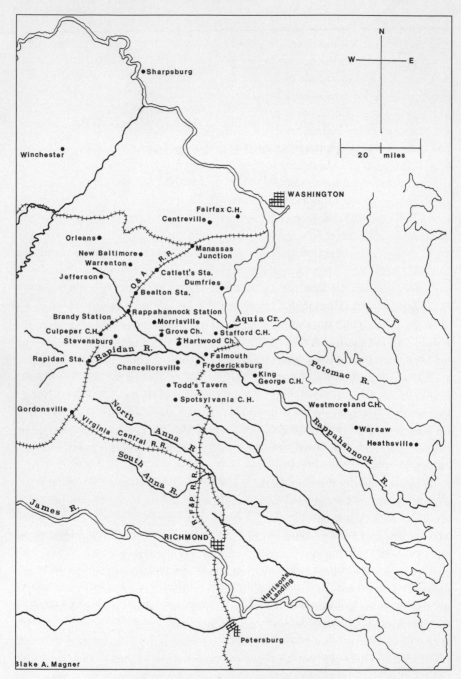

Theater of Operations, Spring 1863

Stoneman, Jr., of New York, McClellan's friend and West Point classmate, served as the Army of the Potomac's first chief of cavalry until he took command of an infantry division, leaving the post of chief of cavalry vacant.

During the 1862 Peninsula Campaign, Confederate cavalry commanded by Maj. Gen. J. E. B. Stuart rode all the way around the Army of the Potomac to great fanfare and to the everlasting embarrassment of Stuart's father-in-law, Brig. Gen. Philip St. George Cooke, field commander of McClellan's horse soldiers. Stuart actually escaped the Federal cavalry, which arrived too late to stop him, and a great hue and cry went up throughout the North. Although he was commonly known as the "Father of the United States Cavalry," General Cooke was relieved of command and never led horse soldiers in the field again. That fall, after the Battle of Antietam, Stuart led his horsemen on a second ride around McClellan, venturing into south central Pennsylvania. Again, the Army of the Potomac's cavalry could not stop the ride, but the Federal horsemen gave a good account of themselves in scattered fighting in the Loudoun Valley of Virginia once McClellan advanced into the Old Dominion in late October. In spite of that solid performance, the country still perceived that the Confederate mounted arm was far superior to that of the Federals. "Our organization was so incomplete that the operations of the cavalry during the Antietam campaign were almost insignificant," recalled an officer of the 5th U.S. Cavalry years later, "so much so that at that time in our history it was a joke to offer a reward for a dead cavalryman."[3]

There were legitimate reasons for that feeling. McClellan believed that it required two years to adequately train volunteer cavalry, and few in 1861 expected that the Rebellion would last that long. Consequently, the Federal high command vigorously debated the question of how to properly use and arm the many volunteer cavalry regiments raised after the defeat at Bull Run. McClellan was biased against volunteer cavalry, and believed in late 1861 that "for all present duty of cavalry in the upper Potomac volunteers will suffice as they will have *nothing to do but carry messages & act as videttes.*" A week later, McClellan requested that no more volunteer cavalry regiments be raised throughout the North, since their role was unclear, and questions remained about the army's ability to mount and arm the new recruits.[4]

The traditional role of saddle soldiers was well defined, even if McClellan did not make good use of it. "Reliable information of the enemy's position or movements, which is absolutely necessary to the commander of an army to successfully conduct a campaign, must be largely furnished by the cavalry," wrote Brig. Gen. William Woods Averell, a West Point graduate, in defining the traditional role of cavalry in the conventional doctrine taught at the Military Academy and as practiced at the beginning of the war. "The duty of the cavalry when an engagement is imminent is specially imperative—to keep in touch with the enemy and observe and carefully note, with time of day or night, every slightest indication and report it promptly to the commander of the army. On the march, cavalry forms in advance, flank and rear guards and supplies escorts, couriers and guides. Cavalry should extend well away from the main body on the march like antennae to mask its movements and to discover any movement of the enemy."

Averell continued, "Cavalry should never hug the army on the march, especially in a thickly wooded country, because the horses being restricted to the roads, the slightest obstacle in advance is liable to cause a blockade against the march of infantry." Moreover, "in camp it furnishes outposts, vedettes and scouts. In battle it attacks the enemy's flanks and rear, and above all other duties in battle, it secures the fruits of victory by vigorous and unrelenting pursuit. In defeat it screens the withdrawal of the army and by its fortitude and activity baffles the enemy." Averell concluded, "In addition to these active military duties of the cavalry, it receives flags of truce, interrogates spies, deserters and prisoners, makes and improves topographical maps, destroys and builds bridges, obstructs and opens communications, and obtains or destroys forage and supplies."[5] Although these functions were well defined, McClellan did not use his saddle soldiers for all of them, meaning that the cavalry was not used as effectively as it might have been.

On the Peninsula, McClellan parceled out his volunteer cavalry regiments to specific infantry brigades, primarily using the horsemen as messengers and orderlies. This was a poor use for an expensive arm of the service like cavalry. The government invested millions of dollars into raising and equipping its mounted units, and McClellan frittered them away. However, McClellan wisely formed the Cavalry Reserve, consisting of most of the Regular Army mounted units. "As to the regular Cavalry," wrote McClellan, "I have directed all of it to be concentrated in one mass that the numbers in each company may be increased & that I may have a reliable and efficient body on which to depend in a battle."[6] McClellan relied heavily on the Cavalry Reserve during the Peninsula Campaign. His Regulars captured the first Confederate flag taken in combat, and they made a magnificent but disastrous charge into Southern infantry at Gaines Mill, saving the V Corps from destruction. The Regulars performed well, foreshadowing better days to come for the Northern horsemen. The spectacle of Stuart's escape overshadowed their solid service.

The Army of the Potomac's volunteer cavalry regiments did not have an opportunity to serve together as a cohesive command until the Maryland Campaign that fall. McClellan had to incorporate Pope's beaten, demoralized army into the Army of the Potomac, and he had to reorganize the army's command structure while it marched to meet Robert E. Lee's invasion of Maryland. With Buford as chief of cavalry and Brig. Gen. Alfred Pleasonton in tactical command of the horse soldiers, they performed competently if not spectacularly. Better things clearly lay ahead if inspired leadership emerged.

Buford served as chief of cavalry throughout the fall of 1862, and still filled that role during the December 1862 Fredericksburg Campaign. During Buford's tenure as chief of cavalry, the mounted arm faced significant obstacles. While the troopers were competent to perform their duties, the high command of the Army of the Potomac chose not to use these men in the most efficient or effective way. In McClellan's case, his belief that it would take too long to train volunteer cavalry units doomed these men to mundane tasks. However, he allowed his cavalry to operate in cohesive units during the Army of the Potomac's slow advance into Virginia that fall, and the horsemen performed very well, giving Stuart and his cavalry battle in the Loudoun Valley on several occasions. Further, the combination of terrain and tactical situations prevented McClellan and his successor, Maj. Gen. Ambrose E. Burnside, from making effective use of their mounted forces.

As an example, during the Battle of Antietam, the bloodiest single day of the Civil War, the Army of the Potomac suffered nearly 13,000 casualties, but only twenty-eight of them were in the cavalry. Burnside, who had no background in the effective use of horse soldiers, assigned cavalry forces to each of his Grand Divisions, which consisted of two infantry corps, at least a brigade of cavalry, and artillery batteries, meaning that each Grand Division was a separate combined-arms army. The organization of the Army of the Potomac's mounted forces during Burnside's tenure in command of the army is found in Appendix 1.

During the equally bloody Battle of Fredericksburg in December, the Army of the Potomac's cavalry suffered only two killed and six wounded. Unfortunately, one of those two was Brig. Gen. George D. Bayard, a promising and dashing young officer who, with Buford, had capably commanded a cavalry brigade in Pope's Army of Virginia. Bayard was sitting on his horse at the headquarters of Maj. Gen. William B. Franklin, commander of the Left Grand Division and received a mortal wound when a fragment of an artillery shell struck him.[7] Bayard, who had great promise, was a tremendous loss to the Army of the Potomac's mounted arm.

The Army of the Potomac's cavalry was never used efficiently or effectively during the first two years of the war. This system placed "the cavalry at the disposal of generals without experience, who still further divided it, so that each brigade, almost, was provided with its troop or squadron whose duty it was to add to the importance of the general by following him about, to provide orderlies for dashing young staff officers and strikers for headquarters."[8] As one Federal officer recalled, "The smallest infantry organization had its company or more of mounted men, whose duty consisted in supplying details as orderlies for mounted staff officers, following them mounted on their rapid rides for pleasure or for duty, or in camp acting as grooms and bootblacks." He continued, "It is not wonderful that this treatment demoralized the cavalry."[9] A trooper of the 1st Maine Cavalry summed up the feelings of the Northern horse soldiers quite effectively. They served "a little here, and a little there," leading the men to wonder aloud, "Whose kite are we going to be tail to next?"[10] Since McClellan himself had held a captain's commission in the cavalry and had designed the so-called "McClellan saddle" (the primary saddle used by Union horsemen), his ineffective use of his horse soldiers was a mystery to all.

The Army of the Potomac's poor utilization of the cavalry quite naturally bred unhappiness among the ranks of the soldiers, officers, and politicians responsible for funding the war effort. Because of the need to acquire, equip, and feed horses, cavalry was the most expensive arm of the military service, and the government had invested tremendous sums of money into raising the cavalry.[11] The Confederate cavalry had rather literally ridden rings around McClellan, much to the embarrassment of all involved, and now little was being done to change the perception that the cavalry was good for little beyond serving as messengers and orderlies. For the first year and a half of the war, the government had not gotten much in the way of results for its investment, and the White House and the War Department were growing impatient and increasingly unhappy not only with the performance of the cavalry, but also with its misuse. Both President Lincoln and Secretary of War Stanton made their displeasure abundantly clear to all those who cared to listen.

In the fall of 1862, when President Lincoln intervened in a dispute over providing additional mounts to the Army of the Potomac's cavalry, the President, known for his biting, acid wit, inquired, "Will you pardon me for asking what the horses of your army have done since the battle of Antietam to fatigue anything?"[12] Wesley Merritt, who was the final commander of the Army of the Potomac's Cavalry Corps in 1865, summed things up nicely when he observed that McClellan had demonstrated "ignorance of the proper use of cavalry," and had utterly failed to provide "a fit management of this important arm of the service."[13]

Buford inherited a daunting task when he assumed the role of chief of cavalry. Having just completed the Second Bull Run Campaign, he knew the wretched state of the cavalry horses of his own brigade. The mounts of Bayard's and Col. John Beardsley's brigades were in equally poor condition. The Army of the Potomac's cavalry horses had fared no better on the Peninsula and during the march north. The new chief of cavalry had to locate adequate numbers and quality of horses for a cavalry force already pursuing Lee's army into Maryland.

Well after the end of the campaign, McClellan complained, "When I marched this army from Washington on the 8th day of September, it was greatly deficient in cavalry horses, the hard service to which they had been rendered in front of Washington having rendered about half of them unserviceable." He pointed out that most of the horses received during the fall of 1862 merely replaced unserviceable mounts, but also noted that he had not received enough new mounts to provide for his entire mounted arm. Instead, wrote McClellan, the entire Army of the Potomac had received only 1,964 horses as of November 1862, *after* the conclusion of the Antietam Campaign. Those horses were "much inferior to those first obtained, and are not suitable for the hard service of cavalry horses."[14]

McClellan stated the dilemma facing John Buford very succinctly in his official report of the Battle of Antietam. "My cavalry did not amount to one-twentieth part of the army, and hence the necessity of giving every one of my cavalry soldiers a serviceable horse. Cavalry may be said to constitute the antennae of the army. It scouts all the roads in front, on the flanks, and in the rear of the advancing columns, and constantly feels the enemy."[15] Without adequate mounts, McClellan's cavalry could not fulfill the mission he ascribed to it.

After Antietam, Buford joined the fray with the War Department to obtain more and better horses for the Army of the Potomac's cavalry. McClellan bitterly argued with Chief Quartermaster Montgomery Meigs regarding the number and quality of horses sent to him during the Maryland Campaign. On October 15, 1862, Buford wrote to Meigs, "From my own experience I am satisfied that we are daily reporting horses as inserviceable which if rested, cared for and fattened would render more hard service a second time than had they never been used." Buford observed, "[W]e have many good horses that came to us young and unbroken which from bad horsemanship and mismanagement, are almost worn out before they are called upon to do any severe work." Buford opined that much of the army's problem with horses breaking down resulted from improper care and the lack of adequate forage. He closed the letter by stating, "I respectfully recommend that the horses which have proved themselves to be good ones, but are unserviceable at present, be put into the hands of some responsible persons to be recuperated, instead of being sold at auction."[16] The War Department rejected this suggestion as uneconomical. Unfortunately, many good cavalry horses were wasted, and good advice was rejected.[17]

On December 1, 1862, Pleasonton penned a detailed memorandum regarding the state of Burnside's cavalry. This document, which may have been Pleasonton's single most important contribution to the Union cause, accurately reflects the problems handicapping a cavalry commander's understanding of the role and mission of his combat arm. After examining the organizational structure of the Confederate cavalry, Pleasonton suggested that the cavalry be organized into brigades and divisions, and that the army's commanding general should issue orders directly to the commanders of the cavalry divisions. Further, Pleasonton suggested that the cavalry be formed into a corps, under a single commander.

A strong organization, observed Pleasonton, was crucial for the cavalry in order to ensure the uniformity of the intelligence and scouting reports forwarded to the commanding general and to alleviate the rivalries and confusion faced by independent commanders in the field. "Our cavalry can be made superior to any now in the field by organization," he stated. "The rebel cavalry owe their success to their organization, which permits great freedom and responsibility to its commanders, subject to the commanding general." Finally, Pleasonton recommended that eight batteries of horse artillery be assigned to the nascent cavalry corps.[18] While these points had great merit, Pleasonton had a transparent motive—he obviously manipulated the system in order to be named commander of the proposed cavalry corps, succeeding Buford, as chief of cavalry, in the process.

At the end of December, Brig. Gen. William Woods Averell, who commanded the cavalry brigade assigned to the Army of the Potomac's Center Grand Division, proposed a daring cavalry raid on Richmond.[19] Averell wanted 1,500 of the Army of the Potomac's best mounted elements to demonstrate along the upper Rappahannock River while Averell led an expedition of 1,000 picked men from a variety of units, including the U.S. Regular cavalry regiments. He wanted to cross the Rappahannock River at Kelly's Ford, advance to the Rapidan, cross it at Raccoon Ford, and then cross the upper James River. He expected to destroy the railroads, bridges, and telegraph lines between the Army of the Potomac's position and Richmond, and intended to live off the land during his raid.[20] Averell wanted to dash to the crucial railroad junction at Petersburg and then on to Suffolk, disrupting lines of communication and supply in the Confederate rear. In the meantime, while Averell's horsemen wreaked havoc in the Southern rear, Burnside would take the main body of the army, cross the river, and either sever Lee's lines of supply, or defeat him in battle. Averell proposed the North's first large-scale cavalry raid of the Civil War.

Burnside enthusiastically approved the plan, and instructed Averell to make the necessary preparations. However, Stuart had set out on a raid of his own, the Christmas 1862 raid on Dumfries, near the army's rear. President Lincoln told Burnside to call off Averell's raid, stating, "I have good reason for saying you must not make a general movement of the army without letting me know." Lincoln may have scotched the planned raid in order to make certain that adequate mounted forces remained to chase after Stuart.[21] Averell devised a bold and dashing plan that planted the seed for future raids on Richmond by the Union cavalry. Stuart's Christmas raid would cost the Union cavalry the initiative, and instead of a glowing triumph, the Federal army faced another embarrassment at the hands of their plumed rival, Stuart.[22] However, Averell's audacious plan marked an important first for the mounted forces assigned to the Army of the Potomac. Averell's proposal would have taken an aggressive stance, something that the Union cavalry had not done to date. It also marked the beginning of a long-term dream of the Federal cavalry, the idea of a large-scale cavalry raid on the Confederate capital.

President Abraham Lincoln had been dissatisfied with the organization and use of the mounted arm since McClellan's failure to make an aggressive pursuit after

Antietam. He had stated his displeasure in no uncertain terms in addressing the brouhaha over replacement mounts, and his complaints went unheeded. Then, in the wake of Stuart's Christmas raid, the President, struggling to find a more effective way of using his expensive horse soldiers, suggested the formation of a "reserve cavalry corps of, say, 6,000 for the Army of the Potomac," to be culled from the cavalry detachments of the 11th and 12th Army Corps. Because the War Department and the President were unhappy with the performance of the army's mounted arm, change became inevitable.[23]

The stagnant and defeated army's morale plummeted. "1862 gone! 1863—the present is ours! Ours. What for?" inquired a trooper of the 3d Indiana Cavalry.[24] "Oh, I wish this war would end, so we could all return home once more," complained Thomas M. Covert of Company A, 6th Ohio Cavalry, on January 2. "It makes me feel sick at heart when I think of the prospects of the war, for it does not look any nearer a close than it did when I enlisted."[25] A few days later, he wrote, "We have had reverses enough to discourage most any one and then the men that the army had the most confidence in is removed from command and next there is a great deal too many Foreigners in command of our army and last and greatest of all there is so many Traitors in the army, and many of them in command. I never look for any great victory from the Army of the Potomac as long as it is organized as it is."[26]

On January 5, Lt. Thomas B. Lucas of the 1st Pennsylvania Cavalry observed, "There will be an end to this war sometime. A constant dripping will wear away the hardest stone and, although we can see no visible results one way or the other from the many hard fought fields of the last year, yet it is against the nature of things to suppose that they will not have an effect either for or against us. The terrific slaughter and unprecedented expense will eventually wear both governments down, and the one with the greater resources with proper care and management will certainly conquer."[27] Lucas had no idea how accurate his predication would prove.

"We could live here very comfortably all winter if the powers that be would only suffer us to remain inactive for so long a time," groused a trooper of the 1st Pennsylvania Cavalry. "But the country is still clamorous for a forward movement of this army, and our rulers, not being able or not having the moral courage to resist the clamors of the dominant party, will of course do something to check the criticism of the press, if nothing to suppress the rebellion. On to Richmond is the cry of the northern press still."[28] Discontent festered.

Trying to redeem himself after the crushing repulse at Fredericksburg, Burnside attempted a winter campaign along the Rappahannock. The Army of the Potomac would try to flank Lee out of his strong positions above Fredericksburg. However, the campaign quickly bogged down in the horrendous January weather.

"Mud up to horses' knees. Army stuck in the mud," observed Capt. Isaac Ressler of the 16th Pennsylvania Cavalry.[29] "An indescribable chaos of pontoons, wagons and artillery . . . supply wagons upset by the roadside, artillery stalled in the mud, ammunition trains mired by the way," recalled a member of the 6th Pennsylvania Cavalry. "Horses and mules dropped down dead, exhausted with the effort to move their loads. . . . A hundred and fifty dead animals, many of them buried in the liquid muck, were counted in the course of a morning's ride."[30] As the Confederates watched and waited for the Army of the Potomac to slog through the mud, they had a good laugh at the expense of the Northerners. Near army headquarters at Falmouth, the Rebels posted a banner with the inscription, "Burnside's army stuck in the mud six miles above Falmouth."[31]

"On the other side of the river, the Rebels enjoyed themselves immensely at the sight, shouting helpful advice across the stream, offering to come over and help, and putting up hastily lettered signs pointing out the proper road to Richmond," reported a bitter Pennsylvanian.[32] "The jovial Rebels on picket at the fords, seeing the plight we were in, kindly volunteered to 'come over and help us,'" glibly noted an officer of the 1st U.S. Cavalry, "The conditions favorable to a surprise were evidently not present."[33] Apparently, nobody in Washington had the moral courage to resist the calls for the Army of the Potomac to press on toward Richmond, no matter what the consequences for doing so.

The sullen and angry Northerners felt humiliated. Burnside himself wrote, "I moved the greater part of the command, with a view to crossing above, but owing to the severe storm which began after the concerted movement commenced, we have been so much delayed that the enemy has discovered our design. The roads are almost impassable, and the small streams are very much swollen. I shall try not to run any unnecessary risks. It is most likely that we will have to change the plan." A second storm soon followed, and more than six inches of snow covered the ground, making the movement of an army impossible.[34] Instead, the Army of the Potomac settled back into the tedium of its winter encampment.

Morale in the Federal cavalry reached its nadir after the Mud March. The men sank into the depths of despair when they realized that they were being misused and wasted. "Army matters in general appear blue," reported Capt. George N. Bliss of the 1st Rhode Island Cavalry. "There have been 10,000 deserters from the army since the battle of Fredericksburg. Some of our leading generals appear determined to ruin General B[urnside] at any cost. It is always darkest just before day, ergo our day ought to be near at hand. Every dog has his day, I hope we have not had ours."[35] A trooper of the 3d Indiana Cavalry ominously noted in his diary, "A dissatisfaction making its appearance in the North which promises serious results."[36]

Capt. Charles Francis Adams, Jr., of the 1st Massachusetts Cavalry, grandson and great-grandson of American presidents, inherited the Adams family talent for the written word. "The Army of the Potomac . . . will fight yet, but they fight for defeat, just as a brave, bad rider will face a fence, but yet rides for a fall," he reported on January 26. "There is a great deal of croaking, no confidence, plenty of sickness, and desertion is the order of the day. This arises from various causes; partly from the defeat at Fredericksburg and the failure, but mostly from the change of commanders of late. You or others may wonder or agree, as you choose, but it is a fact that McClellan alone has the confidence of this army. They would fight and rally under him tomorrow and under him only. Burnside has lost, and Hooker never had their confidence."[37]

Sgt. Nathan Webb, a young theology student, kept a diary of his service with the 1st Maine Cavalry. "There is no disguising the fact that the Army of the Potomac is of very little consequence about this time," he noted. "Even among ourselves it is regarded as of little account. . . . Yet out of this all, from our seeming bitterness and apathy, I hope an army shall grow which shall ultimately crush the Rebellion. As I have said before all we want is a leader."[38] The words of one trooper of the 6th U.S. Cavalry sum up the attitudes of the Army of the Potomac's cavalry at the end of the January 1863: "I am actually beginning to lose hope. The army seems to be disheartened. . . . Large numbers of the married men receive letters from home describing the destitute conditions of their families. The army has not been paid for some six or eight months. . . . The old soldiers curse and growl about politicians generally."[39] A sergeant of the 12th Illinois demonstrated the depths of his despair. "Mother, I am very sorry to say that our Army is becoming very much demoralized," wrote William H. Redman on January 20, "and that our once glorious Union must be severed. I say, and fearless of any contradiction too, that the South will yet establish her independence. Mother, I would vote today to give her what she wants."[40]

Rumors flew. The men still adored McClellan and enthusiastically embraced even the slightest hint that he might return. In mid-January, a trooper of the 16th Pennsylvania Cavalry noted, "It is reported that Genl. McClellan had been appointed commander-in-chief of the Armies."[41] Just the name sent electric chills up the collective spines of the Northern soldiers. However, the high command had other ideas for the army.

On January 26, at his own request, Burnside was relieved of command of the Army of the Potomac. "I have a great deal of sympathy for General Burnside. I think he deserves no blame," observed Sergeant Webb. "Although he may not be capable of handling 150,000 men to the best advantage, yet he is an honest man, one who tries to quench this Rebellion, which cannot be said of all the Generals we have had in this Army." He concluded, "What we want is a mighty man, who will cut adrift from Washington and lead this Army to glorious victory. We may not have the man in this nation, or if we have it may take years of war yet to show the one. Here is as fine a body of men as ever formed an army." And so it was. All it needed was the right leadership.[42]

Maj. Gen. Joseph Hooker succeeded Burnside. Lieutenant Lucas observed, "Burnside, my especial favorite, has been taken from us. Still I don't grumble at that. McClellan, the soldier's friend, was taken from us, but his place was filled. I didn't grumble. But who, now, will fill the place of Burnside? 'Old Joe' is emphatically a fighting man but has to prove his ability yet to command the Army of the Potomac. I hope, *sincerely* hope, that he will prove himself equal to the task."[43] Captain Bliss, a lawyer by training, had a keen eye. "A new broom sweeps clean and Hooker appears to be moving with vigor but whether he is competent to command so large an army time alone can show," he noted a few days after Hooker's appointment.[44]

That remained to be seen. Joseph Hooker, grandson of a Revolutionary War captain, was 48 years old in the winter of 1863. He graduated midway in the West Point Class of 1837, and had an outstanding career in the Regular Army. He demonstrated both leadership and administrative abilities, and received brevets of all grades through lieutenant colonel for gallant and meritorious service in the war with Mexico, a record not surpassed by any first lieutenant in the U.S. Army. After the end of the Mexican War, he served as assistant adjutant general in the Pacific Division of the Army and finally resigned his commission in February 1853. Regretting this decision, he unsuccessfully sought reinstatement five years later. On August 6, 1861, he received a commission as brigadier general of volunteers, making his date of rank senior to that of even U. S. Grant.

The following spring, during McClellan's Peninsula Campaign, Hooker's division fought several hard battles, and Hooker received the moniker "Fighting Joe," taken from a newspaper headline. During the coming months, Hooker demonstrated solid leadership skills, and commanded a corps at Antietam and a Grand Division at Fredericksburg. In the aftermath of the Mud March, Hooker led a cabal scheming for the removal of Burnside as army commander. When he learned of the cabal's efforts, Burnside preemptively tried to relieve Hooker. When that failed, Burnside requested that he be removed from command himself, a request quickly and happily granted by Lincoln and Stanton.[45]

The new army commander was brash, brave, and arrogant. Hooker was a gifted administrator who understood the importance of logistics. He firmly believed that the nation needed him to lead it to victory, and he energetically set about overhauling the Army of the Potomac for a grand campaign to end the war that spring. "Fighting Joe" immediately instituted sweeping reforms. He made sure that the men had ample rations, including fresh bread and vegetables, and they also received all of the clothing they needed. He instituted a system of furloughs, allowing the men to go home and see their families for a few precious days, and he made a strong effort to recruit replacements to fill the ranks of regiments depleted during the brutal fighting of 1862. He eliminated Burnside's ponderous Grand Divisions system, and instituted corps badges to develop *esprit de corps* in the ranks. Army hospital facilities improved dramatically, and the new commanding general held frequent inspections and reviews to restore the men's pride. He ordered that regular drills be held, and soon, the morale of the entire Army of the Potomac soared. "Our new commander took hold of the reins with a firm hand, and the army, if not united in believing his nomination to the position the best that could have been made, was at least ready and anxious to obey his orders, and to do its whole part in the solutions of the problems all were called upon to face," observed a Regular cavalry officer.[46]

"'Old Fighting Joe' appears to be running this 'Machine' now pretty much to the liking of soldiers generally," reported a contented officer of a Pennsylvania cavalry regiment.[47] "I believe the general tone and feeling of the army to be improving and can see much improvement which is due entirely to Hooker. I begin to feel a great deal of faith in Hooker," announced Capt. George N. Bliss, less than two weeks after proclaiming his skepticism at "Fighting Joe's" appointment to command, "and hope he will give the rebels hell one of these days."[48]

Rumors swirled through the army. "It is reported here that you will be made new chief of cavalry in this army," wrote an officer to Averell on February 3. "I hope it is so if you would prefer it. The brigade cannot spare you because it does not know when it can get a commander."[49] Another rumor held that the Army of the Potomac would be broken up and its horse soldiers sent to South Carolina. A few days later, Averell received a letter from his old friend Capt. William Redwood Price stating, "General Rosecrans's army is greatly in need of Cavalry. I thought it might be of interest to you under existing circumstances. If the Army of the Potomac is to be divided up, you might feel inclined to make efforts to come to the Western Army."[50] Fortunately, Hooker put an end to the rumors, crystallized his plans, and announced them to the army. When he did, they changed everything within the Army of the Potomac's mounted arm. Things would never be the same again.

On February 6, 1863, Hooker issued his General Orders Number 6, which consolidated all of the Army of the Potomac's horse soldiers into a single corps under the command of the army's senior cavalry officer, Maj. Gen. George Stoneman.[51] Although "Fighting Joe" had no experience in the cavalry himself, he understood how important a role it could play with a clearly defined mission and good leadership. "For the first time it was realized what a capital mounted force there was," observed a captain of the 6th Pennsylvania Cavalry. "Superb regiments seemed to creep out of every defile within the lines of the army."[52]

In forming the new Cavalry Corps, Hooker adopted nearly all of the recommendations made in Pleasonton's December memorandum to Burnside, even though there is no evidence that Hooker had read Pleasonton's memorandum, or that he was guided by anything other than implementing ideas whose time had come.[53] This order had far-reaching implications for the balance of the Civil War. Two days later, Stoneman reported 8,943 cavalrymen and 450 horse artillerists present and fit for duty.[54] Capt. George B. Sanford of the 1st U.S. Cavalry noted that the Cavalry Corps "certainly owes to General Hooker a debt of gratitude, which it would be difficult to repay. From the date of its reorganization by him until the close of the war, its career was constantly growing more and more glorious, until the end of the rebellion nothing could stand before the rush of its squadrons."[55] It also meant that the bypassing of Pleasonton set the stage for intrigue by the dapper cavalryman that continued for months.

Stoneman was a career horse soldier. An 1846 graduate of West Point, the crusty, hard-bitten Stoneman served with distinction in the Indian and Mexican wars. He had spent his entire career in either the dragoons or the cavalry. "Lieutenant Stoneman was an universal favorite with all the officers," recalled a fellow old Army horse soldier, "and likewise beloved by the private soldiers . . . when a detachment was ordered out for scouting or other purposes, the men all wanted to go if Lieutenant Stoneman was in command."[56] In 1846–47, Stoneman served as quartermaster for a battalion of 500 Mormons who marched to California to assist in the U.S. war with Mexico. The Mormon Battalion made a monumental journey of 2,000 miles from Council Bluffs, Iowa, to San Diego, California, the longest infantry march in history. Arriving there, the Mormons were mustered out of service.

With the coming of war in 1861, Stoneman was the third-ranking captain in the 2d U.S. Cavalry, later redesignated the 5th U.S. Cavalry. This regiment included some of the most famous army officers of the era, including Col. Albert Sidney Johnston, then–Lt. Col. Robert E. Lee, Maj. George H. Thomas, Capts. Edmund Kirby Smith and Earl Van Dorn, then–Lt. Fitzhugh Lee, and Lt. John Bell Hood, all of whom became general officers during the Civil War, and five of whom commanded armies. Stoneman immediately received a promotion to major, and after serving on the staff of his old friend and West Point classmate McClellan in West Virginia, Stoneman received an appointment as the Army of the Potomac's first chief of cavalry. After the Peninsula Campaign, Stoneman took command of a division of infantry, and led the III Corps at Fredericksburg. On November 29, 1862, Stoneman received a promotion to major general of volunteers, giving him rank equivalent to the responsibilities of a corps commander.[57]

The Union horse soldiers generally approved of Stoneman's appointment. He was a no-nonsense, rigid Regular with "an air of habitual sadness" and "an austere, dignified bearing that was somewhat repellant."[58] He suffered from a severe case of hemorrhoids, a condition that made every moment spent in the saddle a living hell, perhaps explaining his dyspeptic nature. However, in spite of his off-putting manner, the men had great confidence in him. As a career saddle soldier, Stoneman understood cavalrymen, and he knew how to make the best use of their unique talents. "Stoneman we believe in," wrote Capt. Charles Francis Adams of the 1st Massachusetts Cavalry, "We believe in his judgment, his courage and determination. We know he is ready to shoulder responsibility, that he will take good care of us and won't get us into places from which he can't get us out."[59] "All cavalry are to be under command of Gen. Stoneman," reported an Ohioan, "He can dispose of them as he sees fit."[60]

Stoneman set about organizing his new command, which consisted of three divisions and an independent reserve brigade made up of the regiments of Regular Army cavalry assigned to the Army of the Potomac. The 6th Pennsylvania Cavalry, also known as Rush's Lancers for their unique weapons, nine-foot-long wooden lances, would serve as an independent command attached to Cavalry Corps headquarters. "This will give [the 6th Pennsylvania] a much better chance of seeing service than when attached to Headquarters, which is a lazy, loafing sort of duty," announced Maj. Gen. George G. Meade, whose son George served in the regiment.[61] Stoneman also had a brigade of veteran horse artillery at his disposal, and these Regular Army cannoneers gave the Army of the Potomac a trump card to play in almost every engagement. All regiments, squadrons, and troops of cavalry scattered about the Army of the Potomac received orders to report to the division or brigade to which they had been assigned. From that moment on, each of the seven infantry corps would have assigned to it only one squadron of cavalry "to act as orderlies, messengers, &c.," when whole regiments had previously performed the same duty.[62]

Brig. Gen. Alfred Pleasonton received the First Division. Born in Washington, D.C., on July 7, 1824, Pleasonton attended local schools and received an appointment to West Point in 1840. He graduated seventh in the class of 1844, and was commissioned into the 2d Dragoons. In 1846, he received a brevet to first lieutenant for gallantry in the Mexican War and served on the Indian frontier and in Florida against the Seminoles. While serving in the West, Pleasonton met and befriended John Buford, who played a major role in the drama that unfolded in 1863. In 1861, while a captain, Pleasonton commanded the regiment on its march from Utah to Washington in September and October. In the winter of 1862, he was promoted to major and distinguished himself during the Peninsula Campaign. On July 18, he was promoted to brigadier general of volunteers, and had field command of the Army of the Potomac's cavalry during the 1862 Maryland Campaign and at Fredericksburg.[63]

Many believed Pleasonton to be a conniver, a manipulator, and a man desperate to advance his own cause. Active and energetic, he swaggered like a bantam rooster, exuding self-confidence. He was something of a dandy, preferring fancy uniforms, a straw hat, kid gloves, and a cowhide riding stick. "Pleasonton is small, nervous, and full of dash," reported a war correspondent, "dark-haired and finely featured with gray-streaked hair."[64]

Pleasonton's courage in battle was suspect; he was "notorious" among those "who have served under him and seen him under fire."[65] Captain Adams, who possessed the acid pen of his great-grandfather, John Adams, correctly noted, "Pleasonton . . . is pure and simple a newspaper humbug. . . . He does nothing save with a view to a newspaper paragraph."[66] In spite of these unattractive personality traits, Alf Pleasonton had demonstrated competence in the field, and the Army of the Potomac's Cavalry Corps badly needed competence and experience.

Pleasonton's division had two brigades. Thirty-one year-old Col. Benjamin F. "Grimes" Davis commanded the First Brigade. Davis, born in Alabama and raised in Mississippi, had five brothers and a sister. He was a cousin of Confederate president Jefferson Davis, who also hailed from Mississippi. Two of Davis's brothers served in the 11th Mississippi Infantry during the Civil War, and both were killed in battle before war's end. When young Benjamin's parents died, probably as a result of an outbreak of smallpox, he became the ward of a wealthy uncle who lived in Aberdeen, Mississippi. Another uncle was involved in politics, and arranged an appointment to West Point for Davis, who entered the academy in 1850. "He was a youth of exceptional character and fine abilities, and . . . he had good size, pleasing appearance, strictly brave, and every way honorable." He received the nickname "Grimes" at the academy, and served as captain of the cadets during his senior year. Along with Jeb Stuart, Davis graduated in the class of 1854.[67]

Upon graduation, Davis joined the 5th U.S. Infantry, but transferred to the 1st Dragoons in 1855. In 1857, he suffered a wound while fighting Indians on the Gila River Expedition. Davis spent most of his Regular Army career in New Mexico and California. He was promoted to first lieutenant in January 1860. At the beginning of the war, he sought and obtained a commission as colonel of the 1st California Cavalry, but deserted his unit to rejoin the Regulars when they marched east.[68] On July 31, he was promoted to captain of Company K of the 1st Dragoons, which had been redesignated as the 1st U.S. Cavalry. He first drew the attention of his superiors during the 1862 Peninsula Campaign, when, at the Battle of Williamsburg on May 2, his squadron charged a larger force of Confederate cavalry and routed it, drawing the praise of his superiors.[69]

In spite of his Southern roots, "Col. Davis was emphatically a son of the Union."[70] "He was a gallant man, an ambitious soldier, a courtly gentleman," recalled Wesley Merritt, who had a distinguished forty-three-year career in the Regular Army. "A Southerner . . . he stood firm by the flag under which he had received his qualifications and commission as an officer."[71]

As a result of his good service on the Peninsula, Davis received an appointment as colonel of the 8th New York Cavalry in July 1862. He became famous in the aftermath of Jackson's capture of Harpers Ferry during the 1862 Maryland Campaign. Refusing to surrender, Davis led 1,500 Union cavalry on a dangerous escape, capturing Maj. Gen. James Longstreet's wagon train along the way. This feat led to his appointment to brigade command, and he served in that capacity with distinction.[72]

Davis was a veteran Regular, and not afraid to lead men into a fight.[73] "When Colonel Davis found the rebels, he did not stop at anything, but went for them heavy," recalled a member of the 8th New York Cavalry. "I believe he liked to fight the rebels as well as he liked to eat."[74] The hard-fighting colonel was also a martinet. "Davis was a . . . proud tyrannical devil," recalled the regimental surgeon of the 3d Indiana Cavalry.[75] Another Hoosier recalled Davis as "a strict disciplinarian. Prompt in the performance of his own duties and exacting of his inferiors. Brave and audacious. Much esteemed by his own regiment and respected by the whole command."[76] His veteran brigade consisted of the 8th New York Cavalry, the 9th New York Cavalry, the 8th Illinois Cavalry, and six companies of the 3d Indiana Cavalry.

Colonel Thomas C. Devin of New York commanded Pleasonton's 2d Brigade. Devin was a house painter prior to the war, and received his military training in the New York militia, where he commanded a company of cavalry. Two days before the First Battle of Bull Run, Devin mustered into the Federal service as a captain in the 1st New York (Lincoln) Cavalry. He was commissioned colonel of the 6th New York Cavalry, also known as the 2d Ira Harris Guards, on November 18, 1861. The 6th New York performed good service during the Antietam Campaign, and, after the Battle of Fredericksburg, Devin assumed command of a brigade under Pleasonton, who regularly and fruitlessly urged his promotion to brigadier general.[77] Devin's "command was long known in the Army of the Potomac as one of the few cavalry regiments which in the earlier campaigns of that Army, could be deemed thoroughly reliable," observed an early historian of the Cavalry Corps. A healthy mutual respect and attachment developed between Buford and Devin.[78]

"I can't teach Col. Devin anything about cavalry," Buford once said. "He knows more about the tactics than I do."[79] Another said of Devin that he was "of the school of Polonius, a little slow sometimes in entrance to a fight, but, being in, as slow to leave a point for which the enemy is trying."[80] Perhaps the finest accolade paid him was that "Colonel Devin knew how to take his men into action and also how to bring them out."[81] At 40, Devin was older than the other cavalry commanders, but he had experience and was always reliable under fire. "His blunt soldiership, sound judgment, his prompt and skillful dispositions for battle, his long period of active service, his bulldog tenacity, and his habitual reliability fully entitled him to the sobriquet among his officers and soldiers of the old 'war horse,' 'Sheridan's hard hitter,' and the like," observed one of Sheridan's staff officers after the end of the war.[82] Devin's brigade consisted of his 6th New York, the 8th Pennsylvania, and the 17th Pennsylvania.

Brig. Gen. William Woods Averell received command of the 2d Division. Averell was born in Cameron, New York, on November 5, 1832. He came from hardy stock—his father had been one of the first settlers of the area, and his grandfather had fought in the Revolutionary War. His great-grandfather, Josiah Bartlett, was the first constitutional governor of New Hampshire and signed the Declaration of Independence.[83] Young William spent his youth in school and working as a drugstore clerk. He received an appointment to West Point in 1851, graduating in the bottom third of the class of 1855. Averell's superb skills as a horseman made him a natural for the cavalry. He was commissioned as a lieutenant in the Regiment of Mounted Rifles, later the 3d U.S. Cavalry. While at the Military Academy, Averell befriended cadet Fitzhugh Lee, who was a nephew of the Academy's superintendent, Lt. Col. Robert E. Lee. Fitz Lee also wanted to serve in the cavalry, and the two grew as close as brothers, even though they were a year apart at the Academy.[84]

Not long after being commissioned, Averell attended the Cavalry School at the Carlisle Barracks, and spent a tour of duty as the adjutant to the commanding officer. In 1857, he transferred to a post in New Mexico, where he fought Indians and received a serious leg wound that nearly forced him to leave the service. He spent two years on recuperative leave. Averell went to Washington with the coming of war in April 1861. After a stint as a staff officer that placed him on the battlefield at First Bull Run in July 1861, Averell became colonel of the 3d Pennsylvania Cavalry.

Although an ambitious man, Averell was a conservative commander. He believed that troops needed constant training and did not want to take them into the field if he did not believe them to be ready. As a result of his efforts, the 3d Pennsylvania soon gained the reputation of being one of the best-trained and best-disciplined volunteer cavalry regiments assigned to the Army of the Potomac. "He was an excellent drillmaster, with proper views of what constituted proper discipline," recalled an admiring trooper. "Instruction in a systematic manner, with a view of preparing these men for the service expected of them, was commenced and persistently followed in the most industrious and painstaking manner."[85]

Under McClellan's leadership, Averell commanded a brigade of cavalry during the 1862 Peninsula Campaign. He fell victim to the so-called "Chickahominy Fever," a nasty and persistent malarial fever, in the aftermath of the Peninsula Campaign, requiring five weeks of recuperation. A relapse of the fever forced him to miss the Antietam Campaign in the fall of 1862. In spite of the persistent illness, Averell assumed command of a division later that fall.[86]

Averell's personality mirrored that of the army's commander, Maj. Gen. George B. McClellan, a trait that cost him dearly. "McClellan and Averell would take time to reorganize, reequip and retrain their forces even if it meant stopping the momentum of battle. Lack of a visceral desire to aim for the jugular of a defeated enemy eventually would cost both men their commands," observed a modern historian.[87] Like McClellan, Averell was a Democrat. Averell did not trust politicians, and he certainly did not trust the Republican administration, whose bungling he blamed for the war. He also did not believe that amateur soldiers and politicians had any role in the army, believing that only professional soldiers like him should command large bodies of troops in the field. His haughtiness greatly hindered his military career in the highly politicized environment of the Army of the Potomac.

Col. Alfred Napoléon Alexander Duffié, of the 1st Rhode Island Cavalry, commanded Averell's 1st Brigade. Born Napoléon Alexandre Duffié, he carried the nickname "Nattie." Duffié was born in Paris, France, on May 1, 1833, the son of a well-to-do bourgeois French sugar refiner who distilled sugar from beets.[88] At age 17, Duffié enlisted in the French 6th Regiment of Dragoons. Six months later, he was promoted to corporal, and received a second promotion, this time to sergeant, in March 1854. He served in French campaigns in Africa and in the Crimean War from May 1, 1854, to July 16, 1856, and received two decorations for valor during this period.

In 1854, the 6th Regiment of Dragoons, along with two other mounted units, made a brilliant cavalry charge at the Battle of Kanghil, near the Black Sea port of Eupatoria in the Ukraine, leading to the issuance of Duffié's decorations. In February 1858, Duffié became first sergeant in the 6th Dragoons and then transferred to the 3d Regiment of Hussars. Although he would have been eligible for discharge from the French Army in 1859, Duffié signed on for another seven-year enlistment that spring after being graded "a strong man capable of becoming a good average officer."

On June 14, 1859, Duffié received a commission as second lieutenant in the 3d Regiment of Hussars. Just two months later, Duffié tried to resign his commission, stating a desire to go into business. He had met thirty-two-year-old Mary Ann Pelton, a young American woman serving as a nurse in Europe's charnel houses. Duffié's regimental commander rejected the attempted letter of resignation, stating his "regrets that this officer so little appreciates the honor of recently having been promoted sous-lieutenant, and that he would prefer a commercial position to that honor."[89] When the French army refused to allow Duffié to resign, he deserted and fled to New York with Miss Pelton. He was listed as absent without leave and court-martialed in 1860. He was convicted and sentenced to dismissal without benefits for desertion to a foreign country and stripped of his medals. On December 20, 1860, by decree of Emperor Napoléon III, Duffié was sentenced, in absentia, to serve five years in prison for deserting and was dishonorably discharged from the French army.[90]

After arriving in New York, he adopted the first name Alfred, perhaps trying to disguise his true identity from prying eyes. He also married Miss Pelton, the daughter of a wealthy and influential New York family. Mary Ann Duffié's father was a dealer in boots and shoes and shoemakers' supplies, and was "an energetic and successful businessman" who lived in an enclave of strong abolitionists in Staten Island.[91] When the Civil War broke out, Duffié received a commission as a captain in the 2d New York Cavalry. He quickly rose to the rank of major, and was appointed colonel of the 1st Rhode Island Cavalry in July 1862.[92]

Duffié took great pains to hide his military history, spinning an elaborate web of lies, convincing all that cared to hear his story that he was the son of a French count, and not a humble sugar refiner. He changed the reported date of his birth from 1833 to 1835. He claimed that he had attended the preparatory Military Academy at Vincennes, that he had graduated from the prestigious military college of St. Cyr in 1854, and that he had served in Algiers and Senegal as lieutenant of cavalry.[93]

Duffié also claimed that he had been badly wounded at the Battle of Solferino in the War of Italian Independence in 1859, a conflict between the forces of Austria on one side and the allied forces of Piedmont, Sardinia, and France on the other. Solferino was a huge and bloody affair, involving more than 300,000 soldiers and nearly 40,000 casualties. However, his unit, the 3d Hussars, was not part of the Army of Italy and did not fight at Solferino. Although Duffié said that he had received a total of eight wounds in combat, his French military records do not suggest that he ever received a combat wound. He also asserted that he had received the Victoria Cross from Queen Victoria herself.

Finally, Duffié claimed that he had come to the United States to take the waters at Saratoga Springs, not because he had deserted the French army and fled to America in the company of a woman who was not his wife. Perhaps the Peltons created the myth of Alfred Duffié, French nobleman and war hero, to make their new son-in-law more palatable to their prominent social circles. Because of his martial bearing, he soon persuaded both his superior officers and the men who served under him that he had noble roots and a superb military pedigree.[94]

"Confronting us, he presents the aspect of the beau ideal soldat . . .with his tall symmetrical form erect in saddle and severe facial expression emphasized by a mustache and goatee of formal cut waxed to a point a la militaire," observed a war correspondent. "A Frenchman I judged him on sight, from his tout ensemble, and his first utterance, which launched without instant delay, proved my surmise correct."[95] He wore an unusual uniform of his own design, based closely upon the attire of the French Chasseurs, knee boots, and an ornately embroidered cap patterned after the French Chasseur design.[96]

Duffié spoke fractured English. "His attempts were interlarded with curious and novel expletives, which were very amusing."[97] In assuming a new command, the Frenchman would say, "You no like me now. You like my bye and bye." He was right. Before long, they would follow him when he ordered a charge. "Once, in preparing to make a charge where the situation looked a little desperate," recalled a New Yorker, Duffié "encouraged his men, who were little more than boys, by saying, 'You all have got to die sometime anyway. If you die now you won't have to die again. Forward!' His charge was successful."[98]

Although the Gallic colonel got off to a rough start with his Rhode Islanders, he soon won them over. The men of his brigade liked him. "Duffié is in command of the Brigade. He is a Frenchman," observed Albinus Fell of the 6th Ohio Cavalry, "he is a bully little cuss."[99] Another predicted that the Frenchman would quickly receive a promotion and leave the 1st Rhode Island. "He is a bully man," observed Sgt. Emmons D. Guild of the 1st Rhode Island Cavalry. "I tell you he will not stay long, so you will have to look out if you want to see him. His name is A. N. Duffié."[100] Duffié's experience showed, and he performed competently if not spectacularly. "Whatever may have been the faults of Colonel Duffié," recorded his regimental sergeant major, "there is no gainsaying the fact that he was probably the best regimental cavalry drill-master and tactician in the army."[101] His veteran brigade, which saw heavy action during the Second Bull Run Campaign of 1862, consisted of the 1st Rhode Island, the 1st Massachusetts, 6th Ohio, and 4th New York. Later in the spring of 1863, Duffié briefly commanded the division.

Col. Horace Binney Sargent of the 1st Massachusetts Cavalry briefly succeeded Duffié in command of Averell's 1st Brigade when an injury restricted the Frenchman to camp. Sargent was born on June 30, 1821, in Quincy, Massachusetts, and attended Harvard University. Graduating in 1843, he enrolled in Harvard's law school, completing his legal training in 1845. Sargent began his legal career shortly thereafter, practicing law until the coming of war in 1861. He was appointed lieutenant colonel of the newly formed 1st Massachusetts Cavalry in September 1861, and took command of the regiment when its original colonel, Col. Robert Williams, resigned his commission in October 1862. Sargent "was a superb horseman, very enthusiastic about cavalry service, and a student of military matters, although of no experience."[102]

Col. John Baillie McIntosh led Averell's 2d Brigade. McIntosh, aged thirty-four, was the son of a Regular Army officer, and served in the prewar navy. A brother, Confederate Brig. Gen. James M. McIntosh, had been killed in the 1862 Battle of Pea Ridge. Although not a West Pointer, McIntosh received a commission as lieutenant

in the 2d U.S. Cavalry in 1861 and compiled a distinguished record of service in the
Civil War. He received a brevet to major for his service during the 1862 Peninsula
Campaign and was appointed colonel of the 3d Pennsylvania Cavalry in November. With the formation of the Army of the Potomac's Cavalry Corps in the spring
of 1863, McIntosh assumed command of Averell's 1st Brigade.[103] He was a "born
fighter, a strict disciplinarian, a dashing leader, and a polished gentleman," although
the men of his brigade did not particularly like him.[104] McIntosh proved himself a
reliable and competent brigade commander, perhaps the finest in the Army of the
Potomac.

By June, Col. Luigi Palma di Cesnola commanded Duffié's brigade. Born to an
ancient, ennobled Italian family, the thirty-year-old colonel had a glittering reputation. His father had fought for Napoléon. Di Cesnola was educated at the Royal
Military Academy at Turin, and entered the mounted arm of the Sardinian army.
At age seventeen, the young count fought against powerful Austrian armies in
Italy's war for independence. He also fought in the Crimea in the late 1850s. Finally,
in 1860, di Cesnola emigrated to the United States, settling in New York. He
married the daughter of an American naval officer and served as the director of a
700-student military school in New York.

With the coming of war, he offered his services to the 11th New York Infantry,
and received a commission as major as a result of his prior military service. He was
promoted to lieutenant colonel in 1862, before accepting an appointment as
colonel of the 4th New York Cavalry.[105] The 4th New York was a polyglot unit.
"Other field officers included Americans and Germans, Frenchmen, Italians,
Spaniards, Hungarians, and perhaps men of other countries. Most of them could
speak only their own languages. They were sad rogues, and the regiment lacked
cohesion and unity. . . . In some battles they fought very well, but generally they
were not considered reliable, and there were scandals of frequent occurrence."[106] In
February 1863, the dashing count was dismissed from the service for allegedly
stealing six pistols, but he was exonerated, reinstated, and returned to his regiment.[107] He assumed command of Duffié's brigade when the Frenchman became
division commander in May. Di Cesnola's tenure as a brigade commander would
be short.

Brig. Gen. David McMurtrie Gregg led the 3d Cavalry Division. He was born
in Huntingdon, Pennsylvania, on April 10, 1833, a first cousin of the wartime governor of Pennsylvania, Andrew Gregg Curtin. His paternal grandfather, Andrew
Gregg, served in both the U.S. House of Representatives and the Senate during
1791–1813, so Gregg came from a family with a long history of public service. He
was educated at various private schools and at Bucknell University. In 1851, Gregg
received an appointment to West Point, and graduated with Averell in 1855. He
was commissioned into the 2d Dragoons, serving in various posts in the West. In

September 1855, he was promoted and transferred to the 1st Dragoons, and served out the balance of his antebellum career in California, working as regimental adjutant. When war broke out, Gregg was a captain in the newly formed 3d U.S. Cavalry, which was redesignated as the 6th U.S. Cavalry. When volunteer units were organized, he was elected colonel of the 8th Pennsylvania Cavalry.[108]

Gregg served well on the Peninsula and in the Antietam Campaign. Accordingly, he was promoted to brigadier general of volunteers on November 20, 1862. David Gregg was remembered fondly as "tall and spare, of notable activity, capable of the greatest exertion and exposure; gentle in manner but bold and resolute in action. Firm and just in discipline he was a favorite of his troopers and ever held, for he deserved, their affection and entire confidence." Gregg knew the principles of war and was always ready and eager to apply them. Endowed "with a natural genius of high order, he [was] universally hailed as the finest type of cavalry leader. A man of unimpeachable personal character, in private life affable and genial but not demonstrative, he fulfilled with modesty and honor all the duties of the citizen and head of an interesting and devoted family."[109] A former officer later commented that Gregg's "modesty kept him from the notoriety that many gained through the newspapers; but in the army the testimony of all officers who knew him was the same. Brave, prudent, dashing when occasion required dash, and firm as a rock, he was looked upon, both as a regimental commander and afterwards as Major-General, as a man in whose hands any troops were safe."[110] His men called him "Old Reliable."[111]

Hugh Judson Kilpatrick, a native of New Jersey, was born the son of a farmer on January 14, 1836. He had little education but still received an appointment to West Point in 1856, and graduated in the May class of 1861. Ever vigilant for opportunities for self-promotion, Kilpatrick realized that the fastest route for advancement lay in the volunteer service. With the assistance of Lt. Col. Gouverneur K. Warren, one of Kilpatrick's instructors at West Point, Kilpatrick obtained a volunteer's commission as captain of Company H, 5th New York Infantry, also known as Duryee's Zouaves. He was the first Regular Army officer wounded in combat at the 1861 Battle of Big Bethel. Kilpatrick returned to duty later that year as lieutenant colonel of the 2d New York Cavalry and served capably during the campaigns of 1862. By December 1862, he was colonel of the regiment and assumed command of one of Gregg's brigades during the spring of 1863.[112]

Later in 1863, Kilpatrick earned the unflattering moniker "Kill Cavalry" for his penchant for using up men and horses. He had the reputation of being "flamboyant, reckless, tempestuous and even licentious."[113] An officer of the 1st Massachusetts Cavalry wrote, "Kilpatrick is a brave, injudicious boy, much given to blowing, and surely will come to grief."[114] Another Federal staff officer called Kilpatrick "a frothy braggart without brains."[115] He was one of those characters that men either loved or hated. There was no middle ground when it came to Judson Kilpatrick. His brigade consisted of the 1st Maine, 2d New York, and 10th New York.

Col. Sir Percy Wyndham, a rakish twenty-nine-year-old English soldier of fortune, led Gregg's 2d Brigade. He was born on the ship *Arab* in the English Channel on February 5, 1833, while his parents were en route to Calcutta, India. Capt. Charles Wyndham, his father, served in the British Fifth Light Cavalry. With that pedigree, the boy seemed destined to be a horse soldier. However, fifteen-year-old Percy Wyndham entered the French navy instead, serving as a midshipman during the French Revolution of 1848. He then joined the Austrian army as a sublieutenant and left eight years later as a first lieutenant in the Austrian Lancers, resigning his commission on May 1, 1860, to join the Italian army of liberation being formed by the famed guerrilla leader Giuseppe Garibaldi. Wyndham received a battlefield promotion to major in the great battle of Milazzo, Sicily, on July 20, 1860, where Garibaldi's army defeated the Neapolitans, consolidating the guerrilla's hold on the island. A grateful King Victor Emmanuel knighted the dashing cavalryman. With the conquest of Italy complete, the soldier of fortune went hunting for another opportunity, and found one in the United States in 1861. Largely as a result of his reputation in Italy, Wyndham received an appointment as colonel of the 1st New Jersey Cavalry in February 1862.[116]

A Federal horseman recalled, "This officer was an Englishman, an alleged lord. But lord or son of a lord, his capacity as a cavalry officer was not great. He had been entrusted with one or two independent commands and was regarded as a dashing officer. . . . He seemed bent on killing as many horses as possible, not to mention the men. The fact was the newspapers were in the habit of reporting that Colonel or General so-and-so had made a forced march of so many hours, and it is probable that 'Sir Percy' was in search of some more of that kind of cheap renown."[117]

One Confederate trooper noticed that Sir Percy, who wore a spectacular mustache nearly two feet wide, was "a stalwart man . . . who strode along with the nonchalant air of one who had wooed Dame Fortune too long to be cast down by her frowns."[118] A Federal officer called Wyndham "a big bag of wind."[119] Another Northerner, remembering his first encounter with Wyndham, compared him to a bouquet of flowers, noting, "You poor little lillies, you! You haven't the first chance with the glorious magnificence of his beauty. He's only been in Camp for two hours, and he now appears in his third suit of clothes!"[120] Wyndham's brigade included his own 1st New Jersey Cavalry, the 12th Illinois Cavalry, the 1st Pennsylvania Cavalry, and the 1st Maryland Cavalry.

John Buford outranked everyone in the Army of the Potomac's Cavalry Corps but Stoneman and Pleasonton. His seniority entitled him to command of one of the new divisions. However, the thirty-seven-year-old Kentuckian had other ideas that kept him from assuming command of a division until June 1863. John Buford,

Jr., was born near Versailles, Kentucky, on March 4, 1826. He was the first son of John and Anne Bannister Howe Watson Buford. Young John Buford came from a large family—he had two full brothers, as well as thirteen half brothers and sisters from the first marriages of both of his parents. His grandfather, Simeon Buford, had served under Col. Henry "Light Horse Harry" Lee, father of Gen. Robert E. Lee, in the Virginia cavalry in the Revolution. John Buford's mother died in a cholera epidemic in 1835, and the family relocated to Rock Island, Illinois. He was "a splendid horseman, an unerring rifle shot and a person of wonderful nerve and composure."[121]

Buford received an appointment to West Point in 1844. His performance there was solid, if unspectacular. He graduated sixteenth in the class of 1848. Upon graduation, and at his request, Buford was commissioned into the 1st Dragoons as a brevet second lieutenant. He only remained with the 1st Dragoons for a few months, and transferred to the newly formed 2d Dragoons in 1849. Buford served as quartermaster of the 2d Dragoons from 1855 through the beginning of August 1858, fighting in several Indian battles along the way, including the Sioux Punitive Expedition under command of Brig. Gen. William S. Harney. That engagement culminated in the Battle of Ash Hollow in 1856. Col. Philip St. George Cooke, commanding officer of the 2d Dragoons, cited Lt. Buford for his "good service" at Ash Hollow, as did Harney himself.

Buford participated in quelling the disturbances in Kansas during the mid-1850s, and served on the Mormon Expedition to Utah during 1857. Buford won high praise from Cooke for his service during the arduous march west, and served in Utah until the outbreak of the Civil War in 1861. When the war began, Buford was torn between his loyalty to his native Kentucky and his loyalty to the government he had served for thirteen years. John Gibbon recalled, "One night after the arrival of the mail we were in his [Buford's] room, talking over the news . . . when Buford said in his slow and deliberate way, 'I got a letter by the last mail from home with a message in it from the Governor of Kentucky. He sends me word to come to Kentucky at once and I shall have anything I want.'" Anxious, Gibbon asked, "What did you answer, John?" Gibbon was greatly relieved to hear Buford's reply: "I sent him word I was a captain in the United States Army and I intend to remain one."[122]

Reporting to Washington with his regiment, Buford requested, and received, an appointment as a major in the inspector general's office. He served in that position until June 1862, when Maj. Gen. John Pope, commanding the Army of Virginia, who knew Buford's talent and special affinity for the enlisted man, promoted Buford to brigadier general of volunteers, and gave him command of a brigade of cavalry in the Army of Virginia. Buford served with great distinction during the Second Bull Run Campaign, providing superior scouting and intelligence services, and also going toe-to-toe with the vaunted troopers of J. E. B. Stuart's

Confederate cavalry on two different occasions. His men nearly captured both Stuart and Robert E. Lee at different points during the campaign, and his intelligence saved Pope's army from destruction shortly after the August 9, 1862, Battle of Cedar Mountain. Buford commanded the Union forces in a little-known but important phase of the Second Battle of Bull Run, the cavalry melee at the Lewis Ford on August 30, 1862, where Buford enjoyed some success against Stuart's men, and bought time for the beaten Army of Virginia's retreat. Buford himself was slightly wounded in this engagement, leading to his appointment as chief of cavalry under McClellan.[123]

When Stoneman took command of the new-formed Cavalry Corps, Buford was serving on court-martial duty in Washington, D.C. He remained trapped on this unwelcome duty until the third week of March, despite repeated requests for his release. On February 9, 1863, Buford penned a revealing letter to his old friend Stoneman. "I have heard that all of the cavalry of the Army of the Potomac is to be massed under your command. I take it for granted that I am to have a command under you," wrote Buford. "Being absent while you are making your organizations, I am a little afraid that the different brigade commanders being on the ground may succeed in getting the fighting regiments leaving me the less desirable ones. There is a great difference in the Reg'ts—some will *stay* while others will not under any circumstances. If I can have my choice I would prefer Western troops. If the Regulars are to be put together, I believe they would prefer me to either of the other cavalry commanders."[124]

Buford had correctly evaluated the feelings of the Regulars. One Regular officer reported to his father that the army's cavalry was to be formed into a corps, and that the Regulars were to be brigaded together, to form the army's cavalry reserve under Buford's command. "We are all glad enough, I assure you, of the change, specially so on account of getting away from the volunteers," he wrote. The thought of serving under one of their own pleased the Regulars.[125] During the third week in March, Buford assumed command of the Reserve Brigade, consisting of the 1st, 2d, 5th, and 6th U.S. Cavalry regiments. The Reserve Brigade served as an independent command.

His new corps structure in place, Stoneman set about changing the way that things were done. First, he inspected his Cavalry Corps, trying to ascertain its condition and morale.[126] He intended to do away with ponderous cavalry wagon trains, replacing them with mule trains. Stoneman also ordered that the mounted units be made ready "for the most vigorous and rapid movements." Further, all disabled or lame horses were to be turned in for replacement. The Cavalry Corps would be outfitted properly at last, validating Buford's earlier efforts to find quality horses.[127] Stoneman also appointed a promising young officer, Capt. Wesley Merritt of the 2d U.S. Cavalry, as his ordnance officer. Merritt supervised the arming of the Cavalry Corps. Until the fall of 1862, Northern cavalry companies had only ten carbines per company. That fall, he instituted a policy of issuing a carbine to every trooper. Each trooper received a single-shot breech-loading carbine. Most of the horse soldiers got Sharp's carbines, highly prized for their ability to be re-loaded quickly while on horseback or prone, although some also received the Burnside carbine, a popular weapon designed by the former army commander. These new weapons played a significant role in the improvement of the Union cavalry.[128]

Once the men had received new weapons, both commissioned and noncom-missioned officers went to work studying cavalry tactics, and regular recitations occurred nightly by the flickering light of candles. Noncommissioned officers recited their lessons to the senior captain of each squadron, the commissioned officers recited to the majors, and at certain times, the majors reported to their colonels for a quiz of their knowledge of tactics. Duffié, for example, introduced a regimen of written tests and oral examinations in order to make sure that his men learned the important lessons offered by the assigned cavalry tactics manuals.[129]

In addition to the book learning, most regiments underwent rigorous daily drilling in squadron, battalion, and regimental drill, with occasional brigade and divisional reviews. "The study and drill of the winter produced a cavalry corps which was ever after respected in our own army and dreaded by the enemy," proudly recalled a Rhode Island horse soldier.[130]

An Ohio trooper described this training regimen in a letter home. "The daily routine I follow is 'reveille' 6 o'clock in the morning & roll call. Feed horses and care for them[,] get breakfast. Company drill at 9. Water call at 11. Feed at noon. Company drill at one[,] water call at 3. Dress parade at 5[,] feed horses at 6[,] get supper and then play poker or euchre until 8 o'clock at night. Then fall in for roll call & from that time until 6 o'clock in the morning we have to ourselves." The routine varied on Sunday. After chapel, the brigade commanders reviewed the commands on dress parade. While monotonous, this routine quickly paid substan-tial dividends.[131] Another Ohioan noted in his diary, "Our time is occupied in drilling and inspection, when not on picket duty. The orders are very strict and no one is allowed to shirk."[132] The men learned discipline that paid dividends later that summer, and for the rest of the war.

Colonel Duffié focused his attentions on the 4th New York Cavalry in par-ticular. The New Yorkers did not perform their drills to the Frenchman's satisfac-tion, as "there were said to be fifty-three different languages and dialects spoken in that regiment." Duffié, whose English was not the greatest either, explained his dilemma. "The colonel of the Fourth New York," announced the Frenchman in his fractured English, "he give an order, all the officer they stick up their head, they holler like one geese."[133]

With the coming of the Civil War, the newly formed volunteer regiments elected their own officers. This practice meant that the person responsible for raising the regiment usually ended up being elected colonel whether he was qualified for that important position or not. As a result, a lot of politically influential but incompetent officers had to be winnowed out, a painful and lengthy process. The Cavalry Corps was not exempt.

The saga of Col. John Beardsley of the 9th New York Cavalry provides an excellent illustration of the point. Born on October 12, 1816, in Fairfield, Herkimer County, New York, John Beardsley was appointed to the U.S. Military Academy in 1837. He graduated 17th in the class of 1841, which included such future luminaries as Don Carlos Buell, Richard Garnett, Robert Garnett, Nathaniel Lyon, John F. Reynolds, and Israel Richardson, all of whom became generals in the Civil War.

Upon graduation, Beardsley joined the 8th Infantry, serving in the Seminole War in Florida from 1841 to 1842, and in Mexico. In 1846 Beardsley participated in the Battle of Palo Alto and in the Battle of Resaca de la Palma. On June 18, Beardsley was promoted to first lieutenant. The 8th Infantry served with the expeditionary force of Maj. Gen. Winfield Scott, then preparing for an amphibious landing at Vera Cruz. When the invasion began, the 8th Infantry participated in the Siege of Vera Cruz and in the Battle of Cerro Gordo, where their division played an important role in routing the Mexican forces.

Fighting alongside his comrade in the 8th Infantry, Lt. James Longstreet, Beardsley fought in the Battle of Churubusco and at the Battle of Molino del Rey, where he was severely wounded in action while leading an assault on the Mexican works. His conduct at Molino del Rey caught the eye of his superiors, and Beardsley received a brevet to captain for gallant and meritorious service. It took him more than a year to recover from his wound, and he did not return to active duty until 1849, when he was promoted to captain and company command in the 8th Infantry. After several more garrison assignments, and as a result of visual impairment and lingering problems resulting form his combat wound, Capt. John Beardsley resigned his commission on December 31, 1853, thus ending a twelve-year career in the Regular Army marked by regular promotions and meritorious service.[134]

The decorated war hero returned home to New York and took up farming. He led a quiet life on his farm near Athens, New York, until the storm clouds of civil war gathered in 1861. In October of that year, the governor of New York appointed Beardsley as colonel of the 9th New York Cavalry, and gave him the task of recruiting, arming, and training the regiment. His commission was dated November 21, 1861, meaning that he was one of the most senior colonels in the mounted service.[135]

Beardsley seemed a good choice to command a brigade in Maj. Gen. John Pope's Army of Virginia. Surprisingly, his brigade played a limited role in the campaign, its principal contribution being the capture of the Waterloo Bridge, near Warrenton, Virginia, on August 25. Beardsley's command had the hopeless task of trying to stem the stampede to the rear after his old comrade in arms, Maj. Gen. James Longstreet, launched his massive counterattack against the Union left on the afternoon of August 30. Thereafter, Beardsley ordered his men to form line of battle (in a single rank) to the east of Henry House Hill, astride the Warrenton Turnpike, covering the retreat of the army. Beardsley's brigade eventually followed the broken Army of Virginia off the field.[136]

After the ignominious defeat at Second Manassas, Beardsley's brigade returned to Washington, D.C., with the XI Corps, where the unit served in the city's defenses during the Antietam Campaign. Beardsley and his brigade rejoined the reconstituted Army of the Potomac in November. Sometime in late 1862, Col. Beardsley took command of the cavalry branch's Convalescent's Camp near Hall's Farm in northern Virginia, where he remained until late February 1863.

On March 10, 1863, Maj. Charles McLean Knox of the 9th New York Cavalry preferred court-martial charges against Colonel Beardsley, claiming disloyalty, cowardice, and conduct unbecoming an officer and a gentleman resulting from a series of incidents occurring between August 6 and November 4, 1862. Major Knox alleged that, on August 6, 1862, Beardsley proclaimed, in the presence of enlisted men of his command that "we have no government that we are fighting for—no government; Congress is a mean, abolition faction; the Constitution is broken—we have no Constitution; the abolitionists of the North brought on this war; the Republicans are abolitionists." Similarly, on September 12, when he learned that Gen. Robert E. Lee had invited the conservative portion of the North to join Lee in putting down the administration in Washington, Beardsley allegedly said, "I would rather fight under Lee than under an abolition leader."[137]

Major Knox preferred more serious military charges regarding Colonel Beardsley's actions in the face of the enemy. Knox alleged that Beardsley left his command while it was skirmishing with the enemy on September 1, 1862, when the brigade acted as the army's rear guard near Fairfax Court House, Virginia. Knox similarly alleged that, on November 4, 1862, during the XI Corps advance from Centerville, Virginia, toward Warrenton, near New Baltimore, Beardsley precipitately retreated when his command first encountered enemy resistance. Beardsley, "manifest[ing] trepidation and fear . . . placed himself at the head of the retreating column and finally ordered the column to trot . . . ." Knox pointed out that forty men of the 9th New York Cavalry stopped the enemy advance and drove the Rebels back to New Baltimore while Beardsley conducted his retreat.[138]

Knox's most serious charge related to Beardsley's conduct on the battlefield at Second Bull Run. Knox alleged that on August 30, 1862, Beardsley publicly berated Lt. Col. William Sackett, commanding Beardsley's own 9th New York Cavalry, while Sackett tried to form line of battle "to stop a stampede that had commenced on the battlefield." Beardsley allegedly interrupted Sackett's dispositions of the troops, stating, "[W]hat in Hell are you doing with the Regiment there—bring it around here—bring it here, I tell you—by file, march—trot—march—by God, you do not know how to handle a Regiment—I will put someone in command of it that does form a line."

Knox believed that Beardsley's words and actions indicated that Beardsley "was too much excited to know what he was doing." Knox further alleged that Beardsley then left the 9th New York and went to the rear, leaving the command under fire without orders. Sackett kept his command in place until no more stragglers came his way, and then retired the regiment across Bull Run until he found Beardsley, from whom Sackett requested instructions.

Knox alleged that Beardsley told Sackett to form on one side of the road, but then ordered the 9th New York to the other side of the road while retreating artillery was passing. Knox alleged that Beardsley used the subsequent chaos in the road to abandon his command once again, and that the colonel then rode off to Centerville, leaving the 9th New York formed but without orders.[139] Finally, Knox alleged that Beardsley arrested Sackett on September 8, 1862, while Beardsley was under the influence of alcohol and that the inebriated colonel berated Sackett in an abusive and ungentlemanly manner. This episode involved a matter in which Beardsley never preferred charges against Sackett.[140]

Major Knox's charges were sent to the 1st Cavalry Division on March 10, 1863. On March 12, Pleasonton forwarded the charges to Cavalry Corps headquarters, stating that "Colonel Beardsley . . . is not a proper officer to command a brigade, to which his rank entitles him and from the gravity of these charges, it would evidently be of advantage to the service if he was out of it."[141] Pleasonton obviously required no deliberation before deciding that Beardsley should be removed from command.

Beardsley must have realized that he had little chance of retaining his command. He resigned as colonel of the 9th New York Cavalry on March 14, 1863. Divisional headquarters speedily accepted his resignation and forwarded it on to Cavalry Corps headquarters on March 16. Stoneman obviously expected it, because Colonel Beardsley's resignation was accepted immediately, with Stoneman's endorsement: "Respectfully forwarded with the recommendation as strong as English language can express that it be excepted [sic]."[142]

While Beardsley marks an extreme case, he remains a valid illustration of the sort of problems inherited by Stoneman. The incompetents like Beardsley had to be culled and competent officers like Sackett had to be brought forward to assume their rightful places at the heads of their respective regiments. This painful and unpleasant process took time. Nevertheless, it marked another rite of passage for the new Cavalry Corps.

Hooker's reforms greatly increased the confidence and morale of the men serving under him. He challenged his horse soldiers to show their mettle, which had an electric effect on the men of the Cavalry Corps. "When this brave and dashing commander declared that he would give a bonus to any one who would show him a dead cavalryman, he did but express, in an enigmatical form, the idea that the cavalry was capable of doing, and of daring as it had never done."[143] Soon, men who "often felt heartily ashamed of belonging to a branch of the service which it was costing the government so much to maintain, and which was of so little real service" came to believe in themselves and their ability to make a difference in the outcome of the war.[144]

Hooker later wrote, "The cavalry was consolidated in a separate corps and put in the best condition ever known in our service. Whenever the state of the roads and of the [Rappahannock] River permitted, expeditions were started out to attack the pickets and advance posts of the enemy, and to forage in the country he occupied. My object was to encourage the men, to incite in their hearts, by successes, however unimportant they might be, a sentiment of superiority over their adversaries."[145]

This new policy showed immediate results. As one trooper of the 1st New Jersey Cavalry noted, there was "but one opinion as to [Hooker's] management of [the] army in winter quarters. Finding the Army of the Potomac a disorderly, dissatisfied, ill-provided, uncomfortable crowd of men . . . he transformed [them] into a well-disciplined, contented, enthusiastic body of soldiers. . . . Troops soon learn to appreciate this kind of administrative ability . . . and during the winter of sixty-two-sixty-three 'Joe Hooker' held a place in their esteem only second to the man who first organized them into an army."[146] Just a week after Stoneman assumed command of the army's horse soldiers, a Rhode Islander correctly predicted, "Next summer our cavalry intend to make their mark upon the rebs."[147]

"Judging from what I see and hear, I should have no hesitation in saying that the Army of the Potomac is improving every day, and that it was never in as good and efficient condition as at the present time," reported Stoneman in a letter to his old friend McClellan. "The study of the science of war is not permitted to do away with the necessity of a knowledge and practice of the art of war. I think the three requisites to constitute a good military organization, the physical, the moral, and the intellectual, are now in more happy accord than they have ever been before, and I trust and pray that they may remain so; and that this army has ceased to be an engine with which to experiment and to test Generals, or rather men, to find out if they could ever become Generals."[148]

Capt. Wesley Merritt of the 2d U.S. Cavalry observed, "From the day of its reorganization under Hooker, the cavalry of the Army of the Potomac commenced a new life. Before that time it had become so accustomed to meet and be overpowered by superior numbers, that it at times took the numbers for granted, and left some fields to inferior foes. In its new form and numbers it avoided no enemy of any arm of the service; for, while it could contend always successfully with the enemy's cavalry, it was always sufficiently strong and confident of its powers to make a stubborn fight and a dignified retreat in the face of even an army."[149] This new-found confidence and enthusiasm spread throughout the newly created Cavalry Corps. Its time had come.

NOTES

1. *The War of the Rebellion: A Compilation of the Official Records of the Union and Confederate Armies,* 128 vols. in 3 series (Washington, D.C.: U.S. Government Printing Office, 1889), series 1, vol. 19, part 2, 242 (hereinafter, "O.R."; all further references are to series 1, unless otherwise noted).
2. Ibid., vol. 11, part 3, 40.
3. Marcus A. Reno, "Boots and Saddles: The Cavalry of the Army of the Potomac," *National Tribune,* April 29, 1886.
4. Robert F. O'Neill, Jr., "The Federal Cavalry on the Peninsula," included in William J. Miller, ed., *The Peninsula Campaign of 1862: Yorktown to the Seven Days* (Campbell, Calif.: Savas, 1997), 3:87; O.R., series 3, vol. 1, 622.
5. Edward K. Eckert and Nicholas J. Amato, eds., *Ten Years in the Saddle: The Memoir of William Woods Averell, 1851–1862* (San Rafael, Calif.: Presidio Press, 1978), 328–29.
6. O.R., vol. 1, 622.
7. Ibid., vol. 21, 451. Bayard's death was a true blow to the blueclad cavalry. Bayard was young, talented, and extremely popular with the men of his command. He and Buford deserve nearly all of the credit for the dramatic improvements in the quality of the performance of the Union cavalry during the second half of 1862. He was also the senior brigadier general in the mounted arm, outranking all but Stoneman.
8. Moses Harris, "The Union Cavalry," *War Papers* 1, Military Order of the Loyal Legion of the United States, Wisconsin Commandery, 3 vols. (Milwaukee: Burdick, Armitage & Allen, 1891–1903), 351.
9. Wesley Merritt, "Personal Recollections—Beverly's Ford to Mitchell's Station, 1863," included in Theophilus F. Rodenbough, ed., *From Everglade to Canon with the Second Dragoons* (New York: D. Van Nostrand, 1875), 284.
10. Samuel H. Merrill, *The Campaigns of the First Maine and First District of Columbia Cavalry* (Portland, Maine: Bailey & Noyes, 1866), 55; Edward P. Tobie, *History of the First Maine Cavalry 1861–1865* (Boston: Press of Emory & Hughes, 1887), 123.
11. It typically cost approximately $500,000–600,000 to raise, mount, and equip a cavalry regiment. Stephen Z. Starr, *The Union Cavalry in the Civil War,* 3 vols. (Baton Rouge: Louisiana State University Press, 1979), 1:66.
12. O.R., vol. 19, part 2, 485.
13. Merritt, "Personal Recollections," 284.
14. O.R., vol. 11, part 1, 17. This letter, addressed to General-in-Chief Henry W. Halleck, on October 18, 1862, was part of a particularly nasty exchange between McClellan and Q.M. Gen. Montgomery Meigs. This venomous exchange later surfaced again in

McClellan's self-serving and self-laudatory report of the Antietam Campaign. Perhaps seeing an opportunity to use this situation as a justification for moving slowly after Antietam, McClellan may have opportunistically relied upon this situation at Meigs' expense.

15. Ibid., 80.

16. John Buford to Montgomery C. Meigs, October 15, 1862, Letters Sent and Received, Quartermaster's Office, National Archives, Washington, D.C.

17. Ibid. The great irony is that, less than a year later, the War Department created the Cavalry Bureau, which had the task of providing mounts for the cavalry. Many of Buford's recommendations were adopted and incorporated into the operations of the new Cavalry Bureau. Its role included procurement and nursing sick and worn-out animals back to health. It is quite likely that, as the war dragged on, the Cavalry Bureau reacquired some of the horses sold in 1863 as unserviceable.

18. O.R., vol. 21, 815. The soldiers assigned to artillery batteries usually marched on foot. In horse artillery batteries, the artillerists rode horses from place to place so that they could keep up with the cavalry.

19. Bayard had proposed a similar raid in October, in the aftermath of Stuart's circumvention of the Army of the Potomac.

20. Charles D. Rhodes, *History of the Cavalry of the Army of the Potomac, Including That of the Army of Virginia (Pope's), and also the History of the Operations of the Federal Cavalry in West Virginia During the War* (Kansas City, Mo.: Hudson-Kimberly, 1900).

21. O.R., vol. 21, 900; *Charleston Mercury,* January 5, 1863.

22. O.R., vol. 21, 895–96 and 902.

23. Ibid., 954.

24. Samuel J. B. V. Gilpin diary, entry for January 1, 1863, Gilpin Papers, Manuscripts Division, Library of Congress, Washington, D.C.

25. Thomas M. Covert to his wife, January 2, 1863, Thomas M. Covert Letters, U.S. Army Military History Institute, Carlisle, Pa. (hereinafter referred to as "USAMHI").

26. Ibid., January 11, 1863.

27. Thomas Lucas to his wife, January 5, 1863, Thomas Lucas Letters, Dona Sauerburger collection, Gambrills, Md.

28. Andrew W. German, ed., "Picketing along the Rappahannock," *Civil War Quarterly* 8 (March 1987): 33.

29. Isaac Ressler diary, entry for January 19, 1863, *Civil War Times Illustrated* Collection, USAMHI.

30. Samuel L. Gracey, *Annals of the Sixth Pennsylvania Cavalry* (Philadelphia: E. H. Butler, 1868), 127–28.

31. Hillman A. Hall, ed., *History of the Sixth New York Cavalry (Second Ira Harris Guards), Second Brigade-First Division-Cavalry Corps, Army of the Potomac 1861–1865* (Worcester, Mass.: Blanchard Press, 1908), 90.

32. Lucas to his wife, January 23, 1863, Lucas.

33. E. R. Hagemann, ed., *Fighting Rebels and Redskins: Experiences in Army Life of Colonel George B. Sanford, 1861–1892* (Norman: University of Oklahoma Press, 1968), 194.

34. O.R., vol. 21, 752 and 755.

35. George N. Bliss to Dear Gerald, January 23, 1863, George N. Bliss Letters, Rhode Island Historical Society, Providence, R.I.

36. Gilpin diary, entry for January 17, 1863.

37. Worthington C. Ford, ed., *A Cycle of Adams Letters, 1861–1865,* 2 vols. (Boston: Houghton-Mifflin, 1920), 1: 241.

38. Nathan Webb diary, entry for February 13, 1863, Schoff Civil War Collection, Clements Library, University of Michigan, Ann Arbor.

39. Sidney Morris Davis, *Common Soldier, Uncommon War: Life as a Cavalryman in the Civil War,* Charles F. Cooney, ed. (Bethesda, Md.: SMD Group, 1994), 333.

40. William H. Redman to his mother, January 20, 1863, Redman Correspondence, Alderman Library, University of Virginia, Charlottesville.

41. Robert L. Winder, ed., *Jacob Beidler's Book: A Diary Kept by Jacob Beidler from November 1857 through July 1863* (Mifflintown, Pa.: Juniata County Historical Society, 1994), 141.

42. Webb diary, entry for February 14, 1863.

43. Lucas to his wife, January 31, 1863.

44. Bliss to Dear Gerald, February 10, 1863.

45. Ezra J. Warner, *Generals in Blue: The Lives of the Union Commanders* (Baton Rouge: Louisiana State University Press, 1964), 233–34.

46. Hagemann, *Fighting Rebels and Redskins,* 194.

47. Lucas to his wife, February 5, 1863.

48. Bliss to Dear Gerald, February 19, 1863.

49. James K. Kim to William W. Averell, February 3, 1863, William Woods Averell Papers, N.Y. State Library and Archives, Albany.

50. William Redwood Price to Averell, February 19, 1863, Averell Papers.

51. O.R., vol. 25, part 2, 51.

52. Frederic C. Newhall, *With General Sheridan in Lee's Last Campaign* (Philadelphia: J. B. Lippincott, 1866), 41.

53. Starr, *The Union Cavalry in the Civil War,* 1: 327.

54. O.R., vol. 25, part 2, 65–66.

55. Hagemann, *Fighting Rebels and Redskins,* 194.

56. Quoted in David Evans, *Sherman's Horsemen: Union Cavalry Operations in the Atlanta Campaign* (Bloomington: Indiana University Press, 1996), 47.

57. Warner, *Generals in Blue,* 481. For more on Stoneman's service in the West prior to the Civil War, see James R. Arnold, *Jeff Davis's Own: Cavalry, Comanches, and the Battle for the Texas Frontier* (New York: Wiley, 2000).

58. Quoted in Evans, *Sherman's Horsemen,* 50.

59. Ford, *A Cycle of Adams Letters,* 2:8.

60. Albinus Fell to Dear Lydia, February 10, 1863, Civil War Miscellaneous Collection, USAMHI.

61. George Gordon Meade, *The Life and Letters of George Gordon Meade,* ed. George Gordon Meade, 2 vols. (New York: Charles Scribner's Sons, 1913), 1: 354.

62. O.R., vol. 25, part 2, 71–72.

63. Warner, *Generals in Blue,* 373.

64. P. J. Staudenraus, ed., *Mr. Lincoln's Washington: Selections from the Writings of Noah Brooks, Civil War Correspondent* (South Brunswick, N. J.: Thomas Yoseloff, 1976), 210.

65. Jeffry D. Wert, *Custer: The Controversial Life of George Armstrong Custer* (New York: Simon & Schuster, 1996), 75.

66. Ford, *A Cycle of Adams Letters,* 2:8.

67. Allan L. Tischler, *The History of the Harpers Ferry Cavalry Expedition, September 14 & 15, 1862* (Winchester, Va.: Five Cedars Press, 1993), 26. The West Point class of 1854 also included Generals O. O. Howard and John Pegram. *New York Herald,* June 11, 1863.

68. Dan L. Thrapp, *Encyclopedia of Frontier Biography,* 3 vols. (Lincoln: University of Nebraska Press, 1991), 1: 379.

69. O.R., vol. 11, part 1, 425–32. Davis was recommended for a brevet to lieutenant colonel in the Regular Army for this action, but the Senate never confirmed the brevet. *New York Herald,* June 11, 1863.

70. *Rochester Daily Union and Advertiser,* June 20, 1863.

71. Merritt, "Personal Recollections," 285–86.

72. For the only detailed treatment of this adventure, see Tischler, *History of the Harpers Ferry Cavalry Expedition.*

73. Henry Norton, *Deeds of Daring: or History of the Eighth New York Volunteer Cavalry* (Norwich, N.Y.: Chenango Telegraph Printing House, 1889), 30–33.

74. Wert, *Custer,* 78.

75. Elias W. Beck, M.D., "Letters of a Civil War Surgeon," *Indiana Magazine of History* (June 1931): 154.

76. Samuel J. B. V. Gilpin diary, entry for June 9, 1863, Gilpin Papers, Manuscripts Division, Library of Congress, Washington, D.C.

77. Warner, *Generals in Blue,* 124. That promotion did not come until the spring of 1865, and was long overdue when it finally happened.

78. Henry Edwin Tremain, *The Last Hours of Sheridan's Cavalry* (New York: Bonnell, Silver & Bowers, 1904), 37.

79. Edward G. Longacre, *The Cavalry at Gettysburg: A Tactical Study of Mounted Operations during the Civil War's Pivotal Campaign, 9 June–14 July 1863* (Rutherford, N.J.: Fairleigh-Dickinson University Press, 1986), 51.

80. Newhall, *With General Sheridan,* 228.

81. Warner, *Generals in Blue,* 124.

82. Tremain, *Last Hours of Sheridan's Cavalry,* 39.

83. Francis Smith Reader, *History of the Fifth West Virginia Cavalry, Formerly the Second Virginia, and Battery G First West Virginia Light Artillery* (New Brighton, Pa.: Daily News, 1890), 197.

84. Warner, *Generals in Blue,* 12–13.

85. Eckert and Amato, *Ten Years in the Saddle,* 388.

86. Darrell L. Collins, *General William Averell's Salem Raid* (Shippensburg, Pa.: Burd Street Press, 1998), 9.

87. Ibid., 5.

88. His father, Jean August Duffié, served as mayor of the village of La Ferte sous Juarre. At least one contemporary source states that the Duffié family had its roots in Ireland, and that the family fled to France to escape Oliver Cromwell's Reign of Terror. See Charles Fitz Simmons, "Hunter's Raid," *Military Essays and Recollections, Papers Read Before the Commandery of the State of Illinois Military Order of the Loyal Legion of the United States* 4 (Chicago: 1907), 395–96.

89. Napoléon Alexandre Duffié Military Service Records, French Army Archives, Vincennes, France. The author is grateful to Jean-Claude Reuflet, a relative of Duffié's, for making these obscure records available and for providing the author with a detailed translation of their contents.

90. Ibid.

91. Jeremiah M. Pelton, *Genealogy of the Pelton Family in America* (Albany, N.Y.: Joel Munsell's Sons, 1892), 565. The true state of the facts differs dramatically from the conventional telling of Duffié's life, as set forth in Warner's *Generals in Blue.*

92. Warner, *Generals in Blue,* 131–32.

93. A document prepared by Duffié's son indicates that Duffié attended the cadet school at Versailles, that he took and passed the entrance examinations for the military college of St. Cyr, and that he was admitted to St. Cyr in 1851. Daniel A. Duffié claimed that his father dropped out of St. Cyr after a year to enlist in the 6th Regiment of Dragoons. Procuration executed by Daniel A. Duffié, heir of Jean August Duffié, March 16, 1885, Pelton-Duffié Family Papers, Staten Island Historical Society, New York, N.Y.

94. For an example of the elaborate ruse spun by Duffié, George N. Bliss, "Duffié and the Monument to His Memory," *Personal Narratives of Events in the War of the Rebellion, Being Papers Read Before the Rhode Island Soldiers and Sailors Historical Society* 6 (Providence: Rhode Island Soldiers and Sailors Historical Society, 1890), 316–376. Bliss presents a detailed biographical sketch of Duffié that includes all of the falsehoods. Duffié himself apparently provided Bliss with most of his information. See pages 317–20 for the recitation of this litany of falsehoods.

95. James E. Taylor, *The James E. Taylor Sketchbook* (Dayton, Ohio: Morningside, 1989), 134.

96. Gregory J. W. Urwin, *The United States Cavalry: An Illustrated History* (Poole, Dorset: Blandford Press, 1983), 98–99.

97. Benjamin W. Crowninshield, *A History of the First Regiment Massachusetts Cavalry Volunteers* (Boston: Houghton-Mifflin, 1891), 113.

98. William H. Beach, *The First New York (Lincoln) Cavalry from April 19, 1861, to July 7, 1865* (New York: Lincoln Cavalry Association, 1902), 399.

99. Fell to Dear Lydia, March 8, 1863.

100. Emmons D. Guild to his parents, March 20, 1863, Fredericksburg and Spotsylvania National Military Park Archives, Fredericksburg, Va. (FSNMP).

101. Jacob B. Cooke, "The Battle of Kelly's Ford, March 17, 1863," *Personal Narratives of Events in the War of the Rebellion, Being Papers Read Before the Rhode Island Soldiers and*

Sailors Historical Society 4 (Providence: Rhode Island Soldiers and Sailors Historical Society, 1887), 9.

102. Roger D. Hunt and Jack R. Brown, *Brevet Brigadier Generals in Blue* (Gaithersburg, Md.: Olde Soldier Books, 1997), 534; Crowninshield, *First Regiment of Massachusetts Cavalry*, 42.

103. Warner, *Generals in Blue,* 300.

104. Mark M. Boatner III, *Civil War Dictionary* (New York: David McKay, 1959), 534.

105. Robert F. O'Neill, Jr., *The Cavalry Battles of Aldie, Middleburg, and Upperville: Small But Important Riots, June 10–27, 1863* (Lynchburg, Va.: H. E. Howard, 1993), 36.

106. Crowninshield, *First Regiment of Massachusetts Cavalry*, 307–308. In fact, John Buford despised this regiment. He believed they had failed him at Second Manassas, and he would take away their regimental colors in the fall of 1863 as a result of another perceived failure.

107. An interesting and detailed account of this episode can be found in Elizabeth McFadden, *The Glitter and the Gold: A Spirited Account of the Metropolitan Museum of Art's First Director, the Audacious and High-Handed Luigi Palma di Cesnola* (New York: Dial Press, 1971), 40–44.

108. Warner, *Generals in Blue,* 187–88.

109. "David McMurtrie Gregg," Circular no. 6, series of 1917, Military Order of the Loyal Legion of the United States, Commandery of Pennsylvania, May 3, 1917, p. 2.

110. Samuel P. Bates, *Martial Deeds of Pennsylvania* (Philadelphia: T. H. Davis, 1875), 772. There is no satisfactory biography of David M. Gregg available. The only published biography is Milton V. Burgess, *David Gregg: Pennsylvania Cavalryman* (privately published, 1984).

111. Hampton S. Thomas, *Some Personal Reminiscences of Service in the Cavalry of the Army of the Potomac* (Philadelphia: L. R. Hamersly, 1889), 8.

112. Samuel J. Martin, *"Kill-Cavalry": Sherman's Merchant of Terror—The Life of Union General Hugh Judson Kilpatrick* (Madison, N.J.: Fairleigh-Dickinson University Press, 1996), 1–63.

113. Edward G. Longacre, "Judson Kilpatrick," *Civil War Times Illustrated* 10 (April 1971): 25.

114. Ford, *A Cycle of Adams Letters,* 2:44–45.

115. Longacre, "Judson Kilpatrick," 25.

116. Percy Wyndham, "The Wyndham Question Settled," *New York Herald,* September 16, 1863. Wyndham referred to himself as a mercenary, writing in the fall of 1863, "Call me a soldier of fortune, if you will." Ibid.

117. James H. Kidd, *Personal Recollections of a Cavalryman in Custer's Michigan Brigade* (Ionia, Mich.: Sentinel, 1908), 90–91.

118. Edward G. Longacre, "Sir Percy Wyndham," *Civil War Times Illustrated* 8 (December 1968): 12, 14.

119. Samuel Harris, *The Personal Reminiscences of Samuel Harris* (Detroit: Robinson Press, 1897), 14.

120. Walter S. Newhall to My Dear George, October 2, 1863, Newhall Family Papers, Historical Society of Pennsylvania, Philadelphia.

121. John Gibbon, "The John Buford Memoir," copy in the author's collection.
122. Ibid.
123. Warner, *Generals in Blue,* 52–53.
124. John Buford to George Stoneman, February 9, 1863, Letters Sent and Received, First Cavalry Division, Army of the Potomac, National Archives, Washington, D.C.
125. Lt. Frank W. Dickerson to Dear Father, February 17, 1863, Civil War Miscellaneous Collection, USAMHI.
126. Hall, *History of the Sixth New York,* 92.
127. O.R., vol. 25, part 2, 71.
128. Ibid., 93.
129. Bliss, "Duffié and the Monument to His Memory," 13–15.
130. George N. Bliss, "Reminiscences of Service in the First Rhode Island Cavalry," *Personal Narratives of Events in the War of the Rebellion* 1 (Providence: Rhode Island Soldiers and Sailors Historical Society, 1878), 64.
131. Fell to Dear Lydia, March 8, 1863.
132. Wells A. Bushnell diary, February 28, 1863, Western Reserve Historical Society, Cleveland, Ohio.
133. Bliss, "Reminiscences of Service," 64–65.
134. George Washington Cullum, *Biographical Register of the Officers and Graduates of the United States Military Academy at West Point, New York, From Its Establishment in 1802, to 1890, with the Early History of the United States Military Academy,* 3d ed., 3 vols. (New York: Houghton-Mifflin, 1891), 2:29.
135. Beardsley's service records, RG 94, National Archives, Washington, D.C.; see also Frederick Pfisterer, *New York in the War of the Rebellion 1861–1865,* 2 vols. (Albany: J. B. Lyon, State Printers, 1912), 2:905.
136. O.R., vol. 12, part 2, 272.
137. Beardsley service records.
138. Ibid.
139. Ibid.
140. Ibid.
141. Ibid.
142. Ibid. Even more remarkable than the events surrounding Beardsley's resignation are the efforts made by many different people to sweep these ugly incidents under the rug. Instead of elaborating on the reasons why Beardsley left the service, the regimental history of the 9th New York states only, "March 9 . . . Col. Beardsley . . . rejoined the regiment. . . . June 4, Lieut. Col. Sackett returned from Washington with a Colonel's commission for himself and a Lieut. Colonel's commission for Maj. Nichols. Col. Beardsley had resigned." There were no other references to Beardsley in the balance of the 9th New York's fine regimental history. An obituary of Beardsley that appeared in a West Point alumni publication simply stated, "Immediately after [Second Bull Run], he came back to the Regiment and assumed command and remained with it until he resigned his commission at Acquier[sic] Creek, on the Potomac, April 8, 1863." It also said, "Colonel Beardsley was highly respected by all who knew him for his excellent

qualities of mind and heart." The cover-up of the circumstances of Beardsley's resignation from command of the 9th New York Cavalry was complete. Cheney, *History of the Ninth New York Cavalry,* 80 and 93.

143. Merrill, *Campaigns of the First Maine,* 88.

144. Frederic Dennison, *Sabres and Spurs: The First Regiment Rhode Island Cavalry in the Civil War, 1861–1865* (Central Falls, R.I.: First Rhode Island Cavalry Veteran Assoc., 1876), 206.

145. Quoted in Regis de Trobriand, *Four Years with the Army of the Potomac* (Boston: Ticknor, 1889), 415–16.

146. Henry R. Pyne, *The History of the First New Jersey Cavalry* (Trenton, N.J.: J. A. Beecher, 1871), 137–38.

147. Bliss to Dear Gerald, February 13, 1863.

148. Stoneman to McClellan, as reported in *New York Daily Tribune,* March 20, 1863.

149. Merritt, "Personal Recollections," 285.

2

A RESTLESS WINTER:
THE BATTLE OF HARTWOOD CHURCH

The men of the Cavalry Corps did not idle the winter of 1862–63 away with drilling and book learning. Consistent with Hooker's more aggressive approach, the men regularly took the field, raiding and picketing. They spent the winter balancing training and education with hard and active service. The men typically spent ten days out on the picket line and then the next ten days in camp. "It is rather tough, but I guess we can stand it," observed a member of the 1st Pennsylvania Cavalry.[1] A member of the 16th Pennsylvania Cavalry echoed a similar note. "I like soldiering very well yet it is hard," recounted Sgt. Henry W. Owen. "We are exposed to all kinds of weather, to all climates, are called up at all times of night and some times in case of a raid, we march all day and stand by or sit on our horses all night or nights as the case may be."[2] The Yankee horsemen picketed the Rappahannock River from Falmouth to Hartwood Church in Stafford County. They also patrolled the countryside, picketed both flanks from Fredericksburg to Hartwood Church, and guarded the Richmond, Fredericksburg and Potomac Railroad (RF&P) to Aquia Landing. Averell's division picketed along the RF&P near Potomac Creek, Gregg's division handled the left near Belle Plain, and Pleasonton's division remained flexible, filling in where needed.

Hartwood Church marked the far right flank of the Army of the Potomac's position. Located about four miles north of the Rappahannock River and eight miles west of Falmouth, the church sat at the junction of the Warrenton, or Telegraph Road, and the Ridge Road, and provided a conspicuous landmark in the densely wooded countryside. In 1825, the Winchester Presbytery organized the Yellow Chapel Church in Hartwood, using a small eighteenth-century frame structure

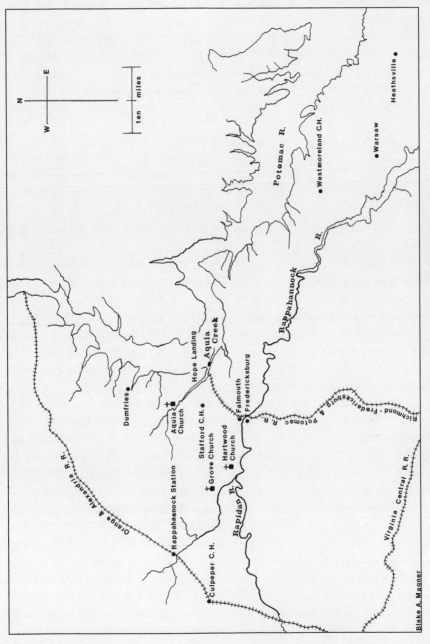

Theater of Operations, February–March 1863

ten miles

N
W   E
S

Heathsville

Potomac R.

Westmoreland C.H.

Warsaw

Rappahannock R.

Dumfries

Hope Landing

Aquia Creek

Aquia Church

Stafford C.H.

Grove Church

Hartwood Church

Falmouth

Fredericksburg

Richmond–Fredericksburg & Potomac R.R.

Orange & Alexandria R.R.

Rappahannock Station

Culpeper C.H.

Rapidan R.

Virginia Central R.R.

Blake A. Magner

that had been an Anglican chapel. In 1858, at the cost of $2,000, a handsome red brick sanctuary was built and renamed Hartwood Church. Both sides, drawn by its location on commanding high ground, had used its grounds for camps, and most of the interior woodwork of the church had been used for firewood during the bitter Virginia winters, leaving the sanctuary barren, and leaving the church useless for worship during the war.[3] The church sat on a divide between streams running south into the Rappahannock River and east into the Potomac River. In the winter of 1862–63, Union outposts dotted the area, and both infantrymen and horse soldiers occupied the church grounds.

The Federal picket lines in the vicinity of Hartwood Church covered nearly eight miles along the north bank of the Rappahannock. Northern saddle soldiers manned the area heavily, spending several days on duty for every day in camp. An officer of the 4th Pennsylvania Cavalry, whose company pulled regular picket duty at Hartwood Church, noted that his unit "had to scout the country in the vicinity of our forces, in order to guard against raids and surprises by any large body of the enemy."[4]

Picket duty was miserable, numbing work that required the men to remain mounted in the face of howling winds and stinging precipitation. When not on actual picket duty, the men had to remain ready to mount up and move at a moment's notice. They were not permitted to sleep while on picket.[5] The line ran along the banks of the Rappahannock, crossing the Northern Neck and running past Hartwood Church. The picketing at the ends of the line tended to be more arduous, because the vedettes were often exposed to guerrilla attacks or raids by roving bands of Southern cavalry.

Sgt. Nathan Webb of the 1st Maine Cavalry reflected the misery of picketing in his diary. After a heavy storm of snow and sleet in January 1863, Webb observed, "The snow was blowing, the wind howling, and we were all hovering over our little fires and not in a very admiring mood of Army life. We failed to see the romance of it, and thought it tough amusement, 'this camping on old Virginia's soil beneath the good skies and under the rustling trees, etc.'" The freezing, miserable Yankees longed for warm meals and cozy family hearths.[6]

The enterprising pickets fraternized with their counterparts on the opposite banks of the river. "The rebs on the opposite bank are shivering around their picket fires peaceably disposed fellows they are and very talkative," noted a Hoosier horse soldier.[7] An informal cartel developed wherein the pickets traded coffee for tobacco and sent newspapers back and forth. Men floated little rafts across the river to facilitate their illegal trading. Good-natured taunts flew across the water along with the goods being bartered. "Picketing in good weather was real pleasure during this state of affairs," observed the regimental historian of the 1st Maine Cavalry, "but matters got to such a pass that it was found necessary to order all communication between the pickets stopped. This order was pretty well obeyed, but occasionally the temptation was too strong to be resisted, and trade was carried on in a small way on the sly."[8] An officer of the 2d New York Cavalry recalled, "Squads of soldiers from both armies may be observed seated together on either side of Rappahannock earnestly discussing the great questions of the day. . . . During these interviews, trading was the order of the day. . . . There was . . . a special demand of the Rebels for pocket knives and canteens."[9]

However, as an officer of the 1st Rhode Island Cavalry pointed out, "Our pickets are the eyes of the army," he wrote. "If they sleep, or are negligent of duty, the whole army is in danger. The neglect of a single duty on picket is liable to the severest punishment. The officers in command of the pickets hold most important and responsible positions, having, as it were, the keys to the gates which separate the two contending armies."

Each brigade patrolled a specific section of the picket line with proportional guard details selected from each regiment of the brigade. These details were divided into small bodies for reliefs and reserves. The reserves typically established their headquarters deep in the nearby woods, hollows, or other concealed places, "where fires are allowed, the men remaining dismounted with the privilege of keeping themselves as comfortable as possible, but always keeping themselves girded for an attack. The horses are kept saddled and bridled, hitched to the nearest trees, that the men may instantly spring to the defensive should the men on their posts give an alarm, or be driven in."

Where a regiment had three battalions, one stood picket and one remained in reserve each day of their three-day tours of duty. They would stand picket, on horseback, with their horses' heads facing in the direction of the enemy, with carbine advanced, for two to four hours at a time, until the corporal of the guard relieved them. They stayed vigilant, their revolvers and carbines at hand and ready to be fired instantly. Pickets challenged anyone approaching their positions, and they raised the alarm by firing if the right countersign was not given. Officers regularly visited the picket posts to inspect and encourage them, and to make certain that all was well along the line. Once relieved, they could then eat and rest, often by a fire, but could not remove their side arms. "Everything is so systematically arranged that, in case of an attack, we could give the rebels a warm reception, holding any force at bay until we could be reinforced from the main army."[10] Picketing, while tedious, was not easy duty in the frigid Virginia winter.

On February 5, a detachment of Duffié's brigade of Averell's division marched up the north bank of the Rappahannock River to burn an important railroad bridge at Rappahannock Station, thirty miles above Falmouth. Maj. Samuel E. Chamberlain of the 1st Massachusetts Cavalry commanded the expedition. The bridge that carried the Orange & Alexandria Railroad across the river had recently been rebuilt by the Confederates, and was a strategic position. A strong detachment of Confederates guarded the sturdy wooden trestle. The Yankee raiders contended with terrible roads made into sheets of ice by the combination of snow and freezing rain. They carried three days' worth of rations for the men and one day of forage for their horses. On the first night, the Federals camped in a pine grove near Grove Church. They built rail fence fires to cook their dinners and had a pleasant evening until the snow turned to rain. After putting out pickets, "we stood around our fires or sat, making ourselves as comfortable as circumstances would permit. I slept none that night, but ate considerable, the long and tedious march giving us good appetites," reported bugler Henry T. Bartlett of the 1st Massachusetts Cavalry.[11]

The next morning, the Federals called in their soggy pickets and resumed the march. That afternoon, the dim winter sun broke through for a few hours of blessed relief. "We continued our course through the woods & valley and across runs of water where your feet would be covered by water if they remained in the stirrups." At midnight, they halted in a thick wood about a mile from the bridge and established a bivouac. No fires were allowed, and the men stood ankle deep in frigid slush until 4:00, when they finally received permission to lay down. The soaked horse soldiers shivered under their blankets, trying to fend off the winter chill that permeated their bones.[12]

While most of his command struggled to stay warm, Chamberlain detailed men with axes and carbines to approach the bridge. "Not three strokes of axe was given, when the sentry at the other end of the bridge fired into the workmen and alarmed the village and troops encamped near there." The alarm spread quickly, and the surprised Rebels scrambled to respond. "Our batteries were planted on the brow of the hill by the light of the moon and the firing of the Rebs, our men kept on working disregarding the shot which came thick & fast around them and did not leave until they had accomplished their object of making the railroad bridge one of destruction, another party tore up the track for some distance and tore down the wires and poles of their telegraph for some three miles."[13]

Amazingly, the roads had deteriorated further, making the return march even more arduous. "The water in the holes and ruts was frozen up, so as to make it very slippery along like a boy trying to use a pair of stilts on ice." Bartlett's horse fell twice, causing the bugler to crash to the icy ground in an undignified heap. Major Chamberlain allowed his column to stop and build fires to warm themselves a bit, and the march resumed the next morning, with the weary horsemen arriving back at camp that afternoon.[14] "Splendid affair, I assure you the 'Rebs' were so mad about it . . . the enemy would fire at our men," recounted Captain Walter S. Newhall of the 3d Pennsylvania Cavalry.[15] The Northern horse soldiers returned after taking only two casualties in a severe firefight and a long march through terrible conditions.[16] "I got in night before last from a 3 days scout and a more uncomfortable 3 days and nights I never passed," reported Cpl. John B. Weston of the 1st Massachusetts. "I was in the saddle 20 hours out of 24."[17]

The combination of picketing, reconnaissances, and raids took their toll on men and animals. "Our regiment has been worked very hard all winter doing picket duty and our horses are in poor condition," recounted Captain Bliss, "but we now have plenty of forage and hope soon to have less work so that we can get up our war horses a little."[18] "The infantry lose more men by the casualties of battle, but the cavalry nearly make it up in excessive duty and exposure," observed an officer of the 1st Pennsylvania Cavalry.[19]

Horses, for all of their size and strength, are fragile beasts. They require a great deal of care and constant attention. They also suffered in the winter cold, perhaps more than the men. "I . . . dare not go and look at my horses," observed Captain Adams in late January. "I know just how they look, as they huddle together at the picket-ropes and turn their shivering croups to this pelting northeaster. There they stand without shelter, fetlock deep in slush and mud, without a blanket among them, and there they must stand—poor beasts—and all I can do for them is to give them all the food I can, and that little enough. Of oats there is a sufficiency and the horses have twelve quarts a day; but hay is scant, and it is only by luck that we have a few bales just now when we most need them." Adams fed his animals four times per day, "and if they have enough to eat, they do wonderfully well, but it comes hard on them to have to sustain hunger, as well as cold and wet. It is all over, however, with any horse that begins to fail, for after a few days, he either dies at the rope, or else glanders set in and he is led out and shot. I lose in this way two or three horses a week."[20] Sgt. Nathan Webb of the 1st Maine Cavalry noted that the morning after a heavy January snowstorm, "the horses have icicles pending from and snow frozen over them. I took pains last night to cover up Hal with one of my blankets and he is not now shivering like most of the others."[21]

"We are still living in our shelter tents, or I might rather say—we live out doors and sleep in our tents for they are not large enough to live in," observed Capt. Delos Northway of the 6th Ohio Cavalry. "They are just high enough so that we can creep in and sit up, that is if we sit on the ground. But they are famous things to sleep under for at night we can be snug as kittens." Northway noted that his regiment had occupied its winter camp at Dumfries for nearly a month. "When we came, we were informed that it was only for temporary duty and so we left baggage and everything else nearly, at Stafford," he noted. After four weeks of hard duty, he and his men grew ragged, as they had only the clothes on their backs. "Mort hasn't changed his clothes for four weeks," he sniffed, "and my pants could be very fitly described by the military command 'To the rear open door.'" In spite of the adverse circumstances, Northway and his command vowed to make the best

of the situation. "We live well, have plenty of soft bread, coffee, pork, beans, pota-
toes, molasses, sugar, can buy fresh oysters for seventy five cents per bushel and on
the whole have lots of things for which to be thankful."[22]

Sgt. William H. Redman of the 12th Illinois Cavalry echoed a similar note. "We
have our tent fixed quite comfortable to live," he reported to his sisters. "We have
a nice fire place to cook by and we have raised our tent about three feet so that
we have plenty of room. We call the whole arrangement 'our shebang.' You would
laugh to see how we live," he concluded.[23]

On February 17, an expedition to break up smuggling on the peninsula between
the Rappahannock and Potomac Rivers set off. The expedition consisted of two
squadrons of the 8th New York Cavalry and of the 2d Wisconsin Infantry. Capt.
Craig Wadsworth, of Maj. Gen. John F. Reynolds's staff, led this expedition. The
New York horsemen visited Westmoreland Court House, Warsaw, Union, the
Hague, and Heathsville, and covered nearly 150 miles in five days, bringing back
twelve prisoners, including a Confederate signal officer, a lieutenant, several smug-
glers, a quantity of contraband goods, four Rebel mails, and a large quantity of
bacon. The raiders also destroyed "a large quantity of whiskey intended for rebel
consumption."[24]

The Northern horse soldiers left a swath of destruction in their wake. The 9th
New York camped near Aquia Church. The church dated to 1751, and had survived the Revolutionary War. It was a handsome place, built in the shape of a cross.
"The walls are badly defaced by soldiers, as everyone seems to think that it is necessary to write his name wherever there is a good place for it. The floor which is
stone has also been torn up in several places, and even those which mark the resting place of the dead are not left undisturbed," observed a member of the 9th New
York in February. "It is a sad sight to see the desolation which marks the track of
the Union army," he continued. "Nothing escapes where the men are allowed to
roam around unchecked. The finest houses are soon reduced to a pile of ruins and
as for fences they disappear as if by magic as soon as a lot of soldiers camp near
them."[25]

On February 21, three squadrons of the 8th New York Cavalry went out on
picket duty near Dumfries. They occupied a desolate stand of scrub oak and pine
trees that offered little shelter from the bitter cold. It snowed all night and most of
the next day, accumulating nearly an additional foot of fresh snow. "If a horse
moved two feet to the right or left, he would go in so deep that it was impossible
to save him from strangling," recorded Pvt. Jasper Cheney in his diary.[26] Several men
had their boots freeze to their feet, meaning that they had to be cut away in order
to remove them. Henry Norton recalled, "It was so cold one night when I was on
picket, that I got off from my horse and walked around to keep my feet from freezing." Norton had received orders not to dismount, but he "thought if the rebels had

as hard a time to keep warm as I did, they would not trouble us any." The men lit a bonfire and piled up fence rails "to keep us out of the snow, and we would roast one side a while, and then turn around and warm the other side."

As long as it stayed bitter cold, Norton was right. However, once it thawed out a bit a few days later, the Confederates grew bolder. Angry locals, dubbed "bushwhackers" by the Northerners, "would steal up in the daytime and shoot men at their posts." A number of men were killed and wounded that way, and the activities of the guerrillas and bushwhackers gave the Confederate high command an accurate picture of the dispositions of the Army of the Potomac. They targeted the members of the 8th New York's three newest companies and captured quite a few of them, gaining all sorts of valuable intelligence from their new prisoners.[27]

Samuel M. Potter of the 16th Pennsylvania Cavalry spent an enjoyable day on February 21, visiting a friendly family near Fredericksburg. He and his companions spotted activity on the south side of the Rappahannock. "After staying there a short time to get a spyglass we went down to Fredericksburg," recounted Potter in a letter to his wife. "We got on the river bank opposite the city & could see them playing ball. Could hear them laughing & talking & we saw a number who had blue overcoats on which they took off our dead soldiers." Potter's host pointed out the killing fields in front of Marye's Heights, chilling the inexperienced Pennsylvania soldier.[28]

On February 22, the Army of the Potomac celebrated George Washington's birthday with a booming 100-gun artillery salute.[29] A heavy snowstorm accompanied by a furious northeast wind amplified the booms of the celebration. Eight inches of fresh snow fell. "Jolly old times in camp this morning," reported Pvt. Albinus Fell of the 6th Ohio Cavalry, "Our tent was drifted over with snow inside and out. Some of the boys could not get out of their tents until the snow was going away. The boys had to halloo as they hunt around in the snow for wood."[30] Thomas Covert, also of the 6th Ohio, noted, "We had orders to move at eight o'clock this morning but it commenced to snow in the night and the snow was about six inches deep this morning and asnowing like the deuce and has snowed all day, and the snow is over a foot deep now, and it is about noon now. We cant move today. If we did we would all freeze to death."[31]

Other Yankee horsemen waxed philosophic that day. The men of the 3d Indiana Cavalry picketed around Washington's boyhood home on the Rappahannock east of Fredericksburg. As they huddled for warmth, talk turned to the brutal winter of 1776 and the ordeal of Valley Forge. "This is Washington's birthday—and all about the old homestead and above his mother's grave, the cannon of his contending sons are celebrating its return! Nonsense. Mockery!" proclaimed Samuel Gilpin in his diary. "If the father was a great and good man, let the sons be ashamed of themselves and go home," he concluded.[32]

Brig. Gen. William Woods Averell did not feel well on Washington's birthday. He suffered from chronic dysentery, which sapped his strength. He spent a quiet day studying Stoneman's orders for the formation of the Cavalry Corps, trying to find shelter from the howling storm in a smoky tent. The decision to divide his brigade in two and form a division from it surprised Averell.[33]

Company I of the 6th New York, as well as all of the 8th Pennsylvania, drew picket duty that day. The freezing soldiers slogged through the miserable conditions for fifteen miles, establishing their picket line along Cannon's Run, near Ebenezer Church. "The suffering and hardship of that march, and later on, the exposure and inactivity while on the lonely picket-post, were such that none but an experienced soldier can fully understand," observed a New Yorker.[34] Colonel Devin, commander of the brigade, used this expedition to identify a suitable site for a bridge over Aquia Creek a mile or so beyond Ebenezer Church.[35]

The Regulars stood picket duty just like their brethren in the volunteer units. Company F of the 6th U.S. Cavalry picketed along the lower Rappahannock just across the river from the camps of Lt. Gen. Thomas J. "Stonewall" Jackson's infantry corps. Men stood picket duty for four hours at a time, and it usually took up to two hours to get to and from picket posts, meaning that the men had only two hours to rest, "if such a thing as sleep were possible under the circumstances." Although they tried to cover themselves with brush, the Regulars suffered along with their volunteer brethren.[36]

The next day, General Averell learned that the enemy had fired on his pickets near Hartwood Church, and the uneasy division commander prepared to act. On the morning of February 24, word of an impending attack upon his pickets reached the New Yorker. Averell's vedettes spotted a squadron of Confederate cavalry lurking about Hartwood Church and reported their findings.[37] Robert E. Lee wanted to know what Hooker's intentions were, and the only way to find out was to penetrate the Army of the Potomac's picket lines with a force of cavalry.[38]

On February 23, Stuart ordered Brig. Gen. Fitzhugh Lee, Averell's old friend, to reconnoiter the Union picket lines at Hartwood Church.[39] "We all loved Fitz Lee," recalled a Southern officer. "His bright, sunny disposition made things happy and pleasant for all who were attached to his headquarters. Fond of fun, yet there was no one who commanded more respect when on duty or whose able services were more pronounced on the field."[40] Thomas L. Rosser sounded a similar note. He described Lee as "brave, buoyant and jolly." His men happily followed Fitz Lee as he set off to make some mischief for his old chum. Fitz's well-known sense of humor played a significant role in the foray he was assigned to lead.[41]

On the morning of the 24th, Lee led 400 selected men of his brigade across the icy waters of the Rappahannock at Kelly's Ford. His command included detachments of the 1st, 2d, and 3d Virginia Cavalry. Recent rains swelled the Rappahannock, and it had snowed heavily just two days earlier. The Confederate horse soldiers contended with mud, rain, and terrible roads in making the march, no small feat in the brutal Virginia winter. "On account of 18 inches of snow roads were miserable and almost impassable," noted Lt. Col. William R. Carter of the 3d Virginia Cavalry in his diary.[42] Carter's adjutant described this journey as "one little expedition which I had like to have forgotten."[43] Lee's little force spent the night of February 24 near Morrisville, a small settlement about five miles from the Ford.[44]

The Federal right flank bent back from the Rappahannock, stretching to the north. The cavalry picket line ran about four miles to the west of an infantry picket line and passed through the intersection at Hartwood Church. The Telegraph Road and the Ridge Road extended to the east of the church, running parallel between one-half and two miles apart, the Ridge Road running north of the Telegraph Road. The infantry picket line crossed these two roads about four miles east of Hartwood Church, in the direction of Falmouth. Since the formation of the Cavalry Corps in January, the Northern cavalry had done a good job of protecting the infantry picket lines and keeping Southern probes from finding that line. Because of his uncertainty about the precise whereabouts of the Army of the Potomac's picket line, Robert E. Lee decided to send a mounted force to try to pierce the cavalry screen and see whether the Army of the Potomac's infantry remained in force in the area around Falmouth.

On the morning of February 25, Fitz Lee moved out again and advanced on the Federal pickets near Hartwood Church, the 1st and 3d Virginia Cavalry leading the way. The Confederates stole up on a group of green pickets of the 16th Pennsylvania Cavalry. Wearing blue Union army overcoats, three Rebels approached a picket post manned by the inexperienced Pennsylvanians. A corporal halted them, but allowed them to pass after only a moment's delay. The three Southerners passed the picket post, abruptly wheeled, ordered the pickets to dismount, and took the unfortunate greenhorns prisoner.[45] A number of Pennsylvanians retreated in the face of the Southern onslaught and were captured. James Roney, a trooper of the 16th Pennsylvania, was "retreating as fast as he could with the rebs close behind when his horse stumbled & threw James & he is a prisoner too."[46] The enemy soon appeared in force, and the situation appeared increasingly desperate.

At about 2:00 in the afternoon, the grayclad horsemen drove in the Federal pickets of the 3d and 16th Pennsylvania near Hartwood Church. Lee split his column, sending it east on both the Telegraph and Ridge Roads. After piercing the main picket line, Lee attacked the picket reserve and main body, striking a sector manned by men of the 3d Pennsylvania Cavalry. "Just as they started, a small squadron of cavalry passed out by us on a dead run," recalled Charles H. Weygant of the 124th New York Infantry, whose regiment manned the infantry picket line several miles farther east. "Presently, they came dashing back, through a piece of woods just in front of us, in utter confusion. Several horses were riderless, and most of the riders hatless. The officers were waving their swords over their heads, vainly endeavoring to rally their men. Every few yards a horse would sink into the mud, and in plunging to extricate himself, would fall with his rider, and together they would wallow in the mire."

Capt. Charles Francis Adams, Jr., of the 1st Massachusetts Cavalry commanded part of the picket line that day. He and a small column of Federal troopers set out early that morning, riding west along the Ridge Road. "We looked on our business as a lark and rode leisurely along enjoying the fine day and taking our time." Just as Lee's troopers prepared to descend upon the Federal pickets, Adams, Maj. Oliver O. G. Robinson of the 3d Pennsylvania Cavalry, and Capt. Benjamin B. Blood of Company G of the 4th Pennsylvania Cavalry (whom Adams described as "a curious nondescript . . . made up of dullness and whiskey") entered the woods near the headquarters of the picket reserve. "Oh, there's a carbine shot," proclaimed one of the officers. A vedette challenged them, and Major Robinson rode forward to explain their business. More shots rang out, prompting Robinson to yell, "Hurry up, there's a fight going on," as he spurred off through the thick, knee-deep mud.

"Well, I can't hurry up in these roads, even if there is," responded Adams. He found a good reason to hurry, though. The rookies of the 16th Pennsylvania and the veterans of the 4th New York came flying back from the direction of Hartwood Church, with Fitz Lee's Confederates in hot pursuit. "Pell-mell, without order, without lead, a mass of panic-stricken men, riderless horses and miserable cowards, our picket reserve came driving down the road upon us in hopeless flight. Along they came, carrying helpless officers with them, throwing away arms and blankets, and in the distance we heard a few carbine shots and the unmistakable savage yell of the rebels." The officers drew their sabers and tried to block the flight of the fugitives—all from the green 16th Pennsylvania Cavalry. "Some only dashed past, but most obeyed us stupidly and I rode into the woods to try to form a line of skirmishers," recalled Adams.

As he tried to cobble together a line, the high-pitched Rebel yell sounded nearby. His line vaporized, leaving the disgusted captain alone. "The panic seized my horse and he set his jaw like iron against the bit and dashed off after the rest." The frantic animal dashed through the thick woods, knocking Adams's feet from his stirrups, smashing him against a tree, and sending his hat flying. "I clung to the saddle like a monkey, expecting every instant to be knocked out of it and to begin my travels to Richmond." A few hundred yards later, he got the frantic animal under control and found Robinson, who proclaimed, "My God, Adams! This is terrible! This is disgraceful!"

"Thank God," replied the battered captain, "I am the only man of my regiment here today."

"Well, you may," responded Robinson.[47]

The Confederates also attacked the position held by Capt. George N. Bliss's pickets. Bliss commanded a section of the 1st Rhode Island's picket line on the south side of the Telegraph Road. At about 1:00, Bliss heard the cheers of the advancing Rebels, and knew that they had cut him off from the main picket line. He had orders to fight his picket posts and not to abandon them, so he made dispositions to do just that, even though his exposed position made him nervous and uncomfortable. He formed his little command of twelve men in a single rank across the road at the top of a hill facing toward the rear and the sounds of the enemy war cries.

As the enemy appeared, one called out to Bliss, "What regiment is that?"

"Advance one," replied the captain.

"What regiment is that?" repeated the Rebel.

"What regiment is *that?*" countered Bliss.

"I ask *you* that question," came the response.

"Advance one," ordered Bliss.

"Are you rebels or Union?" inquired the confused Southerner.

"Union!" proclaimed Bliss with a shout. Stunned, the Confederates fell back, buying Bliss sufficient time to call in his pickets and order their withdrawal. The Confederates gobbled up some of the vedettes, but Bliss and most of the pickets escaped. He cobbled together a line of battle and repulsed two more Rebel forays before Lee broke off the engagement and withdrew. The next morning, Bliss learned that his little force of 12 men had stopped a Confederate column of 150 men, and that the officer in command had reported the road ahead impassable, as an entire regiment of Yankee horsemen held it.[48]

"Those of my men that were taken were on their posts and I know that they fought like the devil before they were taken," recounted Bliss. "I found two of my horses shot in the woods but so far as I know none of my men were killed, that is I could find no bodies so I consider them all prisoners." He concluded, "If I had hesitated the other day I should now be on my way to Richmond. As it was I turned back several hundred men with 12 and escaped."[49]

After pushing through Bliss's pickets, Lee's troopers encountered the Union picket reserve, commanded by Lt. Col. John L. Thompson of the 1st Rhode Island Cavalry. Fortunately, the pickets had just been relieved, and the men had not made their way back to the reserve post, meaning that twice the normal number of Union horse soldiers held the picket line when Lee's foray struck it. Thompson had 600 troopers, consisting of 200 men from the 16th Pennsylvania, and 100 men from each of the 3d and 4th Pennsylvania, 4th New York, and 1st Rhode Island. These 600 troopers had just relieved men under command of Lt. Col. Edward S. Jones of the 3d Pennsylvania Cavalry when the Confederates struck their position. Jones's horsemen heard the infantry picket firing near Hartwood Church and moved out to the west along the Telegraph Road to try to check the Confederate advance.

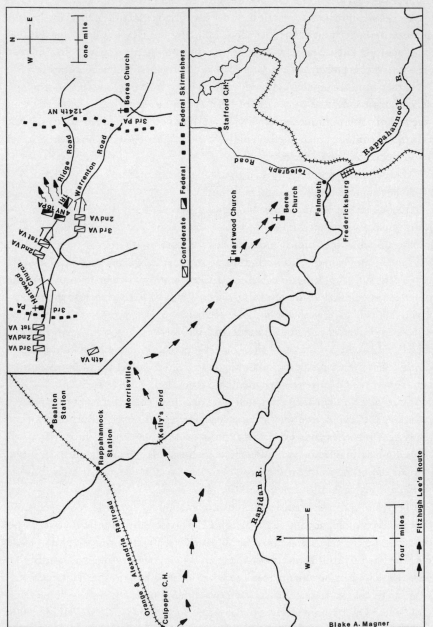

Fitzhugh Lee's Hartwood Church Raid, February 24, 1863

Blake A. Magner

Colonel Jones had ridden out to Hartwood Church to investigate the firing on the picket lines when an officer of the 16th Pennsylvania Cavalry hailed him. The frightened officer shouted that the Rebels were charging down the road. A bend in the road prevented Jones from seeing very far, "and in almost a moment a squad, filling the road and charging at full speed, commenced firing at me." Jones, alone, turned his horse and rode through swampy ground to make his escape, the bog slowing the pursuing enemy horsemen.[50]

Jones ordered his small force of 100 men to fall back slowly until he could find a better defensive position. These men fought hard, "with great gallantry and entirely checked the advance of the enemy, both flanks and threatened to their rear if they continued in that direction." Jones rallied his men, and instructed them to continue their fighting retreat. "As soon as our men turned the enemy charged and the retreat turned into a rout."

Major Robinson of the 3d Pennsylvania, the field officer of the day, arrived on the scene as Jones's command broke and ran, and, with assistance from Adams, "by almost superhuman efforts succeeded in halting and rallying some seventy-five men, whom he formed in line fronting the enemy, and delivered a terrible volley into them, checking their advance completely." The Confederates returned fire, and Major Robinson instructed Adams to bring up his little line of thirty rallied men.

"I clearly can't drive them," thought Adams, "perhaps they'll follow me." Adams spurred his horse forward and called, "Come on, follow me, there they are!" and pointed his sabre at the Confederates. His little column, instead of charging, melted away, to Adams's fury. "Then wrath seized my soul and I uttered a yell and chased them. I caught a helpless cuss and cut him over the head with my sabre. It only lent a new horror and fresh speed to his flight. I whanged another over the face and he tarried a while," recounted the furious captain. "Into a third I drove my horse and gave him pause, and then I swore and cursed them. I called them 'curs,' 'dogs,' and 'cowards,' a 'disgrace to the 16th Pennsylvania, as the 16th was a disgrace to the service,' and so I finally prevailed about half of my line to stop for this time."[51]

After consulting with Adams, Robinson ordered and led a sabre charge at the Wallace farm, known as Ellerslie, on the Ridge Road several miles to the east of Hartwood Church. Robinson had his horse shot out from under him, and his men retreated in confusion, trampling the major and bruising him badly. "He immediately got on his feet, and waving his saber rallied them, and mounting a riderless horse led them again in a charge on the enemy." The charge killed two Confederates and wounded four others. They captured Capt. John Alexander of the 2d Virginia Cavalry, and mortally wounded Lt. Edward W. Horner, capturing Horner and two privates.[52] The Pennsylvanians briefly pursued the fleeing Confederates, but soon called off the pursuit, content with their accomplishments.[53]

Adams found himself alone and isolated in the wake of the charge, his little command having retreated. He had dispatched Captain Blood and six of his men to the left, and the Pennsylvanians were captured.[54] A Southern trooper raised his carbine, drew a bead on Adams, and squeezed off a shot. "I had never had a bead drawn on me before and the sensation was now not disagreeable." As Adams rode off, he thought to himself, "You're mounted, I'm in motion, and the more you aim the less you'll hit." The ball whizzed harmlessly by and his antagonist spurred off. Adams soon saw troops moving, and was greatly relieved to find the men of the 1st Rhode Island advancing in line of battle.[55]

Thompson's Yankee horsemen formed line of battle, in the following order: 1st Rhode Island on the right, 4th Pennsylvania, 4th New York, and 16th Pennsylvania on the left. As they finished aligning, Lee's troopers fell upon them with loud Rebel yells, charging on the Telegraph Road. In response, Thompson wheeled five squadrons to face the Confederates. Two of the squadrons—from the 16th Pennsylvania Cavalry—had never been under fire before, and they quickly broke and ran. The other remaining squadrons soon followed suit in spite of Colonel Thompson's orders to draw sabers and charge.[56]

Capt. Edward N. Chase, who commanded a squadron of the 1st Rhode Island Cavalry, had moved to protect Thompson's rear with his own squadron and a squadron of the 16th Pennsylvania. He wheeled and led his little command over to the Ridge Road, not expecting to find a large force of Confederates charging toward him. To his surprise, Chase heard the clatter of cavalry horses to his rear, "and, to their great anger and mortification, in an instant almost, they were inextricably mixed up with the three retreating squadrons from Lieutenant-Colonel Thompson's line." Chase rallied the men and re-formed his line; Lieutenant Colonel Jones blunted Lee's advance on the Ridge Road, and the Federals began planning a counterattack.[57]

Chase's squadron, along with a squadron of the 4th New York, followed by the balance of the regiment, counterattacked, driving the grayclad horsemen back, exchanging fire the whole way. The Confederates made a stand at the slave cabins along Horsepen Creek on the William Irvine farm on the Telegraph Road about half a mile from Hartwood Church, and heavy skirmishing broke out again. Chase's squadron, weary of the annoying skirmish fire, "gave a cheer for a charge, and away they went for the enemy, and, in less time that it takes to describe the stroke, had possession of the buildings." A squadron of the enemy countercharged, putting Chase's squadron to flight. A heavy volley by the dismounted Federal carbineers blunted the Southern countercharge, which ran out of steam. Chase had his horse shot out from under him, and he was briefly taken prisoner. However, he "was released by reason of the persuasive arguments of a few bullets from his men, who came to the rescue."[58]

The Confederates fought as they retreated, leapfrogging regiments. One regiment made a stand while the others fell back and formed additional lines of battle behind it. The first regiment then pulled back, and so forth. As a result, "the skirmish extended over a good deal of ground," commented a Federal horseman.[59] Lt. Col. William R. Carter's Confederate 3d Virginia Cavalry made a stand and received orders to fall back and form behind the 1st Virginia's line of battle. Carter learned that a Yankee regiment occupied the nearby woods, and made his dispositions accordingly. He spotted an officer alongside the road, waving his handkerchief at the Virginian. "Learning from some stragglers that party probably belonged to the enemy & thinking it merely a ruse for the purpose of disentangling the men from the woods, I threw the Regiment 'left into line' to be ready to meet them in case they attempted to charge & advanced myself to meet the flag of truce," noted Carter in his diary, "whereupon [an officer] of the 3d Penn. Cavalry surrendered himself & no men to me." Another ten Federals also surrendered to the commander of the 1st Virginia. "This proved to be the party that was supposed to be a regiment of the enemy, & I immediately informed Gen. Lee to that effect."[60]

As the Federals advanced, Lee ordered Carter to countercharge. The heavy, wet snow made charging difficult, but the Virginians valiantly rolled forward, charging east along the Telegraph Road.[61] With the Rebel yell resonating, the 3d Virginia crashed into the advancing column, disregarding flanking fire as they bore down. "They continued to move on until we came in 30 yards of them, and then they broke & fled in perfect confusion," proudly noted Carter. "Pursued them ¼ of a mile, killing & capturing several, when thinking we had pursued as far as prudence would permit or was in accordance with the designs of Gen. Lee, we halted the column, formed it 'front into line' & immediately received orders to return to the edge of woods and form in line facing the enemy, which I did." Lee rode up and complimented the Virginians for their ferocious charge, "which compliment the men received with loud cheers."[62] Capt. Richard Watkins, who commanded Company K of the 3d Virginia, lost his horse in the charge. Watkins fell with the animal, and then the horse rose and dashed off toward the Union lines, leaving the bruised captain dismounted and alone.[63]

Early that bright, sunny winter morning, the men of the 124th New York Infantry of the Army of the Potomac's III Corps departed from their camps near Falmouth, headed for their familiar position on the picket lines four miles to the east of Hartwood Church. "It was quite muddy. The roads seemed to be breaking up, and occasionally as we marched along one of the men would step in a hole and sink down almost to his knees," recalled an officer of the 124th New York. When they arrived at Berea Church, four companies of New Yorkers moved toward the front lines to relieve the pickets. A rude surprise awaited them.[64]

Four miles to the east of Hartwood Church, Lt. Col. Francis M. Cummins of the

124th New York, who commanded the infantry picket line, rallied his men and ordered them to advance. They opened fire on a body of Southern cavalry in their front. "The rebels evidently did not expect to meet any considerable force of infantry, for the moment we appeared, they went fours about, and dashed off as wildly as our cavalry had come in."[65] Before long, an entire Union infantry brigade reinforced the picket lines.[66] "An order came for us to be ready to fall in line at a moment's notice as Stuart's cavalry made a raid into our picket lines and they had a very exciting time out there and were driven in," recalled a member of the 118th Pennsylvania Infantry.[67]

"The enemy did not succeed in accomplishing their designs, which were to capture our entire picket force around Hartwood," observed Capt. William Hyndman, commander of Company A of the 4th Pennsylvania. "The command deserved credit for their promptness in rallying for such a sudden emergency, and their conduct was favorably noticed in orders from Hooker."[68]

Fitz Lee realized that, while he had caught Averell's men by surprise, his small force might be overwhelmed if the Yankees rallied and counterattacked. Further, the long-range rifles of the infantry gave the foot soldiers a decided advantage in range. Lee had accomplished his mission—he had found the Northern infantry and confirmed that they still occupied the area in force. Having accomplished his mission, Lee wisely withdrew and marched until late that night, finally encamping near Groveton on the old Second Bull Run battlefield.[69]

In the confused, whirling melee, Lee captured 150 prisoners, including 5 commissioned officers, as well as their horses and equipment. The prisoners included Lt. E. Willard Warren of the 3d Pennsylvania Cavalry, who had just returned to his regiment after a stint in Richmond's notorious Libby Prison. The Rebels captured the lieutenant when his horse fell and he could not get clear before the enemy pounced on him. Poor Warren started back to Libby the next day.[70] Capt. Isaac Ressler's company of the 16th Pennsylvania Cavalry lost four men captured. That regiment lost a total of thirty prisoners.[71] Most of Lee's captives came from the cavalry, and not from the infantry pickets in the vicinity of Hartwood Church.

Members of the 3d Virginia Cavalry captured Lt. Francis D. Wetherill of Company K of the 3d Pennsylvania Cavalry. Wetherill and a detail of twenty men had fought hard, escaping from one enemy trap. They marched along a narrow path through the mud and snow, surrounded by thick woods. Unexpectedly, a party of men in blue overcoats appeared in front of them. Believing them to be friendly, Wetherill did not act. Instead of friends, the men in blue turned out to be the 3d Virginia Cavalry. Wetherill tried to order a charge, but the narrow road did not permit it. In a flash, the Pennsylvanians were surrounded and forced to surrender. They marched some distance to the rear, where they gave up their sabers and gave their names and units. An officer reviewing the list called out, "Who's Wetherill?" The lieutenant presented himself, and the officer asked, "Are you the little Wetherill who used to go to Bolmar's School?" When Wetherill affirmed his identity, the officer identified himself as Brig. Gen. William H. F. "Rooney" Lee, General Robert E. Lee's second son, who had been Wetherill's good chum at Bolmar's School years earlier.[72]

Rooney Lee realized that his old friend was glum about his plight and tried to cheer him up. That night, Lee brought Wetherill a canteen of applejack whiskey and said, "Look here, Wetherill, don't try to escape tonight and we'll have a good time." Without many options, Wetherill readily agreed, and the two spent the night sitting by the campfire, nipping from the canteen of applejack, reminiscing about happier days gone by. "At last, when sleepiness overcame us, we laid down together, in the snow, covered with the same horse blanket. When we awoke and got up the prints made by the bodies of the rebel and the Yankee were side by side in the snow." That day, Wetherill began his long march to the hellish confines of Libby Prison.[73]

Fitzhugh Lee had light losses—four men killed, eight men wounded, and three men captured.[74] The Virginian was pleased with his accomplishments in the terrible conditions. He left Dr. Charles R. Palmore, the regimental surgeon of the 3d Virginia Cavalry, behind to care for his wounded. Lee, who "was the precise and punctilious soldier, with a great regard for all the etiquette of the profession," could not resist tweaking Averell's nose as he prepared to leave.[75] As he departed, Lee left a taunting note and a bag of Virginia tobacco with Dr. Palmore for delivery to his old friend. "Dear Averell," wrote Fitz Lee, "Please let this surgeon assist in taking care of my wounded. I ride a pretty fast horse, but I think yours can beat mine. I wish you'd quit your shooting and get out of my State and go home. If you won't go home, why don't you come pay me a visit. Send me over a bag of coffee. Good-bye, Fitz."[76] Not terribly amused, Averell grimly resolved to answer his old friend's taunting invitation at the earliest possible opportunity.

On hearing the first shots, Colonel Jones sent a galloper to division headquarters to inform Averell that the enemy was attacking the picket lines near Hartwood Church. When Averell heard about the attack on the pickets, he scribbled a note back, instructing Jones, "If the enemy attack, whip them."[77] Averell quickly set his division in motion. "On receipt of the news at camp, we were ordered after the Rebels 'double quick,'" reported Capt. Walter Newhall of the 3d Pennsylvania Cavalry.[78]

Word of the attack quickly reached Hooker. When they deftly evaded the infantrymen camped near Berea Church, Lee's raiders passed within ten miles of Hooker's headquarters east of Falmouth, engendering panic. Army headquarters instructed Averell to meet Fitz Lee's raiders head on. As an incentive, Hooker's chief of staff, Maj. Gen. Daniel Butterfield, wrote, "General Hooker says that a major general's commission is staring somebody in the face in this affair, and that the enemy should not be allowed to get away from us."[79] Averell had his men moving in a matter of a few minutes. "We were startled by the sounding of 'Boots and Saddles,'" recalled a member of the 1st Rhode Island Cavalry, "and learned that the pickets had been driven in and threatened by Stuart's cavalry. In line as quickly as possible, the brigade proceeded to Hartwood Church."[80]

His advance hindered by the sloppy road conditions, Averell finally arrived about 9:00 that night and found "disorder prevailing." He jotted off a note to Butterfield, requesting that the Reserve Brigade be sent to reinforce him, and started looking for Fitz Lee. However, the Confederates had already withdrawn to Morrisville, twelve miles upstream from Hartwood Church and safely out of range.[81] Not long after, a courier reined up, carrying further instructions from Butterfield. "The commanding general directs that you follow the enemy's force; that you do not come in until the force which General Stoneman is directed to send out at 1 A.M. gets up with the enemy, and you have captured him or found it utterly impossible to do so," wrote Butterfield. "Stoneman will endeavor to get between them and the river."[82] Averell's men lit fires and stood to horse, waiting for further orders. They spent a long, cold night.[83] "All the sleep I got last night I got lying on one rail," complained a trooper of the 16th Pennsylvania Cavalry.[84] Pleasonton, with the First Division, was on his way to reinforce Averell. Stoneman directed Pleasonton to march upstream with all possible speed, in the hope of cutting Lee off at the river fords.[85]

"About 2,000 of the enemy's cavalry felt my pickets yesterday afternoon," reported Hooker to Stanton. "Were repulsed, and Stoneman is now after them at full chase, with instructions to follow them to their camps, should it be necessary, to destroy them. These are on the south side of the Rappahannock, and near Culpeper." Although the immediate danger had passed, Hooker grew angry that yet another Confederate foray had found his picket lines so porous.[86]

"That night, in the midst of a heavy rain storm 'boots and saddles' were sounded and the orders were to march," recalled a member of the 8th Illinois Cavalry. "It was rumored that the rebel, General Stuart, was at his old tricks again. The men crawled from under their blankets, mounted their horses and started." Retracing for nearly forty miles the route of Burnside's Mud March, made just four weeks earlier, Pleasonton's blueclad troopers never caught up to the Confederates, who had too much of a head start. "In addition to the severity of the weather, the location of the picket-line was an extremely dangerous one, as the country round was infested with bushwhackers," noted a member of the 6th New York Cavalry.[87]

Pleasonton's division arrived at Aquia Church early on the morning of the 26th after a long, miserable night in the saddle, and halted. They did not push on, as Hooker had wanted.[88] "Stood a few hours in the rain. Started together with three regiments on a wild goose chase after an imaginary Stuart," groused an unhappy Hoosier. "Night found three brigades of us poor fellows shelterless, wet, cold, hungry, without rations or horse feed, shivering in the snow and water."[89]

That morning, Pleasonton reported his whereabouts. "General Stoneman directed me to inform you when I should leave for Aquia Church," he wrote at 3:00. "I have therefore the honor to report that the Second Brigade left its camp at 2:30 this morning and the First is about leaving. I shall move with the latter. One regiment is already at the Church, which is some 8 miles from here by the road which can now be traveled. . . . I shall not move beyond Aquia Church until I hear further concerning the rebel movements."[90] An unhappy Butterfield fired off a stinging note to Stoneman. After quoting Pleasonton's report of his position, Butterfield noted, quite facetiously, "His brilliant dash and rapid movements will undoubtedly immortalize him!" He continued, "It is fair to presume that he failed to receive your orders to push on, otherwise I cannot account for his movements at all." Butterfield then wrote to Pleasonton. "I don't know what you are doing there," he stated. "Orders were sent you at 11 P.M. last night, by telegraph and orderlies, to push for the enemy without delay, and to communicate with General Stoneman at Hartwood. The enemy have recrossed the river, at Kelly's Ford, probably, and Averell is pursuing them."[91]

Butterfield wanted to push out infantry forces to try to cut off the Southern horsemen from the Rappahannock fords. Coaxing, cajoling, and browbeating, Butterfield fired off telegram after telegram to the army's infantry corps commanders trying to spur them to move. As an example, at 11:15 that evening, Butterfield wrote to Maj. Gen. Samuel P. Heintzelman, commander of the forces assigned to the defenses of Washington, D.C., "The force is F. Lee's and Hampton's brigades. . . . Their horses are well tired. We are pushing all out tonight. Can you not push out tonight and push this side of the railroad at Rappahannock Station?" Try as he might, the chief of staff could not coax superhuman effort from the Army of the Potomac's soldiers, and his frustration simmered into a boiling wrath.[92]

Averell's men pursued as far as Morrisville before the general learned that Lee had crossed to safety on the other side of the Rappahannock. "We only seen one rebel & he had no arms, but we took him prisoner," noted a Pennsylvanian in his diary.[93] Lee blockaded the road with felled trees to slow the pursuit, and the tactic worked. The heavy overnight rains caused a "terrible flood," as Averell described it.[94] Pleasonton and his weary division arrived around 5:00 that afternoon, too late to be of any good. The Reserve Brigade, which had also made a forced march, accompanied by General Stoneman and his staff, arrived at nearly 4:30 A.M.

Stoneman roused the weary horse soldiers from their miserable bivouacs, and the entire column moved out, with Averell's division in the lead. Stoneman remained at Hartwood Church, dispatching a few squadrons of Regulars to pursue the escaping Confederates. He soon learned that the Rappahannock was rising quickly and was impossible to cross. He had received orders from Hooker that "in the event of your inability to cut off the enemy's cavalry, you will follow them to their camp and destroy them." However, the river could not be forded. "After no little thought and some misgivings on the subject, I determined to move the whole of my available force down to the river that night, and at daylight the next morning push them at all hazards for the south bank of the Rappahannock, myself, of course, setting the example, a prospect anything but cheering," reported Stoneman.[95]

Stoneman learned that Averell and Pleasonton had arrived at Morrisville. They found no signs of Lee or his brigade. At 4:45, Stoneman received an order directing him "that in case the enemy has re-crossed the Rappahannock and are on the other side, you will return with all your command to camp." Stoneman communicated these orders to Averell and Pleasonton, and once they ascertained for certain that the enemy had, in fact, returned to the other side, Stoneman directed the entire force to head for its camps.[96] By the time Pleasonton's division made its way back to camp, it had traveled nearly eighty miles through horrible conditions, taking a severe toll on men and horses.[97] "We had a hard trip—*accomplished nothing!!*" groused a Hoosier.[98]

Averell welcomed the orders to return to camp, which he gladly did, traversing terrible, muddy roads. "Settled down again into dreary camp life," Averell noted in his diary.[99] In fact, the return march was thoroughly unpleasant for all involved. "Arrived at camp after dark having been in our saddles all day except about 15 minutes at noon," observed a member of the 16th Pennsylvania. "Horses no feed since last night & none since morning. Traveled about 40 miles today & nearly every step in the mud nearly to horses' knees. Many horses gave out entirely & were left sticking in the mud. We are all horses and men completely plastered with Va. mud from head to foot and as tired as need be."[100] Sgt. Henry W. Owen, who also served in the 16th Pennsylvania wrote to his sweetheart, "We have been out five days and nights chaseing the rebs and yet we are willing to soldier. We had a scirmish a short time a go killing several rebs driving them back a cross the Rappahanock River. We lost three killed forty seven taken. I expect we will soon have a nother brush. It may be before this reaches you."[101] Although Owen did not know it, his prediction was correct.

Northern newspapers quickly caught wind of Lee's raid. "Another raid by Stuart's horse thieves," proclaimed a New York newspaper.[102] "The rebels failed in accomplishing their object," claimed a correspondent to the *New York Herald,* "and retreated in great haste across the Rappahannock, felling trees across the roads and placing other obstacles in the way of the pursuing force."[103]

Jeb Stuart, however, saw it quite differently. Praising Lee's command, the Confederate cavalry chieftain noted that Fitz Lee's brief report of the action "shows how skillfully it was executed and how successfully it was terminated." He continued, "Special attention is called to the commendations of the officers and men mentioned, to which I desire to add my high appreciation of the ability and gallantry displayed by Brigadier-General Lee in his prompt performance of the important duty assigned him."[104] Robert E. Lee also viewed the mission as a success. In a letter to President Davis, General Lee reported that his nephew Fitz "penetrated their lines five miles in rear of Falmouth, found the enemy in strong force, fell upon their camps, & brought off about 150 prisoners, killing thirty-six, & losing six of his own men."[105]

"Everything here is perfectly quiet," claimed Stuart in a letter to his brother-in-law. "Fitz Lee, whom I sent on a reconnaissance in rear of Falmouth was very successful indeed—bagging 150 and fighting heavy odds all the time. William H. F. Lee about the same time drove two gunboats out of the Rappahannock with two pieces of the Stuart Horse Artillery." Indeed, it appeared that in spite of all of Hooker's reforms, little had changed.[106]

Capt. George N. Bliss, whose Rhode Islanders had fought hard after their initial surprise, gave an honest appraisal of the Union performance at Hartwood Church. Just a few days later, he wrote, "I am not surprised at the success of the rebels in this affair. Such an event has been predicted by many prophets among us, and unless our Genls. improve this lesson and make better arrangements on this flank of our army, the rebels will do the same thing again."[107] The performance of the Northern horse soldiers did not impress their counterparts in the infantry. "Our frightened cavalry, as an excuse for their disgraceful stampede, had reported a force of the enemy's horse at least three thousand strong, in the act of swooping down on our picket line," sneered an officer of the 124th New York Infantry. "The truth probably was that a strong reconnoitering party, having come across our small body of horse, made a dash at them and accidentally ran into our picket line." Not surprisingly, the infantrymen claimed it was they who repulsed the Confederates, not the horse soldiers who carried the bulk of the day's fighting.[108]

Neither Hooker nor Butterfield considered the expedition a Union success. Upon returning to camp, Stoneman received instructions "to have as soon as possible an exact report of the . . . movements in full of each portion of your command, and the delay of any portion to execute promptly and completely the part assigned it, together with the reasons therefor."[109] Hooker then summoned his cavalry chief to headquarters and exploded. "We ought to be invincible, and by God, sir, we shall be!" bellowed the army commander. "You have got to stop these disgraceful cavalry 'surprises.' I'll have no more of them. I give you full power over your officers, to arrest, cashier, shoot—whatever you will—only you must stop these surprises. And by God, sir, if you don't do it, I give you fair notice, I will relieve the whole of you and take command of the cavalry myself!"[110] Clearly, no major general's commissions could be expected any time soon.

Averell penned his report of the incident, now lost, on March 2, and apparently mentioned the note left by Lee in that missing report.[111] When Hooker learned about Fitz Lee's taunting note to Averell, he paid the division commander a visit. Averell, stung by his old friend's needling, asked for permission to cross the river and settle his score with Lee. Hooker assured Averell that the division commander's request would be granted soon. When Averell expressed confidence in his ability to even the score with Fitz Lee, Hooker said, "If you do there will likely be some dead cavalrymen lying about." Some have misinterpreted this statement as suggesting, "Who ever saw a dead cavalryman?" as is often attributed to Hooker on this occasion. Averell's response is not known, but the New Yorker was now determined to even the score with his old friend. He set about planning a mission to do just that.[112]

On February 28, Stoneman took stock of his command. In a letter to Hooker, he reported having 12,000 men and 13,000 horses fit for duty. His prior report showed 11,955 men and 13,875 horses, meaning that nearly 1,000 horses had been lost in a month.[113] The harsh winter conditions had taken a terrible toll on the Cavalry Corps's mounts, suffered in the cold climate of Virginia. "The cavalry horses look as if they came from Egypt during the seven years' famine," noted a foreign observer during the first week of March. "I inquired the reason from different soldiers and officers of various regiments. Nine-tenths of them agreed that the horses scarcely receive half the ration of oats and hay allotted to them by the government. Somebody steals the other half but every body is satisfied. All this could very easily be ferreted out, but it seems that no will exists anywhere to bring the thieves to punishment."[114] The willingness to turn a blind eye to such corruption would cost the Cavalry Corps dearly later that spring.

The men were also tired. "The line this force has to guard is but little less than 100 miles," explained the Cavalry Corps commander. "One-third on duty at one time gives 40 men to the mile on post at one time, and one-third of these gives 13 to the mile on post at one time. Considering the condition of the roads, it is a good day's march to get out to the line and another to return, so that actually the horses are out one-half the time or more. Added to this the fact that frequently the whole cavalry force is in the saddle for several days together, and it will be perceived that but little more than one-third of the time is allowed the horses in which to recruit." Stoneman apologized if it sounded like he was complaining, and then concluded, "Should the general consider it expedient to diminish the amount of duty at present being performed by the cavalry, either by weakening or contracting the lines as now established, or by substituting a system of patrols for stationary vedettes, or in any other mode he may prescribe, I shall most gladly do so, and consider that the interests of the service have been benefited thereby."[115]

Hooker approved the request. On March 2, Averell and Pleasonton received new instructions for picketing from Stoneman. Stoneman shortened the picket lines, and more frequent mounted patrols took the place of static vedette posts. "Patrols, mounted on the best horses, will be sent out on all the main approaches sufficiently often to keep you well informed of what is going on in your front. These patrols will not only watch all the main approaches, but will examine and thoroughly inspect the intervening country between these approaches." Stoneman gave his division commanders discretion to set the size and strength of these patrols as they saw fit. These changes conserved horseflesh and marked another step in the long and painful process of educating the Army of the Potomac's cavalry.[116]

Turmoil in the officer corps continued. Col. Luigi Palma di Cesnola, the Italian count who commanded the 4th New York Cavalry of Averell's division, was dismissed from the service in the second half of February for allegedly stealing government property. At the time, di Cesnola commanded a brigade of cavalry as well as a detachment of infantry and a battery of artillery. The unhappy colonel protested, and the Judge Advocate General's office launched an investigation. It found that di Cesnola "was most unjustly wronged," and he was reinstated to his former rank and position. Di Cesnola wrote to Averell, asking, "In regard to my former position I heard that my brigade has been broken up & my Regt is under your command now; though I regret my command has gone yet it is gratifying to me to be under the command of a regular officer like you are." Averell returned di Cesnola to command of the 4th New York Cavalry, and the dashing Italian count proved himself a brave man in the coming months.

Although the injustice was corrected, this incident had cut di Cesnola to the quick. "With what aching heart I return to my regiment few persons can appreciate it," he wrote to his congressman a week later. "I tried ever to my utmost in well deserving from my adoptive country and the rewards I received from the Administration I may say were nothing but kicks." He concluded, "I am . . . going to the Regiment with a broken heart to stay there some weeks and then I shall resign as it is incompatible with my character to continue."[117] The dashing count did not resign, and remained with his regiment, which had a troubled history for the duration of its service with the Army of the Potomac.[118]

The 8th New York drew ten days' picket duty under unpleasant circumstances, standing four-hour shifts at a time. "Our duties are very arduous, men on duty 4 hours of 4," observed a trooper on February 27.[119] On the night of March 5, enemy cavalry broke through the picket line of Company K of the 8th New York located near Dumfries, well north of Falmouth, along the picket line in the rear of the army. They killed two men, wounded two, and captured seventeen more in another embarrassment for Stoneman.[120] The next day, Grimes Davis, the brigade commander, directed that mounted patrols be beefed up. "These patrols are to be sent out often, especially at night, and on the best horses," wrote Davis. "Orders from division headquarters require the line thoroughly observed and patrolled; and the colonel directs that if your present force is not sufficient, you make application for the number which you may consider necessary." Davis concluded ominously: "The colonel commanding expects that your command will meet with no disgraceful surprise, such as occurred the other day in the Eighth New York."[121]

Three days later, in a heavy rain, the men of the 6th New York Cavalry of Devin's brigade drew up in line of battle, waiting for yet another enemy foray, picket firing having been heard. This time, though, the enemy was not Confederate cavalry. Instead, "it proved to be nothing more than the pickets firing at bushwhackers," sneered a New Yorker, "a detestable set of cowardly sneaks who should have been shot at sight without challenge." On the 10th, Pleasonton announced that the "noted Stuart" would pay the First Division a visit that night and "deliver a lecture at Ebenezer Church." Eagerly anticipating the bible lesson, and standing to horse on a stormy night, pelted by rain and snow, the 6th New York waited patiently, "with a full supply of tickets, but the lecturer failed to put in an appearance."[122]

The 3d Indiana Cavalry, of Pleasonton's First Division, spent most of the winter picketing near Dumfries, "where the snow was deep and the heavy pine woods was thick with bushwhackers," recalled saddler Augustus C. Weaver. "It was a nightly occurrence for some of our pickets to be fired on. We made good and killed several bushwhackers." Being constantly on the alert and regularly under fire wore on the nerves of even these veteran horse soldiers, who eagerly awaited the coming of spring and the new campaigning season.[123] On March 6, a nervous picket of the 3d Indiana shot a lieutenant of the 8th New York who refused to dismount along the picket line.[124]

The Hoosiers of the 3d Indiana itched for battle. "This command is now in good condition, notwithstanding the hard labor it has to perform and the winter's exposure of the horses," reported Col. George H. Chapman, the regimental commander. "There are few, if any, regiments of cavalry in the service that have worn as well as this, but we are sadly in need of reinforcements to be put on a working par with the regiments with which we are associated." The 3d Indiana, which had elements serving in both the Army of the Potomac and the Army of the Cumberland, was smaller than the other regiments in its brigade. Chapman wanted two new companies raised in the fall of 1862 sent to him to increase the size of his command. "It is because of this disadvantage that I am so desirous the new companies should be sent as I trust I do not annoy you with my importunities and can assure you that my desire is to preserve the reputation of the 3d Inda Cavy and reflect honor upon the State we represent." Chapman, a lawyer with a way with words, concluded, "We have to contend against more or less jealousy on the part of Eastern troops, but we have another western regiment in the Brigade (8th Illinois) and together we hold our own."[125] The Hoosiers had no reason to hang their heads. Although a smaller regiment than most, they fought hard and well and brought great honor on their state over the course of the war.

Things soon returned to the normal tedium of winter camp life. "There is no sign of the Army of the Potomac moving from its present encampment soon that I can see," observed Lieutenant Lucas of the 1st Pennsylvania. "In fact, I don't think it can for a month yet on account of the weather. The roads are very bad yet."[126] Two days later, he observed, "I shall look with interest to the time when the weather will permit a move of the Army of the Potomac, when I hope to hear of our army achieving a most glorious victory. If we don't whip them this summer I shall give up all hopes of ever whipping them."[127] A member of the 6th Ohio Cavalry expressed a similar sentiment. "I expect this army will move ahead just as soon as the roads will admit, and I do hope that we will not meet with any more reverses, for the soldiers are now down hearted enough. We want to gain a great victory to give the men confidence once more, but we must await the result with all the patience we can."[128]

While the Union mounted arm had made strides since the formation of the Cavalry Corps, it still had room for further improvement. The affair at Hartwood Church proved that beyond all doubt. "This dash of Confederate cavalry . . . and the manner in which it was met, are interesting evidence as to the relative efficiency of the two opposing cavalries," observed a Northern historian. "They show that Hooker's and Heintzelman's horsemen, and their commanders, had something to learn before they would be up to the standard of Lee's. It is plain that the country beyond the Federal outposts was not adequately patrolled, and that the troops were not proficient in turning out suddenly and promptly and getting on the march."[129]

The pieces of the puzzle were all in place. It remained to be seen whether the Northern horsemen would be up to the heavy task that lay ahead of them. The Army of the Potomac's new Cavalry Corps would get its chance to prove its mettle just a few days later, and the blueclad horse soldiers proved that they were equal to the task.

NOTES

1. German, "Picketing along the Rappahannock," 35.
2. Henry W. Owen to Dear Emma, March 15, 1863, Howard McManus Collection, Roanoke, Va.
3. *Where 300 Gather* (Hartwood, Va.: Hartwood Presybterian Church, 1998), 2. Hartwood Church remains an active, ongoing, vibrant congregation today, nearly 200

years after its founding. The 1858 sanctuary building remains in use. There are no lingering scars or signs of the vandalism described by so many Union soldiers.

4. William Hyndman, *History of a Cavalry Company: A Complete History of Company A, Fourth Pennsylvania Cavalry* (Hightstown, N.J.: Longstreet House, 1997), 47.

5. *Instructions for Officers and Non-Commissioned Officers on Outpost and Patrol Duty, and Troops in Campaign* (Washington, D.C.: U.S. Government Printing Office, 1863), 56.

6. Webb diary, entry for January 23, 1863.

7. Gilpin diary, entry for February 4, 1863.

8. Edward P. Tobie, *History of the First Maine Cavalry 1861–1865* (Boston: Press of Emory & Hughes, 1887), 109–11.

9. Willard Glazier, *Three Years in the Federal Cavalry* (New York: R. H. Ferguson, 1873), 118.

10. Dennison, *Sabres and Spurs,* 199–200.

11. Henry T. Bartlett to his brother, February 9, 1863, Civil War Miscellaneous Collection, USAMHI.

12. Bartlett to his brother, February 9, 1863; James Burden Weston to his mother, February 9, 1863, in Robert W. Frost and Nancy D. Frost, eds., *Picket Pins and Sabers* (privately published, 1971), 37.

13. Bartlett to his brother, February 9, 1863.

14. Ibid.

15. Walter S. Newhall to his mother, February 9, 1863.

16. Bliss to Dear Gerald, February 10, 1863.

17. Frost and Frost, *Picket Pins and Sabers,* 37.

18. Bliss to Dear Gerald, February 19, 1863.

19. Lucas to his wife, February 26, 1863.

20. Ford, *A Cycle of Adams Letters,* 1:246–47. Glanders is an extremely contagious bacterial disease often fatal to horses. Symptoms include swollen lymph nodes, nasal discharge, and ulcers of the respiratory tract and skin. Glanders is communicable to other mammals, including humans.

21. Webb diary, entry for January 22, 1863.

22. Delos Northway to his wife, February 22, 1863, included in *Souvenir: Fiftieth Annual Reunion of the Sixth Ohio Veteran Volunteer Cavalry Association* (Warren, Ohio: Sixth Ohio Veteran Volunteer Cavalry Association, 1915), 108–10.

23. Redman to his sisters, February 8, 1863.

24. *New York Herald,* February 18, 1863.

25. John Wilder Johnson to his wife, February 15, 1863, Olive Johnson Dunnett Collection, Hanover, Pa.

26. Jasper Cheney diary, entry for February 20, 1863, *Civil War Times Illustrated* Collection, USAMHI.

27. Norton, *Deeds of Daring,* 56–8.

28. Samuel M. Potter to his wife, February 21, 1863, Potter Letters, Pennsylvania State Museum and Library, Harrisburg, Pa.

29. Winder, *Jacob Binder's Book,* 144.

30. Fell to Dear Lydia, February 22, 1863.
31. Covert to his wife, February 22, 1863.
32. Gilpin diary, entry for February 22, 1863.
33. William Woods Averell diary, entries for February 22–23, 1863, Gilder-Lehrman Collection, J. P. Morgan Library, New York, N.Y.
34. Hall, *Sixth New York*, 93–4.
35. O.R., vol. 25, part 2, 95–96.
36. Davis, *Common Soldier, Uncommon War*, 350–51.
37. Averell diary, entry for February 24, 1863.
38. Louis H. Manarin and Clifford Dowdey, eds., *The Wartime Papers of R. E. Lee*, 2 vols. (Boston: Little, Brown, 1961), 1:409. A few days earlier, elements of the 4th Virginia Cavalry had crossed the Rapidan at U.S. Ford. Having crossed the flooded river they soon found a strong force of Union cavalry pickets, which meant that the Virginians could not proceed further, so they withdrew without ascertaining the intentions of the Army of the Potomac.
39. Here is Averell's description of his old friend Fitz Lee, as stated in his postwar memoirs: "Fitzhugh Lee was a sturdy, muscular, and lively little giant as a cadet. With a frank, affectionate disposition he had a prevailing habit of irrepressible good humor which made any occasions of seriousness in him when in '61 he was compelled to choose between his state and the Nation and we came to the parting of the ways, the tears which suffered his eyes and the lamentations that escaped his lips betrayed a depth of feeling which revealed a sincere character beneath his habitual cheerfulness." Eckert and Amato, *Ten Years in the Saddle*, 49.
40. George Wilson Booth, *Personal Reminiscences of a Maryland Soldier in the War Between the States, 1861–1865* (Baltimore: privately published, 1898), 116.
41. Thomas L. Rosser, *Addresses of Gen'l T. L. Rosser at the Seventh Annual Reunion of the Association of the Maryland Line* (New York: L. A. Williams Printing, 1889), 25.
42. William R. Carter, *Sabres, Saddles and Spurs*, ed. Walbrook D. Swank (Shippensburg, Pa.: Burd Street Press, 1998), 46.
43. Robert T. Hubard Memoir, Alderman Library, Special Collections, University of Virginia, Charlottesville, Va.
44. O.R., vol. 25, part 1, 25–26.
45. William Brooke-Rawle, *History of the Third Pennsylvania Cavalry, Sixtieth Regiment Pennsylvania Volunteers, in the American Civil War 1861–1865* (Philadelphia: Franklin Printing, 1905), 190.
46. Potter to his sister, March 2, 1863, Potter Letters.
47. Ford, *A Cycle of Adams Letters*, 1:255–57.
48. Dennison, *Sabres and Spurs*, 204–5.
49. Bliss to Dear Gerald, February 28, 1863.
50. Brooke-Rawle, *Third Pennsylvania Cavalry*, 190.
51. Ford, *A Cycle of Adams Letters*, 1:257–58.
52. *New York Times*, February 28, 1863.
53. *Philadelphia Inquirer*, February 28, 1863.

54. Not surprisingly, Captain Blood resigned his commission after his exchange at the end of May 1863. Samuel P. Bates, *History of the Pennsylvania Volunteers, 1861–1865,* 5 vols. (Harrisburg, Pa.: B. Slingerly, 1869), 2: 550.

55. Ford, *A Cycle of Adams Letters,* 1: 260–63.

56. Dennison, *Sabres and Spurs,* 201–202.

57. Ibid., 202.

58. Ibid., 203.

59. Potter to his sister, March 2, 1863.

60. Carter, *Sabres, Saddles and Spurs,* 46–47.

61. Hubard memoir.

62. Carter, *Sabres, Saddles and Spurs,* 47.

63. Hubard memoir.

64. Charles H. Weygant, *History of the One Hundred and Twenty-Fourth Regiment, N.Y.S.V.* (Newburgh, N.Y.: Journal Printing House, 1877), 85.

65. Ibid.

66. O.R., vol. 25, part 1, 21.

67. John L. Smith to his mother, March 3, 1863, FSNMP.

68. Hyndman, *History of a Cavalry Company,* 51.

69. Ibid.

70. Brooke-Rawle, *History of the Third Pennsylvania Cavalry,* 188 and 194.

71. Ressler diary, entry for February 25, 1863; Norman Ball diary, entry for February 25, 1863, Connecticut Historical Society, Hartford, Conn.

72. Brooke-Rawle, *History of the Third Pennsylvania Cavalry,* 193.

73. Ibid., 193–94.

74. O.R., vol. 25, part 1, 24–25.

75. Frank A. Bond, "Fitz Lee in the Army of Northern Virginia," *Confederate Veteran* 6 (1898), 421.

76. Frank W. Hess, "The First Cavalry Battle at Kelly's Ford, Va.," *National Tribune,* May 29, 1890. Dr. Palmore spent three pleasant weeks at the headquarters of the 3d Pennsylvania Cavalry before he returned to his regiment. In the meantime, he resumed an old friendship with a cook for the Pennsylvania saddle soldiers. Hubard memoir.

77. Brooke-Rawle, *Third Pennsylvania Cavalry,* 189–90.

78. Walter S. Newhall to his father, March 8, 1863.

79. O.R., vol. 25, part 2, 101.

80. Dennison, *Sabres and Spurs,* 200.

81. Averell diary, entry for February 25, 1863.

82. O.R., vol. 25, part 2, 102–103.

83. Ball diary, entry for February 25, 1863.

84. Winder, *Jacob Beidler's Book,* 144.

85. O.R., vol. 25, part 2, 103–104.

86. Ibid., 107.

87. Hall, *History of the Sixth New York,* 94.

88. Abner N. Hard, *History of the Eighth Cavalry Regimen Illinois Volunteers* (Aurora, Ill.: privately published, 1868), 204.

89. Gilpin diary, entry for February 26, 1863.

90. O.R., vol. 25, part 2, 104–105.

91. Ibid., 108.

92. Ibid., 104.

93. Winder, *Jacob Beidler's Book,* 144.

94. Averell diary, entry for February 26, 1863.

95. O.R., vol. 25, part 1, 23–24.

96. Ibid., 24.

97. Hall, *History of the Sixth New York,* 94.

98. Gilpin diary, entry for February 28, 1863.

99. Averell diary, entry for February 26, 1863.

100. Ball diary, entry for February 27, 1863.

101. Owen to Dear Emma, March 15, 1863.

102. *New York Tribune,* February 27, 1863.

103. *New York Herald,* February 28, 1863.

104. O.R., vol. 25, part 1, 26.

105. Manarin & Dowdey, *Wartime Papers of R. E. Lee,* 1: 409.

106. Adele H. Mitchell, ed., *The Letters of Major General James E. B. Stuart* (Richmond, Va.: Stuart-Mosby Historical Society, 1990), 296.

107. Bliss to Dear Gerald, February 28, 1863.

108. Weygant, *History of the One Hundred and Twenty-Fourth Regiment,* 85–86.

109. O.R., vol. 25, part 1, 22.

110. *Boston Transcript,* March 25, 1863.

111. Averell diary, entry for March 2, 1863.

112. John B. Bigelow, Jr., *The Campaign of Chancellorsville* (New Haven: Yale University Press, 1910), 73–74.

113. O.R., vol. 25, part 2, 111.

114. Adam Gurowski, *Diary from November 18, 1862, to October 18, 1863,* 2 vols. (New York: Burt Franklin, 1968), 2:168.

115. O.R., vol. 25, part 2, 111.

116. Ibid., 116.

117. Luigi Palma di Cesnola to Erastus Corning, March 10, 1863, Luigi Palma di Cesnola Papers, Rauner Special Collections Library, Dartmouth College, Hanover, N.H.

118. Luigi P. di Cesnola to Averell, March 4, 1863, Averell Papers. Di Cesnola received a Medal of Honor for gallantry in the days just prior to the Battle of Gettysburg, when, while under arrest, he led a gallant charge at the Battle of Aldie.

119. Cheney diary, entry for February 27, 1863.

120. Norton, *Deeds of Daring,* 58; Henry C. Frost to his sister, March 8, 1863, Lloyd D. Miller Collection, USAMHI.

121. O.R., vol. 25, part 2, 128.

122. Hall, *History of the Sixth New York,* 94–5.
123. Augustus C. Weaver, *Third Indiana Cavalry: A Brief Account of the Actions in Which They Took Part* (Greenwood, Ind.: privately published, 1919), 3–4.
124. Gilpin diary, entry for March 6, 1863.
125. George H. Chapman to Lazarus Noble, Adjutant General of Indiana, March 12, 1863, Indiana Adjutant General's Office, Correspondence File, 3d Indiana Cavalry, Indiana State Archives, Indianapolis.
126. Lucas to his wife, March 10, 1863.
127. Lucas to his brother, March 12, 1863.
128. Thomas M. Covert to his wife, March 3, 1863.
129. Bigelow, *The Campaign of Chancellorsville,* 71.

3

St. Patrick's Day Melee:
The Battle of Kelly's Ford

Fighting Joe" Hooker kept his promise to Averell. On March 12, Hooker instructed Stoneman to send a reconnaissance in force to Kelly's Ford to observe and report on the enemy's dispositions.[1] To the army commander's delight, the scouting expedition found the ford only lightly guarded, presenting an opportunity for Hooker to unleash Averell's quest for revenge. He also wanted to know what sort of defenses awaited the New Yorker's foray across the river.

On March 14, Hooker instructed Averell to take 3,000 horse soldiers and six pieces of artillery, and with that force, attack and rout or destroy "the cavalry forces of the enemy reported to be in the vicinity of Culpeper Court House." The army commander may also have wanted to test the reactions of the Confederate troops occupying the area, so that he would know what to expect when he launched his spring campaign. Hooker informed Averell that he believed that Rebel cavalry was operating north of the Rappahannock near Manassas, and that the strength of this enemy force was between 250 and 1,000 men, with at least one piece of artillery supporting them. Hooker also indicated that the bulk of Fitz Lee's horse soldiers lay near Culpeper.[2] The New Yorker eagerly set about planning his raid, looking to even the score with his old chum Fitz Lee. "Now it came the Yankees' turn to make a raid," recalled Rosser.[3]

Averell intended to cross the Rappahannock at Kelly's Ford. He knew the terrain, and that the Kelly's Ford Road provided the shortest route to the Confederate camps near Culpeper.[4] "Kelly's Ford is a very easy ford, and shallow. A broad, smooth rock covers the bottom to about twenty feet below, where it drops off suddenly to a deep hole, evidently once a fall," recalled a member of the 3d Virginia

Cavalry. "On the north side the bluff is fully eighty feet high with two roads through, both down deep breaks in the bluff. One directly in front of the ford leading out to Zoan Church, and elsewhere. One coming down to the river below the deep hole, then alongside the river to the ford. On the south side, the land slopes up to the timber land for nearly a mile. Cut up with stone fences, a few ditches, and slight hillocks, and extends up and down the river for five miles."[5] However, because of the winter rains and the melting of snow, the water ran unusually fast and deep, and only one man at a time could navigate its tricky passage.[6]

The Army of the Potomac's horse soldiers wanted an opportunity to cross sabers with the enemy, "to prove the superb fighting abilities of our much-maligned cavalry, and illustrate the sabre as the proper weapon for a cavalryman." Anticipating a brawl, Averell instructed the men of his division to sharpen their blades, and ordered them to use them freely. He boldly promised a victory over Fitz Lee.[7] Because he heard that there was Confederate cavalry in his rear, Averell requested that Hooker send a regiment of cavalry to Catlett's Station, to cover the Rappahannock fords and to picket toward Warrenton. Hooker denied the request, prompting Averell to detach nearly 900 men from the 1st Massachusetts and 4th Pennsylvania to guard the fords and watch out for the enemy force thought to be operating in the area on the north side of the Rappahannock. With Averell's ambitious promises ringing in their ears, and with the regimental band of the 1st Rhode Island Cavalry playing martial airs, 2,100 Federals moved out of their camps early on the morning of March 16.[8]

Averell left 900 men, nearly a third of his force, to picket the railroad between Bealeton and Catlett's Station and also left a reserve at Morrisville. Pickets guarded the fords beyond the railroad. He had no wagon train to guard, and he did not need supplies from a depot along the Orange & Alexandria Railroad. He had only his line of retreat to guard, and his command was certainly large enough to force it open if the Confederates managed to cut it. Perhaps he feared a movement from the Shenandoah Valley. Had he done so, Hooker might have dispatched further troops to watch Averell's flank. However, the New Yorker did not do so. By sending off this large detachment, Averell demonstrated his cautious nature. It also meant that he did not go into battle with 3,000 as ordered by Hooker.

Averell's column marched thirty-two miles to Morrisville that day. The men did not know where they were going; some surmised that Warrenton was their ultimate destination, while others guessed that it would be Culpeper. "The roads have froze so hard that it would carry a horse," observed a trooper of the 16th Pennsylvania.[9] Averell arrived at 11:00 that night, "with horses in poor condition for the expedition." His troopers took an hour or so to eat something and to feed their mounts.[10] The men of the 6th Ohio Cavalry stripped an old church of its pews and quickly built large fires to cook coffee. "It seems hard to so desecrate the houses of worship," recorded Capt. Delos Northway of the 6th Ohio in his diary that night, "and yet probably from the pulpit has been preached the Doctrines of Secession and the divine right of one man to own another. Well let it go, it has had its day."[11] Exhausted from the day's long march, the Ohioans quickly fell asleep. They did not get to rest for long. At 1:00 A.M., orders came, "Up boys, feed your horses and get ready to march." The men made hasty preparations, cooked coffee, fed and saddled their horses, and then stood to horse, waiting for orders to move out. However, they did not actually march for another three hours; the column did not start until 4:00 A.M.[12]

As the blueclad column snaked across the countryside, Averell heavily picketed his front, sending small parties ahead on all roads and to the fords, hoping to mask his approach.[13] That night, his men spotted the fires of Confederates camps near Mt. Holly Church, and his scouts heard the Southern drummer boys beating retreat and tattoo from the direction of Rappahannock Station. At least one Federal reported spotting Confederate signal rockets going up for a substantial part of the night.[14] That evening, enemy pickets appeared in Averell's front on the road leading west to Kelly's Ford.[15]

In the inky darkness, five members of Fitz Lee's 1st Virginia Cavalry crossed the Rappahannock below Kelly's Ford in a small boat, intending to capture Averell's pickets. They failed, "but gave them a considerable fright," recounted Pvt. Peter M. Grattan of the 1st Virginia, "but I question whether the party that went over were not as much scared as the Yankees from the present account they gave of their own firing. Only ten or fifteen yards off and did not hit a Yank. Which do you think was the most excited?"[16]

Averell had 775 men from the three regiments of Duffié's brigade. He also had 565 men from the 3d Pennsylvania, the 16th Pennsylvania, and two squadrons of the 4th Pennsylvania of McIntosh's brigade. Capt. Marcus A. Reno also joined the expedition with the 1st U.S. and three squadrons of the 5th U.S. Cavalry, totaling an additional 760 men. The six guns of the 6th New York Light Independent Battery also accompanied the column as it moved out early on the morning of March 17. "Daylight found us pelting through the woods, at a slapping pace," reported a member of the 16th Pennsylvania.[17] The head of the Yankee column arrived at Kelly's Ford at almost 8:00 after a four-hour march. The Federals ushered in St. Patrick's Day with a bugle call, the clang of sabers, and the crack of pistols. Things would never be the same again.

By 11:00 A.M. on March 16, the Confederates knew about Averell's movement. That morning, Robert E. Lee telegraphed his nephew Fitz that "a large body of cavalry has left the Federal army, and was marching up the Rappahannock." By 6:00 P.M., Fitz Lee's scouts had located Averell's column near Morrisville. Lee did not know whether Averell intended to cross at Kelly's Ford or at Rappahannock

Station, or whether he intended to continue northwest toward Warrenton. Fitz reinforced his picket of twenty sharpshooters with forty more men, but only eleven or twelve of them actually reached the skirmish line by morning.[18] "Three thousand Yankee cavalry & artillery reported near Kelly's Ford, and a circular sent to the Regiments to have all their sharpshooters out at daybreak & to send them down the railroad to the road leading from Brandy Station to Kelly's Ford," recorded Lt. Col. William R. Carter of the 3d Virginia Cavalry in his diary that night. "Then to wait for orders, Regiments holding themselves ready to move at a moment's warning."[19]

Fitz Lee's horse soldiers made arrangements to entertain the advancing Federals. They constructed abatis. The Confederates had dug rifle pits along the riverbanks at the ford over the winter, and the sharpshooters held these rifle pits. Two houses overlooking the ford provided shelter for the Southern defenders and substantial obstacles for the advancing Northerners. The grayclad horsemen also occupied the millrace from the large mill at Kellysville, meaning that the small force of Southerners held a formidable defensive position.[20] Capt. James Breckinridge of the 2d Virginia Cavalry commanded the sharpshooters. His force consisted of 45 men from the 2d Virginia and Lt. William A. Moss's Company K, 4th Virginia Cavalry, with eighty-five carbines, putting 130 Southerners at the Ford. Another forty men, under command of Maj. William A. Morgan of the 1st Virginia Cavalry, waited about five miles away at the point where the Orange & Alexandria Railroad and the road to Kelly's Ford diverged, so that these reinforcements could respond to any need quickly.[21]

THE UNION ATTACK OPENS

Duffié's brigade led the way. One hundred men of the 4th New York and 5th U.S. advanced toward Kelly's Ford as an advance guard. At the first glimmer of dawn, these men were to dash across the river and capture the pickets on the other side. They would clear the way for the rest of Averell's division to cross the river unmolested. The balance of the 4th New York, which was not known to be an especially reliable command, would support the advance guard. They took position near the river on the night of the 16th, and moved out early in the morning. Two squadrons of the 4th New York dismounted and opened fire on the enemy sharpshooters and a brisk exchange followed. "Whenever a rebel head appears above the entrenchment it becomes a mark for a hundred balls," noted an officer of the 6th Ohio.[22] The balance of the advance guard attempted to cross the river, but the severe fire of the well-protected Confederates drove them back. The water was to the top of their horses's backs, and the men had to carry their ammunition and pistols around their necks. It was dangerous going.[23] Two additional attempts also failed. "The firing was very sharp and incessant and it seemed as though our men could never cross in the face of that deadly fire," observed a member of the 6th Ohio.[24]

Frustrated, Averell sent a small column one fourth of a mile downriver to try to flank the Southern sharpshooters, but the deep water and steep riverbanks foiled the attempt. After half an hour, Averell, livid because the element of surprise had been lost, sent his chief of staff, Maj. Samuel E. Chamberlain of the 1st Massachusetts Cavalry, to try to force a crossing. Chamberlain ordered the men of the 4th New York to form column of fours and to follow him across the river. They swam across the Rappahannock and ran afoul of the abatis, exposing the men to severe enemy fire from the well-protected rifle pits. Chamberlain had his horse shot in three places, and he was shot in the face. The horse, frantic from its wounds, was impaled on a fallen tree and fell dead as it hit the water. Seeing the major reel in the saddle, the skittish New Yorkers beat a hasty retreat.[25]

Even though he was badly injured, Chamberlain sent to Averell for pioneers and obtained twenty men of the 16th Pennsylvania armed with axes. Chamberlain put these men to work chopping away the abatis, and the major deployed his dismounted carbineers in the road to cover them with rifle fire. Averell brought up a section of guns and unlimbered them but, concerned that opening fire would announce the size of his force, chose not to commit the artillery to the fighting. He contented himself with maintaining a brisk fire to prevent the enemy from drawing a bead on his axemen. Chamberlain ordered the 4th New York to try again. With the injured major leading them, the New Yorkers again swam across the river, but not enough of the trees had been cleared, and severe fire from the rifle pits had driven off the pioneers. Lt. John Domingo of the 4th New York led his men into the frigid waters of the river. He partly turned in his saddle, waved his sword, and was cheering his men on when he received a mortal wound. Another officer riding next to him also had his horse shot out from under him. The remaining New Yorkers rode into a withering volley, turned, and fled.[26]

Averell fumed as he watched these efforts fail. He sat on his horse overlooking the ford. His division, strung out along the road in column of fours, could not advance until the abatis was cleared. The New Yorker realized that with the failure of the attempt to cross downstream, he had no choice but to force a crossing of the Rappahannock. He ordered the dismounted men in the road to increase their rate of fire, and thus protected, the axemen of the 16th Pennsylvania resumed their work. They made some progress clearing the felled trees and opening more of the road to permit the further advance of the Northern horsemen.

Major Chamberlain handed off his valuables to a staff officer and rode up to the main column, calling for volunteers to carry the crossing. He rode over to the 1st Rhode Island and announced, "I want a platoon of men who will go where I tell them."[27] Chamberlain chose Lt. Simeon A. Brown of the 1st Rhode Island to lead this assault, and ordered Brown to either cross or not return. Brown, riding a conspicuous large white horse, would make the dash with eighteen men, to be followed by the balance of the 1st Rhode Island and the 6th Ohio. As he finished giving Brown his instructions, the major said, "If you do that it will be a good thing for you."[28] Away the little assault column went. As soon as they reached the road on the south side of the river, a fusillade met them.

The Rhode Islanders broke and ran, leaving Major Chamberlain alone and exposed. His horse was mortally wounded as it reached the water, and the gallant major received his second wound of the day, striking his left cheek, cutting off the tip of his nose, ranging down through his neck, and knocking him from the saddle. The pioneers dragged him up the bank, and the dazed major, partially blinded by his own blood, emptied his revolver, "firing first, it is said, at the fleeing Rhode Islanders, and then at the enemy on the opposite side of the river."[29] Pvt. Charles Capwell of the 1st Rhode Island recalled, "The first thing that saluted our eyes was Major Chamberlin [sic] coming up the bank with his face a gore of blood. Says he, 'Go on, boys, I am done for.'"[30] An officer of the 3d Pennsylvania noted that Major Chamberlain "was picked up more dead than alive, and carried to camp. His wounds are very bad, but he still lives."[31]

The Rhode Islanders rallied, and with a cheer, advanced again, dashing into the frigid water. They saw a horse, "near the center of the stream, reared up and turned over on his side, with blood spurting from him, crimsoning the water through which we were to pass."[32] This time, the axemen of the 16th Pennsylvania followed close behind them, with their "axes shining and glittering above their heads, the ford and its passengers presented a singularly picturesque scene suggestive of men at arms with their battle axes." The balance of the Rhode Islanders and the Buckeyes of the 6th Ohio followed close behind.[33]

Trooper Truman Reeves of the 6th Ohio was one of the first members of his regiment to make it across the river. "It was a sorry sight, I can assure you, as nearly one half of the men and horses that first went into the river were either killed or wounded, the latter floundering in the rapid current. As fast as we crossed we charged on the mill-race, shooting with our Colt's revolvers, which soon put the enemy to flight," he wrote.[34]

The act of dismounting had reduced the effective strength of the Confederate picket forces by 25 percent. Someone had to hold the horses of the dismounted men fighting, and every fourth man drew that unpleasant duty. They were usually kept near the line, so that they were quickly accessed. "This occasion as well as many others demonstrated the fact that the horse-holders in a cavalry fight should be the coolest and bravest men in the company," observed a Confederate officer. "'Number Four' has no right to be exempt from the perils of the battle. He holds the horses of his comrades only in order that they may more efficiently fight on foot; and he should always be near at hand to give whatever aid the occasion demands."[35] Horse holders were not available to fight, but they nevertheless served an important and necessary role.

Confederate Capt. James Breckinridge faced a challenge. His men recognized the odds facing them. "Four times they charged through our stockades and some of them with drawn sabers mounted the parapets," he recounted. "At last we had fired all of our ammunition, carbines and pistols, but kept our post until almost every hope of escape was past and 12 of my little band were captured by the overwhelming force." Along with two or three others, Breckinridge ran for his horse, hoping to escape. However, the horse holders were not nearby, as they should have been. After a harrowing run of 300 yards, the winded captain "reached a stray horse nearly exhausted, mounted while the Cavalry was almost up to me, and got off safe."

Lieutenant Moss ordered his men to support Breckinridge, "but they had to pass over a wide meadow to reach the pits and no human persuasion could make them go. In vain I ran from the pits to them and back again, coaxed and threatened. They would not follow me. Some of them I got out into the meadow. The balls would plough up the earth around them. They would then fall flat and I suppose never get up until the Yankees picked them up." Breckinridge fired twelve shots from his pistol during his gallant stand. "At one time I saw my men falling back from one of the pits," he recounted. "I rushed over the bank and they rallied and fought with a desperation I never saw excelled."[36]

This left only the eighty-five men of Moss's squadron of the 4th Virginia to face the blueclad onslaught. The suppressing fire that kept his men pinned down ceased in order to avoid hitting friendly targets, allowing Moss and his men to rise and open fire freely. Moss directed all of his available firepower on the gray horse ridden by Brown, the brave young Rhode Islander. If Brown's horse went down, reasoned Moss, so would Brown. Of the eighteen men riding with Brown, only three, Sgt. Emmons D. Guild and Pvts. John A. Medbury and Patrick Parker, emerged on the other side, the others cut down while still in the river. Parker lost his horse in the swirling currents.[37] Two were killed, including Lt. Henry L. Nicolai of the 1st Rhode Island. Five enlisted men were wounded, and fifteen horses were killed or disabled by the galling fire of Moss's defenders.[38]

Brown, somehow untouched, rode up the bank and opened fire on the rifle pits with his revolver. He turned and waved his sword to the main body of his regiment, calling them forward. He rode up to the edge of a rifle pit that held eight Confederates, where every man had his carbine aimed at the lieutenant. However, not one had fired, "so astonished were they at such a spectacle." Brown wheeled his horse, galloped a few yards to the right, and dismounted behind a tree, where two of his men joined him. The three Rhode Islanders opened a galling fire on the rifle pit, killing two men and wounding a third.[39] Later, Lieutenant Brown realized that five bullets had pierced his clothes, and that his horse had been wounded three times. Sgt. Emmons D. Guild, firing at Brown's side, was slightly wounded in the side in the firefight with the Virginians. "I have often wondered how it was that I could have missed the gray horse" ridden by Lieutenant Brown, wrote a frustrated Captain Moss years after the war, "as I fired at him more than at his rider."[40] In consequence of his bravery, Hooker later requested that the lieutenant be promoted to captain for his distinguished service that morning.[41]

AVERELL CROSSES THE RAPPAHANNOCK

Buoyed by Lieutenant Brown's heroic dash, the Rhode Islanders finally crossed the river and broke through the impediments. Two bullets smashed the scabbard of Lt. Jacob B. Cooke of the 1st Rhode Island, and another passed through his coat. The fortunate officer escaped unharmed.[42] When he tried to cross, a bullet hit Colonel Duffié's horse. The wounded animal threw the Frenchman into the river, "considerably bruising one of his legs."[43] Pvt. Bernard Murrin of Company D, 1st Rhode Island Cavalry, made his way through the icy waters. Murrin, a twenty-four-year-old native of New York, was shot through the left elbow by a carbine ball. "He received the wound while in a charge made by his regiment across the Rappahannock River and in which his company was foremost," recalled Lt. Willis C. Capron, Murrin's commanding officer. "He was nobly performing his duty as a soldier when he received the wound which made him a cripple for life." Surgeons amputated Murrin's arm just below the shoulder, and he received a disability discharge that November.[44]

Realizing that their position could not be held, Moss's dismounted men withdrew, many being chased by pursuing Yankees, who captured twenty-five of the Virginians. "Lieutenant Brown obeyed his orders," observed Averell.[45] With the Rhode Islanders to deflect the fire of Moss's Virginians, the axemen veered a bit upstream, climbed the riverbank, and vigorously went to work. It took nearly two hours to remove the remaining obstacles, clear the road, and for the balance of Averell's command to cross the river. Because of the narrowness of the ford, the Northern horse soldiers had to cross it by squadrons in columns of four, engendering long delays. A squadron of horsemen removed the artillery ammunition from the limbers and carried it across to prevent it from getting wet. They dragged the guns through the water, which came up to the top of the limber boxes. Upon reaching the other side, Averell paused to form his troops and to water his horses.

The impatient New Yorker grabbed a detachment of horsemen and rode to the front to make a hasty reconnaissance. He spotted an open plain three quarters of a mile up the road toward Culpeper, near the Wheatley farm, and noted it as the likely place for the expected battle to occur. Averell massed his regiments and waited for his old friend to come out and attack him instead of fanning out across the countryside, searching for scattered Confederate regiments. At 10:15, Averell moved his command out as soon as all was ready. Averell left a squadron to guard the ford and advanced. The Yankee horsemen marched through the little settlement of Kellysville, consisting of a gristmill and six houses, and followed the road northwest toward the Orange & Alexandria. Duffié's brigade led the way, with the 6th Ohio deployed as skirmishers and the 4th New York and 1st Rhode Island following as supports. They moved slowly and cautiously, with ground scouts dismounting to search the nearby woods for flankers. McIntosh's brigade formed line of battle along the woods and along a stone wall, while Reno's Regulars stayed in reserve.[46]

"About midway in a narrow strip of woods, the rebels became belligerent and drove in our skirmishers rapidly on the reserves, following up with a charge," observed Capt. Walter S. Newhall of the 3d Pennsylvania. Lt. George Browne, Jr., commander of Averell's battery, unlimbered a section of guns, and "the first volley changed the aspect of affairs, and gave us a chance to push beyond the woods, where we formed in column of echelon, ready for the charge." As the Federals cautiously advanced, they spied Fitz Lee's brigade drawn up in line of battle on the other side of a wide field.[47]

FITZ LEE RESPONDS TO THE THREAT

Averell had correctly measured his old friend. When Averell first attempted to cross the river, a courier rode for Culpeper to warn the brigade commander, but the message never arrived. At 7:30, a second courier informed Lee that the enemy had crossed and had captured twenty-five of his pickets. As the courier dashed up on his lathered horse, he called out that there was "hell to pay,' that the Yankees had crossed the Rappahannock and that they were moving on the abatis in force.[48]

"Boots and saddles" blared in Lee's camps, and his 800 troopers trotted off to meet Averell. Lee had the 1st, 2d, 3d, 4th, and 5th Virginia Cavalry and Capt. James Breathed's battery of horse artillery to oppose Averell's division. These veteran troopers had seen hard marching and harder fighting, and they had humiliated Averell at Hartwood Church just three weeks earlier. The confident Southern cavaliers were ready to meet the Northern upstarts on the field of battle, and they believed that they could whip even a much larger force. Col. Thomas H. Owen called the company commanders of his 3d Virginia Cavalry around him and "asked them to do their duty & see that their men did the same."[49] Lee assumed a position at Dean's Shop, located at a road junction a mile and a half from the ford, and three miles from Brandy Station on the Orange & Alexandria Railroad. He sent his wagons and disabled horses back to Rapidan Station, and waited for Averell to arrive.[50] As they formed, "truly a fearful sight we saw," noted a member of the 3d Virginia. "Down near the river were fully 3,000 men drawn up, with two pieces of artillery."[51]

Jeb Stuart followed Lee's brigade that morning. The Southern cavalry chieftain, who had gone to Culpeper for the court-martial of one of his officers, also heard the sound of the firing. Stuart and his chief of horse artillery, Maj. John Pelham, borrowed horses and accompanied Lee's brigade to Kelly's Ford. "Being charged by [Robert E. Lee] specially with 'preparations to meet Stoneman,' I was present on this occasion, because of the responsibility which would necessarily attach to me for what was done; but having approved of Brig. Gen. Fitzhugh Lee's plans, I determined not to interfere with his command of the brigade as long as it was commanded so entirely to my satisfaction, and I took special pride in witnessing its gallant conduct under its accomplished leader."[52]

Fitz Lee sat watching Averell's deployment. Pvt. William B. Conway of the 1st Virginia Cavalry carried a message to Lee from Maj. William A. Morgan. Conway delivered the message and started to ride off, but Lee told him to wait. One of Lee's staff officers inquired why the general had detained Conway. Perhaps anticipating that his orders might be changed, and that Conway might have to carry new instructions to Morgan, Lee raised his field glasses and said, "He is coming now." Fitz Lee's eyes sparkled as he watched a rider approach. "It is Jeb Stuart!" he proclaimed.[53] Moments later, Stuart and his giant Prussian aide, Maj. Heros von Borcke, rode up. "General, I am truly glad to see you. We are in a tight place. I turn over command to you," said Lee.

"No you don't," replied Stuart. "I came as a volunteer and brought all the reinforcements I could. Fitz, this is your fight. Command and I obey."[54] Stuart spent the day watching the action unfold. He saw quite a show.

Lee turned to Stuart and said, "General, I think there are only a few platoons in the woods yonder. Hadn't we better 'take the bulge' on them at once?" Stuart agreed that Lee should order the attack, and the ball opened.[55]

FITZ LEE ATTACKS AVERELL
AT THE STONE WALL ON THE WHEATLEY FARM

When the Yankees did not appear, the impatient Virginian rode toward the Wheatley farm buildings. Believing that he faced only an advance guard, Lee deployed a dismounted squadron, hoping to check the Northern advance. About noon, as Averell's skirmishers emerged from a stand of woods about a mile from Kelly's Ford, they met a volley from Lee's small force of dismounted troopers. Reacting, Averell deployed the dismounted 4th New York on the right (north) side of the road and the 4th Pennsylvania on the left, placed a section of artillery between them, and instructed his line to advance to the edge of the woods and to open fire with their carbines.

"The Fourth Pennsylvania and Fourth New York, I regret to say, did not come up to the mark at first," complained Averell, "and it required some personal exertions on the part of myself and staff to bring them under the enemy's fire, which was now sweeping the woods." With the general's curses ringing in their ears, these horse soldiers "soon regained their firmness, and opened with effect with their carbines." However, as the 4th New York and 4th Pennsylvania rallied, Averell spotted two or three columns of Confederates trotting toward his right. "I immediately went to the threatened point, and found that it was a question which should obtain possession of [the Wheatley] house and outbuildings," recalled the New Yorker.[56]

McIntosh dispatched a contingent of dismounted troopers of the 16th Pennsylvania and a section of artillery to secure these buildings. As the Pennsylvanians rode up, a slave woman approached, wailing at them not to fight there.[57] With his guns roaring, McIntosh advanced his right beyond the house and into the open fields in front. With Col. J. Irvin Gregg's 16th Pennsylvania leading the way, McIntosh attacked the Confederate left. The 4th New York and 4th Pennsylvania advanced with a cheer against the stone wall while 100 of Gregg's Pennsylvanians crashed through the woods to attack the rear of the stone wall. The determined attack drove the Southern defenders from the wall, and the 4th New York and 4th Pennsylvania assumed a stout position behind the wall.

FITZ LEE COUNTERATTACKS

Lee counterattacked with his whole brigade. The men of the 3d Virginia Cavalry threw down a rail fence and formed line of battle. The Virginians charged in column of fours, directing them toward the stone wall on the Wheatley property. Fitz hoped to flank Averell's right, but the Virginians rode into a hail of carbine fire and veered to their left, turning their flank to the Union line, looking for an opening and firing their pistols at the well-protected Yankees. They dashed for the Wheatley house, hoping to outflank the Northerners from their strong position behind the stone wall.[58]

Platoon Sgt. Robert S. Hudgins of the Old Dominion Dragoons of the 3d Virginia Cavalry recalled, "Giving the old Rebel yell, we hit them and went through their advance guard nearly up to the Stevensburg Road." St. Patrick's Day did not mark the sergeant's first fencing match with a Northern horseman—he had been involved in another melee on the Peninsula in 1862. Now, Hudgins squared off with a big Yankee mounted on a magnificent sorrel horse. "As we drew near he raised his sabre and, as before, I threw mine into a parry with a prayer that I could stop his blow, or at least turn it. Again my opponent tore the sabre from my grasp, breaking the leather thong around my wrist. As I wheeled in my saddle I saw my opponent throw up his hands and topple to the ground." Someone had shot the blueclad horseman. Hudgins escaped and rejoined his unit. Later, Sergeant Hudgins saved his regiment's battle flag from capture.[59]

The 5th Virginia, commanded by Col. Thomas L. Rosser, joined the 3d Virginia as they came opposite the Union right, and the two regiments headed for the Wheatley house, where they would try to gain the Federal rear, cutting Averell off from his route of retreat to Kelly's Ford. "Seeing the situation in which we were and thinking we might get at the enemy through a lane on our left, [Owen and Rosser] resolved to try it," recalled the adjutant of the 3d Virginia Cavalry. "Wheeling to the left by fours, the 5th trotted into the lane and we followed." However, the 100 men of the 16th Pennsylvania dispatched by McIntosh to protect the Federal flank opened a withering fire on the Virginians and forced them to withdraw. "The enemy now advanced a regiment dismounted to the fence and poured a hot fire into our flanks," continued the adjutant of the 3d Virginia.[60] "They then made a charge upon our center & were handsomely repulsed in several charges," observed a member of the 16th Pennsylvania.[61] Another member of the same regiment noted, "The charge was a desperate one, riding up to the muzzles of our carbines, and attempting to force their way through the lane. All to no avail. Reduced in numbers, they were once more driven back to their cover."[62]

Fitz Lee sent one of his staff officers, Capt. Harry Gilmor, to Rosser with an order to charge with the 5th Virginia on the extreme left near the river, sweep around the enemy, get between him and the ford, and attack the Union rear. Gilmor rode a gauntlet of sharpshooters and delivered his message. Rosser, who was moving out in column when Gilmor reined in, replied that he was starting his new errand. Gilmor accompanied the charge. As they dashed across the fields, the entire column drew heavy fire as the Virginians negotiated the difficult terrain. Rosser tried to keep his column together, but could not. Gilmor heard Rosser call out to Maj. John W. Puller of the 5th Virginia, "Major Puller, why, in the name of God, don't you assist me in rallying the men?"

Gilmor turned and saw Puller, bent forward on his horse's neck, coming up behind him. Puller weakly raised his head and said, "Colonel, I'm killed."

Mortified, Rosser responded, "My God, old fellow, I hope not; bear up, bear up!" Rosser spurred off to rally the troops, but Gilmor stayed behind to tend to the mortally wounded major. When Rosser told him to bear up, Puller tried to straighten himself in the saddle, but he was too weak to do so and toppled from it. Puller died a few minutes later from a chest wound. Gilmor then rode off to report the results of the charge to Stuart.[63]

As the 3d Virginia charged the stone fence, looking for an opening to pass through, a squadron of Yankee troopers broke and ran. Their commander tried to rally them, but failed. Drawing his pistol, the blueclad officer emptied every chamber at the advancing Southerners. "Everyone honors a brave man," noted a member of the 3d Virginia, "and we cheered him. Understanding our cheer, he raised his

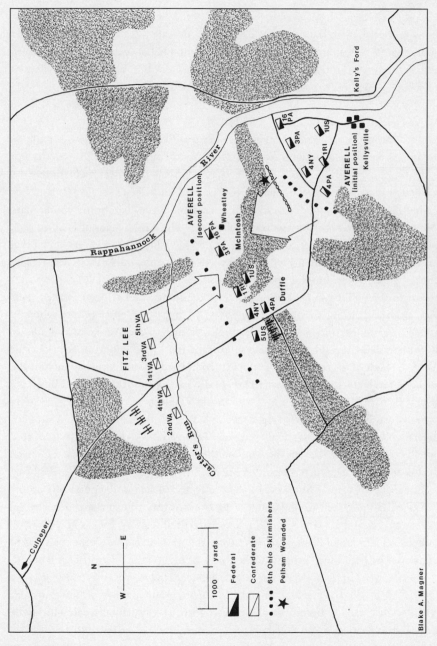

The Battle of Kelly's Ford, March 17, 1863

Blake A. Magner

hat, gave a salute and rode off." The Virginian sniffed, "He was worthy to lead better men."[64]

As the 3d Virginia leapt a ditch, Pvt. William H. Ware spotted a dismounted Federal lying in the ditch. Ware wheeled his horse and called back, asking the Northerner what he was doing. The Yankee replied that the bullets were too thick for him
there, so he was hiding. Ware captured the man and sent him back into the safety of
the woods, where his trip to Richmond's Belle Isle prison camp began.[65]

DEATH OF THE GALLANT PELHAM

Twenty-four-year-old Maj. John Pelham served as Stuart's chief of horse artillery.
Born in Alabama, Pelham was a member of the West Point class of 1861, but did not
graduate. Along with his classmate and friend Thomas L. Rosser, Pelham left the
Academy two weeks before graduation to join the Confederate service. Pelham had
bright blue eyes and blonde hair, and was considered a very handsome young man.
Young ladies all over Virginia swooned over him. "He was . . . a young man of high
tome and decided character, and his proficiency in military exercise and in all that
pertained to a soldier's life made him a cadet noncommissioned officer and a cadet
officer," recalled a classmate. The young cannoneer caught Stuart's eye shortly after
the Battle of Bull Run in 1861, and Stuart made him his chief of horse artillery. Pelham's extraordinary performance earned him the respect of every officer who saw
him. "General, if you have another Pelham, give him to me," remarked an admiring Stonewall Jackson. He was promoted to captain in 1862 and to major later that
year. As a result of his courageous performance in holding off Union infantry at the
Battle of Fredericksburg, Robert E. Lee praised the young man, called him "the
Gallant Pelham," and requested his promotion to lieutenant colonel.[66]

Pelham was in Orange visiting a young lady and inspecting Capt. Marcellus
Moorman's battery of horse artilley when Confederates in the vicinity reported
that 3,000 cavalrymen had left the Army of the Potomac and ridden west. He made
his way to Culpeper, where he joined Stuart. Since Pelham also had a sweetheart
in Culpeper (Miss Bessie Shackelford, the pretty and vivacious daughter of a prominent local judge), Pelham seized upon the opportunity to call upon her. On the
morning of March 17, 1863, Pelham and Stuart's aide, Maj. Heros von Borcke,
were laying a wooden plank walkway across the main street in Culpeper, so as to
avoid tracking mud into Judge Shackelford's house. As the two officers labored,
word came that the Yankees were trying to force a passage at Kelly's Ford.[67]

Pelham paused to scribble a note to Moorman, whose battery of horse artillery
remained in Orange. "Be on the alert. Large force of cavalry between Morrisvlle
and Bealton Station," scrawled Pelham, "If everything is quiet here I will be at
Rapidann Station tomorrow." A courier spurred off to deliver this message to
Moorman. This was the last order Pelham ever wrote.[68]

The artillerist then borrowed a horse, and rode to the sound of the guns with Stuart. He assisted Captain Breathed in bringing up his guns. Pelham sighted a gun himself, and then turned over command of the battery to his subordinate. The major was in good spirits that morning. Gilmor recalled that Pelham looked "as fresh, and as joyous, and rosy as a boy ten years old."[69] He rode off to find Lee and Stuart, and arrived as Lee ordered his first charge. Impulsively, the Gallant Pelham joined the charge. He drew his saber, spurred his horse into line with the charging Virginians, and dashed forward. When he reached the stone wall, he rose in his stirrups, turned his head to the troopers following him and cried, "Forward! Let's get them!"[70]

At that moment, a Union artillery shell exploded on the wall, spraying lethal shrapnel. A chunk of metal about the size of a ripe cherry entered the back of Pelham's skull, and the gallant artillerist toppled from the saddle. When he failed to rise, Captain Gilmor rode over to him, saw the glazed, unblinking eyes of a mortally wounded or dead man, and instructed two of Fitz Lee's staff officers to take the body back to Culpeper. The two officers lifted Pelham's limp body and draped it over the front of a horse, his feet hanging down on one side and his head on the other. They carried the unconscious artillerist to safety. Although Gilmor thought the artillerist was dead, Pelham was barely still alive.

Gilmor, covered in Pelham's blood, rode up to report the loss to Stuart. "I shall never forget his look of distress and horror," recalled Gilmor. "We were almost cut off from our own troops by a sudden advance of a strong body of the enemy, and were making our way rapidly through a dense wood to regain our line, when he halted, and made me repeat all about his death, or rather wound. Then he bowed his head upon his horse's neck and wept. 'Our loss is irreparable!'" wailed Stuart.[71]

At Stuart's behest, Gilmor then dashed off to Culpeper. Along the way, he encountered the two troopers he had placed in charge of Pelham, and was appalled to find the desperately wounded artillerist still draped across the horse, his hands, face and hair caked and clotted with mud and blood. "Overwhelmed with horror, I had him laid on the grass in a fence corner, and then, to my astonishment, found him still alive. Imagine my indignation and vented wrath when I learned that, instead of looking for an ambulance, they had moved on toward Culpeper, a distance of eight miles, four of which they had already accomplished." Gilmor sent for an ambulance. He went to his grave believing that prompt and proper medical care might have saved Pelham's life.

When Pelham arrived in Culpeper, three surgeons attended him and removed the shell fragment. They pronounced the young artillerist hopeless and left him in the care of Bessie Shackelford and Captain Gilmor. About 1:00 A.M. on the 18th, his eyes opened, he moved his head slightly, closed his eyes, drew a long breath, and died quietly. "We dressed him in his best uniform, and had but just laid him out on

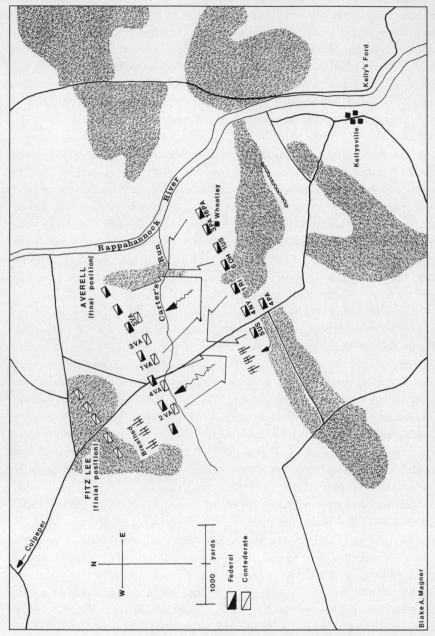

The Final Engagement at Kelly's Ford, March 17, 1863

Blake A. Magner

the bed," recalled Gilmor, "when the door was gently opened, and Stuart entered, having returned from the fight at Kelly's Ford. Great tears rolled down his cheeks as he silently gazed upon the lifeless form, and then retired."[72]

AVERELL COUNTERATTACKS

Averell had no troops close enough to follow up on the repulse of the 3d and 5th Virginia, and he also did not know how large a force lay in his front. Uncertain and not wanting to expose himself to a strong counterattack, Averell could not exploit McIntosh's success. He allowed the Virginians to withdraw to safety, badly shaken, but still intact and dangerous.

As McIntosh regrouped, Duffié formed the 1st Rhode Island, 4th Pennsylvania, and 6th Ohio in front of the left of the Federal line, and ordered the charge. Spotting Duffié forming for the attack, Averell called for Reno to advance three squadrons of Regulars to support the Frenchman's assault. Duffié's decision to attack without orders incensed Averell, but it was too late to stop the Frenchman from making the charge. "The temptation to pitch into men who so boldly threw themselves at [Duffié] was too much . . . and he was resolved at all hazards to try his hand at the charging too." Reno and Averell galloped to the left to watch Duffié's charge. The balance of the Regulars remained in reserve, waiting for the right opportunity to pitch into the fray.[73]

Duffié, who was a fine swordsman, "advanced in splendid order and charged the enemy," his sabers flashing in the bright morning sunlight. Perhaps carried away with the moment, the Frenchman held back only the 4th New York as a reserve. "It was our turn to yell now," reported a member of the 4th New York, "and such a shout as burst along our whole line is not often heard."[74] Two squadrons of Reno's 5th U.S. dashed to Duffié's support, McIntosh's left flank also rolled forward, "and the enemy were torn to pieces or driven from the field in magnificent style," praised Averell. However, the impetuous charge was made three minutes too soon, and without arranging any support for it. "Had it been possible to reach the enemy's flank when Duffié charged with the Fifth United States or Third Pennsylvania, 300 to 500 prisoners might have been captured, but the distance was too great for the time, the ground was very heavy," observed Averell.[75]

THE SECOND CONFEDERATE ATTACK

Fitz Lee led the 1st, 2d, and 4th Virginia forward to meet Duffié's charge, their blades glinting along a line of woods. The Frenchman's command halted, waiting. When the enemy came within 100 yards of the Frenchman's position, his Rhode Islanders dashed ahead to meet Lee's horsemen in the open field. The 6th Ohio and two squadrons of the 4th Pennsylvania followed on the right while two squadrons of the 5th U.S. trailed on the left, supporting the attacking Rhode Islanders. "All eyes watched the encounter," recalled an officer of the 3d Pennsylvania. "On they went, erect in saddle, horses well in hand, sabers flashing in the sunlight." The command "charge" rang out, and "the earth trembles as these two regiments thunder at each other. They meet—the shock is terrible. Amidst the slashing of sabers and firing of pistols, we could hear the cry, 'You Yankees, use your pistols, fight like gentlemen.'"[76]

Trooper Reeve of the 6th Ohio recalled, "It was like the coming together of two mighty railroad trains at full speed. The yelling of men, the clashing of sabers, a few empty saddles, a few wounded and dying, and the charge is over. One side or the other is victorious, perhaps, only for a few minutes, and then the contest is renewed. A charge of this kind is over almost before one has time to think of the danger he is in."[77]

Northern steel did its job with cold efficiency. "The sight of blood gushing from ghastly sabre-slashes is too much for our opponents; they waver, break, and give way, and the victory is that of Saber over Pistol."[78] Maj. Preston M. Farrington of the 1st Rhode Island received a dangerous and serious wound when a pistol ball passed through his neck. After having his wound dressed at a field hospital, the major returned to his regiment and led it in two more charges.[79] Sgt. Emmons D. Guild of the 1st Rhode Island also had a lucky escape. "The nearest I got to getting hit was a ball passed through my overcoat jacket, vest & shirt, just above my pants on my right side, but it did not touch the flesh, that was near enough to sute me, I tell you."[80]

Lt. George W. Wilson of the 6th Ohio Cavalry sat on his horse at the head of his company, his orderly sergeant by his side, their knees touching. A well-placed Confederate artillery shell exploded at an angle of about forty-five degrees in front of them, and ten feet from their heads, scattering shrapnel in all directions. "The sulphur in the shell, bursting so close to our heads, took the power of speech from Wilson, and he did not speak a loud word for more than a week. The bridle reins were cut entirely from his hands, we were both slightly wounded, he in his left leg, and I in my right leg and left wrist, but neither severely."[81]

Lt. Robert B. Isbell of Company B, 2d Virginia Cavalry, joined the charge. He lost his horse during this first melee when the animal was shot through the head. "It fell on the field and died without a struggle." Isbell was unhorsed less than fifty yards from the Yankees, and he was in a precarious situation. The lieutenant realized that he did not have time to try to save his saddle, other equipment, or dry clothes. He abandoned all, losing "every item of clothing I had except what I had on my back." The Federals drew a bead on the fleeing lieutenant. A bullet tore through his boot and broke the skin on his ankle, but the thick cavalry boots slowed the ball enough that it did not enter his leg. Badly bruised, he staggered back to safety. "All I want is a good horse and I will be after the Yanks again," he vowed the day after the battle.[82]

The 3d Pennsylvania, of McIntosh's brigade, assumed the position previously held by the 3d and 5th Virginia on the Union right, to the west of the Wheatley farm buildings, threatening Lee's flank. Outnumbered, and in danger of being flanked, Lee's men squeezed off a few shots, wheeled irregularly by fours and platoons to the right, and fled, with the victorious Rhode Islanders in hot pursuit. The Rhode Islanders swept up a number of prisoners.[83] Lt. Jacob B. Cooke of the 1st Rhode Island joined this charge. "My horse carried me through the Confederate lines," he recalled, "and I escaped by making a detour to the left, jumping a fence into a by-road which ran into the Culpeper road, and turning to the left again jumped a fence back into the field where the regiment was." Cooke remembered the wild and perilous ride for the rest of his life.[84]

However, the enthusiasm of the Rhode Islanders carried a few of them too far. A fresh squadron of Southerners met their charge, and a running fight broke out, costing the Northerners two officers and eighteen enlisted men captured. Two squadrons of the 5th U.S. countercharged, and a wild saber-swinging melee erupted. "At the second attempt of the enemy to rally, the [5th U.S.] seized the opportunity and made a brilliant charge which forced them into a rapid retreat and won the commendation of General Averell."[85]

Twenty-three-year-old Lt. Nathaniel "Nat" Bowditch of the 1st Massachusetts served as an assistant adjutant general on Duffié's staff. Bowditch, who rode a powerful horse, surged ahead of the main column. "Raising himself erect in his saddle, throwing aloft his glittering sabre, he called on us to follow; and immediately dashed forward without a look behind." He captured and sent two Virginians to the rear and cut down three more Southern horsemen with his saber. Alone and surrounded, he attempted to hack his way free, but a saber blow to the head and a ball to his shoulder knocked him from his horse. A flurry of bullets killed the beast, leaving Bowditch trapped. The Confederates quickly encircled the dismounted adjutant, demanding his surrender. When he refused, the Southerners opened fire on him, and Bowditch took a mortal wound to the abdomen. Desperately hurt, the adjutant finally yielded his pistol and the Confederates seized his belt and scabbard. For some reason, they left his saber in his bloody hand, instead focusing their attention on a small gold ring. "That I will never surrender," proclaimed Bowditch, "so shoot away!"

Duffié's troops rallied and drove back the Confederates, leaving Bowditch in no-man's land. Soon a Union straggler came up and stripped off the bridle from the adjutant's dead horse. Thinking him dead, the straggler left Bowditch alone. Soon another came by and saluted the critically wounded man. Bowditch indicated that with assistance, he might be able to mount, but that he could not move without help. The soldier hoisted Bowditch into the saddle and led him back to safety. Two surgeons examined him and quickly realized that the wound was mortal. "Well," replied the adjutant, "I hope I have done my duty. I am content."

The surgeons loaded him into an ambulance for the trip back. When Lt. Col. Greeley S. Curtis of the 1st Massachusetts Cavalry learned that Bowditch occupied the ambulance, he rode up alongside and asked the adjutant if he had been badly injured. "He said that he had a saber-cut on the head, and a shot in his shoulder, neither of which he thought serious; but that he had a bullet in the pit of his stomach, which, if it had gone upwards, 'had done for him;' but that he couldn't tell exactly what direction it had taken. He said that he was perfectly comfortable, and felt no pain, only that he was very thirsty; so I rode off and got him a cup of water." The colonel helped Bowditch into a house and sat with him a while. The lieutenant related his adventures modestly. Bowditch lingered for a couple of days and died in a Union field hospital at Morrisville.[86]

The Federals lamented the loss of the popular Bowditch. "Your gallant son fell *like a soldier,*—respected, lamented, and beloved," wrote Col. Horace B. Sargent of the 1st Massachusetts Cavalry in a letter to Bowditch's father.[87] More tellingly, a private of the 1st Massachusetts wrote, "There was not a single officer in the regiment who was so universally loved by both officers and men. I had learned to love him myself. Well, he died like a soldier; bravely fighting the enemy, first and foremost. His death is an example which the whole army might be proud of."[88]

Another officer of the 1st Massachusetts, Lt. Henry T. Davis, also served on Duffié's staff. Lieutenant Davis pitched into the fray, and had a Confederate ball strike the clasp of his sword belt. Fortunately, the ball bent the clasp squarely, doubling it up like a cup, but doing no harm to the lucky staff officer, who, unlike Bowditch, escaped unharmed.[89]

Unable to resist joining the melee, a squadron of the 3d Pennsylvania, previously held in support, drew sabers and joined the pursuit. Furious at his subordinates for launching charges without orders to do so, Averell recalled the Pennsylvanians immediately. The angry New Yorker insisted that once troops were assigned a position in line, they were not to leave it under any circumstances without orders from Averell or some other officer designated by him. Averell stripped his horsemen of all latitude to act on their own initiative. As historian John B. Bigelow put it, "Such an order is prohibitive of effective cavalry action."[90]

The 3d Pennsylvania crossed the field in echelon of squadrons at a walk, harassing the retreating Southerners with carbine fire. As the Pennsylvanians neared the wood line, they turned and formed front into line of battle at a trot, ready to charge. They fell in alongside the 16th Pennsylvania, impatiently waiting for someone to give them the order to charge.

Wisely, Fitz Lee withdrew a mile or so in order to rally his troops and forge a new line. The Virginian assumed a blocking position on the road near Carter's Run, placing mounted skirmishers in front. Lee also brought up Breathed's battery of four guns and planted it behind his main line. He had plenty of time to form his new line. "Our position here was very good," recalled an officer of the 3d Virginia. "The level ground in our front was 600 yards across, bordered on the other side by woods. The road to Kelly's Ford ran through the center, from us directly across, with a cap-and-stake fence on either side. At right angles to this road, a plank fence crossed the center of this plateau."[91] Averell was in no hurry to press his advantage. Although Averell had seized the initiative, the tricky terrain hindered his troopers.

A LULL IN THE ACTION WHILE AVERELL RE-FORMS HIS LINES

"A little reorganization was requisite before advancing farther," reported Averell. "It was necessary to form my line again and get stragglers from the Fourth New York and other regiments out of the woods behind, to assemble the sections of the battery, bring up the reserve, and give orders with regard to the wounded and prisoners. These duties occupied me half an hour or more," concluded the New Yorker. Two of Averell's guns ran out of ammunition and went to the rear. He renewed the battle with only four of his six guns. Upon reconnoitering, Averell discovered that the ground to the left of the road was marshy and unsuited to mounted operations. He placed his left on the road, and spread his line to the right, to the edge of the woods.[92]

Once Averell felt comfortable with his dispositions, he moved out again, this time with Lt. Robert Sweatman's squadron of the 5th U.S. leading the way. Averell cautiously advanced through the woods in line of battle for about three quarters of a mile before drawing the fire of Lee's artillery. The New Yorker rode in front of his lines, and pointing to the enemy guns, proclaimed, "Boys, you mustn't mind the fire from those guns; it won't hurt you; its effect is only a moral one." At that moment, a shot struck a few feet from Averell's horse, prompting the general to wheel and gallop off to the right to inspect his lines there.[93]

As the Federal skirmishers advanced, the Virginians could discern their positions by the puffs of smoke from their carbines. "After a while they became bolder and advanced steadily out into the open field," recalled the adjutant of the 3d Virginia Cavalry. "They were mounted about five yards apart in single file and extended along our entire front of half a mile. The skirmish now became very brisk indeed." Although the Confederate line was long and thin, the Virginians held their ground firmly in the face of the Federal advance.[94]

Averell called a halt, and the two opposing forces glared at each other across an open field of some 600 yards, sloping gently down from each side toward Carter's Run. Averell discovered that he had left the marshy ground, so he took a moment to extend his line of battle to the left of the road. The men of the 5th U.S., demonstrating the strict discipline expected of Regulars, extended the left in a tricky parade ground maneuver while taking heavy artillery and small arms fire.

THE FINAL CHARGE OF THE CONFEDERATES

Even though he greatly outnumbered Fitz Lee, Averell did not press his advantage. Instead, he invited his old friend to attack him. He did not have long to wait.

Fitz rode along his line of battle, telling his colonels that immediately after two shots by Breathed's guns, "he should command a charge on the extreme right and wished the regiments to gallop off in columns of squadrons, their front into line en echelon."[95] Lee would keep no reserve, meaning that if Averell followed it up with a counterattack, there would be nothing to prevent the Federals from steamrolling over Breathed's artillery. Evidently, Lee based his dispositions on his familiarity with his foe, and Fitz suspected that the cautious Averell would not make such a dash.

Breathed's signal guns boomed, and the Virginians heard the loud voice of Fitz Lee commanding, "Forward, gallop, march!" The 1st, 3d and 5th Virginia aimed for the center of the Union right, while the 2d and 4th Virginia attacked Averell's left. "It was a beautiful, splendid charge, the prettiest I ever witnessed," recalled the adjutant of the 3d Virginia.[96] After crossing Carter's Run, the men of the 1st, 3d, and 5th Virginia bore down on three squadrons of the 3d Pennsylvania which were posted on either side of a small stand of trees. Recognizing the threat, Averell brought up the 1st U.S. Cavalry of Reno's command, and placed it about 100 yards to the left of the 3d Pennsylvania. The Northern horsemen deployed in double ranks. The first rank advanced carbines, and the second rank waited, the cold steel of their sabers at the ready. The Virginians slogged through the soft, muddy ground, taking flanking fire from elements of the 16th Pennsylvania, located on the far left of Averell's line. These impediments shattered the cohesion of the Southern line, and many had either halted completely or were proceeding cautiously through the muck.

"On they came yelling and swinging their sabers and revolvers thinking no doubt the Yankees would turn and run at the terrible array," recalled a member of the 6th Ohio Cavalry. "Our line stood fast, and our boys with sabers drawn awaited the word of command to move forward. It was a thrilling moment and the excitement was intense. On the rebels came, and as they drew nearer, and see no sign of commotion or disorder in our ranks, their yell died away and they began to hesitate when within a hundred yards."[97]

Colonel Carter of the 3d Virginia watched as his horsemen bore down on the Federal guns, looming large in his front. "A battery of 3 of the enemy's guns was playing on us from the moment we commenced the charge," he noted. "Some of the men passed several hundred yards beyond the Battery, causing the most of the gunners to desert their pieces, & were only prevented from capturing the guns by a double fence which intervened & a heavy line of sharpshooters posted in the edge of the woods." Finding that they could not break this heavy line of sharpshooters, the 3d Virginia retreated to the charge's starting point, Carter's Run, and rallied.[98]

The lead elements of the Confederate charge came within twenty-five yards of the position of the 3d Pennsylvania. The Keystone Staters unleashed volley after volley of withering carbine fire into the faces of the attackers, forcing them to pull up, turn about, and retire in small squads. "At last they charged down in three columns," recalled Captain Newhall, "We held our carbine fire till we could almost see the whites of their eyes, and away they went and we after them."[99] Undaunted, the Virginians rallied and prepared to charge again.

Averell had intended to countercharge with Reno's Regulars once the Virginians made contact with the line of the 3d Pennsylvania, but the Confederates were repulsed before making contact. A few blueclad soldiers spurred forward to engage in saber duels, violating Averell's stern orders about staying in their designated places. "Since the crossing of the river there had been many personal encounters—since horsemen dashing at each other with full speed, and cutting and slashing with their sabers until one or the other was disabled," observed a correspondent. "The wounds received by both friends and foes in these single combats were frightful—such as I trust never to see again."[100]

Reno and the Pennsylvanians desperately wanted to counterattack, but Averell's orders locked them in place, so the frustrated Northerners sat and watched as the Confederates fell back to the cover and safety of their guns. As the grayclad horsemen rallied, the Pennsylvanians received orders to charge. Slinging their carbines and drawing their sabers, they dashed forward with a yell, driving the Virginians back toward Breathed's guns. "There was a moment of wild clamor, the ring and flash of sabers, the crack of revolvers, as our men met the rebels and then they turned and fled, then a cheer went up from our boys that made the heavens ring. The rebels could not stand yankee steel," claimed a proud member of the 6th Ohio.[101] A shell fragment tore through the fleshy part of Colonel McIntosh's horse's buttocks, leaving an open, ugly wound. However, the sturdy animal did not go down. The brigade commander remained mounted in spite of his horse's nasty injury.[102]

Sgt. George Reeve of the 6th Ohio charged. As the two sides clashed, a big trooper of the 1st Virginia Cavalry loomed in front of Reeve. The diminutive Reeve faced a superbly proportioned man more than six feet tall. Reeve came up on his right side, and their sabers clashed, the Virginian's at right hand cut and Reeve's at parry. "He delivered a powerful blow, but, thanks to a good saber guard, I saved my head," recalled Reeve. "In passing him I wheeled my horse so as to come up on his left side, at the same time hitting him over the head and back; and at each strike of my sabre I called to him to halt, which he did not do, and after hitting him five or six times, without apparently doing him much damage, I tried a tierce point on him with the result that a thrust through the neck brought him to the ground." The big Virginian survived. Later that evening, the two men resumed their acquaintance; this time, the Confederate was a prisoner of war. The disgusted Rebel sized up his foe and asked, "Are you the little cuss that unhorsed me?"[103]

While this scene played out, the 2d and 4th Virginia, making up Fitz's right, attacked Averell's left, trying to turn the Union flank. The Southerners advanced in column of squadrons, starting at a trot, going to a gallop and finally to the charge, the grayclad horse soldiers dashing ahead and loosing the Rebel yell. Some of the regiment's lead elements dismounted to throw down a worm rail fence obstructing their line of attack. They did so under heavy artillery fire, coolly removing the obstacle. "Firing an occasional shot from a pistol or carbine, [they] swept on toward the ranks of motionless figures with drawn sabers silently awaiting them."[104] The four Union guns opened on them, belching shell, shrapnel, and finally double-shotted canister as the Southerners bore down on them. The Federal artillerists laid down a very effective fire. "I seen one man cut in two, another with his head taken off & one with part of the head off," observed a member of the 16th Pennsylvania.[105] The concentrated artillery fire caused the lead Confederate squadron to waver, and as files peeled off to the right and left, the cry "Charge!" rang up and down the Union line.

Duffié sat quietly on his horse, watching the action unfold. When a nervous Rhode Islander discharged his carbine, the Frenchman spoke. "Steady men; don't you stir; we fix 'em; we give 'em hell!" A moment later, he cried, "Sling carbines! Draw sabers!!" Empty scabbards clinked against saddles as the blades flew out, "and a line of cold steel flashed in the waning sunlight." Lieutenant Cooke turned to inspect the line of the Rhode Islanders. "Never shall I forget their appearance," he wrote. "Every sabre was grasped as with a hand of iron; every eye was looking straight to the front; every knee was gripping its owners saddle with a vice.[sic] They sat indeed like a veritable stone wall; they appeared as immutable as fate," waiting for the order to charge. Finally, Major Farrington, back in command of the Rhode Islanders after having his wound dressed, gave the order.[106]

With a cheer, the blueclad horsemen of the 1st Rhode Island and parts of the 1st and 5th U.S. and 6th Ohio surged forward and crashed into the Virginians, "giving sudden vent to their pent-up feelings and energy."[107] A member of the 4th New York Cavalry described this charge as a "terrible onslaught."[108] "With a line like a stone wall our boys rushed upon the foe and routed them as though they had been sheep," recorded Capt. George N. Bliss of the 1st Rhode Island. Averell later told the Rhode Islanders that they had made the best charge he had ever seen.[109] Capt. Alan Baker, Jr., of the 1st Rhode Island received a wound to his hand in this charge. That night, the surgeons amputated his forefinger.[110] Capt. Delos Northway of the 6th Ohio was unhorsed in the melee and lost his mount, pistols, and all of his equipment, but avoided capture.[111]

Sgt. William J. Kimbrough of Company G, 4th Virginia Cavalry, was wounded during Lee's first charge, but refused to leave the field. When Lee ordered the second charge, Kimbrough gamely dashed off with his regiment, and he sprang from his horse to help remove the fence that blocked the 4th Virginia's route of march. The sergeant remounted and sped on at the head of his regiment. For his troubles, he was twice sabered over the head, had his arm shattered by a bullet, was captured and carried over the river, escaped, and made his way back to his regiment after a twelve-mile hike through jet blackness, his mangled arm painfully hanging useless by his side.[112]

Outnumbered, some of the Virginians broke and ran in disorder, leaving dead and wounded men behind. In the confusion, the Federals captured Maj. Cary Breckinridge of the 2d Virginia Cavalry, a man whom his commanding officer, Col. Thomas T. Munford, described as "modest as a woman, but resembled a volcano covered with snow, when called to action, was dangerous to meet in a road."[113] When the Confederate charge started, Breckinridge did not like the attack formation, a column of fours, because the men were exposed to artillery fire the whole way. They also took flanking fire from the dismounted men in the wood line. "When we passed over about two-thirds of the distance a wide ditch was encountered which completely broke the force of the charge," recalled Breckinridge. "I got across the ditch and a part of the way on towards the stone fence followed by the broken front of the regiment when my horse was shot. The enemy seeing the condition of my command made a countercharge with a mounted regiment and I was forced to surrender."[114]

The Yankees completely surrounded Breckinridge. The major fired "right and left, his horse wounded and broken down." His men, who could not cut their way through to rescue their commander, saw him lift his hat in surrender, and watched as a Yankee trooper led him off by the arm. A civilian from the north side of the Rappahannock spotted Breckinridge "riding very composedly along with one Yankee close by him and ten more following some distance behind, the rest of our prisoners were compelled to walk."[115]

Reno and his Regulars charged the fleeing Southerners. Reno finally halted his command at Carter's Run, the starting point of Lee's charge. The rest of Averell's division joined the Regulars there. The artillery dueled, with shells whistling back and forth. All factors were now in Averell's favor, and the Confederates were on the retreat.

AVERELL FAILS TO PRESS HIS ADVANTAGE
Instead of following up on the repulse of the Confederate charge, Averell contentedly let his artillerists speak for him. "The enemy opened three pieces, two 10-pounder Parrotts and one 6-pounder gun from the side of the hill directly in front of my left," he reported. "No horses could be discovered about these guns, and from the manner in which they were served it was obvious that our artillery could not hurt them. Our ammunition was of miserable quality and nearly exhausted. There

were 18 shells in one section that would not fit the pieces," complained Averell. "The fuses were unreliable, 5-second fuses would explode in two seconds, and many would not explode at all." The Confederate artillerists, on the other hand, were "exceedingly annoying. Firing at a single company or squadron in line, they would knock a man out of the ranks very frequently."[116] The fact that his artillerists had the wrong ammunition was, ultimately, Averell's fault as the commanding officer of the expedition. He was as much to blame for his lack of effective artillery support as the commander of that section of guns.

The 3d Pennsylvania formed for a final charge, but the Southern gunners quickly got their range. Shell after shell raked the massed Pennsylvanians. A piece of shrapnel cut the throat of Maj. J. Claude White's horse and entered the side of Capt. Charles Treichel's mount, gouging a piece out of the tall captain's leg. Both horses fell, pinning their riders to the ground. The entrails of Treichel's mortally wounded horse spilled all over the dazed captain, who said, "Goodbye, boys; I'm done for. Leave me; don't you see my bowels are all out?" The men trying to free him burst into laughter, "for the fellow was six feet two inches tall and no fatter than a match, and could not possibly have had more than one bowel extending through him."[117]

Capt. James Breathed's grayclad gunners were superb that day. As they awaited Averell's anticipated charge, Breathed brought up his ammunition wagons and "soon that little hill with its six guns became a veritable volcano." The Southerners worked their guns as if on the drill ground. Men shuttled back and forth to a nearby pond to bring water to cool the barrels of the brass Napoleons. They worked long and hard, and their intense and accurate fire helped to dissuade the cautious Averell from pressing his advantage.[118]

Lee's men tried to rally behind swales and in woods nearly half a mile away, but "for a considerable time there was not a formed body of Confederate cavalry on the field."[119] Averell had beaten Fitz's vaunted horsemen on the field of battle, but a greater opportunity lay in front of him. The officers of the scattered Virginians frantically tried to rally their forces. Averell had only to press the attack with his entire force, and he would have swept Lee from the field. However, someone told the New Yorker that infantry had been spotted at a distance to his right, moving toward his rear, and Averell claimed that he could hear railroad cars running on the Orange & Alexandria, presumably bringing Lee reinforcements.[120] In fact, there were no reinforcements, and the nearest Southern infantry lay in the Army of Northern Virginia's winter camps at Fredericksburg. Averell also believed that he faced stout Confederate earthworks, another chimera. In fact, the flat terrain offered no protection for the Southerners. The dim winter sun dipped behind the hills to the west of Culpeper. "It was 5:30 P.M., and it was necessary to advance my cavalry upon their entrenched positions, to make a direct and desperate attack, or to withdraw across the river," reported Averell. "Either operation would be attended with immediate hazard. My horses were very much exhausted. We had been successful thus far. I deemed it proper to withdraw."[121] Averell was in enemy territory, on the wrong side of a flooded river, with no support, low ammunition, and night was rapidly falling. He made the only decision that made sense, even if it meant accepting less than a complete victory over the Southern cavalry.

An officer of the 3d Pennsylvania defended Averell's choice. "Being an isolated enterprise of a single small cavalry division, whose horses had been weakened by an arduous and engrossing picket duty throughout the Winter, and unsupported on this occasion by any cooperation of the army, from which it was separated by a distance of over 30 miles, with a dangerous river in between, it is difficult to imagine any sense of duty which would have prompted its commander to have gone farther."[122]

He deployed horsemen in front of his artillery and the division began retiring toward Kelly's Ford. Reno, with his Regulars, covered the rear. "His task was anything but an easy one, the battery having almost exhausted its ammunition, and having therefore to fire very slowly." The Confederates shelled the retreating Northerners and tentatively pursued. On several occasions, Reno drew up, inviting the Southerners to charge him, but they declined, instead trying to drive off the horsemen with concentrated carbine fire so that they could instead charge an undefended battery. The disciplined Regulars stood their ground, taking heavy fire, allowing the cannoneers to take their guns to safety in spite of heavy losses in horses. Averell ordered Capt. George B. Sanford's squadron of the 1st U.S. to support the battery. Sanford held his fire, waiting in line of battle. "By careful maneuvers of my squadron, the demonstration of the enemy was foiled," recalled Sanford, "and I succeeded in bringing off the battery entire." That night, Averell praised Sanford for his success in this delicate operation.[123]

Captain Reno lost his horse during one of these stands. When the mortally wounded animal fell on top of him, the captain suffered a hernia that caused him considerable pain and forced him to take sick leave in Harrisburg, Pennsylvania.[124] Averell praised Reno's performance: "Captain Reno, whose horse was wounded under him, handled his men gallantly and steadily."[125] Reno received a brevet to major in the U.S. Army for his "gallant and meritorious service" at Kelly's Ford.[126]

After crossing, Lt. Browne, commander of the New York battery, placed two guns in position on the northern bank of the Rappahannock to cover the crossing of the remaining cavalry. "It was with difficulty that many of [the Federals] could be persuaded to return," observed a newspaper correspondent.[127] Browne sent his other two guns to Morrisville with the 1st Rhode Island. Over the course of the day, the Northern gunners fired 247 rounds. They fought as hard as the horse soldiers. With the artillerists protecting them, the balance of Reno's force of Regulars made it to safety after a trying ordeal. The Battle of Kelly's Ford was over.[128]

AVERELL'S RETURN MARCH

Averell brought his prisoners with him. Pvt. Rufus Peck of the 2d Virginia Cavalry was with Capt. James Breckinridge in the millrace, and he was captured early in the engagement. Now a prisoner of war, Peck slowly trudged along. When he reached the Rappahannock, he waded it along with a handful of other prisoners of war. "The water was just over our shoulders," remembered Peck with a shudder, "I remember how the mush-ice and water ran down my coat collar. You can imagine how pleasant that would be, in March and zero weather." Peck was a good sport about it. He remembered that Fitz Lee had made his prisoners do the same thing on the way back from Hartwood Church and figured that turnabout was fair play.[129]

As Averell prepared to depart, he left two badly wounded officers at a farmhouse with a surgeon and some medical supplies. He left a sack of coffee and a note with the doctor, who gave it to Fitz Lee that evening, when the Southern commander paid a call on the two wounded officers. "Dear Fitz," wrote the New Yorker, "Here's your coffee. Here's your visit. How did you like it? How's that horse? Averell."[130] A few weeks later, Lee sent a message across under flag of truce. "Your two officers are well enough to go home, where they ought to be," wrote Fitz. "Send an ambulance to Kelly's and you can have them." Averell complied, and the officers came across the Rappahannock without giving their paroles.

The weary Northerners returned to Morrisville that night, arriving about 11:00. "We have not had an opportunity to cook coffee or anything else from the time we left camp until after we returned to Morrisville," complained a member of the 16th Pennsylvania. "Then I walked about ½ a mile for water & made coffee. So ended our first fight." After a short night, the men were in the saddle again at 6:00 A.M. on March 18, marching twenty-two miles back to camp. They halted at familiar Hartwood Church to eat lunch, as provisions had been sent forward from the division's camps.[131] The weary horsemen arrived in their camps at 4:00 that afternoon. They deserved a rest after marching more than forty miles and fighting a pitched battle.[132]

AN ASSESSMENT OF THE BATTLE OF KELLY'S FORD

Averell crossed the Rappahannock with a force nearly three times the size of Fitz Lee's. Averell's men carried four days' supplies and orders to seek and destroy an enemy half their size. The enemy found him, and the New Yorker repulsed them, but Averell failed to defeat Lee's force in detail. After twelve long hours, Averell's horsemen covered about three miles and did not destroy Lee's brigade. Averell justified his actions. "The principal result achieved by this expedition has been that our cavalry has been brought to feel their superiority in battle; they have learned the value of discipline and the use of their arms," he wrote. "At the first view, I must confess that two regiments wavered, but they did not lose their senses, and a few energetic remarks brought them to a sense of their duty. After that the feeling became stronger throughout the day that it was our fight, and the maneuvers were performed with a precision which the enemy did not fail to observe."[133]

While that was undoubtedly true, Averell contentedly remained on the defensive, ceding the initiative to Fitz Lee. On three separate occasions, Averell assumed a defensive posture and waited for Lee to attack him, instead of pressing his advantage. On the final instance, had the Union horsemen pushed ahead, if they had made one more determined charge, they would have fulfilled their objective for the mission—they would have scattered Lee's forces about the Virginia countryside. Further, by ordering his men to remain in position until ordered to attack, Averell stripped his brigade and regimental commanders of the ability to show any initiative in taking the fight to the Confederates. Clearly, Averell's cautious nature cost him a decisive victory over his old friend. His force of 2,100 men suffered 1 officer and 5 enlisted men killed, 12 officers and 38 enlisted men wounded, and 2 officers and 20 enlisted men missing or taken prisoner. The total reported losses were 78, representing less than 4 percent of his total force.[134]

However, Kelly's Ford worked marvels for the morale of the blueclad horse soldiers. "Permit me to congratulate you on the effect and result of our tramp," wrote Marcus Reno two days after the battle. "It is apparently a *big thing*, & I am glad of it."[135] "I believe it is the universal desire of the officers and men of my division to meet the enemy again as soon as possible," claimed Averell when he wrote his report a few days later.[136] As recounted by an Ohioan, the New Yorker later told his men that Kelly's Ford marked "the most galent cavalry fight of the war."[137]

"Here was an opportunity—so long sought for—of meeting the rebel cavalry in a fair and square fight in an open field," wrote Duffié, who had every right to be proud of his Rhode Islanders.[138] Years later, an officer of the 3d Pennsylvania recorded, "This was a square stand-up fight, on fairly open ground, away from either army, between nearly equal numbers, and convinced our Confederate foes that henceforth they would no longer have a holiday when they met Federal cavalry." Even then, he did not realize that Averell had outnumbered Lee better than two to one.[139]

The men of the 16th Pennsylvania Cavalry unburdened themselves of the taint of Hartwood Church. They fought well at Kelly's Ford, and their repulse of the Southern flank attack earned them the respect of their fellow horsemen. "The rebs were severely chastised in this engagement, for the raids they had made on our picket lines," proudly observed Norman Ball of the 16th Pennsylvania. Averell commended the Pennsylvanians for their fine performance and for their promptness and coolness under fire.[140]

The men came to believe in themselves. "It is not considered to be much of a disgrace to belong to the 6th [Ohio] since the fight at Kelley's Ford," wrote a Buckeye, "although our regt. does not get credit for what it realy done. It stood the brunt of the fight. It repulsed the rebles alown. The seckond charge that was made, but in the papers, the first R. Island cavalry get the credit that belongs to our regt."[141] Another Ohioan noted, "It has been a hard trip, but feel it a victory for we have met the enemy and beaten him on his own ground."[142] Twelve days later, the Federals still basked in the afterglow of their fine performance. "Everything is quiet about hear," reported trooper William Bard to his wife, "the rebels have not troubled our men since they got that last thrashing from Billy Avrills men they will begin to think that our men means fight."[143]

"It was a square, stand-up, cavalry fight of over four hours duration, and the result proves that our cavalry, when well handled, is equal if not superior to the enemy," claimed an ebullient member of the 4th New York Cavalry. "In every instance they fled before the impetuous charge of our men. . . . Our Regiment and the whole Division are in great spirits over the affair, which they claim to be the greatest hand-to-hand cavalry combat that ever took place on this continent, and only excelled by one fight in Europe."[144] Kelly's Ford marked the largest all-cavalry fight on the North American continent to date.

"At last our regiment has had the opportunity so long wished for of meeting the rebel cavalry in a fair field fight and the result has far surpassed our expectations. . . . This fight has shown that the rebel cavalry cannot stand the cold steel," observed Captain Bliss. "They will stand so much shooting as any soldiers but when it comes to crossing sabers they break and run."[145] Perhaps most telling, a Confederate horseman declared, "Your men never fought with the sabre so well as they did at Kelly's Ford."[146] A member of the 2d Virginia Cavalry noted that his regiment "was very badly used up" during the Kelly's Ford fight.[147] "The rebels acknowledged that they 'never knew that Yankee cavalry could fight so well,'" reported the *New York Tribune* a few days after the battle.[148] "For once during this war, there was a fair cavalry fight," echoed the *New York Times,* "and the result was just what everybody predicted it would be—a Union triumph."[149]

Butterfield reported on the fight to several of the infantry corps commanders. Averell "sent in a large number of prisoners, including 1 major. Captain Moore, of General Hooker's staff, who accompanied him, reports it as a brilliant and splendid fight—the best cavalry fight of the war—lasting five hours, charging and recharging on both sides, our men using their sabers handsomely and with effect, driving the enemy 3 miles into cover of earthworks and heavy guns."[150] Secretary of War Edwin M. Stanton heard the reports of the fighting and wrote to Hooker, "I congratulate you on the success of General Averell's expedition. It is good for the first lick. You have drawn the first blood, and I hope now soon to see 'the boys up and at them.' Give my compliments and thanks to Averell and his command."[151]

Word of the great fight at Kelly's Ford quickly spread throughout the rest of the Cavalry Corps. Several days later, Col. Richard H. Rush, commander of the

6th Pennsylvania Cavalry, encountered Capt. Walter S. Newhall of the 3d Pennsylvania. Newhall's brother Fred was Rush's adjutant, and the two officers were well acquainted. Rush spoke highly of "our little affair over the River. He said if the object of the reconnaissance was mainly to prove the superiority of our officers and men, it was eminently successful and, he was glad that everybody found it in the light of a splendid cavalry fight, resulting so entirely in our favor." Newhall commented, "He appeared to understand the whole thing from beginning to end, and only asked how many I thought the Rebels lost during the engagement."[152]

Despite these laudatory comments, Hooker was not satisfied. "After the brigadier general commanding had permitted one third of his force to remain on the north bank of the Rappahannock, his passage of the river with the residue of his force appears to have been eminently soldierlike, and his dispositions for engaging and following the enemy, up to the time of his recrossing of the river were made with skill and judgment," wrote the army commander in May, after his defeat at Chancellorsville. "Had he followed his instructions and persevered in his success, he could easily have routed the enemy, fallen upon his camp, and inflicted a severe blow upon him. The enemy was inferior to the command he had in all respects." Hooker concluded with a strong condemnation of Averell's performance. "The reason assigned—that he heard cars arriving at Culpeper, and not knowing but that they might be bring reinforcements to the enemy—is very unsatisfactory, and should have had no influence in determining the line of that officer's conduct. He was sent to perform a certain duty, and failed to accomplish it from imaginary apprehensions." Thus, Hooker's festering dissatisfaction with Averell, which began at Hartwood Church, grew.[153]

Hooker was correct. Averell possessed the strength to steamroll over Lee's lone brigade and reach the Orange & Alexandria and the railroad bridge at Rappahannock Station, but his cautious nature prevented him from seizing the opportunity, which slipped away. Although the Northerners claimed victory, Kelly's Ford represented a Southern triumph. By most measures of the day, the contestant left in possession of the battlefield at the end of the day was considered the winner, and Fitz Lee and his battered brigade remained on the field at the end of the day. Second, Averell only managed to advance fewer then three miles. He failed to fulfill Hooker's orders for the expedition: he utterly failed to rout or destroy Fitz Lee's force, although he possessed the means to do so.

The Confederates seemed to understand this. "The expedition itself was barren of results, unless, as some claim, it improved the morale of the Federal cavalry," observed Stuart's adjutant, Maj. Henry B. McClellan. "It certainly added nothing enviable to the reputation of the brigadier-general in command." McClellan concluded, "We cannot excuse General Averell's conduct. He ought to have gone to Culpeper Court House."[154] Rosser offered a facetious view in a postwar speech.

"The fact of the business was, Averell became frightened, mistook the wild beating of his timid heart for drums.... No doubt he took safe advice—the counsel of his fears."[155]

By comparison, Fitz Lee reported 3 officers and 8 enlisted men killed, 11 officers and 77 enlisted men wounded, and 1 officer and 33 enlisted men captured, for losses of 133, or about 11 percent of his total engaged forces. The loss exchange ratio for Kelly's Ford was two men for every man lost by Averell, as well as 10 percent more of his total strength.[156] Maj. John W. Puller of the 5th Virginia was killed during the melee, prompting Lee to lament the loss of a "gallant and highly efficient" officer who was "a heavy loss" to his regiment and country.[157] Lee's heavier losses can be attributed to the fact that he was the aggressor throughout the day's fighting, pressing the attack at every opportunity. Although badly outnumbered, Lee took the fighting to Averell, and his men performed quite well under adverse circumstances. Fitz's skillful choices of terrain, picketing the river and at Carter's Run, also saved his command from taking greater losses at Kelly's Ford.

His men recognized that they had been in a tough fight. "Great cavalry fight. Lee's (Fitzhugh) brigade against three Yankee brigades," noted one Virginia horseman.[158] "A memorable day in my life," was the laconic description by an officer of the Little Fork Rangers of the 4th Virginia Cavalry.[159]

"By this little fight we defeated an expedition designed to reach and destroy Gordonsville," observed one Fitz's saddle soldiers. "I always regarded it as one of the best cavalry fights during the war. A fight which reflected credit on the men and no less credit on the gallant young officer who, without support, relying on the moral effect of a charge such as he knew his command could make under his lead, hurled his 800 against 4,000 with the result of so far discouraging and demoralizing the latter as to induce them to retreat from the field and abandon a carefully prepared for and elaborately planned expedition!" He concluded, "This fight won for our brigade a high reputation, a reputation which it successfully strove to maintain ever afterward."[160]

Rosser took a dimmer view of Averell's expedition. "The Federal cavalry had at last made a raid," he observed. "It had ventured beyond the infantry lines of its own army, and had penetrated the rebel lines, and without infantry support, had made an attack on the enemy! It had done even more; it had captured 34 prisoners—34 live rebel cavalrymen, and escaped back to their infantry!" Drolly, Rosser concluded, "A wonderful achievement for the Federal cavalry, we must admit, and Gen. Averell deserved great credit."[161]

The most prominent Southern casualty was Pelham. "The noble, the chivalric, the gallant Pelham is no more. He was killed in action yesterday," reported Stuart to the artillerist's family. "His remains will be sent to you today. How much he was beloved, appreciated and admired, let the tears of agony we have shed, and the

gloom of mourning throughout my command bear witness. His loss to the country is irreparable."[162] Two days later, he issued General Orders Number 9, lamenting
the loss of his chief of artillery. Stuart ordered his command to wear the military
badge of mourning for thirty days in memory of his lost friend.[163] Newspapers all
over the South mourned the passing of the gallant Pelham, and many a young
woman wore mourning clothes in his honor.[164] Von Borcke obtained an appro-
priate coffin for the fallen artillerist and escorted the body home to Alabama for
burial.[165]

Two weeks later, Stuart wrote to his pregnant wife, Flora. "If a boy, I wish him
to be called John Pelham Stuart. I have thought of it much—it is my choice. His
record is complete and it is spotless. It is noble. His family was the very best. His
character was pure, his disposition as sweet and innocent as our own little Flora's.
You have no idea how I will feel to know that if a boy, I will have an heir named
John Pelham. Think of it, my darling. If a girl, name it Maria Pelham Stuart, and
thus combine two lovely natures in the name of our little one. There can never be
anything to regret in either case, and she or he will be grateful while she or he
lives." Their daughter, born not long after, was named Virginia Pelham Stuart in
honor of the slain artillerist.[166]

"Pelham is now a tradition of the Southland, nay more, of the American
people," wrote the historian of the Army of Northern Virginia's artillery branch
years after the war. "His fame is the heritage of a united country and an inspira-
tion for all time to the soldier of whatever race."[167]

After leaving Pelham's bedside on the night of March 17, Stuart fired off a telegram to Robert E. Lee. "Enemy is retiring," he wrote, "We are after him. His dead
men and horses strew the roads."[168] The next day, he forwarded a more detailed
report. "I telegraphed you last night enemy had retired north bank of Rappahannock. From the best information it was Averell's division, 3,000 in the saddle. Pork
and hard bread packed in boxes. He was very badly hurt, and left a hospital on this
side. It was undoubtedly intended as a great expedition, but thanks to the superior
conduct of General Fitzhugh Lee and his noble brigade it has failed; not, however,
without the loss to us of such noble spirits as Majors Pelham and Puller."[169]

A few days later, a defiant Fitz Lee congratulated his brigade. "The general
commanding the brigade announces to his command his high gratification and
proud appreciation of their heroic achievements upon the ever memorable 17th
instant," he began. "Confident in numbers and equipment, it was their purpose to
penetrate the interior, to destroy our railroads, to burn, rob, and devastate, and to
commit their customary depredations upon the property of our peaceful citizens."
He continued, "Rebel cavalry have been taught that Yankee (would-be) horsemen, notwithstanding their numbers, can be confronted and hurled back, and
their infamous purposes, however well planned in security, in the open, fair field

frustrated. Rebel cavalry have been taught that a determined rush upon the foe is the part of sound policy as it is the part of true courage. Rebel cavalry have taught an insolent enemy that, notwithstanding they may possess advantages of chosen position, superiority in numbers and weapons, they cannot overwhelm soldiers fighting for the holiest cause that has ever nerved the arm of a freeman or fired the breast of a patriot."[170]

Stuart echoed his subordinate. "On no occasion have I seen more instances of individual prowess—never such heroic firmness in the presence of danger the most appalling," wrote the Southern cavalier. "The enemy, afraid to contest the palm as cavalry, preferred to rely upon his artillery, ensconcing his cavalry, dismounted, behind stone fences and other barriers, which alone saved him from capture or annihilation, thus converting the long-vaunted raid, which was 'to break the back-bone of the rebellion,' with preparations complete for an extensive expedition, into a feeble advance and a defensive operation." He concluded, "Commanders will take care to record while fresh in their memories the instances of personal hero-ism for future use, and the brigade will have the battle of Kellysville inscribed on its banner as its greatest achievement."[171] At the same time, Stuart acknowledged pri-vately that Kelly's Ford was the hardest cavalry battle he had ever seen.[172]

Robert E. Lee was impressed with his nephew's performance at Kelly's Ford.. "As far as I learn Fitz Lee & his Brigade behaved admirably, & though greatly out-numbered stuck to the enemy with a tenacity that could not be shaken off. The report of our scouts north of the Rappk place their strength at 7000," wrote Gen-eral Lee in a letter to his brother a few days after the battle. "Stuart does not put it so high, while Fitz did not have with him more than 800. But I grieve over our noble dead! I do not know how I can replace the gallant Pelham. So young so true so brave. Though stricken down in the dawn of manhood, his is the glory of duty done! Fitz had his horse shot under him but is safe."[173]

The Southern horsemen also understood the importance of this fight. "The fight at Kellys is thought to be one of the hardest cavalry fights of the war," wrote Pvt. Peter Grattan of the 1st Virginia Cavalry. "Charge after charge was the pro-gramme of the day."[174] "Our men with vastly inferior numbers & with horses which had not been fed in some time," observed Lt. Col. William R. Carter of the 3d Virginia Cavalry in his diary that night, "held the insolent foe in check."[175] Eight hundred Southern horse soldiers stopped a force nearly three times larger. Nevertheless, a New York newspaper noted that Confederate prisoners character-ized the conduct of the Northern horsemen "as one of the ablest and most gal-lantly fought cavalry raids of the whole war, and admit that their own troops were totally demoralized by the gallant sabre charge of our cavalry."[176]

"Unimportant as this action may appear, so far as the numbers engaged, it must be taken as a decided success for us," claimed a Richmond newspaper. "It was the advance guard of the enemy and it was his first stop in his 'On to Richmond.' The preparations he had made and his packed provisions show that he was prepared for a long march, and that it was no mere reconnaissance. Had they been successful, there is no doubt that they would have been soon followed up by the whole of Hooker's army." The article continued, "The affair is therefore important in its result, and will no doubt have an effect on the enemy's plans in his meditated advance on Richmond. Foiled and driven back, he is now disconcerted in his plan and farther from Richmond than ever."[177]

While this clearly overstated the case, the point remained well taken. Determined fighting by the Confederates stymied Averell, preventing him from fulfilling Hooker's orders. The critical question was whether Averell would learn anything from his experiences on March 17.

A Regular summed up the results of the Battle of Kelly's Ford nicely. "The dead cavalrymen that General Hooker had so much desired to see had been on view on many hardly contested fields in which the cavalry had taken a distinguished part," he noted. "Between February 1st and St. Patrick's Day, a little more than a month and a half, there had been fourteen contacts in which the Cavalry of the Army of the Potomac had taken an important part and in some of which serious losses had been sustained. Properly regarded, these afforded visible, convincing testimony to the fact that the Union cavalry was undergoing a process of development, which was as rapid as was permitted by the conditions under which it served." Kelly's Ford represented another important step in the development of the Army of the Potomac's Cavalry Corps. Only time would tell what the final result would be.[178]

NOTES

1. O.R., vol. 25, part 2, 136.
2. Ibid., part 1, 47 and 1073.
3. Rosser, *Addresses*, 34.
4. O.R., vol. 25, part 1, 48.
5. W. H. Ware, *The Battle of Kelley's Ford, Fought March 17, 1863* (Newport News, Va.: Warwick Printing, n.d.), 4.
6. Delos Northway diary, entry for March 17, 1863, in *Souvenir*, 111.
7. David M. Gilmore, "Cavalry: Its Use and Value as Illustrated by Reference to the Engagements of Kelly's Ford and Gettysburg," *Glimpses of the Nation's Struggle*, 2d series (St. Paul, Minn.: St. Paul Book and Stationery, 1890), 41–43.
8. Delos Northway diary, entry for March 16, 1863, in *Souvenir*, 111; O.R., vol. 25, part 1, 47.
9. Winder, *Jacob Beidler's Book*, 146.
10. Ball diary, entry for March 16, 1863.
11. Northway diary, entry for March 16, 1863, in *Souvenir*, 111.
12. Wells A. Bushnell diary, entries for March 16 and 17, 1863, Wells A. Bushnell Papers, Western Reserve Historical Society, Cleveland, Ohio.
13. Cooke, "Battle of Kelly's Ford," 14.

14. William Bard to his wife, March 22, 1863, William Bard/Arthur Martin Papers, USAMHI.

15. O.R., vol. 25, part 1, 47.

16. Peter M. Grattan to Dear Mary, March 22, 1863, Mary E. Grattan Papers, Southern Historical Collection, Wilson Library, University of North Carolina, Chapel Hill.

17. *Philadelphia Press,* March 24, 1863.

18. O.R., vol. 25, part 1, 61.

19. Carter, *Sabres, Saddles, and Spurs,* 49.

20. O.R., vol. 25, part 1, 48.

21. Henry B. McClellan, *The Life and Campaigns of Major General J. E. B. Stuart* (Boston: Houghton-Mifflin, 1895), 207.

22. *Ashtabula Sentinel,* March 22, 1863.

23. Ware, *Battle of Kelley's Ford,* 5.

24. Bushnell diary, entry for March 17, 1863.

25. Frank W. Hess, "The First Cavalry Battle at Kelly's Ford, Va.," part 1, *National Tribune,* May 29, 1890; Cooke, "Battle of Kelly's Ford," 17.

26. *Litchfield Enquirer,* April 30, 1863.

27. Bliss, "Reminiscences of Service," 65.

28. Ibid.

29. Bigelow, *Campaign of Chancellorsville,* 93.

30. *Naragansett Weekly,* April 2, 1863.

31. Newhall to his father, March 18, 1863, Newhall Papers.

32. *Naragansett Weekly,* April 2, 1863.

33. Bigelow, *Campaign of Chancellorsville,* 93–94.

34. Truman Reeves memoir, copy in files, FSNMP.

35. McClellan, *Life and Campaigns,* 207–208.

36. Mary D. Robertson, ed., *Lucy Breckinridge of Grove Hill: The Diary of a Virginia Girl, 1862–1864* (Kent, Ohio: Kent State University Press, 1980), 108–109.

37. Cooke, "Battle of Kelly's Ford," 18.

38. O.R., vol. 25, part 1, 48.

39. Bliss, "Reminiscences of Service," 66–67.

40. Frank W. Hess, "The First Cavalry Battle at Kelly's Ford, Va.," part 2, *National Tribune,* June 5, 1890.

41. O.R., vol. 25, part 1, 1074.

42. Bliss to Dear Gerald, March 21, 1863, Bliss Papers; Cooke, "Battle of Kelly's Ford," 23.

43. *Providence Journal,* March 23, 1863.

44. Bernard Murrin Certificate of Disability, author's collection; Bernard Murrin pension file, Affidavit of W. C. Capran, RG 94, National Archives, Washington, D.C.

45. O.R., vol. 25, part 1, 1074.

46. Ibid.

47. Newhall to his father, March 18, 1863.

48. Garland C. Hudgins and Richard B. Kleese, eds., *Recollections of an Old Dominion*

Dragoon: The Civil War Experiences of Sgt. Robert S. Hudgins II, Co. B, 3d Virginia Cavalry (Orange, Va.: Publisher's Press, 1993), 63.

49. Carter, *Sabres, Saddles and Spurs,* 49.
50. O.R., vol. 25, part 1, 59 and 61.
51. Ware, *Battle of Kelley's Ford,* 5.
52. O.R., vol. 25, part 1, 58.
53. William B. Conway, "The Battle of Kelly's Ford, Va.," *Confederate Veteran* 27 (September 1919): 330.
54. Ware, *Battle of Kelley's Ford,* 6.
55. Harry Gilmor, *Four Years in the Saddle* (New York: Harper & Brothers, 1866), 66.
56. O.R., vol. 25, part 1, 49.
57. Winder, *Jacob Beidler's Book,* 145.
58. Carter, *Sabres, Saddles and Spurs,* 50.
59. Hudgins and Kleese, *Recollections of an Old Dominion Dragoon,* 64–65.
60. Hubard memoir.
61. Ball diary, entry for March 17, 1863.
62. *Philadelphia Press,* March 24, 1863.
63. Gilmor, *Four Years in the Saddle,* 68–70.
64. Ware, *Battle of Kelley's Ford,* 7–8.
65. Ibid., 8.
66. Emmie Martin Hunt, "John Pelham of Alabama," *Confederate Veteran* 30 (September 1922): 329; William Woods Hassler, *Colonel John Pelham: Lee's Boy Artillerist* (Chapel Hill: University of North Carolina Press, 1960), 142–51. There are two other full-length biographies of Pelham: Philip Mercer, *The Gallant Pelham* (Macon, Ga.: J. W. Burke, 1958); and Charles G. Milham, *Gallant Pelham: American Extraordinary* (Washington, D.C: Public Affairs Press, 1959).
67. Heros von Borcke, *Memoirs of the Confederate War for Independence* (Philadelphia: J. B. Lippincott, 1867), 346–47.
68. Milham, *Gallant Pelham,* 229.
69. Gilmor, *Four Years in the Saddle,* 65.
70. Hassler, *Colonel John Pelham,* 164.
71. Gilmor, *Four Years in the Saddle,* 71–72.
72. Ibid., 73–74.
73. Hess, "First Cavalry Battle," part 1.
74. *Litchfield Enquirer,* April 30, 1863.
75. O.R., vol. 25, part 1, 49.
76. Hess, "First Cavalry Battle," part 1.
77. Reeve memoir.
78. Gilmore, "Cavalry," 43.
79. Bliss, "Reminiscences of Service," 68.
80. Guild to his parents, March 18, 1863, FSNMP.
81. Reeve memoir.

82. Robert B. Isbell to Dear Anna, March 18, 1863, Lewis Leigh Collection, USAMHI.

83. O.R., vol. 25, part 1, 49.

84. Cooke, "Battle of Kelly's Ford," 24.

85. George F. Price, *Across the Continent with the Fifth Cavalry* (New York: D. Van Nostrand, 1883), 114–15.

86. Henry Ingersoll Bowditch, *Memorial for Nathaniel Bowditch* (Boston: John Wilson & Son, 1865), 38–44, 56–58.

87. Ibid., 55.

88. Ibid., 70.

89. Crowninshield, *History of the First Regiment,* 116.

90. Bigelow, *Campaign of Chancellorsville,* 98.

91. Hubard memoir.

92. O.R., vol. 25, part 1, 49.

93. Cooke, "Battle of Kelly's Ford," 27–28.

94. Hubard memoir.

95. Ibid.

96. Ibid.

97. Bushnell diary, entry for March 17, 1863.

98. Carter, *Sabres, Saddles and Spurs,* 51.

99. Newhall to his father, March 18, 1863.

100. *New York Times,* March 20, 1863.

101. Bushnell diary, entry for March 17, 1863.

102. Brooke-Rawle, *Third Pennsylvania Cavalry,* 226.

103. Reeve memoir.

104. Bigelow, *Campaign of Chancellorsville,* 99.

105. Winder, *Jacob Beidler's Book,* 147.

106. Cooke, "Battle of Kelly's Ford," 30–31.

107. Bigelow, *Campaign of Chancellorsville,* 100.

108. *Peoples Press,* April 2, 1863.

109. Bliss to Dear Gerald, March 19, 1863.

110. Alan Baker, Jr., diary for 1863, entry for March 17, 1863, Civil War Miscellaneous Collection, USAMHI.

111. Northway diary, entry for March 17, 1863, in *Souvenir,* 112.

112. McClellan, *Life and Campaigns,* 217.

113. Thomas T. Munford to John B. Bigelow, Jr., January 7, 1907, John B. Bigelow, Jr., Papers, Manuscripts Division, Library of Congress, Washington, D.C. The Bigelow Papers are a treasure trove for those interested in primary source materials on the Chancellorsville Campaign.

114. Robert J. Driver, Jr., and Harold E. Howard, *2d Virginia Cavalry* (Lynchburg, Va.: H. E. Howard, 1995), 75.

115. Robertson, *Lucy Breckinridge of Grove Hill,* 109.

116. O.R., vol. 25, part 1, 50.

117. Gilmore, "Cavalry," 44.

118. Ware, *Battle of Kelley's Ford,* 8.

119. Bigelow, *Campaign of Chancellorsville,* 100.

120. O.R., vol. 25, part 1, 50.

121. Ibid.

122. Hess, "First Cavalry Battle," part 2.

123. Hagemann, *Fighting Rebels and Redskins,* 196.

124. By the time that Reno returned to duty, the Confederates had already invaded Pennsylvania, and Reno was assigned to the defenses of Harrisburg. As a result, he missed the entire Gettysburg Campaign.

125. O.R., vol. 25, part 1, 52; Ronald H. Nichols, *In Custer's Shadow: Major Marcus Reno* (Fort Collins, Colo.: Old Army Press, 1999), 53.

126. Nichols, *In Custer's Shadow,* 53. Reno, of course, receives the lion's share of the blame for the disaster that befell Lt. Col. George A. Custer's 7th U.S. Cavalry at the battle of Little Big Horn in 1876. Custer was a staff officer at the time of Kelly's Ford, and had he been with the army on March 17, he might have been assigned to serve under Reno. The irony of that would have been remarkable.

127. *New York Times,* March 20, 1863.

128. O.R., vol. 25, part 1, 55–56.

129. Rufus H. Peck, *Reminiscences of a Confederate Soldier of Co. C, 2d Va. Cavalry* (Fincastle, Va.: privately published, 1913), 23–24.

130. *New York Times,* March 22, 1863.

131. Bushnell diary, entry for March 18, 1863.

132. Winder, *Jacob Beidler's Book,* 147.

133. O.R., vol. 25, part 1, 50.

134. Ibid., 53.

135. Marcus A. Reno to William Woods Averell, March 19, 1863, Averell Papers.

136. O.R., vol. 25, part 1, 53.

137. Covert to his wife, March 21, 1863, Covert Letters.

138. Dennison, *Sabres and Spurs,* 315.

139. Gilmore, "Cavalry," 44.

140. Ball diary, entries for March 17–18, 1863.

141. Covert to his wife, April 1, 1863, Covert Letters.

142. Northway diary, entry for March 18, 1863, in *Souvenir,* 112.

143. Bard to his wife, March 29, 1863.

144. *Peoples Press,* April 2, 1863.

145. Bliss to Dear Gerald, March 19, 1863.

146. Bliss, "Reminiscences of Service," 69.

147. Isbell to Dear Anna, March 18, 1863.

148. *New York Tribune,* March 23, 1863.

149. *New York Times,* March 18, 1863.

150. O.R., vol. 25, part 2, 147.

151. Ibid., 148.

152. Walter S. Newhall to his father, undated, March 1863, Newhall Papers.

153. O.R., vol. 25, part 1, 1073.

154. McClellan, *Life and Campaigns,* 203 and 216.

155. Rosser, *Addresses,* 34.

156. Applying the conventional doctrine, where a two-to-one or greater loss exchange ratio exists, the force inflicting those casualties is considered the winner of the battle.

157. O.R., vol. 25, part 1, 63.

158. Anonymous diary, entry for March 17, 1863, Eleanor S. Brockenbrough Library, Museum of the Confederacy, Richmond, Va.

159. Woodford B. Hackley, *The Little Fork Rangers: A Sketch of Company D Fourth Virginia Cavalry* (Richmond, Va.: Press of Dietz Printing, 1927), 83.

160. Hubard memoir.

161. Rosser, *Addresses,* 35.

162. Mitchell, *Letters of Major General James E. B. Stuart,* 299.

163. O.R., vol. 25, part 1, 60.

164. See, as an example, the *Richmond Enquirer* for April 2, 1863, which ran a lengthy obituary of Pelham on its front page. Today, a handsome monument marks the spot where Pelham fell, a fitting tribute to a gallant warrior.

165. Von Borcke, *Memoirs,* 350–51.

166. Mitchell, *Letters of Major General James E. B. Stuart,* 309–10.

167. Jennings Cropper Wise, *The Long Arm of Lee: The History of the Artillery of the Army of Northern Virginia,* 2 vols. (Lynchburg, Va.: J. P. Bell, 1915), 1:435.

168. O.R.., vol. 51, part 2, 685.

169. Ibid., 686.

170. Ibid., vol. 25, part 1, 64.

171. Ibid., 59.

172. Lucius Haney to his sister, Click Family Papers, Perkins Historical Library, Duke University, Durham, N.C.

173. Robert E. Lee to Carter Lee, March 24, 1863, FSNMP.

174. Grattan to Dear Mary, March 22, 1863, Grattan Papers.

175. Carter, *Sabres, Saddles and Spurs,* 54.

176. *New York Herald,* March 19, 1863.

177. *Richmond Daily Examiner,* March 19, 1863.

178. George B. Davis, "The Cavalry Combat at Kelly's Ford in 1863," *Journal of the U.S. Cavalry Association* 25 (January 1915), 401.

4

STUCK IN THE MUD:
PRELUDE TO CHANCELLORSVILLE

While Averell planned his revenge against Fitz Lee, John Buford suffered through two months of court-martial duty. The Kentuckian eagerly looked forward to assuming command of his beloved Regulars. On February 21, Hooker requested that Buford be relieved and report to the army. However, general-in-chief Maj. Gen. Henry W. Halleck denied the request, stating, "General Buford is on a court for the trial of an officer of your command and cannot be relieved till trial is over."[1] Given Buford's naturally aggressive tendencies, sitting through dreary days of testimony before the court-martial panel undoubtedly rankled him.

The Kentuckian finally shook himself free on March 4, and reported to the Army of the Potomac for duty. Once Buford took command of the Reserve Brigade, he set about restoring the Regulars to a high state of readiness and efficiency. He drilled them daily while incorporating new recruits into their ranks, raising the Reserve Brigade's effective strength to 900. The spirits of the Regulars had slumped during the winter, but having one of their own leading them immediately restored the élan of old. Before long, they were ready to assume a leadership role within the nascent Cavalry Corps. They would soon have their chance to do so.

While the fighting raged at Kelly's Ford, Gregg's division remained active, picketing the left of the army along the Rappahannock. The 1st Pennsylvania Cavalry did picket duty at King George Court House. On March 17, two squadrons of the 1st Pennsylvania scouted the area, destroying barges and boats engaged in smuggling contraband goods across the Rappahannock. Two days later, another detachment made a similar foray, destroying a large boat and capturing a smuggler's

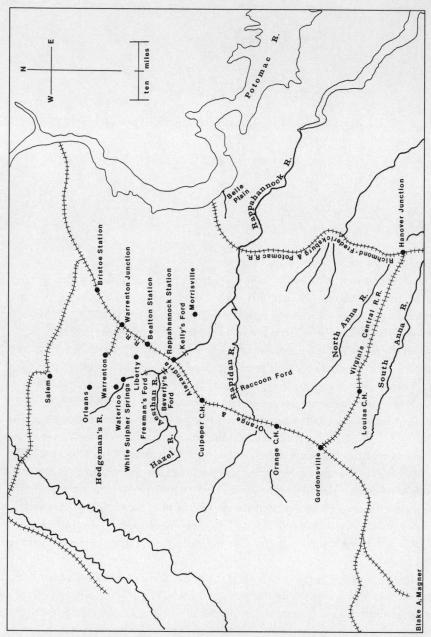

N
W — E
S

ten miles

Potomac R.

Belle Plain

Rappahannock R.

Bristoe Station

Warrenton Junction

Bealton Station

Rappahannock Station

Kelly's Ford

Morrisville

Richmond–Fredericksburg & Potomac R.R.

Hanover Junction

Warrenton

Salem

Orleans

Hedgeman's R.

Waterloo

White Sulpher Springs

Liberty

Freeman's Ford

Beverly's Ford

Hazel R.

Bethan R.

Alexandria &

Rapidan R.

Raccoon Ford

Culpeper C.H.

Orange &

Orange C.H.

Gordonsville

North Anna R.

Virginia Central R.R.

Louisa C.H.

South Anna R.

Theater of Operations, April–June 1863

Blake A. Magner

wagon loaded with "silks, shows, fancy goods and imperial teas." Elated with their windfall, the Pennsylvanians loaded all that they could carry on their saddles and destroyed the rest. "The party returned the next day to headquarters, having more the appearance of a travelers' caravan, than a squadron of Yankee cavalry."[2]

Hooker planned his grand spring campaign for the Army of the Potomac while the men engaged in all sorts of activities intended to keep their morale high. "The Army of the Potomac is becoming quite a sporting institution of late, as you may probably have learned by the papers," recounted a member of the 1st Pennsylvania Cavalry. "Horse racing, pig-racing, climbing greased poles &c. are becoming quite popular among the leaders of the army."

A major horse race was scheduled. "Tomorrow there is to be a 'big' race for a 'purse' at which Gen. Stoneman, Gen. Gregg, and many of the subordinate officers of our cavalry division have entered horses. I don't know whether it will take place in front of our camp or not, but I hope it will." Although the Pennsylvania soldier wanted to watch the festivities, he remained unconvinced of their benefit. "Yet still I do not think such things are beneficial to the discipline, 'esprit du corps' etc of any army, but they are very well in their place. And our commanding generals being sporting men of course they must indulge in their favorite amusements." He concluded by reporting that a soldier was badly injured when his horse fell on him during a race. "But nothing is thought of a man's life or limbs here," he sniffed. "He might as well be killed one way or another."[3]

"I hope that it will come warm weather before long, for I want to see this war pushed along," observed a member of the 6th Ohio Cavalry on March 21. "I see the papers state there has been a peace proclimation offered by the rebles to the reble Congress. I don't know what will come of it but not much I expect, but I wish the war would end one way or the other," he proclaimed.[4]

Capt. Charles Francis Adams of the 1st Massachusetts Cavalry, always a keen observer, speculated that the army's campaign would closely resemble McClellan's 1862 Peninsula Campaign. He noted that the army's morale was higher than ever, and predicted an overwhelming success. "As for the cavalry, I think that we shall do one of two things: either push after Lee, if he allows himself to be caught in a tight place; or, which to my mind is more probably, if he slips off, be sent up towards Culpeper to operate on his left flank and annoy him." Regardless of the precise mission, Adams realized that they had their work cut out for them.[5]

The Confederates continued probing the Federal lines for weakness. On March 25, Stuart's horsemen dashed on Stoneman's pickets. At 4:00 that morning, the men of the 6th Ohio Cavalry received orders to be ready to march at reveille to chase the Southerners. The order was countermanded, and the men spent the day in mounted and dismounted drilling, honing their skills for their next encounter with the enemy.[6]

The men of the 12th Illinois Cavalry, part of Grimes Davis's brigade, also spent the entire day drilling on March 25. They then went out on picket duty. The tedious routine of the winter encampment dragged on, seemingly endlessly. However, the intense, repetitive drilling soon paid dividends for the Northern horse soldiers.[7]

The night of the 25th, Capt. George N. Bliss of the 1st Rhode Island recounted his activities since Kelly's Ford. "When the roads become good Hooker will astonish the rebels," he predicted. "I don't believe Hooker means to be 'stuck in the mud' as Burnside was last January. This army is now in splendid shape. The men are full of life and spirit, well clothed and armed, and are now improving fast by long daily drilling. Give me 1000 veterans and I will whip 5000 raw recruits," he bragged.[8]

The Federal commanders, however, remained unproven in the eyes of the men of the Cavalry Corps. "Averell and Stoneman and Duffié have all excellent reputations and have claim to them in my belief," noted Maj. Henry L. Higginson of the 1st Massachusetts Cavalry, "tho' I've never seen them do anything yet."[9] The men knew that their leaders would soon get the chance to prove themselves.

The 1st Pennsylvania Cavalry drew picket duty during the last week of March. "We had a good time generally on picket the last time, and had the extreme pleasure of receiving eight deserters from the enemy," reported Lt. Thomas Lucas. "The rebels are worse whipped now than ever I saw them. They argue in this way, that their friends that are inside of our lines get along so much better than those outside, inasmuch that these inside get the necessaries and comforts of life at reasonable prices, while those outside are abused and have to pay enormous prices for everything." Lucas observed that the citizens of Virginia were bitter about the war's duration and the privations visited on them as a result, and that they wanted peace at almost any cost.[10]

Averell's division returned to its routine in the days after Kelly's Ford. Averell entertained Stoneman and his wife for dinner on March 30, and a chorus of cavalrymen serenaded the group. Averell was pleased with his command's performance at Kelly's Ford. He waited impatiently for another opportunity to pitch into his old classmate.[11]

"Word has reached the right of my line that there is 5000 cavalry with 6 pieces of artillery on the Hartwood Church Road about three miles out in front of our line," reported an officer of Pleasonton's division on March 31st. "At 1 ock[sic] last night we were aroused and ordered to be ready to move out on a moment's notice," recorded a sergeant of the 16th Pennsylvania Cavalry, "At 9 this A.M. all was quiet—and normal."[12] Worried, Pleasonton immediately shifted troops to meet the threat, which proved to be nothing more than a probe. The Southerners came no closer than 1,000 yards from the Northern pickets.[13]

The Federal troopers remained alert, waiting for the next Confederate foray across the river. "Three fourths of my time has been spent on the outposts watching the enemy who at first was very troublesome but lately he has let me alone," reported Maj. Peter Keenan of the 8th Pennsylvania Cavalry on March 31, "though my friends on my right and left suffer more or less daily. My old regiment has always proved too much and too wide awake for our rebel friends. They would no more think of attacking us with equal force than they would fly." Rumors flew that Stuart had gone off on another raid. "I doubt much if he will be as successful as he has been heretofore," noted a confident Keenan.[14]

The morale of the Yankee troopers remained high. They got into the spirit of tomfoolery that normally marked the first day of April. "Called up very early and ordered to pack and saddle," scrawled a member of the 8th New York in his diary on April 1. "After standing in line for 5 hours found that we had been 'April fooled' so we unsaddled and put up our tents."[15] Having been skunked, the New Yorkers waited for an opportunity to get revenge upon their tormenters.

On April 6th, President and Mrs. Lincoln and their son Tad came to the army's camp to review the entire Army of the Potomac. The review was conducted in full sight of the Confederate camps around Fredericksburg, with colors snapping proudly in the breeze. Preceded by a twenty-one-gun salute, the blueclad horse soldiers paraded past the president in a grand review. It took three or four hours for the entire Cavalry Corps of twenty-five regiments to pass Lincoln's reviewing stand.[16] The Yankee horsemen spread out across a broad plain three miles wide and arrayed themselves in double ranks. They passed the president's reviewing stand with "naked swords reversed, the usual method of salutation in such occasions."[17] Daniel Peck of the 9th New York Cavalry noted, "I suppose we had the largest and most magnificent military display ever gotten up on the American Continent. The President was accompanied by his Lady & little son. The little Lincoln rode a pony beside his father during the reviews. Mrs. Lincoln remained in a carriage."[18]

A member of the 6th U.S. Cavalry recalled, "Of reviews there were but few. There was a grand one, however, in which nearly the entire army participated. The display was magnificent, the men looking hearty and cheerful, executing their maneuvers with a precision that showed a high state of discipline, yet with the peculiarly graceful nonchalance and dash that is so characteristic of American soldiers in the field." He continued, "I felt, as I stood upon a hill overlooking the scene, an unutterable pride in the grand old Army of the Potomac, whose sturdy columns had covered themselves with glory amid the fearful trials through which they had passed during the last two years."[19] Stoneman had every reason to be proud of his troopers. "Nobody was more astonished than the troops themselves when they saw the face of the country swarm with cavalry," observed one of the corps commander's staff officers, "and apparently an endless stream of horsemen pouring from every avenue leading to the parade-ground."[20]

The men slogged through the mud and melting snow just to get to the parade grounds near Falmouth. One member of the 8th Illinois Cavalry jotted in his journal, "Grand review of the Cavalry. Mud knee deep, but we marched the best we could. Lincoln and his wife were here. The President looks tired but he is as handsome as ever."[21] "This was the first good sight I ever had of the President," observed a Pennsylvanian, "and cannot but say that, notwithstanding the prejudices against him, he looks really the great man that he is."[22]

"It was a grand sight to look upon this immense mass of cavalry in motion with banners waving, music crashing, and horses prancing, as the vast columns came on and on, winding like a large serpent over hills and dales, stretching far away out of sight," gushed a newspaper correspondent. "Never before upon this continent was there such a sight witnessed, and probably never again will there be in our country so great a number—17,000, assembled together, men and horses, and all looking in excellent condition and admirably fit for service." The sight inspired confidence in the correspondent, who observed, "This arm of our service has been of little account heretofore, owing to the mismanagement and imbecility of General McClellan, but now, educated by experience and allowed a latitude of operations by the present commander of the Army of the Potomac, it promises to make a brilliant record for itself when the time comes, and already the gallant Averell, one of the more modest and quiet officers in the army, has inspired the whole cavalry corps with a feeling of emulation which will tell when it is called into action."[23]

Another bluecoat noted that the president looked "pale, haggard and careworn, as though there was a heap of trouble on the old man's mind."[24] "Old Abe . . . looks as though he was just ready to die," echoed a Maine horse soldier, "don't know when I have seen a man look so miserable."[25] A member of the 8th New York was surprised that "the President made a better appearance on horseback than I would have expected to see, but looks extremely thin and careworn, as if his strength would scarcely carry him to the end of his term."[26]

Buford and his gallant Irish aides, Capts. Myles W. Keogh and Joseph O'Keeffe, led the Cavalry Corps in the grand review before President Lincoln. Bringing up the rear of Buford's Reserve Brigade was Rush's Lancers, sunlight dancing off their polished lances as they trotted past the reviewing stand. "Rush's Lancers are presenting a perfect picture like effect in beautiful order," reported a Pennsylvania officer. "They side wheeled into line, forming as they came up on the left of the preceding company at a gallop—it was with the Artillery, the most brilliant part of the whole affair."[27]

David M. Gregg's big bay horse grew nervous when a regimental band started playing loudly next to him. Riding alongside the President as Lincoln inspected the Second Division, General Gregg's restive mount bolted. The general left Lincoln struggling along behind as the animal sprang over ditches. Gregg, a fine horseman, had to use all of his considerable strength to turn his fiery mount at the end of the line. To make matters worse, when the President presented Gregg to Mrs. Lincoln, the bay reared and had to be brought back under control, much to the Pennsylvanian's embarrassment. Both Lincolns spoke kindly to Gregg about "the exciting ride" and the "magnificent horse," but the horse's antics had infuriated the general for making him look like a show-off in front of the presidential reviewing party. Gregg, who typically used only a light bit, acquired a heavy bit in order to control the big bay, which served him well for two years after this episode.[28]

The Philadelphia Inquirer reported that "[t]he finest cavalry display ever witnessed in the United States, was that of the review of cavalry to-day by the President. Every regiment turned out in its largest possible numbers, and the display was most imposing."[29] As a result of the reforms and the morale boost created by the reviews, the Federal troopers, for the first time, began to believe that they were the equals of the Confederate cavalry.

The next night, Averell called on the Lincolns at army headquarters. He "saw and talked horse awhile with the President." He also related the story of the taunting note left him at Hartwood Church by Fitz Lee, and recounted his adventures at Kelly's Ford to the President. Lincoln expressed regret that the war had driven a wedge between Averell and his old school chum and stated that he hoped that the war would soon end so that the two men could resume their friendship.[30]

In the wake of the grand review, the Army of the Potomac's morale soared. "Any one that says the Army of the Potomac is not in a good condition now knows nothing about [it] or else tells a knowing falsehood," observed a Pennsylvania horse soldier. "I never saw the army in better condition, better clothed, better equipped, better fed, nor in better spirits or in more confidence of the ability of its leader."[31] "General Hooker is a splendid looking man and I have all confidence in him to command our army," announced a sergeant of the 12th Illinois Cavalry the day after the grand review. "I believe him to be as good a General as we have in the Nation."[32] The winter's despair gave way to unprecedented high spirits.

The Northern saddle soldiers speculated about what the spring campaigning season might bring. "There are different objects spoken of in connection with the increase of Cavalry here. I think it looks somewhat suspicious, and all of the talk of raids may be true," guessed another member of the 12th Illinois Cavalry. "I confess I cannot see why out of the present force of cavalry here there could not [be] a sufficient number spared to overwhelm any force the enemy could bring against them, and lay waste the country to the west and south of Richmond, renting the railroad and telegraph communications all around. Could such a thing be done it would do more towards our cause I think than the addition of 20,000 men to our Army in front of Fredericksburg." The Illinois trooper had no way of knowing how accurate his prediction was about the high command's intentions for the Cavalry Corps.[33]

Adapting Burnside's plan for the Mud March, Hooker intended to sneak a march around Lee's left flank near a crossroads called Chancellorsville, located a few miles to the east of a tangled, dense forest of undergrowth known as the Wilderness. Time was crucial. A large portion of his army consisted of nine-month and two-year enlistments, and many of those enlistments were about to expire. Further, Lt. Gen. James Longstreet's Corps of the Army of Northern Virginia had been detached to besiege Suffolk, meaning that Hooker enjoyed a nearly three-to-one numeric advantage over Lee's army. Clearly, this disparity would not last long as enlistments expired and Longstreet made his way back to the Army of Northern Virginia for the spring campaigning season. Hooker had to move soon.

He intended to march up the Rappahannock River past its confluence with the Rapidan River, cross the two rivers at a number of fords and on pontoon bridges, and move on the Virginia Central and Richmond, Fredericksburg and Potomac Railroads, destroying Lee's main supply line. Once these rail lines were out of commission, Hooker believed that Lee would have to abandon his strong lines at Fredericksburg, where Hooker could fall upon the Army of Northern Virginia at a time and place of his choosing. Nearly half of his massive army would cross the Rappahannock at Fredericksburg and assault Lee's lines there, in the hope of hiding the movement of the main body from prying Confederate eyes. Hoping that the assault on Fredericksburg would pin down Lee's army, Hooker and the balance of the Army of the Potomac would deliver a crushing flank attack on the Army of Northern Virginia.

If the plan worked, Hooker would get around Lee's flank, moving between the main Rebel army and the Confederate capital of Richmond. Lee would have to come out and fight Hooker on ground of his choosing. To create a diversion, Hooker intended to send the Cavalry Corps, save for one brigade, on a far-ranging raid on Richmond, leaving his army's advance largely unscreened. The cavalry would cut Lee's lines of communications with Richmond, and destroy, to the extent possible, the RF&P Railroad. This would be the first major raid of the Cavalry Corps, and the stakes were very high as the plans were finalized.

On April 11, Hooker summoned Stoneman to his headquarters to instruct the cavalry commander on his role in the coming campaign.[34] Hooker ordered Stoneman to move the next morning "for the purpose of turning the enemy's position

on his left, and of throwing your command between him and Richmond and iso-
lating him from his supplies, checking his retreat, and inflicting on him every possible injury which will tend to his discomfiture and defeat." The army commander
gave explicit direction to his cavalry chief. "Let your watchword be fight, and let
all your orders be fight, fight, fight," proclaimed Hooker. The ante was high in
Hooker's intricate game. "It devolves upon you . . . to take the initiative in the forward movement of this grand army, and on you and your noble command must
depend in great measure the extent and brilliancy of our success."[35]

That night, Stoneman sent for his subordinates and explained to them the
objects of the expedition. He assigned each his allotted tasks and duties. "The
commanders had hardly left my Headquarters when . . . the sky suddenly became
overcast, the darkness almost subterranean, and the rain began to fall," recounted
Stoneman after the raid, "and, of course, our bright hopes and high expectations,
than to which no command ever started with brighter or higher, began to be
dimmed and lowered."[36] "It has commenced raining tonight as it always does when
our army advances," reported a trooper of the 9th New York Cavalry. "It seems as
though the elements were against us and always in favor of the rebels."[37]

Nevertheless, orders to march were issued. The men received eight days' rations
and five days' forage. As they prepared, rumors buzzed through their camps. Men
speculated about where they were going. "Well, this looks like business," said many.
"You bet," would be the reply. The men bundled up their excess winter baggage
and shipped it home. They hastily scribbled letters to parents and sweethearts. "I
hasten to write you a few lines today. We have just received orders to be ready to
march tomorrow morning at daybreak with three days' rations," reported Sergeant
Redman of the 12th Illinois. "I think that means that something is to be done. I
hope so anyway. We have all the sick at the Division Hospital and take nothing with
us but what we can carry on the horses and pack mules. I am well and ready for
action. I hope that we may meet with success," he concluded.[38]

However, "while every one was busy, no one seemed excited," observed a soldier
of the 16th Pennsylvania Cavalry. "Discipline had done much to make us soldiers.
A few months before, whining and complaints would have been numerous. Now
nothing of the kind was heard. Sensations new and strange were being experienced.
Where we were going no one seemed to know, nor was there anything to indicate
what was to occur. All hoped for a march to victory," he concluded.[39]

Early on the morning of April 13, the Cavalry Corps broke camp and moved
out, nearly 10,000 strong, supported by 275 supply wagons and mule trains carrying supplies.[40] Each officer was allowed one valise in his regiment's wagon train, but
the men had to carry their possessions on their mounts.[41] This would be the first
long march for some of the Northern regiments. Still suffering from the injuries he

sustained at Kelly's Ford, Col. Alfred Duffié remained behind. His senior colonel, Horace B. Sargent of the 1st Massachusetts Cavalry, took command of the Frenchman's brigade. Duffié assumed command of the dismounted elements of the Cavalry Corps.[42]

A New England trooper left behind an especially vivid account of the load carried by the mounts. "Just imagine your house, your bed, your cooking utensils, your rations, and the feed for your horse, all on the horse's back." He continued, "On each saddle there are three straps in front and three behind; on front is strapped the overcoat, two pieces of shelter tent, and a rubber talma; behind is carried the nose-bag and saddle-bags, containing curry-comb and brush, extra ammunition, knife, fork and spoon; over these hangs the haversack, containing rations; shirt and stockings extra are rolled in the shelter tent; the blanket is put under the saddle on top of the saddle blanket; the carbine is slung from the left shoulder and hangs on the right side; the revolver, in a holster attached to the belt, is on the right hip; the sabre hangs by the left side; each man has a quart cup for making coffee, and a tin plate; perhaps each fourth man carries a little frying pan." As the march wore on, the heavier items disappeared first, followed by the unnecessary smaller items until they carried only the bare minimum to fill their needs. This hard lesson stayed with them for the rest of the war.[43]

"The whole cavalry force is said to be on the march," observed a Hoosier of Grimes Davis's brigade.[44] Unaccustomed to such activity by the Cavalry Corps, the Army of the Potomac's fascinated infantry watched them depart. A member of the 118th Pennsylvania Infantry thought he saw 40,000 horsemen depart. "They had picks, ropes, tar and everything to rip up railroads and burn bridges. Everyone had a quart of camphene they needed to burn bridges at Gordonsville," he noted.[45] The foot soldiers had high expectations for their mounted comrades, knowing that they would follow them into the field a few days later.

John Follmer of the 16th Pennsylvania Cavalry was assigned to his regiment's mule train. This marked Follmer's first exposure to the troublesome beasts, which did pretty much as they pleased. He observed that when they wanted to rid themselves of their loads, they would "resort to many devices." Some rubbed against fences, trees, or other mules in an effort to loosen their loads. When all else failed, the obstinate animals would lie down and roll. "The last resort generally did the business," observed Follmer. As a result, oats, corn, hardtack, pots, kettles, pans, and the like lined the Cavalry Corps's route of march. The mules also resorted to kicking. "I do not remember how many times we were compelled to repack these pesky varmints' loads, but patience deserted pretty early in the march," concluded the exasperated trooper.[46]

Sgt. Samuel Cormany, also a member of the 16th Pennsylvania, had been ill for several days when the marching orders arrived. He noted, "Heard cannonading frequently frontward and leftward." After moving about twenty miles, the 16th Pennsylvania fought a slight skirmish about 4:00 P.M. and then camped for the night. The unfortunate Cormany drew picket duty. "Alert for the night—I sat on my saddle—leaned against a tree," he noted in his diary, "took little naps holding my horse's rein in my hand." He had a sore throat and a throbbing headache; picket duty proved to be a trying ordeal for the sick soldier.

Morning light brought a different perspective. In spite of the scratchy throat and aching head, Cormany "felt perfectly calm and willing, almost eager to go into a fight." Instead, after the column advanced ten miles, it went into camp, and the sergeant spent a pleasant afternoon basking in the warm sunlight. That night, as he recorded the day's activities in his diary, Cormany ominously predicted, "Looks like rain."[47]

Gregg's division spent an unpleasant night. The 3d Pennsylvania Cavalry did picket duty all night. "Had no sleep and no fires last night," noted Lt. W. F. Potter in his diary. "It was quite cold and we were obliged to keep walking up and down that we might be warm." A heavy frost settled across the shivering men, who eagerly awaited the arrival of morning.[48]

About 2:00 A.M. on April 13, an orderly brought orders to the 6th U.S. Cavalry to saddle up and get ready to march. Buford and the rest of the Reserve Brigade moved out about daybreak. They marched to Kelly's Ford. "A farewell cheer was given to our old camping ground as the regiment moved out," noted a member of the 6th Pennsylvania Cavalry.[49] When they arrived at Kelly's Ford, they found enemy pickets guarding the river crossing. One company of the 6th U.S. dismounted and advanced to the riverbank as skirmishers, and drove off the grayclad pickets. When some of the Southerners halted to occupy the rifle pits along the millrace, Buford drew the entire Reserve Brigade up into line of battle in plain view of the enemy. "The object in view at Kelly's Ford was to make a demonstration in favor of the portions of the corps that were to cross the river higher up," commented Buford, who claimed that these demonstrations were a success.[50]

"We remained in this position hour after hour, every moment expecting the order to charge and cross the ford," wrote Lt. Louis H. Carpenter, "but time passed and no order came." Carpenter sat and watched as the Confederates continued moving troopers about, and the grayclad horsemen opened fire on the Federal skirmishers along the riverbank. The Regulars opened a severe carbine fire on them. "Two dropped from their saddles and the riderless horses galloped away over the field. The rest of the party retreated in double quick time." About 3:00, Buford discovered that the Southerners were moving artillery into position, and wisely withdrew out of range of the guns. "Before we were underway, the rebels opened upon us from 2 six pounders, the shot and shell flew rather thick for a short time, but we were soon under shelter."[51]

The main body of the Cavalry Corps proceeded to the familiar ground around Morrisville, where it camped for the night. The men could hear cannonading up-river from Averell's selected crossing point. Davis's brigade continued riding that night, intending to cross the Rappahannock well upstream of White Sulphur Springs. He would then march along the south bank, clearing the critical crossings at Beverly's Ford and Rappahannock Bridge for the rest of the Cavalry Corps.[52] "The [river] which commonly was about 18 inches high swelled up the horses sides," recalled Daniel Pulis of the 8th New York. "It carried one man down the stream and to cap all when the storm was at its highth it began to haile like great guns."[53] The soggy horsemen also had to ford the swollen Hazel River, a tribu-tary that flows into the Rappahannock just upstream of Beverly's Ford, where the frigid water reached the level of their saddles.[54] "We have not met serious opposi-tion," noted a member of the 3d Indiana Cavalry.[55] They covered about fifteen miles that day.[56]

The Confederates noticed the passage of such a large mounted force immedi-ately. Southern scouts detected the movement within hours. Brig. Gen. William H. F. "Rooney" Lee, commanding the Confederate forces in that sector, dispatched reinforcements to cover the crossing at Kelly's Ford, where they would await the arrival of Stoneman's column.[57] However, an intricate scheme of deception by Hooker confused the Southerners, who were tricked into believing that the fertile Shenandoah Valley and the strategic city of Winchester were the actual target, not Lee's rear. Stuart and the Lees made their dispositions accordingly, knowing that the Federal horsemen were stuck in the mud, leaving gaps in their picket lines to be exploited by the Federal forces.[58]

Davis and his men swam across the Rappahannock at two places on April 14, while the balance of the Cavalry Corps moved to the vicinity of Beverly's Ford, several miles upriver from the familiar crossing at Kelly's Ford. Gregg's troopers skirmished with elements of the 9th and 13th Virginia Cavalry of Rooney Lee's brigade. Men of Col. John Chambliss's 13th Virginia occupied the rifle pits at Kelly's Ford. The Federal advance drove the Virginians from their rifle pits, wound-ing Lt. William T. Gary, the commander of the Southern sharpshooters.[59]

Gregg sent eighty members of the 1st Maine Cavalry to seize the railroad bridge at Rappahannock Station. The bridge was about 60 feet above the river and nearly 400 feet long, presenting a significant undertaking. Lee's men obstructed the river by winding telegraph wire around stakes driven in the bottom of the river that had to be removed before the Federal horses could safely cross. The delay permit-ted the Confederate pickets to escape and spread the word of the Federal advance. The alerted Virginians charged and drove the Maine men back across the river. Southern horse artillery opened fire on the retreating Maine troopers. "Their first shot struck the bank. The second, the first end of the bridge and the third passed under and took away a brace in front of me under the bridge," recounted Nathan Webb of the 1st Maine Cavalry in his diary. "They shelled us pretty briskly but we lay on the bank all day while our artillery replied." They stayed there until it was nearly dark, taking fire from Southern sharpshooters and waiting for an opportunity to make their way to safety.[60]

Although he greatly outnumbered Rooney Lee's little force, Stoneman elected to wait until morning to push across. His cautious decision had far-reaching implications for the coming campaign.[61] That night, a heavy rainstorm blew in, raising the level of the Rappahannock River by seven feet in just a few hours, turning little rivulets into raging torrents and the roads into impassably soupy mud. "Owing to the intensity of the storm and the certainty that all the streams in our front would soon [necessitate] swimming should the rain continue many hours, and the roads impassable for artillery and wagons," recounted Stoneman, "I determined to postpone crossing for a time and await results—a most fortunate delay as, had we crossed, we should have been surrounded by streams impassable except by swimming, and in the presence of an enemy who could have assembled against us, over his railroads and turnpikes in his rear, any force he might have thought proper."[62]

"Our whole Command was . . . to eclipse Stuart's famous raid around McClellan's army," wrote Edward W. Whitaker of the 6th New York Cavalry. He speculated that the Cavalry Corps was to destroy the crucial railroad junction at Gordonsville. Whitaker had served in this area in 1862 and knew the terrain. As a result of Whitaker's familiarity with the area, Stoneman sent for the New Yorker, and instructed him to take a sergeant and ten men, carrying verbal orders to bring Davis's brigade back to safety "before they were whipped, being alone, or the river got too high for them to recross." Whitaker found the men of Davis's brigade fighting and driving Rooney Lee's Confederates, following the Southerners as they retired. "Seeing the trouble we had in recrossing [the Confederates] charged down our last squadron over which was in line on the bank down which both were rushed into the boiling river and a scene of tangled horses and men drowning rebs and unionist all together," he recounted.[63]

Unfortunately, by the time the orders arrived, the Rappahannock had already started to rise, and the rear of Davis's column had to swim their horses across the raging river. The swirling, frigid waters trapped two companies of the 3d Indiana Cavalry on the banks. With Jeb Stuart leading the way, troopers of Rooney Lee's 9th Virginia Cavalry fell upon them, sabers drawn. "The little band of twenty or thirty looked small beside the column that we saw coming down the road with the reb flag flying and sabers drawn," recounted an Indiana trooper.[64] Elements of the 8th New York, guarding the ford, tried to help, but they were too little, too late in the face of the grayclad onslaught. The Confederates fired upon the fourth squadron of the 8th New York, wounding an officer of Company I. "They threw a few shells, but they did no damage," recalled a member of the 8th New York.[65]

"Brigade recrossed . . . leaving us," noted Trooper Samuel Gilpin of the 3d Indiana. "Reb forces surrounded us. 8th New York failed. We were forced back across Rap. River high. *Gave us fits* while crossing."[66] "We charged them and drove them pell-mell into the river," reported Col. Richard L. T. Beale of the 9th Virginia, "capturing fourteen prisoners and drowning several." Beale noted that his command suffered only one man wounded and one man missing in the melee.[67]

Maj. Heros von Borcke, one of Stuart's staff officers, desperately wanted to join the charge, but Stuart forbade it. The Prussian dashed toward a group of dismounted Indiana carbineers popping away at him at a range of 100 yards. He reined in and demanded their surrender. The Indianans responded with a flurry of balls that clipped a lock of von Borcke's hair. The Prussian spurred his horse and leapt into the creek that separated them, the frigid waters reaching his shoulders. With great effort, the horse reached the other side and climbed the muddy, slippery bank. Von Borcke drew his blade and fell upon them, slashing and hacking at a corporal and a private of the 3d Indiana.

Terrified, the Northerners threw away their weapons and begged for mercy. "In the first excitement, I felt but little inclined to heed their prayers," recalled von Borcke, "seeing that but a few minutes before they had shot down one of our men, and had spent their last cartridge in the attempt to do the like for me; but the poor wretches were so terror-stricken, and begged so hard for their lives, that I was content to commute the penalty of death to treating them to just such a cold bath as I had had; and so I sent them through the water to the other side." The Prussian turned his new charges over to a courier and rode back to Stuart's position. The cavalry chieftain watched the entire episode, and "was much amused at the plight in which I returned, soaked through, and beplastered with mud." Laughing, Stuart indicated that he never expected to see von Borcke emerge after his plunge in the creek, and that his soggy aide resembled a tortoise crawling up the bank once he finally did emerge.[68]

Sgt. Willis H. Stapp of the 3d Indiana Cavalry spotted a Virginian bearing down on him with his saber drawn. He jumped to the side and let the horseman pass. He raised the hammer of his revolver, waiting for the Virginian to return. "When he got within five yards of me, I took good aim at him. He dropped his head on his horse's neck and my pistol only snapped the cap. While his head was down and my pistol failed me, I had to jump to one side to save myself; and one of the Sergeants of Company F seeing the danger I was in, came to my assistance." The other sergeant fired at the Virginian, scaring Stapp's horse, which bolted. "He jumped into a mud hole about four feet deep and threw me," recalled Stapp.

Tangled in his stirrups and covered with thick, gooey mud, Stapp found himself with a pistol to his head and a demand for surrender ringing in his ear. "I was surrounded and about drowned out," he glumly observed, "so I had to pull off a sabre that I had captured from one of the rebels. My pistol I threw away to keep them from getting it." He lost his horse and personal effects, including his spare clothing. Stapp's journey to Richmond as a prisoner of war began.[69]

The captured Hoosiers were initially forced to walk but when the Southerners learned that these men belonged to the 3d Indiana Cavalry, they returned their horses out of respect for their fighting ability and courage. For many unhappy Indianans, it would be a long time until their next ride on a cavalry horse.[70]

Some of the Federals drowned in the raging torrent as they fought their way back across the angry Rappahannock. The 3d Indiana lost twenty-six men killed, wounded, or captured in this fiasco.[71] "The operations of Davis's Brigade, as far as they went through, delayed somewhat by darkness and the rain in the distribution and packing of supplies and in reaching Freeman's Ford, were most satisfactory and were performed with the vigor and enterprise which was a sure presage of success," praised Stoneman.[72]

Pleasonton's men also had to force their way across the Hazel River. Capt. Elon J. Farnsworth led a scouting party toward Warrenton, including his own squadron of the 8th Illinois Cavalry plus one from the 9th New York Cavalry. "We took the road to Warrenton, and there had a nice little skirmish with the enemy; but the Ninth New York Captain pitched in without orders and so spoiled the beauty of the fight," noted an Illinoisan. "If he had followed Captain Farnsworth's orders, we might have taken thirty or forty of the [1st Virginia Cavalry]; whereas we took but half a dozen." After defeating the Virginians, Farnsworth withdrew to White Sulphur Springs to await further orders from Grimes Davis. At nightfall, Farnsworth, concerned that it might be too dangerous to remain in place after dark and missing his rearguard squadron, crossed the Rappahannock at a mill, obtained fodder for his horses, and camped for the night, "so tired that we did not cook any supper."[73]

The little command awoke soggy and miserable on April 15. "One of the most rainy days of the season. The rain falling in torrents all day," noted a glum Illinoisan. Farnsworth sent to Liberty for orders and found the missing rearguard squadron there. The captain of the missing squadron, Capt. J. G. Smith, carried orders from Davis for Farnsworth to rejoin the brigade. Farnsworth impressed an old man, once a militia colonel, into guide service. The old colonel "was a plucky old fellow, and offered 'to whip Captains Hynes and Farnsworth both,' at a fist fight." The tired horsemen rejoined Davis at Kelly's Ford in time for the brigade's retrograde movement.[74]

When the Confederates charged Davis's rearguard at Kelly's Ford, Farnsworth ran a gauntlet of enemy skirmishers to inform Davis of the location of the contingent of the 8th Illinois. Davis said that the Illinois would be "gobbled up" unless they crossed the river immediately. Farnsworth "made his mustang do some tall running up the river six miles and down the opposite side; and taking us by a circuitous route, we were enabled to join the brigade without loss." The captain's coolness and foresight had saved his command from capture. Stoneman, in relating this incident, called Farnsworth "a very excellent officer." The high command of the Union cavalry marked the young man for advancement.[75]

The fact that Stoneman had to funnel thousands of men over a long bridge in column of twos necessarily delayed his advance at Rappahannock Station and stranded his large force on the wrong side of the river, meaning that the Cavalry Corps could not fulfill Hooker's orders or his timetable for the expedition. That night, Hooker telegraphed Washington to report on the progress of the raid. "I am rejoiced that Stoneman had two good days to go up the river, and was enabled to cross it before it had become too much swollen," noted Hooker. The army commander also sent a stern note to his cavalry commander. "The commanding general desires me to call your attention to your letter of instructions," wrote Hooker's chief of staff, Maj. Gen. Daniel Butterfield. "The tenor of your dispatches might indicate that you were maneuvering your whole force against the command of Fitz. Lee, numbering not over 2,000 men. The commanding general does not expect, nor do your instructions indicate, that you are to act from any base or depot."[76]

John McIntosh's brigade advanced at 5:00 A.M. on the morning of April 15, and marched about five miles upriver. Orders to prepare to fight on foot rang out, and two squadrons of the 16th Pennsylvania Cavalry dismounted and formed line of battle. "We threw off our Overcoats and sabers," recorded Sergeant Cormany, "and fell into ranks. Stood two hours in heavy rain—Kept ammunition dry." Finally, the Pennsylvanians received orders to move out, and drove in the Confederate pickets, who fled. "We followed a short distance—firing on them at ¼ mile range—No casualties on our side," observed Cormany. The Federals then fell back and formed a picket line, "wet to the hide."[77]

The men of the 1st Maine Cavalry spent a miserable day escorting the wagon train. "The rain still poured, the roads were very muddy, progress, which would have been slow at best, was rendered more so by the difficulties that beset the train, and the boys began to feel thoroughly blue," noted an officer. "One comrade offered a large premium to whoever would say something that would make him laugh, but to no purpose." They stopped to rest and spotted a nearby rail fence. "They went for those rails, filled with the idea that there was heat and comparative comfort in them. In a minute there was not a rail left on the fence. All had been transferred to little piles in rear of the several companies, ready to be made into cheerful fires." To their great disappointment, orders came down not to start fires in the hope that the enemy across the river would not spot their presence. The disappointed men named their pathetic bivouac "Camp Misery."[78]

The rest of Duffié's division spent the day in a different way. "We marched before daybreak, having been roused 2½ o'clk, and the roads were horrid," noted Maj. Henry Higginson of the 1st Massachusetts Cavalry in his diary. "Halted after some five miles, in a wood, and dismounted . . . the crossing was given up on account of the storm and we encamped in the woods. It rained all day and all night tremendously, and wet everything and everybody. 'Tis odd how well one can sleep between damp blankets in wet clothes and boots soaked thro' and thro'; yet we did very well." The men spent a quiet next day in camp, reading and wait- ing for the waters to recede.[79] Many broke apart hardtack boxes and used the pieces for bedding in the hope of avoiding sleeping in the cold mud.[80]

Later that evening, Brig. Gen. Seth Williams, the Army of the Potomac's adjutant general, chided Stoneman. "If it is practicable to carry into execution the general instructions communicated to you on the 12th instant, the major-general com- manding expects you to make use of such means as will, in your opinion, enable you to accomplish them, and that as speedily as possible. The army is now awaiting your movement." Williams concluded, "I am directed to add that in view of the swollen condition of the streams it is not probable, in the event of your being able to advance, that you will be troubled by the infantry of the enemy." Williams for- warded a copy of this dispatch to the White House.[81]

The delays concerned Lincoln. He responded, citing his "considerable un- easiness." Noting that bad weather in Virginia during April was predictable, the President said, "General S. is not moving rapidly enough to make the expedition come to anything. He has now been out three days, two of which were unusually fair weather, and all three without hinderance from the enemy, and yet he is not 25 miles from where he started. To reach his point he still has 60 to go, another river [the Rapidan] to cross, and will be hindered by the enemy." The frustrated chief executive concluded, "I do not know that any better can be done, but I fear it is another failure already. Write me often. I am very anxious."[82]

While Hooker and Lincoln fretted, the rains continued falling and the already swollen river continued to rise. The frustrated horse soldiers spent their time pick- eting the river and moving their camp from place to place. Stoneman concen- trated his force at Warrenton Junction, where the Orange & Alexandria Railroad provided a steady stream of supplies. On the 16th, he responded to the letter from Williams. "I cannot say what has been the state of affairs away from this vicinity," he wrote, "but here, at the hour of my last dispatch, the condition of things may be judged of when I tell you that almost every rivulet was swimming, and the roads next to impassable for horses or pack-mules, not to speak of artillery and wagons, the latter of which had in the morning all been started for the rear." The cavalry commander reported that the flooded waters of the Rappahannock had carried away part of the railroad bridge at Rappahannock Station, that the river was out of its banks, and that it continued rising. "Three hours ago Gregg's division, which was directed to move back from the river to higher ground, began crossing a bed nearly dry yesterday morning, and its rear is not over yet. This morning the same bed was swimming, and a squadron in attempting to cross it lost 1 officer and 2 men, swept off, and several horses drowned."

He noted that the whole Cavalry Corps was on the north bank of the Rappahannock, and that he felt more comfortable with the flooded river in his front and not his rear. Stoneman reported that the river would not be fordable for several more days, and that "up to midnight, night before last, everything had worked as well as could have been wished, and my dispatch was based upon the expectation that we were to be favored with a continuation of fair weather. It certainly was not predicated upon the expectation of being overtaken by one of the most violent rainstorms I have ever been caught in, and that, too, in a country where streams rise as rapidly as do the rivers in our front." The frustrated commander concluded, "To cross the swollen streams in our front at present, with any chance of meeting with a success, is an undertaking I consider, as a military operation, almost certain to meet with failure." He reassured Hooker that his men were ready to move as soon as conditions permitted.[83]

Hooker defended Stoneman when he transmitted this report to Lincoln. "His failure to accomplish speedily the objects of his expedition is a source of deep regret to me, but I can find nothing in his conduct of it requiring my animadversion or censure. We cannot control the elements." He also noted that army headquarters had no reason to believe that the enemy had divined the intention of Stoneman's expedition, and reassured the anxious President. "No one, Mr. President, can be more anxious than myself to relieve your cares and anxieties, and you may be assured that I will spare no labor and suffer no opportunity to pass unimproved for so doing."[84] In the meantime, Hooker sent a large train of supplies to the stranded men.

But the element of surprise was gone. On April 16, Robert E. Lee reported Stoneman's movement to Jefferson Davis. "On Monday evening they were seen moving up the Rappahannock, and on Tuesday morning they appeared at Kelly's Ford with an intention to cross," wrote General Lee. "They were however repulsed by our dismounted skirmishers, but forced a passage at the Rappahannock Bridge where they were soon driven back. From information which I received I was led to believe that their destination was the Shenandoah Valley." As a result, Lee alerted Brig. Gen. William E. "Grumble" Jones, whose cavalry patrolled the valley district, to be alert for the approach of a large force of Union cavalry. The delays engendered by the rains meant that Stoneman lost the advantage gained by marching quickly to the Rappahannock.[85]

On the morning of April 16, Buford's brigade shifted its camp to be closer to the rest of the Cavalry Corps. When "Boots and Saddles" sounded, the column moved out in the driving rain, slogging its way through horrible roads on the way to Kelly's Ford.

After marching several miles, the Regulars "were then dismounted in the middle of the road and ordered to stand to horse. I think I never saw it rain as hard as it did about this time. I was wearing a cap and the water poured over my face and trickled down my back in streams," complained Lieutenant Carpenter. "I should have preferred a seat by the fire in the front parlor at home, as you may imagine." After a number of frustrating failures, Carpenter and several of his other fellow officers managed to get a little fire going in spite of the rain, and they were able to warm a little of the chill from their bones. Carpenter concluded, "No one knows what we are to do next."[86]

Another Regular officer, Capt. George B. Sanford, echoed a similar note. "The rain fell almost constantly during the whole time and the country was like a sea," he observed. "We marched all day in the rain and lay down at night in the mud in our wet clothes, often unable to get even a cup of coffee owing to the impossibility of making fires with the wet wood." Sanford recalled that his clothes never got completely dry until the middle of May. He soon fell very ill, nearly succumbing to the fevers that racked his body.[87]

On April 17, Gregg dispatched scouting parties toward Warrenton to deal with local bushwhackers. They failed to find them, and the scout squadron returned without incident. The Yankee troopers quickly grew bored with these frustrating tasks.[88]

The 1st Pennsylvania Cavalry, which had not accompanied the raiders, occupied Cleve Place, a handsome plantation owned by a family named Lewis. "Mrs. Lewis told me yesterday that she supposed this country would be completely yankeeised and observed that she hated to see the inroads of other times, as the good old southern life suited her so well," noted a Pennsylvanian. In spite of their obvious reluctance to part with their old way of life, the locals treated the Northern horse soldiers kindly, sending them milk and inviting them to dine with their families. This was comfortable, pleasant duty, and the men enjoyed themselves, even if the duty bored them. Their duty greatly contrasted the hardships undergone by the rest of the Cavalry Corps.[89]

The Southern high command understood that each day that the rivers ran high delayed the beginning of the Northern campaign. "I do not think that General Hooker would venture to transfer his army to the Pamunkey or James River, and thus uncover Washington, unless the troops in front of Alexandria and in and around Washington are as numerous as stated by your signal officer," wrote Robert E. Lee to Stuart on April 17. "If his movement on the Upper Rappahannock was not intended against [the cavalry force of Brig. Gen. William E. 'Grumble' Jones, operating in the Shenandoah Valley], it may have been designed to draw us out from our present position, either to disclose our force, or enable them to seize upon Fredericksburg, rebuild the bridge across the river, etc." Lee continued, "I am very much gratified at your having repulsed all efforts made by the enemy to cross the Rappahannock, and at the arrangements generally you have made. I hope you may yet be able to deal him a damaging blow, but request that you will not necessarily expose yourself or men."[90]

On April 18, Hooker cajoled, "The difficulty of supplying your command in its present position, in addition to other reasons, renders it necessary for you to resume your forward movement at the earliest possible moment." He instructed Stoneman to carry six days' supplies when the Cavalry Corps finally moved, and to remain watchful for Confederates who might have taken the opportunity presented by the rain to block the route of march. He told Stoneman that the Cavalry Corps should live off the land wherever possible. Hooker's impatience and frustration were boiling to the surface, and it showed.[91]

The Confederate high command had divined Stoneman's intentions. "The interval was fruitful of heavy skirmishes, the greatest of which, terminating so lately at Kelly's Ford, proves to have been only an intended raid, more for plunder and devastation than for a reconnaissance having in view a determined effort to retrieve the disaster at Fredericksburg," reported a Richmond newspaper on April 18.[92]

On April 19, elements of Davis's brigade conducted another scouting expedition well up the Rappahannock. The 8th Illinois charged some enemy cavalry near Orleans. They chased the Southerners to within six miles of Salem but broke off their pursuit at Clover Hill and headed back toward Warrenton, stopping for the night at the plantation of a local farmer named Morgan, where they found abundant supplies. The woman of the house, described as a "perfect Amazon," used all of her powers of persuasion to save her chickens and other valuables, but her entreaties failed and the chickens became prisoners of war, soon to meet their fate at the hands of their Northern captors. The 3d Indiana brought in several prisoners and the men spent a pleasant evening.

About 10:00 P.M., word arrived that a large force under Confederate partisans Capt. John Singleton Mosby and Lt. Col. Elijah V. White was gathering, so Maj. John L. Beveridge of the 8th Illinois, commanding the expedition, mounted up and moved out. The Federals camped two miles from Warrenton. In heavy rain, the expedition marched to Bealton the next day and rejoined the rest of Davis's brigade. "This is but a specimen of what a scouting party has to endure," noted an

Illinois trooper in his diary. "Is it any wonder that men and horses fail under such trials?"[93]

Duffié's brigade spent the day picketing along the river. "A little more firing, but no signs of the enemy until 12 o'clk, when some 200 cavalry (rebel) were seen at a distance over [the upper fork of the Rappahannock]," noted an officer of the 1st Massachusetts. "Made a sketch of the picket line. Relieved at 6 o'clk P.M. and returned thro' the mud to Bealeton Station, where I found the preparations for a six-days' jaunt making."[94]

On April 19, a trooper of the 10th New York Cavalry of Gregg's Division scrawled an ominous note in his diary. "Considerable force of Confederates on opposite side of river now," he observed. The loss of the element of surprise meant that once the Federals could ford the swollen river, they would have to fight their way through a strong line of pickets deployed by the enemy. The wretched weather not only foiled Hooker's plan, it sentenced the Northern horsemen to battling their way across the Rappahannock.[95] That night, Stoneman transmitted his instructions to the Cavalry Corps.

Stoneman's "part of the move is by this time fully known to Lee as a matter of course," wrote Col. Charles S. Wainwright, who commanded the artillery battalion attached to the I Corps, in his diary that night. "Even the privates seem well informed about it, so that we get as late news through Rebel deserters as we do direct; while their pickets call across the river to ours, asking what is the matter with our cavalry that it does not get across."[96] "From all we can learn the enemy is concentrating in our front," agreed Stoneman. An impatient trooper bitterly noted in his diary, "What are we waiting for?" Since the men had not been told the details of their mission, none of them knew for sure. They simply waited and grew increasingly frustrated.[97]

That night, Robert E. Lee penned instructions to Jeb Stuart. "I have been able as yet to learn nothing which goes to show the real intention of the enemy," stated Lee. He reiterated his opinion that Hooker would not expose Washington to Confederate attack, and proclaimed, "It appears to me that he is rather fearful of an attack from us than preparing to attack. His operations in front of you look rather to prevent your moving against his right or getting in his rear." The Confederate commander admonished his cavalry chief. "I am aware that from the superior strength of the enemy he will be able to overpower you at any one point, but believe, by your good management, boldness, and discretion, you will be able to baffle his designs." So far, the combination of Stuart's diligent picketing and the heavy rains had done just that. It remained to be seen how long it would last.[98]

On April 20, the rain finally stopped. "Stood in the rain (in line) during the morning and marched through the rain during the afternoon encamping at night at Carters Run near Waterloo," near the upper crossing of the Rappahannock, noted a Hoosier horse soldier in his diary.[99] "The rebels may gobble us though I think we can hold this position as they will soon have something to do across the river," recounted a trooper of the 6th Ohio Cavalry. "No fighting has taken place yet."[100] "We marched in expectation of crossing the river at Waterloo Bridge which was held by a smaller force than any other crossing," observed Edward W. Whitaker of the 6th New York Cavalry, "but again the rain impeded our advance and we were halted for the rain to 'dry up.'"[101]

Expecting the river to be fordable on April 21, the next day, Stoneman wrote out marching orders.[102] He expected to cross the river at Kelly's Ford, Beverly's Ford, and at Rappahannock Station, and then concentrate his force between Culpeper and Orange. Once his command had assembled at the rendezvous site, Stoneman intended to turn on Rooney Lee's cavalry brigade, disperse it, push on to Gordonsville, and get out as best as they could. "The idea of trying to carry out our original instruction to its full extent, owing to the state of the roads, the rage of water in the streams, and the condition of our supplies, had, I was sorry to think, to be abandoned," noted Stoneman.[103] Unfortunately, it started raining again, and continued all night.

Left with no choice, Stoneman canceled the movement again, as the water at the fords ran deeper than ever. He dispatched a couple of couriers to Hooker, looking for instructions from the army commander. The Federal horsemen spent a quiet day in camp on April 21, awaiting further orders.[104] Those orders arrived the next morning. Hooker directed Stoneman to fall back to the Orange & Alexandria Railroad, where the Cavalry Corps would be resupplied. Hooker also instructed Stoneman to "husband your resources and the strength of your animals as much as possible."[105]

On April 22, Averell's division and Davis's brigade marched along the railroad from Warrenton to Warrenton Junction. Gregg's division, Buford's brigade, and the 6th Pennsylvania Cavalry, riding with Cavalry Corps headquarters, met them there. Stoneman dispatched pickets to observe the enemy's actions along the river and to watch the railroad all the way to Bristoe Station. Hooker telegraphed Stoneman, instructing him to cross the river the next morning if the fords permitted. "The general does not look for one moment's delay in your advance from any cause that human effort can obviate, and directs me to add that this army is awaiting your movement," concluded the telegram.[106]

"Here we are in the woods and it is raining like hell," complained a Rhode Islander on April 23. "Ten days ago we started for a brush with the rebs but just as we were going to cross the river the river raised it so high we could not ford." He recounted his regiment's travails and stated, "We shall probably stay here until the roads again become fit for military operations." The next day, he reported, "Still it rains and God only knows when it will stop."[107]

The rains continued unabated until April 24. "The whole country has been inundated and the water in the small streams has been such that it has been almost impossible to communicate with the different portions of the command, and a portion of the time, utterly so, except by swimming numerous streams," complained a frustrated Stoneman. He concluded, "There never was a command freer from encumbrances of all kinds than is this Corps at the present time, or one more eager to take the field at the very earliest moment."[108]

On the 24th, a Maine horseman wrote, "It rains and it has been raining ever since night before last and it seems as if it was going to rain always. There is nothing but mud mud & rain all the time. I am tired of it." He continued his complaint, "It aint much fun when it rains. There aint much fun in being out 24 hours in the rain paddling around in the mud and water when it is so dark you cannot see anything but it aint so very bad after a fellow gets used to it."

The same soldier graphically described both the ordeal faced by the Cavalry Corps and the men's efforts to lighten the mood as they languished in the mud. "Just think of about 12 men out in the roads all setting around a low fire or place where there had been a fire and all looking at the coals, the rain coming down on their rubber blankets and they are all leaning forward resting their elbows on their knees and their heads on their hands. By the by one gets to breathing hard when some bugger tickles his nose with a piece of brush and after brushing a while he wakes up to be laughted at, then all look at the coals again." He continued, "Now and then the order comes Hault from some sentinel off at a distance then every head comes up and listens and if it is repeated every man looks for his Rifle but as yet we have had no occasion to use them and I don't care if we don't."[109]

The men's morale, so high when they left their camps, plummeted as they remained stuck in the thick Virginia mud. "This lying still is horrid," noted Major Higginson. "Read and wrote and washed. It would be a relief to get answers to some of my letters before starting, tho' waiting for something seems to be the normal state of men."[110] Lieutenant Carpenter, with his tongue placed firmly in his cheek, reported that after the rains began yet again, "in very short order, the elegant and accomplished gentlemen of the Sixth [U.S.] Cavalry resembled nothing so much as a company of drowned rats."

An unsympathetic local woman mocked the plight of the Yankee troopers lying in wait at Warrenton Junction. She suggested to Lieutenant Carpenter that the heavens were on the side of the Confederates and remarked, "Let the Yankees but attempt an advance and those heavens are opened to prevent it." Carpenter smiled wanly, and suggested that "the showers were what was required to lay the dust for the Yankees."[111]

The Cavalry Corps ran out of rations, forcing the men to forage in the surrounding countryside. "We are entirely out of rations today," noted a Maine trooper on April 24, "so we killed some pigs and a beeve." Until the army resupplied the horse soldiers, they would have to fend for themselves. The pickings were slim, and when the Yankees helped themselves to the property of the local citizens, the populace naturally became angry and joined the growing ranks of bushwhackers operating along the fringes of the Federal Cavalry Corps.[112]

In addition, the wet weather had taken its toll on the animals. Most of the mules were getting sore backs from their burdens. The packs were usually placed on saddles to protect the mules, but in the soggy conditions, the teamsters and horse soldiers were unable to place dry saddle blankets on the mules, and they suffered mightily under their burdens. Some were already unserviceable and required replacement. Considering that the raid had never even gotten started, the prospects for the pack animals looked bleak.[113]

Hooker's purpose having been frustrated by the torrential rains and thick mud, the army commander reformed his plans for the cavalry expedition. Late in the evening of April 22, General Williams had composed a new set of orders for Stoneman. They drastically changed the cavalry's mission—Hanover Junction was no longer the expedition's object, and neither was blocking the routes of retreat for Lee's army. Instead, Hooker instructed Stoneman to "subdivide your command, and let them take different routes, and have some point of meeting on your line of general operations. These detachments can dash off to the right and left, and inflict a vast deal of mischief, and at the same time bewilder the enemy as to the course and intentions of the main body."

Hooker told Stoneman to march without most of his artillery or wagons, to stick to the railroads, and to make long night marches if necessary. Only six guns would accompany the expedition. "You have officers and men in your command who have been over much of the country in which you are operating; make use of them," exhorted Hooker. "You must move quickly and make long marches. The experience of your march up the river will, doubtless, satisfy you of what can be accomplished by celerity."[114] These orders haunted Hooker in the years after the Civil War.

By April 25, General Lee had concluded that Stoneman did not intend to cross the Blue Ridge and threaten the Shenandoah Valley, as he had originally feared. "I think it probable that among the considerations that prevent Stoneman from crossing the Blue Ridge is the apprehension that you will plunge into the rear of his army," wrote Lee to Stuart. Lee instructed his cavalry chief to pursue the enemy into the valley if they crossed the Blue Ridge, as "nothing would call him back sooner than such a move on your part, and it is worthy of your consideration how you could, in that event, most damage him." Lee suggested that Stuart unleash Mosby's guerrillas on the Federal rear, something that would undoubtedly pull the Yankee horsemen back from a foray into the Confederate breadbasket.[115]

During the standstill, Averell's provost marshal placed a guard for the protection of the local citizens and households near his camp. On April 26, Southern guerrillas attacked the guards at two different houses. One Federal was captured while one of the guerrillas was mortally wounded during the ensuing firefight. "I have sent out a party to find the men who perpetrated this outrage," reported an indignant Averell.[116]

That day, Capt. Charles F. Adams of the 1st Massachusetts led sixty men toward White Sulphur Springs to relieve the 4th Pennsylvania of picket duty along the upper Rappahannock. An officer of the 4th Pennsylvania showed Adams the picket line and assured him that he would not have much to worry about until the level of the river dropped enough for men to cross it. "As for guarding the army, I gave that idea up at once and perforce ran for luck," he noted. He made his dispositions, but concluded that they were unsatisfactory, given the small picket force available. Fortunately, the enemy did not bother him, and the next morning, one of his men tested the Rappahannock and reported that the waters had dropped enough to allow the Federals to ford it. Adams then rode out to study the terrain until his unit could be relieved. "Our picket duty is made immensely more difficult by the state of the population," he observed. "The enemy know the country and we don't, and every man is a citizen or a soldier, as the occasion offers. We feel no single man is safe and so our posts have to be double, and we feel at any time that these may be picked off and thus our reserves and the army exposed to surprises." Adams gladly relinquished this unpleasant duty.[117]

The 1st Maine Cavalry did picket duty near Cedar Run. Trooper Nathan Webb, his sergeant, and a handful of men visited a "fine looking house" to chat with the owners. "A young woman was very vehement in her denunciations of our government in allowing its men to roam around so insulting and disturbing the people." The woman of the house's husband served with the Confederate army. He was "doing wonders for their cause" and his "name was a terror to the Yankee horde," she claimed. Webb thought she might be the wife of some famous Southern general, and asked who he might be. The woman was afraid to say for fear that identifying her husband might bring retribution on her and her home. After some additional encouragement from Webb, she drew "herself up to full strength, her eyes flashing, her arms proudly folded, and stepping back a step she says, 'I have the distinguished honor of being the wife of the gallant Major Mosby.'"

"Oh! Ah!" proclaimed Webb. "I thought that you were at least the wife of some brave and open-handed officer, but instead, I find you to be the spouse of that plundering, prowling, thieving, bushwhacking Mosby."

The woman grew angry at Webb's response. She "ranted fiercely about our abuse of him. She seemed desirous of making herself a heroine. She presumed upon her sex to protect her in her epithets heaped upon us, and cried out somewhat after the manner of the Spartan mothers, 'O, that I were a man!'" Webb bantered with Mrs. Mosby for a few moments before moving on, feeling quite satisfied with himself.[118]

That same night, a correspondent attached to the Cavalry Corps penned his regular dispatch to the *New York Daily Tribune*. "We shall doubtless move at the earliest practicable moment, but probably with new plans. The enemy have become aware of our proximity, have changed their positions, and prepared a reception," he observed. "It is to be hoped . . . that Gen. Stoneman will be allowed to use his own judgment, and not be fettered with orders based solely upon advices received [from army headquarters at Falmouth]."[119] Whether Hooker granted his cavalry commander that much discretion remained to be seen.

On April 28, Col. Thomas C. Devin's small brigade of Pleasonton's division was detached from the Cavalry Corps and sent to report to Maj. Gen. Henry W. Slocum's XII Corps. Pleasonton accompanied Devin's three regiments back to army headquarters. Hooker finally realized that his daring plan would have left the Army of the Potomac without any cavalry screens at all, and when the army commenced its movement on April 26, it moved blindly. "Fighting Joe" ordered Stoneman to detach the brigade and send it back to the main army for service with the V and XII Corps. Although these men missed Stoneman's great expedition, they had plenty of harrowing adventures of their own.[120]

Also on the 26th, the waters receded enough to permit passage at the river fords. Finally able to exploit the change in the weather for the better, Hooker sent orders to Stoneman on April 28, again altering his concept for the raid. His orders reverted to the original concept of April 12, that the horse soldiers were to gain the Richmond, Fredericksburg and Potomac Railroad in Lee's rear. The cavalry would "cut off the retreat of the enemy" after uniting in the vicinity of the confluence of the North Anna and South Anna Rivers. One wing of Stoneman's corps would move against enemy forces near Culpeper and the rest of the column would head for Raccoon Ford on the Rapidan River. From there, they would head for Louisa Court House on the Virginia Central Railroad. Hooker ordered Stoneman to attempt the crossing that night, or, at the latest, by 8:00 A.M. on the morning of April 29.[121]

As early as April 16, a runaway slave had come into the camp of the 10th New York Cavalry and "reported that his master knew of the movement of our cavalry from the time it left camp at Belle Plain, and had gone to Richmond to inform the authorities."[122] The alarm quickly spread across the Virginia countryside as confirmation of the early reports of the Northern movement filtered in. "The enemy have occupied the county of Fauquier in large force, reported from twenty to thirty thousand," recounted one of the Richmond newspapers on April 27. "They are said to have fifteen thousand infantry and eight thousand cavalry." The article also noted that the Federal cavalry picketed the Rappahannock from Waterloo down.[123] If surprise were a critical element of Hooker's grand plan for the expedition, there was no chance of it happening at this late stage of the game.

Stoneman spent the rest of the day gathering his troopers and preparing to march. Some men negotiated nearly thirty miles of sloppy, muddy roads to rejoin the main column by 8:00 the next morning. Changes in the organization of the Cavalry Corps continued to occur. Col. Richard Henry Rush of the 6th Pennsylvania Cavalry was as much a blue blood as any Philadelphian could be. His great grandfather, Dr. Benjamin Rush, was not only a prominent physician and educator, he was also a well-known patriot who signed both the Declaration of Independence and the Constitution. His father, Richard Rush, had served as the U.S. minister to England. Young Richard received an appointment to the U.S. Military Academy at West Point in 1842, and graduated with the legendary class of 1846. This was probably the greatest class to ever grace the halls of the academy and included his fellow Philadelphians George B. McClellan and John Gibbon, Cavalry Corps commander George Stoneman, Virginians Thomas Jonathan "Stonewall" Jackson, Ambrose Powell Hill, and George E. Pickett, as well as a number of other officers who achieved the rank of general during the Civil War.[124]

Rush served honorably in the Mexican War and was well respected for his service in the artillery during his eight-year career in the Regular Army. Responding to President Lincoln's initial call for volunteers, Rush sought a commission as a brigadier general and command of the Commonwealth of Pennsylvania's volunteer artillery units in May 1861. When Gov. Andrew Curtin denied that request, Rush asked for permission to raise a regiment of light artillery. Ten days later, Rush learned that "the Governor would raise no artillery reg't. & if I desired active service, he would advise me to apply to the War Department." When those efforts were also rebuffed, Rush asked for permission to raise a cavalry regiment, a request finally granted by the governor.[125]

Rush raised the Philadelphia Light Cavalry, which eventually became known as either the 70th Regiment of Pennsylvania Volunteers or the 6th Pennsylvania Cavalry. McClellan asked Rush to arm his regiment with lances, and Rush's Lancers, as they became known, served with distinction, bestowing great credit on their commander. Although Rush led his regiment out of its winter camp with the rest of the Cavalry Corps on April 13, an illness he had contracted years earlier in Mexico flared up in the miserable weather conditions, driving the colonel to his sickbed. Rush took sick leave on April 25 while his regiment remained stuck in the mud. "The Boys are all disgusted with Colonel Rush," reported Capt. Walter S. Newhall of the 3d Pennsylvania Cavalry, who served as one of Stoneman's staff officers, and whose brother Fred was the Lancers's regimental adjutant. He "has another sick leave of twenty days."[126] The colonel's days with the regiment were numbered. On April 25, he wrote, "I am mortified that . . . I have not the physical endurance to retain my health under the vicissitudes of our cavalry campaign."[127]

At regimental dress parade on the evening of April 27, Colonel Rush addressed his men, "deeming it very doubtful that he should be able to rejoin the command this campaign. He expressed great regret at being compelled to leave just at this juncture, but the severe exposure of the last three weeks had revived a chronic disease contracted while serving in Mexico." With that Rush took leave of the regiment that proudly bore his name and left for Washington. "The honorable position attained by the regiment in its later campaigns, is doubtless due to the military skill and knowledge, and the superior qualities of Colonel Rush as an organizer and disciplinarian," lamented regimental Chaplain Samuel L. Gracey.[128] Maj. Robert Morris, Jr., another blue-blooded Philadelphian, the ranking officer in the regiment, assumed command, as Lt. Col. C. Ross Smith was serving on Stoneman's staff at Cavalry Corps headquarters. When the great raid finally kicked off, Rush's Lancers marched without their namesake.

After terrible frustration, horrific weather conditions, and the towering impatience of the army's commanding general, Stoneman's great expedition was finally ready to begin in earnest. The raid had spent two full weeks stuck in the mud. It had lost the element of surprise, and its mission had changed. Whether its new mission would succeed remained an open question.

NOTES

1. O.R. vol 25, part 2, 93.
2. William P. Lloyd, *History of the First Reg't Pennsylvania Reserve Cavalry, from Its Organization, August 1861, to September 1864, with List of Names of All Officers and Enlisted Men* (Philadelphia: King & Baird, 1864), 44–45.
3. German, "Picketing along the Rappahannock," 35.
4. Covert to his wife, March 21, 1863, Covert Letters.
5. Ford, *A Cycle of Adams Letters,* 1: 266.
6. Bushnell diary, entry for March 25, 1863.
7. Diary of Abner Frank, entry for March 25, 1863, Civil War Miscellaneous Collection, USAMHI.
8. Bliss to Dear Gerald, March 25, 1863, Bliss Papers.
9. Bliss Perry, ed., *Life and Letters of Henry Lee Higginson* (Boston: Atlantic Monthly Press, 1921), 184.
10. Lucas to his wife, March 30, 1863, Lucas Letters.
11. Averell diary, entry for March 30, 1863.
12. Mohr, *Cormany Diaries,* 304.
13. George A. Brumby to Josiah H. Kellogg, March 31, 1863, Peter Keenan Papers, FSNMP.

14. Peter Keenan to Patrick Keenan, March 31, 1863, Keenan Papers.

15. Jasper Cheney diary, entry for April 1, 1863.

16. Willard Glazier, *Three Years in the Federal Cavalry* (New York: R. H. Ferguson, 1873), 162–63.

17. *New York Daily Tribune,* April 9, 1863.

18. Daniel Peck, *Dear Rachel: The Civil War Letters of Daniel Peck,* ed. Martha Gerber Stanford and Eleanor Erskin (Freeman, S.D.: Pine Hill Press, 1993), 30.

19. Davis, *Common Soldier, Uncommon War,* 356.

20. Newhall, *With General Sheridan,* 41.

21. Silas D. Wesson, Diary 1861–1864, entry for April 6, 1863, *Civil War Times Illustrated* Collection, USAMHI.

22. Lucas to his wife, April 7, 1863, Lucas Letters.

23. Staudenraus, *Mr. Lincoln's Washington,* 152–53.

24. Alfred G. Sargent to "Dear Folks," April 22, 1863, Alfred G. Sargent Letters, Center for American History, University of Texas, Austin.

25. Alvin N. Brackett to Dear Friend, April 7, 1863, Gregory A. Coco Collection, Harrisburg Civil War Roundtable Collection, USAMHI.

26. *Rochester Daily Union and Advertiser,* April 7, 1863.

27. Alexander Biddle to Julia Biddle, April 6, 1863, Rush/Williams/Biddle Family Papers, Rosenbach Library, Philadelphia, Pa.

28. Milton V. Burgess, *David Gregg: Pennsylvania Cavalryman* (State College, Pa.: privately published, 1984), 44.

29. *Philadelphia Inquirer,* April 8, 1863.

30. Averell diary, entry for April 7, 1863.

31. Lucas to his wife, April 10, 1863.

32. Redman to his mother, April 7, 1863.

33. Winthrop S. G. Allen, *Civil War Letters of Winthrop S. G. Allen,* ed. Harry Pratt (Springfield, Ill.: Phillips Brothers Printing, 1932), 24.

34. George Stoneman to Joseph Hooker, undated letter from 1863, Box 12, Folder B, Joseph Hooker Papers, Albert P. Huntington Library, San Marino, Calif. This letter may also be found in the *Supplement to the Official Records of the Union and Confederate Armies,* 100 vols. (Wilmington, N.C.: Broadfoot, 1993–99), 1: 536 (hereinafter referred to as "O.R. Supp.").

35. Joseph Hooker to Samuel P. Bates, April 2, 1878, Samuel P. Bates Papers, Pennsylvania State Archives, Harrisburg, Pa.; O.R., vol. 25, part 1, 1066.

36. Stoneman to Hooker, undated 1863 letter.

37. John W. Johnson to his sister, April 12, 1863.

38. Redman to his sister, April 12, 1863.

39. John Follmer diary, entry for April 12, 1863, FSNMP.

40. O.R., vol. 25, part 1, 1067.

41. Brooke-Rawle, *History of the Third Pennsylvania Cavalry,* 227.

42. Dennison, *First Rhode Island Cavalry,* 220.

43. Ibid., 219.

44. Gilpin diary, entry for April 13, 1863.
45. J. L. Smith to his mother, April 16, 1863, FSNMP.
46. Follmer diary, entry for April 13, 1863.
47. Mohr and Winslow, *Cormany Diaries,* 305–306.
48. Brooke-Rawle, *History of the Third Pennsylvania,* 228.
49. Gracey, *Annals of the Sixth Pennsylvania,* 133.
50. O.R., vol. 25, part 1, 1088.
51. Louis H. Carpenter to his father, April 14, 1863, Louis Henry Carpenter Letters from the Field, 1861–1865, Historical Society of Pennsylvania, Pa. Carpenter had a forty-year career in the Regular Army. He won a Medal of Honor for his gallantry in leading the 10th Cavalry, known as the "Buffalo Soldiers," during the Indian Wars. He served as a brigadier general of volunteers in the Spanish-American War, and later received a promotion to brigadier general in the Regular Army. Carpenter's long and notable service is remarkable, considering that he had no military training prior to his commission as a lieutenant at the outbreak of the Civil War.
52. O.R., vol. 25, part 1, 1067–68.
53. Daniel Pulis to his parents, May 1, 1863, Daniel W. Pulis Letters, Rochester Public Library, Rochester, N.Y.
54. *Madison Daily Evening Courier,* May 2, 1863.
55. Gilpin diary, entry for April 14, 1863.
56. Frank diary, entry for April 13, 1863.
57. O.R., vol. 25, part 1, 85.
58. The deceptions included sending out false dispatches indicating that the Shenandoah Valley was the real target, as well as false wigwag signals by Union Signal Corps officers intended to deceive the Confederates about Northern intentions. The deceptions were wildly successful. One of Hooker's strengths was his understanding and use of clandestine intelligence-gathering services to great advantage. Col. George H. Sharpe was Hooker's intelligence chief, and Sharpe and his staff of crack officers performed admirably during the entire Chancellorsville Campaign. For a detailed examination of their campaign of misinformation, see Edwin C. Fishel, *The Secret War for the Union: The Untold Story of Military Intelligence in the Civil War* (Boston: Houghton-Mifflin, 1996), 340–59.
59. O.R., vol. 25, part 1, 88.
60. Webb diary, entry for April 14, 1863; Stoneman to Hooker, undated letter.
61. McClellan, *Life and Campaigns,* 219–22.
62. Stoneman to Hooker, undated letter.
63. Edward W. Whitaker to his sister, April 23, 1863, FSNMP.
64. *Madison Daily Evening Courier,* May 2, 1863.
65. Norton, *Deeds of Daring,* 60–61.
66. Gilpin diary, entry for April 15, 1863.
67. O.R., vol. 25, part 1, 88.
68. Von Borcke, *Memoirs,* 357–58.
69. *Madison Daily Evening Courier,* May 2, 1863. Stapp was exchanged a few weeks later and returned to his regiment in time for the Gettysburg campaign.

70. Vevay, *Indiana Reveille,* June 4, 1863.

71. *Rochester Daily Union and Advertiser,* May 29, 1863.

72. Stoneman to Hooker, undated letter.

73. Hard, *History of the Eighth Cavalry Regiment,* 228–29.

74. Ibid., 229.

75. Ibid., 230; Stoneman to Hooker, undated letter.

76. O.R., vol. 25, part 2, 213.

77. Winslow and Mohr, *Cormany Diaries,* 306.

78. Tobie, *History of the First Maine Cavalry,* 129.

79. Perry, *Life and Letters,* 184.

80. Follmer diary, entry for April 13, 1863.

81. O.R., vol. 25, part 2, 214.

82. Ibid.

83. Ibid., 220–21.

84. Ibid., 220.

85. Manarin and Dowdey, *Wartime Papers of R. E. Lee,* 1:434–35.

86. Louis H. Carpenter to his mother, April 17, 1863.

87. Hagemann, *Fighting Rebels and Redskins,* 197.

88. O.R., vol. 25, part 2, 223.

89. Lucas to his wife, April 17, 1863.

90. O.R., vol. 25, part 2, 731.

91. Ibid., 228–29.

92. *Richmond Daily Enquirer,* April 18, 1863.

93. Hard, *History of the Eighth Cavalry Regiment,* 230–31.

94. Perry, *Life and Letters,* 185.

95. Noble D. Preston, "Gregg's Cavalry: Its Participation in the Stoneman Raid of 1863," *National Tribune,* July 28, 1887.

96. Charles S. Wainwright, *A Diary of Battle: The Personal Journals of Colonel Charles S. Wainwright, 1861–1865,* ed. Allan Nevins (New York: Harcourt, Brace & World, 1962), 182.

97. George Stoneman to Seth Williams, April 17, 1863, Order Book of the Chief of Cavalry for 1863, Civil War Miscellaneous Collection, USAMHI; Perry, *Life and Letters of Henry Lee Higginson,* 184–86.

98. O.R., vol. 25, part 2, 737.

99. Gilpin diary, entry for April 20, 1863.

100. Alcinus Ward Fenton to his mother, April 21, 1863, Alcinus Ward Fenton Papers, Western Reserve Historical Society, Cleveland, Ohio.

101. Whitaker to his sister, April 23, 1863.

102. These marching orders may be found at O.R., vol. 25, part 2, 232.

103. Stoneman to Hooker, undated letter.

104. Ibid.

105. O.R., vol. 25, part 2, 237.

106. Ibid., 242–43.

107. Bliss to Dear Gerald, April 23, 1863.

108. Stoneman to Hooker, undated letter.

109. Brackett to Dear Aunty, April 24, 1863.

110. Perry, *Life and Letters*, 186.

111. Louis H. Carpenter to his father, April 25, 1863.

112. Peter Carl Haskell, ed. *To Let Them Know: The Civil War Diaries of Sumner Ansel Holway, Pvt., Company H, 1st Maine Cavalry* (Acadia, Maine: Acadia Lodge Press, 1990), 66.

113. Carpenter to his father, April 25, 1863.

114. O.R., vol. 25, part 2, 244–45.

115. Ibid., 749–50.

116. Ibid., 264–65.

117. Ford, *A Cycle of Adams Letters*, 1: 284.

118. Webb diary, entry for April 27, 1863. There is no proof that this woman was actually Mrs. Mosby, but the author accepts Webb's account of this incident as true.

119. *New York Daily Tribune*, April 24, 1863.

120. O.R., vol. 25, part 2, 274–75. Their exploits are the subject of the next chapter of this book.

121. Ibid., part 1, 1065.

122. Preston, *History of the Tenth Regiment*, 68.

123. *Richmond Daily Inquirer*, April 27, 1863.

124. John C. Waugh, *Class of 1846—From West Point to Appomattox: Stonewall Jackson, George McClellan and Their Brothers* (New York: Warner Books, 1994), xiv–xvi.

125. Statement of Richard Henry Rush, W. M. Meredith Papers, Misc. Correspondence, Historical Society of Pennsylvania, Philadelphia.

126. Walter S. Newhall to his father, April 26, 1863, Newhall Papers, Historical Society of Pennsylvania, Philadelphia.

127. Richard H. Rush to Capt. Andrew J. Alexander, April 25, 1863, Richard H. Rush service records, National Archives, Washington, D.C. Rush resigned his commission in the 6th Pennsylvania on September 30, 1863, after accepting a commission as colonel in the Invalid Corps, which he commanded for most of the rest of the war. Richard H. Rush to Lorenzo Thomas, September 30, 1863, Richard H. Rush service records.

128. Gracey, *Annals of the Sixth Pennsylvania*, 135.

5

Two Costly Charges: The Cavalry at Chancellorsville

While most of the Cavalry Corps remained stuck in the mud, Hooker finalized his plans and set the Army of the Potomac in motion. It must be remembered that the actions of the Cavalry Corps were adjunct to, and in support of, the actions of the main body of the Army of the Potomac. A brief overview of the infantry campaign will assist the reader in placing these actions in their proper context. What follows is not intended to be an exhaustive study of the Battle of Chancellorsville, but is rather intended to provide some factual backdrop for the actions of the horse soldiers, including those few that remained with Hooker's main body as the campaign unfolded.

The Army of the Potomac broke its winter camps and began marching on April 27. Three corps, V, XI, and XII, marched to Kelly's Ford, where they crossed the Rappahannock and swung southeast toward Germanna Ford on the Rapidan River. While III Corps remained at Falmouth, I and VI Corps started moving toward the river crossings at Fredericksburg. Hooker had more than 133,000 infantrymen in motion by the afternoon of April 28. By the night of April 29, Maj. Gen. George G. Meade's V Corps was poised to enter the Wilderness from Ely's Ford on the Rapidan while Maj. Gen. Darius N. Couch's II Corps crossed the Rappahannock at U.S. Ford and moved toward Chancellorsville, a handsome tavern at a critical road intersection on Lee's left flank. By the night of April 30, four Union infantry corps were concentrated around Chancellorsville, ready to move against Lee's flank. Lee did not know they were there, and was unprepared to fend them off, as his attention was focused on the large force in front of Fredericksburg. However, instead of pressing his advantage, Hooker halted and ceded the initiative to the wily Lee, who shifted most of his army to meet the threat when he became aware of it.

The battle around Chancellorsville began in earnest on May 1. Hooker's troops attacked the outnumbered Confederates of Stonewall Jackson's Corps and shoved them back. Over the vehement objections of his subordinates, Hooker pulled back to a defensive position at Chancellorsville and waited for Robert E. Lee to attack him. That attack came on the afternoon of May 2. Lee gambled, dividing his out-numbered force and sending Jackson's Corps on a seventeen-mile flank march, leaving fewer than 20,000 men to contend with Hooker at Chancellorsville. In spite of warnings and evidence indicating that Jackson's Corps was on the move, Hooker refused to act, and the Confederates crashed into the XI Corps flank and broke it, sending its routed elements streaming back toward Chancellorsville late in the afternoon of May 2. That night, Jackson was shot by his own troops while out scouting. He died a few days later. However, his flank attack shattered Hook-er's confidence and cast the die for the Army of the Potomac's campaign in the Wilderness.

Hooker pulled back into a tight defensive position centered on Chancellorsville. On the morning of May 3, Jackson's weary infantrymen, now commanded by Jeb Stuart, resumed the assault on Hooker's left. About 9:00 that morning, a Southern artillery shell struck the porch where Hooker stood, stunning and probably con-cussing the army commander, who was incapacitated. Couch, the senior corps commander, found himself in de facto command of the Army of the Potomac, and he fought a superb defensive action against Jackson's determined veterans, who were joined by the rest of Lee's army. Couch was wounded twice in the action, and his horse was shot out from under him. The Army of the Potomac withstood the onslaught with heavy losses.

Meanwhile, the Union VI Corps had crossed the Rappahannock River at Fredericksburg and driven the Confederate defenders from their strong position along a sunken road at Marye's Heights. They pressed on, hoping to link up with Hooker from the east, but a stout stand by Maj. Gen. Lafayette McLaws's Con-federate infantry at Salem Church on May 4 repulsed this attack, preventing the VI Corps from reinforcing the Union position at Chancellorsville. Southern rein-forcements then drove the VI Corps back toward Fredericksburg, ending any hope of linking up with the Army of the Potomac's main body.

Hooker then pulled back into prepared defensive positions around the Chan-cellor house, with his flanks anchored on both ends on the banks of the Rappa-hannock River. The two battered armies spent May 5 glaring at each other, but there was not much fighting. On the morning of May 6, Hooker finally admitted defeat and began pulling the Army of the Potomac back across the Rappahannock at U.S. Ford. Lee let them go, knowing that his outnumbered army had already done as much as he might have hoped. Hooker's magnificent campaign, which had begun with so much hope, ended with a fizzle, a victim of the commander's own hesitation at the critical moment on May 1.[1]

Colonel Devin's cavalry brigade broke its camp on the morning of April 28. By that time, the Federal infantry was in motion, headed for the crucial river fords. Devin's three regiments, accompanied by Pleasonton, marched to Grove Church on the road to Morrisville. Devin immediately threw out pickets to screen his advance. The New York horse soldier established his headquarters at the church and sent out parties to scour the countryside, arrest all civilians encountered, and watch the river from Banks's Ford to the bridge at Rappahannock Station. His horsemen arrested a number of civilians and kept them locked up until the entire Army of the Potomac had safely passed on its way to the Rappahannock River fords.[2]

Devin faced real danger that morning. They passed two divisions of the XI Corps between Hartwood Church and Deep Run. Devin, known to his fellow horse soldiers as "The Old War Horse," made a personal reconnaissance to Ely's Ford while his men watered and fed their horses. However, Devin awoke the sleeping Federal infantry, "who came down into the rifle-pits and drew bead on us. They sent one shot at a picket I left." After persuading the skittish infantrymen that his men were actually friends and not the enemy, Devin picketed the fords and covered the XI Corps flank. Devin also sent Maj. Peter Keenan, with two squadrons of the 8th Pennsylvania Cavalry, to scout the flank.[3]

That night, Devin received orders to send the 17th Pennsylvania Cavalry to report to Maj. Gen. O. O. Howard, the commander of the XI Corps, and to withdraw his pickets and concentrate his remaining two regiments near Mt. Holly Church. The 17th Pennsylvania spent the next few days picketing and scouting the way for the advance of the XI Corps as it made its way to Kelly's Ford. The relatively inexperienced Pennsylvanians skirmished with a force of Rooney Lee's brigade as the Federal infantrymen made their way to the riverbank. "The regiment did not lose a man," noted Devin, "killing several of the enemy and taking 1 prisoner."[4]

However, Col. Josiah H. Kellogg, commander of the 17th Pennsylvania, had misunderstood his orders. The 17th Pennsylvania should have been escorting the XI Corps wagon train, but they had not joined the column. Brig. Gen. Adolph von Steinwehr, commander of a division of the XI Corps, sent for the Pennsylvanians, who rode back—only to meet a force of the enemy just as it bore down on the rear of the wagon train. Colonel Kellogg found at least 300 well-armed Rebel horsemen dismounted and supported by a section of horse artillery. Uncertain as to the status of the wagon train and without carbines to engage the enemy, Kellogg reconnoitered the strength of the Southern force and returned to Germanna Ford.

Kellogg was ordered to communicate with the train, and finally learned that it was bringing up the rear of the XI Corps column. Spurring off, the Pennsylvanians returned to where they had seen the dismounted enemy troopers, charged, and drove them down the road for a quarter of a mile. However, the same horrible weather that plagued Stoneman's column also hindered the Pennsylvania horse soldiers. Kellogg called off the pursuit when his men encountered a barricade of felled trees across the road. Having lost eight horses and being unable to see in the rainy, inky darkness, Kellogg waited until morning. As the first fingers of daylight crept across the horizon, Kellogg and his men withdrew toward the rear. The Pennsylvanians received orders to return to the front of the column, cross the Rapidan River, scout to the right, and cover the infantry column marching toward Chancellorsville.

The 17th Pennsylvania spent the night of April 30 picketing all roads to the right and rear of the infantry column, and reported back to brigade headquarters on May 1, just as the fighting at Chancellorsville intensified. After leaving two squadrons with General Howard, the rest of the regiment spent the balance of the battle picketing to the right and front of the XI Corps, observing the country toward Orange and Spotsylvania Court Houses.[5] They played no role in the drama unfolding in the woods near Chancellorsville. Had they remained on Howard's flank, they might have detected the passage of Jackson's Corps and given enough warning of the impending flank attack to give the XI Corps a better opportunity to defend itself.

THE FIGHT OF THE 6TH NEW YORK CAVALRY
AT ALSOP'S FIELD

Lt. Col. Duncan McVicar, a ruddy-faced, red-haired Scot, commanded the 6th New York Cavalry. McVicar served as a gunner's mate in the British Army before moving to Canada. With the coming of war in 1861, McVicar resided in Rochester, New York, and had helped Frederick Douglass smuggle runaway slaves into Canada. He joined an artillery unit in New York City and went to Rochester looking for recruits. Through Douglass's influence with Horace Greeley, the publisher of the *New York Tribune*, McVicar received a commission as lieutenant colonel of the 6th New York Cavalry, serving under Devin's tutelage. "No one was more active than he in raising these regiments, and none better deserved the honor he wore," noted a New York newspaper. "So successful was he as a recruiting officer, that he was detained on that service until after his regiment went into squadrons."[6]

He was a capable and popular officer, although he was excitable and "apt to see mountains in mole hills," periodically subjecting him to the taunts of the Army of the Potomac's infantry, who viewed the Scot as a bit of an alarmist.[7] A newspaper correspondent described him as "a man of sterling qualities, a gallant officer, and a

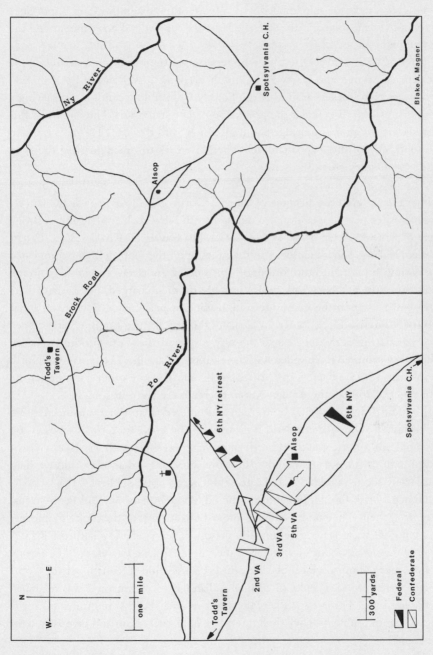

The Fight at Alsop's Field, April 30, 1863

Blake A. Magner

genial companion."[8] Another wrote that he "was in every magnitude a loyal and zealous officer, thoroughly imbued with a sense of the magnitude and importance of the interests involved in the struggle between the Federal government and the absolution of Jeff Davis."[9]

On April 27, McVicar led his troopers out of their camp and marched via Stoneman's Switch and Hartwood Church, arriving at Kelly's Ford at 4:00 P.M. When the New Yorkers arrived at the Ford, they found a pontoon train laying a bridge across the river under the protection of Union artillery. The engineers finished laying the pontoon bridge about 11:00 P.M., and the army began crossing to the south side of the Rappahannock. The New York troopers guarded the Ford while the infantry crossed the river.[10]

At 8:00 on the morning of the 28th, the New Yorkers crossed the pontoon bridge and covered the advance of the XII Corps as it moved toward Chancellorsville. After marching about two miles, the 6th New York crashed into a strong force of about 150 men of the 1st North Carolina Cavalry at Crook's Run. "A part of them had stationed themselves in the pines upon the bluffs which commanded the narrow approach to the ford upon this side of the river," recalled Sgt. Frank Saunders of the 6th New York.[11] McVicar and his men charged, and "a sharp skirmish ensued, when the enemy retired, leaving as prisoners 1 lieutenant and 1 private."[12] The Tar Heels dispersed, clearing the way for the Empire Staters. They drove the Confederate pickets all the way to Germanna Ford on the Rapidan, where they captured three vedettes of the 1st North Carolina. The remaining North Carolinians retreated across the bridge to the safety of the other bank under the protection of 200 Southern infantrymen guarding the river crossing.

McVicar dismounted fifty of his men and ordered them to advance to the ford as skirmishers. They were to hold it if possible. The New Yorkers took possession of an old mill on the banks of the river, exchanging shots with the North Carolinians until the infantry came up.[13] "Our fire was rapid and accurate and we soon completely silenced them," noted one of the Scot's horse soldiers.[14] His troopers laid down a brisk fire until infantry of the 2d Massachusetts and 73d Pennsylvania reinforced them. The combined force proved too strong for the pesky Confederates, who fell back, leaving behind 100 prisoners. Carried away with the excitement of the moment, McVicar grabbed the carbine of J. N. Crawford of Company C and squeezed off several shots. Lt. John F. Ramsey and three troopers of Company E were wounded, and Cpl. Samuel A. Fanshaw of Company I was wounded in the left knee. The New Yorkers picketed an area about three miles from the Rapidan until midnight. They then moved to Wilderness Run and bivouacked for the night.[15]

The next morning, April 29, the regiment crossed Wilderness Run and continued on for several miles. They engaged Southern infantry, but the Rebel infantrymen retired. The New Yorkers pursued, skirmishing with the enemy the entire way, driving them and capturing a number of prisoners. They advanced to Louisa Run, where they found twenty dismounted men picketing the Ford. Spotting an entire mounted regiment bearing down on them, these pickets retired into the woods, clearing the way for the New Yorkers to advance toward Chancellorsville, where they camped for the night.[16] A corporal of Company M of the 6th New York was killed during this engagement with the Confederate pickets.[17]

The 254 officers and men of the 6th New York Cavalry set out again on the morning of April 30. "The Sixth had been our advanced skirmishers upon Slocum's front during our entire march," recalled a member of the regiment. "They were few in number, and the duty required was very fatiguing, but they had stood up to the work manfully and had achieved for themselves a reputation for dash, pluck, and efficiency rivaled by no other regiment in the service. So well were they appreciated, that detail after detail, had been made from among them until but about two hundred and fifty men were left; but these were tried men and true."[18]

Pleasonton ordered McVicar to report to Maj. Gen. Henry W. Slocum, the commander of the Army of the Potomac's right wing, which included the V, XI, and XII Corps. The Scotsman and his adjutant, Lt. Fergus A. Easton, reported as directed and received a verbal order from Slocum. Like most of the Army of the Potomac's corps commanders, Slocum "thought the Cavalry of little account except to furnish mounted orderlies for the Infantry generals," as a Federal horseman noted.[19] This attitude explains Slocum's handling of McVicar's concerns that night.

"You will proceed with your command to Spotsylvania Court House," instructed Slocum, "where you will be joined by others of our troops. Should you meet the enemy in force and offering resistance, you will gradually fall back and report to me by couriers. Meeting no resistance, you will continue the march." McVicar repeated the order to make certain that he had understood it, saluted, and retired. Slocum wanted the New Yorkers to screen the army's advance, but intervening events would prevent them from doing so.

The colonel and Easton had ridden only a short distance when McVicar said, "I wish for more definite information as to the troops we shall meet at Spotsylvania, and to whom I shall report." Worried, McVicar turned back to ask Slocum for additional information. Reining in, he began his request. Slocum interrupted him, snapping, "You have your orders, sir; go."[20]

The corps commander's waspish response concerned the cautious McVicar, who grew saddened and serious in the wake of the retort. McVicar commented that the mission indicated a "dusty job, with results uncertain and perilous." Nevertheless, he rode back to his regiment and prepared it to march. The New Yorkers marched about half a mile before the Scotsman called a halt and drew up his regiment in close formation. He addressed the officers and men, "admonishing them to a full performance of their duty as soldiers and Christians." Concluding, he declared, "Tomorrow, we shall meet in Fredericksburg or heaven." Although the speech was intended to inspire the men, it had the opposite effect. "We felt impressed with coming disaster," recalled Adjutant Easton. "The ranks fell silent, and it required no close observer to note the look of dogged determination that settled on their countenances. It was not with our usual gaiety and dash that the march was resumed."[21]

McVicar evidently misunderstood his orders, which he believed directed him to continue on until he met some large force of the enemy. Slocum sent a courier after the New Yorkers, carrying a modification of those orders, but the courier never arrived. Considering how far behind enemy lines they had forayed, the courier was probably captured. McVicar "was becoming a little disturbed about his position, knowing that he was a long way from any support, and in a country where the rebels were likely to come down upon him at any moment. But he would not disobey orders."[22]

Leading the way for the Army of the Potomac's right wing, the advancing horse soldiers periodically scattered Rebel picket posts. The Southern vedettes fled without offering resistance. The New Yorkers found the road clear; no Confederate wagon trains blocked their way.[23] The few Confederates they encountered were undoubtedly sizing up the Northerners, looking for an opportunity to fall upon them. "Mile after mile was passed, yet we saw no signs of any great force of the rebels. Citizens whom we picked up told us there had been a hundred troopers along a short time before, but they were not now to be found."[24] The New Yorkers splashed across a wide but shallow stream, and stopped short, hearing a shot ring out in their rear. The nervous horsemen wheeled and started searching for the culprits in the gathering dusk. When they heard no further shots after a few minutes, the men concluded that they had made a mistake, that there were no enemy in their front. Several shots rang out a moment later, shattering their reverie. McVicar worried that the men engaged with his rear guard were actually part of a Federal column on its way to Spotsylvania Court House. That notion was about to be dispelled.

The vanguard of the 6th New York rested at a road junction roughly halfway between Todd's Tavern and the Court House, near Hugh Alsop's house and shops. "After marching until dark we halted in a clearing surrounded by woods where two roads intersected."[25] The regiment drew up in the narrow road, closed up ranks, and dismounted, awaiting further developments. The road barely accommodated a column of fours. Heavy woods lined both sides. A half moon brightened the dark evening sky as the New Yorkers waited to see what would happen next.[26] Alsop's large and open field was used primarily for grazing animals. It had gentle folds in the terrain and a ravine where a small creek cut through it. In the daylight, it would have made good ground for cavalry operations. At night, however, it might as well have been heavily wooded. McVicar swung from his saddle near the stout rail fence lining Alsop's field and engaged "an intelligent looking colored man" in conversation, trying to find out whether there were any enemy nearby. He also sent a small detachment forward to reconnoiter the road ahead.[27]

Maj. Gen. J. E. B. Stuart, his Prussian aide, Maj. Heros von Borcke, and a few other staff officers happened to be riding along the road between Chancellorsville and Todd's Tavern as the New Yorkers advanced. "Stuart had been feeling his way to get around the Federal troops," recalled Col. Thomas T. Munford of the 2d Virginia Cavalry. "It was when he left us & rode with his staff to report to Genl. Robert E. Lee."[28] "No one suspected any enemy to be in front of us," recalled a sergeant of the 2d Virginia Cavalry. The inky blackness of the night made it difficult to see anything along the dark, narrow, densely wooded road.[29] As the Southern cavaliers marched, they heard a pistol shot ring out in their rear. A courier dashed back and informed Stuart that Yankee pickets had fired on him just a few yards up the road. "Stuart, perfectly convinced that the courier was deceived, and had taken some of our own men for the enemy, requested me to ride ahead and investigate the matter," recalled von Borcke.[30]

Accompanied by another of Stuart's staff officers, von Borcke spurred ahead. They spotted a group of about thirty New Yorkers, barely discernable in the pale moonlight, up ahead. The two grayclad officers rode to within fifty yards of the Northerners and inquired what regiment they belonged to. "You shall see that soon enough, you damned Rebels," came the response. The New Yorkers dashed forward. Von Borcke squeezed off a few shots with his revolver before wheeling and riding back toward Stuart and the rest of the staff. "Resistance when so completely outnumbered would have been folly; and accordingly I had the pleasure of seeing our General, who had now lost all doubts about the real character of these cavalrymen, for once run from the enemy," noted an amused von Borcke.[31]

Colonel Munford of the 2d Virginia watched as Stuart, "a bold, self-reliant, dashing horseman . . . led the way, with only a handful of couriers, when suddenly he stumbled on the advance guard of the Sixth New York Cavalry, and he was so careless that he liked to have ridden into them unaware of their presence. He wheeled, but it became a matter of 'legs' between their horses, and with great difficulty he extricated himself." Stuart rode back to Fitz Lee's brigade and called for the lead regiment, the 5th Virginia Cavalry, to charge. It took a few moments for the Virginians to form, but they did not charge.[32] Instead, they put up "an unearthly howl."[33]

Cpl. Edward W. Pratt of Company I of the 6th New York rode back toward Chancellorsville along with four troopers of Company M and some prisoners rounded up during the march. After turning over their prisoners, the little band of Empire Staters wheeled and headed back toward Alsop's Field. Pratt had nearly made it back to the regiment when the Confederate rear guard fell upon him. The little band of five Yankee troopers repulsed this attack and captured a Virginia captain. A countercharge by the Virginians freed the captain and, in turn, captured the New Yorkers. However, in the resulting confusion, Pratt escaped and rejoined the main body of his regiment.[34]

Lt. J. Hamilton Bell, with a squad of twenty New York horsemen, rode ahead to reconnoiter the road to Spotsylvania Court House. A fusillade of carbine fire in their rear halted them in their tracks. Bell wheeled and returned, reporting that enemy troops blocked their way. "The road is full of rebs!" cried Bell.[35] Without awaiting orders, the New Yorkers mounted. "We must have room to fight! Down with that gate!" cried McVicar. "Forward!" With the gate out of their way, the New Yorkers entered Alsop's Field. They drew up in line of battle, regimental front near the center of the field, and facing what had been their rear.

No sooner had they formed line of battle than more shots rang out upon their front, rear, and right flank. Only a ravine on their left prevented the 6th New York from being completely encircled. A familiar foe, Fitzhugh Lee's Brigade, bore down on their position, although many of the New Yorkers clung to the notion that they faced friendly fire. To settle the question, Lieutenant Bell rode to the front, and in a direct but inquisitive voice, demanded, "Who are you, anyway?"

"Third Virginia," responded several voices.

"Oh! I thought so," replied Bell, who galloped back to report on their predicament. For some reason, the Confederates did not fire on the fleeing officer, whom they believed was one of their own. "Colonel, there is no doubt, it is the enemy," reported the lieutenant. When he found McVicar, the New Yorkers could not distinguish a friendly from a hostile uniform from a distance of less then thirty feet in the blackness of the night. The New Yorkers taunted the Confederates to "come out and give us a square fight."[36]

Accepting the proffered invitation, the Confederate bugles called "charge," and above the clatter of hooves and small arms fire, the Rebel yell sang out. Col. Thomas L. Rosser's 5th Virginia Cavalry charged toward the gate, where a heavy volley drove them back. "For a few moments the zip, zip, z-z-z of the Minie balls and the sharp ring of the sabers were heard above the noise of the shooting."[37] Lt. Justus Schiebert, another Prussian serving on Stuart's staff, recalled, "Our horsemen came roaring back pell-mell through the woods."[38]

The victorious New Yorkers resumed their taunts, crying out, "Let us at them, Colonel!" "To hell with the Johnnies," and other similar challenges. The Confederate bugles sang out again, and the Empire Staters heard the Southern officers exhorting their men. The charge never materialized, and the Northerners responded by calling the Virginians cowards. "No soldier, be he Federal or Confederate, could tamely submit to this, and with a yell and dash they came for us in gallant style."[39]

The 3d Virginia had followed the 5th Virginia at a walk, expecting to support their attack. When Colonel Rosser's men were repulsed, the 3d Virginia drew sabers and, at a brisk trot, dashed forward to make an attack of their own. "We fell in with the enemy at the forks of two roads, a half-mile below Alsop's gate," recorded Lt. Col. William R. Carter of the 3d Virginia in his diary. "Finding they were the enemy, I ordered the Regiment to charge, whereupon the enemy fled in every direction through the woods."[40] The 3d Virginia charged through the same opening in the fence used by the New Yorkers to enter the field, but the barking of the Federal carbines drove them back.

Pvt. Joseph Ragland of Company C, 3d Virginia Cavalry, rode ahead to reassure the 5th Virginia that help was on its way. Ragland drew his saber and went only a short distance before a New Yorker halted him. The blueclad horseman asked Ragland which regiment he belonged to, and the private answered, "The 3d." The Northerner raised his pistol and aimed it at Ragland. "I am your prisoner," proclaimed the Virginian, and handed his sabre to the Northerner. A moment later, the 6th New York opened fire on Carter's approaching column, killing Carter's horse. "I found they were not paying any attention to me," recalled Ragland, "as I asked them to 'please take me back to the rear. I do not want to be killed by my own men.'" As Ragland made his way back into the woods, he lost his hat to a low-hanging branch. He bent down to pick it up and realized that nobody was guarding him, so he escaped and returned to his regiment, his stint as a prisoner of war quite short.[41]

McVicar realized that even though they had repulsed the first two charges, his New Yorkers were in an extremely precarious position. He and his men had strayed far beyond the safety of the Army of the Potomac's lines, and he had no idea just how large an enemy force lay in front of him. Staying there meant that they would have to surrender. "At this stage of the game it seemed as if every man of our gallant regiment considered himself a soldier hero, determined to bravely do his duty in this emergency," recorded an officer of the 6th New York in his diary that night.[42] McVicar turned to Lieutenant Easton and said, "Adjutant, go down the rear line and order the men to take nothing but the saber." Easton galloped off. McVicar closed his ranks and cried, "Men of the Sixth New York we must never surrender to the rebels! Right forward, fours right!" Rising in his saddle with saber raised, the Scotsman exclaimed at the top of his voice, "Sixth New York, follow me. CHARGE!" Bugles called and "like a catapult the column thundered forward, and now, with a definite purpose, gave vent to soul-stirring 'hurrahs' that thundered and reverberated through those old Virginia pines."[43]

Mounted on his large gray horse, the colonel offered a conspicuous target for the Southern carbineers. "In the darkness it seemed as though a sheet of fire belched forth from their carbines," recalled a New Yorker.[44] As he reached a spot about seventy feet from the gate, McVicar fell dead, shot through the heart. "He died as he would have wished," lamented a New York newspaper correspondent, "cutting his way through the enemy."[45]

Although the gallant Scot met a noble end, his men remained in a dangerous situation, hemmed in by both fences and swarming Confederates. The first squadron, now leaderless, halted, uncertain what to do next.[46] Twenty-six-year-old Capt. William L. Heermance of Kinderhook, New York, the regiment's next ranking officer, took command. He instructed Lt. George W. Goler to lead the men out. However, Goler was dismounted moments later when his horse was shot out from under him.[47] More than twenty of the blueclad horse soldiers fell during this fusillade.[48]

"I commanded the right squadron, & leading the first section of fours, struck the enemy massed in our front, being a horse's length or more in advance, as I struck them, I was for a moment surrounded," recalled Heermance. He squared off with a lieutenant of the 5th Virginia, slashing at him with his blade, practically severing the Virginian's nose from his face. Capt. Reuben Boston of the 5th Virginia dashed up and pressed his pistol into Heermance's left side. Before Boston could fire, Heermance hacked at him with his sabre, knocking the pistol from the captain's hand just as it discharged. The bullet passed through Heermance's arm and into his stomach. At the same time, a Rebel blade crashed down on the back of Heermance's head and unhorsed him. The Confederates took him prisoner and sent him off to Libby Prison.

"I most firmly believe, from my own personal knowledge of affairs, at the front of the Regt. on the eventful night, while riding near the Colonel and close to the right of the line, as was my place," proclaimed chief bugler Thomas M. Wells, "while we were preparing for the charge, and during the onset, that the coolness and bravery displayed by Capt. Heermance, at the right and head of the regiment in repeating the command to his squadron to charge and that he would lead them, to a yell and cheer loud and long, and ride down and cut through the enemy in our front, gave such confidence and courage to the men of the 1st Squadron, at the start, that it was taken up by the whole Regt. enabling all to move together riding down the enemy and defeating them at all points."[49] Lieutenant Goler echoed a similar chord, writing, "In my judgment, Captain Heermance won immortal fame at that time and deserves the Medal of Honor."[50] In 1893, with the endorsements of Colonel Devin and Wesley Merritt, Heermance received the Medal of Honor for his valor that night.[51]

Lt. Col. William R. Carter of the 3d Virginia could not find his way through the inky darkness, and worried about slamming into the 5th Virginia instead of the enemy. Carter halted his regiment 100 yards below the fork in the road to await further orders and to see what circumstances would bring. "Presently there was another advance," he noted, "& we killed 10 & wounded a number, among whom was their Lt Col. & 2 Capts. Soon a cry arose that we were shooting our friends & finding some of the 5th Regiment mixed up among us, I ordered the men to cease firing. This was done & we moved back slowly down the road to ascertain if we were mistaken & to prevent a flank movement from a road leading off in the direction of the enemy."[52] One of Stuart's staff officers recalled, "[A] scene of indescribable confusion occurred." Cries of "Don't shoot! Don't shoot! We're friends!" filled the air as the melee spread.[53]

The New Yorkers pressed on, striking the Confederates at the fork of the road and shoving them back toward Todd's Tavern. Lieutenant Bell, now the ranking officer, faced a difficult choice: should he follow the Confederates toward Todd's Tavern, or proceed on to Spotsylvania? The Empire Staters desperately needed leadership, but the lieutenant was afraid of the responsibilities of command. Finally persuaded that there were no other superior officers left with this portion of the regiment, and that he was in charge, Bell decided to form the men in line with their right resting on the road to Spotsylvania.[54]

Adjutant Easton sent a man to the rear to bring up a superior officer to take charge of the situation. Capt. George M. Van Buren, who had heard the firing while still in Alsop's Field, galloped up to investigate. His comrades paralyzed by the heavy casualties in the regiment's officer corps, Sgt. Frank T. Saunders felt that because "the work is half accomplished . . . the ice must be broken." Saunders spurred to the front to lead the charge. Captain Van Buren came up just behind Saunders.[55] Van Buren arrived at the intersection, took stock of the situation, rode to the front of the line, and called out, "Fours right, charge, and yell like hell!" Stuart saw the enemy ahead and drew his saber. He turned in his saddle and ordered the attack, taking the lead himself. "For once our horsemen refused to follow their gallant commander; they wavered under the thick storm of bullets; soon all discipline ceased, and in a few minutes the greater part of this splendid regiment, which had distinguished itself in so many battlefields, broke to the rear in utter confusion." So, too, did Stuart and the rest of the staff, the New Yorkers pursuing. Stuart and von Borcke became separated, finding each other in the dark woods an hour or so later.[56]

Sergeant Saunders did not notice the bullets buzzing by him. Later, when he finally had a chance to take stock of his situation, he noticed that his right stirrup had been hit. "Had not the leather been very dry and hard and a little convex, it would have taken effect on my leg," he reported to his brother. For now, though, all that mattered was reaching the safety of the Army of the Potomac's guns.[57]

Van Buren led most of the survivors to safety at Chancellorsville, but a significant portion of the men faced another challenge that dark spring night. Because the road was so narrow, the New Yorkers were strung out along it for about half a mile. As a result, some of them remained in Alsop's Field.

Stuart rode over to Munford and ordered him to open the road, if possible, as Stuart had orders to report to Robert E. Lee near Spotsylvania Court House. Stuart told Munford that unless his 2d Virginia drove the New Yorkers away, Stuart would have to find a different route.[58] Munford had seen the battered and bloodied troopers of the 3d and 5th Virginia fall back after their repulse at the gate to Alsop's Field, and realized that his men faced a difficult task. Munford thought that his men were equal to the task. "I believe that I had as good a regiment as America has ever produced," he proudly proclaimed nearly fifty years after the Civil War.[59]

Even though it was extremely dark, Munford saw an opportunity. After instructing his men to maintain absolute silence, they moved out. "We moved in promptly," recalled Munford. "The road was sandy and nothing but the click of a scabbard or the snorting of the dust from the horses's noses would indicate that 500 mounted men were again advancing against an unknown force as to numbers." They bore down on the unsuspecting Yankee troopers.[60]

Arriving at the intersection, Lt. Col. James W. Watts, second in command of Munford's regiment, heard someone call out in the darkness, "Who comes there?" Watts replied instantly, "2d Va. Cavalry, charge!" Uncertain of what lay in front of them, the 2d Virginia "moved promptly not knowing what number we had to meet." They encountered the thin picket line deployed by the 6th New York "when the charge was ordered, and gallantly made, scattering the command in our front," recalled Watts. Stuart drew his pistol and dashed forward with Watts. He remained "until the danger was over, ready to charge with me at the head of the regiment. There was considerable firing and yelling around us," recalled Watts, "but little damage done; a few men and horses were shot. Major von Borcke, of Stuart's staff, had his horse killed very near the head of the regiment" as he joined the charging Virginians.[61]

"With a yell which is said to have had more effect than sabers or pistols," the 2d Virginia's charge cut off and demoralized those New Yorkers still trapped in the field, dividing what remained of their column.[62] Some of the Federals took shelter behind the Alsop house, hoping to escape the 2d Virginia's onslaught.[63] "The silent and desolate spot, the moonlight glancing from the sabers, the excitement of the struggle," recalled a participant, "recalled some scene of knightly glory."[64]

Capt. William Beardsley, the next senior Union captain, brought up the rear of the column. He tried to escape with a few men, the regiment's wounded officers, and a dozen prisoners. However, the charge of the 2d Virginia drove off his small command, forcing him to leave McVicar's body, his prisoners, and his wounded officers behind. On the morning of May 1st, Beardsley, gathering a few stragglers along the way, found a local black man who guided them to safety near Chancellorsville. Lt. Richard O'Neil, of Company C, who had lost his mount during the melee, found another horse, gathered up sixty stragglers, and led them to safety through enemy lines. The regiment rallied at Louisa's Run and then withdrew to the main line of infantry pickets on the Plank Road, where it remained until it received orders to rejoin the rest of the brigade.[65] "But for the darkness & fear that we were firing upon our own men (5th Reg.) we could have killed or captured the whole party," observed Lieutenant Colonel Carter of the 3d Virginia Cavalry.[66]

The 1st Virginia Cavalry brought up the rear of the Confederate column. Stuart had not intended to commit the 1st Virginia to the fight, as its men had been in the saddle for hours without a break, and they were exhausted. Fitz Lee approached Stuart and said, "Let the First rest tonight, they were in their saddles all night long last night, and all day today; and it is too hard on them to make them go again tonight."

"Can't help it Fitz," responded Stuart, "they are bound to go tonight."

With the commanding general's specific order in place, the men of the 1st Virginia set off to find the enemy. Sgt. Benjamin J. Haden of the 1st Virginia rode toward the sound of the firing. Along the way, they found evidence of the rout of Rosser's men. Abandoned guidons and other debris lined the route of march, only to be retrieved by disgusted members of the 1st Virginia. "We mounted and started to [the 5th Virginia Cavalry's] relief, and soon met members of the Fifth, some on foot, some minus hats, guns, and sabers, and some wounded, telling us to go ahead boys, they have torn our Regiment to pieces!" These words steeling them, the men of the 1st Virginia drew their pistols and spurred ahead to join the pursuit of the 6th New York.[67]

The victorious men of the 1st and 2d Virginia Cavalry pursued the fleeing New Yorkers along parallel roads. "We had gone about a mile when some of the scattered men of [the 6th New York] who had been bewildered when they ran off," recalled Munford, "ran into the advance of the 1st Va. Cavalry." They exchanged shots, and the New Yorkers withdrew in confusion. "When the firing commenced, I wheeled my regiment about facing by fours to the rear, and all of Stuart's and Lee's couriers and staff officers who were riding at the head of my column, dashed back to the rear, when Stuart was with my regiment questioning the prisoners, and a pandemonium arose as the 1st Va. fired into our rear, and the staff officers and couriers dashed back, running against everybody in the road, and cursing and swearing was the order of the moment, until by good luck we discovered that we were friends, but the prisoners had a rough time, not knowing who were friends or foes." Munford finally restored order and led his small column of prisoners to Spotsylvania Court House.[68]

Colonel Owen of the 3d Virginia called for his adjutant, Capt. Robert T. Hubard. Owen instructed Hubard to send a dispatch to General R. E. Lee informing him that a strong force of Union cavalry had gotten between the Southern horse and Lee's headquarters. Hubard selected a reliable courier, and "wrote the dispatch on the side of the road, my knee serving for a writing desk, on a scant slip of paper, all I had left, as we left our camp expecting to go at once into action. I gave Colonel Taylor, A.A.G., all the information we had of the two columns moving from Germanna and Ely's ford." The courier delivered the dispatch to Lee's headquarters sometime between 12:00 and 1:00 A.M. on May 1. The courier informed Hubard that this message "was the first intelligence received that morning at army headquarters from the direction of Chancellorsville. Orders were immediately issued for General Jackson's corps to move toward Chancellorsville." After pausing to feed their horses at Todd's Tavern, the 3d Virginia Cavalry reported to Brig. Gen. Ambrose Wright, of Maj. Gen. George T. Anderson's division, at Tabernacle Church, eight or nine miles west from Fredericksburg. Drawing on this valuable intelligence, Wright moved forward that evening, and finding nothing but cavalry in his front, "was disposed to regard the whole movement as a feint and a 'big scare.'" The Virginians bivouacked for the night on the roadside, behind Wright's lines.[69]

The Southerners, impressed by McVicar's courage, cared for his remains. They returned his sword and personal effects and carried his body to a nearby house, where Mr. Alsop's son tended to it.[70] On May 1, Fitz Lee stopped at the log house, and "learning that the body of the gallant leader of the little band which had driven back his whole brigade lay unburied on the field of battle, he had it brought in, a coffin made from the material that could be had, and buried it there."[71] Fitz Lee sent the chaplain of the 1st Virginia Cavalry, Rev. Dabney Ball, to Alsop's house to pray over McVicar's remains. Jeb Stuart also paid his respects, patting the Scotsman's forehead and saying, "Brave man, brave man." A few days later, after the Battle of Chancellorsville, the Confederates permitted the New Yorkers to recover the body of their fallen commander under a flag of truce.[72]

The 6th New York managed to slash its way through more than three times its numbers in making its way to safety. "The prisoners captured, but who afterward escaped during the second attack, were from the Second, Third, Fifth, and Ninth Virginia Cavalry, showing that the regiment was evidently surrounded by a brigade," observed Devin.[73] The Empire Staters lost several officers and fifty men killed, wounded, or captured in the engagement, or more than a quarter of their numbers.[74] The Confederates lost only one man captured.[75] However, the 6th New York delayed the arrival of Stuart and his cavalry at the Army of Northern Virginia's headquarters until May 1, once the fighting had already begun at Chancellorsville.[76]

On May 10, 1863, after the end of the Battle of Chancellorsville, Pleasonton praised their valor. "The heroism of the Sixth New York Regiment in cutting its way back to our own lines through treble its force of the enemy's cavalry on the 1st inst . . . have excited the highest admiration," wrote the division commander.[77] "That Col. McVicar made a most spirited and gallant defense," observed Munford, "no one denies, and with his small regiment, he delayed Stuart nearly a whole night," persuading Stuart that he had faced an entire brigade and not a single regiment.[78] The battered New Yorkers, who suffered substantial losses, withdrew to Hartwood Church and rejoined the rest of Devin's brigade. Although they did not participate in the bloody fight at Chancellorsville, these men had earned their spurs in Hugh Alsop's field.

MAJOR PETER KEENAN'S CHARGE AT CHANCELLORSVILLE

Colonel Devin accompanied the 8th Pennsylvania Cavalry as it advanced to Chancellorsville. The Pennsylvanians spent April 29 and 30 picketing along the Rapidan River, guarding the crucial fords used by the infantry to move toward Chancellorsville. On April 30, Lt. J. Edward Carpenter, leading the 8th Pennsylvania's vanguard, spotted Confederates on the road from Chancellorsville to U.S. Ford. The horsemen charged the enemy, capturing an entire company of the 12th Virginia Infantry and all three of the officers assigned to that company. The rest of the Virginians retreated to their rifle pits, and "some severe skirmishing ensued, when, by a brilliant charge, they were driven from their works to a wood in the rear." The fire of the Confederates increased in intensity as the Pennsylvanians advanced. Capt. Alexander McCallum, commander of Company E of the 8th Pennsylvania Cavalry, lost his horse when it was shot out from under him during the second charge.[79]

When the rest of the regiment came up, Devin directed his skirmishers to advance. They cleared the woods, and the horse soldiers dashed into Chancellorsville, driving out the Southern pickets guarding the crucial road intersection at the tavern. They captured six prisoners in this charge. Devin reported to Meade that he held the road intersection, and asked that the infantry occupy the place in force. As a result, Meade himself rode over and positioned his pickets at the tavern.[80]

This freed the Pennsylvanians to ride east toward Banks's Ford and determine whether the enemy held that crossing in force. Devin proceeded down the old Fredericksburg Turnpike and realized that Brig. Gen. William Mahone's Virginia infantry brigade blocked his way. On reaching the foot of a hill overlooking the intersection of the roads to Banks's Ford and U.S. Ford, Devin slammed into Mahone's pickets, who retired slowly, resisting all the way, suggesting that they expected reinforcements.

Major Keenan, leading the advance with two squadrons, dismounted part of his command and deployed them as skirmishers on either side of the road. They advanced through the thick woods that led to the crest of the hill and drew fire from Southern artillery. As the dismounted horse soldiers neared the crest, the Virginians opened a heavy volley of musketry, forcing the Pennsylvanians to withdraw. Keenan lost three men wounded during this skirmishing. Realizing that one regiment of cavalry could not take the stoutly defended hill, Devin reported his plight to Meade, who sent Maj. Gen. Charles Griffin's infantry division to relieve the Pennsylvania cavalrymen.[81]

Griffin sent a brigade of infantry into the woods, and then, receiving orders from Meade, withdrew toward Chancellorsville without seriously engaging Mahone's infantry. As darkness fell, Devin also withdrew half a mile and bivouacked, leaving a strong line of vedettes in front.[82] The Pennsylvanians had a short night.

At sunrise on May 1, Devin received orders to report to Hooker. Soon after, the Confederate advance drove in the pickets, the 8th Pennsylvania went to their support, and "severe skirmishing ensued." With the Keystone State horsemen leading the Union advance to the Joseph Alsop house along the Orange Turnpike, it is quite likely that a member of the 8th Pennsylvania fired the Army of the Potomac's first shots at the Battle of Chancellorsville. Their advance to the Alsop homestead marked the farthest eastward advance of the Army of the Potomac during the Battle of Chancellorsville.[83] As two divisions of Confederate infantry pressed west from Fredericksburg, the Pennsylvania horsemen delayed their advance by making several mounted charges, and they held their position until Brig. Gen. George Sykes's infantry division relieved them along the picket line at the Alsop house.

As the advancing Southerners drove Sykes's infantry back toward Zoan Church, Capt. Charles Wickersham and his battalion of Pennsylvania horsemen occupied the small two-story Ann Lewis house, about a tenth of a mile from Zoan Church.[84] Mrs. Lewis, who was sixty-three years old, grew excited as she saw the large body of Confederate infantry moving toward her house. In an agitated state, Mrs. Lewis called to Wickersham "to go upstairs and look at the rebels." The captain ran up the steps, "and looking out of the windows saw a line of skirmishers, with short intervals, arms at a trail, coming slowly toward my line, and followed by three solid lines of infantry." Wickersham rushed outside and called for his men to mount and hold their ground.

"I rode out rapidly to my picket line, which had just begun exchanging shots with the enemy, and, telling the sergeant in command to stay there as long as he could and then fall back at a gallop." He then rode back to his reserves, dismounting all of his men, save five or six, whom he directed to corral the horses and to take them to the shelter of a small stand of woods not far behind their position. "The enemy soon came within easy carbine range when we commenced firing, to which they promptly replied and a lively skirmish was soon in progress."[85]

Other elements of the 8th Pennsylvania occupied the 157-acre farm of John Leitch, situated between the opposing lines on May 1. Mr. Leitch later recalled that "the whole cavalry of the enemy grazed our lands" late on April 30 and early on May 1. Shortly before noon, the 12th Virginia Infantry, advancing west from Zoan Church, engaged pickets of the 8th Pennsylvania. One Virginian recalled, "We got

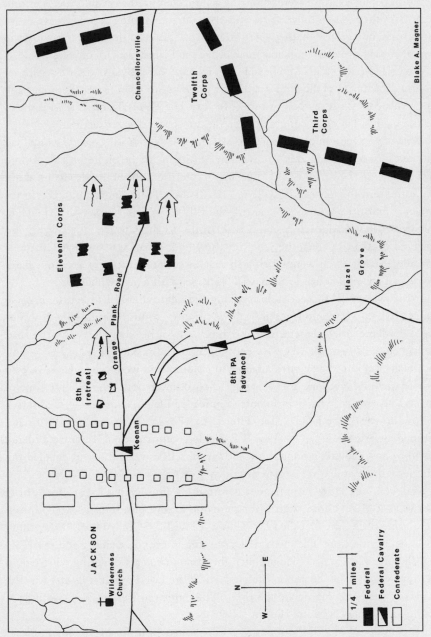

The Charge of the 8th Pennsylvania Cavalry at Chancellorsville, May 1, 1863

Blake A. Magner

to the top of a hill, and then the Yanks were some two hundred yards off on another elevation deployed, as we were across the road facing us, they would fire at us, and then make their horses move about and keep us from aiming accurately, we drove them back, but I must say they were stubborn fellows to deal with." Finally, the overwhelming size of the infantry force drove the Pennsylvanians off. Soon, Sykes's Regulars came forward and relieved the pickets.[86] After Sykes's infantry relieved them, a detachment of the 8th Pennsylvania went out to reconnoiter the right flank and returned with seventeen prisoners in tow. The Pennsylvanians then camped for the night.[87] They had conducted a classic, successful delaying action.

With the exception of one squadron of the 6th New York Cavalry, which had rejoined Devin's brigade after its ordeal in Alsop's Field, the entire brigade moved to the front, just behind the XI Corps line, and to the right of the III Corps, about one mile from the Chancellorsville tavern. As the column moved out, Devin received additional orders to report with the 6th New York Cavalry to Brig. Gen. David Birney's headquarters, about three miles to the left. Devin reported and received orders to determine whether the Plank Road was open at Chancellorsville. Birney's men were retiring in that direction because of a vicious flank attack by Lt. Gen. Thomas J. "Stonewall" Jackson's Confederate infantry.

Devin wrote, "[I] succeeded in reaching the field where I had left the brigade under General Pleasonton, and found the infantry about forming line. I immediately ordered a detachment to make their way to the Plank Road by the road we had come. When half-way, we were fired upon from skirmishers in the woods, and finally ran into the enemy's infantry, in column, and were driven back." Devin formed the 6th New York in line facing the road, and reported his plight to one of Birney's brigade commanders. Infantry reinforced Devin, who then retired into a hollow in rear of the Federal line. There, the 17th Pennsylvania Cavalry finally rejoined his brigade. Maj. Gen. Daniel E. Sickles, commander of III Corps, ordered Devin to post vedettes around the woods at Hazel Grove, and Devin detailed the 6th New York Cavalry to perform this duty.[88]

Maj. Pennock Huey, commander of the 8th Pennsylvania, spent most of the afternoon at Hazel Grove, waiting for someone to give him orders. "We had been there some little time," recalled Lt. Andrew B. Wells of Company B. "Everything was quiet on the front. The men were gathering in groups, chatting and smoking, and the officers were occupied in much the same manner, wondering what would turn up next."[89] The afternoon dragged on as the horse soldiers listened to the sounds of the battle raging around them. They grew concerned as the sounds of the fighting came closer and closer.

Huey rode off to find Pleasonton, seeking instructions for his regiment. Pleasonton was at Sickles's headquarters when a panicked staff officer spurred up, dispatched by Howard to report that the XI Corps had been flanked and was in serious danger. This news stunned Sickles. Sickles, Pleasonton, and Huey wheeled and started back toward Hazel Grove. Another staff officer, sent by the Army of the Potomac's chief engineer, now—Brig. Gen. Gouverneur K. Warren, rode up and confirmed the news of the rout of the XI Corps and suggested that a regiment of cavalry be sent to try to check the movement. Sickles ordered Pleasonton to send a regiment.

Pleasonton turned to Huey and told him to report, with his regiment, to Howard as quickly as possible. Neither officer knew where to find Howard, and when Huey asked where to go, Pleasonton responded, "I suppose you will find him at or near the Old Wilderness Church; there is where he was." Huey spurred off to find his regiment.[90]

About 4:00, Lieutenant Wells of the 8th Pennsylvania suggested a game of draw poker. Wells, Major Keenan, the regimental adjutant, Lt. J. Haseltine Haddock, and Capt. William A. Daily turned over a hardtack box, threw a blanket over it, and started playing cards. They played for nearly two hours, and "the game was a big one." A mounted officer dashed up and asked, "Who is in command of this regiment?"

Keenan, who was sitting next to Wells, turned his head and said, "I am, what's the trouble?"

The officer replied, "General Howard wants a cavalry regiment." At that, the staff officer dashed off before further questions could be asked. Major Huey arrived and ordered the men to mount up, prompting Keenan to quip, "Major, you have spoiled a damned good game." The game ended immediately as the five officers stood up to prepare the regiment to move out. "The sleepers, as well as the talkers, sprang to their saddles, and a regiment of cavalry was seen in place of a lounging crowd."[91]

Huey and Keenan led the column, followed by Capt. Charles Arrowsmith, commander of the first squadron, Carpenter, and Haddock. The Pennsylvanians trotted out of Hazel Grove in column of twos. "This road was too narrow due to over hanging shrubbery, to accept more than four men abreast," recalled a horse soldier, "indeed uncomfortable for this column of fours. This formation had to continue until the Plank Road was reached. On this narrow road we met a considerable mass of the Eleventh Corps." Dense undergrowth hid the fact that a heavy enemy battle line lay nearby at the intersection of the Plank Road.[92]

Lt. J. Edward Carpenter recalled that "until after the 8th Pennsylvania had left the place there was not the slightest evidence that the enemy was in the immediate neighborhood, excepting, perhaps, that the musketry-firing seemed to be drawing closer."[93] The Keystone Staters marched through the woods toward the Plank Road, wondering what awaited them. "Nobody in the regiment, with the exception of myself, knew where we were going or for what purpose," recalled

Huey. None of the Pennsylvanians had any idea that they were riding right into the midst of Jackson's Corps, attacking the XI Corps flank. Accordingly, the men rode with their sabers safely ensconced in their scabbards and their pistols in their holsters, totally unprepared for the gauntlet that awaited them.[94] "Caps are raked off by the brushwood, faces are scratched and torn by the hanging briars," but the Pennsylvanians rode as fast as they could.[95]

When the column reached the Plank Road, Huey realized that they had ridden right into Jackson's flank, "that we were completely surrounded, the woods at that point being filled with the flankers of Jackson's column, who were thoroughly hidden from our view by the thick undergrowth." Seeing no other options, Huey cried, "Draw sabers and charge," which order Keenan repeated. "Never before did three hundred cast themselves with such true aim and so impetuously against twenty thousand victorious and advancing veterans," noted a Pennsylvanian.[96] The horsemen dashed forward, reaching the Plank Road and finding it "packed about as closely with the enemy as it possible could be."[97] The sudden onslaught stunned the Southern foot soldiers. "An attack from, or an encounter with, cavalry in that dense country seemed about as unlikely as an attack from a gunboat," correctly observed one Confederate soldier.[98] Believing that all of the Union cavalry had fallen upon them, many grayclad infantrymen cried out, "I surrender!"

The cavalrymen veered to the left, facing the Confederate column, trying to hack their way through to safety. They made it almost 100 yards through the shocked foot soldiers. The panicked horses trampled those unfortunate Rebels unable to get clear. A heavy volley of musket fire greeted them, killing Keenan, Arrowsmith, and Haddock, "three of the noblest and most gallant officers of the war, besides a large number of men, all of whom are entitled to equal honor from a grateful nation in whose service they laid down their lives." Keenan toppled against Major Huey and dropped to the ground under Huey's horse. Arrowsmith rode a big bay horse, and fell with his horse, animal and rider toppling together on the right side of the road, not far from Keenan. The 8th Pennsylvania left thirty men and eighty horses dead at the intersection.[99]

Lt. J. Edward Carpenter saw Keenan fall. "He was actually among the bayonets of the enemy, in their line of battle, which was badly thrown out of order by our charge. He fell forward, pitching headlong in the direction of the enemy, and in the direction in which his horse was moving," recalled Carpenter. "Captain Arrowsmith rode a bay horse, and fell with his horse, both horse and rider striking down together." "Keenan was a powerful man, and just before he fell he was flourishing his saber with unexampled rapidity in the very midst of, and hand-to-hand with the enemy."[100] At that moment, a Confederate ball struck Carpenter's terrified horse squarely in the breast, cutting the breast strap, and causing the horse to rear and turn around.

Lieutenant Wells rode with Capt. William A. Corrie and the second squadron. "When we passed out of the clearing there were no officers or men on our flank, all was in order ahead, and the command was moving at a walk, when, at the distance of about one mile from where we had mounted, Captain Corrie and myself saw the first squadron take the trot, leaving a space between us of about twenty-five yards." The command "draw sabers" rang out, and Wells and Corrie saw the blades of the first squadron spring from their scabbards. Then, they heard the ominous sound of musketry cracking nearby.[101]

Corrie gave the order for the squadron to draw sabers and charge, and away they went at a trot. They found a bend in the road, turned the corner onto the Plank Road, and "a sight met our eyes that it was impossible for me to describe. After charging over the dead men and the horses of the first squadron we charged into Jackson's column, and, as luck would have it, found them with empty guns—thanks to our poor comrades ahead. The enemy was as thick as bees, and we appeared to be among thousands of them in an instant."[102]

Slashing right and left, Wells recalled, "the enemy were as much surprised as we were, and thought, no doubt, as they now say, that the whole cavalry corps of the Army of the Potomac was charging them. I distinctly remember hearing a number of them call out, 'I surrender! I surrender!' We did not stop to take any prisoners for fear of being captured ourselves." After one stint at Libby Prison, Wells was not eager to return.[103]

Captain Wickersham, who commanded a battalion of the 8th Pennsylvania Cavalry, rode alongside Capt. Alexander McCallum, who led a company. The two officers watched the squadron in front draw their sabers and take the trot. "The men, comprehending the greatness of the moment, lifted their sabers high in the air." McCallum turned in his saddle as they trotted along, and spotting the massed enemy in their front, declared, "I think this is the last of the 8th Pennsylvania Cavalry."

Wickersham replied, "I think so too, but let us go down with our colors flying." They were quickly closing in on Keenan's beleaguered battalions, "and from the dreadful fire we were receiving, I feared the road ahead would be obstructed by Keenan's dead and wounded men and horses, and I raised my saber to check the men of my battalion for a moment. At this juncture the fight became, if possible, more furious, the entire command using sabers vigorously while pressing forward. At no time did the regiment lose its formation, the only gaps being caused by those who fell."[104]

Trooper John L. Collins knew that a difficult task lay ahead of the 8th Pennsylvania. He could see a small band of grayclad officers ahead, and realized that the Pennsylvanians were about to crash into a large force of Confederate infantry. "We struck it as a wave strikes a stately ship," he recalled, "the ship is staggered, maybe thrown on her beam ends, but the wave is dashed into spray, and the ship sails on as before." Collins attempted to turn to the right, but his horse was shot out from under him, and he pitched over the animal's neck onto the roadside. "When I jumped to my feet, I had time to take only one glance at my surroundings. My sole thought was to escape capture or death." Strong lines of Southern infantry doubled and bent the charge, with the survivors trying to hack their way to safety out of reach of the Southern rifles.

"By instinct I turned toward the woods on the right of the Plank Road as the best way out," recalled Collins, "and made a mad dash at the lines, which had just recovered from their surprise that a cavalry regiment should have ridden over them, and were firing after it." Waiting until the Southerners reloaded, Collins dashed through their ranks, ducking to avoid the bullets flying in pursuit. "The Plank Road, and the woods that bordered it, presented a scene of terror and confusion such as I had never seen before. Men and animals were dashing against one another in wild dismay before the line of fire that came crackling and crashing after them. The constantly approaching rattle of musketry, the crash of shells through the trees, seemed to come from three sides upon the broken fragments of the Eleventh Corps that crowded each other on the road." Cavalry horses, joined by terrified pack mules from the broken infantry ranks, dashed through the woods, searching for safety. Collins vainly tried to corral one.

Collins soon abandoned the idea of finding a new mount when Confederate artillery killed some nearby mules, and instead decided to try to find shelter on foot. "Once, when throwing myself down to escape the fury of the fire, I saw a member of my own regiment, whose horse had also been shot, hiding in a pine top that had been cut away by a shell. He had thrown his arms away that he might run the faster, and he begged me to do the same. This I refused to do, and I got in safely with my arms, while he was never seen again." Collins fell in with a large group of refugees of the 8th Pennsylvania, all of whom had thrown away their arms. The terrified horse soldiers slashed their way to safety, passing Major General Howard, who, with tears streaming down his face, was trying to halt his broken and demoralized troops by clutching the national colors under the stump of his missing arm and calling out to them to rally on the colors (he had lost the arm in 1862 from a wound received at Fair Oaks). Collins and his comrades eventually found the survivors of the regiment huddled behind some hastily deployed artillery blocking the pursuit of the Rebel infantry.[105]

The swarming Confederates completely cut off Capt. Joseph W. Wistar's squadron, bringing up the rear of the 8th Pennsylvania, before they could even reach the Plank Road. Wistar's men had to cut their way through Jackson's infantry in another direction, escaping into the open space between Hazel Grove and Chancellorsville. As they tried to escape, they had to jump over hastily constructed

Maj. Gen. Ambrose E. Burnside's lack of experience in the handling of cavalry forces and his dispersion of them amongst his "Grand Divisions" continued the inefficiencies begun under Maj. Gen. George B. McClellan. The Union cavalry was completely ineffective in the battles of Fredericksburg and Antietam and throughout the first two years of the war.

LIBRARY OF CONGRESS

Maj. Gen. Joseph Hooker succeeded Burnside in command and, implementing a plan advocated by Maj. Gen. Alfred Pleasonton, consolidated the cavalry into a single corps under the command of Maj. Gen. George Stoneman. NATIONAL ARCHIVES

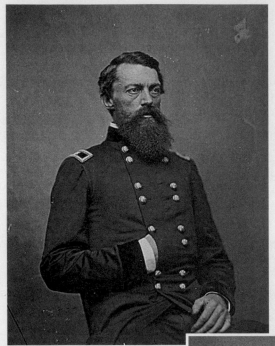

Maj. Gen. George Stoneman's appointment in 1863 to command Fightin' Joe Hooker's cavalry corps was generally supported by the men under his command. Stoneman, an 1846 graduate of West Point and a career horse soldier, was a veteran of the Indian and Mexican wars. NATIONAL ARCHIVES

Maj. Gen. Alfred Pleasonton was known to be something of a show-off and a self-promoter. Nonetheless, he demonstrated competence at administration and command at a time when the cavalry corps was in desperate need of a leader. Pleasonton's memorandum suggesting the subsequently enacted reorganization of the cavalry into one corps was probably his greatest contribution to the service. NATIONAL ARCHIVES

Brig. Gen. William Woods Averell commanded a division under Pleasonton. He was known for a haughty personality that rubbed many the wrong way and stunted his career. Averell was said to mirror the overly cautious nature of Maj. Gen. George McClellan, often losing momentum because of a penchant for treating a battlefield like a chessboard. NATIONAL ARCHIVES

Brig. Gen. David M. Gregg led Pleasonton's Third Cavalry Division. Nicknamed "Old Reliable" by his men, Gregg was considered to be intelligent, modest, honorable, genial, if not demonstrative, and of unimpeachable character. UNITED STATES ARMY MILITARY HISTORY INSTITUTE (USAMHI)

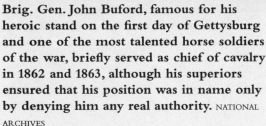

Brig. Gen. John Buford, famous for his heroic stand on the first day of Gettysburg and one of the most talented horse soldiers of the war, briefly served as chief of cavalry in 1862 and 1863, although his superiors ensured that his position was in name only by denying him any real authority. NATIONAL ARCHIVES

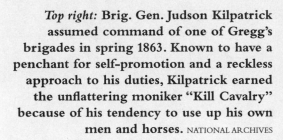

Top right: Brig. Gen. Judson Kilpatrick assumed command of one of Gregg's brigades in spring 1863. Known to have a penchant for self-promotion and a reckless approach to his duties, Kilpatrick earned the unflattering moniker "Kill Cavalry" because of his tendency to use up his own men and horses. NATIONAL ARCHIVES

Center right: The French-born Col. Alfred N. A. Duffié claimed that he was the son of a count and had compiled a decorated combat record as a cavalryman in Europe, but the historical record suggests otherwise. During the Civil War, he performed competently if not spectacularly.

NATIONAL ARCHIVES

Col. Benjamin F. "Grimes" Davis of Mississippi was a cousin of
Confederate president Jefferson Davis but remained loyal to the Union.
He served as a brigade commander under Pleasonton and was mortally
wounded in the opening minutes of the Battle of Brandy Station. USAMHI

Left: Col. Thomas C. Devin commanded a brigade
under Pleasonton. Considered a reliable and
trustworthy leader, perhaps the best reflection on
Devin was John Buford's observation, "I can't teach
Col. Devin anything about cavalry." USAMHI

Col. Luigi Palma di Cesnola was the son of Italian nobility. A
veteran of the Crimean War, he emigrated to the U.S. in the 1860s,
married the daughter of an American naval officer, and directed a
seven-hundred-student military school in New York City. He
succeeded Duffié as a brigade commander when the Frenchman
was promoted to divisional command. MICHAEL MCAFEE

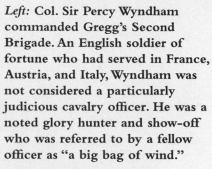

Left: Col. Sir Percy Wyndham commanded Gregg's Second Brigade. An English soldier of fortune who had served in France, Austria, and Italy, Wyndham was not considered a particularly judicious cavalry officer. He was a noted glory hunter and show-off who was referred to by a fellow officer as "a big bag of wind."

NATIONAL ARCHIVES

Above: Lt. Col. Duncan McVicar, commander of the Sixth New York Cavalry, who was born in Scotland, was known as a brave man and competent officer. He was killed in action in the fight at Alsop's Field during the Battle of Chancellorsville, on April 30, 1863.

USAMHI

Lt. Col. Hasbrouck Davis, a Universalist minister, commanded the Twelfth Illinois Cavalry. Davis, who had helped lead the cavalry breakout from Harpers Ferry in 1862, led one of the columns that participated in Stoneman's Raid. His troopers came closest to Richmond. ROGER HUNT

Maj. Peter Keenan of the Eighth Pennsylvania Cavalry was killed in action at Chancellorsville while leading his regiment in a desperate charge into Lt. Gen. Thomas J. "Stonewall" Jackson's infantry. USAMHI

Capt. Wesley Merritt (pictured as a brigadier general) became one of the finest cavalry officers in the history of the U.S. Army. He commanded a detachment during Stoneman's Raid, and led the Second U.S. Cavalry at Brandy Station. He received a promotion to brigadier general of volunteers on June 28, 1863. NATIONAL ARCHIVES

Capt. Elon J. Farnsworth of the Eighth Illinois Cavalry. Considered "a most excellent officer," Farnsworth was known for being a bold and daring leader. He commanded a regiment at Brandy Station and received a promotion to brigadier general of volunteers on June 28, 1863. He was killed at Gettysburg while leading a brave but futile charge. USAMHI

Capt. Ulric Dahlgren was the son of Union admiral John A. Dahlgren. A talented and motivated officer, the twenty-two-year-old Dahlgren was killed on a controversial 1864 raid on the Confederate capital of Richmond. Confederates who recovered his body claimed to find papers ordering him to assassinate Jefferson Davis. It is a controversy that still rages to this day. NATIONAL ARCHIVES

Lt. William Heermance of the Sixth New York Cavalry was awarded a Medal of Honor for his valor in the fight at Alsop's Field, April 30, 1863. USAMHI

Lt. Nathaniel P. Bowditch, First Massachusetts Cavalry. Bowditch, a brave and popular officer, was mortally wounded at Kelly's Ford, Virginia on March 17, 1863. This photograph was taken in May 1861, about a month before Bowditch enlisted. AUTHOR'S COLLECTION

Maj. Gen. J. E. B. Stuart of Virginia commanded the cavalry forces assigned to the Army of Northern Virginia. LIBRARY OF CONGRESS

Brig. Gen. Fitzhugh Lee, Gen. Robert E. Lee's nephew, was Stuart's favorite subordinate. Known as the "laughing cavalier," Fitz Lee had a fun-loving nature. He was also a hard fighter who engaged the Union cavalry numerous times during 1863. USAMHI

Brig. Gen. W. H. F. "Rooney" Lee, Robert E. Lee's second son, was a Harvard-educated farmer who became a competent cavalry commander. His brigade dogged Stoneman's Raid. Rooney Lee was badly wounded at Brandy Station and was captured a few days later. USAMHI

Brig. Gen. Wade Hampton of South Carolina. Hampton, reputedly
the wealthiest man in the South, proved to be a very competent
commander of cavalry. After Stuart's death in 1864, he became
commander of Robert E. Lee's cavalry corps. LIBRARY OF CONGRESS

Brig. Gen. William E. "Grumble" Jones of Virginia. The plain-spoken and profane Jones was a career horse soldier and a West Point classmate of John Buford. Jones and Stuart did not get along, which greatly hindered Jones's career. Nevertheless, he was competent and earned Stuart's begrudging respect. USAMHI

everly
, who
nded a
derate cavalry
ade, had been called
Stuart "the most
ifficult man in the
army." Robertson did
poorly at the Battle of
Brandy Station. USAMHI

Col. Thomas L. Rosser,
commander of the Fifth Virginia
Cavalry, was a favorite of Stuart.
The Texan, who was a West Point
classmate and friend of George
Custer, rose to division command
as a result of Stuart's unwavering
affection and support.

AUTHOR'S COLLECTION

Maj. John Pelham of Alabama commanded the Stuart Horse Artillery Battalion. The dashing and handsome Pelham earned a reputation as a gifted artillerist and ladies' man and was mortally wounded while leading a cavalry charge at Kelly's Ford, March 17, 1863. Stuart wept when he learned of Pelham's death.

ALABAMA DEPT. OF ARCHIVES AND HISTORY

earthworks, adding yet another obstacle to their already nerve-jang[...]
Trooper William H. Bentz came through the gauntlet unharmed. Ho[...]
horse "received two severe wounds which put him *hors de combat* for som[...]
three months."[107]

As the Pennsylvanians mingled with the grayclad infantrymen, "sabre bl[o...]
thick and fast; some threw down their guns and raised their hand beseech[...]
Soon the lines behind them opened fire, and horses and riders tumbled headl[...]
for several hundred yards the cavalry column ploughed its way through more t[...]
one line of Confederate infantry before it lost its aggressive force." Captain Wic[...]
ersham recalled, "During this charge it seemed as though the enemy were firin[g...]
almost in our faces, so close were their lines to us, and in one instance where our
horses were checked a moment by those in our front, a rebel officer caught [my]
bridle, and pointing a revolver at [me], ordered [me] to surrender. The reply was
what is known in the sabre exercise as 'left cut against infantry.' The rebel officer
did not respond to roll call the next morning." In just a few minutes, it was over,
but the horse soldiers had suffered extremely heavy losses.[108]

Most of the 8th Pennsylvania emerged from the woods on the north side of
the Plank Road. Huey formed the remnants of his regiment in the rear of XII
Corps batteries being deployed along the Plank Road to resist Jackson's savage
flank attack. Huey intended to support the artillery, and to prevent the gunners
from opening ranks before the rest of the horsemen could dash to safety. The sudden and unexpected appearance of the blueclad horsemen confused the pursuing
Confederates, who stopped their pursuit to form and defend against cavalry. By
the time the Confederates realized that there would be no grand Napoleonic cavalry charge, it was too late for them to press their advantage, meaning that many
more men of the XI Corps made it to safety than otherwise might have.[109]

Chaos reigned. "Tennyson's 'Light Brigade' is more truly applicable to the charge
at Chancellorsville than to Balaklava," observed an officer of the 8th Pennsylvania
in a postwar letter, "as the former had passed through two lines of the enemy and
into their reserve there was veritably enemy to the right, left, front and rear of
them. I can understand how many did not know of an order to go into squadron
from the clatter of the hoofs, the clanking of scabbards, the rustle of foliage, being
continuously brushed aside by the troopers, the explosion of fire arms to the left
and front, made it difficult to hear an order even when passed from squadron to
squadron by officers or from troop to troops, as was done on this fatal march."[110]

"The effect of the charge was immediate: it scattered that portion of the enemy's
line and made great confusion," claimed Carpenter after the war, "so much so that
their advance was checked and the regiment was not followed when it retired to
rally. Ample time was thus secured to form not only the Eighth Pennsylvania Cavalry, which was immediately formed on the left of the Plank Road, but also some

of the reserve artillery, which took position on our left; and later our infantry force formed on the same line and on a prolongation thereof on the right of the Plank Road."[111] The survivors retired behind the guns, enabling them to see muzzle flashes in the valley below. Finally, the firing petered out as night fell over the bloody, chaotic battlefield.[112]

The 8th Pennsylvania had survived its ordeal, but with severe losses. It had crashed into Brig. Gen. Alfred H. Colquitt's Georgia infantry brigade, which was part of Maj. Gen. Robert Rodes's division, and it had paid the price.[113] "The whole affair was accidental," observed Lieutenant Wells. "We were on our way to report to General Howard, some three miles from where we were camped, and the country that General Howard's staff officer had just passed over in quest of the cavalry had in the meantime been crossed by Stonewall Jackson's troops, and in following the same tracks we naturally ran into them. The officers who were at the head of our column, seeing the situation, had only an instant to determine what was to be done. We could not turn around and get out in the face of the enemy, and the only thing left for us was to go through them, 'sink or swim.'" He concluded, "Can any man who was a soldier for one moment imagine an officer deliberately planning a charge by a regiment of cavalry, strung out by twos in a column half a mile long in a thick wood?"[114] Indeed. No sane officer would.

In fact, Huey later claimed, "Had the real condition of affairs been known, or even suspected, by Sickles when he ordered Pleasonton to send a regiment of cavalry to Howard, such an order would never have been given. As it is, he certainly would not have ordered three hundred men right into certain destruction without one word of caution to their commanding officer."[115] However, circumstances pitched the 8th Pennsylvania Cavalry into a crucible along the Plank Road, and it paid dearly. The accidental charge of the Pennsylvanians broke up part of the Confederate pursuit and allowed a lot of panicked Northern infantrymen to reach safety.

As dusk fell, and the crisis passed, the 8th Pennsylvania withdrew to Chancellorsville as the XI Corps tumbled back, routed by Jackson's infantry. "General Howard not being in that part of the field, and circumstances having changed since I was ordered to report to him, I made no effort to find him, but formed the regiment across the plaint," recalled Major Huey, "covering the road that led toward the river and fords, where the regiment did service all night in stopping the stampeded and scattered soldiers, and assisted in reforming them."[116]

Because the tide of stampeding soldiers slowed to a trickle by 4:00 A.M. on May 3, Huey rode to Hooker's headquarters for orders. As Huey arrived at army headquarters, Pleasonton reined in, and Huey reported to him instead. Pleasonton expressed "great surprise and pleasure on seeing me, and said 'that he was afraid we had all been captured or killed,' and 'that it was almost miraculous that we had been able to extricate ourselves from the perilous position.'" Huey thought it was "very evident" that Pleasonton "thought we *had* been surrounded and captured, and that he had lost a regiment from his small command."[117]

Pleasonton instructed Huey to cross the Rapidan and Rappahannock Rivers and picket the road from Hartwood Church toward Kelly's Ford. That night, Huey received orders to return, and the regiment bivouacked for the night near U.S. Ford on the army's far left. On May 4, instead of the blare of bugles calling reveille, the sound of Confederate artillery awoke Huey's weary horse soldiers. The shells killed two horses. After shaking themselves free of the troublesome artillerists, the Pennsylvanians moved a short distance downstream and reported to Maj. Gen. John Sedgwick at Banks's Ford. Sedgwick was withdrawing to the river after his repulse at Salem Church prevented him from joining forces with Hooker's army at Chancellorsville. Sedgwick sent Huey on to support Brig. Gen. Albion P. Howe's hard-pressed VI Corps division, and the 8th Pennsylvania lost two more horses to the heavy fire. "Lieutenants Garrett and Baker, with companies C and I of my regiment, brought up the rear, and swam their horses across the river, the pontoons having been removed," concluded Huey.[118]

These two hard-fought cavalry actions directly contributed little to the outcome of the Battle of Chancellorsville. The action in Alsop's Field delayed Stuart's advance to Todd's Tavern, and Keenan's Charge temporarily disrupted a portion of Jackson's crushing flank attack. The Federals tried to put as favorable a spin on things as possible. "I regret to add that [McVicar] lost his life in [charging the Confederates at Alsop's Field], yet such was the dash and spirit of the affair that comparatively few were lost or captured," announced Pleasonton, "and the movement, as has since been ascertained from the enemy, perplexed them not a little."[119]

Likewise Pleasonton wrote, "I immediately ordered the Eighth Pennsylvania Cavalry to proceed at a gallop, attack the rebels, and check them until we could get the artillery in position. This service was splendidly performed by the Eighth, but with heavy loss, and I gained some fifteen minutes to bring Martin's battery into position, reverse a battery of Sickles's corps, detach some cavalry to stop runaways, and secure more guns from the retreating column."[120] Unfortunately, Pleasonton credited the late Major Keenan with leading the charge, and not Major Huey, who had actually commanded the regiment that day. The slight offended Huey, who spent years trying to correct the record to reflect that he had led the charge that day, and not the ill-fated Keenan.[121]

Keenan's Charge had consequences for the battle that nobody could have foreseen. The sudden and unexpected appearance of a large force of horses on their flank badly rattled the Confederate infantrymen. Fearing the possibility of another mounted charge, the Southern pickets became especially nervous as night fell over the thick woods. Although it was moonlit, the night was very dark. Uneasy about their situation, the distinctive sounds of a body of horsemen made the Confederate vedettes nervous, and they fired on anything that moved, including Stonewall Jackson and A. P. Hill, who were out reconnoitering the Orange Turnpike in front of Jackson's corps. They hit Jackson three times, costing Jackson his arm that night, and his life a few days later. If the 8th Pennsylvania had not made its costly charge, the pickets might not have fired on Jackson. The ultimate outcome of the war might have changed as a result of Jackson's ride that night.[122]

Devin, whose small brigade lost two high-ranking officers, noted, "The regimental commanders, Colonel Kellogg, Major Huey, and Captain Beardsley, were cool, prompt, and ready in carrying out my orders, and in no one case failed in their execution while under my command." He continued, "Of those that we have lost their reputation belongs to the whole command. The daring bravery of McVicar and the splendid fighting of Keenan will not soon be forgotten by those who witnessed it."[123]

On one hand, these two unrelated and accidental cavalry actions demonstrated just how far the Federal cavalry had come since the beginning of the year. The action in Alsop's Field was hard fighting, pure and simple. Lt. Col. Duncan McVicar, a brave, popular, and competent officer, lost his life trying to lead his men out of a trap. "His death is a serious loss to the service and to the country of his adoption," mourned a Rochester, New York, newspaper.[124] Only by heroism and hard fighting did his regiment escape intact.

Likewise, Keenan's Charge demonstrated that the Union cavalry could show courage and resourcefulness under the most difficult of circumstances, and that the Northern horse soldiers could make a difference on the battlefield if given the opportunity to do so. Both the 6th New York and 8th Pennsylvania took heavy losses—in men and horses. Further, the Pennsylvanians fought a spirited and stubborn delaying action against the Virginia infantry near Zoan Church on May 1, holding off the advancing enemy until Sykes and his Regulars came up to relieve them. This foreshadowed the magnificent stand of the Union cavalry at Gettysburg sixty days later.

On the other hand, these two episodes demonstrated that hard lessons still remained to be learned by the Army of the Potomac's Cavalry Corps. First, Devin's small brigade was split up and its three regiments acted as independent commands, meaning that all three might have been an effective unit if used as a cohesive brigade. However, using these three regiments piecemeal was ineffective and inefficient. In some ways, it almost seemed like a throwback to the McClellan days, when the cavalry was not used as well as it could have been. "I let you know that we had very hard times during the fight," recounted Peter Boyer of the 17th Pennsylvania. "We had to follow the generals wherever they went and some times they took us in the thickest of the fight."[125] Second, the presence of both Pleasonton and Devin created chain-of-command problems. With only three regiments involved, either Pleasonton should not have been in field command, or Devin should not have been in command of his brigade. Three regiments had to do the work of at least a full division, and the task proved too great for one small brigade to handle. Devin's men paid dearly for Hooker's decision to strip the army of its cavalry screen.

The savage mauling caused by sending a single regiment of cavalry headlong into a large body of enemy infantry also should have taught a valuable, albeit painful and costly, lesson, but it did not. Another, more costly lesson remained to be learned two months later at Gettysburg. Finally, and most significantly, these two episodes demonstrate that the high command of the Army of the Potomac still had not learned how to make the best use of its potent mounted arm. Those difficult lessons remained to be learned. In the meantime, Devin's little brigade suffered mightily for that education.

NOTES

1. Obviously, it is not possible to chronicle fully a four-day battle the size and scope of the fight at Chancellorsville in a few paragraphs, and doing so goes beyond the scope of this book. For an excellent and well-balanced study of the campaign, see Ernest B. Furgurson, *Chancellorsville 1863: The Souls of the Brave* (New York: Alfred A. Knopf, 1992). For a study of the campaign that defends Hooker's conduct of the battle, see Stephen W. Sears, *Chancellorsville* (Boston: Houghton-Mifflin, 1996).
2. O.R., vol. 25, part 1, 777.
3. Ibid., part 2, 275.
4. Ibid., part 1, 778.
5. Ibid., 778–79.
6. *Rochester Democrat,* May 5, 1863.
7. Edward P. McKinney, *Life in Tent and Field, 1861–1865* (Boston: Richard G. Badger, 1922), 86–87; Milo S. Quaife, ed., *From the Cannon's Mouth: The Civil War Letters of General Alpheus S. Williams* (Detroit: Wayne State University Press, 1959), 182.
8. *New York Herald,* May 4, 1863.
9. *Rochester Democrat,* May 5, 1863.
10. Hall, *History of the Sixth New York,* 98.
11. Frank Saunders to his brother, May 10, 1863, Sue Martin Collection, Fairport, N.Y.
12. O.R., vol. 25, part 1, 778.
13. *Fifth Annual Reunion of the Veteran Association 6th New York Cavalry* (New York: Russell Brothers, 1891), 10.
14. Saunders to his brother, May 10, 1863.
15. Hall, *History of the Sixth New York,* 98; O.R., vol. 25, part 1, 778. The exact number of prisoners is open to debate. Colonel Devin's report states that the New Yorkers captured 100 prisoners, while the regimental history indicates that 60 prisoners were taken.
16. Ibid.

17. *New York Daily Tribune,* May 4, 1863.

18. *New York Times,* May 4, 1863.

19. McKinney, *Life in Tent and Field,* 87.

20. Hall, *History of the Sixth New York,* 101–102.

21. Ibid., 102.

22. *New York Times,* May 4, 1863.

23. Cary Breckinridge to Thomas T. Munford, January 2, 1907, John Bigelow, Jr., Papers, Manuscripts Division, Library of Congress, Washington, D.C.

24. *New York Times,* May 4, 1863.

25. Saunders to his brother, May 10, 1863.

26. Hall, *History of the Sixth New York,* 103.

27. Thomas M. Wells diary, entry for April 30, 1863, included in William L. Heermance Medal of Honor file, 825 U.S. 1880, R G 94, Entry 496, Box 300, Office of the Adjutant General, Volunteer Service Branch, National Archives, Washington, D. C.

28. Thomas T. Munford to John B. Bigelow, Jr., December 24, 1907, Bigelow Papers.

29. C. E. Adams to Thomas T. Munford, undated 1909 letter, Bigelow Papers.

30. Von Borcke, *Memoirs,* 364.

31. Ibid.

32. Hall, *History of the Sixth New York,* 115–16.

33. Saunders to his brother, May 10, 1863.

34. *New York Times,* May 4, 1863.

35. Bigelow, *Campaign of Chancellorsville,* 226.

36. Hall, *History of the Sixth New York,* 104.

37. *New York Times,* May 4, 1863.

38. Justus Scheibert, *Seven Months in the Rebel State during the North American War, 1863,* ed. William Stanley Hoole (Tuscaloosa, Ala.: Confederate, 1958), 57–58.

39. Hall, *History of the Sixth New York,* 104.

40. Carter, *Sabres, Saddles, and Spurs,* 59.

41. Thomas P. Nanzig, *3d Virginia Cavalry* (Lynchburg, Va.: H. E. Howard, 1989), 33.

42. Thomas M. Wells diary, entry for April 30, 1863.

43. Hall, *History of the Sixth New York,* 105.

44. *Fifth Annual Reunion,* 14.

45. *New York Times,* May 5, 1863.

46. Ibid., May 4, 1863.

47. George W. Goler to Russell A. Alger, November 15, 1897, Heermance Medal of Honor file.

48. *Fifth Annual Reunion,* 14.

49. Affidavit of Thomas M. Wells, November 20, 1897, Heermance Medal of Honor file.

50. Goler to Alger, November 15, 1897.

51. William L. Heermance to Col. H. E. Ainsworth, December 11, 1893, Heermance Medal of Honor file.

52. Carter, *Sabres, Saddles, and Spurs,* 59.

53. McClellan, *Life and Campaigns of J. E. B. Stuart,* 230.

54. Hall, *History of the Sixth New York,* 105.

55. Saunders to his brother, May 10, 1863.

56. Von Borcke, *Memoirs,* 365–66.

57. Saunders to his brother, May 10, 1863.

58. Adams to Munford, undated 1909 letter.

59. Munford to Bigelow, November 15, 1911, Bigelow Papers.

60. Hall, *History of the Sixth New York,* 117.

61. Driver and Howard, *2d Virginia Cavalry,* 76.

62. Bigelow, *Campaign of Chancellorsville,* 226.

63. Adams to Munford, undated 1909 letter.

64. M. T. Rucker to William E. Graves, January 18, 1909, Bigelow Papers.

65. Hall, *History of the Sixth New York,* 106; O.R., vol. 25, part 1, 779.

66. Carter, *Sabres, Saddles, and Spurs,* 59.

67. Benjamin J. Haden, *Reminiscences of J. E. B. Stuart's Cavalry* (Charlottesville, Va.: Progress, 1912), 18.

68. Thomas T. Munford to William L. Heermance, October 29, 1897, Heermance Medal of Honor file.

69. Robert T. Hubard, "Operations of General J. E. B. Stuart before Chancellorsville," *Southern Historical Society Papers* 8 (1880): 253–54.

70. *New York Herald,* May 4, 1863.

71. *Fifth Annual Reunion,* 10.

72. Hall, *History of the Sixth New York,* 106.

73. O.R., vol. 25, part 1, 779.

74. Thomas M. Wells diary, entry for April 30, 1863.

75. McClellan, *Life and Campaigns,* 231.

76. Cary Breckinridge to John B. Bigelow, Jr., February 12, 1907, Bigelow Papers.

77. Hall, *History of the Sixth New York,* 119.

78. Munford to Heermance, October 29, 1897.

79. O.R., vol. 25, part 1, 780; Charles I. Wickersham, "Personal Recollections of the Cavalry at Chancellorsville," *War Papers,* Military Order of the Loyal Legion of the United States, Wisconsin Commandery, vol. 3 (Milwaukee, Wis.: 1891), 454.

80. O.R., vol. 25, part 1, 780.

81. Ibid.

82. Ibid., 780–81.

83. Noel. G. Harrison, *Chancellorsville Battle Sites* (Lynchburg, Va.: H. E. Howard, 1990), 26.

84. Ibid., 35.

85. Wickersham, "Personal Recollections," 456–57.

86. Harrison, *Chancellorsville Battle Sites,* 40.

87. O.R., vol. 25, part 1, 781.

88. Ibid. These men made a stand in the face of the crushing Confederate flank attack that afternoon. This was the introduction to combat for the green horsemen of the 17th Pennsylvania, but they stood the assaults well. Years later, the regimental historian

noted, "Considering that this was really the first baptism of blood for the regiment, the heroic manner in which it met the mad assault of Stonewall Jackson's army by a single line of cavalry, virtually with no support, certainly reflected great credit upon the regiment. It was a trying position, but the firm front presented, saved the day, and enabled General Hooker to reform his shattered troops, and once more present an unbroken line." Henry P. Moyer, *History of the Seventeenth Regiment Pennsylvania Volunteer Cavalry* (Lebanon, Pa.: Sowers Printing, 1911), 39.

89. Andew B. Wells, "Charge of the 8th Pennsylvania Cavalry," Arnold C. Franks Collection, Tucson, Ariz.

90. Charles C. Kelsey, *To the Knife: The Biography of Major Peter Keenan, 8th Pennsylvania Cavalry* (Ann Arbor, Mich.: privately published, 1964), 38.

91. Pennock Huey, *A True History of the Charge of the Eighth Pennsylvania Cavalry at Chancellorsville* (Philadelphia: Porter & Coates, 1883), 11; Wickersham, "Personal Recollections," 460.

92. J. E. Giles to John B. Bigelow, Jr., November 1, 1908, Bigelow Papers.

93. J. Edward Carpenter, "The Charge of the 8th Pennsylvania Cavalry," Franks Collection.

94. Huey, *A True History*, 13.

95. "At Chancellorsville: The Spot Where 'Stonewall' Fell," *National Tribune*, August 27, 1882.

96. Ibid.

97. Huey, *A True History*, 13–14.

98. Bigelow, *Campaign of Chancellorsville*, 317.

99. Huey, *A True History*, 14–15; Bates, *Battle of Chancellorsville*, 232.

100. Bates, *Battle of Chancellorsville*, 232–34.

101. Wells, "Charge of the 8th Pennsylvania Cavalry."

102. Ibid.

103. Ibid.

104. Wickersham, "Personal Recollections," 460.

105. Collins, "When Stonewall Jackson Turned Our Right," 3:183–85.

106. Huey, *A True History*, 15–16.

107. William H. Bentz, "From One of Keenan's Men," *National Tribune*, October 22, 1881.

108. Wickersham, "Personal Recollections," 461–62.

109. O.R., vol. 25, part 1, 942. When he penned his report of the Battle of Chancellorsville, Rodes recorded, "During this glorious victory and pursuit of more than 2 miles, I had only three brigades really engaged. General Colquitt, soon after starting, was misled by the appearance of a small body of the enemy's cavalry, and, notwithstanding the instructions to himself and General Ramseur, halted his brigade to resist what he supposed to be an attack on his flank. This error was discovered too late to enable him to do more than follow the victorious troops of Doles over the field they had won. Ramseur, being ordered to follow Colquitt and watch his flank, was necessarily deprived of any active participation."

110. Giles to Bigelow, November 1, 1908.

111. Huey, *A True History,* 72–73.

112. Collins, "When Stonewall Jackson Turned Our Right," 3:185.

113. In fact, Colquitt wrote that he had expected to encounter Federal cavalry during Jackson's flank attack, and that he had made his dispositions accordingly. "Intelligence was communicated to me by the skirmishers that a body of the enemy was on my right flank. I ordered a halt, and called back the Sixth Georgia, which had continued to advance. The regiment upon the right [the Nineteenth Georgia] was quickly thrown into position to meet any demonstration upon the flank, and ordered to advance about 100 yards to the summit of a hill. The enemy's force proved to be a small body of cavalry, which galloped away as soon as the regiment advancing toward them was discovered, and a picket of infantry, which was captured by my skirmishers. All apprehension in this quarter being allayed, we advanced again to the front, to renew connection with the line that had preceded us. As we emerged from the woods into an open field, I discovered Doles's brigade hotly engaged with the enemy at his first works. With a shout, and at a double-quick, we moved to his support, but before we reached musket-range the enemy broke in confusion and fled. I halted in the open field, and brought up two of my regiments which had been delayed in crossing a creek and in climbing its steep banks. It was now nearly dark, and too late for further action." O.R., vol. 25, part 1, 975.

114. Wells, "Charge of the 8th Pennsylvania Cavalry."

115. Huey, *A True History,* 48.

116. Ibid., 17.

117. Ibid., 17–18. In the years following the Civil War, Major Huey, who eventually was promoted to colonel and received a brevet to brigadier general of volunteers, grew indignant at Pleasonton's treatment of the episode. When Pleasonton testified before the Committee on the Conduct of the War, he indicated that he had ordered Keenan to lead the charge, and not Huey, the regimental commander. When this rumor persisted for many years, an angry Huey penned a pamphlet to clear his name and to ensure that he received proper credit for leading the charge. Pleasonton's tendencies to stretch the truth were well known. "His account of the charge of the 8th Penn. Cav. has of course been proved without foundation and I am inclined to think there is very little truth in his account of the gathering and service of guns at Hazel Grove on the evening of the 2d May," observed a Federal officer. C. P. Morse to John B. Bigelow, Jr., February 1, 1912, Bigelow Papers. I have drawn on that pamphlet heavily in my discussion of these events.

118. O.R., vol. 25, part 1, 784.

119. O.R., vol. 25, part 1, 774.

120. Ibid., 775.

121. See Alfred Pleasonton, "The Successes and Failures of Chancellorsville," in *Battles and Leaders of the Civil War,* edited by Robert U. Johnson and Clarence C. Buel, 4 vols. (New York: Century, 1884–1888), 3:179 ("[A]s I rode forward, Major Keenan of the 8th Pennsylvania came out to meet me, when I ordered him to take the regiment, charge into the woods, which, as we had previously stood, were to our rear, and hold

the enemy in check until I could get some guns into position. He replied, with a smile the size of the task, that he would do it and started off immediately"). Pleasonton also claimed that he positioned and rallied the Federal artillery, preventing the entire Army of the Potomac from breaking and running. While Pleasonton deserves credit for being in the right place at the right time, he greatly overstated his own role. Historian Frank A. O'Reilly described Pleasonton's wild exaggerations about his role at Chancellorsville as "toxic fiction." See introduction by Frank A. O'Reilly in Augustus C. Hamlin, *The Attack of Stonewall Jackson at Chancellorsville* (Fredericksburg, Va.: Sgt. Kirkland's, 1997), viii. This is a classic example of just the sort of glory seeking that alienated Pleasonton from the men who served under him and with him. Huey wrote a book to refute Pleasonton's contention and to claim his rightful place at the head of the ill-fated charge.

122. "I have no doubt but that this extraordinary combat in the dense thicket with Huey's cavalry at about seven o'clock had kept our men in the highest state of excitement," noted a Confederate staff officer, "and the slightest movement in their front, and especially the appearance of men on horseback, caused them to be unduly apprehensive of another attack, and thus led to the greatest calamity that could have befallen the Confederate army at that time, the wounding by his own men of Stonewall Jackson." Randolph Barton, "A Cavalry Charge at Chancellorsville," *Confederate Veteran* 13 (1905), 453. For the most complete discussion of the circumstances surrounding the wounding of Stonewall Jackson, see James I. Robertson, *Stonewall Jackson: The Man, the Soldier, and the Legend* (New York: Macmillan, 1997), 724–36.

123. O.R., vol. 25, part 1, 783.

124. *Rochester Democrat,* May 5, 1863.

125. Peter Boyer to his father, May 1863, Peter Boyer Letters, USAMHI.

6

THE ELEMENT OF SURPRISE IS LOST:
A FALSE START FOR STONEMAN'S RAID

On April 28, the men of the Cavalry Corps drew five days' rations and three days' forage for their horses. They received orders to be ready to move out at a moment's notice. They struck their tents, loaded their wagons, saddled their horses, and waited. Near midnight, a hard rain resumed, drenching men and beasts as they stood waiting for orders to march.[1] All of the men whose horses could not withstand great fatigue or the coming ordeal were sent to Pleasonton.[2] The great raid finally began on April 29, after the level of the river briefly dropped low enough to permit a crossing by Stoneman's command.[3] "As we filed out last night from our old camp in silence," recorded Nathan B. Webb of the 1st Maine, "everything had a weird somber look. All were mute. We knew we had started in earnest and no one was inclined to make any remarks at least before morning."[4]

"We have undoubtedly some pretty hot work before us," recounted Sgt. Christian Geisel of the 6th Pennsylvania, "where we are going is not publicly known, but the general opinion is here that we are to get into the rear of the rebel army of the Rappahannock and cut off their communication from Richmond, while General Hooker will attack them with the Infantry."[5] Capt. Charles Francis Adams of the 1st Massachusetts Cavalry doubted "whether we ever should get across that miserable little river."[6]

Buford and the Regulars slogged out of their camp to the accompaniment of their band, which played "Listen to the Mocking Bird."[7] Each man carried three days' rations for himself and his horse, while a supply train of pack mules carried an additional three days' rations for the men and two for their horses. No wagon trains burdened the raiders.[8] The troopers were told to carry only those items that would fit in saddlebags or rolled up in a blanket. The typical trooper's inventory included a shirt, a pair of socks, a needle and thread, some paper and envelopes, a tin cup, and a bag each of coffee and tobacco. Some few carried a towel and soap, but for the most part, they were learning to travel light. "At first the soldier thinks he must have this article of luxury and the other, until he finds that they are positive burdens to himself and horse, and gradually he throws off this weight and that encumbrance until his entire outfit is reduced to nearly 'the little end of nothing, whittled to a point!'" noted an officer of the 2d New York Cavalry. "Possessed of a coffee-bag, and a cup of hard tack or biscuit, the most essential things, he seldom now borrows much trouble about his surroundings."[9]

The passage of three divisions of cavalry, something never seen before on the North American continent, was quite a spectacle. The Yankee saddle soldiers were not used to moving together in large masses, and it showed. "A cavalry column was a sight to behold, as it straggled along in uneven paces, keeping none for more than a minute," recalled a captain of the 6th Pennsylvania Cavalry who served on Stoneman's staff. "When from a decorous walk, which was easy to man and beast, they would break into a furious gallop, while officers shouted 'Close up! Close up!' and tin pans rattled, and sabers swung dangerously to and fro, blankets slipped, backs galled into shocking sores, feedbags split open, and oats were sowed on the trampled highway; then there would be a shock as if two railroad trains had collided and pulled up with a sudden halt, the panting horses would gasp for breath, while the riders wonder whatever had happened to the head of the column, to which nothing had happened at all."[10] The Northern horsemen had a lot of lessons to learn, and going off on an extended raid was a new experience for them. The Stoneman Raid offered them the first opportunity to do so. They presented quite a spectacle as they struggled to work as cohesive units.

AVERELL'S DIVISION

After finally crossing the Rappahannock, Stoneman detached Averell's division, along with Grimes Davis's brigade of Pleasonton's division and some horse artillery, to march by way of Brandy Station and Culpeper, where they would engage Brig. Gen. W. H. F. "Rooney" Lee's Confederate cavalry brigade. Averell received his orders on the morning of April 28, and immediately sent an officer to reconnoiter Beverly's Ford. His mission was to defeat the Confederate cavalry force in Culpeper County, operate against the Orange & Alexandria Railroad, and then rejoin the rest of Stoneman's column at the Anna Rivers near Richmond to block the Richmond, Fredericksburg and Potomac Railroad.[11]

Averell and McIntosh, commanding one of Averell's brigades, conducted their own reconnaissance. The two officers decided that high waters made the ford unusable. Averell then marched his division downstream to Kelly's Ford, and had to wait for the III Corps infantry to finish crossing before his column could move out. The high waters made the crossing of the foot soldiers tricky, but they managed as the horsemen sat and watched. "We are waiting," scrawled a Hoosier in his diary. "What awaits us time will tell."[12]

"It was an exciting time," recorded a member of the 6th Ohio Cavalry. "Several horses and men were swept down stream and were drowned. Everyone received a thorough wetting."[13] Three columns crossed the Rappahannock simultaneously, one swimming, one fording, and one on the pontoon.[14] An officer of the 4th Pennsylvania Cavalry recalled that the Kelly's Ford Road presented "one of the grandest sights" he had ever seen. "For miles over the face of a perfectly level country stretched our line of mounted skirmishers, steadily advancing in most excellent order, and driving back the enemy's skirmishers," he continued. Averell's skirmishers led the way while flankers and the main body followed, using the open fields on either side of the road to facilitate the movement.[15]

Averell's men encountered a small body of troopers from Rooney Lee's 13th Virginia Cavalry near the old Kelly's Ford battlefield. At Col. Horace B. Sargent's order, the Rhode Islanders drew sabers and drove the Virginians from the field after a brief but sharp skirmish. "A huge concentration of Yankee cavalry struck our picket at Kelly's Ford with such force that we had to retire," recalled a Virginia horse soldier. "Stuart immediately relayed this information on to Gen. [Robert E.] Lee who had anticipated the enemy advance for some time. We began intensive scouting to gather all information that might be of service to Gen. Lee."[16]

This engagement had "almost the dignity of a battle," recalled one Rhode Islander. "The dispute was short. They retired to their old position of March 17th, not caring to meet again, as on that sorely remembered day, the charge and steel of the Yankees." Three members of the 1st Rhode Island Cavalry were captured, and one horse was killed in this brisk skirmish.[17] The rest of the blueclad horsemen finally made their way across the Rappahannock at 5:00 that afternoon and pushed on until dark, stopping short of Brandy Station, their objective for the day.[18] The men of the 16th Pennsylvania kept their horses in line all night, and many of them slept at the heads of their mounts, the animals tied to their wrists.[19] "Halted some time in the night and spent the remainder of it in line in rain and mud and Morpheus' arms," recorded an Indiana trooper in his diary.[20] That night, Averell heard from a deserter that Jeb Stuart and four brigades of Confederate cavalry and fifteen pieces of horse artillery waited for him near Brandy Station.[21]

The 13th Virginia was "nearly surrounded at Brandy Station, but the main body succeeded at passing the enemy during the night. The remainder cut their way through with no loss," recalled a Southern officer.[22] "General Lee, with his small force, fell back before Averell's advance, one squadron being kept near the enemy to retard his progress, until the Rapidan was crossed, when he disposed his men and one gun above the station, to give battle if the attempt to cross was made," noted another.[23]

On April 30, "the boys were up at sunrise and groomed and fed their horses," recalled a member of the 8th New York.[24] After breakfast, the regimental commanders inspected their men, and every trooper riding an unserviceable horse was sent to the rear before the balance of the division moved out.[25] Several members of the 16th Pennsylvania Cavalry plundered the Kelly house. "He is said to be a rank rebel, who fired on our men as they were crossing," rationalized trooper John Follmer. "Plundering does not seem to be right. The house was entered and ladies insulted. The men also broke into a sick lady's chamber, and insulted the husband in her presence. The men claim to come from an enlightened country, but are a disgrace to the army."[26] In the meantime, the 1st Rhode Island briefly visited the grave of Lt. Henry S. Nicolai, killed during the Battle of Kelly's Ford. During the battle, they had hastily buried the lieutenant in the middle of the battlefield and had to depart without marking the grave. His comrades respectfully placed a stone, marked with an "N," over the fallen lieutenant's grave. After paying their respects, the 1st Rhode Island moved out again.[27]

Because Averell had sent his wagon and mule trains back at the beginning of the expedition, his men had to live off the land.[28] "We certainly calculated on a fight that morning," recalled Capt. Charles Francis Adams of the 1st Massachusetts, "but when morning came the rumor crept round that the enemy was gone and so it proved. It had stolen away like a thief in the night and left open to us the road to Culpeper."[29] At 7:00 A.M., still expecting to run into at least two full brigades of enemy horsemen, Averell and his 3,400 horsemen moved out toward Culpeper, arriving about 11:00 A.M. "A column in the road and one each side in the fields were moved all day," observed an officer of the 1st Massachusetts Cavalry, "Sometimes by fours, sometimes by squadrons."[30] In order to guard against any lurking enemy horsemen, the three columns kept three quarters of a mile between them. Stoneman had instructed Averell to "push the enemy as vigorously as possible, keeping him fully occupied, and, if possible, drive him in the direction of Rapidan Station."[31]

As his men entered the town where the gallant Pelham died, Averell learned that Stuart had taken part of the Confederate cavalry force toward Stevensburg while the two Lees headed toward the Rapidan River crossings. Fanning out through the streets of Culpeper, the Northerners captured a large quantity of meat, flour, and other supplies intended for the Army of Northern Virginia. Without a means to cart away their booty, the Union horse soldiers put it to the torch, leaving a roaring bonfire in their wake.[32]

Averell arrived at Cedar Mountain about 4:00 P.M. on April 30. "The enemy was pursued rapidly beyond Cedar Mountain toward the Rapidan," reported Averell.

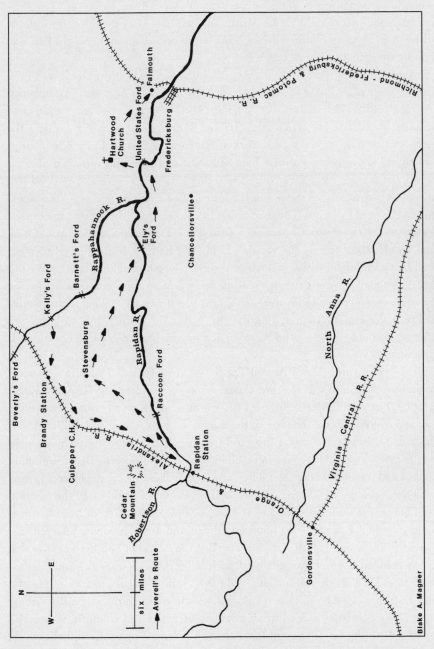

Averell's Expedition, April 29–May 6, 1863

Blake A. Magner

"From all that could be learned from prisoners, contrabands, and citizens, it was believed that two brigades of the enemy's cavalry were flying before us." The Federals marched past the old Cedar Mountain battlefield, seeing the grim sight of "many of the bones of human beings lying about on the ground," a sight that sent chills up the spines of Averell's men.[33]

It started raining again, slowing Averell's advance and raising the level of the Rapidan once more. "One of the hardest days rides we have ever seen," complained a member of the 3d Indiana Cavalry.[34] The Northerners did not reach the Rapidan until after dark. "The rebels threw two or three shells at us, which brought the regiment to a halt," noted a New Yorker. His men bivouacked in a heavy forest that night.[35] The enemy gunners harassed their camp and pickets all night.[36] A member of the 8th New York complained that he and his comrades camped in a mud hole that night.[37] A New Englander recalled that this site was "the worst camping ground I ever saw. The mud and water stood everywhere up to the horses' fetlocks and our ankles and it seemed a dead flat."[38] Had it rained, they would have been flooded. Fortunately, the weather held. "We had not been allowed to build fires during the night, which was damp and cold," recounted an officer of the 6th Ohio. "You may imagine that our situation was not in all respects agreeable. But the boys did not grumble any for they thought it was necessary."[39] That night, Stoneman sent Averell a message stating that he "turns the enemy over to you," and ordering Averell to move toward Rapidan Station, driving the grayclad horsemen as he went.[40]

The next morning, May 1, Averell, Davis, and Capt. John C. Tidball, a fine horse artillerist and Buford's West Point classmate, reconnoitered the Rapidan River crossings. The three officers observed the enemy's works on the other side of the river and concluded "the defenses of the enemy . . . were strong and skillfully constructed. Nothing but a direct fire could be brought to bear upon their works from the north side. Their pits were filled with sharpshooters, who completely commanded the ford and bridge." They saw four artillery pieces deployed to command the crossings. "It was my opinion at the time that I could carry the position by a charge, the same as was done at Kelly's Ford on the 17th of March, but it would require the sacrifice of a hundred officers and men," concluded Averell.

Averell, Davis, and Tidball were surprised by a squadron of Southern cavalry that "nearly gobbled" them, as Averell described it in his diary. Rooney Lee had directed Col. Richard L. T. Beale, commander of the 9th Virginia Cavalry, to take a squadron and break through Averell's line of skirmishers in order to draw out the enemy force. The Virginians charged in an effort to ascertain the strength of Averell's force.[41] "With drawn sabers, and our Adjutant's clerk, William Campbell, taking the lead, the squadron charged with a yell," recounted Colonel Beale.

The Northern commander waved his saber and urged his men forward, but the blueclad horse soldiers wheeled and fled. The "gallant fellow, leaping his fine charger over the fence to our right, held his ground till abreast of us, and then after emptying his pistol on us, retreated unscathed by the dozen bullets which were fired at his person." The Virginians pursued until they came upon Averell's main body. "Enough was discovered to satisfy us that the force in front of our little command was overwhelming," recorded Beale. The Virginians withdrew with two casualties. They captured a captain of the 8th Illinois Cavalry when they overran a picket post.[42]

On the night of April 30, Colonel Sargent, his brigade commander, summoned Lt. Daniel H. L. Gleason of the 1st Massachusetts Cavalry to headquarters. "Mr. Gleason, you know the weakest part of the picket line is usually where two regiments meet; you will take two good men, well mounted, and go out and see that the vedettes are doing their duty, and that the whole front is well protected," ordered Sargent. Gleason and two noncommissioned officers spent much of the night wandering about checking on the pickets. They arrived at Rapidan Station about 7:00 on the morning of May 1, where they discovered that a force of enemy cavalry was about to charge across the river.

Sure enough, the Southerners dashed across the river and drove in Averell's pickets. Gleason found himself facing the enemy with only a rail fence dividing them. "Drawing my Colt, I fired six shots into or at them, then with a Smith and Wesson began a second round." Somehow, the lieutenant missed his targets, and five of the alerted Southerners tore a hole in the fence and spurred after him. "My security was at an end, and putting spurs to [my horse] I headed for home, over a fence and into another field," said Gleason. A deep gully blocked his way, and two grayclad horsemen were hot on his tail. With only two shots left, Gleason looked for an opportunity to make the best of them. He wounded one of his pursuers but missed the other.

Out of ammunition, Gleason tried to draw his saber, but his heavy overcoat made it difficult. When he could not free the blade, the pursuing Rebel officer, a lieutenant of the 6th Virginia Cavalry, "ordered me in choice language to surrender, or he would shoot." Gleason stared down the barrel of the Southerner's pistol and saw that there were no bullets visible, meaning that it was also empty.

"What, with that pistol?" Gleason inquired.

"Yes, damn you, it's loaded," came the reply.

Gleason laughed and said, "I've got two in my holsters in the same condition," and declined to surrender. The Rebel drew up alongside Gleason and the two men, still mounted and moving, wrestled each other, all the while struggling to stay in their saddles. The Southerner struck Gleason with the pistol, gashing his forehead above his eyes.

Soon, a ditch faced them, and Gleason's horse, which did not like getting wet, stopped short. Both horsemen were dismounted while their horses ran away. Gleason drew his saber and ran at his pursuer, who fled. Later that day, Gleason found the Virginian lying wounded on the side of the road. He tried to make the man as comfortable as he could. The Southerner asked Gleason why he did not surrender when ordered, saying, "If my pistol had been loaded I would have blown your brains out."

"No doubt," replied Gleason, "but you wouldn't have been fool enough to tell me it was loaded if it had been." The two men had a good laugh, and Gleason left his wounded foe behind.[43]

"A squad of rebel cav charged across but were repulsed with a loss of several of their number captured," noted a trooper of the 16th Pennsylvania in his diary.[44] Averell "got sharpshooters at work from the houses and the battery playing on the pits, but could not drive them out." The Federals advanced cautiously, prompting the Confederates to try to burn the bridge and open on the Federals with their artillery; this triggered a severe counterbattery duel. However, the constant rains had waterlogged the timbers of the bridge. In spite of their best efforts, the Virginians could not cause it to catch fire.

Averell sent a dismounted squadron of the 9th New York Cavalry of Davis's brigade toward the bridge. The New Yorkers carried kindling and kerosene to fire the trestle. At about noon they advanced, and a tremendous volley greeted them, driving them back and forcing the New Yorkers to seek cover in a nearby cemetery. Using headstones for cover, they returned fire. Scattered firing continued for most of the afternoon. As darkness fell on May 1, the Confederates broke off the engagement and finally managed to set the bridge on fire, saving the New Yorkers the trouble.[45] "The enemy thought we wished to preserve it so they fired it first," explained a member of the 3d Pennsylvania Cavalry.[46]

Averell had no way of knowing that his force outnumbered the Confederates by nine regiments to one. Well-positioned Southern carbineers on high ground overlooking the swollen river laid down a heavy fire. The New Yorker responded by shifting troops to the right. They waded across the flooded Robinson River and approached Barnett's Ford on the Rapidan about four miles upriver from the railroad crossing. By burning the bridge, Rooney Lee forced Averell to find another crossing farther east. His men had to make a forced march in the inky blackness of a cloudy night.

Averell interviewed two prisoners from the 9th Virginia Cavalry. One of them informed him that he faced Rooney Lee's horsemen, but that infantry, artillery, and cavalry reinforcements were hurrying from Gordonsville. "Precisely what effect this answer had on the mind of General Averell cannot be definitely stated," recounted an officer of the 9th Virginia. "All the circumstances seem to indicate that it had great weight, for no attempt was made to push his command farther."[47]

However, Stuart had ordered Rooney Lee to break off from Averell and to ride off toward Gordonsville to confront the main body of Stoneman's raiders.[48] Thirty men of the 9th Virginia Cavalry stayed behind to create a distraction for the Federals. Although the Virginians captured more then two dozen troopers and a captain, a counterattack freed the prisoners and drove off the intrepid little band of Virginians, costing Colonel Beale two casualties of his own as the railroad bridge blazed in the gathering darkness. One Federal was killed and two or three other men were wounded in the exchange before the Southern horsemen finally withdrew after twelve long hours.[49]

The men of the 6th Ohio captured a captain of the 4th Virginia Cavalry, who was returning to his regiment after a visit home. "He had no idea that the Yankees were in that part of the country," recorded Capt. Delos Northway of the 6th Ohio, "and when he saw our boys coming toward him with orders for his surrender, he said he thought it was some of his own men trying to play a trick on him." The captain surrendered and the Ohioans moved on, surprising the local populace, which was unaccustomed to the sight of large parties of Northerners riding about the countryside unhindered.[50]

Hooker, whose army was engaged in mortal combat at Chancellorsville, recognized that his flank was largely uncovered due to the lack of a strong force of cavalry. When Hooker learned that Averell's force was not far off on its raid, he concluded that Averell had not fulfilled his orders, and that his 3,400 men had neither brought the enemy cavalry to battle nor joined Stoneman's main body. As a result, Hooker grew livid. He fired off a testy dispatch to Averell, having an aide write, "I am directed by the major-general commanding to inform you that he does not understand what you are doing at Rapidan Station. If this finds you at that place, you will immediately return to United States Ford and remain there until further orders, and report in person." Averell retorted, "I have been engaged with the cavalry of the enemy at that point and in destroying communications," and enclosed a copy of Stoneman's April 30 orders to support his position.[51]

The next day, May 2, Averell decided to cross the Rapidan at Raccoon Ford and try to join Buford's command. He drew in his pickets on the right and prepared to march. Averell was surprised to receive an order from Hooker directing him to "report in person with your entire command, save one regiment." The single regiment left behind was to patrol the area between the RF&P Railroad and the Orange and Alexandria Railroad, and "must be kept well thrown out, for the purpose of giving timely notice of any raids and destroying any guerrilla parties that may invade that district."[52] Averell and his division marched to Ely's Ford via Stevensburg. "To our immense surprise, [we] found ourselves on the back track," reported Adams. "They said that we had accomplished all we came for, but we couldn't see it, and we didn't relish our march."[53] "Long march," noted Hoosier Samuel Gilpin in his diary, "Many horses played out."[54]

They stopped to graze their horses at Stevensburg for a couple of hours before moving on toward the Rapidan.[55] As the Northern horsemen advanced, they heard the heavy infantry battle raging around Chancellorsville. Stonewall Jackson's Corps blocked Averell's way, making the advance more challenging. They arrived at Ely's Ford at 10:30 that night, and pitched their camp. As a result of careless dispositions, the blueclad horsemen failed to push out pickets to the other side of the river, leaving their camp open to surprise attack.

After dark that evening, Jeb Stuart, bored and without anything to do, proposed that he take a regiment of infantry and some cavalry to take and hold the Ely's Ford Road. Jackson approved the request, and Stuart set out with the 16th North Carolina Infantry of Maj. Gen. William Dorsey Pender's division and the 1st Virginia Cavalry in tow. About an hour later, Stuart and his little column arrived on the crest of the high hill overlooking the ford.[56] "Calling a halt, the General and I rode cautiously forward to reconnoiter the enemy a little more closely, and we managed to approach near enough to hear distinctly the voices and distinguish the figures of the men sitting round their fires, or strolling through the camp," recalled Maj. Heros von Borcke. "The unexpected presence of so large a body of the enemy immediately in our path entirely disconcerted our previous arrangements." Instead Stuart decided "on giving them a slight surprise and disturbing their comfort by a few volleys from our infantry." While the North Carolinians formed a line of battle, a messenger arrived to inform Stuart that Jackson had been wounded and that the cavalryman was to take command of his corps. Stuart left von Borcke in command of the expedition, and as Stuart rode off, the North Carolinians opened fire on Averell's sleeping camp. As Stuart planned, the unexpected volleys by the Tar Heels had the desired result.[57]

"A hail of bullets rattled through the forest, and as volley after volley was fired, the confusion and dismay occasioned in the camp was indescribable," recalled von Borcke. "Soldiers and officers could be plainly seen by the light of the fires rushing helplessly about, horses were galloping wildly in all directions, and the sound of bugles and drums mingled with the cries of the wounded and flying, who sought in the distant woods a shelter against the murderous fire of their unseen enemy." After keeping up the firing for half an hour, von Borcke ordered the North Carolinians to break off and withdraw. As the infantrymen marched back toward the main Confederate body, von Borcke spurred ahead in order to find Stuart.[58]

"About 10 pm while I was cleaning my horse a regiment of rebs fired 3 volleys into us from the opisite side of the river," recalled Jacob Beidler of the 16th Pennsylvania. "Killed 1 man out of Company A of our regiment & wounded some, I know not how many. I was taken very cool, only our Lieut. Col. Robison, he did not know what he was doing. He would give one command at one time, then again something else. Our horses run every direction. But we let the horses run &

formed a line & gave them a few volleys, then gathered up our horses & fell back about one mile & there halted."[59]

Maj. Henry Lee Higginson of the 1st Massachusetts Cavalry roused his men quickly as the Southerners attacked Averell's camps. "I went out with some carbineers into a wood on foot to hold it," he recorded in his diary. "Great confusion in the arrangement of our brigade. Col. [Sargent] knew nothing of his regiment or of the ground. General Averell decided it was a mistake of our own infantry." Accordingly, Higginson left a small picket and went back to sleep, the crisis past.[60] Fortunately, the presence of Averell's division meant that the escape route offered by Ely's Ford remained available to the Army of the Potomac.

On the morning of May 3, Averell sent a party of men to reconnoiter the enemy's left, to see whether his horse soldiers might make an impact on that side. The scouting party returned with nine prisoners in tow. They then destroyed a bridge over the Rapidan River, and Averell rode off to report to General Hooker.[61] "Found him prostrated with energy," noted Averell. "Talked with Slocum and others, found that we had met a severe check—lost 10,000."

After consulting with "Fighting Joe" at U.S. Ford on May 3, Averell returned to his division. The rest of Averell's men were not heavily engaged at Chancellorsville. They sat in the soaking rain and listened to the booming of the guns as the battle raged.[62] Even with the rains, the day of rest was welcome. "We made a long march yesterday, and our horses are getting weak from want of feed," observed a Pennsylvanian in his diary.[63] "A thousand doubtful stories are in circulation as usual," recorded a Hoosier, "The great number of wounded tells of the fierceness of the struggle. Riding along the lines and where they are collected and seeing their condition makes me tired of the war."[64]

On May 4, Averell's division crossed the Rappahannock River on pontoons at U.S. Ford. They marched to the familiar grounds around Hartwood Church, where they formed a picket line to protect the main body of Hooker's army, which began a full retreat after its defeat at Chancellorsville on May 5. The miserable and demoralized Northern troopers suffered on the picket line while the rains started anew. By May 6, they had returned to their original camps near Falmouth. It seemed like nothing had changed, in spite of all that they had accomplished since Hooker took command of the Army of the Potomac in January.[65]

A little after sunrise, Capt. George Bliss, with sixty men of the 1st Rhode Island and forty men of the 6th Ohio, commanded by Maj. Preston M. Farrington, who had recovered from his wound at Kelly's Ford, reported to Maj. Gen. John F. Reynolds on the right of the Union line at Chancellorsville. Reynolds sent the horse soldiers to Ely's Ford to hold the Rapidan River crossing, as it appeared that the Army of the Potomac would be retreating in the wake of its defeat at Chancellorsville. The little column moved out, and fought its way through Fitz Lee's cavalry, taking nearly three hours to do so. This intrepid band of Union horse soldiers finally made their way to the Ford and held it, standing in line with drawn sabers, keeping the Army of the Potomac's line of retreat open. The gallant group then fought their way back to safety and rejoined the rest of the division.[66]

A livid Hooker relieved Averell of command on May 4, sending Pleasonton to deliver the bad news in person. Hooker claimed that Averell had entirely disregarded his orders for the expedition, "in consequence thereof, the services of nearly 4,000 cavalry were lost, or nearly lost, to the country during an eventful period, when it was his plain duty to have rendered services of incalculable value. It is not excuse or justification of his course that he received instructions from General Stoneman in conflict with my own, and it was his duty to know that neither of them afforded an excuse for his culpable indifference and inactivity. If he disregarded all instructions, it was his duty to do something. If the enemy did not come to him, he should have gone to the enemy." Hooker noted that Averell's force greatly outnumbered any enemy forces in the area, that his march was largely unopposed, and that Averell's division covered more than fifty miles without fighting the enemy's cavalry. Hooker's greatest complaint, however, was, "It is unnecessary for me to add that this army will never be able to accomplish its mission under commanders who not only disregard their instructions, but at the same time display so little zeal and devotion in the performance of their duties. I could excuse General Averell in his disobedience if I could anywhere discover in his operations a desire to find and engage the enemy."[67]

Twelve years after the war, Hooker remained bitter about Averell's conduct during the Stoneman Raid. "If he had attempted to give my orders a flagrant and full disobedience, he could not have made his dispositions to accomplish that purpose more complete," he complained in a letter to historian Samuel P. Bates. "He did not strike the Rail Road on the 3rd and encountered a train filled with prisoners and wounded men, but doing the Rail Road no damage, beyond a temporary delay. . . . On the 3rd of May, hearing that Genl. Averell was not one day's march from me, I ordered him in, his loss having been two men wounded and one killed."[68]

Col. William E. Doster of the 4th Pennsylvania Cavalry spotted Averell sitting alone in his headquarters tent on the day before the disconsolate general departed for Washington. Averell sat "quite alone," Doster observed, "with his head resting on his hand . . . dejected." Doster thought that the deposed division commander appeared "much like a condemned cavalry horse."[69]

Averell's removal from command was unjustified, and he knew it. Hooker had ordered him to operate along the Orange & Alexandria Railroad and against the Confederate cavalry defending it. In fact, had Hooker called for Averell's division sooner, Jackson's flank attack might not have gone undetected, and it also might not have been as successful with a full division of cavalry to guard the flank.

When he arrived at Culpeper on May 1, Averell did just as Hooker ordered, directing his attentions to the Confederate railroads. He chased off the Southern defenders and obeyed the orders of his direct superior, Stoneman, who had instructed Averell to push the Confederates to Rapidan Station and keep them fully occupied. Again, Averell did just as he was instructed. He obeyed both the letter and the spirit of his orders. If Hooker had not recalled him, Averell undoubtedly would have reached Gordonsville by dark on May 2, but he never got the chance. Stoneman, Averell's direct superior, had given the division commander differing orders from those given by Hooker. Averell did what good soldiers do—he obeyed the orders of his direct superior. Averell realized that if he took care of his troopers, they would take care of their mission. His instinct to protect his command is often misconstrued as undue caution and lack of aggressiveness. The New Yorker was keenly aware of his duty to protect the lives of the soldiers entrusted to his command, and he always acted accordingly. Undoubtedly, Hooker's inability to communicate with Averell aggravated the situation further.

In his zeal to find scapegoats for the disaster that befell him at Chancellorsville, Hooker directed his wrath at the unfortunate Averell. When he reported to the Adjutant General of the army in Washington, D.C., Averell did not go quietly: "[A]s the orders seem to be unjust towards him, he asks for an enquiry respecting his conduct."[70] His request for a court of inquiry was swept under the rug, and nothing more came of it.

Whether he deserved it or not, Averell was finished with the Army of the Potomac. The officer who had proposed an ambitious and aggressive cavalry raid just a few months earlier was exiled in disgrace. He was banished to Wheeling, West Virginia, where he took charge of a ragtag band of cavalry that desperately needed Averell's firm and guiding hand. In time, he whipped them into an effective and efficient mounted command that pulled off a daring raid, relieving pressure from besieged Federal forces in Knoxville. This division became a solid and reliable command that played an important role in the Shenandoah Valley Campaign of 1864.

On May 14, Averell noted in his diary, "Tried to gain some satisfaction at War Dept. did not succeed." A few days later, he recorded, "[C]ould get no explanation of the causes of my being relieved from my command in the Army of the Potomac."[71] He tried to get a court of inquiry to find out the reasons for his relief, but the request was never approved.[72] Averell knew that Hooker intended to make him a scapegoat for the loss at Chancellorsville, and he resisted it to the best of his ability, making sure that the official records reflected his protest and declarations of innocence.[73] The experience crushed Averell, who never forgave Hooker for the treatment he received at the commanding general's hands.

"Averell was an experienced soldier and, within limits, an excellent division commander. But he was lacking in aggressiveness; his division on the whole was well commanded; his dispositions were always skillful; he never met with disaster but he never inflicted serious damage upon the enemy," observed a Regular officer years after the war.[74] "Our brigade was with Averell's division during the late advance," complained a member of the 8th New York Cavalry of Grimes Davis's brigade, "and the boys are all regretting that owing to that officer's neglect to join Stoneman, they were unable to accompany the expedition to Richmond."[75]

Lt. Louis H. Carpenter of the 6th U.S. reported on the rumors flying about the camps of the Cavalry Corps on May 13: "General Stoneman asserts that Averell willfully disobeyed position orders. He was directed to advance his column upon Gordonsville, but when he arrived at the Rapidan, he allowed our column to advance into the enemy's country and retired himself to the Rappahannock."[76] While certainly untrue, these rumors destroyed any chance Averell might have had for reinstatement. The men did not want to see him go. "He's the best we have," observed Charles Francis Adams a few days after the raid.[77] A few days later, Duffié, the senior brigade commander, took over the division, even though he was only a colonel. The French sergeant soon proved that divisional command was beyond his competence. Col. Luigi Palma di Cesnola of the 4th New York succeeded Duffié in command of the brigade.

Averell's relief nearly cost the Cavalry Corps an important officer. Col. John B. McIntosh, who learned his trade under Averell's tutelage during the early days of the 3d Pennsylvania Cavalry, remained fiercely loyal to his former commander even after Averell's relief. He complained about the misuse of his horse soldiers after his mentor left.[78] McIntosh, enraged by Hooker's action, threatened to resign his commission several times over the coming weeks, only to be talked out of it by his more cool-headed wife.[79] McIntosh was, perhaps, Averell's most important legacy, and his decision not to resign preserved his service for the Union. He became one of the finest tactical commanders in the Army of the Potomac's Cavalry Corps.[80]

THE REST OF STONEMAN'S COLUMN MOVES OUT

While Averell's command marched on the morning of April 28, Gregg's division and Buford's reserve brigade, with Stoneman at the head, went to Stevensburg, where the disparate elements of the command would sortie in different directions. The cavalrymen halted for the night in a freshly ploughed farm field, "and without fire, or shelter from a cold merciless storm, we spent the night," recalled Chaplain Gracey. "It was dark and dreary in the extreme; no bugle calls were sounded, and strict silence was observed, as we were supposed to be in proximity to the rebels. The vivid flashes of lightning alone illuminated the scene." A New Englander noted, "We sat in the saddle drawn up in line of battle, all night, raining as hard as it would, and dark as Egypt."[81] The misery of the Yankees increased during the night when straggling bands of Confederate cavalry charged their pickets. Moreover, they did not know what their mission or destination was. This uncertainty increased their unease.[82]

Dr. John B. Coover, the regimental surgeon of the 6th Pennsylvania Cavalry, recalled that morning as "the most disagreeable one I have ever seen."[83] That day, the blueclad horse soldiers fanned out across the countryside. Foraging parties emptied corncribs and barns and helped themselves to the rich bounties of the area. "Every smokehouse and farmyard near the line of march was made to contribute to our comfort," noted Chaplain Gracey. "Chickens, ducks, and hams, in great numbers, were secured."[84]

Stoneman's objective was the important transportation center of Louisa Court House. The Virginia Central Railroad passed through Louisa, and several major arteries cut through or near the town, including the Marquis Road, an ancient route of commerce named for the Marquis de Lafayette. The soggy Northerners mounted and moved out toward Raccoon Ford. "All felt as though they were going forward to the accomplishment of an object of the greatest importance to the army and the country," observed an optimistic Stoneman.[85]

The advance elements of Buford's brigade reached Raccoon Ford on the Rapidan about noon on April 30. Capt. Charles L. Leiper of the 6th Pennsylvania Cavalry led a reconnaissance and encountered a rebel force not far from the ford. Leiper scattered the enemy with a lance charge, returning with eleven prisoners, but losing Lt. Thompson Lenning of Company M, captured by the Confederates. Buford learned the condition of the surrounding country from these prisoners and hurried his command across the Rapidan. Stoneman and Gregg sat up on the riverbank, exhorting their men to press on while Col. Judson Kilpatrick urged his command to "keep closed up, keep well upstream."[86] One of Kilpatrick's officers recalled, "The water being much above the fording mark and very rapid, we had an exciting time. Several horses and men were swept down the stream by the swift current and were drowned; and none of us escaped the unpleasant operation of getting wet."[87]

Stoneman expected an attack by Rooney Lee's lurking troopers, so he sent out pickets in all directions and ordered his men to spend the night standing to horse in line of battle on a high plateau overlooking the river crossing. The Federals did not know where the Southern horsemen were, and "It was a season of considerable anxiety to all, and of great fatigue especially to those of us who had been in the saddle several consecutive days and nights." The men got little rest that night. Many either defied their orders or, exhausted, sank to the ground, trying to grab a few moments of sleep at the heads of their faithful horses.[88] With a staunchly

Unionist local man named G. S. Smith as his guide, Stoneman made his headquarters at Willis Madden's tavern between Stevensburg and Germanna Ford, nine miles east of Culpeper. Although Madden was a loyal Union man who regularly provided valuable intelligence to the Union high command, Federal troopers nevertheless helped themselves to two of Madden's horses and fifty bushels of corn.[89]

"Stoneman, with his full corps of cavalry, is sweeping down in a wide circle, determined, with skill, energy, and dash, to retrieve the liquidated laurels of the past fortnight," reported a correspondent of the *New York Daily Tribune* traveling with the Cavalry Corps. "He delayed, dilly-dallied, and finally failed in his expedition to an extent that would have defeated the entire plan of operation but for the double resources of the commanding General." Prophetically, the correspondent concluded, "What the infantry has now accomplished Stoneman should have done with his cavalry ten days ago, by a bold dash across the rivers and a sweep to the enemy's rear. It is to be that he now covers over the disgrace of the past two weeks, by a brilliant success in a raid on the Rebel lines of communication, he may regain the confidence of his friends; if not, his reputation will be lost, and his career as a commander of cavalry at an end."[90]

After crossing and joining the rest of the column, Buford's Reserve Brigade established a miserable bivouac. "Hungry, wet, and fatigued, we were illy prepared to spend a night standing to horse, but such were our orders," remembered Chaplain Gracey. "[A]nd without unsaddling, the regiment was drawn up in close column of companies, the men dismounted, and ordered to stand at their horses' heads all night. No fires could be kindled, and as a dense fog settled down in the valley during the night, it became very cold, and our clothing being wet, we suffered greatly before morning." Stoneman forbade fires among the ranks, but his staff officers soon kindled a raging bonfire outside his headquarters. A number of members of the 1st New Jersey Cavalry spotted the dancing flames, approached with their coffee cups in hand, and begged permission to boil their coffee and dry their soggy clothes by the bonfire before they fell asleep in the flickering light of the fire.[91]

At 2:00 A.M., the Federals swung into the saddle, but the thick fog hindered their progress. Finally, Gregg's division, along with the Lancers and Buford's Regulars, marched southwest through Orange Springs and then on to Louisa Court House. Periodically, the Yankees found and chased Confederate soldiers along the way. The 1st New Jersey, leading the Yankee column, pounced upon a Confederate picket post, capturing a major and twelve other Southerners, as well as a supply of boots and shoes they found in Louisa Court House.[92] With no rations left, columns of foragers fanned out across the countryside, slowing the pace of march while hungry men sought rations and fodder for their mounts. That afternoon, the Yankee horsemen tore up five miles of railroad track, all the way to an obscure depot

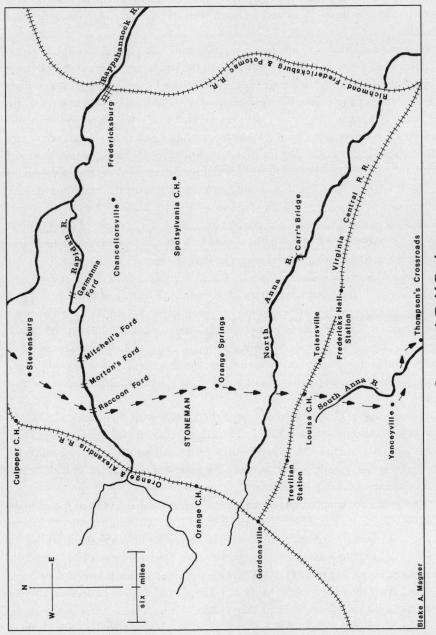

Stoneman's Raid Begins

Blake A. Magner

to the west called Trevilian Station. The Yankee horsemen also destroyed a water tank and some commissary stores, in addition to damaging public buildings. These men would visit the same ground again thirteen months later with much deadlier results.[93]

Gregg heard that a Confederate wagon train had rushed through Orange Springs headed toward Spotsylvania earlier in the day. Gregg dispatched Col. Percy Wyndham's brigade to chase the train. The British knight's men set off in high spirits, but after a five-mile wild-goose chase, Wyndham called off the pursuit and returned to Orange Springs without his prize.[94] The rest of Gregg's command caught a few hours' rest until the Pennsylvanian gave orders to march at 6:00 P.M. His men pressed on, marching for nine long hours, finally halting a mile north of Louisa Court House. "We were all very sleepy and as we rode along we would sleep . . . while . . . nodding and swaying, first one side then the other and making all sorts of gyrations," recalled a sergeant of the 1st Maine.[95] Later that night, Buford's Regulars splashed across the North Anna River and joined Gregg's division on the south bank of the narrow river at 3:00 A.M., unsaddling their horses and building fires for the first time since leaving Warrenton.

Gregg expected the Confederates to defend Louisa, so he made his dispositions accordingly. He deployed Capt. James M. Robertson's battery of horse artillery in a commanding position on high ground and supported it with Wyndham's troopers. Kilpatrick's brigade advanced in three columns aimed at the town and points one mile above and one mile below it. Kilpatrick's men dashed into the town and were surprised to find it undefended. They burned the depot and storehouses, sleeper cars, and tore up the tracks of the Virginia Central Railroad for nearly five miles.

While most of Gregg's men occupied themselves with their tasks of destruction, a few mischievous New Yorkers occupied the town's telegraph office. They spent a couple of enjoyable hours trading telegrams with Richmond until the Southerners finally realized that something was wrong and signed off with "some very decided remarks of approbation."[96]

The sudden onslaught stunned the local citizenry, which had been spared from Yankee visits so far in the war. "The inhabitants were . . . considerably at a loss to know where we came from so suddenly," observed Sgt. Nathan Webb of the 1st Maine Cavalry. "No doubt some thought we came from the clouds and looked for our wings, horns, and forked tails." Although the blueclad horde spared the homes of the locals, their food stocks were fair game, and many a Federal saddlebag was filled with tasty treats. "A huge slice of ham in one hand, a fritter in the other, the utter abjuration of knives and spoons, faces all grease or wiped off with their jackets sleeves and all laughing and jolly as kings in their palaces," Stoneman and his men enjoyed the bounty of the countryside, largely emptying the town of provisions.[97] The marauding Northerners spared hardly a family. Women poured out liquor to prevent drunken Yankees from becoming more dangerous or destructive. The Yankees stripped local planters of their clothes and left them naked in the surrounding woodlands just to punish them for supporting the Confederacy.[98]

Stoneman dispatched two companies of the 1st Maine to ride west along the Gordonsville Stage Road, toward Trevilian Station. The New Englanders encountered and scattered Rooney Lee's pickets not long after starting. They soon found the 9th Virginia Cavalry's main line of battle and broke off after losing nearly half their number captured. One squadron of Virginians drew their revolvers and charged down the road, while the next squadron dismounted and took position in the railroad cut, lying in ambush. A third squadron took position a couple of hundred yards back, while the balance of the regiment remained in reserve near the Trevilian depot. "Before these dispositions were completed squads of the party charging began to return. A few of the enemy had been killed—some three or four—and one mortally wounded was brought in. About forty-five prisoners were taken," reported Colonel Beale. Interrogation of these prisoners persuaded Beale that all of Stoneman's force lay in front of him. The Virginian sent a courier to Rooney Lee while Beale's men hunkered down to wait for Stoneman's main body to advance.[99]

"After waiting a short time we began to withdraw," recalled Beale, "when a feeble yell was heard, and a small squad of troopers charged past our dismounted men, and received their fire at very short range, but without any injury to them." Before the Federals could wheel, the mounted Virginians fell upon them, driving back the Yankee horsemen. The uncertain Federals did not advance in force, and skirmishing occupied the afternoon.[100] Rooney Lee reported that he "sent the Ninth Virginia in that direction; their videttes were driven in by the enemy; they charged and drove them three miles, killing and wounding a number, and took thirty-two prisoners, one lieutenant; my loss was three or four wounded; four prisoners taken represented three different regiments." Lee dispatched the 13th Virginia and two pieces of horse artillery to support the 9th Virginia, and then waited for Stoneman to attack. When he did not, Lee "learned that General Stoneman with his whole corps was at Louisa Court House, moving towards James River." Lee correctly surmised that Stoneman intended to tear up the railroad, and waited for the Yankees to approach. When the blueclad troopers did not come, wrote Lee, and "men and horses being worried out by four days' fighting and marching, left out my pickets and withdrew to Gordonsville."[101]

Not knowing how large an enemy force lay near Gordonsville, and not wanting to take unnecessary chances, Stoneman continued the march southeast, destroying the railroad as far as Fredericks Hall Station. Capt. Andrew J. Alexander, Stoneman's able assistant adjutant general and the architect of the great raid, urged

Stoneman to dash into Richmond and free the thousands of Yankee prisoners of war suffering in horrible conditions at Libby Prison and Belle Isle. "I know damned well we can do it," grumbled Stoneman, "but my orders are not to go to Richmond." A Federal horse soldier who overheard the exchange observed, "My impression then was that Stoneman was too much of a Regular of the old school to disobey an order even if he knew it would result in great good to his cause."[102] The rigid West Pointer pressed on, determined to fulfill his orders to the best of his ability, even if doing so meant that a golden opportunity to capture the Confederate capital slipped away.

Buford sent Capt. Richard S. Lord's 1st U.S. to destroy the train tracks and public buildings of the Virginia Central Railroad, and to burn Carr's Bridge over the North Anna River, six miles north of the town of Fredericks Hall. Lord, a West Pointer from Ohio, took fourteen officers and 251 enlisted men, the only portion of his regiment still riding serviceable horses, and destroyed the railroad tracks, culverts, switches, water houses, water cars, telegraph depot, and storehouses located at Tolersville. They also rendered a fifteen-mile stretch of the Virginia Central impassable. Finally, Lord and his men torched the bridge over the North Anna before returning to the main column of the Reserve Brigade. Lord's foray prevented the pursuit of Confederate cavalry forces at Spotsylvania.[103]

No longer encumbered by the supply wagons, the column headed for Mitchell's Ford on the Rapidan River. Lt. Julius W. Mason's squadron of the 5th U.S. swam the ford and reconnoitered the ground beyond, capturing thirteen prisoners, scouring the country as far as Morton's and Raccoon Fords, and reporting back to Buford. Meanwhile Buford's aristocratic young aide, Lt. Peter Penn-Gaskell, a direct descendant of William Penn, led a contingent of troopers of the 5th U.S. that drove the Confederate pickets from Raccoon Ford, securing it for the advance of the Regulars. Penn-Gaskell and his men chased the fugitives along the road to Orange Court House for nearly five miles before calling off the pursuit. They captured a lieutenant and nine artillerists during the pursuit.[104]

In the meantime, the main column proceeded to Yanceyville, crossed the South Anna River, and marched on to Thompson's Crossroads on the right bank of the South Anna River at the intersection of the Old Mountain Road running west from Richmond to the Blue Ridge, and the Cartersville Road, connecting Spotsylvania Court House and the James River. Stoneman's column arrived late in the day on May 2. Buford's Regulars captured a train of twenty-six wagons with four-mule teams assigned to each wagon, and this prize slowed down the column's advance. The captured wagon train carried an unexpected bounty—a section of recent and accurate topographical maps Stoneman would use to guide his forces through enemy territory. "We were now in the very heart of the enemy's country, and what was to be done must be done quickly, as the enemy were known to be concentrating all the force they could get together to prevent the accomplishment of our designs."[105] Buford sent the wagons to the rear to avoid being slowed down by this burden.

Unable to cross at Mitchell's Ford, Stoneman's command crossed the Rapidan upriver at Morton's Ford, with the 6th Pennsylvania in the vanguard of the column. Once across the Rapidan, the horse soldiers rested for a few hours. The entire Cavalry Corps then formed line of battle, and stood to horse all night, awaiting further orders.[106] "It was a season of considerable anxiety to all, and of great fatigue especially to those of us who had been in the saddle several consecutive days and nights," wrote a Federal officer. "Standing to horse as we were compelled to do, very little rest could be obtained, though many were so exhausted that, dropping to the earth, with bridle and halter in hand, they fell asleep, while their comrades wished for the morning, which came at last."[107]

While standing picket duty near the ford, Bugler William H. Leeser of Company B, 5th U.S., became an early casualty when he accidentally shot himself. The commander of the 5th U.S., Capt. James E. Harrison, left two men with Leeser at a nearby farmhouse. The raid certainly ended ignominiously for these three Yankees, who were subsequently captured.[108]

The miserable weather and the resulting lack of surprise meant that Stoneman could not fulfill Hooker's objectives for the raid. Instead, the Cavalry Corps commander now had to find a way to do the most damage possible while getting his horsemen safely back to the Army of the Potomac. This proved to be no small task, and many harrowing adventures remained for the already weary Union horse soldiers.

NOTES

1. Gracey, Annals of the Sixth Pennsylvania Cavalry, 136.
2. Carpenter to his father, May 9, 1863, Carpenter Letters from the Field, 1861–1865, Historical Society of Pennsylvania, Pa.
3. O.R., vol. 25, part 1, 1057.
4. Webb diary, entry for April 29, 1863.
5. Christian Geisel to his sister, April 27, 1863, Christian Geisel Papers.
6. Quoted in Edward G. Longacre, Mounted Raids of the Civil War (South Brunswick, N.J.: A. S. Barnes, 1975), 157.
7. Theophilus F. Rodenbough, "Personal Recollections—The Stoneman Raid of '63," in From Everglade to Canon with the Second Dragoons: An Authentic Account of Service in Florida, Mexico, Virginia, and the Indian County, 1836–1875, ed. Theophilus F. Rodenbough (New York: D. Van Nostrand, 1875), 274–75.
8. O.R., vol. 25, part 1, 1067–68.
9. Glazier, Three Years in the Federal Cavalry, 170.
10. Newhall, With General Sheridan, 191–92.

11. O.R., vol. 25, part 1, 1074, and part 2, 471; Norton, *Deeds of Daring,* 62.
12. Gilpin diary, entry for April 29, 1863.
13. Bushnell diary, entry for April 29, 1863.
14. Perry, *Life and Letters,* 187.
15. Hyndman, *History of a Cavalry Company,* 53.
16. Hudgins and Kleese, *Recollections of an Old Dominion Dragoon,* 71.
17. Dennison, *Sabres and Spurs,* 221–22.
18. Averell diary, entry for April 29, 1863; Dennison, *Sabres and Spurs,* 221–22.
19. Winder, *Jacob Beidler's Book,* 150.
20. Gilpin diary, entry for April 29, 1863.
21. O.R., vol. 25, part 1, 1078.
22. Daniel T. Balfour, *13th Virginia Cavalry* (Lynchburg, Va.: H. E. Howard, 1986), 15.
23. Beale, G. W. *A Lieutenant of Cavalry in Lee's Army* (Boston: 1918; reprint, Baltimore: Butternut & Blue, 1994), 70.
24. Norton, *Deeds of Daring,* 62.
25. Bushnell diary, entry for 30, 1863.
26. Follmer diary, entry for April 30, 1863, USAMHI.
27. Dennison, *Sabres and Spurs,* 222.
28. Delos Northway to his wife, May 16, 1863, in *Souvenir,* 114.
29. Ford, *A Cycle of Adams Letters,* 1:287.
30. Perry, *Life and Letters,* 187.
31. O.R., vol. 25, part 1, 1078.
32. Hyndman, *History of a Cavalry Company,* 55.
33. Ball diary, entry for April 30, 1863. Capt. Charles Francis Adams of the 1st Massachusetts reported, "We looked over the field and saw the graves of our troops, but there are few signs of a battlefield left. I noticed that our horses would not eat the grass, and as we passed one ditch, some of my men hit upon a skull, apparently dug up and gnawed on by the swine. Such it is to die for one's country!" Ford, *A Cycle of Adams Letters,* 1:288.
34. Gilpin diary, entry for April 30, 1863.
35. Averell diary, entry for April 30, 1863; O.R., vol. 25, part 1, 1078.
36. Norton, *Deeds of Daring,* 62.
37. Cheney diary, entry for April 30, 1863, USAMHI.
38. Ford, *A Cycle of Adams Letters,* 1:289.
39. Northway to his wife, May 16, 1863, in *Souvenir,* 114.
40. O.R., vol. 25, part 1, 1075.
41. George W. Beale, "The Story of General Averell's Interview with a Confederate Prisoner Retold," *Richmond Times-Dispatch,* March 4, 1906. Lieutenant Beale's father was the commander of the 9th Virginia Cavalry.
42. Beale, *History of the Ninth Virginia Cavalry,* 63; Hard, *History of the Eighth Cavalry Regiment,* 232.
43. Crowninshield, *A History of the First Regiment,* 123–24.
44. Ball diary, entry for May 1, 1963.

45. Cheney, *History of the Ninth New York,* 91–92, MOH.
46. Brooke-Rawle, *History of the Third Pennsylvania Cavalry,* 231.
47. Beale, "The Story of General Averell's Interview."
48. Cheney, *Ninth New York,* 91–92, MOH; Hard, *History of the Eighth Cavalry Regiment,* 232.
49. Averell diary, entry for May 1, 1863; O.R., vol. 25, part 1, 1079.
50. Northway to his wife, May 16, 1863, in *Souvenir,* 114.
51. O.R., vol. 25, part 1, 1079–80.
52. Ibid., part 2, 356.
53. Ford, *A Cycle of Adams Letters,* 1:290.
54. Gilpin diary, May 2, 1863.
55. Norton, *Deeds of Daring,* 62.
56. O.R., vol. 25, part 1, 887.
57. Von Borcke, *Memoirs,* 376–77.
58. Ibid., 377–78. Von Borcke arrived and found Stuart, who informed him that both Jackson and his senior division commander, Maj. Gen. A. P. Hill, had been wounded by friendly fire, and that Jackson had wanted Stuart to take command of his corps instead of the inexperienced officers commanding his other two divisions.
59. Winder, *Jacob Beidler's Book,* 151.
60. Perry, *Life and Letters,* 188.
61. O.R., vol. 25, part 1, 1076.
62. Norton, *Deeds of Daring,* 63.
63. Brooke-Rawle, *History of the Third Pennsylvania Cavalry,* 231.
64. Gilpin diary, entry for May 4, 1863.
65. Winder, *Jacob Beidler's Book,* 151; Brooke-Rawle, *History of the Third Pennsylvania Cavalry,* 231.
66. Bliss to Dear Gerald, May 8, 1863, Bliss Papers; Dennison, *Sabres and Spurs,* 223.
67. O.R., vol. 25, part 1, 1072–73.
68. Joseph Hooker to Samuel P. Bates, April 2, 1877, Samuel P. Bates Papers, Pennsylvania State Archives, Harrisburg, Pa.
69. William E. Doster, *Lincoln and Episodes of the Civil War* (New York: G. P. Putnam's Sons, 1915), 200–201.
70. Note of the Adjutant General of the Army, May 7, 1863, William Woods Averell file, Letters Received by the Appointment, Commission, and Personal Branch of the Adjutant General's Office, 1871–1894, M1395, National Archives, Washington, D. C. ("Averell ACP File").
71. Averell diary, entries for May 14 and May 17, 1863.
72. Robert B. Boehm, "The Unfortunate Averell," *Civil War Times Illustrated* 5 (August 1966): 32.
73. O.R., vol. 25, part 1, 1076–77. Averell wrote, "The form and tenor of the order and its mode of communication are extraordinary. No cause is or has been assigned for its issue, to my knowledge. Issued at the close of the unsuccessful engagement of Sunday, May 3, and destitute of history or explanation, its effect is to place upon me, by impli-

cation, an indefinite share in the responsibility for whatever there may have been of failure in the operations of the Army of the Potomac in the recent attack upon the enemy's forces. I therefore deem it my duty to make you acquainted with the history of the recent cavalry operations in which I took part, to ask your consideration of the inclosed orders, marked A, B, C, D, and E, which controlled my conduct, and to ask that an inquiry be made as to the causes for my removal, and that I may be informed of their nature." Averell continued, "If the execution of my orders was faulty, it cannot be attributed to a misunderstanding of them, as the cavalry, in their recent operations, were engaged in carrying out a part of the plan originated by myself previous to the first battle of Fredericksburg, and which I once set out to execute about the beginning of the year. The major-general commanding the Army of the Potomac also did me the honor to invite my opinion upon the details of these operations before they were ordered, and I believe I thoroughly understood the project of the general commanding, so far as the cavalry was concerned."

74. George B. Davis, "The Stoneman Raid," *Journal of the U.S. Cavalry Association* 24 (1917), 544.
75. *Rochester Daily Union & Advertiser,* May 29, 1863.
76. Carpenter to his mother, May 13, 1863, Carpenter Letters from the Field.
77. Ford, *A Cycle of Adams Letters,* 1:295.
78. McIntosh to Averell, May 8, 1863, Averell Papers.
79. McIntosh to his wife, May 13, 1863, John B. McIntosh Papers, Brown University Library, Providence, R.I.
80. William Brooke-Rawle to his mother, June 12, 1863, William Brooke-Rawle Papers, Civil War Museum and Library, Philadelphia, Pa.
81. Frank W. Dickerson, "Letter from a Maine Cavalry Officer in Stoneman's Raid," *Bangor Daily Whig & Courier,* May 20, 1863.
82. Gracey, *Annals of the Sixth Pennsylvania Cavalry,* 137.
83. John B. Coover to John B. Coover, May 22, 1863, John B. Coover letters, George F. Scott Collection, Mt. Carmel, Pa.
84. Gracey, *Annals of the Sixth Pennsylvania Cavalry,* 139–40.
85. O.R., vol. 25, part 1, 1059.
86. Nathan B. Webb diary, entry for April 30, 1863.
87. Glazier, *Three Years in the Federal Cavalry,* 177.
88. Ibid.
89. Affidavit of G. S. Smith, Willis Madden Reparations Claims File, Southern Claims, National Archives, Washington, D.C. Smith played a major role in the Union's efforts to gather intelligence about the large concentration of Confederate cavalry in Culpeper County at the beginning of June 1863 that led up to the Battle of Brandy Station. See also Wainwright, *A Diary of Battle,* 271, for further confirmation of Smith's role in guiding the Cavalry Corps across the central Virginia countryside.
90. *New York Daily Tribune,* May 2, 1863.
91. Henry R. Pyne, *The History of First New Jersey Cavalry* (Trenton, N.J.: J. A. Beecher, 1871), 141–42.

92. Ibid., 142.

93. Ben F. Fordney, *Stoneman at Chancellorsville* (Shippensburg, Pa.: White Mane, 1998), 31.

94. *New York Herald,* May 11, 1863; O.R., vol. 25, part 1, 1082.

95. Webb diary, entry for May 2, 1863.

96. O.R., vol. 25, part 1, 1082; Gracey, *Annals of the Sixth Pennsylvania Cavalry,* 140–41.

97. Webb diary, entry for May 2, 1863.

98. Walbrook D. Swank, *The War & Louisa County 1861–1865* (Charlottesville, Va.: Papercraft Printing & Design, 1986), 18.

99. O.R., vol. 25, part 1, 1060 and 1082; Beale, *History of the Ninth Virginia Cavalry,* 64.

100. Beale, *History of the Ninth Virginia Cavalry,* 64–65.

101. "Report of Brig. Gen. W. H. F. Lee," *Southern Historical Society Papers* 3 (1877), 181.

102. "The Stoneman Raid," *National Tribune,* June 14, 1888.

103. O.R., vol. 25, part 1, 1091.

104. *New York Times,* May 11, 1863.

105. Gracey, *Annals of the Sixth Pennsylvania Cavalry,* 142.

106. O.R., vol. 25, part 1, 1060.

107. Glazier, *Three Years in the Federal Cavalry,* 177.

108. O.R., vol. 25, part 1, 1092.

7

THE BURSTING SHELL:
STONEMAN'S RAID FINALLY BEGINS

Stoneman realized that his two small, tired divisions could not stop the entire Army of Northern Virginia if it withdrew or retreated intact after its encounter with Hooker's army. He also realized that Lee probably would not withdraw all the way to Richmond even if Hooker defeated him. Stoneman decided to inflict as much damage as possible, and targeted key bridges and logistics centers in Lee's rear, hoping to wreak havoc. Accordingly, Stoneman called his subordinates together to give them their new assignments. "At this point, the James and South Anna Rivers are less than 12 miles apart, and here I determined to make the most of my 3500 men in carrying out my previously conceived plan of operations," recalled Stoneman. "I called together my regimental commanders, showed and explained to them the maps, and gave them an idea of what I wished done. I gave them to understand that we had dropped in that region of the country like a shell, and that I intended to burst it in every direction, expecting each piece or fragment would do as much harm and create nearly as much terror as would result from sending in the whole shell, and thus magnify our small force into overwhelming numbers and the results of this plan satisfied my most sanguine expectations."[1]

After the conference ended, Lt. Col. Hasbrouck Davis of the 12th Illinois approached Stoneman to seek out specific details. His regiment would approach the outskirts of Richmond, hoping to cut vital railroad links. "Where then, General?" he inquired.

"God only knows," replied Stoneman. "If you succeed in getting down the Peninsula, you had better continue on, if possible, and report to Gen. Rufus King at Yorktown. It will be a tough proposition at best, and I fear you won't make the trip without some pretty hard fighting." Ten minutes later, about 2:30 A.M., the bugles called "Boots and Saddles," and the corps marched again.[2]

This plan, while clever, deviated from Hooker's carefully drawn strategic raid. Although Stoneman's scheme would have fulfilled Hooker's orders of April 22, it did not meet the requirements of the April 30 orders. It meant that the fragmented command would not be able to block a retreat by the Army of Northern Virginia, and it also meant that its scattered columns offered a tempting target for marauding Confederate cavalry to defeat them in detail. Instead of operating against Lee's lines of supply and communications, Stoneman intended to scatter his horsemen across the countryside, spreading destruction in their wake. The cavalry chief also had no way of knowing what was occurring on the battlefield at Chancellorsville.

On April 30, an optimistic Hooker issued a General Order to the army that proved hollow. "It is with heartfelt satisfaction the commanding general announces to the army that the operations of the last three days have determined that our enemy must ingloriously fly," he boasted, "or come out from behind his defenses and give us battle on our own ground, where certain destruction awaits him."[3] Only the part about the Confederates coming out from behind their defenses proved true.

The Battle of Chancellorsville was fought on May 1–4, 1863. Although he had stolen a march on Lee, and despite his great numerical advantage, Hooker lost the fight badly. After a day of fighting on May 1, Hooker suspended the action and assumed a defensive posture. He announced to Maj. Gen. Darius N. Couch, commander of the II Corps, that he had "Lee just where I want him; he must fight me on my own ground." Couch later wrote, "The retrograde movement had prepared me for something of the kind, but to hear from his own lips that the advantages gained by the successful marches of his lieutenants were to culminate in fighting a defensive battle in that nest of thickets was too much, and I retired from his presence with the belief that my commanding general was a whipped man."[4]

On the morning of May 2, Confederate cavalry chieftain Stuart discovered that the Federal flank was "in the air," meaning that it was entirely unprotected; the withdrawal of the Federal cavalry for the great raid left inadequate mounted support to screen Hooker's flanks. Capitalizing on the opportunity, Robert E. Lee ordered Lt. Gen. "Stonewall" Jackson to make a flank march around Hooker's right flank, find the exposed flank, and strike the Union right. Jackson shocked the Union XI Corps while its men were cooking their dinners late in the afternoon of May 2. A rout ensued, and only a spirited stand by Couch's II Corps saved Hooker's army from complete destruction.

However, the victory at Chancellorsville cost Robert E. Lee the services of Stonewall Jackson when he died a few days later. Despite the loss of Jackson,

Chancellorsville was a huge victory for the Confederates. Although Hooker out-numbered Lee by a margin of more than two to one, he suffered a crushing defeat in a long and bloody battle. The Federals sustained more than 17,000 casualties in the battle, and the Confederates nearly 13,000.[5] Hooker had originally intended for his horsemen to interdict Lee's lines of supply and communications. However, the results of the battle meant that there would be no retreat. There was nothing for Stoneman to interdict.

Stoneman intended to send Wyndham, the 1st New Jersey, and most of the 1st Maryland Cavalry to Columbia in Fluvanna County, where they would dismantle the James River and Kanawha Canal aqueduct over the Rivanna River. Wyndham would then proceed eastward along the canal, "doing all the harm possible." Col. Judson Kilpatrick and the 2d New York Cavalry would head toward Richmond and the railroad bridges over the Chickahominy River, while Lt. Col. Hasbrouck Davis and the 12th Illinois would operate against the Richmond, Fredericksburg and Potomac Railroad at Ashland and the Virginia Central Railroad at Atlee Station. Gen. David Gregg would take the 1st Maine and the 10th New York down the South Anna to "destroy all the road bridges thereon, and, if possible, the two railroad bridges across that river." Capt. Thomas Drummond and the 5th U.S. Cavalry would follow along behind, mopping up any unfinished business. Capt. Wesley Merritt, Stoneman's gifted twenty-eight-year-old ordnance officer, was already leading a "flying party" of the 1st Maryland Cavalry on a ride "to do what he thought he could accomplish in the way of destroying bridges, &c." Finally, Stoneman would remain at Thompson's Crossroads with a reserve of 500 picked men of Buford's brigade. They would act as a rallying point when the disparate columns drew back together.[6]

Stoneman, who suffered from a terrible case of hemorrhoids, undoubtedly relished the chance to spend some time out of the saddle, resting near Thompson's Crossroads. Every moment spent riding a horse was sheer agony for the cavalry-man, but he gamely hung on. However, his uncertainty about the whereabouts and safety of his far-flung columns caused him to spend May 3 "in no little anxi-ety." Tense days still lay ahead before the ordeal of the Federal cavalrymen ended.[7]

JUDSON KILPATRICK'S MARCH TOWARD RICHMOND

Col. Judson Kilpatrick's cavalry column of 450 troopers aimed for Hungary Station on the Richmond, Fredericksburg and Potomac Railroad. Worried about close observation of his route by unfriendly eyes, Kilpatrick decided to march at night. His men enjoyed the respite from their labors, but wondered what their leader's orders to discard extra clothing, blankets, and baggage meant for their prospects. The 2d New York, Kilpatrick's own regiment, moved out at three o'clock on the morning of May 3. "The silence which reigned during this movement was painful," recounted a newspaper correspondent who rode with the 2d New York. "Not a loud word or boisterous laugh gave token of the presence of the brave men who were afterwards to enter the massive works before Richmond."[8] They reached the depot at Hungary Station, about fifteen miles away, by daybreak. Two Southern pickets spotted the advancing column and dashed off to raise the alarm, meaning that they left the station and telegraph lines to the tender mercies of the New Yorkers, who also tore up several miles of track.

Once his command was within five miles of the spires of Richmond, Kilpatrick advanced cautiously. "There was good reason for this, for our condition was critical," recalled an officer of the 2d New York. "There we were, only a remnant of a regiment, many miles away from any support, with no way to retreat, as we had burned all the bridges and ferries in our rear, nearer to the Confederate capital than ever any Union troops had been before, and ignorant of the forces that garrisoned it."[9]

The 2d New York pushed on to the Brook Turnpike, a main artery leading into Richmond from the north. To their great surprise, they encountered no resistance from the outer defenses of Richmond, chasing off a battery of artillery before it fired a shot. Kilpatrick pressed on, wondering if he would be able to enter the Southern capital unmolested. Lt. R. W. Brown, one of the Confederate staff officers assigned to the provost marshal of Richmond, Brig. Gen. John H. Winder, along with a squad of a dozen men, trotted up to the dusty column and inquired, "What regiment?"

"The Second New York Cavalry," responded Kilpatrick, "and you, sir, are my prisoner."

"You're a mighty daring set of fellows," replied the shocked lieutenant, "but you will certainly be captured before sundown." Kilpatrick acknowledged the possibility, but told Brown that he intended "to do a mighty deal of mischief first."[10]

Kilpatrick paroled the lieutenant and his men and rode forward until they could see the main defenses of the Southern capital. He planted the American flag on some earthen defensive works, so that the grayclad defenders across the way could plainly see the Stars and Stripes waving.[11] Examining the stout enemy defenses bristling with artillery pieces, Kilpatrick wisely decided to change directions. Reaching the Meadow Bridges over the Chickahominy, near the old Seven Days' battlefields, Kilpatrick burned the four spans across the river, captured a train loaded with supplies, torched the cars, and pushed the flaming train onto the ruined bridge. The bridge collapsed, pitching the fiery wreckage into the Chickahominy "until the whole thing well-nigh disappeared in the deep mud and water."[12]

The 2d New York paid an unexpected and unwelcome visit to the home of a prominent local physician of Hanover Town named Brockenbrough. Hearing that a large force of Yankees was bearing down on his home, Brockenbrough came outside, just in time to face a mounted New Yorker with a drawn pistol. "Who are you?" inquired the doctor. "A member of the 2d New York Cavalry," came the response.

"The devil you say," replied the physician. However, a glance at the mass of blue-clad horsemen drawn up in the road gave the doctor pause, and he reconsidered his hostile stance. The mounted trooper took the doctor to Kilpatrick. "Do you intend to take my horse, colonel?" he inquired.

Kilpatrick smiled and said, "A military necessity, sir." A trooper spurred up and announced that there was also a supply of grain at the doctor's home. Brocken-brough told Kilpatrick that his slaves would suffer more than he would if the Yan-kees took the grain, but his plea fell on deaf ears. Kilpatrick again cited military necessity as his justification for seizing the grain. The unhappy physician watched the raiders head for his barn.

A few moments later, they spurred off, having emptied the grain house and seized all of the horses of both the doctor and his neighbor. They camped just below his home, "where I had the unhappiness of seeing the creatures remain till seven o'clock in the evening, smoking, many reclining in the grass and others rid-ing about with their legs over the pommels of their saddles—every act displaying the most perfect assurance of gaiety and contempt for authority in Richmond," proclaimed the doctor. Once the Yankees left, Brockenbrough went off to report his experiences with them, but he could not find a force of Southerners adequate to bring the Yankees to bay.[13]

Fearing that whatever force might be defending Richmond might pursue him, "Little Kil," as the men sometimes called him, turned north, perhaps hoping to unite with Hasbrouck Davis's column of raiders. He decided to continue down the Peninsula to Yorktown, nearly sixty miles away. Using a local guide, the New Yorkers crossed the Pamunkey at Hanover Town, where they commandeered a local flatboat, which ferried the entire column across at the rate of twenty men and horses per trip. After the last of them reached safety on the other side of the Pamunkey, the New Yorkers burned the ferry and moved out into the dense woods of King William County. As the ferry burned, Confederate cavalry from the de-fenses of Richmond glared helplessly across the deep, wide river. "Cheer after cheer now rent the air," recalled a New Yorker, "and the skillful manner in which their leader conducted the hazardous enterprise gave him such a hold on the hearts of his men, and such a feeling of confidence in him was inspired, as to raise their enthusiasm to the highest point of admiration."[14]

Flushed with his success, Kilpatrick captured and destroyed thirty wagons loaded with bacon and then bivouacked five miles from the Pamunkey. They moved out on May 5, reaching Aylett on the Mattapony River, surprising 300 enemy troopers, capturing 2 officers and 33 enlisted men. "About four o'clock in the afternoon a cold rainstorm set in, borne on the flapping wings of a chilly wind," remembered a captain of the 2d New York. "Cold, hungry, and fatigued, we still pressed onward, suffering not a little." They stayed on back roads and byways in an effort to avoid any pursuing Confederates.[15]

After burning fifty wagons and a depot filled with grain and other provisions, Kilpatrick crossed the river ahead of pursuing Confederate horsemen. Kilpatrick called for a council of his officers, and they voted to try to make it to Gloucester Point, opposite Yorktown, which they knew to be safely in Union hands. That night he reached the Rappahannock near the small village of Tappahannock. Finding a wagon train laden with hams and other delicacies, the famished New Yorkers helped themselves to all that they could carry away, and destroyed the train before leisurely pressing on to the southeast toward King and Queen Court House, skirmishing with bushwhackers and Confederate cavalry the entire way.[16]

As darkness fell on May 6, Kilpatrick spotted a line of horse soldiers drawn up in front of King and Queen Court House. Kilpatrick shook out a line of skirmishers and advanced in column of squadrons, expecting to give battle. "Our opponents were not idle," recounted a newspaper correspondent, "but quickly formed in line of battle, and threw out their skirmishers in return to meet ours." Everything beckoned a sharp fight, when an officer rode forward from the opposite side with a flag of truce and asked, "Who are you?" "Who are you?" retorted the New Yorkers. "The Twelfth Illinois Cavalry, Colonel Davis," responded the officer. "Then a scene of rejoicing and mutual congratulations occurred that baffles description," noted the relieved newspaper correspondent.[17] "This reencounter was very pleasing," noted one of Kilpatrick's men. "We needed this stimulus exceedingly, for we had been marching all day through a cold drizzling rain, which had dampened our ardor somewhat, and chilled our blood."[18]

Kilpatrick realized that he was out of touch with the army and was uncertain about what to do next. He decided to send a staff officer off to find a telegraph station with which to communicate with Hooker's headquarters. Lt. Llewellyn G. Estes of Kilpatrick's staff spurred off with a squad of ten volunteers. About five miles into his journey, he encountered a force of 150 local militiamen blocking his route. Estes and his little force charged them, capturing a major, a captain, and 16 men, whom he paroled. The little column resumed its march and soon met an even larger force of militia, this time consisting of 200 cavalry and 500 infantry. Their commander sent out a flag of truce, stated the size of his force, and demanded that the Northerners surrender. "Come and take me," replied Estes.

While the flag of truce remained out, Estes and his men dashed down to the shores of the Tappahannock River and hid in a swamp. The militia pursued them, and with the aid of bloodhounds, brought the Federals to bay. The Northerners destroyed their weapons and those of their prisoners and surrendered. When they refused to give their parole, the militia commander sent them on to Richmond under guard. A detachment of Union cavalry dashed on the prisoners and their guard, freeing Estes and his men, who rejoined Kilpatrick's column at Gloucester Point a few days later.[19]

HASBROUCK DAVIS'S ADVENTURE

Thirty-three-year-old Lt. Col. Hasbrouck Davis came from a prominent Massachusetts family. His father served as governor and U.S. Senator for the Bay State. Davis graduated from Williams College in Williamstown, Massachusetts, and also attended the University of Heidelberg in Germany. After a stint as a teacher, he briefly served as a Unitarian minister before studying law in the 1850s. Davis settled in Chicago in 1855, and became a prominent and well-respected lawyer. In 1861, he was commissioned lieutenant colonel of the 12th Illinois Cavalry. Col. Arno Voss, the regimental commander, was in poor health, and Davis had field command of the regiment. Along with Grimes Davis, Hasbrouck Davis led the daring escape of more than 1,000 Federal cavalrymen from Harpers Ferry in September 1862. He demonstrated that he was a competent and daring leader of horsemen through the first months of the Civil War. Davis eventually became colonel of the regiment, and received a brevet to brigadier general of volunteers at the end of the Civil War.[20]

The 12th Illinois marched out of Thompson's Crossroads before dawn on May 3, heading toward Ashland Station on the Richmond, Fredericksburg and Potomac Railroad. Davis's men destroyed a bridge across the South Anna River and dispersed a band of guerrillas before reaching Ashland that morning. Lt. Frederick W. Mitchell led the Illinois men in their dash into the town.[21] "Words cannot describe the astonishment of the inhabitants at our appearance," reported Davis.[22] The women of Ashland were like "baboons and monkeys peeping out of the windows and over the fences," observed Sergeant Redman.[23]

Encountering no resistance, Davis's men cut the telegraph wires, tore up the railroad, and wrecked more bridges. An ill-timed train arriving from the north fell victim to Davis's men, who captured 250 wounded men from the Chancellorsville battlefield, including Lt. Joseph G. Morrison, Stonewall Jackson's aide and brother-in-law, who was en route to Richmond to escort his sister to the sickbed of her mortally wounded husband. Morrison escaped and completed his mission once the Northern raiders resumed their ride. Jackson's wife reached his side before he expired on May 10.[24] A courier carrying dispatches from General Lee to Richmond also escaped, protecting the vital intelligence he carried. Colonel Davis ordered that the engine be destroyed. They uncoupled it and superheated the engine's boiler until it burst. One of the Richmond newspapers noted, "The Yankee colonel was disposed to be very chatty. He said he knew the country round about Ashland like a hook; that he had fox hunted over it many times."[25]

Their advance on Ashland raised havoc among the local populace. Another Virginian, who lived in Richmond, reported, "On Sunday night [May 3] news came that a body of Yankee Cavalry were at Ashland—had burnt the place destroyed the railroad & captured the train with wounded—a call was made on the citizens who immediately assembled on the Square & by 10 o'clock they had formed ten or twelve companies averaging about 100 men each. Among them were Congressmen—Colonels, Captains, Lieutenants, &c. serving as privates." He continued, "They spent the night waiting for orders—one company in the Senate—two others in the City Hall & the rest scattered around loose. The next day, having been supplied with arms, was spent marching about town & around about some of the batteries & by night having had glory enough they dispersed & went quietly to their homes." Richmond residents had turned out to defend their city, but no Federal horse soldier came closer than about four miles.[26]

Davis then turned east toward Hanover Station on the Virginia Central Railroad. He arrived about 8:00 that evening, burning more than 100 wagons loaded with supplies and scattered nearly 1,000 sacks of flour and corn. His men then turned their attention to the rails, telegraph, stables, bridges, and storehouses at Hanover Station, cutting the Virginia Central. Completing their work at Hanover Station, Davis's exhausted men moved out, passing through Hanover Court House. They came within ten miles of the outer defenses of Richmond before finally calling a halt and bivouacking for the night.[27]

Davis intended to head down the Peninsula toward Williamsburg. The 12th Illinois marched along the south bank of the Pamunkey River on May 4. They met a train from White House Landing near Tunstall's Station on the Richmond & York River Railroad. A regiment of Confederate infantry, supported by three pieces of artillery, rode the train with the specific assignment of bringing the raiders to bay. Davis tried to engage the infantrymen and skirmished along the railroad embankment. He lost two men killed and several wounded, and the Confederates also suffered casualties in the sharp firefight. Recognizing that he lacked sufficient firepower to defeat an entire regiment of veteran Southern infantry, Davis broke off the engagement and withdrew across the Pamunkey at Plunkett's Ferry, near Hanover Town. Employing a small ferry as Kilpatrick's men did, Davis crossed the river and marched to Walkerton, where he also crossed the Mattapony without incident. A squad of eighteen Southern horse soldiers of the 15th Virginia Cavalry sat glaring helplessly at the Federals as they made their way across the river, but their force was too small to engage Davis's men.[28]

On May 5, the Illinoisans fell upon twenty-four Southern wagons. After burning the wagons, they captured an officer and chased away the Southern waggoners. They marched to Urbana and Gloucester Court House, encamping at 8:00 that night.[29] The next day, he joined Kilpatrick's regiment and the combined forces continued on together.[30]

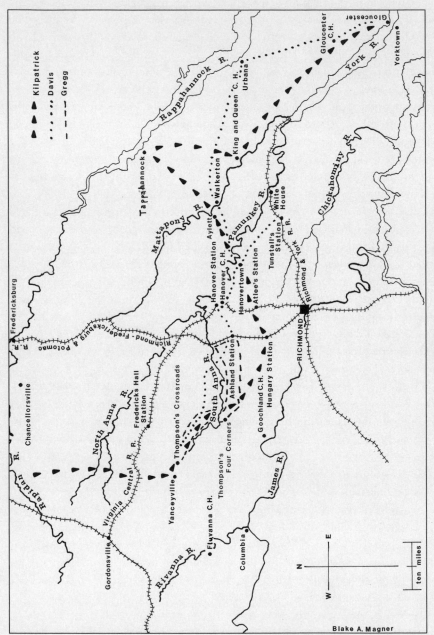

The "Bursting Shell," Stoneman's Raid

Blake A. Magner

Angry local citizens buzzed around the fringes of the Federal column as it made its way to Gloucester Point. The bushwhackers took potshots at the moving column the whole way, but inflicted no casualties. Their presence only made the march of the Northerners more unpleasant as they struggled their way to safety.[31] On May 7, the combined regiments of Kilpatrick and Davis made their way into the Union lines at Gloucester Point.

Kilpatrick had covered nearly 200 miles in just over 100 hours with losses of only one officer and thirty-seven enlisted men. Their ride rivaled Jeb Stuart's legendary "Ride Around McClellan" during the Peninsula Campaign, and was as much of an accomplishment. The men of the 2d New York Cavalry burned two bridges of the Richmond, Fredericksburg and Potomac Railroad along the way and raised a panic in Richmond. Likewise, Davis's men had cut both the RF&P and the Virginia Central, and they also inflicted serious damage on the Confederates. The Illinoisans lost two officers and thirty-three enlisted men in their expedition, which also covered more than 200 miles. "We brought in with us 100 mules and 75 horses captured from the enemy," claimed a proud Hasbrouck Davis, "We captured on the course of our march a much larger number, which we could not bring in. The amount of property destroyed is estimated at over $1,000,000."[32] A defiant Richmond newspaper claimed, "The damage they accomplished was very slight. The buildings burned were small structures and will be replaced with little cost and but an immaterial delay. The only real inconvenience is occasioned by the want of facilities for transportation of the wounded in the recent battle."[33]

On May 9, Davis inspected his regiment to ascertain what was lost during the course of the long and arduous raid, which had taken a severe toll on the regiment's mounts.[34] Kilpatrick received orders to assume command of all Federal cavalry at Yorktown, and to remain there until ordered to move.[35]

Kilpatrick's men conducted a short excursion toward Matthews Court House to scour the local countryside for fresh mounts and other provisions that only added to the Southerners' hardships. "We got near three hundred and they were the best of horses, too," proudly reported a member of the 12th Illinois. "Got about 200 head of cattle and a great many sheep and etc. We have won the honorable name now of 'Horse Thieves' and we are pretty good at the business you may bet but we saw no Rebbs this time except a few bushwhackers, which we captured." They destroyed a fair amount of property, including several gristmills filled with wheat and flour.[36] Although these two regiments did not return to the main body of the Army of the Potomac until the end of May, they achieved a remarkable accomplishment. When they safely arrived at Yorktown, Secretary Stanton cabled, congratulating them for "an achievement unsurpassed for daring and success."[37]

Kilpatrick assumed hero status in the eyes of his men. They believed that he had done a superb job of leading them to safety through their long ordeal, and they wrote a letter to President Lincoln, asking that their colonel be promoted to brigadier general. Seventy-six of the brigade's officers signed the letter, stating that "Little Kil" had conducted the most "daring feat of the war, leading his command within, through, and out of the fortifications of Richmond."[38] The promotion came through on June 14, 1863, so this letter undoubtedly influenced President Lincoln's decision.

WESLEY MERRITT'S RIDE

Stoneman selected his chief ordnance officer, Capt. Wesley Merritt, to lead one column of his bursting-shell strategy. Merritt, at age twenty-nine, was just embarking upon a spectacular military career that had few parallels in American history. He graduated twenty-second out of forty-one in the West Point class of 1860, and was commissioned into the 2d Dragoons. The young subaltern had the good fortune to be assigned to serve in Capt. John Buford's Company G in Utah. At the outbreak of the Civil War, Merritt came east with his regiment and served as aide-de-camp to Brig. Gen. Philip St. George Cooke, Jeb Stuart's father-in-law, and the man known as the Father of the U.S. Cavalry. Merritt performed ably in that role, and when Stoneman assumed command of the newly formed Cavalry Corps, he selected Merritt to be his ordnance officer.[39]

Wesley Merritt was "a pleasant, handsome young fellow" who possessed "the right temperament for a cavalryman."[40] He was "tall, slender and intellectual-looking. He had a constitution of iron, and under a rather passive demeanor, concealed a fiery ambition."[41] Capt. Theophilus F. Rodenbough, who served with Merritt in the 2d U.S. Cavalry, recalled his friend as "the embodiment of force. He was one of those rare men whose faculties are sharpened and whose view is cleared on the battlefield. His decisions were delivered with rapidity of thought and were as clear as if they had been studied for weeks." Rodenbough continued, "He always said that he never found that his first judgment gained by time and reflection. In him a fiery soul was held in thrall to will. Never disturbed by doubt, or moved by fear, neither circumspect nor rash, he never missed an opportunity or made a mistake."[42] Quiet, unassuming, and modest, Merritt was very much John Buford's protégé. The young man was marked for greatness. However, this would be his first independent combat command.

After receiving his assignment from Stoneman, Merritt took a contingent of approximately fifty members of the 1st Maryland Cavalry led by Capt. W. H. Griffin and a few pioneers from the 12th Illinois Cavalry to destroy as many bridges and fords as possible along the South Anna River below Yanceyville. Merritt left two bridges intact at Yanceyville and a few miles south, and then commenced his wave of destruction, meeting up with David Gregg's column. Gregg lent Merritt a few additional pioneers, as well as his aide, Capt. Henry C. Weir, and Merritt then set out once again. They destroyed two additional bridges, one above Ground Squirrel Creek and the so-called Factory Bridge, with Captain Weir, zealously accomplishing the expedition's objects. "These bridges were all strongly built," observed Merritt, "and averaged fifty feet in length. The work of destroying them was necessarily arduous, and consumed time. They were all effectually destroyed by fire and the axes of the pioneers, so that they cannot be rebuilt save by preparing new material for their construction."[43]

After demolishing these bridges, Merritt and his men continued their march. About an hour after sundown on May 3, he found Gregg's column of raiders and joined them. Merritt had done well in his first independent command. He praised the Maryland men and their leader, Captain Griffin, as well as the Illinois pioneers, for their performance during the expedition. "The command marched two days and nights, after having passed through the same hardships on the preceding two days as the rest of the expedition, without any sleep save what they got in their saddles, and little if any food," wrote Merritt. "The distance marched was over 100 miles, and during the halts the men, without exception, were all hard at work destroying the bridges, felling trees, and rolling logs, to render the fords impracticable." About the pioneers from the 12th Illinois, Merritt claimed, "These men worked and endured beyond my preconceived notions of human capacity without a murmur."[44]

GEN. DAVID M. GREGG'S MARCH

General Gregg led the largest detachment away from Thompson's Crossroads on May 3. He marched two regiments down the South Anna "for the purpose of destroying the several bridges between Thompson's Four Corners and the [Virginia Central] Railroad."[45] Not far into their march, Merritt and his squadron of the 1st Maryland fell in with the 1st Maine and the 10th New York, and the combined force destroyed five bridges across the South Anna. Late that afternoon, they arrived at Rocky Mills, fifteen miles from Richmond. Gregg stopped there to feed his horses and give his men a rest. While there, the Pennsylvanian heard a report that only a handful of enemy cavalry held the bridge carrying the RF&P over the South Anna River, and ordered Lt. Col. Charles H. Smith to select 100 men from each of the two regiments, along with Merritt's Marylanders, to destroy the bridge, which would cripple critical lines of supply for the Confederates.[46]

Smith found a local black man to act as a guide. Unfortunately, the man's knowledge of the terrain left a lot to be desired. Smith waited until dark to mask his approach and had quite an adventure. "It was a wild ride of several miles, mainly through woods, with no road, and it seemed in no particular direction, and most of the way at a trot," recalled the regimental historian of the 1st Maine. "There was a lively dodging of the lower branches of the trees, and more than one of the boys found himself nearly, if not quite, brushed from his saddle by a heavy branch, which he did not see in time to dodge, in his rapid ride."[47]

They struck the tracks near Ashland about 9:00 P.M., targeting "several culverts, 4 large RR buildings, 400 cords of wood, repairing tools of eight men, three locomotives, cut the wire, and damaged things generally." "We had a grand fire," described one of the Maine men.[48] Another recalled, "We set a station house, depot, lots of Government stores and a mighty lumber pile on fire, and you better believe we made one rousing blazer. You would have thought the whole Confederacy was on fire if you had seen it."[49] Stopping by a nearby house, they also rounded up a few unfortunate Confederates whom Sgt. Nathan Webb thought were "sparking" the girls inside. "Such a sheepish, woebegone, forsaken lot of mortals I never saw," recounted Webb.[50]

The Yankee horsemen found the destruction of the South Anna Bridge a difficult task. They learned that "the enemy had sent a force of infantry and artillery for its protection, this protection doubtless having resulted from Lieutenant-Colonel Davis's operations at Ashland," noted Gregg. One member of the 6th Ohio speculated that 500 Southern infantrymen guarded the bridge, preventing the Federal horsemen from getting to it.[51] "We moved out and fired a volley into their ranks, but could not draw them out," noted a Maine horse soldier, "so the Colonel concluded that 200 poor, tired, sleepy cavalrymen were not equal to the task, and I think that he was right, for we were entirely worn out by hard marches and lack of sleep."[52]

With the excitement of the wild ride over, Smith's exhausted horsemen headed toward Rocky Mills as "tired nature began to assert its sway." Most of Smith's men nodded off in the saddle, trusting their horses to find their way. Because the sleeping troopers exercised little control over their horses, their column was strung out across the Virginia countryside "to almost indefinite length, with large gaps in it; and the utmost efforts of officers and the wakeful men were insufficient to keep the men anywhere except straggling along in single file."[53] A handful of alert Confederates could have bagged the entire column, and the nervous Union officers knew it. They finally arrived at Rocky Mills about 2:00 A.M. The discipline of the exhausted and frustrated horsemen broke down completely, as "arguments, orders, curses, loud and frequent, and even blows could not keep the men awake."[54]

Gregg typically liked to ride alone, at the head of his troops, although he would periodically invite his divisional medical director to join him. Pvt. Henry C. Meyer of the 2d New York Cavalry, clerk to one of Gregg's staff officers, rode a fine horse that happened to be a fast walker. Meyer often fell asleep in the saddle, and when his grip on the bridle reins slackened, the horse forged ahead. Instead of trying to rein in the horse, Meyer's amused comrades opened ranks and urged him along.

The soundly sleeping soldier was soon riding alongside the commanding general, and sometimes even passed him. Gregg would grab him by the arm and say, "Meyer, wake up." The embarrassed and sleepy horseman returned to his rightful place in line to the laughs and catcalls of the staff officers and orderlies.

At one point while marching, Meyer nodded off and his horse strayed from the road and followed a fence up a bank until he could go no farther. Gregg spotted Meyer, and with a laugh, called out, "Wake him up, he will break his neck." As the horse slid back down the slope toward the road, the jolt startled Meyer from his slumber, although he somehow managed to stay in the saddle. According to Meyer, "The incident happened so frequently on this raid that it evidently made an impression on the general, because meeting him some twenty years after the war at a reunion in Philadelphia he, on greeting me, introduced me to a group of officers and immediately recalled the feat of my so often being asleep on horseback." Meyer continued, "The only penalty I suffered from sleeping on horseback was the occasional loss of a cap and the scratching of my face by the branches of trees, but it undoubtedly had much to do with my being able to withstand the fatigue incident to our campaigns, since the fact is that I never was off duty for a single hour, by reason of sickness, during my whole term of service."[55]

Somehow, Smith spurred them on, and they caught up to the rest of Gregg's column about an hour later. The entire column rested briefly, then the tired horsemen swung back into their saddles before dawn on May 4. "We did not unsaddle our horses," recalled a Maine trooper, "but just had a few moments to rub them down and rest their backs. We got very little sleep. We would just turn out into the field or woods, dismount, hitch the halter to our wrists and lie down for an hour's sleep." Rumors of large enemy forces waiting for them on the banks of the Pamunkey River sent chills up the spines of the weary Federals, but they pressed on anyway.[56] "Our rations were hardtack and raw pork. We had no time to make coffee. We finally got so sleepy that we would go to sleep on our horses and the last night of this raid if the Johnnies had come onto us they would have captured a lot of us. As it was, there were quite a number got so sleepy that they fell out of the column in the night and were gobbled up by guerrillas. We did not meet with any regular forces of the enemy, just a few home guards and they did not give us much trouble."[57]

Gregg and his men reached Stoneman's base at Thompson's Crossroads about noon. "We started back with our plunder which consisted of horses, mules, niggers besides what flour, bacon, grain and tobacco we could well carry," recounted a Maine trooper. "On the whole we had a big time though suffered much from want of sleep."[58] By the time Gregg's command made its way back to Thompson's Crossroads, its men had spent nearly two full days in the saddle, and they had marched about 100 miles. It had been quite an adventure.[59]

SIR PERCY WYNDHAM'S EXPEDITION

Departing at 3:00 A.M. on May 4, Wyndham and 400 horse soldiers of two regiments took a southerly route. After marching fifteen miles, they crossed Byrd Creek and burned the bridge. Two squadrons of Southern cavalry greeted the raiders, but the advance guard of Wyndham's column drove away the little enemy force that escaped across the James River; the bridge they crossed was later destroyed by Wyndham's men. The Federals reached Columbia on the James about 10:00 in the morning.[60]

A local citizen marked their route of march and rode nearly ten miles ahead to warn the skeptical town populace that a strong force of Yankee horsemen was headed their way. "What? Yankees near Columbia?" cried one citizen. "It is impossible," proclaimed another, "Jeff Davis would not permit such an invasion." The citizens threw dirt and rocks at the messenger, and were threatening to run him out of town on a rail when the vanguard of the 1st New Jersey Cavalry clattered in. There were no Southern soldiers there, and the citizens scattered quickly, several of them reaching safety on the far side of the James River.[61]

A local man, thinking that Stuart commanded the approaching column, sent his son out to greet the horse soldiers. The boy rode a fine horse. As he approached, the boy asked whether the Yankees had been whipped. "Whipped!" replied one of the Federals. "I reckon they will never want to be worst whipped!" The Union trooper eyed the boy's fine mount, and said, "By the way, my horse is just about played out, and I want yours instead." The lad, still thinking they were Confederate cavalrymen and wanting to do his part to help the cause, made the exchange. He returned home with a worn-out nag while the New Jersey trooper rode off with a fine new mount.[62]

The Jerseymen, commanded by Lt. Col. Virgil Brodrick, immediately set to work destroying everything they could. Some of the Federal troopers tried to drill a hole in the aqueduct wall, hoping that it would spring a leak that would eventually breach it. They gave up after the drill penetrated to a depth of six inches and instead placed two kegs of black powder in the river next to the aqueduct, hoping that the resulting explosion would destroy it. They ran a long fuse, but it fizzled out. Thwarted, the Federals contented themselves with the destruction of half a dozen bridges and the seizure of all available horses.[63] They destroyed five locks on the canal, as well as three barges loaded with supplies intended for the Army of Northern Virginia.[64] "I attempted to destroy the aqueduct crossing the canal at this point," reported Wyndham, "but failed to accomplish my purpose on account of not having sufficient time and the proper materials, as it is an immense structure, and would require a large amount of labor and at least forty-eight hours' time to accomplish it."[65]

Confederate soldier J. Kent Langhorne had narrowly missed being captured by Union troopers in Louisa Court House a few days earlier. Langhorne and his traveling companions rode to Columbia, hoping to escape from the Federal horse soldiers swarming across the central Virginia countryside. They arrived at Columbia just in time to see the vanguard of Wyndham's column arriving. Langhorne and his comrades tried to escape on the James River Canal towpath, but instead found themselves on top of the Federal raiding party. "I thought then I would be a prisoner in 10 minutes," recounted Langhorne, "but we crossed the small part of the James R. and got over on the island and happened to come to a man's private ferry who got us over and saved us from their mercy. They have burned all the bridges over the canal and all the barns and stables and everything like food on the other side of the River from here."[66]

About 4:00 that afternoon, Wyndham's column headed down the canal bank for about five miles to Cedar Point and destroyed the bridge to Elk Island. They also wrecked the canal at four different places and chopped to pieces the locks and gates, "rendering the canal irreparable and impracticable for a long time at least," he claimed. Wyndham wanted to destroy the depot at Appomattox Station, but he felt that the march was too long, and he worried about Confederates rumored to be pursuing him. Indeed, horse soldiers commanded by Fitzhugh Lee hovered close enough to the rear of Wyndham's retreating column that they passed still-burning campfires used by the Northerners to boil their coffee.[67] Rooney Lee's saddle soldiers arrived too late to catch Wyndham. Instead they turned toward Thompson's Crossroads. "I thought it expedient to retire to the cross roads, which I did without meeting any interruption whatever on the way."[68] Wyndham's men forded Byrd Creek, and continued on to Thompson's Crossroads, arriving there safely at 10:00 that night, covering fifty miles in sixteen hours with no casualties. They captured several hundred horses along the way, and were joined by several hundred escaped blacks.[69]

THE ENGAGEMENT AT SHANNON HILL

On the 3d, as the desperate battle whirled around the Chancellor house, Buford's Regulars pressed on to Thompson's Crossroads, where the Old Mountain and Cartersville Roads intersected below the South Anna River, in Goochland County. Buford reported to Stoneman, who still had his headquarters there. There, the 200 men of Capt. Thomas Drummond's 5th U.S. received instructions to examine the fords above Allen Creek, to burn the bridge on the Goochland Court House Road over the South Anna River, and to proceed to Goochland Court House. Along the way, they captured horses, mules, ham, bacon, flour, and a number of Southern prisoners. "The inhabitants were panic stricken," recounted a Regular who accompanied Drummond. "They fled their homes in the greatest haste, leaving everything they could not take away with them in their hurried flight. The greatest consternation prevailed. In some houses the tables were all spread ready to sit down to, and these meals our soldiers had the pleasure of eating."[70] Drummond fulfilled his orders "to the satisfaction of the general commanding [Buford]," and safely returned to the main column. Later that night, Lt. Julius W. Mason's detachment of the 5th U.S. reconnoitered the bridge over the South Anna at Yanceyville, leaving Drummond with only 109 men in camp. Drummond scouted the territory in the direction of Gordonsville, Fluvanna, and Columbia, and established contact with Mason.[71]

Rooney Lee, with 800 men of the 9th and 13th Virginia Cavalry, carefully followed Stoneman's command west toward Gordonsville, moving parallel and west of Stoneman. With his vigilant scouts constantly feeling for the Northern advance, Lee avoided a pitched battle against an adversary that greatly outnumbered him.[72] Early on the morning of May 3, Lee and his command left Gordonsville and rode south through Green Springs and on to Palmyra. A trooper of the 9th Virginia remembered the march as "very fatiguing to both men and horses."[73] They went on to Columbia, arriving too late to catch Wyndham's raiders. Frustrated, Rooney Lee gave chase, heading east on the River Road and then north on the Cartersville Road.

Aware that a large force of Confederate cavalry operated in the area, Stoneman sent Capt. James E. Harrison's 5th U.S. Cavalry to Fleming's Crossroads, where a handsome farm called Shannon Hill sat.[74] Harrison was to guard against surprise by the Confederate cavalry operating nearby. John Buford's twenty-nine-year-old nephew Temple, a lieutenant in the 5th U.S. Cavalry, served as an aide on Buford's staff. On the morning of May 4, Lieutenant Buford rode with the 5th U.S. Cavalry.

At 6:00 on the morning of May 4, the 9th Virginia arrived at the crossroads of the Three Chopt and Cartersville Roads, about four miles east of Shannon Hill, where a local farmer informed them that Wyndham's column had passed through several hours earlier.[75] The Southerners stopped to eat breakfast before continuing. Because one of the Virginians had no rations, he asked permission to forage west up the Three Chopt Road in search of something to eat. He came flying back a few minutes later, reporting that a dozen of Harrison's Yankee pickets could be seen about a mile west.

About 6:30, Col. Richard L. T. Beale, the commander of the 9th Virginia, ordered one of his officers to take ten men and try to capture the Federals. The Confederates moved west up the Three Chopt Road, trying to surprise the Regulars. The pickets spotted the Virginians and opened fire on them. These pickets also warned Harrison that the enemy had been spotted moving on his position. After sending out his various scout and picket details, Harrison had only twenty-five men with him as a main body. He reinforced the picket line with nine additional men, who charged and shoved the Confederates back. Beale committed two companies, approximately sixty men, to the growing fight, while the rest of Lee's men quickly finished their breakfasts and prepared for action. The opposing columns charged each other in the road, four abreast.[76] The overwhelming Confederate force drove the Regulars back toward Shannon Hill, with the balance of Lee's command in pursuit.

Harrison decided to make a stand at the crossroads until he could get word to Stoneman. Fourteen men of the 5th U.S. charged the onrushing Confederates, blunting their approach. They "came up to the charge manfully," noted a Confederate officer.[77] Beale's 9th Virginia Cavalry attacked Harrison's thirty-man battle line, drawn up in the road. Harrison's men charged the Confederates, and a "spirited hand-to-hand sabre fight" took place.[78] As the Virginians came up to join the fray, one of Beale's officers recalled, "[V]ery quickly we saw the men ahead of us flashing their sabers in the morning light, and meeting a charge by a Federal squadron."[79]

"When the enemy discovered Captain Harrison had no reserve they also charged," noted the regimental historian of the 5th U.S., "and the combatants met on an open plain, near the edge of a wood, in a shock in which the foremost horses were knocked down like ten-pins in a bowling alley."[80] To his consternation, Harrison realized that he faced two full regiments of Confederates, not a squadron or two. After a whirling ten-minute engagement, sabers clanging in the afternoon sunlight, the Federal commander wisely broke off the action and looked for an avenue of escape. Harrison reported, "I fought them as long as I deemed prudent, and finding that I was overpowered by numbers, I wheeled about and retreated on the road to Yanceyville." They dashed up Shannon Hill with Rooney Lee's troopers in hot pursuit.[81]

Harrison's small command lost 33 prisoners in the engagement out of fewer than 100 men engaged, among them Temple Buford, whom Rooney Lee mentioned by name in his after-action report.[82] At least one Federal was killed, and another was shot through the shoulder. One of Harrison's Regulars, Pvt. George W. Burch, received seven saber wounds in the chaos. A number of Lee's horse soldiers also suffered saber cuts in the melee.[83] "Unfortunately, in one of these charges, we lost our regimental standard, the old color which we have carried through all the battles of the war, which was tattered and torn by grape shot and pierced by musket balls—our pride and our glory," lamented one of the Regulars.[84]

After interrogating his prisoners, Lee learned that Stoneman's main column was nearby. Lee realized that they were severely outnumbered and that his men and horses were at the limits of their endurance. Satisfied with his victory over Harrison's little command, Rooney Lee broke off the engagement and withdrew to Gordonsville.[85] In fact, when word of the engagement at Shannon Hill reached Stoneman, he dashed off with the rest of Buford's Regulars in tow, hoping to rescue Harrison's men. They arrived in time to capture a couple of stragglers, but not in time to bring on a general engagement with Lee's troopers.[86]

"Capt. Harrison speaks in the highest terms of the officers and men with him in this engagement, and he deserves the highest praise for his coolness and gallantry displayed in extricating his command from the clutches of a force that was more than ten times superior in numbers," noted Buford. "I feel confident that had he had the 200 men of his regiment with Captain Drummond, he would have dispersed the force that attacked him."

Several days later, after the end of the raid, Buford found time to write to his half-brother, Brig. Gen. Napoléon Bonaparte Buford, about his son Temple's fate. "On the 3d a picket of the 5th Cavalry was attacked by over 1000 of the enemy. Capt. Harrison met their charge with 30 men, checked them long enough to call in his different parties, and made good his escape. Your son, Temple Buford, was the lieutenant," reported John Buford, who noted that Temple "had been sent down a by road with 6 men, and while there the rebel cavalry charged past the mouth of the road, thus cutting his party off. I feel confident he is safe. This was near Shannon Hill, 8 miles from the James river." Buford concluded, "We had a terrible march—constantly on the go, night and day. All speak well of Temple. Poor fellow, I guess he has found the cavalry service rougher than he dreamed of."[88]

THE REST OF BUFORD'S COLUMN ADVANCES

Departing from Thompson's Crossroads on May 4, elements of the Cavalry Corps fanned out across the countryside, foraging vigorously as they went. "The next three days are long to be remembered," observed Dr. John B. Coover of the 6th Pennsylvania Cavalry, "for we were in the enemy's country far enough away from reinforcements & our command considerably cut up by separation for various expeditions."[89]

Edgar B. Strang, saddler for Company E of the 6th Pennsylvania Cavalry, went out foraging with a few of his comrades. They rode up to a farm where the owner greeted them at the gate. Rubbing his hands and smiling, the farmer said "he was glad to be able to look in the face of Union men again," but indicated that he had no food to spare. Suspicious, Strang and his fellow Lancers forced the man to open his smokehouse, where "there were huge hams like apples on a tree." The hungry Lancers quickly confiscated their prize and escaped, with cries of "You Yankee thieves!" echoing behind them. Unfortunately for Strang and his comrades, their expedition soon came to naught, as Rooney Lee's men captured them near the North Anna River, where they were searching for more supplies. They then marched off to Richmond's notorious Libby Prison.[90]

The 1st U.S. Cavalry had a different mission that morning—destroying the warehouses, depot, and railroad at Fredericks Hall Station. Capt. Isaac R. Dunkelberger of the 1st U.S. approached the burning depot. He spotted the legs of a man sticking out from under a straw stack. Dunkelberger noticed that the man wore blue pants but figured that the man was a Confederate trying to hide. One of the Regulars pulled the man out, and Dunkelberger realized that he was a member of his company, named Flaherty. "Bejabers, I found a barrel of apple whiskey," slurred Flaherty. He had found a cask of the stuff, poked a hole in it, and filled half a dozen canteens. Dunkelberger realized that he could not afford to have drunken men roaming about the unfriendly countryside, so he confiscated the whiskey and moved on. That night, he passed around the canteens so that every man in his company got some. His men slept well that night, their stomachs warmed by the contraband whiskey.[91]

Meanwhile, the balance of Stoneman's command was off raiding Confederate railroad and telegraph positions. Some contingents approached the very suburbs of Richmond. As word of the Yankee threat spread, sirens blared in the city of Richmond. Contingents of old men, young boys, and convalescents deployed to defend the Confederate capital.[92] In the chaos following the Army of the Potomac's defeat at Chancellorsville, Stoneman's men were now completely cut off from all communication with Hooker's headquarters. They did not even know that the battle had been fought, let alone that Hooker's army had suffered a crushing defeat. Stoneman fretted about being cut off, and began reuniting the disparate elements of his command.[93]

Stoneman's troopers drew the attention of the Confederate high command. Confederate Secretary of War James Seddon reported the day's events to Lee, noting that the Federals "have been hovering around [Richmond] with two or three regiments, apparently menacing attack, probably covering escape of all down the Peninsula. We have a force to protect the bridges over the Annas and to defend the city, but want cavalry to punish the marauders. Hood's division is expected here this evening. The railroad communications shall be opened at the earliest practicable moment." Two regiments of Rooney Lee's cavalry brigade were ordered to Richmond, and part of Longstreet's Corps prepared for the defense of the Confederate capital, if necessary.[94]

THE IMPACT OF THE BURSTING SHELL

Stoneman's bursting shell had the predicted outcome. As a result of the threat posed by the Yankee cavalry, Brig. Gen. Wade Hampton's cavalry brigade, which had been on detached recruiting duty, was recalled to reinforce the defenses of the Confederate capital. Small parties of Hampton's troopers harassed Stoneman's rear, blocking the Northerner's routes of march. Hampton used every means of detaining the enemy possible, hoping to buy time for the Confederate high command to send out a large force to destroy Stoneman's column. Hampton's and Rooney Lee's men felled trees to block the roads.[95] One Confederate noted in his diary that if the Yankee cavalry were, "not back on the north side of the Rappahannock by this time, it is probable that they will reach Richmond in a few days without arms, and on foot."[96] Stoneman's bedraggled Union troopers had to find their way back to the Army of the Potomac quickly, lest the now-alerted Confederates intercept them and bag the whole lot.

THE MARCH BACK TO THE ARMY OF THE POTOMAC

Stoneman had heard whispers from runaway slaves and local citizens of a catastrophic Union defeat at Chancellorsville. This information, along with Harrison's repulse at Fleming's Crossroads, decided the issue. Stoneman retired to Shannon Hill on May 4. The next day, he moved to Yanceyville and began working on a plan to make his way back to the main body of the Union army and safety. Stoneman was "determined to make our way back to the Army of the Potomac," convinced that "all that we were sent to perform" had been accomplished.[97]

The Cavalry Corps commander realized that "to take the enemy by surprise and penetrate his country was easy enough, but to withdraw from it was a more difficult matter." Confederate forces positioned near Gordonsville to prevent him from marching on Charlottesville presented the most serious threat to the Northern cavalry.[98] "It was known that this point was garrisoned by a large force of Rebel infantry, and as it was a very important point, it was taken for granted that if it was threatened the enemy would concentrate all his available cavalry in that neighborhood," remembered an officer of the 1st U.S. Cavalry. "This would give Gen. Stoneman and our main body an opportunity to push straight for the Rapidan, and if that stream was fordable to cross it and make for the Rappahannock." Buford would be left to his own devices. "It was a forlorn hope, but it was the only [one] left us, and Buford was the man of all others to be entrusted with such an undertaking," concluded the Regular.[99]

On May 5, Stoneman sent Buford, with 646 handpicked men from the Reserve Brigade and the 6th Pennsylvania Cavalry, on their forlorn mission. Buford left Fleming's Crossroads, crossed the South Anna on the Yanceyville Bridge, and tried to go west cross-country to Gordonsville. However, the dense woods and poor ground prohibited him from doing so. The march was not pleasant. The rain had commenced again, and it increased in intensity as the day wore on. The men were in unfamiliar country, trying to navigate increasingly poor roads. As horses became hopelessly mired in the thick muck, their riders often left them foundering. The dismounted trooper, his saddle slung across his back, tried to make better progress on foot. If he was unable to find another mount, he often collapsed from sheer exhaustion, "would wrap himself in his horse blanket and sleep by the roadside until morning. Many of our men thus dropping out by the way, were captured by the enemy," reported one Lancer.[100]

With a freed slave as his guide, Buford now headed north for Louisa Court House.[101] The second Federal visit in a week found telegraph service restored, so the Yankee troopers again put the telegraph out of commission and seized the post office. Buford then moved west along the railroad to Trevilian Station, hoping to find out whether Confederate cavalry held Gordonsville, six miles away. There, his horse soldiers destroyed water tanks, rails, pumps, handcars, arms, ammunition, and a large supply of provisions. "I little thought then that thirteen months later I was to be engaged in a terrible battle at this very spot, but so it was," observed Capt. George B. Sanford of the 1st U.S. Cavalry.[102]

The Kentuckian's weary troopers then advanced toward Gordonsville. In the process, they captured several horses belonging to Confederate Maj. Gen. Isaac Trimble, as well as an entire warehouse of tobacco, a much-welcomed treat for the men of the 1st U.S. "When within two miles of Gordonsville, we found a large force of infantry and artillery in our front," recalled Sanford, "and it looked very much as if our time had come."[103] As they marched, an aide galloped up to inform the Regulars that the head of the column was under attack. "Hundreds of pounds of tobacco was thrown away by the men to lighten up; but before we came to where the fight had been, it was over," noted an officer. "The enemy had been beaten back." All of that good tobacco had gone to waste.[104] Repulsed, Buford forded the North Anna River at Mallory's Ford just in time—its waters were rising from the constant rain. His rear guard had to cross on rafts.[105]

By now, Buford's Regulars were nearly at the limits of their endurance. "The mud was deep, and worked into a very soft condition. From the unceasing splash of liquid mud, one would suppose we were marching in a stream of water to our horses' knees," recalled Gracey. "Our clothing being thoroughly saturated for more than two days, and a keen wind and cold driving rain in our faces, rendered this night's ride anything but pleasant." Exhausted men slept on their horse's necks as their faithful mounts struggled along to keep up with the rest of the column. Occasionally, "a weary rider and jaded beast were passed on the roadside, having marched to the point of possible endurance for that night." Relying on the good instincts of their horses in the cold darkness, men could only hope to keep up with the column, trusting their steeds to bring them to safety.[106]

While Buford's men made their feint, Stoneman, with the rest of the Union cavalry, numbering fewer than 2,000 men, rested at Yanceyville. On May 5, near Yanceyville, Rev. A. O. Brickman, chaplain of the 1st Maryland Cavalry, officiated at services for the entire Cavalry Corps. "A patriotic and fervent prayer was offered by Major Charles H. Russell of the same regiment," inspiring the horse soldiers to finish their journey.[107] That same day, Stoneman sent a separate column of 300 selected troopers, under command of Capt. Theophilus F. Rodenbough of the 2d U.S. and Capt. Thomas Drummond of the 5th U.S., to cross the South Anna downstream to create an additional diversion. "Our march was somewhat delayed by the darkness of the night and the mixed 'convoy' of contraband Negroes and captured horses and mules," recalled Rodenbough, "making our column fully one-half mile long. At Louisa Court House the roads were knee deep in mud, destroying all trails, and being without a map or information as to the direction taken by the main body, I was somewhat puzzled as to my further movements."[108]

As dusk fell, these horsemen mounted and crossed the river, burning the bridge behind them. With miserable weather plaguing their march, they crossed the Virginia Central at Tolersville and the North Anna River near the Victoria Iron Works. "It was a dismal ride, made more so by the sound of an occasion shot from a guerrilla," noted a member of the 1st Maine Cavalry, "and the doleful note of a single whippoorwill that followed the column all night long."[109] Cold, wet, and weary to the bone, Sergeant Webb trembled "till my flesh was as tender as raw meat" as he continued his march.[110] Rodenbough was worried. He did not know where the main body lay, and he also did not know where to go. Just as Rodenbough's level of concern grew, one of Stoneman's staff officers reined in, saying, "We thought you had been captured and had about given you up." With the staff officer to lead them, the relieved Rodenbough and Drummond made their way back to Stoneman and main body of the Cavalry Corps.[111]

Gregg's division marched all night on May 4. They did not halt until morning on May 5, when they finally fed their horses and themselves and moved out again. That night it rained heavily once more, and the troopers, suffering greatly from the elements, continued their advance, Gregg and Stoneman relentlessly spurring them on. The two officers were afraid of being cut off and captured wholesale by the enemy. Their fears forced the men on to superhuman exertion. "Many of the men slept in their saddles on the march and when the column stopped you could hear snoring all along the line," observed an Ohioan. "It sounded comical enough, though in reality there was not much sport in it. For myself, I managed to keep conscious while marching, but when we halted I sometimes slept."[112]

Early on the 6th, as Buford's Reserve Brigade prepared to march again, Stoneman and Gregg arrived, reuniting the column. The entire command rested for several hours, setting out for Raccoon Ford toward evening. Stoneman pointedly observed that "[a]dded to the severe duty performed by the command previous to its return, the men had been almost constantly in the saddle for two nights, and a day, and we were all wet, cold, tired, and hungry."[113] After fording the Rapidan at Raccoon Ford, Stoneman realized that both men and animals were approaching the end of their endurance. He ordered the horses unsaddled and fed, and permitted the troopers to cook whatever rations they could forage. "Fires were soon started, coffee prepared, and after a light lunch, we wrapped ourselves in wet blankets and were soon asleep," recorded one Federal trooper.[114] At ten that morning, the column set out for Kelly's Ford. They arrived that night, only to find the Rappahannock once again too flooded to ford.[115] "The rain pouring in torrents, and so dark that at times I could not see my horse's ears," reported Capt. John Robertson, who commanded a battery of horse artillery, "and with the mud so deep that it was with difficulty my saddled horse could extract his feet."[116]

On the night of the 6th, the 1st U.S. Cavalry arrived at Raccoon Ford. Unable to cross and exhausted, Captain Dunkelberger settled down to take a nap on a nearby log. He dozed off quickly, but got only a few minutes of shut-eye. His adjutant shook him awake with orders to reconnoiter Raccoon Ford in order to make certain that no Confederates held it. "It was a cruel awakening as I had not slept for nearly a week," recalled Dunkelberger, "but I mounted my squadron and off I went. I found the Ford clear of the enemy. I forded the stream and found it fordable. I then moved back with my squadron towards the command about three miles from the Ford. I saw the head of the column approaching me." By the time that the Regulars returned to the ford, it was dark and raining hard. All night, the bedraggled column of cavalry struggled across the Rappahannock. Many of the exhausted Yankees slept, but still held their balance on their sturdy mounts. Other horses wandered off into the woods with their riders. "It was estimated that we lost 300 men that night. The men could keep awake no longer," observed Dunkelberger.[117]

Buford had orders to join Stoneman the next day at Orange Springs. The Kentuckian waited for the rest of the corps to arrive for several hours and was just about to give up and ride for Raccoon Ford when Stoneman and the rest of the column arrived at midnight on May 7. In a pelting rain, the soggy Federal troopers began the long march back to the Army of the Potomac. "The night was very dark, and much of the way led us through dense woods, intensifying the darkness," recalled a member of the 6th Pennsylvania Cavalry. "For several hours it was utterly impossible for one to see the person riding immediately in advance, or even the head of the animal upon which he was himself mounted."[118] Moving through the black night, navigating swamps, impenetrable woods, and cowpaths, the blueclad troopers avoided the main roads.

On May 7, Stoneman confirmed that Hooker had suffered a crushing defeat at Chancellorsville, meaning that further raiding would serve no purpose. He would have to withdraw across the Rappahannock River to reach safety. Stoneman dashed off a letter to Hooker. "We shall move on today, as fast as the nature of the roads and the broken down, worn out condition of the men and animals will permit, towards Germanna, from which point I am in hopes of to communicate directly with Headquarters." Stoneman closed by pleading for rations for horses and men, "We can meet them at any point on the Rappahannock as far up as Bealeton Station, but not beyond."[119]

Stoneman sent Lt. Edwin V. Sumner, Jr., son of the former Army of the Potomac corps commander, and an escort of sixteen handpicked men to carry dispatches to Hooker. The little force marched by way of Germanna Bridge, hoping to reach U.S. Ford. Local residents told Sumner what had happened at Chancellorsville and advised him to find another route, as he would be heading into a large force of Confederates if he continued on. They charged an enemy picket post, scattering the Southern vedettes. In a few minutes, the alerted Confederates were pursuing, and it became a race for whom would reach Kelly's Ford—eight miles away—first. Sumner and his troopers turned on their pursuers, dismounting several of the Southerners, and escaping. Sumner reached his objective just before dark. Leaving a few of his men behind, Sumner plunged into the flooded river and crossed while the Confederates shot at him. "Being deep in the water by the side of his swimming horse, he made a difficult target, and the Confederate fire was distracted by that of a strong Federal picket on the opposite side of the river."

Sumner made his way to Army of the Potomac headquarters after a cold, wet ride of twenty-two miles. The weary officer nodded off in the saddle, but his stead-fast mount continued on. The horse carried him straight to Hooker's tent, and the noise brought a staff officer out to investigate. "Why, this is Lieutenant Sumner, of General Stoneman's staff," proclaimed the staff officer. They lifted Sumner from his saddle, wrapped him in blankets, and left the exhausted officer to sleep a bit. Papers stored in his boot were taken to Hooker. The rest of Sumner's little column safely rejoined Stoneman's command the next day.[120]

After feeding and watering their horses, Stoneman's bedraggled cavalrymen pressed on to Orange Springs and crossed the Rapidan at Raccoon Ford.[121] "When we emerged on the bank of the river and found the coast clear we felt greatly relieved," recorded Webb. "The Col. had told us we were to remain here six hours. Six long hours! What a time in which to sleep. More than we've had at any one time since we started." Webb and his comrades quickly hunkered down and made the best of the opportunity.[122]

That night, the horsemen, who had spent two long nights in the saddle, were cold, tired, and hungry. They still had to make their way across the Rappahannock at Kelly's Ford. After unsaddling, they built fires and rested, cooking and eating whatever they had. The troopers then moved down to try to cross the swollen river, arriving about 9:00 P.M. on May 7. Learning that they could not cross, they stood to horse all night. "Few doubted that with the rising of the sun, Stuart with his horsemen would be upon us in force, and every precaution was taken to guard against surprise." Luckily, the dreaded attack never happened; the Confederate cavalry were nearly as used up as the Union men.[123]

The Union riders waited until morning, and found that they could only cross the river by swimming part way. "The river was a swollen torrent and too deep for fording," recalled an officer of the 2d U.S. "On the opposite bank a group of staff and line officers, with their backs towards a comfortable fire of rails and logs, were shouting the location of the ford, how to enter the stream, swim over, and land on the opposite bank. The water was very cold and, not inclined to get wet to the waist if I could avoid it, I crossed my legs on the pommel of my saddle." The staff officers immediately warned the cavalryman to be careful, that he would drown if he did not put his feet in the stirrups. "Preferring drenching to drowning, I obeyed. My horse entered the stream, moving up current until almost beyond his depth, then made a sharp turn to the right, then down the stream heading for the guide who stood to direct my course. As my horse turned, he lost his footing and began to swim low in the water, with his head and nostrils just above the surface. I landed safely, spoke to my horse and gave him a caress for his good behalf, raised my boot for the sacred water of Virginia to flow out, and received the congratulations of my fellow officers as we stood around the fire."[124] Stoneman himself was the last Union cavalryman to cross the Rappahannock.[125]

Almost the entire command made it to safety on the north bank of the Rappahannock, although one man and six horses drowned in the process of crossing the swollen stream. They moved to Bealeton Station on the Orange and Alexandria Railroad, where they found supplies and a safe place to halt.[126] The grateful Federals enjoyed several boxes of hardtack, which had been left for them on the north side of the Rappahannock. The men had been without rations for three days. As one soldier put it, "I never enjoyed a meal more than I did my hardtack that morning."[127] According to one of Buford's Regulars, "We had gained experience and earned the right to sleep in a tent for a day or two."[128] The long ordeal of the Yankee troopers was over. After nearly a month of extreme hardship and accomplishment, they were right back where they had started on April 13.

On May 8, a Richmond newspaper noted, "Whether Stoneman still lies upon the Central railroad or had returned North by Raccoon Ford is the question. We think he has, like the sensible cavalry officer he is said to be, done the latter. It seems impossible that he could have subsisted the force he is reported to have had on the exhausted country along the railroad."[129] However, the Confederate high command knew precisely where they were. Rooney Lee reported that they had recrossed the Virginia Central Railroad and were heading toward Raccoon Ford on May 7. The Southerner allowed them to go unmolested. "Down to the ford we have been operating on his flank and rear with some success," reported Rooney Lee, "but his main body has been too large for me with my small body of cavalry to make any impression."[130] One of Wade Hampton's officers expressed his frustration. "Our brigade was so much scattered and so far off we could not make a strike at Stoneman's Cavalry," complained Capt. Leonard Williams, who commanded a squadron of the 2d South Carolina Cavalry. "The other brigades were engaged more or less at Fredericksburg, consequently the raiders were unmolested. As soon as they heard of Hooker's defeat, they ran for dear life. I am annoyed at their escape but circumstances saved them."[131]

That day, Stoneman's commissary officer rode to Hooker's headquarters at Falmouth, where he received a cool reception. Hooker's chief of staff, Maj. Gen. Daniel Butterfield, told the officer, "From your account, I don't see but that you

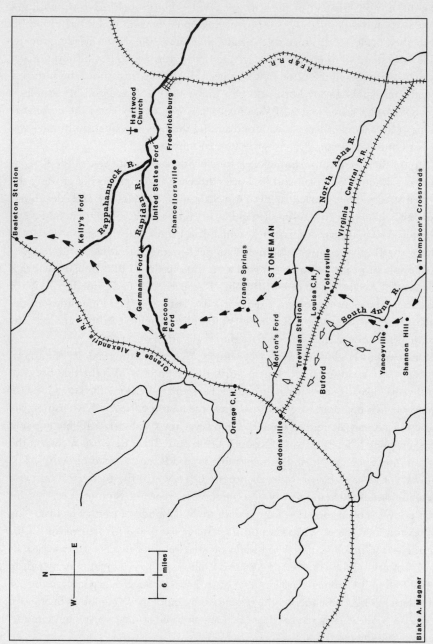

Stoneman's Raid Ends

Blake A. Magner

are ready to start out on another expedition right away." Offended by the remark, the Yankee officer bristled, "Perhaps, sir, your long experience with infantry has unfitted you to form a fair estimate of the work of the cavalry."[132]

Capt. Charles Francis Adams of the 1st Massachusetts wrote to his mother, "The air of Virginia is literally burdened today with the stench of dead horses, federal and confederate. You pass them on every road and find them in every field, while from their carrions you can follow the march of every army that moves."[133]

Elements of the Union Cavalry Corps were scattered all over Virginia, and it took time for the entire command to make its way back to the Army of the Potomac. "This is indeed a twice told tale and of the weariest at that," continued Adams. "Here am I once more picketing Hartwood Church after another battle of Fredericksburg, just as I did last December! I did on the fifteenth of last month confidently hope never again to see this modest brick edifice, but the wisdom of Providence differently ordained and here I am once more."[134] After two grueling weeks in the saddle, Stoneman's weary troopers finally rejoined the Army of the Potomac on May 16. Sgt. Christian Geisel of the 6th Pennsylvania Cavalry noted that "from the 29th of April to the 9th of May we only had our horses unsaddled about three hours, after the provisions had run out we carried along we lived on ham and corncakes of which we found a large quantity stored away in some places."[135]

THE CONSEQUENCES OF THE STONEMAN RAID

The raiders destroyed three railroad bridges, canal locks, stage bridges, and a number of railroad stations, as well as miles of railroad track, depriving the Confederacy of vital supply lines. When he penned his report of the expedition on May 13, Stoneman claimed, "Not one of the least valuable among other results of this expedition is the influence it has had upon the cavalry arm of the service, both in showing us what we are able to accomplish if we but have the opportunity and in convincing the country that it has not spent its men and money in vain in our organization."[136] Despite the damage done to the Virginia Central Railroad, the Confederates had repaired and restored it to service by May 11, when a Richmond newspaper reported that the railroad was open and operating to Gordonsville. All of the destroyed bridges were back in service within a matter of a few days.[137] Further, Hooker's defeat at Chancellorsville rendered those valiant efforts moot. "Unfortunately, our withdrawal across the Rappahannock will prevent advantage being taken of the cavalry success," wrote General Meade, "as they will now have time to repair damages before we can get at them again."[138]

The escape of the raiders frustrated the Confederate high command. "All our reports represent the enemy's main cavalry force returning to the Rappahannock by the same or nearly the same route as that they came [by]," complained James

Longstreet. "I fear that no effort has been made by our forces or citizens to obstruct his routes."[139] The *Richmond Daily Dispatch* echoed a similar frustration, claiming, "[T]he Yankees are very imitative. Our cavalry raids have stimulated 'them' to the effort at imitation. . . . Not a bridge worthy the name was destroyed. . . . So the Yankee cavalryman with his long sword, saddle, bridle, cavorting around, has done nothing.—save to get away, for which he has to thank the stars, or somebody else." The editor concluded, "Altogether, it is the most remarkable affair of the war. For deliberate prolonged planning, elaborate equipment and contemptible achievement; for the magnitude of its promises and the poverty of its performances is without parallel. It is not in the nature of things that the Yankee should achieve anything great on horseback. . . . Such a raid and such an escape have no parallel in history."[140] The editor eventually rued those words. For the time being, however, his assessment was accurate.

The commander of the Cavalry Corps had to defend himself from harsh criticism. Hooker believed that Stoneman had failed to follow his orders, and held him responsible for Averell's retreat. Stoneman felt that he had followed Hooker's orders to the letter, and so stated in his after-action report. "To the pecuniary loss in the destruction of the bridges over rivers, railroads, telegraphs, canals, wagon and railroad trains, public stores of all kinds, horses and mules captured, and those brought out by escaped slaves, corn, meal, and bacon consumed by the animals and men, etc., there must be added the money value of some 450 negroes, who came out of the country with the various parties," claimed the cavalry chieftain. "Several thousand more could have obtained their freedom through us could they have procured the means of transportation. Added to all this and much more is the moral effect the expedition has produced in the minds of both the white and black man, not only in that region but throughout nearly the entire South."[141] The Cavalry Corps suffered a total of 4 men killed, 7 wounded, and 139 captured or missing during the raid, for total casualties of 150.[142]

In fact, Stoneman's Raid was a success. First, the raid represented the first time that two divisions of cavalry came together and operated as a cohesive fighting force under the direction of a single commander. Second, the raiders successfully interdicted the Army of Northern Virginia's lines of communication during the Battle of Chancellorsville and for a week or so after the end of the battle, carrying "consternation everywhere," as one New York newspaper correspondent put it.[143] Third, the passage of the large raiding force prevented at least two divisions of Lt. Gen. James Longstreet's Corps from reinforcing the Army of Northern Virginia at Chancellorsville, perhaps saving Hooker's army from an even worse defeat than the one received. Fourth, and in stark contrast to future expeditions, the Cavalry Corps went out on a long and arduous mission and came back safely, with minimal losses. While terrible weather and events on the battlefield prevented Stoneman from carrying out Hooker's original concept for the expedition, Stoneman nevertheless fulfilled the spirit of the army commander's orders, and brought his force out safely. Stanton and Lincoln quite correctly hailed Stoneman's mission as a success.

However, Stoneman's Raid stripped the Army of the Potomac of its cavalry screen at a crucial time. The lack of a cavalry screen on the flanks permitted the Confederates to discover that the Union right flank was "in the air," a fact easily discovered by Stuart's vigilant and active cavalry. Because of this, Jackson completed his Chancellorsville flank march largely unmolested. As Buford's West Point classmate artillerist John Tidball wrote, "The enemy advanced and immediately commenced feeling Hooker's position, during which operation there was considerable desultory artillery practice. 'Jeb' Stuart, with his cavalry, closely reconnoitered the whole of Hooker's line from left to right, and reported to Lee the vulnerable condition of Hooker's right flank; that it was entirely in the air and easily reached."[144]

No less than Stonewall Jackson himself, while riding in an ambulance to his sickbed at Guinea Station, blamed Hooker's defeat at Chancellorsville on the lack of an adequate cavalry screen. "It was, in the main, a good conception, sir, an excellent plan," observed Jackson. "But he should not have sent away his cavalry; that was his greatest blunder. It was that which enabled me to turn him, without his being aware of it, and to take him by his rear. Had he kept his cavalry with him, his plan would have been a very good one."[145] It was Hooker who made the choice to send off virtually all of his cavalry, not Stoneman. That choice cost him dearly.

Fifteen years after the battle, Hooker admitted, "At this juncture, I felt that I had made a mistake in dispatching the greater part of my cavalry force, to sever Genl. Lee's communication with Richmond."[146] Hooker's bold gamble in trying to turn Lee's flank contributed to the turning of his own flank, causing the defeat at Chancellorsville. Confederate diarist John B. Jones wrote that Stoneman's raid "was the mad prank of a desperate commander. Hooker cast all upon the hazard of the die—and lost."[147]

Scout James Rodney Wood of the 1st Massachusetts Cavalry believed that the great raid "was a failure strategically. . . . It nearly crippled us as a cavalry command. Our horses returned from the raid in a ruinous condition, and the condition of the men was scarcely any better." He concluded, "[N]o good results attended this raid commensurate with the officers and labor involved; the loss of efficiency was keenly felt and was impossible to repair in the brief time which elapsed before Lee started on his march to Gettysburg."[148] A member of the 8th New York Cavalry observed that the Union horsemen "were compelled for nearly a month, to be engaged in constant and severe duty, with frequent skirmishes, loss of sleep, short rations for man and beast, which disabled some of the most vigorous of our men and horses both."[149]

"The real weakness of the whole raid was that it only exasperated, without ter-rifying the enemy, and gave color to the accusations that the Federal cavalry were merely mounted robbers," bitterly complained an enlisted man of the 6th New York Cavalry. "Had Stoneman destroyed W. H. F. Lee's brigade, which he might well have done, it would have been of far more value to the cause he represented than all the plunder and destruction that attended his path. As it was, it entirely failed to retrieve the disgrace of Chancellorsville, in public estimation, at the time, and the fact that Stoneman never attacked Richmond, which he might easily have done, as it was almost undefended, added to the unfavorable impression produced by his conduct of the raid."[150]

"During Stoneman's absence the sanguinary battle of Chancellorsville was fought by the Army of the Potomac, and as the success of the raid depended in great measure upon a Federal victory at Chancellorsville, it was not, strategically at least, a success," accurately observed Charles Rhodes, an early historian of the Army of the Potomac's Cavalry Corps. "The detachment of the Union troopers deprived General Hooker of cavalry at a time when he particularly needed a screening force to conceal his movements by the right flank; and it is probable that if Stoneman's cavalry had been present with the Army of the Potomac, it would have given ample warning of Stonewall Jackson's secret concentration opposite the Union right, which well nigh caused a decisive defeat for the Union army."[151]

"On April 29 we moved out of camp, crossed the Rappahannock and Rapidan Rivers, pushed boldly into the enemy's country, and soon came back faster than we went," facetiously claimed Capt. Hampton S. Thomas of the 1st Pennsylvania Cavalry. "As a stupid failure, 'Stoneman's Raid' was a complete success. Our only accomplishments were the burning of a few canal-boats on the upper James River (at Columbia), some bridges, hen-roosts, and tobacco houses."[152] Captain William L. Heermance of the 6th New York Cavalry, whose heroism at Alsop's Field even-tually earned him a Medal of Honor, later stated that Stoneman's Raid "accom-plished nothing."[153] "Raids are grand humbugs," groused Lt. Charles B. Coxe of the 6th Pennsylvania Cavalry.[154] Perhaps they were. Yet many more long and ardu-ous raids lay ahead for the Army of the Potomac's Cavalry Corps.

In spite of the temporary nature of its successes, the raid did have some real ben-efits. While many have criticized the way it was conducted, it severely tested the men's endurance and morale for the first time. It proved that Union troopers, if properly organized, could make a formidable raiding force capable of disrupting daily life in the Confederate capital. The men persevered through horrendous weather conditions, weak command leadership, and nearly indescribable hardship. They finished the raid with their heads held high, finally confident in their ability to hold their own against the best that the Confederate cavalry could throw at them. Trooper Sidney Davis of the 6th U.S. wrote home on May 17, "I have just been over to see the boys in the regiment, who have returned from the raid. Though worn out from fatigue and from want of sleep, and dusty and greasy, they are just full of fun. They seem to imagine that the enemy's cavalry is nothing now—they were victorious in every encounter."[155] A proud New Yorker, reflecting on the trials and tribulations of the recent expedition, commented, "There is but little rest for the cavalry at any time, and it is probably the most arduous branch of the service, still the thorough trooper prefers it to anything else, and considers it a shocking imposition if he is compelled to walk a half mile."[156]

Their participation in the raid became a matter of great pride to the men who endured its hardships. "We had a short but successful campaign as far as cavalry is concerned from April 29th to the 9th of May. It lasted but a short time, much shorter then I expected when we started," commented Sergeant Geisel to his sister, "but long enough for us to be going night and day getting but little rest or sleep and to do a great deal of destruction in rebeldom." He continued, "I would not have believed that we could have gone as near to Richmond as we did without encountering and being opposed by some portion of the rebel army. I have no doubt that Jeff Davis himself was alarmed about his safety in Richmond." Geisel came through his ordeal safely, although he lost his horse and two caps in the process. Fortunately, he found both a new mount and replacement headgear along the way.[157]

A Maine trooper summed up the feelings of the Cavalry Corps quite simply. "It was ever after a matter of pride with the boys that they were on 'Stoneman's Raid,'" he wrote.[158] A New Jersey trooper echoed a similar sentiment. "For the first time the cavalry found themselves made useful," he wrote, "and treated as something better than military watchmen for the army. They saw that the long desired time had come when they would be permitted to gain honor and reputation, and when they would cease to be tied to the slow moving divisions of infantry without liberty to strike a blow for the cause of the nation. . . . It gave our troopers self-respect, and obliged the enemy to respect them."[159]

A Pennsylvanian sounded a similar note. "But with the disaster at [Chancellorsville] comes the news of Stoneman's successful Cavalry Raid in the rear of Lee's Army destroying a vast amount of Rebel property without scarcely any loss," he recounted, "and it is one of the greatest cavalry exploits of the war, far outstripping Stewart's in Pennsylvania, and for once the Cavalry have done something to merit the praise of the Country and in fact the Infantry for the present think the Cavalry can do something towards helping to whip the enemy, in fact the Cavalry are the lions for the time."[160] "It was undoubtedly the greatest cavalry raid made during the war," proclaimed an officer of the 5th U.S., "and could not have been conducted better than it was by General Stoneman."[161] Another Pennsylvanian reported, "Stoneman's Cavalry did a big thing in their raid against Richmond, fully ahead of anything that the rebels did in that line, and let me assure the people at home that it will take harder fighting to whip the noble Army of the Potomac by far than ever."[162] The change in morale was quite welcome.

Groups of contrabands, runaway slaves who attached themselves to Union soldiers in the hope of gaining their freedom, hindered their marches. Stoneman's raiders were the first Yankees ever seen by many of these slaves. "As for the darkies, they were perfectly wild with joy," reported Capt. Delos Northway of the 6th Ohio Cavalry. "Some of them would dance, some would sing and some cry. Some of the boys passed one old fellow who was rolling his eyes, clapping his hands and making every demonstration of joy, and one of them said, 'What's the matter old man?' 'De grace ob God massa,' answered the old Negro." In an effort to discourage them from running away, many slave owners taught their slaves that the Yankees would kill all their children, so the blacks tried to hide them. An Ohioan entered a slave hut to get some bread and saw a cradle piled full of what appeared to be blankets. Curious, the Federal horseman upset the cradle and was shocked to find it filled with three black babies. In spite of their fear, the slaves often followed the blueclad horse soldiers, trudging along on foot through the mud without a word of complaint, jubilant about the prospect of gaining their freedom.[163]

THE CONFEDERATE RESPONSE TO STONEMAN'S RAID
Confederate cavalry chief Jeb Stuart largely dismissed Stoneman's Raid. In his official report of the Chancellorsville Campaign, the Confederate cavalry leader wrote, "That Stoneman, with a large cavalry force, was allowed to penetrate into the heart of the State, though comparatively harmless in results is due to the entire inadequacy in numbers of the cavalry of the Army of Northern Virginia." He continued, "The enemy has confronted us with at least three divisions of cavalry, more or less concentrated, which we oppose with one division, spread from the Chesapeake to the Allegheny; yet had not the approach of a battle below made it necessary to divide the force of the two Lees, I feel very confident that Stoneman's advance would have been prevented, though with great sacrifice of life, owing to the disparity of numbers."[164] However, not all of the Southern horse soldiers saw things the same way. "Stoneman has taken the shine off of Stuart," observed a captain of the 13th Virginia Cavalry. "[T]hat raid beat anything the Yankees ever done."[165]

The Union horsemen had created a great deal of disruption behind Lee's lines. "The enemy's Cavalry have gotten between [Berryville] and Richmond, cut the R. Road at Louisa Cth. and other points below," reported a trooper of the 1st Virginia Cavalry, "penetrated to the James River and are running wild over this country plundering and robbing."[166] One of Wade Hampton's Confederates, reporting on the raid on May 4, noted, "One thing is certain that they are making a great raid and if they get away it will be one of the finest of the war. I have no definite idea what the Yankees have been doing, but there has been considerable fighting, at a time like this you know there are a thousand rumors that are not reliable."[167]

THE RAID'S TOLL ON THE ARMY OF THE POTOMAC'S CAVALRY CORPS

The long ordeal took a savage toll on the Cavalry Corps' mounts. "Day after day, with but little resistance, horses had been captured, bridges, warehouses, and car-loads of provisions and clothing had been burned or otherwise destroyed, and the end of our raid seemed almost in sight," recalled a trooper. "But six days and nights in the saddle, with but slight rest or sleep, had exhausted the little command, and those of the men who had not been fortunate enough to capture fresh horses were wearily struggling along on foot, liable at any moment to be captured by the citizen soldiery who were gathering in squads from all sides."[168]

Buford's brigade alone abandoned 365 horses during the expedition. At the end of May, Pleasonton, then in temporary command of the Cavalry Corps, claimed that 6,000 horses were lost during the raid. Pleasonton reported that only 4,677 horses were serviceable in the entire Cavalry Corps. The March return for the Cavalry Corps showed an effective strength of more than 12,000 men and horses. "It is now one-third of that strength, and, so far as I can ascertain, is not fit-ted to take the field," wrote Pleasonton.[169] As a result of all the time spent slogging through the thick Virginia mud, the horses developed a condition known as "mud fever" that disabled many. Many others had sore backs as a consequence of not having been unsaddled for a week at a time. The Stoneman Raid left much of the Cavalry Corps *hors de combat* just when the Army of the Potomac needed it most. "I shall use every exertion to bring it to a state of efficiency at the earliest possible moment, but the responsibility of its present state, it is proper the major-general commanding should know, does not belong to me."[170] Pleasonton would not get much of an opportunity to prepare his command for further service in the field.

In losing the Battle of Chancellorsville, Hooker conceded the initiative to Robert E. Lee. The men were losing faith in Hooker. "Gen'l Hooker is a bold and fighting Gen'l," noted a Pennsylvania horse soldier, "but not one to plan out maneuvering of a large Army."[171] A New Englander noted, "If Hooker had done his part as well as we had done ours, he would have won the Battle of Chancel-lorsville."[172] A member of the 9th New York wrote, "As for our taking Richmond, I think there is about as much hopes of that as there is of the Rebels taking Phila-delphia."[173] The New Yorker had no way of knowing just how close to fruition his jest about the Confederates taking Philadelphia would come just a few weeks later.

Hooker, searching for a scapegoat, decided that Stoneman had caused the deba-cle and blamed him for the defeat at Chancellorsville. On May 10, Hooker told

Secretary of War Edwin M. Stanton, "[T]he raid does not appear to have amounted to much." As time passed, Hooker became even more convinced that Stoneman had caused the disaster at Chancellorsville. In a letter to historian Samuel P. Bates years after the war, Hooker claimed, "I consider Stoneman as justly answerable for my failure at Chancellorsville as Howard." He continued, "The cavalry did not march as they were ordered—did not obey their orders while marching, and did not return as they were ordered. They disregarded their orders from beginning to end, in letter and in spirit."[174]

Bates picked up Hooker's cudgel. "The purpose of General Stoneman was not to seek the enemy and fight, as his instructions required him to do, but the object of his strategy was, how 'to get out' without meeting an armed foe," sneered the well-respected historian in his 1882 study of the Chancellorsville Campaign, "and to that end to steal away 'under cover of night,' by 'the middle road.'"[175] This perception, which is grossly unfair to Stoneman and to his troopers, continues to plague modern analyses of the campaign, since it ignores Hooker's role in creating the problems that brought his grand plan to failure in the Virginia wilderness.

At a dinner party several months later, Hooker told Lincoln's secretary, John Hay, "I sent [Stoneman] out to destroy the bridges behind Lee. He rode 150 miles and came back without seeing the bridges he should have destroyed. . . . His purposeless ride had all the result of a defeat." Hooker conceded that Stoneman "is a brave good man, but he is spoiled by McClellan and the piles."[176] Stoneman harbored similar sentiments, stating that Hooker "was the most brilliant of all the generals up to a certain point, but when his limitation was reached he was utterly helpless."[177] In a postwar interview, Hooker admitted that his plan for his cavalry failed during the Chancellorsville Campaign, but persisted in blaming Stoneman and Averell: "I had to put Stoneman in command, and neither he nor Averell were of any account. I sent them to cut off Lee's connections and the devils went so far around to avoid an enemy that they never accomplished anything they were sent for. If John Buford had been given the command the result would have been different."[178]

Hooker's need for someone to blame was obvious to those who bothered to look. Capt. Frederic C. Newhall of the 6th Pennsylvania, who served on the staff of the Cavalry Corps, observed, "After Chancellorsville, there was a good deal of bad blood in military quarters; a great promise had been followed by but small fulfillment, and scapegoats were needed on whom to fasten blunders," observed Newhall in 1866. "Generals Stoneman and Averell figured in that capacity."[179] Just after the end of the raid, Captain Adams sounded a similar note, reporting that Hooker was "angrily casting about for someone to blame for his repulse and has, of all men, hit upon Stoneman. Why was Stoneman not earlier? Why did he not take Richmond?"[180]

Throughout the raid, Stoneman's hemorrhoids made every minute spent in the saddle sheer agony. Averell, who served with Stoneman on the Peninsula in 1862, observed that the cavalry chief's maladies "would have kept a man of lesser fortitude in the hospital."[181] However, Stoneman had an iron will, and he suffered through countless hours of misery while doing his duty. Stoneman left the Army of the Potomac on his own initiative. On May 20, the embattled cavalry chieftain took medical leave to try to recuperate. "Stoneman is off on leave, and I don't think will return here again," reported General Meade, "He does not want to, and Hooker does not want him back."[182]

During his absence, Hooker appointed Alfred Pleasonton to assume temporary command of the Cavalry Corps. Stoneman never again commanded any of the Army of the Potomac's cavalry. Pleasonton's appointment became permanent later that summer when Stoneman was appointed to head a new bureau being formed to provide for the logistics of the Federal government's large mounted force.[183]

But Hooker did not particularly want Pleasonton, either. He offered command of the Cavalry Corps to Maj. Gen. Winfield Scott Hancock, a career infantry officer. Buford and Grimes Davis encouraged Hancock to accept the position, and Hancock reluctantly agreed to do so. However, before Hancock could accept the offer, Maj. Gen. Darius N. Couch asked to be relieved of command of the Army of the Potomac's II Corps. As senior division commander in the II Corps, Hancock assumed II Corps command instead, opening the door for Pleasonton's long-desired promotion.[184]

The men of the Cavalry Corps were not excited about the prospect of Pleasonton taking overall command. "Gen'l Stoneman, upon his return, finds that his rivals have been intriguing against him and have been trying to have him superseded in the command of the cav'y corps," wrote Lt. Frank Dickerson of the 5th U.S. "Averell, who has fizzled out by not doing the part of the work assigned him, and Pleasonton, who was left behind altogether in charge of the dismounted and sick horses on account of his incompetency, did their utmost to get Stoneman relieved while he was gone." He continued, "Gen'l Hooker, glad to find some one, if he could, to saddle the responsibility of his ignominious failure upon, had actually made out the order relieving him of his command for *incompetency* and offering the command to Gen'l Meade, who refused to take it because he thought Gen'l Stoneman was the best cav'y officer in the USA."[185]

Capt. Walter S. Newhall of the 3d Pennsylvania Cavalry scribbled in his diary on May 14, "We all feel blue about Stoneman's treatment and Averell being relieved, but hope it will turn out all right in the end."[186] "Poor little pusillanimous Pleasonton wants to command the Army Corps," groused the regimental surgeon of the 3d Indiana Cavalry, "& he is about as fit for it as any 2d Lieutenant in the Command."[187] Col. John B. McIntosh did not much care for Pleasonton. "I never had such a disgust before," he wrote in a letter to his wife.[188] "Pleasonton is working my command to death," he complained in a letter to Averell, "there is no reason or sense in his orders, & I have already remonstrated with him about it & requested him to have a little system about his cavalry operations."[189] Brig. Gen. John Gibbon, an old and dear friend of Buford's, complained, "[Stoneman] has not been a great success & I believe it is understood Pleasonton is to be his successor which is absurd when they have such men as Buford and [Grimes] Davis to put in the place."[190] Pleasonton outranked Buford, so there was no way that the Kentuckian could have assumed command of the Cavalry Corps as long as Pleasonton blocked the way. However, Pleasonton's promotion to corps command opened the door for Buford to assume command of the First Division, a role in which he excelled in the coming months.

Stoneman and Averell, two close friends and protégés of McClellan, contributed a great deal to the organization, training, and development of the Army of the Potomac's Cavalry Corps. Hooker made both men the victims of his loss of nerve, and both quickly faded away from the Army of the Potomac. However, they left their indelible mark on the Cavalry Corps, which owed them much of its confidence and future success. Using the Stoneman Raid as a stepping-stone, the Army of the Potomac's Cavalry Corps conducted at least five strategic cavalry raids in the spring and summer of 1864.[191] That is, perhaps, Stoneman's and Averell's greatest legacy to the horse soldiers of the Army of the Potomac.

NOTES

1. O.R., vol. 25, part 1, 1060.
2. New York Times, May 11, 1863; Frederick W. Mitchell, "A Personal Episode of the First Stoneman Raid," War Papers, no. 85, Military Order of the Loyal Legion of the United States, Commandery of the District of Columbia, Read December 6, 1911, 3. Mitchell was captured during the raid, and spent an unfortunate stint in Richmond's notorious Libby Prison.
3. Glazier, Three Years in the Federal Cavalry, 171.
4. Darius N. Couch, "The Chancellorsville Campaign," in Battles and Leaders of the Civil War, ed. Robert U. Johnson and Clarence C. Buel, 4 vols. (New York: Century, 1880–1901), 3:161.
5. Ernest B. Furgurson, Chancellorsville 1863: The Souls of the Brave (New York: Alfred A. Knopf, 1992), 364–65.
6. O.R., vol. 25, part 1, 1060–61.
7. Ibid., 1061.
8. New York Herald, May 12, 1863.
9. Glazier, Three Years in the Federal Cavalry, 180–81.
10. Ibid.; Bigelow, Campaign of Chancellorsville, 448.
11. New York Times, May 12, 1863.
12. O.R., vol. 25, part 1, 1084; Glazier, Three Years in the Federal Cavalry, 181–82.
13. Richmond Daily Enquirer, May 12, 1863.
14. James Moore, M.D., Kilpatrick and His Cavalry (New York: W. J. Widdleton, 1865), 50–51.

15 Glazier, *Three Years in the Federal Cavalry,* 183.

16. O.R., vol. 25, part 1, 1084; Glazier, *Three Years in the Federal Cavalry,* 184.

17. *New York Herald,* May 12, 1863.

18. Glazier, *Three Years in the Federal Cavalry,* 184–85.

19. *New York Herald,* May 12, 1863.

20. Hunt and Brown, *Brevet Brigadier Generals in Blue,* 149.

21. Samuel M. Blackwell, Jr., *In the First Line of Battle: The 12th Illinois Cavalry in the Civil War* (DeKalb: Northern Illinois University Press, 2002), 75.

22. O.R., vol. 25, part 1, 1086.

23. *Mount Carroll Weekly Mirror,* June 8, 1863.

24. Furgurson, *Chancellorsville 1863,* 325.

25. *Richmond Daily Examiner,* May 5, 1863.

26. Charles H. McKnight to William P. McKnight, May 6, 1863, FSNMP.

27. O.R., vol. 25, part 1, 1086–87.

28. *Richmond Daily Enquirer,* May 8, 1863.

29. Frank diary, entry for May 5, 1863.

30. O.R., vol. 25, part 1, 1087.

31. *New York Herald,* May 12, 1863.

32. O.R., vol. 25, part 1, 1087.

33. *Richmond Daily Enquirer,* May 6, 1863.

34. Frank diary, entry for May 9, 1863.

35. O.R., vol. 25, part 2, 477.

36. Redman to his brothers, May 23, 1863.

37. O.R., vol. 25, part 2, 452; Glazier, *Three Years in the Federal Cavalry,* 184–85.

38. Samuel J. Martin, *"Kill-Cavalry": Sherman's Merchant of Terror—The Life of Union General Hugh Judson Kilpatrick* (Madison, N.J.: Fairleigh-Dickinson University Press, 1996), 89.

39. Warner, *Generals in Blue,* 321.

40. Davis, *Common Soldier, Uncommon War,* 427.

41. Hagemann, *Fighting Rebels and Redskins,* 321.

42. Theophilus F. Rodenbough, "Some Cavalry Leaders," in *Miller's Photographic History of the Civil War,* vol. 4 (New York: Review of Reviews, 1911), 278.

43. O.R., vol. 25, part 1, 1071. Capt. Henry C. Weir was awarded a Medal of Honor for his valor at the Battle of Samaria Church, fought on June 24, 1864. Weir was a brave and intrepid officer who served David Gregg admirably.

44. Ibid., 1072.

45. Ibid., 1082.

46. Tobie, *First Maine Cavalry,* 138.

47. Ibid., 138–39.

48. William B. Baker to Dear Mercie, May 10, 1863, William B. Baker Papers, Southern Historical Collection, Wilson Historical Library, University of North Carolina, Chapel Hill.

49. "Cavalryman," "Pistol and Saber: A Stoneman Raid and the Cavalry Fight at Aldie," *National Tribune,* September 13, 1900.

50. Webb diary, entry for May 3, 1863.

51. Covert to his wife, May 11, 1863, Covert Letters.

52. Cavalryman, "Pistol and Saber."

53. Tobie, *First Maine Cavalry,* 139.

54. O.R., vol. 25, part 1, 1082; Tobie, *First Maine Cavalry,* 139–40.

55. Henry C. Meyer, *Civil War Experiences under Bayard, Gregg, Kilpatrick, Raulston, and Newberry, 1862, 1863, 1864* (New York: Knickerbocker Press, 1911), 24–26.

56. Haskell, *To Let Them Know,* 69.

57. Gardner, *Three Years in the Cavalry,* 31.

58. Baker to Dear Mercie, May 10, 1863.

59. Northway to his wife, May 16, 1863, included in *Souvenir,* 115.

60. O.R., vol. 25, part 1, 1085.

61. *New York Times,* May 11, 1863.

62. Merrill, *Campaigns of the First Maine,* 99.

63. *Richmond Daily Enquirer,* May 7, 1863.

64. *New York Times,* May 9, 1863.

65. O.R., vol. 25, part 1, 1085.

66. Langhorne to his mother, May 4, 1863.

67. Pyne, *Ride to Glory,* 145.

68. O.R., vol. 25, part 1, 1085.

69. *New York Times,* May 11, 1863.

70. Dickerson, "Letter from a Maine Cavalry Officer."

71. O.R., vol. 25, part 1, 1092–93.

72. Bigelow, *Campaign of Chancellorsville,* 443.

73. Beale, *A Lieutenant of Cavalry,* 73.

74. In 1863, Shannon Hill was the name of a farm situated a half-mile west of what is today called Shannon Hill. The reports of the participants placed the fight east of the present-day location of Flemming's Crossroads, where the fighting started. Richard Bowles, Jr., "Shannon Hill Encounter," *Goochland County Historical Society Magazine* 17 (1985): 47, n. 32.

75. Beale, *History of the Ninth Virginia Cavalry,* 65.

76. Ibid.

77. Balfour, *13th Virginia Cavalry,* 15.

78. Beale, *History of the Ninth Virginia Cavalry,* 65.

79. Beale, *A Lieutenant of Cavalry,* 73.

80. Price, *Across the Continent with the Fifth Cavalry,* 117.

81. O.R., vol. 25, part 1, 1093.

82. "Memoranda of Operations of Brig. Gen. W. H. F. Lee's Command during General Stoneman's Raid into Virginia," *Southern Historical Society Papers* 3 (1877): 181. After his capture, Temple Buford was sent to Libby Prison in Richmond for about one month. He was then exchanged and returned to the 5th U.S. where he fought in the entire Gettysburg Campaign, including the Battle of Brandy Station. In 1864, he was reassigned to the 5th Kentucky Mounted Infantry, and participated in a second raid under the command of George Stoneman into Tennessee and west Virginia. He then

was assigned to scouting duties and to the pursuit of guerrillas until fall 1865, when his term of service expired and he was mustered out of the service. See Military Records of Rock Island County, Rock Island Historical Society, Rock Island, Ill.

83. Balfour, *13th Virginia Cavalry,* 16; Bowles, "Shannon Hill Encounter," 44.

84. Dickerson, "Letter from a Maine Cavalry Officer."

85. Bowles, "Shannon Hill Encounter," 44–45.

86. O.R., vol. 25, part 1, 1063.

87. Ibid., 1089.

88. Napoléon Bonaparte Buford to Col. Danforth, May 18, 1863, included in *Rock Island Argus,* May 21, 1863.

89. Coover to Coover, May 22, 1863, Coover Letters.

90. Edgar B. Strang, *General Stoneman's Raid, Or, The Amusing Side of Army Life* (Philadelphia: privately published, 1911), 17–18, 24–25.

91. Isaac R. Dunkelberger, "Reminiscences and Personal Experiences of the Great Rebellion," unpublished manuscript, Michael Winey Collection, USAMHI, 13–14.

92. John B. Jones, *A Rebel War Clerk's Diary,* ed. Earl Schenck Miers (Baton Rouge: Louisiana State University Press, 1993), 199.

93. O.R., vol. 25, part 1, 1062.

94. Quoted in Bigelow, *Campaign of Chancellorsville,* 451–52.

95. Bigelow, *Campaign of Chancellorsville,* 453.

96. Jones, *A Rebel War Clerk's Diary,* 203.

97. O.R., vol. 25, part 1, 1063 and 1067.

98. Ibid., 1062.

99. Hagemann, *Fighting Rebels and Redskins,* 202.

100. Gracey, *Annals,* 149.

101. Bigelow, *Chancellorsville Campaign,* 450.

102. Hagemann, *Fighting Rebels and Redskins,* 202. As Sanford noted, the Regulars paid another visit to Trevilian Station in June 1864, where they carried the bulk of a tremendous, bloody, two-day fight that climaxed Maj. Gen. Philip H. Sheridan's second raid, also known as the Trevilian Raid. The fact that they were on familiar ground undoubtedly helped them. The Trevilian Raid covered most of the same terrain as that covered by this portion of the Stoneman Raid. For more on the Trevilian Raid and the Battle of Trevilian Station, see Eric J. Wittenberg, *Glory Enough for All: Sheridan's Second Raid and the Battle of Trevilian Station* (Dulles, Va.: Brassey's, 2001).

103. Hagemann, *Fighting Rebels and Redskins,* 202. This force was actually Rooney Lee's dismounted cavalrymen and the local home guards of Gordonsville.

104. Dunkelberger, "Reminiscences," 14.

105. O.R., vol. 25, part 1, 1089.

106. Gracey, *Annals,* 150.

107. *New York Times,* May 11, 1863.

108. Theophilus F. Rodenbough to John B. Bigelow, Jr., September 10, 1907, Bigelow Papers.

109. Tobie, *First Maine Cavalry,* 140.

110. Webb diary, entry for May 5, 1863.

111. Rodenbough to Bigelow, September 10, 1897.

112. Northway to his wife, May 16, 1863, included in *Souvenir,* 115.

113. O.R., vol. 25, part 1, 1089 and 1063.

114. Gracey, *Annals,* 149.

115. O.R., vol. 25, part 1, 1063.

116. Ibid., 1096.

117. Dunkelberger, "Reminiscences," 14.

118. O.R., vol. 25, part 1, 1089.

119. George Stoneman to Joseph Hooker, May 7, 1863, Box 12, Folder B, Hooker Papers.

120. *New York Times,* May 11, 1863; Bigelow, *Campaign of Chancellorsville,* 454–55.

121. O.R., vol. 25, part 1, 1063.

122. Webb diary, entry for May 7, 1863.

123. Hagemann, *Fighting Rebels and Redskins,* 203.

124. William H. Harrison, "Personal Experiences of a Cavalry Officer, 1861–66," *Military Essays and Recollections of the Pennsylvania Commandery of the Military Order of the Loyal Legion of the United States* 1 (February 6, 1895): 244–45.

125. Bigelow, *Campaign of Chancellorsville,* 456.

126. O.R., vol. 25, part 1, 1063.

127. Dunkelberger, "Reminiscences," 14.

128. Theophilus F. Rodenbough, "Personal Recollections—The Stoneman Raid of '63," in *From Everglade to Canon with the Second Dragoons: An Authentic Account of Service in Florida, Mexico, Virginia, and the Indian Country, 1836–1875,* ed. Theophilus F. Rodenbough (New York: D. Van Nostrand, 1875), 282.

129. *Richmond Daily Examiner,* May 8, 1863.

130. O.R., vol. 25, part 2, 784.

131. Leonard Williams to My Dear Anna, May 11, 1863, Leonard Williams Letters, David G. Douglas Collection, Ridley Park, Pa.

132. Bigelow, *Campaign of Chancellorsville,* 456–57.

133. Ford, *A Cycle of Adams Letters,* 2:5.

134. Ibid., 1:282.

135. Christian Geisel to Dear Sister, May 20, 1863, Geisel Letters.

136. O.R., vol. 25, part 1, 1064.

137. *Richmond Daily Examiner,* May 11, 1863, and *New York Times,* May 14, 1863.

138. Meade, *Life and Letters,* 1:371–72.

139. Bigelow, *Campaign of Chancellorsville,* 456–57.

140. *Richmond Daily Dispatch,* May 6, 1863.

141. O.R., vol. 25, part 1, 1064.

142. Ibid., 1073.

143. *New York Times,* June 20, 1863.

144. John C. Tidball, "Artillery Service in the War of the Rebellion," *Journal of the Military Science Institution* 13 (1892): 283.

145. Douglas Southall Freeman, *Lee's Lieutenants: A Study in Command,* 3 vols. (New York: Charles Scribner's Sons, 1944), 2:639.

146. Hooker to Bates, April 2, 1877.

147. Jones, *A Rebel War Clerk's Diary,* 200.

148. James Rodney Wood, Sr., "Civil War Memoirs," Maud Wood Park Papers, Manuscripts Division, Library of Congress, Washington, D.C., 30.

149. *Rochester Daily Union & Advertiser,* May 29, 1863.

150. Frederick Whittaker, *A Complete Life of General George A. Custer* (New York: Sheldon, 1876), 144–45.

151. Charles R. Rhodes, "Federal Raids and Expeditions in the East," in *Miller's Photographic History of the Civil War,* vol. 4 (New York: Review of Reviews, 1911), 122.

152. Hampton S. Thomas, *Some Personal Reminiscences of Service in the Cavalry of the Army of the Potomac* (Philadelphia: L. R. Hamersly, 1889), 9.

153. Heermance, "Cavalry at Chancellorsville," 225.

154. Charles P. Coxe to John B. Cadwalader, Jr., May 12, 1863, Charles B. Coxe Papers, Historical Society of Pennsylvania, Philadelphia.

155. Davis, *Common Soldier, Uncommon War,* 385.

156. *Rochester Daily Union & Advertiser,* May 29, 1863.

157. Geisel to his sister, May 30, 1863, Geisel Papers.

158. Tobie, *History of the First Maine Cavalry,* 144.

159. Pyne, *History of First New Jersey Cavalry,* 147.

160. German, "Picketing along the Rappahannock," 36.

161. Dickerson, "Letter from a Maine Cavalry Officer."

162. Lucas to his wife, May 11, 1863, Lucas Letters.

163. Northway to his wife, May 16, 1863, included in *Souvenir,* 115–16.

164. O.R., vol. 25, part 1, 1047.

165. Balfour, *13th Virginia Cavalry,* 16.

166. Phillip H. Powers to his wife, May 6, 1863, FSNMP.

167. George S. Dewey to his mother, May 4, 1863, George Stanley Dewey Papers, Southern Historical Collection, Wilson Historical Library, University of North Carolina, Chapel Hill.

168. Mitchell, "A Personal Episode," 2.

169. O.R., vol. 25, part 2, 533.

170. Ibid.

171. Hoffman to his mother, May 17, 1863, Hoffman Letters.

172. Gardner, *Three Years in the Cavalry,* 27.

173. John W. Johnson to his sister, June 7, 1863, Johnson Letters.

174. O.R., vol. 25, part 2, 463 and 468–69; Joseph Hooker to Samuel P. Bates, December 24, 1878, Bates Papers.

175. Samuel P. Bates, *The Battle of Chancellorsville* (Meadville, Pa.: Edward T. Bates, 1882), 80.

176. John C. Waugh, *Class of 1846—From West Point to Appomattox: Stonewall Jackson, George McClellan and Their Brothers* (New York: Warner Books, 1994), 413.

177. Hebert, *Fighting Joe Hooker,* 225–26.

178. *San Francisco Chronicle,* May 23, 1872.

179. Newhall, *With General Sheridan,* 43.

180. Ford, *A Cycle of Adams Letters,* 2:8.

181. Averell, "With the Cavalry on the Peninsula," *Battles and Leaders,* 2:430.

182. Meade, *Life and Letters,* 1:381.

183. See O.R., vol. 25, part 2, 513, and vol. 27, part 3, 11, for the orders granting Stoneman his medical leave and placing Pleasonton in temporary command of the Cavalry Corps. On June 5, 1863, Hooker directed Stoneman to report to the adjutant general of the army for further instructions. On July 28, Stoneman was appointed chief of the newly formed Cavalry Bureau, an administrative post similar to the old position of chief of cavalry.

184. C. H. Morgan, "Narrative of the Operations of the Second Army Corps, from the time General Hancock assumed command, June 9, 1863, until the close of the Battle of Gettysburg," in Almira Hancock, *Reminiscences of General Hancock by His Wife* (New York: Charles L. Webster, 1887), 182–83. Ironically, Hancock assumed command of the Second Corps on the day that the Battle of Brandy Station was fought, wherein much of Pleasonton's fame arose.

185. Frank Dickerson to Dear Father, May 23, 1863, Frank Dickerson Letters, Civil War Miscellaneous Collection, USAMHI.

186. Sarah Butler Wister, *Walter S. Newhall: A Memoir* (Philadelphia: Sanitary Commission, 1864), 100.

187. Beck, "Letters of a Civil War Surgeon," 152.

188. McIntosh to his wife, May 13, 1863.

189. McIntosh to Averell, May 8, 1863, Averell Papers.

190. John Gibbon to My Dearest Mama, June 2, 1863, John Gibbon Papers, Box 1, Folder 8, Historical Society of Pennsylvania, Philadelphia.

191. Those raids included the Kilpatrick-Dahlgren Raid, the May Richmond Raid, the Trevilian Raid, the Wilson-Kautz Raid, and the First Deep Bottom Raid of August 1864.

8

BRANDY STATION:
BUFORD'S MORNING FIGHT FOR THE GUNS
AT ST. JAMES CHURCH

Following a series of meetings held in Richmond after the Battle of Chancellorsville, Robert E. Lee persuaded the Confederate leadership that the time had come for another invasion of the North. A northward thrust would serve a variety of purposes: First, it held the potential of relieving Federal pressure on the beleaguered Southern garrison at Vicksburg. Second, it would provide the people of Virginia with an opportunity to recover from "the ravages of war and a chance to harvest their crops free from interruption by military operation." Third, it would draw Hooker's army away from its base at Falmouth, giving Lee an opportunity to defeat the Army of the Potomac in the open field. Finally, Lee wanted to spend the summer months in Pennsylvania in the hope of leveraging political gain from such an invasion.

In the meantime, as the Confederate high command crystallized its summer plans, Capt. Ulric Dahlgren, a dashing twenty-one-year-old who served on Hooker's staff, proposed a daring cavalry raid of his own. Dahlgren, a native of Philadelphia, was the son of Rear Adm. John Dahlgren, a brilliant Naval officer known as the "Father of Naval Ordnance."[1] The young man had already made a reputation for himself for courage and dash, and seemed destined for greatness. He had Lincoln and Stanton for patrons, and his father was well known throughout the military. "The rebel cavalry are again feeling along our lines, probably to find a weak point to enter at, as is their custom," wrote Dahlgren. "If they should attempt a raid, this would offer a fine chance for a small body of cavalry to penetrate their country." His plan closely mirrored the one proposed by Averell in December 1862.

If the Southern horsemen launched a raid, Dahlgren proposed a counterpunch. He would take the 6th U.S. Cavalry across the Rappahannock and Rapidan Rivers, march on Louisa Court House, pass between Columbia and Goochland, and cross the James to destroy the arsenal at Bellona. Then they would either burn the bridges across the James at Richmond, dash through the city and on to White House Landing on the Pamunkey River, or, after burning the bridges, go on to the crucial railroad junction town of Petersburg and then into the Federal lines at Suffolk. "The greatest obstacle would be passing their picket line on the Rappahannock," commented Dahlgren, "which, if accomplished without being discovered, would leave the roads open before us; but I know several men in the provost-marshal's service who feel confident of guiding such an expedition." The aggressive young captain knew that his plan could only succeed if the Confederate cavalry went off on a raid of its own. "The object of the expedition would be to destroy everything along the route, and especially on the south side of the James River, and attempt to enter Richmond and Petersburg," he concluded.[2]

On May 26, General Hooker visited Washington, taking Dahlgren with him. This expedition undoubtedly occupied part of the agenda for Hooker's meeting with Stanton and Lincoln and the young man may have presented his plan directly to the President and the Secretary of War. The Union high command did not approve the proposed raid, and the two officers returned to Army of the Potomac headquarters the next day. Although his grand scheme had been rejected, Ulric Dahlgren remained undaunted. The day for his proposed raid would come, although Dahlgren would not live to see the results of his grand scheme to raid the Confederate capital. In the meantime, the young man had a lot of heroics ahead of him.[3]

CONTINUED UNION CAVALRY OPERATIONS IN THE AFTERMATH OF THE STONEMAN RAID

The Northern cavalry remained active and vigilant in the aftermath of the Stoneman Raid. On May 14, reports of Confederate raiders in Hooker's rear brought action. With a ten-year-old boy named Bertram E. Trenis as their guide, elements of seven different Northern mounted units set out in pursuit, rousting a group of Southern guerrillas. Maj. J. Claude White of the 3d Pennsylvania Cavalry led the chase, scouting the country to and around Brentsville. The Federals took a few prisoners, resulting in three horses killed and several of the enemy severely wounded by saber cuts.[4]

On May 17, Lt. Col. David R. Clendennin's 8th Illinois Cavalry received orders to go out on a lengthy reconnaissance into the so-called Northern Neck between the Rappahannock and Potomac Rivers, in King George, Westmoreland, Richmond, Northumberland, and Lancaster Counties.[5] Clendennin divided his command into three battalions, which traversed the entire length of the Neck, making their way to the confluence of the two rivers. They arrived at Leed's Ferry, and determined that it was used for smuggling contraband across the Rappahannock. Clendennin decided to destroy the ferry. Six of the Illinois saddle soldiers dressed themselves in gray, took two prisoners with them, and called out to the men on the opposite bank to bring the boat across. The deception worked famously, and when the ferrymen brought the boat across the river, they were promptly captured and the boat burned.[6]

Pleasonton reported that the Illinois saddle soldiers "destroyed 50 boats, and broke up the underground trade pretty effectually, having destroyed some $30,000 worth of goods in transit. They bring back with them 800 contrabands, innumerable mules, horses, &c., and have captured between 40 and 50 prisoners, including a captain and lieutenant." Pleasonton claimed that his horse soldiers caused more than $1 million in damage to the enemy war effort at the cost of one man severely wounded and two slightly injured. "Considering the force engaged and the results obtained, this is the greatest raid of the war," proclaimed Pleasonton.[7] The regimental historian of the 8th Illinois noted, "It was found that some of the wealthiest citizens on 'the neck' were engaged in the smuggling business, or contributing in some way to the support of the rebellion; and these gentlemen were made to pay dearly for their secession sympathies."[8]

Several infantry regiments also went on this expedition, raiding deep into the heart of Virginia. A squadron of the 3d Indiana Cavalry, led by Maj. George H. Thompson, accompanied them, making a lengthy march and successfully completing a dangerous crossing of the Rappahannock in leaky boats. The Northern saddle soldiers covered forty-five miles in just five hours that day. "We hid in the woods till next morning," reported Bvt. Capt. George A. Custer of the 5th U.S. Cavalry, one of Pleasonton's staff officers, who accompanied the expedition. "With 9 men and an officer in a small canoe I started in pursuit of a small sailing-vessel." They pursued for nearly ten miles until the Southerners ran their boat aground, jumped overboard, and ran for the shore. "We captured boat and passengers," continued Custer, "They had left Richmond the previous morning and had in their possession a large sum of Confederate money." Custer and a handful of men waded ashore, and headed for the nearest house. He spotted a man in Confederate uniform lying on the piazza, reading a book. Although worried that he might be falling into a trap, Custer took the man prisoner. "Then, with twenty men, in three small boats, I rowed to Urbana on the opposite shore. Here we burned two schooners and a bridge over the bay, driving the rebel pickets out of town. We returned to the north bank where we captured 12 prisoners, thirty horses, two large boxes of Confederate boots and shoes, and two barrels of whiskey, which we destroyed." Custer captured two horses himself.[9]

The Hoosiers successfully completed their march, capturing a handful of prisoners, a stash of Confederate money, and fifteen horses, which they turned over to Pleasonton.[10] Custer, a scant two years out of West Point, was beginning to attract attention with his exploits. Hooker sent for him and complimented him highly on his conduct of the expedition, saying it could not have been better done and that he would have more for Custer to do.[11]

Several days later, Michigan Gov. Austin Blair visited the camps of his state's troops. The colonelcy of the 5th Michigan Cavalry was vacant, and Custer craved it. Custer asked Pleasonton to write a letter of recommendation for him, something that Pleasonton happily did. "Captain Custer," wrote Pleasonton, "will make an excellent commander of a cavalry regiment and is entitled to such promotion for his gallant and efficient services in the present war of rebellion. I do not know anyone I could recommend to you with more confidence than Captain Custer." Hooker gladly endorsed the recommendation. "I cheerfully concur in the recommendation of Brig Genl Pleasonton. He is a young officer of great promise and uncommon merit."[12] Although the appointment instead went to Lt. Col. Russell A. Alger of the 6th Michigan Cavalry, Pleasonton nevertheless had great expectations and plans for Custer.

UNION INTELLIGENCE-GATHERING EFFORTS

Once the Confederate leadership approved Lee's audacious plan to invade Pennsylvania, the Southern commander began shifting troops west for a strike up the Shenandoah Valley set to commence on June 3. Almost immediately rumors of this activity trickled into Union headquarters. On May 27, Col. George H. Sharpe of the Provost Marshal General's office and chief of intelligence for the Army of the Potomac, reported, "There are three brigades of cavalry 3 miles from Culpeper County Court House, toward Kelly's Ford. . . . These are Fitz. Lee's, William H. Fitzhugh Lee's, and Wade Hampton's brigades. . . . The Confederate army is under marching orders, and an order from General Lee was very lately read to the troops, announcing a campaign of long marches and hard fighting."[13]

A few days later, a local citizen named G. S. Smith, who was known as a reliable source of intelligence, correctly reported to Pleasonton, "this movement of General Lee's is not intended to menace Washington, but to try his hand again toward Maryland, or to call off your attention while General Stuart goes there. I have every reason for believing that Stuart is on his way toward Maryland. I do not positively know it, but have the very best of reasons for believing it." Pleasonton added his own incorrect analysis of the situation. "It is my impression the rebel army has been weakened by troops sent west and south, and that any performance of Stuart's will be aflutter to keep us from seeing their weakness."[14]

These reports provided the impetus for Hooker, in order to "send all my cavalry against" the assembling mass of Confederate horse, in an attempt "to break . . . up [the offensive] in its incipiency."[15] It may also have been the reason why Lincoln and Stanton decided not to implement Dahlgren's bold plan for a counterraid. Accordingly, Pleasonton ordered John Buford, now commanding the First Division, to join Gregg at Bealeton and reconnoiter the area to try to determine the true object of the Confederate movement.

On the 28th, Pleasonton received a report from Gregg, advising that four brigades of Confederate cavalry had encamped in the vicinity of Culpeper Court House. Alarmed, Pleasonton asked Hooker for permission to send Buford's Reserve Brigade and a battery to reinforce Gregg at Bealeton.[16] Hooker wasted no time in approving the request, and ordered Buford to assume command of all cavalry forces operating in the area. Reports also indicated that enemy patrols were operating on the north side of the Rappahannock near Warrenton, so Hooker gave Buford permission to engage the Rebels and push them back across the river.

The army commander concluded with the critical instruction. If Buford "should find himself with sufficient force, to drive the enemy out of his camp near Culpeper and across the Rapidan, destroying the bridge at that point." Hooker rightly guessed that the Rebel horsemen were gathering there to mask a Confederate advance down the Shenandoah Valley. Hooker specifically ordered Buford to spare no effort to find out the objective of the enemy movement, stating that "[a]t all events, they have no business on this side of the [Rappahannock]."[17]

Later that day, Pleasonton instructed Buford to drive the Confederates from Warrenton, stating, "The advance of the enemy's cavalry in the vicinity of Warrenton may have for its object to conceal a movement in force up the Valley. Spare no effort to ascertain the true object of the movement." On the 29th, Buford tersely announced, "The command is in motion for Bealeton."[18]

Buford's force arrived at Warrenton Junction after a grueling thirty-hour march. The Kentuckian immediately assumed command of the Union forces assembled there. After hearing that the Confederates had burned a nearby railroad bridge, Buford marched his troopers up the Orange and Alexandria Railroad. He discovered that no bridge had been destroyed, but that Capt. John S. Mosby's Confederate guerrillas had torched a ten-car train of supplies, generating the smoke that triggered the erroneous report. The independent cavalry division of Maj. Gen. Julius Stahel, which was not under the authority of the Army of the Potomac, pursued the guerrillas, inflicting a number of casualties. By interdicting the railroads and interfering with the flow of supplies and communication, the Rebels had disrupted lines of supply and communication in both Stahel's area of authority and in Buford's.

Buford tackled the tasks of removing the carcass of the train from the tracks and restoring telegraph communications. He reported that there was a good supply of water and grass for the horses near Warrenton and concluded, "I can hear of no rebel force. None has crossed the river below Waterloo Bridge. The horses and pack mules of the Second and Third Divisions are in wretched condition."[19] The next day, both the railroad and the lines of communication were fully restored.

On June 2, Buford learned that three brigades of Stuart's cavalry had entered the Shenandoah Valley for unknown purposes. Pleasonton instructed the Kentuckian to "aid in the fixing the locality and numbers of the enemy's cavalry especially, with a view to our future movements. Send us by telegraph all the news obtained, and have scouting parties active. The capture of prisoners, contrabands, etc., may give much information."[20] Buford cabled Pleasonton that he intended to establish his troops along a new and shorter line anchored at Catlett's Station, and that "no enemy save some of Mosby's are on this side of the Rappahannock. Orleans, Waterloo, Warrenton, and New Baltimore were visited yesterday." He concluded by stating that his entire command was "packed into an area 2 or 3 miles wide."[21]

Buford gathered his horsemen and set out to obey Pleasonton's instructions. On June 4, after a couple of futile days, army headquarters reported that a portion of the Confederate forces opposite the Union left had disappeared. Hooker ordered Buford to "keep a sharp lookout, country well scouted, and advise us as soon as possible of anything in your front or vicinity indicating a movement."[22] Uncertain of the enemy's whereabouts or plans, Hooker had every reason to be worried.

Buford's labors bore fruit the next day. "I have just received information, which I consider reliable, that all of the available cavalry of the Confederacy is in Culpeper County," announced the vigilant Kentuckian. "Stuart, the two Lees, Robertson, Jenkins, and Jones are all there. Robertson came from North Carolina, Jenkins from Kanawha, and Jones from the Valley. Jones arrived at Culpeper on the 3d, after the others."[23] Buford was incorrect in part of his report—the brigade of Brig. Gen. Albert G. Jenkins was not present. Buford correctly noted that the strength of the Rebel cavalry had increased, but wrongfully suggested that, instead of bringing new units into service, Stuart had instead mounted infantrymen. "My informant—a refugee from Madison County—says Stuart has 20,000; can't tell his instructions, but thinks he is going to make a raid."[24] While the informant's estimate of the number of Confederate cavalry was about twice as large as Stuart's force really was, Buford provided Army headquarters with insightful intelligence of the enemy's whereabouts and dispositions, and Hooker made good use of the information.

A correspondent of one of the New York newspapers accurately observed, "This force is the largest body of cavalry that the enemy has ever got together." He continued, "It is not the intention of this force to fight, unless compelled to do so. They go on a rail-ripping, horse-stealing expedition, and to 'bring the horrors of war to our own doors'—as they express it. Once well on the wing and pursuit, as is always the case, will be well nigh useless. [The Army of the Potomac] may well be depleted of its cavalry and fail to capture more than a few drunken stragglers." He concluded prophetically, "Stuart will doubtless move in a very few days, and the only way to effectually interfere with this dashing arrangement is to pitch into him where he is."[25]

On June 5, Pleasonton notified Hooker that the enemy's cavalry pickets extended to Front Royal, nearly sixty miles west of Falmouth. Pleasonton instructed Buford to "make a strong demonstration without delay upon the enemy in your front toward Culpeper, and push them as far as possible without jeopardizing your command." Pleasonton also informed the Kentuckian that the Confederate forces were in motion in front of Fredericksburg, and that a portion of the enemy army had already moved toward Orange Court House.[26] Buford obeyed the order immediately.

The following day, a nervous Hooker cabled Buford, "Information has been communicated to me that three brigades of the enemy's cavalry are posted at Jefferson." Hooker further inquired how such a turn of events was possible, and asked Buford if his pickets could shut down the Confederate lines of communication across the Rappahannock. Buford responded that Hooker's "information is incorrect about the number of cavalry at Jefferson," and that he would attempt to keep the Confederate lines of communication across the river closed. He concluded, "I have a large force in the neighborhood of Jefferson, reconnoitering."[27]

That same day, Hooker, nervous about the large concentration of Southern cavalry gathering in Culpeper County, asked Halleck whether Major General Stahel's independent division of cavalry assigned to the defenses of Washington, D.C., would be sent to reinforce him. These reinforcements would not come. A few days earlier, Capt. Mosby's guerrillas had captured a train on the Orange & Alexandria Railroad near Catlett's Station, creating great consternation in Washington. Stahel's division could not be sent to reinforce Pleasonton, because Stahel's troopers were protecting the vital rail link. These additional horsemen may well have made the difference at Brandy Station.[28]

On June 7, after collating all of the raw data from the field, Col. Sharpe reported his conclusions to Hooker. Sharpe concluded that the Confederates intended to launch a massive cavalry raid, "the most important expedition ever attempted in this country." He estimated the size of Stuart's force at 12,000–15,000 saddle soldiers, and announced, "[T]here were strong indications that the enemy's entire Infantry will fall back upon Richmond and thence reinforce their armies in the west." Although Sharpe's conclusions about Stuart's ultimate objective were wrong, his analysis that there would be a large expedition into the north was correct.[29]

Uneasy, Hooker proceeded cautiously. Pleasonton belayed the orders for Buford to pitch into the Confederate cavalry at Culpeper until further notice. Instead, Pleasonton instructed Buford to "[r]eport everything as it occurs."[30] Buford responded, "Your dispatch just received. I have sent to recall Colonel Duffié, who had your instructions to carry out. I fear he has gone too far."[31] That afternoon, Buford reported that Duffié had already crossed the Rappahannock at Sulphur Springs with 2,500 men. He announced that "[t]he information sent yesterday has been partly corroborated; none of it denied. Yesterday cannon firing was heard toward Culpeper. I suppose it was a salute, as I was told Stuart was to have had that day an inspection of his whole force." Buford noted that Confederate Maj. Gen. John Bell Hood's infantry division was camped on the Rapidan at Raccoon Ford, but that he could not determine whether any Confederate infantry were stationed in the area north of the Rapidan. Ominously, Buford reported, "[T]here is a very heavy cavalry force on the grazing grounds in Culpeper County."[32]

Now persuaded that Sharpe's estimates were correct, Hooker cabled Lincoln of his "great desire to 'bust [Stuart's contemplated raid] up' before it got fairly under way."[33] The army commander began planning an expedition to do just that.

THE GRAND REVIEW

Buford was correct. Stuart staged the second grand review of his cavalry in a two-week period on the 5th. The first review occurred on May 22, amid much ceremony. On the night of June 4, in anticipation of the next day's pageantry, Stuart and his dashing cavaliers romanced the local belles at a grand ball.

Confederate Secretary of War James A. Seddon attended the second review, along with a large entourage of local ladies. As Stuart's adjutant, Maj. Henry B. McClellan, described it: "Eight thousand cavalry passed under the eye of their commander, in column of squadrons, first at a walk, and then at the charge, while the guns of the artillery battalion, on the hill opposite the stand, gave forth fire and smoke, and seemed almost to convert the pageant into real warfare. It was a brilliant day, and the thirst for the 'pomp and circumstance' of war was fully satisfied."[34]

"It was observed that General Stuart's personal charms never showed to better advantage than on that day," observed a Southern horse soldier. "Young, gay, and handsome, dressed out in his newest uniform, his polished sword flashing in the sunlight, mounted on his favorite bay mare in gaudiest trappings, his long black plume waving in response to the kisses of the summer breeze, he was superb in every movement, and the personification of grace and gallantry combined."[35] A trooper of the 12th Virginia Cavalry observed, "The officers & men were exceedingly well mounted & dressed."[36]

The spectacle of the grand review did not enthrall all of the Southern horsemen. Brig. Gen. William E. "Grumble" Jones's brigade had only arrived at Brandy Station on June 3 and 4 after completing a long and taxing raid in western Virginia, and his men and horses were tired and tattered. "Many . . . grumbled about the use-less waste of energy, especially that of the horses; and when it was announced a few days afterward that there was to be another grand review on the 8th, the grumblers were even more numerous and outspoken." Nearly all of the grumbling ceased, however, when Stuart announced that it was Robert E. Lee who had ordered the review for June 8, and that he planned to attend in person.[37] The Confederate troopers began preparing their equipment and horses. Their attention distracted, the Southerners seemed unaware of Buford's presence in the area.

As a result of his accurate report of the Confederate activities, Pleasonton ordered Buford to send all of his transportation, excepting his pack mules and one wagon per regiment, to the supply depot at Potomac Creek, a sure sign that a major movement by the Union cavalry loomed. Buford dispatched part of his force toward the concentration of Confederate cavalry at Culpeper. He remained at Warrenton Junction, readying the balance of his command for a meeting with their unsuspecting foes at Brandy Station.[38]

Vigilant Union horsemen probed Stuart's pickets, attempting to ascertain the precise whereabouts and intentions of the Rebel cavalry. Buford sent Duffié's divi-sion into northern Culpeper County. The Frenchman reported that he marched south, that he came within four and a half miles of Culpeper, taking no casualties, and that the Confederates seemed to be avoiding a fight. At 3:00 A.M. on June 7, Buford forwarded this intelligence to Pleasonton, who was on his way to Warren-ton Junction to assume field command of the Cavalry Corps.[39]

Pleasonton passed this information on to Hooker with a note of caution. "Col-onel Duffié only reconnoitered the road from Sulphur Springs toward Culpeper," wrote the cavalry chief. "Does not know what cavalry is on the Brandy Station or Stevensburg roads. It is on those roads the bulk of the enemy's cavalry are reported." He continued, "Let us act soon, and please telegraph my instructions. My people are all ready to pitch in. Let me have discretion to cross at the best positions as determined by latest information."[40]

PLEASONTON'S PLAN FOR HIS RAID

When he arrived at Warrenton Junction, Pleasonton knew only of the great con-centration of enemy cavalry near Culpeper. He did not know that Confederate infantry was also camped there. Pleasonton and Hooker did not know that Stuart's cavalry had gone to Brandy Station to cover the northward march of the infantry corps of Lt. Gens. Richard S. Ewell and James Longstreet. Lee had ordered that the march north resume on June 10.[41] Pleasonton worried about the whereabouts of the Southern foot soldiers, and requested infantry support for his cavalry.

Responding, Hooker notified Pleasonton that two brigades of handpicked infantry under the command of Brig. Gens. David A. Russell and Adelbert Ames would report to Pleasonton at Kelly's Ford. Each brigade consisted of 1,500 selected foot soldiers. These regiments came from all of the corps of the Army of the Poto-mac, and represented the best marching and some of the best fighting regiments of the army. The foot soldiers considered it a great honor to be selected for this mis-sion. "The infantry force selected challenged particular admiration," reported a newspaper correspondent. "The regiments were small, but they were *reliable*—such for instance as the Second, Third, and Seventh Wisconsin, Second and Thirty-third Massachusetts, Sixth Maine, Eighty-sixth and One Hundred and Twenty-Fourth New York, and one or two others of like character."[42]

Disregarding Pleasonton's note of caution about the extent of Duffié's recon-naissance, Hooker fired off instructions that would send the Federal horsemen directly into the area where Pleasonton believed the bulk of the Southern cavalry lay waiting. "From the most reliable information at these headquarters, it is recom-mended that you cross the Rappahannock at Beverley [*sic*] and Kelly's Fords, and march directly on Culpeper," instructed Hooker. "For this you will divide your cav-alry force as you think proper, to carry into execution the object in view, which is to disperse and destroy the Rebel force assembled in the vicinity of Culpeper, and to destroy his trains and supplies of all description to the utmost of your ability." The army commander continued, "Shortly after crossing the two fords, the routes you will be likely to take intersect, and the major-general commanding suggests that you keep your infantry force together, as in that condition it will afford you a moving point of d'appui to rally on at all times, which no cavalry force can be able to shake." He concluded, "It is believed that the enemy has no infantry. Should you find this to be the case, by keeping your troops well in hand, you will be able to head in any direction." If the strike succeeded and the Confederates were routed, Hooker wanted Pleasonton to vigorously pursue the Southern cavalry, and to use all available means to destroy Stuart's corps once and for all.[43]

If Pleasonton had correctly assessed the whereabouts of the Confederate cav-alry, Hooker's plan would carry the Northern saddle soldiers right at them. Nev-ertheless, orders were orders, and Hooker had been very specific in his instructions to Pleasonton. The cavalry chief set about planning his expedition.

Gregg's division spent June 7 preparing for the coming excursion. "Haversacks were stored, cartridge-boxes filled, horses shod, the sick sent back, and all the usual preparations for active campaigning gone through with," recalled a member of the 1st Pennsylvania Cavalry. "Then commenced the irksome and wearying delays incident to the moving of troops. Momentarily expecting the order to move, hour after hour passed, and still we were not yet off. Evening came and night passed, and reveille awoke us to another day's expectancy."[44]

On June 8, Pleasonton ordered Duffié to march his division to Kelly's Ford, where he would join Gregg's command for the crossing. The Frenchman had to move from the far right, near Warrenton, down to Kelly's Ford, an impractical move for the division that was supposed to lead the way on the left. "Slowly pursuing our way through the heat and clouds of dust raised by the march of a division of cavalry over parched and arid fields, we at length reached the vicinity of the river, and at nine P.M., bivouacked for the night about a mile from Kelly's Ford," continued the Pennsylvania horse soldier.[45] Thus, the pieces fell into place for the great cavalry battle at Brandy Station. Nine thousand Union cavalrymen and 3,000 infantrymen were prepared to pounce on the unsuspecting Confederates the next morning.[46]

Pleasonton formulated an excellent plan for his foray across the river. Buford would command the right wing of the operation, including the First Division and Ames's brigade of selected infantry regiments. In addition, several batteries of Federal horse artillery would also accompany the columns, adding firepower to the already potent Union force. Gregg would command the left wing, which included Russell's infantry brigade, Gregg's Second Division, and Duffié's Third Division.

Under Pleasonton's plan, Buford's men would cross the Rappahannock at Beverly's Ford, and ride to Brandy Station, where they would rendezvous with Gregg's Second Division. Gregg's division would cross the Rappahannock at Kelly's Ford. Duffié's small division would also cross at Kelly's Ford, and would proceed to the small town of Stevensburg, to secure the flank east of Culpeper. Buford and Gregg would then push for Culpeper, where they would fall upon Stuart 's unsuspecting forces and destroy them. In case there was Confederate infantry in the area, the Federal infantry would support the attacks. Pleasonton had his men pack three days' rations because he intended to chase the routed Confederates. Careful timing would be required to pull off the attack as planned.[47]

The rolling terrain around Brandy Station featured mostly fields and woods. Its well-defined road network lent itself to rapid movement by large bodies of mounted troopers. The Beverly Ford Road, which crossed the Rappahannock two miles north of St. James Church, was a major artery for commerce. A long north-south ridge called Fleetwood Hill rose above the railroad station that gave the settlement its name. "Fleetwood Heights is a beautiful location," observed an officer of the 6th Virginia Cavalry. "Being an elevated ridge . . . it commands the country and roads leading north and south from Brandy Station."[48] Stuart's headquarters crowned this prominence overlooking the area around Brandy Station, the plumed cavalier's personal guidon fluttering in the gentle breezes. One of Stuart's staff officers described the area: "The country is open for miles—almost level without fences or ditches and the finest country for cavalry fighting I ever saw."[49]

The Northern horse soldiers did not have much faith in their new commander. "Stuart is in our front with a big force of cavalry," observed a member of the 6th U.S. Cavalry on the night of June 8. "I only wish Stoneman was here. I have no confidence in Pleasonton."[50] Pleasonton's plan assumed that the Confederate cavalry was concentrated at Culpeper, five miles from Brandy Station. A rude surprise awaited the Federals the next day, when they discovered that the Rebel cavalry lay just across the Rappahannock.

THE JUNE 8TH CONFEDERATE REVIEW

While the Union troopers prepared to attack them, Stuart's unsuspecting troopers held another grand review, this time in front of Robert E. Lee himself. Fitz Lee also invited Major General Hood, a former cavalryman who commanded a hard-fighting infantry division in Longstreet's corps, to attend the review and "to bring any of his friends." Hood appeared with his entire division, announcing that these were "all his friends" and that he thought he should bring them along.[51] "This was a business affair, the spectators being all soldiers," observed one of Stuart's staff officers. "Many men from Hood's Division were present who enjoyed it immensely. During the charges past the reviewing stand the hats and caps of the charging column would sometimes blow off, and then, just as the charging squadron passed and before the owners could come back, Hood's men would have a race for them and bear them off in triumph."[52]

General Lee well knew his cavalry chief's propensity for pomp and circumstance. He watched as the local ladies adorned Stuart and his horse with garlands of flowers. Covered with blossoms, Stuart presented himself to the commanding general. Lee surveyed his cavalier from head to foot, and quietly warned, "Do you know General that Burnside left Washington in like trim for the first battle of Manassas. I hope that your fate may not be like his." But Lee's understated warning did not prepare Stuart for the rude surprise he would face the next day.[53]

The twenty-two regiments of Confederate cavalry arrayed themselves along either side of a straight furrow plowed into the adjacent farmland owned by John Minor Botts, a well-known local Unionist. Stuart's famed horse artillery crowned nearby Fleetwood Hill, sixteen guns of four batteries of fine artillery. Capt. Daniel Grimsley of the 6th Virginia Cavalry noted, "It was a splendid military parade; Stuart's eyes gleamed with peculiar brightness as he glanced along this line of cavalry in battle array, with men and horses groomed their best, and the command arrayed with military precision, with colors flying, bugles sounding, bands playing, and with regimental and brigade officers in proper positions."[54]

General Lee sat watching the glorious spectacle atop a low rise near the railroad bed. The sight of the Southern commander impressed all who saw him. "It was my first sight of the great chieftain," proudly recalled William L. Wilson of the 12th Virginia Cavalry. "Even his personal appearance indicates great mental endowment and nobility of soul." Wilson noted that the review passed quietly and with "less éclat than that of last Friday."[55]

Confederate Gen. William Pendleton recalled that Lee and his staff "had a ride of it, some six miles at full run for our horses, down the line and up again, and then had to sit our horses in the dust half the day for the squadrons to march in display backward and forward near us."[56] In an effort to conserve ammunition, Lee ordered that no artillery rounds be fired in this review.[57] The Southern commander and his staff rode rapidly along the entire line, inspecting the proud gray troopers as they went.

Then, Lee resumed his position, and "at the sound of the bugle, taken up and repeated along the line, the corps of horsemen broke by right wheel into columns of squadron, and moving south for a short distance, the head of the column was turned to the left, and again to the left, moving in this new direction, whence it passed immediately in front of the commanding general. It was a splendid military pageant, and an inspiring scene, . . . as this long line of horsemen, in columns of squadron, with nearly ten thousand sabers flashing in the sun light . . . passed in review before the greatest soldier of modern times." The column advanced at a walk "until it came within some fifty or one hundred paces of the position occupied by the reviewing general, when squadron by squadron would take up first the trot, then the gallop, until they had passed some distance beyond, when again they would pull down to the walk. After passing in review, the several brigades were brought again to the position which they occupied in the line, whence they were dismissed, one by one, to their respective camps."[58] Stuart's magnificent display lasted several exhausting hours.

At the end of the pageant, Stuart pointed out to Lee a significant problem the troops were experiencing. The saddles and carbines manufactured in Richmond for the Army of Northern Virginia had proven themselves defective and inadequate. That night, Lee wrote to Col. Josiah Gorgas, the Confederacy's talented chief of ordnance. "My attention was thus called to a subject which I have previously brought to your notice, viz., the saddles and carbines manufactured in Richmond," noted the army commander. The general noted that he had not inspected these items himself, but that he had been assured that the saddles ruined the backs of horses and that the carbines were so defective as to be demoralizing. "I am aware of the difficulties attending the manufacture of arms and equipments, but I suggest that you have the matter inquired into by your ordnance officers, and see if they cannot rectify the evils complained of. It would be better, I think, to make fewer articles, and have them serviceable." This problem continued to plague the Army of Northern Virginia Cavalry Division for the balance of the war.[59]

"I reviewed the cavalry in this section yesterday," noted Robert E. Lee in a letter to his wife. "It was a splendid sight. The men and horses looked well...Stuart was in all his glory. Your sons and nephew were well and flourishing." He noted that his nephew Fitz was not on horseback while watching his men pass in review. A severe case of rheumatism prevented him from climbing into the saddle, so Fitz sat with "some pretty girls in a carriage," cheering his men. Fitz's disability meant that Col. Thomas T. Munford of the 2d Virginia Cavalry was in command of his brigade, and that Fitz would miss the great cavalry battle that loomed. The general's son Rooney presented a handsome sight on his proud black charger. As he penned this letter on the morning of June 9, little did the Southern commander realize that things were about to change dramatically.[60]

"Grumble" Jones, described by one of his men as "that stern old warrior," was most unhappy with the show—he felt it a foolhardy waste of resources.[61] "No doubt," muttered Jones, "the Yankees, who have two divisions of cavalry on the other side of the river, have witnessed from their signal stations, this show in which Stuart has exposed to view his strength and aroused their curiosity. They will want to know what is going on and if I am not mistaken, will be over early in the morning to investigate."[62] Jones's estimate of the Yankee intentions proved right on target.

BUFORD'S ASSAULT AND THE DEATH OF "GRIMES" DAVIS

The entire Union Cavalry Corps marched on the afternoon of June 8, arriving at the Rappahannock fords about midnight.[63] Buford's men camped on the north side of the Rappahannock, just above Beverly's Ford. High bluffs overlooking the river protected them from the prying eyes of the enemy on the other side. One of his troopers later recalled, "[W]e marched that night to within a mile or two of the fords, and awaited the approach of dawn."[64] The chaplain of the 6th Pennsylvania Cavalry recalled, "Late in the night we arrive behind the wood nearest the river, and bivouac for the night. No fires are allowed, and we make our supper on cold ham and hard tack, spread our saddle-blankets on the ground, and with saddles for pillows, prepare for a night's rest. Our minds are full of the coming battle on the morrow, and various speculations are indulged in regard to our prospects of success."[65]

The Yankee horsemen fully understood that they would face combat the next day. "Our men are confident of success, and eager for the fray. A group of officers are eating their cold supper, perhaps the last they shall all take together. The morrow will soon break upon us, full of danger and death. Messages are committed to friends to be transmitted to distant loved ones, 'in case anything should occur.' And after solemn and earnest prayer we are all sleeping soundly."[66] Even though he served on Pleasonton's staff, Captain Custer was nervous but excited. "I never was in better spirits than I am at this moment," he proclaimed. In case "something happens to me," he told his sister in a letter penned about 2:00 A.M. that night, he had arranged for his chest and personal effects to be shipped to her in Monroe, Michigan. "If such an event occurs, I want my letters burned."[67]

At two in the morning, the Federal troopers awakened to hushed orders; the command "to horse" was whispered, instead of blared by the division's buglers. Buford's troopers quietly mounted up and moved stealthily toward Beverly's Ford, arriving at 4:30. That night a thick fog settled across the river, and a ghostly haze covered the approach of the Union troopers; shapes were difficult to discern across the river in the cool and pleasant dawn.[68] Trooper Sidney Davis of the 6th U.S. recalled that "[t]he dull gray dawn gave a weird shadowy appearance to the landscape and those morning figures."[69] Capt. Frederic C. Newhall of the 6th Pennsylvania, who served on Pleasonton's staff, could see a cluster of officers standing by the riverbank through the ghostly fog. One among them, John Buford, acknowledged the passage of his command "with his usual smile. He rode a gray horse, at a slow walk . . . and smoked a pipe . . . [and] it was always reassuring to see him in the saddle when there was any chance of a fight."[70]

The water at Beverly's Ford was three-and-a-half feet deep, with narrow openings atop the steep riverbanks, meaning that the Union troopers had to cross the river in column of fours. "Grimes" Davis's brigade led the way. One of Davis's staff officers sat at the Ford, and as each company commander passed by, he received the whispered order, "Draw sabers!" Davis's horse soldiers waded the Rappahannock, his 8th New York in the lead, followed by the 8th Illinois and the 3d Indiana.[71] Once across the river, Buford ordered Davis to push any enemy vedettes back from the Ford a mile or so.[72] "We dashed rapidly across, the foremost squadrons receiving a sharp fire from the enemy's rifle pits," reported a member of the 8th New York.[73]

A company of Jones's 6th Virginia Cavalry picketed the area, and the sudden appearance of Davis's soldiers surprised them. Unbeknownst to the Federals, Jones's men had constructed a stout barricade of rails across the river and along the edge of a wood.[74] "Captain Gibson, who was a brave and prudent officer, had already blockaded the road as best he could with the material at hand, and waited patiently to receive them," recalled a Virginia horse soldier. "When at close range the captain gave the word and a sheet of fire flashed in their faces and the shower of lead poured into their ranks, emptied many saddles and caused the advance to recoil, but the head of the main body advancing rapidly to the support of their advance. Capt. Gibson was compelled to fall back, the Yankees pressing close on his rear."[75] Trooper Luther W. Hopkins of the 6th Virginia looked behind, called to the captain, and told Gibson that the pursuing Yankees were closing in on them, and just as Hopkins spoke, two bullets hissed by his head. Gibson yelled to his men to move forward, and bending low on the necks of their horses, Hopkins and Gibson dashed away to safety.[76]

"I hitched my horse, and, wrapped in a blanket, lay down to sleep," recalled an exhausted member of the 6th Virginia Cavalry. "But I was soon rudely awakened by the watchman, who shouted that the enemy was crossing the river. We all jumped up and mounted our horses."[77] Day was breaking, and the grayclad pickets scurried up from the banks of the river in every direction, firing their pistols to raise the alarm.

Many of the Confederates were either still asleep or cooking their breakfasts when Davis's onslaught caught them. "The Company was surprised, yet contended for every foot of ground between them and the camp of Jones's and W. H. F. Lee's brigades, near St. James Church, with the battalion of horse artillery," recalled a member of the 6th Virginia. "The 6th Regiment, which was out on the road, got off first; the 7th Regiment next, just as the Federals were getting up into our midst. Many of our men had not finished their breakfast and had to mount their horses bareback and rush into the fight."[78]

As Davis's horsemen closed in on their camps, Confederate officers quickly turned out their commands and ordered them "to horse."[79] A New Yorker recounted, "We had not gone a quarter of a mile when suddenly a heavy fire was poured into our ranks by their skirmishers who filled the woods on each side of us. At the same time a strong force of cavalry appeared coming down the road in front of us, and a battery of artillery could be seen through an opening, ready to open fire as soon as we should advance a little further. It was rather a tight place, for it was almost impossible to form in line of battle under such circumstances."[80] One Regular observed, "There were lively times for a few minutes."[81]

Gibson's company retired slowly, their retreat protected by ditches in the low ground on either side of the Beverly Ford Road, thereby preventing the Union troopers from flanking them, and limiting their attack to the 6th Virginia's front. "The enemy came pouring up from the river, and we opened fire on them, checking them for the moment," recalled Luther W. Hopkins of the 6th Virginia Cavalry. "Two of our men were killed, several wounded, and two horses killed."[82]

Gibson's delaying action permitted Maj. Cabell E. Flournoy, the regimental commander, to scrape together a force of 150 men with which to blunt the Union onslaught. The sleepy Southern troopers sprang to horse after being awakened by the crack of gunfire coming from the vicinity of the ford. "There being no information or apprehension of an attack, our men had, carelessly, turned their horses out to graze." Only forty horses were haltered and ready for action, so the camp soon became a beehive of activity.[83] Flournoy led a hasty countercharge, many of his men dashing off without their coats or saddles.[84]

The two forces collided in the road, and a brief but savage saber fight occurred, as sabers clanged and pistols echoed. "The fight was at close quarters, and for a short time was fierce and bloody," recalled a member of the 6th Virginia.[85] "It seemed as if the whole air was alive with rebel bullets," recounted a member of the 8th Illinois.[86] "The roar of the guns in the woods at that early hour in the morning was terrific," concurred a Virginian.[87] During this altercation, the 6th Virginia sustained approximately thirty casualties, or 20 percent of the total force engaged. Flournoy yielded to the sheer weight of numbers.

However, Lt. Robert Owen Allen, Company D of the 6th Virginia, riding at the rear of Flournoy's retreating column, spotted "Grimes" Davis, alone and approximately seventy-five yards ahead of the rest of his column. Seeing an opportunity, Allen dashed up to Davis, who was facing his men, urging them on. Davis's last words were, "Stand firm, Eighth New York!" Even as he yelled this, Davis evidently sensed that he was in danger, for he turned upon Allen with a swing of his saber. Allen ducked this blow by throwing himself on the side of his horse while at the same time firing his pistol. Davis was killed instantly. Sgt. John Stone of Company D of the 6th Virginia rode forward to Allen's assistance. Enraged by the loss of their beloved commander, the Union troopers charged Stone, and mistaking him for Davis's killer, attacked him ferociously. A savage saber blow split Stone's skull "midway between eyes and chin," killing him instantly as well.[88]

The loss of Davis hit the Union troopers hard. "The success was dearly bought, for among the noble and brave ones who fell was Col. B. F. Davis, 8th N.Y. Cav. He died in the front giving examples of heroism and courage to all who were to follow," lamented Buford. "He was a thorough soldier, free from politics and intrigue, a patriot in its true sense, an ornament to his country and a bright star in his profession."[89] Wesley Merritt, who had a long and nearly unparalleled career in the U.S. Army, wrote years later that Davis "was dearly beloved throughout the [Reserve Brigade], and many a veteran of the First, Second, and Fifth drew his chin more grimly to his breast and with clenched teeth awaited the shock of battle, anxious to avenge the death of this hero."[90]

The 8th New York lost its way in the woods and pulled back to regroup. "The 8th New York Cav. crossed ahead and went about a mile when the rebels charged them. They broke and ran like a flock of sheep, and we, being close in their rear, now found ourselves among the rebels, who thought they were just doing it, and true enough, they were," observed a member of the 8th Illinois Cavalry. "But it was played out when they met us . . . the frightened New Yorkers came rushing on and we were obliged to draw our sabres and threaten to split their heads, to bring them back to their senses."[91]

The 8th Illinois, next in the Union column, held off the Confederate counterattack, permitting the rest of the column to regroup and prepare to resume the charge. Command of the brigade devolved upon Maj. William S. McClure, commanding the 3d Indiana. "When the sad news of Davis's fall reached me, I crossed and pushed to the front to examine the country and to find out how matters stood. I then threw the 1st Division on the left of the road leading to Brandy Station with its left extending toward the R[ail] Road." Buford brought up Ames's infantry brigade and posted the Reserve Brigade on the right, all connecting from right to left.[92]

The 6th Pennsylvania Cavalry of the Reserve Brigade was coming up as a rough litter bearing a wounded officer came down the Beverly Ford Road. "Who is that, boys?" inquired Chaplain Samuel L. Gracey.

"Colonel Davis, sir," came the response.

"Is it possible! Noble fellow! Is he wounded badly?"

"A Minie ball through his head, sir."

Gracey paused a moment to pray for Davis. "He is insensible, his hair matted and clotted with blood," recalled the chaplain. "God have mercy on the brave, noble, patriot-soldier, the hero of Harpers Ferry!"[93]

At the same time, the 7th Virginia Cavalry, under the command of Lt. Col. Thomas Marshall, arrived and joined the 6th Virginia's counterattack. Confederate troopers surrounded and nearly captured three full companies of the 8th Illinois. "To the right a large party of the enemy tried to force our cavalry back," recalled an Illinois trooper, "and actually got possession of the road in our rear, but the part of the Eighth Illinois regiment not engaged in the fight here had an opportunity to display their courage, and the conflict was severe, but the enemy were forced to yield the ground, after a bloody encounter."[94] In the end, the Rebels gave way after buying precious time for the rest of the grayclad horsemen to react.

Capt. Alpheus Clark, commander of the 8th Illinois, engaged Flournoy in a pistol duel that ended when Fluornoy wounded Clark in the hand. This seemingly inconsequential wound proved fatal when Clark contracted lead poisoning and died. Capt. George Forsythe, the next ranking officer, was also wounded during this fighting.[95] The regiment's next senior captain, Elon J. Farnsworth, took command of the 8th Illinois and led it for the rest of the day, earning praise from both Buford and Pleasonton. The corps commander marked the talented and ambitious young man for advancement.

Capt. George A. Custer came across the river with Davis's horsemen and charged with them. Although at least one of Custer's biographers claims that Custer assumed command of Davis's brigade and rallied it after Davis fell, those claims are unfounded. However, the dashing young man did earn Pleasonton's praise for his courage. He was knocked from his saddle when his horse could not clear a stone wall. Later that day, he delivered the captured headquarters flag of the 12th Virginia Cavalry to Hooker's headquarters. When he wrote his report of the battle, Pleasonton stated that Custer was "conspicuous for gallantry throughout the fight."[96]

After making his way back to report Davis's death, Custer spent the rest of the day at the Cavalry Corps commander's side. "The time was coming and very near at hand," noted one of Custer's many biographers, "though he knew it not, for him to win his star, and emerge from the inconspicuous position of a staff officer to one in which he could command public attention." And so it was.[97]

Although the surprise of the original Union assaults nearly bagged four batteries of Confederate horse artillery, quick thinking by Capt. James F. Hart of the Washington (South Carolina) Artillery saved them. Buford dispatched the 3d Indiana to rescue the New Yorkers, and the Hoosiers drove the Confederates back. McClure's men then joined the running battle. The fully roused Confederate cavalry and horse artillery pressed McClure's troopers hard as they attempted to form lines of battle.

"Our camp . . . was in the edge of a woods, and this morning at daylight, just as we were rounding up the last sweet snooze for the night, bullets fresh from Yankee sharpshooters came from the depths of the woods and zipped across our blanket beds, and then such a getting up of horse artillerymen I never saw before," recalled Sgt. George M. Neese of Capt. Roger P. Chew's fine battery of horse artillery. "Blankets were fluttering and being rolled up in double-quick time in every direction, and in less than twenty minutes we were ready to man our guns, and all our effects safely on the way to the rear. Before I got out of bed I saw a twig clipped from a bush by a Yankee bullet not more than two feet above my head."[98] Another Southern gunner recalled, "We were aroused about daylight from our dreams of home, wives and sweethearts by the firing of our pickets a few hundred yards from us and the whizzing of musket balls all around us. The enemy had made a sudden dash across the ford and were driving our pickets back into our camp, where they were met by our cavalry and our battalion and checked for the time."[99]

Seeing the Union onslaught, Hart unlimbered one of his guns, drawn by hand, on the Beverly Ford Road to cover the retreat of the Confederate troopers and the other horse artillery batteries. This action slowed the Yankee approach long enough for "Grumble" Jones to deploy his entire brigade in line of battle to protect the guns from the Union attack.[100]

The rattling of gunfire awoke Jones, and he dashed off to the head of his troops, wearing neither his coat nor his boots.[101] Once safely out of range of the stalled Yankees, Stuart's batteries unlimbered again east of St. James Church, approximately a mile and a half from Beverly's Ford, defending a ridge which they held for much of the morning's fight. These Confederate batteries kept up a steady fire, helping to repulse repeated Union attacks on the St. James Church position.[102] One of the Confederate gunners noted, "It was a close call and brilliant dash on the part of the enemy."[103]

The 8th Illinois charged into the 6th and 7th Virginia, driving them back. As one Confederate trooper succinctly put it, "Quicker than some of us came we went."[104] Col. Thomas C. Devin's Second Brigade was close behind the 8th Illinois, coming up to join the action. "As Colonel Devin approached the skirmish line, he at once became the target for the Rebel sharpshooters and, the way the minie balls were whizzing around him, it was the next thing to a miracle that he was not killed," recalled a member of the 17th Pennsylvania Cavalry. "One of the skirmishers hailed him and said, 'Colonel, this is no place for you.' He replied by saying, 'Those fellows across the ravine could not hit an elephant if they would try.'" Moments later, the Confederate sharpshooters shot Devin's horse, which was smaller than an elephant.[105]

Seeing the approaching Union troopers and recognizing the extreme danger facing his lone brigade, "Grumble" Jones committed the last of his reserves to the fight. "The men, worn out by the military foppery and display of the previous day's review, were yet under their blankets," recalled Capt. Frank Myers of the 35th Battalion of Virginia Cavalry, which later became known as White's Comanches.[106] In an effort to secure his flanks and rear, Jones sent the 11th and 12th Virginia regiments, along with the Comanches, to join the battle line centered at St. James Church.[107] Jones ordered the 35th to charge the approaching Yankees before the Comanches could even form line of battle as the blueclad horsemen repulsed the charge of the 12th Virginia. A member of the 12th Virginia described the charging Yankees "as thick as angry bees from a hive."[108]

The 35th Battalion of Virginia Cavalry slammed into the lead elements of the Federal charge near the Mary Emily Gee house, staggering them. After a brief melee, the Virginians drove the Union troopers back into the woods, where they received reinforcements. Rallying, the Union troopers again charged and this time shoved the 35th back into the woods from which they had come. In the meantime, the 12th Virginia was also heavily engaged. One member of Company H of the 12th Virginia exclaimed, "It was then warm work, hand to hand, shooting and cutting each other in desperate fury, all mixed through one another, killing, wounding, and taking prisoners promiscuously." This stalemate lasted a while, with each charge being met by a countercharge. Another member of the 12th Virginia recalled, "For hours this seesawing was kept up. Finally, after we had driven them the fourth or fifth time to their rallying point [the nearby woods], they showed no disposition to charge again, and we fell back to the hill."[109]

In the meantime, as the foes traded saber licks, the Reserve Brigade, commanded by Maj. Charles J. Whiting, a stodgy old Regular, crossed the Rappahannock and rode toward the sound of the firing. Advancing, the Regulars met little resistance for the first mile of their approach. Near an old farmhouse, Trooper Sidney Davis of the 6th U.S. and his companions spotted something: "[P]artially covered by an army blanket, lying prone on his back, was the dead body of one of our officers, from whose death wound the warm blood of life still dripped over his dark blue uniform." The sight of "Grimes" Davis's corpse chilled the Regulars, causing many of them to pray for safety in the coming battle.[110]

At 7:40, surprised by the stout resistance of the Confederates, Pleasonton decided to ride to the front. He took a few minutes to scrawl a dispatch to Washington before heading for the ford. "The enemy is in strong cavalry force here," he wrote. "We have had a severe fight. They were aware of our movement, and were prepared." Things did not bode well for the success of Pleasonton's ambitious expedition.[111]

THE FIGHT FOR THE GUNS AT ST. JAMES CHURCH

Buford did not know the size or strength of the force guarding the Confederate guns at St. James Church. He deployed the guns of Lt. Samuel S. Elder's battery of horse artillery. Buford sent a messenger to Maj. Robert Morris, Jr., the commander of the 6th Pennsylvania Cavalry. "General Buford sends his compliments to Major Morris," panted the courier, "and directs him to clear the woods in his front."[112] The Lancers stared across a field nearly half a mile wide, intersected by four ditches. The ground rose steadily to the woods, and upon the ridge sat a small house that became the Confederate headquarters, as well as the site of the Southern artillery.[113] The 6th Pennsylvania made a "dash of conspicuous gallantry" across the wide meadow, directly into the teeth of sixteen pieces of Confederate horse artillery at St. James Church.[114] Indeed, the performance of the 6th Pennsylvania that day so impressed John Buford that he henceforth called them "my Seventh Regulars."[115]

The 6th Pennsylvania "charged the enemy home, riding almost up to the mouths of his cannon," nearly capturing two of the Confederate guns.[116] "The Sixth fell upon these with great gallantry," reported a Northern correspondent who witnessed their valiant dash, "and regardless of the chances of flank attacks from the other battalions, drove them, fighting hand to hand, through the brigade in reserve, and then wheeling about, passed round the battalion on the right and resumed position for another charge."[117]

"We dashed at them, squadron front with drawn sabres, and as we flew along— our men yelling like demons—grape and cannister were poured into our left flank and a storm of rifle bullets on our front," recalled Maj. Henry C. Whelan of the 6th Pennsylvania. "We had to leap three wide deep ditches, and many of our horses and men piled up in a writhing mass in those ditches and were ridden over. It was here that Maj. Morris's horse fell badly with him, and broke away from him when he got up, thus leaving him dismounted and bruised by the fall. I didn't know that Morris was not with us, and we dashed on, driving the Rebels into and through the woods, our men fighting with the sabre alone, whilst they used principally pistols. Our brave fellows cut them out of the saddle and fought like tigers, until I discovered they were on both flanks, pouring a cross fire of carbines and pistols on us, and then tried to rally my men and make them return the fire with their carbines."[118]

When the Lancers charged, Capt. Ulric Dahlgren joined them. On June 7, Hooker had sent Dahlgren to carry his orders for the raid to Pleasonton. The ambitious captain remained with the Cavalry Corps to observe and report on the actions of the horse soldiers. The aggressive youth was unable to resist pitching into the fray. He rode alongside Major Morris and reported, "just as we were jumping a ditch, some canister came along, and I saw his horse fall over him, but could not tell whether he was killed or not, for at the same instant my horse was shot in three places." The wounded horse fell, throwing Dahlgren. "Just then the column turned to go back,—finding that the enemy had surrounded us. I saw the rear passing me, and about to leave me behind, so I gave my horse a tremendous kick and got him on his legs again. Finding he could still move, I mounted and made after the rest,—just escaping being taken. I got a heavy blow over the arm from the back of a saber, which bruised me somewhat, and nearly unhorsed me," recounted Dahlgren. The young man rallied the Lancers and led them to safety. The wounded horse had to be put down.[119]

A newspaper correspondent reported, "Captain Dahlgren, of General Hooker's staff, a model of cool and dauntless bravery, charged with the regiment, and his horse was shot in two places."[120] Pleasonton informed Hooker that Dahlgren had "been baptized in fire" and that the young man was a "capital aid."[121] Dahlgren found another mount after the battle and rode back to Hooker's headquarters to report on the day's activities. He had had a very long and trying day, and was flushed with exuberance. Impressed, Hooker marked Dahlgren for advancement. Assigned to Cavalry Corps headquarters in the days following Brandy Station, the courageous captain performed magnificently in the coming weeks.[122]

As the Lancers reached the Confederate artillery, it opened up, raking the Union line. "Never rode troopers more gallantly than those steady Regulars, as under a fire of shell and shrapnel, and finally of canister, they dashed up to the very muzzles," recalled Captain Hart, "then through and beyond our guns, passing between Hampton's left and Jones's right."[123] A member of the 6th Pennsylvania recalled, "What an awful fire! So close that we are almost in the smoke of the battery. Many of our saddles are emptied, and the horses, freed from the restraint of their riders, dash wildly away; and at the same moment, hundreds of carbines fend their charges of death into our never-wavering ranks." He continued, "Our color sergeant reels, and falls from his horse; another sergeant catches the colors before they reach the ground; and on through the storm of death our weakened lines advance until they meet the enemy, and hand to hand the conflict rages. Though we are outnumbered two to one, we break their ranks, and pursue them into the woods. Now the enemy on our right begin to close upon us: our commander has fallen. Major Whelan assuming command, attempts to withdraw us from our terrible position. But how are we to retreat? The enemy have completely surrounded us—all is lost!"[124]

Spotting the predicament facing the 6th Pennsylvania, four squadrons of the 6th U.S. charged in support of the gallant Lancers.[125] Lts. Louis H. Carpenter and Andrew Stoll led their squadrons out of the woods. Carpenter called for the charge, and away they went. As they charged, Carpenter watched the Lancers break and scatter. "As we went along at headlong speed, cheering and shouting it seemed to me, that the air was perfectly filled with bullets and pieces of shell, shells burst over us, under us, and alongside," recounted Carpenter. The Regulars crossed a wide ditch and continued on. The Virginians retreated to the cover of the woods, where they opened a heavy carbine fire.[126]

The Regulars arrived just as the Confederates were about to fall upon the bloodied Pennsylvanians. Horse soldiers of both sides merged into a wild melee among the guns. "The warlike scene was fascinatingly grand beyond description, and such as can be produced and acted only by an actual and real combat," recalled Confederate gunner Neese. "Hundreds of glittering sabres instantly leaped from their scabbards, gleamed and flashed in the morning sun, then clashed with metallic ring, searching for human blood, while hundreds of little puffs of white smoke gracefully rose through the balmy June air from discharging firearms all over the field in front of our batteries . . . [T]he artillerymen stood in silent awe gazing on the struggling mass in our immediate front."[127] Another survivor remembered "a mingled mass fighting and struggling with pistol and saber like maddened savages."[128] The lines of battle ebbed and flowed like the waves of the ocean, prompting an officer of the 12th Virginia Cavalry to write, "These charges and countercharges continued until noon, without any decisive advantage to either side, but with considerable loss to both, in men and horses."[129]

The men of Carpenter's and Stoll's squadrons laid down a heavy fire with their pistols and carbines for several minutes until their position became untenable and the Regulars retired. "As we turned, a rebel made a dash close to me; I cut at him twice and missed him," recounted Lieutenant Carpenter. "[A]s he passed he threw his saber at me. One of my men almost thrust his carbine against the breast of the rebel and shot him dead."[130] The Lancers and the Regulars retreated across the same fields toward the main Union line. They withstood heavy Confederate artillery fire, sometimes from a range as short as fifty yards. Both the Lancers and the Regulars demonstrated superb leadership at the company and squadron levels. Their officers did a fine job of regaining control of their scattered commands, which resulted in the combat units remaining effective.

The air whistling with the sounds of shrapnel and minie balls, the beleaguered Federal horse soldiers clung to the necks of their horses as they dashed across the fields toward friendly lines in the woods. As the 6th U.S. attempted to re-form in the woods, "the timber on the left was so dense that, but for the coolness of the officers and men, the formation of squadron would have been an impossibility."[131] "The Rebel Battery then advanced and opened on my position and for two hours rained a storm of shot, shell, grape, and canister through the woods," recalled Colonel Devin.[132]

Buford ordered Elder's battery to open on the Confederate artillery. Firing from a range of 1,500 yards, Elder found that the terrain protected the Confederate batteries and that his efforts at counterbattery fire were futile. Instead, Elder opened on the Confederate cavalry, occupying the Confederate battery by sending an occasional shot arching toward the Confederate gunners. The weight of the Yankee cavalry charges soon drove off the Southern guns, and Elder moved forward to better support the attacking cavalrymen. Elder later wrote, "In my frequent changes of position, [I] was never alone, nor did my support flinch, although compelled to sit in their saddles under the most severe artillery fire."[133]

Buford had wanted the 2d U.S. Cavalry to support the charges of the 6th Pennsylvania and 6th U.S. However, the 2d U.S., under Merritt's command, received different orders from the Reserve Brigade commander, Major Whiting, and did not join the charge. While the valiant charges of the Lancers and the 6th U.S. relieved the pressure on Buford's left, which had been pressed by Jones's counterattack, they exposed the Kentuckian's right flank. Seeing an opportunity, Jones pressed Buford's right. Shifting the 17th Pennsylvania and 6th New York of Devin's brigade, as well as a section of Capt. William M. Graham's battery of horse artillery, forward to relieve the pressure, Buford drove the Confederates from his right flank. He anchored his right flank along a tributary of the Rappahannock called the Hazel River and the left flank along the Rappahannock, spread across the Cunningham farm. He now occupied a solid and defensible position.

Recognizing that he was about to be overrun, and hoping that Stuart would arrive with reinforcements, Jones sent the 35th Battalion and the 11th Virginia charging into the midst of the Federal attackers. McClure's bluecoats faltered in the face of the determined charge and fell back through the woods onto the oncoming columns of Devin's Second Brigade. McClure's troopers eventually retired all the way to the Rappahannock before regrouping. The charge of the 35th Battalion also drove Devin's supporting troopers 100 yards back into the woods.[134]

Devin's brigade then rallied, and formed a dismounted line of battle in the woods. Charging the Virginians on foot, Devin's men drove the gray cavalry back toward St. James Church. The fight in the woods around St. James Church was severe, and hand-to-hand in many places. One of Devin's staff officers, Lt. Henry E. Dana of the 8th Illinois, engaged two Rebel troopers in a hand-to-hand fight. "After discharging the contents of their pistols they used them as clubs. The lieutenant finally threw his at one of his antagonists, striking him in the face and inflicting a severe wound; then, warding off the other's blow with his arm, escaped with no further injury than a lame arm and a face well powder-burned."[135] The Comanches of the 35th Battalion captured and sent more than twenty-five Union officers and enlisted to the rear. The fight proved much tougher than any of the

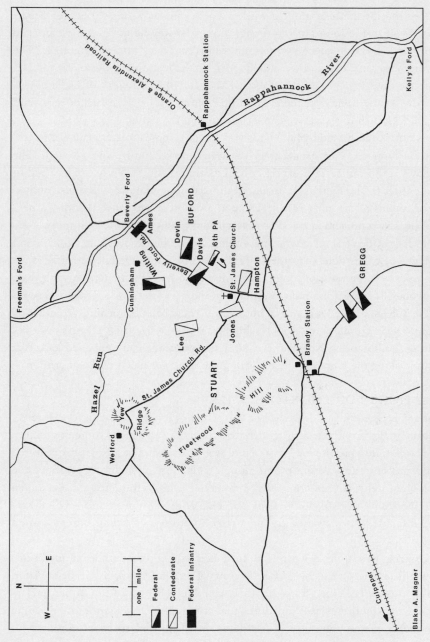

Buford's Morning Fight at Brandy Station, June 9, 1863

Blake A. Magner

Union officers could have anticipated, and Buford was surprised to learn that Brig. Gen. Wade Hampton's command had come onto the field.[136]

Hearing the crash of gunfire while savoring his morning coffee, Jeb Stuart hurried off to the sound of the firing. Along the way he dodged the panicked teamsters of the Confederate wagon trains hurrying away from the fighting: "The wagon trains came first and went thundering to the rear mid clouds of dust—then came the cavalry regiments at a trot with here and there a battery of artillery,—all hurrying to the front with the greatest possible speed."[137] Stuart galloped toward St. James Church to assume personal command of the fight.

As Stuart and his aide, Maj. Heros von Borcke, approached St. James Church, they encountered Confederate stragglers from Jones's Brigade, who shouted, "The Yankees are in our rear! Everything back there is lost!"[138] While Stuart tried to bring order to the fight at St. James Church, Rooney Lee's brigade also rushed to the sounds of the guns from its camp at a nearby estate called Welford. Jones's hard-pressed command received crucial reinforcements at a critical moment.

Seeing the fierce combat whirling around Maj. Robert F. Beckham's guns, Stuart took charge of the fight and ordered Hampton's men into the line of battle, at the Gee house on the right of Jones, facing north. To flush the Federal cavalry from the woods, Hampton dismounted some of his horse soldiers and sent them forward as skirmishers. Before long, several hundred of Hampton's command were fighting against Devin's dismounted troopers. Hampton tried to outflank Devin's position, shifting steadily to the New Yorker's left. Thus stymied, Devin remained locked in position along the Union right, anchoring the flank, for much of the afternoon.[139]

THE FIGHT FOR THE STONE WALL

Rooney Lee's command fell into line to the left of Jones, extending to the north. A stone wall that offered a strong defensive position ran parallel to Lee's position. The wall, following the lay of the land, was L-shaped. Lee posted dismounted troopers along the wall and others along a ridge directly behind and above the wall. These defensive positions offered excellent fields of fire, affording Lee's men an opportunity to enfilade the flank and rear of the Union position. The determined Confederates awaited the next attack with some of their best troops on line.[140]

Utilizing this strong defensive position, Lee fended off a number of uncoordinated, piecemeal attacks by Buford's cavalry. The 5th U.S. made the first assault, trying to drive Lee's men from the stone wall. The 5th, under Capt. James E. Harrison, had only three small squadrons that day, and was understrength. Keeping one squadron to support a section of Graham's battery, Harrison dismounted his remaining two squadrons and pushed them forward as skirmishers. Their Sharp's carbines blazing, the Regulars seized and held a portion of the wall, fending off a number of ferocious Confederate counterattacks. They remained in place until the Regulars completely exhausted their ammunition. Finally, these two hard-pressed squadrons were relieved, and Harrison's men retired to support Graham's battery. The 5th U.S. sustained thirty-eight casualties—a high percentage of their small force involved in the fighting—demonstrating the intensity of the fighting for the stone wall.[141]

Emboldened by Harrison's limited success, Buford decided to commit the rest of the Reserve Brigade. He ordered the Regulars forward, supported by Elder's battery and Ames's infantry brigade. Buford deployed the dismounted Regulars in line of battle alongside McClure's and Devin's brigades, the infantry regiments protecting the flanks. While the fresh troops were being organized, Buford called up his artillery.

A vigorous artillery duel erupted between Beckham's and Elder's guns. Beckham's guns soon found the range of Elder's battery, and disabled several pieces manned by Batteries B and L, 2d U.S. Artillery. The counterbattery blasts kept the Confederate artillery occupied, making an assault easier. Now protected by artillery, Buford's lines surged forward, supported by the deadly fire of the longer-ranged rifled muskets of Ames's infantry. They attacked the wall, but the steady fire of Lee's dismounted troopers drove them back. A lull settled across the battlefield as the two sides regrouped.

At 11:30 A.M., Pleasonton, who had finally arrived on the battlefield, wired Hooker: "All the enemy's force are engaged with me. I am holding them until Gregg can come up. Gregg's guns are being heard in the enemy's rear."[142] Buford's tired horse soldiers had been fighting constantly since dawn. Although Gregg's attack was supposed to have been coordinated with Buford's, Buford had fought alone for nearly six hours.

Nobody had expected a battle of such magnitude, but neither side was willing to quit. Both Stuart and Buford used the lull to redeploy and to recover dead and wounded comrades. At that moment, as Stuart prepared for a full-scale counterattack, the sound of fighting to his rear shifted his attention away from Buford. Finally, about 11:30, as one member of the 8th New York recorded in his diary, Buford's men "heard the booming of distant cannon which told us that Gen. Graig [sic] had arrived from Kelly's Ford and was engaging the enemy."[143]

Hearing Gregg's guns, Buford "resolved to go to him if possible." With that goal in mind, Buford took all of his force, except for the 5th U.S., which anchored the right and supported Graham's battery.[144]

The men of the 124th New York marched to the sound of the guns. "As we moved forward, wounded men began to straggle back past us," recalled a New York infantryman. "Some of these were on horseback, others with pale faces and blood-stained garments came staggering along on foot, and occasionally one was borne hurriedly by on a stretcher, or in the arms of, apparently tender-hearted, but really cowardly, comrades. A little farther on we began to pass over, and saw lying on either side of us, lifeless bodies of men, dressed, some in grey and some in blue, which told unmistakably that the tide of battle was with the Union line." Steeled, the New York infantrymen formed line of battle and prepared to meet the enemy. They finally drove off the dismounted Southerners after a fierce twenty-minute engagement.[145]

"Both parties fought earnestly and up to 12 o'clock the enemy held his position," observed one of Buford's Hoosiers, "but after that hour saw fit to fall back."[146] Late in the morning, Alfred Pleasonton finally came across the Rappahannock River and established his headquarters in Mary Emily Gee's large brick house near St. James Church.[147] A second front was about to break out. The brute force of Gregg's attack on Fleetwood Hill was about to crash onto Stuart's headquarters with the savage power of a tidal wave.

NOTES

1. Admiral Dahlgren invented a powerful naval gun and was highly esteemed for his soaring intellect. Dahlgren was also well connected politically, enjoying favored status with both Lincoln and Stanton.
2. O.R., vol. 25, part 2, 517–18.
3. John Dahlgren, *Memoir of Ulric Dahlgren* (Philadelphia: J. B. Lippincott, 1872), 142.
4. Fishel, *The Secret War for the Union,* 414; O.R., vol. 25, part 1, 1109.
5. Hard, *History of the Eighth Cavalry Regiment,* 228.
6. Ibid., 239.
7. O.R., vol. 25, part 1, 1112.
8. Hard, *History of the Eighth Cavalry Regiment,* 241.
9. Margeurite Merington, ed., *The Custer Story: The Life and Letters of General George A. Custer and His Wife Elizabeth* (New York: Devin-Adair, 1950), 53–54.
10. O.R., vol. 25, part 1, 1116.
11. Merington, *Custer Story,* 54.
12. Alfred Pleasonton to Austin Blair, May 30, 1863, George A. Custer Letters, Special Collections, U.S. Military Academy Library, West Point, N.Y.
13. O.R., vol. 25, part 2, 528. This was just one of a number of extremely accurate intelligence reports that Colonel Sharpe would generate over the course of the coming Gettysburg Campaign. Even in the Civil War, good military intelligence was critical to an army's success.
14. Ibid., vol. 27, part 3, 3.
15. Ibid., 32.
16. Ibid., vol. 25, part 2, 536. The Confederate concentration observed by Gregg's scouts was the beginning of the great massing of Confederate cavalry at Brandy Station. The brigades were the commands of Generals Fitz Lee, Rooney Lee, Hampton, and Beverly Robertson, although the report claimed Brig. Gen. Charles Field commanded it.

17. Ibid., 537.
18. Ibid., 538; John Buford to Capt. A. J. Cohen, May 29, 1863, Letters Received, Telegrams, Reports, and Lists Received by Cavalry Corps, 1861–1865, National Archives, Washington, D.C.
19. O.R., vol. 25, part 2, 571–72.
20. Ibid., 595.
21. Buford to Lt. Col. A. J. Alexander, June 2, 1863, Letters Received, Telegrams, Reports, and Lists Received by Cavalry Corps, 1861–1865, National Archives, Washington, D.C.
22. O.R., vol. 27, part 3, 5.
23. Buford referred to the brigade of Brig. Gen. Albert G. Jenkins, a Harvard-trained lawyer who commanded a rough-and-tumble brigade of Confederate mounted infantry.
24. O.R., vol. 27, part 3, 8. The Jones referred to by Buford was Brig. Gen. William Edmondson "Grumble" Jones, a classmate from the West Point class of 1848. Buford and Jones tangled many times in the coming months. Ironically, neither survived the war—Buford died of disease in December 1863 and Jones died in action in early 1864. Their careers and personalities, even their deaths, paralleled each other in many ways.
25. New York Times, June 10, 1863.
26. O.R., vol. 27, part 3, 10.
27. Ibid., 12.
28. John S. Mosby, Stuart's Cavalry in the Gettysburg Campaign (New York: Moffatt, Yard, 1908), 10.
29. Fishel, Secret War for the Union, 426–28.
30. O.R., vol. 27, part 3, 13.
31. Ibid., 14.
32. Ibid.
33. Fishel, Secret War for the Union, 429.
34. McClellan, Life and Campaigns, 261; see also, Blackford, War Years with Jeb Stuart, 211–12.
35. George H. Moffat, "The Battle of Brandy Station," Confederate Veteran 14 (February 1906), 74.
36. Festus P. Summers, ed., A Borderland Confederate (Pittsburgh: University of Pittsburgh Press, 1962), 71.
37. William N. McDonald, A History of the Laurel Brigade (Baltimore, Md.: Sun Job Printing Office, 1907), 132.
38. O.R., vol. 27, part 3, 14 and 18.
39. Ibid., 24–25.
40. Ibid., 24 and 27.
41. Heros von Borcke and Justus Scheibert, The Great Cavalry Battle of Brandy Station, trans. Stuart T. Wright and F. D. Bridgewater (1893; reprint, Gaithersburg, Md.: Olde Soldier Books, 1976), 35.
42. New York Times, June 11, 1863.
43. O.R., vol. 27, part 3, 27–28.

44. William F. Moyer, "Brandy Station: A Stirring Account of the Famous Cavalry Engagement," *National Tribune*, March 20, 1884.

45. Ibid.

46. Preston, *History of the Tenth Regiment*, 82.

47. Alfred Pleasonton to John Buford, June 8, 1863, Order Book of the Chief of Cavalry for 1863, Civil War Miscellaneous Collection, USAMHI. The only evidence of Pleasonton's intention to turn his raid into a chase for Stuart is a letter by Capt. George A. Custer to his sister, written on the eve of battle, wherein he indicated that Pleasonton had instructed the men to pack three days' rations for a pursuit of the enemy. George A. Custer to Anne Reed, June 8, 1863, Lawrence Frost Collection of Custeriana, Monroe County Library System, Monroe, Mich.

48. Grimsley, *Battles in Culpeper County, Virginia*, 3.

49. Chiswell Dabney to Dear Father, June 14, 1863, quoted in Robert J. Trout, *With Pen and Saber: The Letters and Diaries of J. E. B. Stuart's Staff Officers* (Mechanicsburg, Pa.: Stackpole Books, 1995), 213; Eric J. Wittenberg, "John Buford and the Gettysburg Campaign," *Gettysburg: Historical Articles of Lasting Interest* 11 (July 1994), 27.

50. James S. Brisbin to Dearest Wife, June 8, 1863, *Civil War Times Illustrated* Collection, USAMHI.

51. John Esten Cooke, *Wearing of the Gray, Being Personal Portraits, Scenes & Adventures of the War* (New York: E. B. Treat, 1867), 227.

52. Blackford, *War Years with Jeb Stuart*, 212–13.

53. Peter Wellington Alexander, *Writing & Fighting the Confederate War: The Letters of Peter Wellington Alexander, Confederate War Correspondent*, ed. William B. Styple (Kearny, N.J.: Belle Grove, 2002), 146.

54. Grimsley, *Battles in Culpeper County*, 8.

55. Summers, *A Borderland Confederate*, 71.

56. Daniel E. Sutherland, *Seasons of War: The Ordeal of a Confederate Community, 1861–1865* (New York: Free Press, 1995), 241–42.

57. McClellan, *Life and Campaigns*, 262.

58. Grimsley, *Battles of Culpeper County*, 8.

59. O.R., vol. 27, part 3, 872–73.

60. Capt. Robert E. Lee, *Recollections and Letters of Robert E. Lee* (Garden City, N.Y.: Garden City, 1924), 96.

61. J. E. Copeland, "The Fighting at Brandy Station," *Confederate Veteran* 30 (1922), 451.

62. John Blue, *Hanging Rock Rebel: Lt. John Blue's War in West Virginia and the Shenandoah Valley*, ed. Dan Oates (Shippensburg, Pa.: Burd Street Press, 1994), 198.

63. Gilpin diary, entry for June 8, 1863.

64. Hard, *History of the Eighth Cavalry Regiment*, 242.

65. Gracey, *Annals of the Sixth Pennsylvania Cavalry*, 156–57. Evidently, not all of the Union troopers were permitted to sleep as they waited to cross at Beverly's Ford. See, e.g., Hall, *History of the Sixth New York Cavalry*, 127 ("No fires were permitted at night, the men standing 'to horse,' noiseless and alert").

66. Ibid.

67. Custer to Anne Reed, June 8, 1863.

68. Frank Moore, ed., *The Rebellion Record: A Diary of American Events, with Documents, Narratives, Illustrative Incidents, Poetry, etc.*, 11 vols. (New York: D. Van Nostrand, 1864–68), 7:16.

69. Davis, *Common Soldier, Uncommon War,* 391.

70. Frederic C. Newhall, "The Battle of Beverly Ford," in *The Annals of the War as Told by the Leading Participants* (Dayton, Ohio: Morningside, 1988), 138–39.

71. Hard, *History of the Eighth Cavalry Regiment,* 243.

72. John Buford to Lt. Col. A. J. Alexander, June 13, 1863, Hooker Papers. For some reason, Buford's official report of the Battle of Brandy Station never made it into the Official Records of the Civil War.

73. *Rochester Daily Union & Advertiser,* June 18, 1863.

74. Hard, *History of the Eighth Cavalry Regiment,* 243.

75. Blue, *Hanging Rock Rebel,* 198.

76. Luther W. Hopkins, *From Bull Run to Appomattox: A Boy's View* (Baltimore, Md.: Press of Fleet-McGinley, 1908), 90–91.

77. Ibid., 89–90.

78. McDonald, *History of the Laurel Brigade,* 134; T. J. Young, "The Battle of Brandy Station," *Confederate Veteran* 23 (April 1915): 171–72.

79. Norton, *Deeds of Daring,* 65. According to the regimental historian of the 8th New York, the surprise in the Confederate camps was complete, and mass confusion resulted from their being caught unaware.

80. *Rochester Daily Union & Advertiser,* June 18, 1863.

81. Reno, "Boots and Saddles."

82. Hopkins, *From Bull Run to Appomattox,* 90.

83. John N. Opie, *A Rebel Cavalryman with Lee, Stuart, and Jackson* (Chicago: W. B. Conkey, 1899), 147.

84. Maj. James F. Hart, in the *Philadelphia Weekly Times,* June 26, 1880, quoted in McClellan, *Life and Campaigns of Major-General J. E. B. Stuart,* 266.

85. McDonald, *History of the Laurel Brigade,* 134.

86. Hard, *History of the Eighth Cavalry Regiment,* 243.

87. Hopkins, *From Bull Run to Appomattox,* 91.

88. Norton, *Deeds of Daring,* 65; McClellan, *Life and Campaigns of Major-General J. E. B. Stuart,* 265; Edward G. Longacre, *The Cavalry at Gettysburg: A Tactical Study of Mounted Operations during the Civil War's Pivotal Campaign, 9 June–14 July 1863* (Rutherford, N.J.: Fairleigh-Dickinson University Press, 1986), 67.

89. Buford to Alexander, June 13, 1863.

90. Merritt, "Recollections of the Civil War," 286.

91. P. J. Kennedy to Dear Parents, June 11, 1863, *Morrison-Whiteside Journal,* June 25, 1863.

92. Buford to Alexander, June 13, 1863.

93. Gracey, *Annals of the Sixth Pennsylvania Cavalry,* 158.

94. Hard, *History of the Eighth Cavalry Regiment,* 244.

95. Ibid., 244–45; O.R., vol. 27, part 1, 1046–47.

96. O.R., vol. 27, part 1, 1046. The myth of Custer assuming command of Davis's brigade began with an earlier biographer and has been repeated a number of times. See, e.g.,

Gregory J. W. Urwin, *Custer Victorious: The Civil War Battles of General George Armstrong Custer* (East Rutherford, N.J.: Associated University Presses, 1983), 53 ("... Custer took command of the [8th New York] and two other [regiments], the 8th Illinois and 3d Indiana, leading them through the surrounding Confederates in a smart saber charge that brought them out safely"). Historian Jeffry D. Wert, who has written the most balanced biography of Custer to date, specifically refutes that myth. Wert, *Custer,* 78.

97. Whittaker, *A Complete Life of General George A. Custer,* 147.

98. George M. Neese, *Three Years in the Confederate Horse Artillery* (New York: Neale, 1911), 171.

99. John J. Shoemaker, *Shoemaker's Battery, Stuart Horse Artillery, Pelham's Battalion, Army of Northern Virginia* (Memphis, Tenn.: privately published, n.d.), 38.

100. O.R., vol. 27, part 2, 748.

101. Moffat, "Battle of Brandy Station," 74. Moffat stated that Jones "gave the enemy such a stiff fight that he held them in check until the remainder of the corps could be mounted and Gen. Stuart form his line of battle." Ibid. This may be a bit of an over-statement.

102. O.R., vol. 27, part 2, 772–73.

103. Shoemaker, *Shoemaker's Battery,* 38.

104. Clark B. Hall, "Buford at Brandy Station," *Civil War* 8 (July–August, 1990): 16.

105. Henry P. Moyer, *History of the Seventeenth Regiment, Pennsylvania Volunteer Cavalry* (Lebanon, Pa.: Sowers Printing, 1911), 45; Hall, *History of the Sixth New York Cavalry,* 127.

106. Frank M. Myers, *The Comanches: A History of White's Battalion, Virginia Cavalry* (Baltimore: Kelly, Piet, 1871), 181.

107. O.R., vol. 27, part 2, 749.

108. Dennis E. Frye, *12th Virginia Cavalry,* 2d ed. (Lynchburg, Va.: H. E. Howard, 1988), 36.

109. Myers, *Comanches,* 182; Frye, *12th Virginia Cavalry,* 36. Lt. Col. Elijah Veirs White commanded the 35th, a veteran raiding unit. The Comanches had not seen much classic cavalry combat, and they were largely untested in a stand-up fight. As Jones had no other available reserve, he threw in the 35th, and it performed well.

110. Davis, *Common Soldier, Uncommon War,* 391–92.

111. O.R., vol. 27, part 3, 38.

112. Gracey, *Annals of the Sixth Pennsylvania Cavalry,* 159.

113. Alfred R. Waud, "The Cavalry Fight near Culpeper," *Harper's Weekly,* July 10, 1863.

114. Beale, *History of the Ninth Virginia Cavalry,* 85.

115. Longacre, *Cavalry at Gettysburg,* 73.

116. Buford to Alexander, June 13, 1863.

117. Waud, "Cavalry Fight near Culpeper."

118. Henry C. Whelan to Charles C. Cadwalader, June 11, 1863, Cadwalader Family Collection, Historical Society of Pennsylvania, Philadelphia.

119. Dahlgren, *Memoir of Ulric Dahlgren,* 148.

120. Ibid., 149.

121. Alfred Pleasonton to Joseph Hooker, June 9, 1863, Hooker Papers.

122. For additional information on the critical role played by Ulric Dahlgren in the Gettysburg Campaign, see Eric J. Wittenberg, "Ulric Dahlgren in the Gettysburg Campaign," *Gettysburg Magazine: Historical Articles of Lasting Interest,* no. 22 (January 1999): 96–111.

123. Fairfax Downey, *Clash of Cavalry: The Battle of Brandy Station* (New York: David McKay, 1959), 103.

124. Gracey, *Annals of the Sixth Pennsylvania Cavalry,* 160. Major Robert Morris, Jr., the commanding officer of the 6th Pennsylvania, was captured during the charge. Morris, great-grandson of the financier of the American Revolution, died a prisoner of war in Richmond's notorious Libby Prison, another casualty of this most fratricidal of wars.

125. William H. Carter, *From Yorktown to Santiago with the Sixth U.S. Cavalry* (1900; reprint, Austin, Tex.: State House Press, 1989), 84. One squadron of the 6th U.S. remained on the other side of the Rappahannock in support of the Union guns positioned there.

126. Louis H. Carpenter to his father, June 11, 1863, Carpenter Letters.

127. Neese, *Three Years in the Confederate Horse Artillery,* 172.

128. Hall, "Buford at Brandy Station," 16.

129. George Baylor, *Bull Run to Bull Run; or, Four Years in the Army of Northern Virginia* (Richmond: B. F. Johnson Printing, 1900), 143.

130. Carpenter to his father, June 11, 1863.

131. George C. Cram to Sir, June 10, 1863, Hooker Papers.

132. Thomas C. Devin to Lt. Col. A. J. Alexander, June 1863, Hooker Papers.

133. Lt. Samuel S. Elder to Capt. James M. Robertson, June 20, 1863, Henry Jackson Hunt Papers, Manuscripts Collection, Library of Congress, Washington, D.C.

134. O.R., vol. 27, part 2, 772–73.

135. Abner Hard to Editor Beacon, June 11, 1863, *Aurora Beacon,* June 18, 1863.

136. O.R., vol. 27, part 2, 768.

137. Frank Robertson to My Dear Kate, June 12, 1863, quoted in Trout, *With Pen and Saber,* 208. Captain Robertson was one of Stuart's engineering officers, and traveled with Stuart's headquarters. Thus, he was present when the sounds of the firing reached Stuart's ears that morning.

138. Von Borcke and Scheibert, *Great Cavalry Battle at Brandy Station,* 88.

139. Robertson to My Dear Kate, June 12, 1863, quoted in Trout, *With Pen and Saber,* 209; Devin to Cohen, June 1863.

140. McClellan, *Life and Campaigns of Major-General J. E. B. Stuart,* 267.

141. Buford to Alexander, June 13, 1863; Capt. James E. Harrison to Sir, June 16, 1863, James Harrison Papers, Special Collections, U.S. Military Academy, West Point, N.Y., reference no. 173.

142. O.R., vol. 27, part 1, 903.

143. Diary of Jasper Cheney, entry for June 9, 1863.

144. Buford to Alexander, June 13, 1863.

145. Weygant, *History of the 124th New York,* 145.

146. Gilpin diary, entry for June 9, 1863.

147. Newhall, "The Battle of Beverly's Ford," 141.

9

BRANDY STATION:
CLIMAX ON FLEETWOOD HILL

Brig. Gen. David M. Gregg had not had an easy time of it. Because of the long march from the Warrenton vicinity, Alfred Duffié's division had stopped to rest for a while, and then pushed on. The Frenchman then turned onto the wrong road to Kelly's Ford, a poor decision for an officer who had spent time in the area. His division was nearly three hours late arriving at Kelly's Ford, where Gregg sat and waited impatiently. Finally, some time between 5:00 and 6:00 A.M., Duffié appeared, after taking nearly five hours to cover five miles. The crossing at Kelly's Ford had not gone well. Gregg's crossing was to have coincided with Buford's. However, because Duffié's division was late to the rendezvous, the entire crossing had been delayed for several hours. When Gregg's skirmishers finally got across the river, they unexpectedly found men from the green North Carolina brigade of Brig. Gen. Beverly H. Robertson picketing the ford. Like Buford, Gregg was surprised to find Confederate resistance; Pleasonton's faulty intelligence also failed to disclose the presence of Rebel pickets at Kelly's Ford. Gregg's men captured the Southern vedettes before they could spread word of the Yankee approach, and the Pennsylvanian's column finally splashed across the Rappahannock. He left the 4th New York behind to guard the ford.[1]

General Robertson's brigade was made up of two large but completely inexperienced regiments, which were patrolling the area immediately surrounding Kelly's Ford. When Robertson learned that Yankee troopers were moving on his main body, he sent word to Stuart of the Yankee advance. Robertson was an 1849 West Pointer. He had spent his entire Regular Army career in the 2d Dragoons on the western frontier. Robertson served under Brig. Gen. Turner Ashby in the

Shenandoah Valley, and took command of Ashby's brigade after the legendary cavalier was killed during Jackson's 1862 Valley Campaign. He did well in that position, besting John Buford in the final engagement at Second Bull Run, but Stuart relieved him of command shortly thereafter. Stuart despised him, and once described Robertson as the "most troublesome man in the Army."[2] Stuart thought that he had rid himself of Robertson by banishing him to North Carolina, but his untested brigade was summoned to Culpeper for the forthcoming invasion of the north.

Robertson later claimed that Stuart had ordered him to retreat from Kelly's Ford to Fleetwood Hill, leaving the road to Brandy Station open for the Yankee advance.[3] Stuart then countermanded the order to retreat, and directed Robertson to march his command back to the Kelly's Mill Road position to block the Union route of advance. His North Carolinians immediately encountered Union skirmishers. "Just then the enemy's line of skirmishers emerged from the woods," claimed Robertson, "and I at once dismounted a large portion of my command, and made such disposition of my entire force as seemed best calculated to retard their progress."[4]

Robertson shortly discovered that Gregg had flanked his position, and that the blueclad horsemen were rapidly moving toward Stuart's main position. "I therefore determined to hold the ground in my front should the infantry attempt to advance upon the railroad, and placed my skirmishers behind an embankment, to protect them from the artillery, which had been opened from the woods," proclaimed Robertson in defense of his actions.[5] Robertson did little else to check the Yankee advance, which proceeded largely unhindered. "Brigadier-General Robertson kept the enemy in check on the Kelly's ford road but did not conform to the movement of the enemy to the right, of which he was cognizant," wrote Stuart, "so as to hold him in check or thwart him by a corresponding move of a portion of his command in the same direction. He was too far off for me to give him orders to do so in time."[6]

Robertson claimed that he failed to hinder Gregg's advance because he was trying to check Russell's infantry. He further alleged that his small brigade was an insufficient force to hinder the Yankee advance, so he did not even try to block Gregg's march. His North Carolinians spent the balance of the day jousting with Russell's infantry near Kelly's Ford. They played no role at all in the great cavalry battle raging just a few miles behind them. Their casualties that day totaled four horses killed.[7]

Robertson's failure exposed the Confederate flank to attack, and left Fleetwood Hill completely uncovered. Undisturbed by the North Carolinians, Gregg's Federals enjoyed a pleasant, though slightly longer, march to Fleetwood Hill. While Gregg could plainly hear Buford's guns roaring at St. James Church, he took a longer, more roundabout route instead of brushing Robertson out of his way and marching immediately to the guns over the shortest overland route. This decision permitted Stuart to concentrate the fury of his entire command on Buford. As Gregg marched, Pleasonton sent a galloper to him, informing the Pennsylvanian "of the severity of the fight on the right and of the largely superior force of the enemy." After scribbling a note to Duffié to hurry to Brandy Station, Gregg raced off toward the sound of the guns.[8]

Wyndham's brigade led Gregg's advance on the left, followed by Kilpatrick's brigade just behind and to the right. Some time around 11:00 A.M., nearly seven hours after Buford's initial attack, Wyndham's command finally reached the tracks of the Orange and Alexandria Railroad a half mile from the depot. They spotted a single enemy gun atop Fleetwood Hill and headed straight for it. The Carolina Road, an important route of north-south commerce, ran across the crest of Fleetwood Hill. If Gregg could capture and hold the hill, his position would dominate the line at St. James Church, and Stuart's force would have to abandon its strong position there. He would also interdict Stuart's primary route of retreat to Culpeper.

"Grumble" Jones somehow learned of the Yankee advance, perhaps via one of Robertson's couriers, and sent a messenger to Stuart with this information. Stuart snorted when he heard the courier's report, and responded, "Tell Gen. Jones to attend to the Yankees in his front, and I'll watch the flanks." The courier returned to Jones and repeated what Stuart had said. It was Jones's turn to retort, "So he thinks they ain't coming, does he? Well, let him alone; he'll damned well soon see for himself."[9] This prediction proved correct soon enough.

THE FIGHT FOR FLEETWOOD HILL

Stuart's personal tent-fly still fluttered above Fleetwood Hill as the Yankee wave bore down on it. Two regiments, the 2d South Carolina and 4th Virginia, had picketed the hill, but Hampton had sent these two regiments to Stevensburg to block Duffié's advance. Other than a few miscellaneous staff officers and orderlies, the dominant topographical feature of the area lay unprotected. However, one artillery piece, a 12-pound Napoleon of Capt. Roger P. Chew's battery of horse artillery, which was commanded by Lt. John W. "Tuck" Carter, happened to be present. Carter used almost all of his ammunition in the whirling melee at St. James Church, and pulled back to Fleetwood Hill to refill his limber. Maj. Henry B. McClellan, Stuart's capable adjutant, was the highest-ranking officer in the area.

Major McClellan was a transplanted Philadelphian, and a first cousin of Gen. George B. McClellan. He was a gifted staff officer who found himself in the right place at the right time this day. Just a few minutes after one of Robertson's couriers informed him that the Yankees were advancing in force on his exposed position, the head of Wyndham's column came into view. Seeing the urgency of the situation, McClellan sent a series of orderlies off to warn Stuart. The major, realizing that if he did not take charge, nobody would, sprang into action.

"They were pressing steadily toward the railroad station, which must in a few moments be in their possession. How could they be prevented from also occupying the Fleetwood Hill, the key to the whole position? Matters looked serious!" recalled McClellan. "But good results can sometimes be accomplished with the smallest means. Lieutenant Carter's howitzer was brought up, and boldly pushed beyond the crest of the hill; a few imperfect shells and some round shot were found in the limber chest; a slow fire was at once opened upon the marching column, and courier after courier was dispatched to General Stuart to inform him of the peril."[10] The few shots lobbed by Carter's gun caused confusion in the Federal ranks, and they hesitated a moment to evaluate the threat.

This pause made all of the difference for Gregg's assault. "There was not one man upon the hill besides those belonging to Carter's howitzer and myself, for I had sent away even my last courier, with an urgent appeal for speedy help," observed McClellan. "Could General Gregg have known the true state of affairs he would, of course, have sent forward a squadron to take possession; but appearances demanded a more serious attack, and while this was being organized three rifled guns were unlimbered, and a fierce cannonade was opened on the hill."[11]

McClellan's couriers found Stuart directing the fighting at St. James Church. "Ride back there and see what all that foolishness is about," responded Stuart to the messenger.[12] The repeated urgency of McClellan's messages combined with the sound of cannonading finally prompted Stuart to pull two of Jones's regiments, the 12th Virginia Cavalry and the 35th Battalion of Virginia Cavalry, from the St. James Church line, and send them to Fleetwood. "The regiment, in the great haste with which it repaired, to the point designated, became much scattered and lengthened out," recalled a captain of the 12th Virginia.[13] Another member of the same regiment observed, "The enemy gained our rear beautifully but our brigade cleaned them out nicely."[14]

Stuart also dispatched one of his staff officers, Lt. Frank S. Robertson, to find Hampton, with instructions to send a regiment to reinforce Fleetwood Hill.[15] It took a few precious minutes for the Confederate reinforcements to reach the hill. As the head of the small Confederate column reached Fleetwood, it met Carter's withdrawing gun, now entirely out of ammunition. The vanguard of Wyndham's attacking column was just fifty yards from the crest of the hill. The two forces crashed together with tremendous force.[16] "With a ringing cheer," the 1st New Jersey, led by Lt. Col. Virgil Brodrick "rode up the gentle ascent that led to Stuart's headquarters, the men gripping hard their sabers, and the horses taking ravines and ditches in their stride."[17] As Capt. William W. Blackford of Stuart's staff recorded, "There now followed a passage of arms filled with romantic interest and splendor to a degree unequaled by anything our war produced."[18]

As Gregg approached, he could see the fight raging in the distance. The roar of the artillery grew louder as he rode. The Pennsylvanian ordered his troopers to draw sabres, and "their willing blades leaped from their scabbards, and with one wild, exultant shout they dashed across the field, on, over the railroad, and, with Wyndham at their head, rode over and through the headquarters of Stuart, the rebel chief."[19] The swarming Federals presented quite a spectacle. "The heights of Brandy and the spot where our headquarters had been were perfectly swarming with Yankees," recalled Stuart's aide, von Borcke, "while the men of one of our brigades were scattered wide over the plateau, chased in all directions by their enemies."[20]

Stuart sent the rest of Jones' brigade and the balance of Hampton's brigade to McClellan's aid at Fleetwood. The Confederate chieftain rode to the sound of the fighting himself, arriving just behind the 12th Virginia, with Lt. Col. Elijah V. White's 35th Battalion in tow, close behind. Wyndham's lead regiment, the 1st New Jersey, briefly took possession of the hill, but the Confederate onslaught crashed into them, driving the Jerseymen back. White led one charging column while Maj. George M. Ferneyhough led another. "I ordered 20 men to continue the pursuit from which I was thus reluctantly forced to desist," reported White, "and returned with the remainder of my command to renew the contest for the possession of the hill."[21] Ferneyhough's column likewise slugged it out with the Jerseymen atop Fleetwood Hill, saber blades glinting in the bright sun. The Jerseymen began shoving the Comanches back down the hill. "Stuart's headquarters were in our hands," proclaimed a victorious member of the 1st New Jersey, "and his favorite regiments in flight before us."[22]

Seeing Ferneyhough's men falling back, Col. Asher W. Harman of the 12th Virginia tried to provide a rallying point for them at the eastern base of Fleetwood Hill. Meanwhile, elements of the 1st Pennsylvania Cavalry arrived and joined the New Jersey horsemen in the melee. "For God's sake, form! For my sake form!" Harman bellowed as the fighting whirled around him.[23] His men rallied, and Ferneyhough's retreating troopers joined them. They then charged back up the hill, where Flournoy's 6th Virginia, just arriving, joined them in the counterattack. "First came the dead heavy crash of the meeting columns, and next the clash of sabers," recounted a member of the 1st Pennsylvania, "the rattle of pistol and carbine, mingling with the frenzied imprecation, the wild shriek that follows the death blow, the demand to surrender, and the appeal for mercy, forming the horrid din of battle."[24]

An officer of the 1st Pennsylvania Cavalry remembered, "At one time the dust was so thick we could not tell friend from foe."[25] "The scene now became terrific, grand, and ludicrous," recalled a member of the 1st Maryland (Union) Cavalry. "The choking dust was so thick that we could not tell 't'other from which.' Horses, wild beyond the control of their riders, were charging away through the lines of the enemy and back again. Many of our men were captured and escaped because their clothes were so covered with dust that they looked like graybacks."[26]

Indeed, the heavy dust worked to the advantage of the Federal troopers. Sgt. Charles U. Embrey, Company I of the 1st Maryland, was captured, but made good use of his brown shirt. Umbrey pretended to be an orderly to a Confederate colonel for a few minutes until he escaped. Sgt. Philip L. Hiteshaw of the same company was captured and escaped because he wore gray trousers.

Perhaps, though, the best story pertains to Maj. Charles H. Russell of the 1st Maryland. Major Russell found himself cut off from the main body of Gregg's division, but he rallied fifteen men and went to work. He hid his little command in the woods, and every time a group of the enemy came by, the major dashed at them with three or four men, and when close upon them, turned and called out to an imaginary officer to bring up his supporting squadrons from the woods. Then he fell back, always bringing a few prisoners with him. At one time, he had garnered as many as forty or fifty prisoners using this ruse. Finally, the grayclad cavalry charged his position and retook all but fourteen of the prisoners. "The major turned, fired his pistol into their faces, and again called upon that imaginary officer to bring up those imaginary squadrons." The rebels halted to re-form for the charge, and while they were forming, Russell and his little column slipped away to rejoin their regiment. Russell lost his hat in the melee, and now wore a captured Rebel cap. "He looked like a Reb. When he returned through the two divisions of Rebel cavalry, he had so many prisoners and so few men that they doubtless mistook him and his party for their own men moving out to reconnoiter."[27]

Soon the whole plain in front of Brandy Station became a whirling blur of saber swinging duels, with the two sides mixed promiscuously.[28] With complete victory nearly within his grasp, the taciturn David Gregg caught the spirit of the moment. A staff officer noted that the Pennsylvanian "showed an enthusiasm that I had never noticed before. He started his horse on a gallop . . . swinging his gauntlets over his head and hurrahing."[29]

Lt. Thomas B. Lucas of the 1st Pennsylvania Cavalry received a vicious saber slash to his head during the chaos. Lucas's high-spirited mount bolted, and when it hit a muddy spot, Lucas pitched off the horse. The dismounted lieutenant found himself surrounded by enemy cavalrymen. "Kill the Yankee!" demanded one, who crashed his saber down on Lucas's skull. Fortunately, the blade turned broadside just enough for it to glance off the lieutenant's skull instead of cleaving it. A few of his men spotted his peril and rescued him with a savage charge, leaving a grateful Lucas with a painful but not serious wound.[30]

As the Confederates were about to give way, Wade Hampton's brigade arrived, along with the balance of Jones's force. With Hampton himself leading the charge, the Southern cavalry pitched headlong into the Yankee cavalry at the top of Fleetwood Hill, and the melee resumed. Stuart, following along behind Hampton's column, could be heard to yell, "Give them the sabre, boys!"[31] Saber charge after saber charge occurred, and the whirling struggle deteriorated into small, isolated fights among pockets of men; all organization disappeared as the horsemen clashed. "What the eye saw as Stuart rapidly fell back from the river and concentrated his cavalry for the defense of Fleetwood Hill, between him and Brandy," recalled a Confederate staff officer, "was a great and imposing spectacle of squadrons charging in every portion of the field—men falling, cut out of the saddle with the sabre, artillery roaring, carbines cracking—a perfect hurly-burly of combat."[32]

Gregg brought up a battery, Capt. Joseph W. Martin's 6th New York Independent Battery, which deployed in the fields just in front of Fleetwood Hill. From there, Martin's guns greatly harassed the Confederates, taking a toll on the unsupported Confederate troopers using the crest of Fleetwood Hill as their base of operations. "The gallant fellows at the battery hurled a perfect storm of grape upon the Comanches" of the 35th Battalion of Virginia Cavalry.[33]

Finally growing weary of the Yankee artillery, Lieutenant Colonel White ordered his 35th Battalion to charge the battery, making their way through a perfect storm of shot and shell. The unit's historian recorded, "[W]ith never a halt or a falter the battalion dashed on, scattering the supports and capturing the battery after a desperate fight, in which the artillerymen fought like heroes, with small arms, long after their guns were silenced. There was no demand for a surrender, nor any offer to do so, until nearly all the men at the battery, with many of their horses, were killed and wounded."[34] Martin later reported that "Of the 36 men that I took into the engagement, but 6 came out safely, and of these 30, 21 are either killed, wounded, or missing, and scarcely one of the them will but carry the honorable mark of the saber or bullet to his grave."[35]

White and a few of the Comanches attempted to turn Martin's guns on the Yankees, but they received no support, and a Federal counterattack loomed. Capt. Hampton S. Thomas of the 1st Pennsylvania Cavalry, one of Gregg's staff officers, found two companies of the 1st Maryland Cavalry and led them forward to rescue the guns. Joined by other nearby Federals, the Marylanders charged down the hill.[36] Seeing a wall of blue descending on him, White pulled back, leaving the guns for the Yankees.

Meanwhile, parts of McGregor's and Chew's batteries arrived on Fleetwood Hill, near the Carolina Road. Sections of the 1st New Jersey Cavalry still occupied a spur of Fleetwood Hill, and, pressed by Jones's cavalry, had no route of retreat available to them. The Jerseymen had to hack their way through the Confederate guns in a scene reminiscent of the fight at St. James Church. "The unexpected suddenness of this movement seemed to paralyze us all," recalled one of McGregor's section commanders, "friend and foe alike, for the enemy passed at a walk, accelerated to a trot, and did not design to fire upon or charge us, or attempt to make us surrender." As soon as their shock wore off, one of the gunners cried out, "Boys, let's die over the guns!"[37]

"Hart's men beat them with their gun sticks," recalled an officer of the Cobb Legion Cavalry.[38] "Scarcely had our artillery opened on the retreating enemy from this new position than a part of the 1st New Jersey Cavalry, which formed the extreme Federal left, came thundering down the narrow ridge, striking McGregor's and Hart's unsupported batteries in the flank," recalled Captain Hart, "and riding through between guns and caissons from right to left, but met by a determined hand to hand contest from the cannoneers with pistols, sponge staffs, and whatever else came handy to fight with. Lieutenant-Colonel Brodrick, commanding the regiment, was killed in this charge, as also the second in command, Major J. H. Shelmire, who fell from a pistol ball, while gallantly attempting to cut his way through these batteries. The charge was repulsed by the artillerists alone, not a solitary friendly trooper being within reach of us."[39]

The Jerseymen charged three times against an enemy force four times larger. "The fighting was hand to hand and of the most desperate kind," recounted Lt. Thomas L. Cox of the 1st New Jersey. "Col. Brodrick fought like a lion. Wherever the fight was the fiercest his voice could be heard cheering on his men, and his revolver and sabre dealing death to the enemy around him. His bravery and daring conduct is the admiration and praise of everyone in the division. His horse was killed in the first charge, but he immediately mounted another and was soon leading his regiment." The stout Confederate counterattack drove off the Jerseymen, who had to leave their mortally wounded colonel behind. He died a few days later while in Confederate hands.[40]

Three different times during this melee the enemy captured the guidon of Company E of the 1st New Jersey, and twice the Jerseymen retook it. "The third time, when all seemed desperate, a little troop of the First Pennsylvania cut through the enemy and brought off the flag in safety." As the Jerseymen retreated, the Confederates charged their rearguard, but the next unit in line checked their assault, saving the rear of the Federal column.[41] Wyndham fell, badly wounded in the leg. The Jerseymen withdrew with 150 prisoners in tow.[42] With that, the determined Confederates regained possession of Fleetwood Hill.

The regimental historian of the 1st New Jersey Cavalry pointed out that "men and horses had been fighting for over three hours and were now utterly exhausted. . . . There were not a dozen horses that could charge—not a man who could shout above a whisper." The Jerseymen went into battle with 280 officers and enlisted men, and, in a span of three hours, lost 56, including its regimental commander and his second-in-command. They hung on gamely, nursing the fading hope that Duffié's men would come up from Stevensburg to tip the balance in the fight for Fleetwood Hill.[43]

In response, Gregg ordered Kilpatrick to attack with his brigade to the right of Wyndham, and its charge caused the Confederate force to "break . . . all to pieces . . . [it] lost all organization and sought safety in flight."[44] As Kilpatrick's troopers struggled up the crest of Fleetwood Hill, things looked bleak for the Rebel cavalry. Kilpatrick rode over and ordered the 10th New York Cavalry, which was coming up to support his attack, to draw sabers and charge into the Confederates atop Fleetwood Hill. "The rebel line that swept down on us came in splendid order, and when the two lines were about to close in, they opened a rapid fire upon us," recalled a member of the 10th New York Cavalry. "Then followed an indescribable clashing and slashing, banging and yelling. . . . We were now so mixed up with the rebels that every man was fighting desperately to maintain the position until assistance could be brought forward."[45] Lt. Col. William Irvine of the 10th New York had his horse shot out from under him, and was pitched to the ground. Irvine fought alone until the Southerners overpowered and captured him. Maj. Matthew H. Avery, who succeeded Irvine in command of the regiment, fondly recalled, "I never saw so striking an example of devotion to duty. He rode into them slashing with his saber in a measured and determined manner just as he went at everything else, with deliberation and firmness of purpose. I never saw a man so cool under such circumstances."[46]

Capt. Burton B. Porter of the 10th New York tried to rally enough men to free Irvine, but there were not enough available. "Every man had all he could attend to himself," recalled Porter, who found himself with only two or three troopers available. Just then a big Rebel bore down on him with saber raised. "I parried the blow with my saber," he recounted, "which, however, was delivered with such force as to partially break the parry, and left its mark across my back and nearly unhorsed me." One of Porter's men came to his rescue and dismounted his assailant. "It was plain that I must get out then, if ever," observed the captain while a squadron of enemy cavalry bore down on him. Porter dashed up onto the railroad tracks at the foot of Fleetwood Hill, safely out of their reach. The New York captain saw another officer of his regiment shot down in front of him before making good his escape.[47]

A bold charge by the Cobb Legion, supported by Col. John Logan Black's 1st South Carolina Cavalry, cleared the area for the deployment of the Confederate guns. Jeb Stuart dashed up, doffed his hat, its long, black ostrich plume waving, and cried out, "Cobb's Legion, you've covered yourselves with glory, follow me!" and led the charge himself.[48] Col. Pierce M. B. Young, commander of the Georgians, noted in his report, "I immediately ordered the charge in close column of squadrons, and I swept the hill clear of the enemy, he being scattered and entirely routed. I do claim that this was the turning point of the day in this portion of the field, for in less than a minute's time, [a Federal] battery would have been on the hill."[49] Stuart's staff officer, Heros von Borke, turned to Stuart and said, "Young's regiment made the grandest charge I see on either continent."[50] McClellan called this movement "one of the finest which was executed on this day so full of brave deeds."[51]

Colonel Black's 1st South Carolina, charging at the same time as Young's Georgians, slammed into the 2d New York Cavalry, shattering its ranks and scattering its men across the fields. Lt. Col. Henry E. Davies, the regimental commander, admitted that his regiment became disorganized when "by reason of an order improperly given, as is alleged, the head of the column was turned to the left, and proceeded some distance down the railroad." The regiment had only advanced about 100 yards when Black spotted it and angled his charge to inflict the most harm possible. "After the first charge, the command was broken up into detachments, which attacked the enemy in different directions," wrote Davies.[52] The 2d New York scattered and headed for the protection of the railroad embankment, pursued by Black's screeching South Carolinians, who "were cutting down the fugitives without mercy." When another of Hampton's regiments (probably the Jeff Davis Legion) threatened their flank, the terrified New Yorkers fled, much to the consternation of Kilpatrick.[53] The 2d New York was Kilpatrick's old regiment, and "they were repulsed under the very eye of our chief, whose excitement was well-nigh uncontrollable."[54]

The 6th Virginia Cavalry of Jones's brigade, which had opened the fighting that morning, charged headlong into five regiments of Yankee cavalry.[55] Rallying his troopers, Kilpatrick shouted to the 1st Maine Cavalry, "Men of Maine! You must save the day! Follow me!" and personally led a charge by the Maine troopers. As the Maine men followed, they saw a magnificent sight. "The whole plain was one vast field of intense, earnest action. It was a scene to be witnessed but once in a lifetime, and one well worth the risks of battle to witness," recalled one. "But the boys could not stop to enjoy this grand, moving panorama of war."[56]

"In one solid mass this splendid regiment circled first to the right, and then moving in a straight line at a run struck the rebel columns in flank. The shock was terrific! Down went the rebels before this wild rush of maddened horses, men, biting sabres, and whistling balls."[57] "A grander sight was seldom ever witnessed," gushed a newspaper correspondent who watched the Maine men attack.[58] The charge of the 1st Maine saved the Federal guns near Fleetwood Hill from capture. Near Martin's guns, Captain Thomas of Gregg's staff tried to enlist help to protect the abandoned cannons. Thomas spotted Kilpatrick and galloped over to him, begging the colonel to rescue the guns. "To hell with them!" proclaimed Little Kil. "Let Gregg look out for his own guns." Taken aback, Thomas repeated his request. "No! Damned if I will!" came the reply, as Kilpatrick spurred off. Thomas stood his lonely vigil, hoping to salvage Martin's guns.[59]

Some of the Maine men dismounted and opened fire with their carbines. Lt. Col. Charles H. Smith, in command of this contingent, soon found himself alone and almost cut off. "Seconds seemed like minutes," recalled Smith years after the war. He gathered up some nearby men, wheeled them about, and ordered, "Forward!" Slashing his way back through the gauntlet of Southern cavalry, Smith led his troopers to safety. A year later, he was awarded a Medal of Honor and a promotion to brevet brigadier general for his valor at the Battle of Samaria Church.[60]

Kilpatrick squared off with a Confederate officer he had known and disliked at West Point. The Southerner spotted Kilpatrick coming, drew his pistol, took aim, and fired, missing the hard-charging "Little Kil." He drew his saber, and the two officers fenced. "As they met the business commenced. Both men fought like tigers at bay," recalled an observer. The Southerner "gave Kilpatrick a slight cut on the arm," which, instead of disheartening him, only made Kilpatrick "more tigerish." Receiving a vicious slash, the Confederate officer reeled in his saddle. Seeing an opportunity, Kilpatrick killed his injured foe with a slashing cut of his saber. The victorious colonel rejoined his brigade, proclaiming, "That rights a wrong. I have wanted to meet him ever since the war commenced."[61]

The Jeff Davis Legion of Hampton's command attacked to the east of the railroad tracks, while the balance of Jones's brigade charged to the west. They drove the Federals back, "and then, for an hour or more, there was a fierce struggle for the hill, which seemed to have been regarded as the key to the entire situation. This point was taken, and retaken once, and perhaps several times; each side would be in possession for a time, and plant its batteries there, when by a successful charge it would pass into the possession of the other side, and so it continued."[62]

The defeated Federals melted away, with some of Hampton's troopers in hot pursuit. However, Stuart had ordered two of the South Carolinian's regiments to remain on Fleetwood Hill, supporting the Southern artillery. Deprived of a portion of his command, and frustrated by what he perceived as the cavalry chieftain's meddling, Hampton ordered the recall sounded. "No notice of this disposition of half of my brigade by General Stuart had been given to me by that officer, and I found myself deprived of two of my regiments at the very moment they could have reaped the fruits of the victory they had so brilliantly won," complained Hampton in his after-action report. "This division of my command left me too small a force to operate to advantage, and when the other regiments rejoined me, I received orders to assume a position to protect the hill." He watched frustrated as Gregg's battered division withdrew unmolested.[63]

As the blueclad troopers withdrew, they left Lt. Wade Wilson's section of horse artillery exposed about 100 yards north of the railroad tracks, protected only by

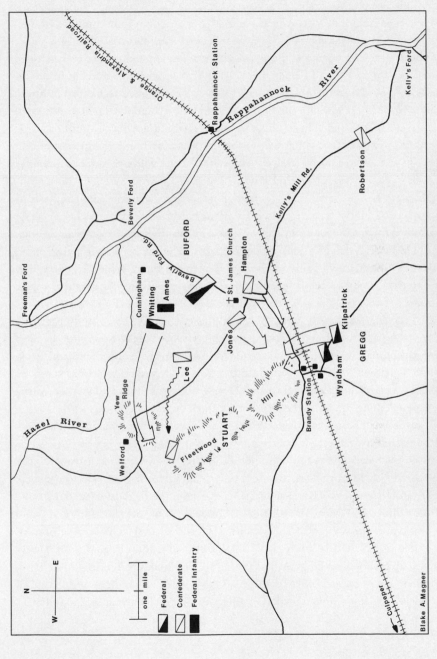

The Fights for Fleetwood Hill and Yew Ridge, June 9, 1863

N

one mile

Federal
Confederate
Federal Infantry

Blake A. Magner

Freeman's Ford

Orange & Alexandria Railroad

Rappahannock Station

Rappahannock River

Kelly's Ford

Robertson

Kelly's Mill Rd.

Beverly Ford

BUFORD

Beverly Ford Rd.

Cunningham

Whiting

Ames

St. James Church

Hampton

Hazel River

Yew Ridge

Welford

Lee

Jones

Fleetwood

STUART

Hill

Brandy Station

Wyndham

Kilpatrick

GREGG

Culpeper

dismounted cavalrymen. These artillerists had had a long, hard day, deploying at eight different positions during the savage fighting for Fleetwood Hill. Kilpatrick ordered the gunners to limber up and retreat, but Col. Lunsford Lomax's 11th Virginia Cavalry came crashing down on them before they could.[64]

These guns had aggravated Stuart all day, and, finally fed up, Stuart had asked Lomax whether he could silence them. "I will do it or lose every man in the attempt," replied Lomax, a West Pointer from a distinguished Virginia family. Stuart ordered him to do so, and Lomax, waving his sword, bellowed, "Men, we want those guns; follow me!" He and his Virginians charged down the Carolina Road "like a whirlwind." Bearing down on the battery at an angle, Wilson shifted his guns, "in which the gunners lost their range, so that the volley of grape and canister was not so effective as it might otherwise have been."[65] Seeing the gray wave coming, Captain Thomas tipped his cap to his approaching adversaries, and finally abandoned his vigil over Martin's guns, leaving them to the victorious Southerners.[66]

The Virginians then slammed into Wilson's guns, fighting it out with the dismounted Federal troopers supporting the artillery, allowing Wilson's gunners to slash their way to safety, bringing their guns off with them. Wilson stopped from time to time, firing an occasional shell to discourage pursuit. The Virginians were not interested in the guns—they were more interested in the dismounted cavalrymen scurrying for their horses.[67] "Lomax and the men of the bloody Eleventh were among them, slashing left and right." After dispersing Wilson's little band of supports, Lomax veered for the railroad, crashing into three of Wyndham's regiments. "I charged, and drove them from the station," claimed Lomax in his report. Lomax sent a small detachment toward Culpeper, in case Federals were operating near there. Taking the rest of his regiment, he briefly pursued Gregg's retreat along the Stevensburg Road, capturing thirty-four before finally breaking off and returning to Fleetwood Hill.[68]

Major McClellan noted, "Thus ended the attack of Gregg's division upon the Fleetwood Hill. Modern warfare cannot furnish an instance of a field more closely, more valiantly contested. General Gregg retired from the field defeated, but defiant and unwilling to acknowledge a defeat."[69] Instead, Gregg reformed his command in the fields to the south of Brandy Station, where he had staged his initial attacks. He noted in his after-action report, "The contest was too unequal to be longer continued. The Second Division had not come up; there was no support at hand, and the enemy's numbers were three times my own. I ordered the withdrawal of my brigades. In good order they left the field, the enemy choosing not to follow."[70]

THE DUEL ON YEW RIDGE

When Stuart sent Jones and Hampton to counter the threat from Gregg, only Rooney Lee's brigade, still positioned behind the stone wall, remained in Buford's front. Under orders from Pleasonton to hold his position, Buford did not move directly around Lee's flank to Fleetwood Hill, but initially remained in a defensive posture along a ridge on the Cunningham farm.

Buford then extended his lines in an effort to outflank Lee along the stone wall. Eventually, his dismounted troopers threatened to envelop Lee's lines.[71] The waist-high wall lay in a valley between two ridges, one of which served as Buford's headquarters. The ground on either side of the wall was cleared, and provided excellent fields of fire for both sides. Because at least a part of the low-lying area was swampy and filled with mud it could not be approached while mounted. Confederate artillery firing from the ridge behind Lee's main line covered the formidable defensive position.

A successful attack by Buford would have placed him in the rear of Stuart's position, poised to roll up the Confederate flank from the side and rear. Some of Rooney Lee's sharpshooters took positions behind the stone wall and peppered away at Ames's infantry brigade, which had moved up to support Buford's planned attack. Visibly "annoyed," Buford approached a group of officers of the 3d Wisconsin of Ames's brigade, and asked of Capt. George W. Stevenson, "Do you see those people down there? They've got to be driven out." One of the Wisconsin officers responded that the enemy's force greatly outnumbered their own. Buford responded, "Well, I didn't order you, mind: but, if you think you can flank them, go in, and drive them off."[72]

Impressed with Buford's calm demeanor and manner of command, the Wisconsin officers ordered several companies of their infantry to advance. Screened from Lee's view by woods and the nature of the terrain, the infantrymen sidled around the Virginian's flank until they reached a position from which they could enfilade the Confederate position. When in position, the flankers unleashed a killing fire on Lee's exposed flank. The foot soldiers then retreated to Buford's original position.

Emboldened by the success of the infantry, Buford ordered Maj. Henry C. Whelan, now commanding the 6th Pennsylvania, to launch a mounted charge against the Confederate position. Supported by Capt. Wesley Merritt's 2d U.S., the Pennsylvanians thundered toward the 10th Virginia through a storm of small arms and artillery fire. Major Whelan, whose horse was shot out from under him, later described the charge as "decidedly the hottest place I was ever in. A man could not show his head or a finger without a hundred rifle shots whistling about. . . . The air [was] almost solid with lead."[73] Spearheaded by the Pennsylvanians, the Federals dashed forward until a vicious countercharge by the 9th Virginia slammed into them.

With sabers drawn, the 9th Virginia crashed into the charging Pennsylvanians, sending the Lancers "into confusion and forcing them back, not along the line of their retreat, but directly on the stone fence through which there was but a narrow opening; and dealing them some heavy blows during the necessary delay in forcing their way through it. They were followed by men of the Ninth at a gallop through the field beyond the fence to the edge of the woods, where a Federal battery was in position. A good many of the prisoners which the Federals had taken were released by this charge."[74]

Elements of the 6th U.S. Cavalry, which were supporting the attacking Lancers, saw an opportunity. The Regulars spotted a large battle flag atop the ridge, and headed for it, Lts. Isaac M. Ward and Christian Balder leading their squadrons forward. Maj. Charles J. Whiting of the 5th U.S. Cavalry described them "twice charging the enemy and each time driving him with severe loss from his position to a hill beyond and holding him in check against heavy odds till withdrawn, with serious loss, by the brigade commander."[75] Trooper Sidney M. Davis of the 6th U.S. watched as Ward positioned his squadron almost at the rear of the 9th Virginia Cavalry. As the Virginians swept past his position, Ward charged the Southern flank, his men cheering wildly as they went. "It was a curious scene," remembered Davis, "this small body so boldly attacking a large force that was at this moment driving from their front quite a strong regiment [the 6th Pennsylvania Cavalry], but the movement was successful. The Confederates halted a moment, gave a startled look backward, and then their regiment broke up and fled by a detour westward to the rear." Although Lieutenant Ward was mortally wounded, his impetuous charge rescued the beleaguered Pennsylvanians. Later, a Virginian said, "From the noise you men made, we thought it was a whole brigade coming out of those woods."[76]

Lieutenants Stoll and Carpenter had been ordered to hold the woods to the 6th U.S.'s right. As Ward's men and the Lancers began withdrawing, the Rebels pursued. The two squadrons of Regulars remained mounted, while the charging Confederates were dismounted. "If I had had command of the squadron, I would have dismounted the men, and fought the enemy equally," reported Carpenter, "but Stoll thought otherwise." Instead, the mounted Regulars waited in the scorching sun. Stoll was badly wounded, and Carpenter took responsibility for withdrawing his beleaguered saddle soldiers.

"I managed in this way, by stopping every minute and fighting the rebels, in getting my men safely out of the wood. The ground sloped downward for 30 or 40 yards and then raised again, just beyond to a little knoll," he continued. "I saw at once that the rebels would have every chance of murdering us, as we crossed this low ground, exposed completely to their fire from behind trees." Carpenter ordered his men to pour in a rapid fire for a few minutes, and then he had them wheel to the right and to gallop at full speed. They obeyed. "The minute we commenced to retreat, the rebels arose in multitudes, as if by magic, and poured in a dreadful fire. The next minute however I had gained the knoll with my squadron, and just behind it, I ordered them to stop, and give it to the rebels. We were completely protected by the ground." The Regulars raked the Confederates from the protection of the woods, and Carpenter saw a number of them drop while the remainder retreated "in great haste." Carpenter's horse was wounded on the inside of the foreleg, and the lieutenant lost his hat in the chaos; he borrowed new headgear from an unfortunate Confederate.[77] Capt. George C. Cram, who commanded the 6th U.S. that day, commended Carpenter for the skillful way he brought Stoll's beleaguered squadron to safety.[78]

The Confederate success was short-lived. No sooner had they driven the 6th Pennsylvania from the hill than the 2d U.S. counterattacked. The 2d U.S. had spent much of the day supporting one of the Federal batteries, and eagerly joined the fray. "At last an order—which we all had hoped and all but asked for, and which General Buford told me he was anxious to give, but had not the authority, but which no doubt he carried—finally came," recalled Merritt. "We were ordered to advance and deal on *their* ground with the batteries and sharpshooters which had wrought such havoc among our men and horses."[79] In addition, Buford ordered Lt. Albert O. Vincent's battery of horse artillery to unlimber within 400 yards of the enemy and to open fire in conjunction with the Regulars' attack.[80]

Following the route of the 6th Pennsylvania's attack, and supported by the fire of Vincent's battery, the 2d U.S. pitched into the flank of the 9th Virginia, driving it back. "Out flew the sabres, and most handsomely they were used," observed Buford.[81] "We rode pell-mell, with sabers in hand at the astonished enemy," recalled Merritt. "The next moment [the Rebel line] had broken and was flying, while horsemen of the 2d mingling with the enemy, dealt saber blows and pistol shots on every side. There was little halting to make prisoners, as friend and foe, mixed inextricably together, rode on in this terrible carnage, each apparently for the same destination."[82] With Merritt leading the way, the determined charge of the 2d U.S. carried up the slope of Yew Ridge, over the plateau, and across the crest.

Capt. Joseph O'Keeffe, one of Buford's staff officers, rashly joined the charge, riding "boot to boot" with Merritt. Merritt and O'Keeffe became separated when the Confederates broke and the sabers began to fly. Sometime during the melee, O'Keeffe was unhorsed, badly wounded in the leg, and captured.[83] Major Whiting, the commander of the Reserve Brigade, later noted, "I have to regret the loss of Captain O'Keeffe, who requested to act with me during the day, and after affording most valuable service could not resist the temptation of charging with the Second United States Cavalry and was wounded and taken prisoner."[84] At that moment, Buford had no time to mourn the loss of his aide—there was more work to do.

Merritt's charge, "in its impetuosity, carried everything before it. It bore up the hill, across the plateau, and to the crest on the other side." The savage attack of the Regulars drove back more than twice their number.[85] "There were discovered in the valley below, fresh regiments of horse moving quietly towards the scene of our combat anxious to strike us while we were in confusion," noted Merritt.[86] Col. Richard L. T. Beale, the commander of the 9th Virginia Cavalry, feared a rout until a courier from Stuart reined in, saying, "The General sends his thanks to Colonel Beale and the men of the Ninth for their gallantry in holding the hill, and if you will hold it five minutes longer he will send reinforcements." Stuart delivered on his promise moments later.[87]

Rooney Lee launched a vicious counterattack, pushing forward his own skirmishers in an attempt to flank Buford's position and sever his lines of communication and retreat across Beverly's Ford. "About 4 o'clock in the afternoon Lee put himself at the head of my regiment which was at the foot of a hill out in the open field, standing in column of fours, and gave the order to charge up the hill, he riding at the head of the regiment," recalled William L. Royall of the 9th Virginia. "I was very near to the head of the column and could see all that took place. When we got to the summit of the hill, there, some two hundred yards away, stood a long line of blue-coated cavalry. Lee did not hesitate an instant but dashed at the center of this line with his column of fours. The Yankees were of course cut in two at once, but each of their flanks closed in on our column, and then a most terrible affray with sabers and pistols took place. We got the best of it, and we had soon killed, wounded, or captured almost all of them. They had a good many more men over beyond the hill, but the thing was over before the others could come to their assistance."[88]

A charge by the 2d North Carolina and the 10th Virginia reached the hill and shoved the Regulars back toward the Union starting point.[89] An unidentified member of Company F of the 10th Virginia, in a letter to the *Richmond Daily Dispatch* written the day after the battle, noted, "The 2d U.S. Cavalry, supported by other cavalry, came up when the 10th Va. Cav . . . were about to charge them. This regiment charged them gallantly, driving them back precipitately, killing many, chopping many over the head, and taking some prisoners. . . . I think it was the hardest cavalry fight of the war."[90]

As the Regulars retreated, Captain Merritt and his aide, Lt. James Quirk, found themselves alone among the Confederates. Merritt, who believed that his entire regiment was still alongside him, carried only his saber and his courage. A nearby group of Confederate officers spotted him, and one yelled, "Kill the damned Yankee!" Riding over to the group of officers, Merritt boldly approached the apparent leader of the group, brought his saber to a point, and declared, "Colonel, you are my prisoner!" The officer was not a colonel, but rather Rooney Lee. Lee proclaimed, "The hell I am!" and swung his saber at Merritt's head. Merritt parried the blow, but the thrust of Lee's saber pierced Merritt's hat and a kerchief that he had tied around his head as a sweatband, nicking Merritt's scalp.

Faced with such immediate peril, Merritt and his aide hastily retreated when other Confederate officers opened fire with their revolvers. With pistol shots and demands for his surrender still ringing in his ears, Merritt safely reached his own lines, where, "a kindly Hibernian gave me the hat off his own head."[91] In the course of the fight on Yew Ridge, Rooney Lee suffered a severe leg wound. Deprived of their senior officers, the Confederates did not press their hard-won advantage and retired to their lines along Fleetwood Hill.[92]

When Buford prepared his report of the battle, he wrote that his men "gained the crest overlooking Brandy Station," but that they could not hold it. He further noted, "The enemy, although vastly superior in numbers was fought hand to hand and was not allowed to gain an inch of ground once occupied. During this fighting, Lt. [Albert O.] Vincent poured his shot into them with terrible execution."[93] Vincent later reported that he maintained his fire for half an hour, and that his battery expended approximately 400 rounds over the course of the day's fighting. Obviously, such heavy fire from a range of only 400 yards took a toll on the Confederates.[94]

Fitz Lee's brigade, commanded in Fitz's absence by Col. Thomas T. Munford, arrived on Yew Ridge as the fighting was winding down. Munford's men were picketing along the Hazel River. Stuart's orders to Munford were vague, meaning that the colonel and his troops advanced slowly and cautiously. Munford arrived at Welford's Ford around 4:00 P.M., and shook out a skirmish line. He could see the battle raging on Yew Ridge, and realized that a very large Federal force lay in front of him. While Capt. James Breathed's battery opened on the Union flank, Munford realized that "the enemy's right flank being protected by infantry, artillery, and twice our number of sharpshooters, made it impracticable at any time to engage them in a hand-to-hand fight."[95] Munford held his position on the flank, engaging in desultory skirmishing until Buford finally broke off the engagement and began withdrawing. Munford's troopers might have made a difference if they had arrived sooner. Rosser, who despised Munford, could not resist sniping at his old rival in a postwar speech. "On the other flank the unfortunate absence of our gallant and wide-awake Fitz Lee from his brigade (he being absent sick), left his splendid regiments and Breathed's battery in less able hands, which, in consequence of a confusion of orders, did not reach the battlefield until very late in the day."[96]

Had Buford and Gregg coordinated their efforts and linked forces, they may very well have driven the Confederates from Fleetwood Hill and Yew Ridge. Also, the addition of Duffié's command to the fray probably would have tipped the balance. However, the Frenchman and his division had their own adventures that day, and did not arrive on the field until the end of the day's fighting.

DUFFIÉ AT STEVENSBURG

Duffié received the order to move his command to Kelly's Ford at 12:15 A.M. on June 9. Gregg instructed the Frenchman to march his division "directly upon Stevensburg, following the road leading to Raccoon Ford. Arrived at Stevensburg, you will halt and communicate with our forces at Brandy Station, and from this point communication will be had with you." Gregg's division would follow along behind on the same road. While the Pennsylvanian moved on Culpeper from Brandy Station, Duffié would advance on Culpeper from the south, after leaving a regiment and a section of artillery at Stevensburg to guard the river crossings. "It is intended that when the right of our line at Brandy Station advances toward Culpeper, your division at Stevensburg will also move upon Culpeper," instructed Gregg.[97]

Reveille sounded in Duffié's camps at 1:00. "It was well past twelve before we got down to sleep and I for one was just dozing off—had not lost consciousness—when reveille was somewhere sounded," recalled Capt. Charles Francis Adams of the 1st Massachusetts. " 'That's too horrid,' I thought, 'it must be some other division.' But at once other bugles caught it up in the woods around." Soon the blue-clad horsemen were stirring and getting ready to march. They had only five miles to cover to reach the rendezvous point with Gregg's division. They had no idea what lay ahead of them as they set off on the five-hour march to Kelly's Ford.[98]

Upon arriving, the Frenchman was to report to Gregg for further orders, cross the river, and advance to Stevensburg, where he was to protect Gregg's flank on the march toward Culpeper.[99] If Duffié controlled the road from Stevensburg to Culpeper, the Frenchman and his troopers would be in a perfect position to cut off Stuart, and either force the Virginian to fight his way out of the trap, or be captured. Gregg ordered the French sergeant not to use guide fires that might give away his position. Because his division had to traverse an unfamiliar road network through a dark night, the march took longer than expected. A local guide insisted that a fork in the road led toward Kelly's Ford, so the column proceeded. After continuing on, Duffié realized that the guide was wrong, and ordered his men to turn around and backtrack. This misstep delayed their arrival even longer as they pressed on through the dense fog. After meeting Gregg, Duffié crossed the river and deployed in line of battle on the Stevensburg Road.[100] "We crossed the Rappahannock without molestation, the Rebs having been driven back early in the morning, about 4 AM," noted an officer of the 3d Pennsylvania Cavalry.[101]

Luigi Palma di Cesnola's brigade led Duffié's advance. The Italian count deployed the 1st Rhode Island and the 6th Ohio on the right, the 1st Massachusetts on the left, and kept the 3d Pennsylvania in reserve. The sound of the guns booming at St. James Church "buoyed us up—tho some got pale—yet every man looked ready for the fray," as a member of the 16th Pennsylvania Cavalry described it.[102]

They waded across fast-moving Mountain Run, a tributary of the Rappahannock that was prone to flooding, near Paoli's Mill and pressed on.

In this array, Duffié advanced slowly toward Stevensburg, sending a battalion of the 6th Ohio forward to scout. At about 8:30, Maj. Benjamin C. Stanhope of the 6th Ohio sent back word that he had reached Stevensburg, that the enemy was in sight, and that he had sent skirmishers forward to meet them.[103] Lt. William Brooke-Rawle of the 3d Pennsylvania Cavalry reported, "From a hill I caught a beautiful glimpse of the advance. The skirmishers deployed in front, supported by their reserves, one column, with the artillery, advancing on our left along the road, & our regiment advancing in echelons of squadrons supporting both the battery & skirmishers. All the guidons flying, & the effect was beautiful."[104] Stanhope's men captured seven pickets, including the lieutenant commanding the vedettes.[105]

Wade Hampton's foresight ensured that Confederate forces guarded Stuart's flank. When he learned that Gregg's command had crossed at Kelly's Ford, Hampton rode to the camp of Col. Matthew C. Butler's 2d South Carolina Cavalry and ordered Butler to mount his regiment and move it to Brandy Station to await further orders. Butler sent a squadron under command of Capt. Leonard Williams to picket Stevensburg, and moved the rest of his regiment to Brandy Station as ordered. No sooner had these pickets arrived than they spotted Duffié's advance guard approaching. "When a regiment and then a brigade of Yankees came in sight and drew up in battle line, I attracted their attention," recounted Williams. "They threw out their skirmishers the length of a mile in front of me. They advanced briskly. I kept out my videttes and placed my squadron back across the stream, dismounted the men to hold them in check as long as possible." Williams sent a galloper to Butler bearing this unwelcome news.[106] Knowing there were no other Confederate forces in the area, and without waiting for orders, Butler ordered his entire regiment to move to Stevensburg.[107]

Matthew Butler was a fine soldier. Born on March 8, 1836, in Greenville, South Carolina, Butler practiced law before the Civil War. When the war broke out, he received a commission as a captain in the Hampton Legion, and was promoted to major after First Bull Run. In August 1862, he became colonel of the 2d South Carolina Cavalry. Young and aggressive, Butler was one of the better regimental commanders. By the end of the war, he wore a major general's stars, and commanded a division under Hampton.[108] This day, he proved to be the right man in the right place.

Protecting the road between Stevensburg and Culpeper was critical—Longstreet's infantry corps was camped around Pony Mountain about midway between Stevensburg and Culpeper, and Ewell's corps was farther north of Culpeper; Brig. Gen. Junius Daniel's infantry brigade could see some of the action on Fleetwood Hill from its camps. The cavalry sought to screen the presence of the Confederate infantry at all costs.[109] Knowing the urgency of the situation, Butler ordered his second-in-command, Lt. Col. Frank Hampton, younger brother of Wade Hampton, to gallop on to Stevensburg with twenty men to do what they could to delay the Yankee advance. Butler wanted Hampton to buy sufficient time for him to deploy his little force on the commanding high ground known as Hansborough's Ridge, just outside of Stevensburg. "The position in which Butler awaited attack was well chosen. The woods concealed the smallness of his numbers, and even on the road the sloping ground prevented the enemy from discovering any but the leading files of Hampton's detachment."[110] Butler's lone regiment of 200 men had to defend a line along Hansborough Ridge that was nearly a mile long, a difficult task at best.

When Hampton and his small contingent arrived at Stevensburg, they learned that although the Yankees had already passed through the town, they had withdrawn after Confederate vedettes fired upon them. Hampton dismounted part of his little force in front of a stately plantation house called Salubria, keeping part of his command mounted and at the ready. With a scratch force of thirty-six men, Lieutenant Colonel Hampton ordered his men to charge the Yankee column, which withdrew instead of engaging. "The fight opened by the rebels, who charged the First Massachusetts Cavalry down a hollow road," recounted Capt. Walter S. Newhall of the 3d Pennsylvania Cavalry. "They came to the conclusion that they 'had the wrong chicken by the tail feathers,' and very shortly changed base, with a loss of twenty-five killed and wounded and a loss of sixty-four prisoners."[111] Thus, Hampton's delaying action bought time for the rest of Butler's regiment to march to Stevensburg and deploy into line of battle.

Captain Williams of the 2d South Carolina found his little command completely surrounded by bluecoats when the sheer weight of Yankee numbers finally forced his squadron back: "I discovered that a Yankee regiment was in front of me, the rear vidette, I suppose, captured. I was thus completely cut off, a brigade in my rear, a regiment on the road in my front and neither more than 500 yards from me." Williams and his thirty men turned into the woods and tried to make their way across country to rejoin Stuart's main body at Brandy Station. "On nearing the place, I halted the column and went towards the road to reconnoiter and found they had passed upon and heard 2 or 3 consecutive charges. On hearing it again, halted to examine."

Williams found no Northerners on the road between Stevensburg and Brandy Station, so he ordered the column forward again. "I discovered that I was encompassed on all sides and then carried my squadron back into the densest wood I could find with the intention of remaining til night and then running the gauntlet through their lines." However, about three o'clock, Williams' vedettes reported that the Yankees had been repulsed and the road between Brandy Station and Stevensburg was clear. "It was universally supposed that we had been captured. I attribute our safety to a divine providence," reported the relieved South Carolinian.[112]

While Butler deployed his troops, the famous Confederate scout, Capt. Will Farley, galloped up with a message from Stuart, informing Butler that a single piece of artillery, along with the 4th Virginia Cavalry under command of Col. Williams C. Wickham, was on its way to reinforce Butler.[113] As the Virginians arrived, Wickham sent Lt. Col. William H. Payne forward to alert Butler that the reinforcements had arrived. Butler responded, "[I] requested Colonel Payne to inform Colonel Wickham of the disposition I had made of the few men at my disposal and to say to him, as he reached me, I would cheerfully take orders from him."[114] Wickham, who was senior to Butler, declined to assume command, so Butler requested that Wickham bring two mounted squadrons of his command forward to support Hampton's squadron. The rest of the 4th Virginia would come into line dismounted alongside the balance of Butler's regiment. By this time, it was approximately 11:00 A.M., and the desperate battle raged at Brandy Station as the first elements of Gregg's command reached Fleetwood Hill.

Duffié approached tentatively. He sent mounted skirmishers forward, but they withdrew after a couple of volleys from Butler's dismounted troopers. "As the first brigade of Duffié advanced, the dismounted men, well protected, fired upon our men, who were mounted, and made the advance uncomfortable," recounted an officer of the 1st Massachusetts. "One carbine in the hands of a dismounted man under cover is certainly worth half a dozen in the hands of men on horseback; and these men of Hampton, on our left of the road, were in the ruins of a large, burned building, a seminary, and delivered a hot fire upon the advance of the 1st Massachusetts, which was opposed to them."[115]

"I sat on my horse skirmishing within 2 rods of the same place for 15 minutes[,] firing as fast as I could get a sight at one[,] they being concealed behind some farm houses and stone walls[.] [W]hen they would step out to fire we would pull," recounted a horse soldier from Massachusetts. "We were in an open field. They had got a good range of us and our men and horses began to fall when our supporters came up in line of battle out of some woods." Taking heavy enemy fire that rattled the rails, the Bay Staters pulled down a split rail fence so that their horses could pass through. Even though Duffié had not ordered an attack, the Massachusetts horsemen drew sabers and advanced. "We charged. They mounted their horses in a hurry and skedaddled toward Culpeper. We followed them about 5 miles and met their batteries coming up and had to retreat."[116]

The grayclad horsemen repulsed a second probing attack, and the Federals shifted the focus of their attack to Hampton's small mounted contingent waiting in the road.[117] "I immediately threw forward the skirmishers of the First Massachusetts, First Rhode Island and Sixth Ohio Cavalry, who immediately became engaged with the enemy, who were strongly posted and partly concealed in the woods," Duffié reported. "Pushing steadily forward, the enemy were quickly dislodged from those dense woods into open fields, where the First Rhode Island Cavalry was ordered to charge on the right, the First Massachusetts on the left, and one squadron of the Sixth Ohio Cavalry on the road, in order to cut off the retreat of the enemy on his flank and check him in his front."[118]

"We drew sabers and started on the charge," recalled Sgt. Albert A. Sherman of the 1st Massachusetts. "The rebels stood until we got within a few yards of them. I thought we had got into a bad fix; but before we got to them, they broke and ran like a flock of sheep toward the village, and we in among them using the sabre. I followed one man and called to him to surrender, but he took no notice of it. I soon reach him and struck him between the shoulders with the staff of the guidon. It knocked the breath out of him and he surrendered." The South Carolinians attempted to make a stand, but the overwhelming force of Union horse soldiers scattered them.[119]

"Imagine my surprise when I learned from the right that a regiment of the enemy's cavalry had charged Colonel Hampton's handful of men and swept him out of the road," recounted Butler. "In the melee, Colonel Hampton received a pistol ball in the pit of his stomach and died that afternoon from the effects of it."[120] Duffié's attack crashed into Butler's line. In the process, the force of the Federal charge cut the 4th Virginia in two, and sent it flying from the field in disorder. The Virginians "broke in utter confusion without firing a gun, in spite of every effort of the colonel to rally the men to the charge."[121] "It was a regular steeple chase," recalled a Federal, "through ditches, over fences, through underbrush."[122] A. D. Payne, a member of the 4th Virginia, lamented, "Oh memorable day . . . A disgraceful rout of the Regiment."[123] Duffié captured more than forty of the Virginians in this charge.[124]

Many years after the battle Butler wrote, "Colonel Wickham not only did not move up his mounted and dismounted squadrons to Colonel Hampton's support, but when the enemy charged they took to their heels toward Culpeper Court House."[125] To his credit, Wickham made no excuses for the conduct of his regiment. "I regard the conduct of my regiment, in which I have heretofore had perfect confidence, as so disgraceful in this instance that . . . the major general commanding, to whom I request that this be forwarded, may have the facts before him on which to base any inquiry that he may see fit to institute."[126]

Duffié re-formed his command on a hill just to the west of Hansborough's Ridge, and pressed forward once again as Butler struggled to rally his small force. Seeing this, Duffié brought up Lt. Alexander C. M. Pennington Jr.'s Battery M, 2d U.S. Artillery, and unlimbered two guns on a small rise. There, the guns opened on Butler's line, wreaking havoc. Butler and Will Farley were the only Confederates still mounted at that time, and they provided a convenient target for the Federal guns. Supported by the artillery, Duffié ordered another charge.

Seeing the approaching Federals, Farley drew his revolver, spurred his horse forward, and opened fire.[127] Butler ordered the officer in command of Company G, positioned next to Farley, not to fire too soon in order to protect men of Butler's regiment who might have gone forward to escape the artillery. "When, however, we discovered the enemy making their way through the bushes and opened fire, I gave the command, 'Commence firing' all along the line. I noticed a mounted cavalryman in blue slide off his horse . . . very easily, and the horse trot back to his rear, and assumed he had dismounted not more than fifty yards down the hill for the purpose of getting the protection of a tree in his future efforts," recalled Butler. "About that time a man wearing a striped hat turned to me and said, 'Colonel, I got that fellow.' I replied by saying, 'Got him, the devil; he has dismounted to get you; load your gun.' It turned out . . . he was right. He had killed this man, who proved to be an officer."[128]

Butler realized that the rout of the 4th Virginia had turned his flank, so he redeployed his command in a valley near Norman's Mill on Mountain Run, just north of Stevensburg. His men cobbled together a second line of battle on the other side of the creek. Butler also deployed his single gun there. It opened counterbattery fire with Pennington's guns atop the hill.

As the artillery duel continued, and as Duffié redeployed his forces, a short lull occurred in the fighting. Farley and Butler sat on their horses, facing opposite directions, laughing as Butler recounted to Farley the anecdote about the Federal officer killed by his men. Butler had his back to the Federal position, not paying much attention to the artillery fire. "Suddenly, [a] twelve pound shell from the enemy's gun on the hill (we had evidently been located by a field glass), struck the ground about thirty steps from our position in an open field ricocheted and passed through my right leg above the ankle, through Farley's horse, and took off [Farley's] right leg at the knee," wrote Butler. "My horse bounded in the air, threw me, saddle and all, flat on my back in the road, when the poor fellow moved off with his entrails hanging out towards the clover field where he had been grazing in the early morning and died there, as I was afterwards informed."

Farley's wounded horse dropped in the road, and Farley fell with his head on the horse's side. "As soon as we discovered what the trouble was my first apprehension was we would bleed to death before assistance could reach us. I therefore directed Farley to get out his handkerchief and make a tourniquet by binding around his leg above the wound. I got out my handkerchief, and we were doing our best in the tourniquet business when Capt. John Chestnut and Lieutenant John Rhett of my regiment came to our relief, soon followed by . . . [the] surgeon and assistant surgeon of the regiment."[129] The surgeon amputated Butler's shattered leg. Farley was carried from the field on a trough. He asked that his leg be brought to him, and he clutched it close as the South Carolinians carried him to safety. He died later that day. That single artillery shot took quite a toll.[130]

With Frank Hampton dead and Butler badly wounded, Maj. Thomas J. Lipscomb assumed command of the 2d South Carolina. In spite of his serious condition, Butler remained calm and collected. "Major Lipscomb, you will continue to fight and fall back slowly toward Culpeper," he instructed, "and if you can save us from capture do it."[131] As Lipscomb attempted to rally his forces, deployed in a thin line in the valley below, Duffié saw that he could carry the position, and ordered the 1st Massachusetts to charge. As the Bay Staters formed, orders reached Duffié from Gregg that he should "return and join the Third Division, on the road to Brandy Station."[132] The Frenchman, standing on the hilltop overlooking the thin line of the South Carolinians along Jonas Run in the valley below, could look straight ahead and see the fight raging on Fleetwood Hill, six miles away.

Instead of ordering his men to overrun Lipscomb's little force and take the direct route to Fleetwood Hill, Duffié obeyed the order explicitly, breaking off and taking a longer, more roundabout route to reach Fleetwood Hill that almost guaranteed that he would arrive too late to be of any assistance to Gregg. Duffié drew off most of his division, leaving the 3d Pennsylvania Cavalry and one section of artillery to watch Lipscomb's men and to keep them from returning to the main Confederate line of battle at Fleetwood Hill.

This small force remained at Stevensburg for about an hour, but seeing no enemy and hearing the heavy firing booming at Fleetwood Hill, the 3d Pennsylvania Cavalry marched to the sound of the guns. "We were ordered to fall back to the support of General Gregg, who was being badly beaten," claimed an officer of the 3d Pennsylvania. "We came up just in time to save the Third Division."[133] The Pennsylvanians arrived at about 4:00 P.M., just as the fighting ended on Fleetwood Hill, and the Federals began withdrawing.[134] "After remaining for about an hour . . . we withdrew to Rappahannock Station," noted a Pennsylvanian, "and crossed the Ford, having moved along the road which our troops had gained."[135] The 3d Pennsylvania then covered the retreat of Duffié's division, squeezing off a few long-range carbine shots at the pursuing Confederate horse soldiers; the Southerners slowly followed the long Northern column toward Rappahannock Station as it withdrew.[136]

As he advanced toward the sound of the guns, Duffié encountered a squadron of the 10th New York Cavalry, fleeing back toward Stevensburg. Learning that a Rebel charge had routed these men, Duffié spent half an hour deploying into line of battle to protect against any Confederate threats. Finally persuaded that the grayclad horsemen were not about to attack, Duffié resumed his march, connected with Gregg, and deployed his guns to cover the retreat of the Cavalry Corps.[137] A member of the 1st Massachusetts offered an alibi for the Frenchman's lack of aggression.

"Their horses were fresh and ours had been marching hard so we did not catch many of them," he claimed.[138] These claims rang hollow.

Thus, the Frenchman and his veteran division played no role at all in the great cavalry fight at Fleetwood Hill. "Duffié went home satisfied to be left alone," claimed Mosby years after the war.[139] The Frenchman had obeyed Pleasonton's orders about guarding the Federal flank, but the flawed premise of the plan meant that an entire division was held out of the great struggle for Fleetwood Hill. "This country is under obligation to Hampton and his brigade," proudly announced one of Butler's officers.[140] Had he not lost an entire day to the stubborn resistance put up by Butler's small but intrepid band, Duffié's 1,900 troopers may very well have tipped the scales in favor of Gregg's men in the fight for Fleetwood Hill. "It so happened that Colonel Duffié's second division went to the left after crossing Kelly's Ford, and only a very insignificant part of one of the brigades was engaged," observed a member of the 1st Massachusetts Cavalry. "The rest of the division, two brigades, was not engaged at all; and the loss was comparatively insignificant."[141]

"We were not very actively engaged or under heavy fire and our loss did not exceed ten or a dozen," reported Captain Adams of the 1st Massachusetts. "The day was clear, hot and intensely dusty; the cannonading lively and the movements, I thought, slow." One thing struck Adams. "I saw but one striking object—the body of a dead rebel by the road-side the attitude of which was wonderful. Tall, slim and athletic, with regular sharply chiseled features, he had fallen flat on his back, with one hand upraised as if striking, and with his long light hair flung back in heavy waves from his forehead." The vision of that dead Southern horse soldier remained with Adams for years.[142]

That they did not play more of a role at Brandy Station bothered Duffié's men. Sgt. Samuel Cormany of the 16th Pennsylvania, who spent the day watching the battle from a nearby hillside, complained, "Am just too sorry that I and our squad could not perform our part in this day's fighting."[143] Thus, the combination of hard fighting by Butler's single regiment and Duffié's undue caution stopped an entire division of Union cavalry. The division's absence made the difference in the ferocious fighting raging around Fleetwood Hill.

THE GREAT BATTLE ENDS

As the fight for Yew Ridge raged, a trooper of the 6th Virginia Cavalry spotted Robert E. Lee "riding across the fields on his gray horse 'Traveller,' accompanied by his staff. He seemed as calm and unconcerned as if he were inspecting the land with the view of a purchase."[144] After receiving a dispatch from Stuart describing Pleasonton's furious assault, Lee had decided to ride to the battlefield to see what all of the noise was. Lee informed Stuart that two divisions of Confederate infantry were nearby, and that Stuart was "not to expose his men too much, but to

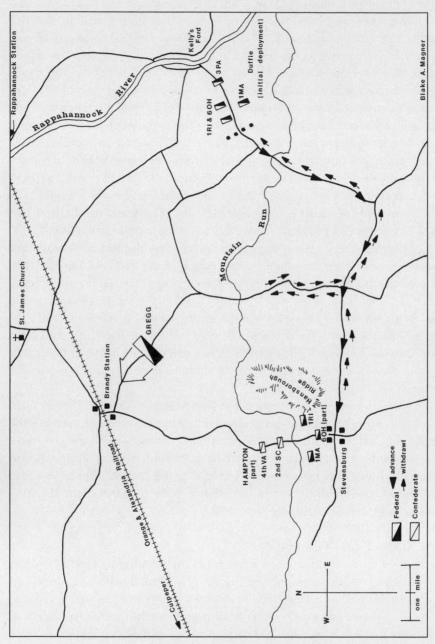

The Action at Stevensburg, June 9, 1863

Rappahannock Station

Kelly's Ford

3PA

1MA

Duffié (initial deployment)

1RI & 6OH

Rappahannock River

Mountain Run

St. James Church

GREGG

Brandy Station

Hansborough Ridge

1RI

6OH (part)

HAMPTON (part)

4th VA

2nd SC

1MA

Stevensburg

Federal

advance

withdrawl

Confederate

Orange & Alexandria Railroad

Culpeper

N
E
W
S

one mile

Blake A. Magner

do the enemy damage when possible. As the whole thing seems to be a reconnaissance to determine our force and position, he wishes these concealed as much as possible, and the infantry not to be seen, if it is possible to avoid it."[145] Lee wanted to avoid tipping his hand regarding the proximity of his infantry. However, as the day dragged on and the fighting grew more desperate, the Confederate commander finally dispatched Confederate infantry to come to Stuart's support.[146]

Earlier in the afternoon, Hooker gave Pleasonton discretionary orders allowing him to withdraw if he felt it was necessary to do so. By 5:00 P.M., Pleasonton's command had been fought out, and upon learning that Confederate infantry was filtering onto the battlefield, Pleasonton exercised that discretion. Concluding that his men had done enough for one day, Pleasonton sent one of his staff officers, Capt. Frederic C. Newhall of the 6th Pennsylvania, to Buford with orders to withdraw from the field. Newhall found Buford "entirely isolated from the rest of the command under Pleasonton . . . but paying no attention and fighting straight on."[147] Buford later wrote that once the firing ceased on Gregg's front along Fleetwood Hill, "I was ordered to withdraw. Abundance of means was sent to aid me, and we came off the field in fine shape and at our convenience. Capt. [Richard S. C.] Lord with the 1st U.S. came up fresh comparatively with plenty of ammunition and entirely relieved my much exhausted but undaunted command in a most commendable style. The engagement lasted near 14 hours."[148]

Covered by the fresh men of the 1st U.S., which supported the artillery most of the day, and by the men of Ames's infantry brigade, Buford withdrew across Beverly's Ford at a leisurely pace. Newhall, who communicated the order to retreat to Buford while the Kentuckian watched the charge of the 2d U.S., recalled that Buford himself "came along serenely at a moderate walk." Buford then climbed the knoll above the river, and joined Pleasonton and a large group of officers to observe the final act of the day's drama as the sun dropped.[149] Pleasonton later noted, "General Buford withdrew his command in beautiful style to this side, the enemy not daring to follow, but showing his chagrin and mortification by an angry and sharp cannonading."[150] About 9:30 that night, Pleasonton scrawled a note to Hooker. "I did what you wanted, crippled Stuart so that he can not go on a raid," claimed Pleasonton, even though the declaration was untrue. "My own losses were very heavy, particularly in officers. I never saw greater gallantry . . . exhibited then on the occasion of the fierce 14 hours of fighting from 5 in the morning until 7 at night."[151]

Their withdrawal perplexed Buford's tired but unbowed troopers. "Our cavalry fell back across the river that night. It was a mystery to the boys why they fell back," wrote a New Yorker.[152] Pleasonton reported to Hooker, "Buford's cavalry had a long and desperate encounter, hand to hand, with the enemy, in which he drove handsomely before him very superior forces. Over two hundred prisoners were captured, and one battle flag. The troops are in splendid spirits, and are entitled to the highest praise for their distinguished conduct." The corps commander later reported Buford's loss at 36 officers and 435 enlisted men killed, wounded, and missing; total casualties in Buford's division were 471, more than 50 percent of the total Union casualties of 866. The 6th Pennsylvania suffered the largest loss, 108, including 8 officers.[153] The 2d U.S. Cavalry suffered 66 killed or wounded out of 225 present for duty during the day's fight.[154] In addition, a great number of horses were killed or wounded in the fierce fighting, leaving many troopers dismounted. "The proportion of horses killed on both sides in this almost unexampled hand to hand cavalry battle was very large," reported a newspaperman.[155]

John Buford had every reason to be extremely proud of the performance of his Regulars that day. "The men and officers of the entire command without exception behaved with great gallantry," wrote Buford. His men acquitted themselves well, matching their foe charge for charge. "No regiment engaged that day on the Union side had more of it than ours," proudly proclaimed a member of "Grimes" Davis's 8th New York Cavalry. "It was first in and last out in our division. It was not later than 4:30 A.M. in going in, and was rear-guard at the Ford."[156] Buford singled out a few officers for commendation, including his protégé, Capt. Wesley Merritt. Finally, he praised two captains of Pleasonton's staff, Ulric Dahlgren of the 1st U.S. and Elon Farnsworth of the 8th Illinois, for their work during the great fight.[157]

When Duffié's division finally arrived, Gregg withdrew about a mile and realigned his position to connect with Buford's northern attack, which was raging on Yew Ridge. Most of the Confederate artillery was concentrated on Fleetwood Hill, and Hampton's and Jones's brigades shifted to meet the Union threat.[158] As Gregg prepared to pitch into the fight once again, Pleasonton ordered the Pennsylvanian to disengage and withdraw. Russell's infantry covered Gregg's retreat. The infantrymen had spent the day pinning down Robertson's brigade, preventing the North Carolinians from reaching the battlefield before the fighting ended. "While Pleasonton was defeated at Brandy Station, he made a masterly withdrawal of his forces," remembered an admiring Virginian.[159] Stuart noted that Buford's attack on the northern end of Fleetwood Hill "made it absolutely necessary to desist from our pursuit of the force retreating toward Kelly's particularly as the infantry known to be on that road would very soon have terminated the pursuit."[160] Thus ended the largest cavalry fight ever seen in the Western Hemisphere.

The day's fighting represented a will-o'-the-wisp of lost opportunities for David Gregg, a veritable litany of "what if's." His command suffered severe casualties. A brigade commander and 2 regimental commanders were wounded or missing, a third field-grade officer wounded, 2 line officers killed and 15 wounded, 18 enlisted men killed, 65 wounded, and 272 missing. His men captured 8 commissioned officers and two sets of colors. Gregg noted, "The field on which we fought bore evidence of the severe loss of the enemy." He singled out Wyndham and Kilpatrick for particular praise, and commended Captain Martin's artillerists for their valiant stand.

At the same time, he squarely and unambiguously placed the blame for his failure to carry Fleetwood Hill on Duffié, both for delaying his crossing, and for the Frenchman's tardiness in arriving on the battlefield.[161] When he realized that the whole Confederate cavalry force lay in front of him, Gregg should have called for Duffié's division immediately. He should have used the Frenchman's division as the hammer to drive Stuart's surrounded troopers against the anvil of Gregg's division, holding the high ground on Fleetwood Hill. He failed to do so, and the opportunity to destroy Stuart's command slipped away. The same opportunity would not present itself again.

For his part, Stuart described the fight for Fleetwood Hill as "long and spirited." He generally praised all of his brigade commanders, singling out Jones and Hampton for particular praise. At the same time, he damned Robertson for failing to delay Gregg's advance. Finally, he heaped particular praise upon Henry McClellan, for without the enterprising major's help, Fleetwood certainly would have fallen and the outcome of the battle would have been very different indeed.[162]

In return, Robert E. Lee praised Stuart. On June 16, after reading Stuart's report, Lee wrote, "The dispositions made by you to meet the strong attack of the enemy appear to have been judicious and well planned. The troops were well and skillfully managed, and, with few exceptions, conducted themselves with marked gallantry. The result of the action calls for our grateful thanks to Almighty God, and is honorable alike to the officers and men engaged."[163] Lee evidently did not realize just how close his cavalry corps had come to being completely destroyed that day; if he did, he did a good job of salving Stuart's bruised pride.

THE CONSEQUENCES OF BRANDY STATION

After a day of savage fighting, Stuart had won a narrow victory by repulsing Pleasonton's foray. The opposing forces ended up precisely where they began. Seemingly, little was accomplished by it, other than heavy casualties. Stuart claimed victory by virtue of retaining possession of the battlefield at the end of the day. Brandy Station was "a passage of arms filled with romantic interest and splendor to a degree unequaled to anything our [Civil War] produced."[164] Rosser, a keen observer, noted, "After Stuart had driven Pleasonton from the field, he could not pursue him, for the country was wooded and the retreat was covered by the infantry, against which cavalry could not operate successfully in such a country, and, as night came on, Pleasonton was not pursued beyond the river, where his infantry made a stand till dark." Rosser concluded, "But had Pleasonton been there without infantry, he could never have got his command safely back to its shelter, for Stuart would certainly have destroyed it."[165] While that probably overstated the case, the infantry undoubtedly provided a substantial hindrance to a pursuit by the Southern horsemen.

For nearly fourteen bitter hours, the Federal troopers battled the Confederates to a standoff. However, they failed in their stated mission of destroying or dispersing Stuart's large force of saddle soldiers. One trooper of the 8th New York wrote, "[T]he Rebels were going to have a review of their cavalry that day, but our boys reviewed them."[166] Brig. Gen. John Gibbon, Buford's old friend, wrote to his wife, "From all accounts, [the fight] must have been a heavy one. Our men behaved well but were overpowered and obliged to come back to this side of the river again, but were not followed."[167]

It seemed that all involved on the Union side tried to claim that their unit had suffered the worst hardships in the long battle. "Today's battle was the heaviest cavalry fight of the war," claimed one of Wyndham's men, "and the brunt of the engagement was born by our brigade."[168]

The Confederates sustained 51 killed, 250 wounded, and 132 missing, while the Yankees suffered 484 killed and wounded and 372 taken prisoner. These casualties speak volumes for the severity of the fighting that day. Perhaps the greatest consequence of Brandy Station was its effect on the morale of the Federal cavalry. As Stuart's aide, Henry McClellan, later wrote, "This battle . . . made the Federal Cavalry. The fact is that up to June 9, 1863, the Confederate cavalry did have its own way . . . and the record of their success becomes almost monotonous. . . . But after that time we held our ground only by hard fighting."[169] Wesley Merritt of the 2d U.S. Cavalry echoed a similar note. "From that day forth the prestige of the Confederate cavalry was broken," he claimed, "and its preeminence was gone forever."[170] Another Confederate, trooper John N. Opie of the 6th Virginia, noted, "In this battle the Federal cavalry fought with great gallantry, and . . . they exhibited marked and wonderful improvement in skill, confidence, and tenacity."[171]

Two days after the great battle, a member of the 8th Illinois recounted, "They had five brigades of cavalry, ten pieces of artillery, and Longstreet's infantry there. It was their intention to make raids into Maryland and Pennsylvania. We spoiled their fun anyway." He continued, "We had about 10,000 cavalry and two 6 gun batteries, and had 6,000 infantry. . . . Our object was accomplished. We had found out their strength and their intentions. They would have commenced crossing the river in an hour if we had not got the start of them."[172] Capt. Willard C. Glazier of the 2d New York observed that Brandy Station "was a glorious fight, in which the men of the North had proved themselves more than a match for the boasted Southern Chivalry."[173]

The historian of the 10th New York claimed that the performance of the blue troopers that day "forever settled the question of superiority as between the gray and the blue cavalry in favor of the latter."[174] Edward P. Tobie of the 1st Maine observed, "[A] higher value attaches to Brandy Station as affecting the regiment. . . . It was . . . the first time it had ever tasted . . . the fruit of victory. The battle aroused its latent powers, and awoke it . . . to a new career. It became self-reliant, and began to comprehend its own possibilities. It became inspired with an invincible spirit that never again forsook it."[175]

On June 11, upon returning to Warrenton Junction, Pleasonton reported to Hooker that he had "just reviewed [the] cavalry. They are in fine spirits and good condition for another fight."[176] That was undoubtedly the case, but some men remained displeased with the way that the battle had ended. Pleasonton failed to disperse the concentration of Confederate cavalry in the area around Culpeper. He also failed, ultimately, to delay the departure of the Confederates on their march north—the great invasion started one day later than originally planned. On June 10, a concerned Hooker wrote to Pleasonton, "I am not so certain as you appear to be that the enemy will abandon his contemplated raid. With this impression I have felt a little hesitation in withdrawing the infantry. Will you be able to keep him from crossing the river with the cavalry and batteries with you? If not, and you consider that the infantry will be of service in preventing a passage, please have it retained until further orders."[177]

After Gettysburg, Pleasonton claimed that he had discovered the Confederate plan to invade the north at Brandy Station, but this argument has little merit.[178] Pleasonton's subsequent actions and communications with army headquarters simply do not support this contention. Capt. Charles Francis Adams, of the 1st Massachusetts—never an admirer of Alfred Pleasonton's—grumbled, "I am sure a good cavalry officer would have whipped Stuart out of his boots, but Pleasonton is not and never will be that."[179]

The Federal troopers had performed admirably in exceedingly difficult circumstances, especially Buford's command, which carried the brunt of the fighting, going it largely alone for a good portion of the day. Not all of the Confederates believed that Brandy Station was a decisive victory, either. "Stuart managed badly that day," proclaimed the ever-diplomatic Wade Hampton, "but I would not say so publicly."[180] The Virginian did not commit Fitz Lee's brigade to the fight until the end of the day; earlier involvement by this veteran command might have tipped the balance.[181] Capt. Charles Minor Blackford, of Stuart's staff, wrote to his family, "The cavalry fight at Brandy Station can hardly be called a victory. Stuart was certainly surprised and but for the supreme gallantry of his subordinate officers and the men in his command, it would have been a day of disaster and disgrace." Another Confederate soldier wrote, "Genl Stuart was beautifully surprised and whipped the other day. He drove them back, but not until he had received a considerable chastising. It is amusing to hear the cavalry fellows trying to bluff out of it."[182] John B. Jones, a clerk in the Confederate War Department, noted in his diary, "The surprise of Stuart on the Rappahannock has chilled every heart, notwithstanding it does not appear that we lost more than the enemy in the encounter. The question is on every tongue—have the generals relaxed in vigilance? If so, sad is the prospect!"[183]

Capt. Theophilus F. Rodenbough of the 2d U.S. Cavalry, who was wounded and had two horses shot out from under him at Brandy Station, became the leading early Union cavalry historian of the 19th century. A few years after the battle, he wrote, "Stuart had the advantage of position; the ground, intersected by ravines and low stone fences and interspersed with groves of large trees, rose gradually in the direction of Brandy Station." With such advantages, Stuart should have won decisively, but he did not. Rather, it was too close a margin for the Confederates' comfort. In fact, given the extreme circumstances, Stuart handled his troops well, shifting forces as needed to meet threats. Rodenbough observed that "the Confederate cavalry, caught napping, endeavored to repair its fault with promptness and gallantry; it had, however, been checked upon the threshold of an aggressive movement, and its leader was taught a lesson, which sooner or later is learned by the general who undervalues his enemy."[184]

The Southern newspapers excoriated Stuart for being taken by surprise at Brandy Station. The *Richmond Sentinel* concluded its coverage of the battle by stating, "The fight, on the whole, may be said to have begun in a surprise and ended in a victory. The latter is what we are accustomed to hear of Confederate soldiers; the former we trust never to hear again."

The *Richmond Daily Examiner* had a far harsher appraisal: it referred to Stuart's command as "this much puffed cavalry of the Army of Northern Virginia," and pointed out that, along with the battle at Kelly's Ford three months earlier, it was at least the second time that Stuart had been surprised by the Federals. Its editorial opined, "If the war was a tournament, invented and supported for the pleasure and profit of a few vain and weak-headed officers, these disasters might be dismissed with compassion. But the country pays dearly for the blunders which encourage the enemy to overrun the land with a cavalry which is daily learning to despise the mounted troops of the Confederacy. It is high time that this branch of the service should be reformed." The paper clearly implied that Stuart should be replaced as commander. Continuing, the editorial proclaimed, "The enemy is evidently determined to employ his cavalry extensively, and has spared no pains or cost to perfect that arm. The only effective means of preventing the mischief . . . is to reorganize our own forces, enforce a stricter discipline among the men, and insist on more earnestness among the officers in the discharge of their very important duty."[185]

The harsh criticism stung the proud Stuart. He wrote home to his wife Flora, "God has spared me through another bloody battle, and blessed with victory our arms." He then vented his frustration with the media. "The papers are in great error, as usual about the whole transaction," he declared. "It was no surprise, the enemys [*sic*] movement was known, and he was defeated. I lost *no paper*—no *nothing*—except the casualties of battle." The offended cavalry chief declared the *Examiner*'s account "lies."[186]

The Army of the Potomac's cavalrymen had performed well that day, tangling with the very best that the Confederate cavalry had to offer, and they had more than held their own. While they were largely fought out by the end of the day, the Yankee troopers withdrew leisurely, and without pursuit. Victory lay within their grasp, but they let it slip away because of poor intelligence work and poor planning by Alfred Pleasonton. Moreover, Pleasonton's plan separated his force and prevented the Northern cavalrymen from delivering a knockout blow; had he concentrated his entire force and made a vigorous attack on one front or the other, he probably would have inflicted a decisive defeat on Stuart and his vaunted cavalry. The combination of poor intelligence work and an unduly complex plan doomed his excursion to failure. This, however, does not detract from the performance of the individual troopers, who fought long and hard, earning the respect of their grayclad foes.

The climax on Fleetwood Hill marked the end of the "coming out party" for the Army of the Potomac's Cavalry Corps. Its maturation process was now complete. The Northern horsemen were finally the equals of their Southern counterparts, and they would never look back. Major victories lay ahead.

NOTES

1. *New York Times,* June 16, 1863.
2. Warner, *Generals in Gray,* 259–60. Robertson was Stuart's principal rival for the hand of Flora Cooke, and many historians speculate that rivalry was the root of Stuart's animosity toward Robertson.
3. O.R., vol. 27, part 2, 733.
4. Ibid., 734.
5. Ibid., 736.
6. Ibid., 680.
7. Ibid., 735. For a detailed examination of Beverly Robertson's role in the Battle of Brandy Station, see Patrick A. Bowmaster, "Beverly H. Robertson and the Battle of Brandy Station," *Blue & Gray* 14 (fall 1996).
8. O.R., vol. 27, part 1, 950.
9. Myers, *Comanches,* 183.
10. McClellan, *Life and Campaigns of Major-General J. E. B. Stuart,* 270.
11. Ibid.
12. Ibid., 271.
13. Baylor, *From Bull Run to Bull Run,* 143.
14. Summers, *A Borderland Confederate,* 72.

15. Robert J. Trout, ed., *In the Saddle with Stuart: The Story of Frank Smith Robertson of Jeb Stuart's Staff* (Gettysburg, Pa.: Thomas, 1998), 67.
16. McClellan, *Life and Campaigns of Major-General J. E. B. Stuart,* 271.
17. Pyne, *History of the First New Jersey Cavalry,* 118.
18. Blackford, *War Years with Jeb Stuart,* 215.
19. Moore, *Kilpatrick and Our Cavalry,* 58.
20. Von Borcke, *Memoirs,* 406–07.
21. O.R., vol. 27, part 2, 769.
22. Pyne, *The History of the First New Jersey Cavalry,* 149.
23. Frye, *12th Virginia Cavalry,* 39.
24. Lloyd, *History of the First Regiment Pennsylvania Reserve Cavalry,* 54.
25. Thomas, *Some Personal Reminiscences of Service in the Cavalry,* 9.
26. O.R. Supp., vol. 5, 250.
27. Ibid., 250–51.
28. Moyer, "Brandy Station."
29. Meyer, *Civil War Experiences,* 28.
30. Lucas to his wife, June 14, 1863.
31. Grimsley, *Battles in Culpeper County,* 11.
32. Cooke, *Wearing of the Gray,* 219.
33. Myers, *Comanches,* 185.
34. Ibid.
35. O.R., vol. 27, part 1, 1025.
36. Thomas, *Some Personal Reminiscences of Service in the Cavalry,* 10.
37. Robert H. Moore, *The 1st and 2d Stuart Horse Artillery* (Lynchburg, Va.: H. E. Howard, 1985), 64–65.
38. Howard, *Sketch of the Cobb Legion Cavalry,* 7.
39. James F. Hart, in *Philadelphia Weekly Times,* June 26, 1880.
40. Thomas L. Cox to John S. Brodrick, June 11, 1863, Virgil Brodrick Letters, Blair Gray-bill Collection, Charlottesville, Va. Brodrick was laid to rest in the National Cemetery in Culpeper.
41. Pyne, *History of the First New Jersey Cavalry,* 121.
42. Ibid.
43. Ibid., 122.
44. Opie, *A Rebel Cavalryman,* 153.
45. Preston, *History of the 10th Regiment of Cavalry,* 85.
46. Ibid.
47. Ibid., 86–87.
48. Wiley C. Howard, *Sketch of Cobb Legion Cavalry and Some Incidents and Scenes Remembered* (Atlanta: Atlanta Camp 159, S.C.V., 1901), 8.
49. O.R., vol. 27, part 2, 732.
50. "The Beau Sabreur of Georgia," *Southern Historical Society Papers* 25 (1897): 149.
51. McClellan, *Life and Campaigns of Major-General J. E. B. Stuart,* 277.
52. O.R., vol. 27, part 1, 997.

53. Eleanor D. McSwain, ed., *Crumbling Defenses: Or Memoirs and Reminiscences of John Logan Black, C.S.A.* (Macon, Ga.: privately published, 1960), 133.
54. Tobie, *First Maine Cavalry,* 154.
55. O.R., vol. 27, part 2, 755.
56. Tobie, *First Maine Cavalry,* 148–49.
57. Moore, *Kilpatrick and Our Cavalry,* 59; Glazier, *Three Years in the Federal Cavalry,* 220.
58. *New York Times,* June 14, 1863.
59. Thomas, *Some Personal Reminiscences of Service in the Cavalry,* 11.
60. Tobie, *First Maine Cavalry,* 150–52.
61. George H. Chase, "A Scrap of History: General Kilpatrick's Desperate Encounter with a Rebel Major," *National Tribune,* September 2, 1882.
62. Grimsley, *Battles in Culpeper County,* 11.
63. O.R., vol. 27, part 2, 722.
64. Ibid., part 1, 1027.
65. Moffatt, "Battle of Brandy Station," 75.
66. Thomas, *Some Personal Recollections of Service in the Cavalry,* 11.
67. Moffatt, "Battle of Brandy Station," 75.
68. O.R., vol. 27, part 2, 763.
69. McClellan, *Life and Campaigns of Major-General J. E. B. Stuart,* 279.
70. O.R., vol. 27, part 1, 951.
71. McClellan, *The Life and Campaigns of Major-General J. E. B. Stuart,* 282.
72. Longacre, *Cavalry at Gettysburg,* 84; Sutherland, *Seasons of War,* 248–49.
73. Whelan to Cadwalader, June 11, 1863.
74. Beale, *A Lieutenant of Cavalry in Lee's Army,* 96.
75. Cram to Sir, June 10, 1863.
76. Davis, *Common Soldier, Uncommon War,* 395.
77. Carpenter to his father, June 11, 1863.
78. George C. Cram to Carpenter, June 11, 1863, Carpenter Letters.
79. Merritt, "Recollections of the Civil War," 287.
80. Lt. Albert O. Vincent to Lt. J. Hamilton Bell, June 16, 1863, Hunt Papers.
81. Buford to Alexander, June 13, 1863.
82. Merritt, "Recollections of the Civil War," 287–88.
83. Ibid., 288.
84. Maj. Charles J. Whiting to Capt. Theodore C. Bacon, June 12, 1863, Hooker Papers.
85. Merritt, "Recollections of the Civil War," 289.
86. Ibid.
87. Beale, *History of the Ninth Virginia Cavalry,* 69.
88. William L. Royall, *Some Reminiscences* (New York: Neale, 1909), 13–14.
89. Beale, *A Lieutenant of Cavalry in Lee's Army,* 96.
90. *Richmond Daily Dispatch,* June 15, 1863.
91. Merritt, "Recollections of the Civil War," 289.
92. Robert Driver, Jr., *10th Virginia Cavalry* (Lynchburg, Va.: H. E. Howard, 1992), 37. Two days after the great battle, Robert E. Lee reported on his son's condition in a letter to

his wife, Mary. "I saw him the night after the battle. Indeed met him on the field as they were bringing him from the front," recounted General Lee. "At night he appeared comfortable & cheerful. Neither the bone or artery of the leg I am informed is injured. He is young & healthy & I trust will soon be up again. He seemed to be more concerned about his brave men & officers who had fallen in battle than himself." Manarin and Dowdey, *Wartime Papers of R. E. Lee,* 2:511. Rooney Lee was taken to Williams Wickham's home in Hanover County to recuperate. Northern cavalrymen found out that he was there and captured him. Lee spent the next six months as a prisoner of war before he was exchanged.

93. Buford to Alexander, June 13, 1863.
94. Vincent to Bell, June 16, 1863.
95. O.R., vol. 27, part 2, 737–38.
96. Rosser, *Addresses,* 37.
97. O.R., vol. 27, part 3, 41–42.
98. Ford, *A Cycle of Adams Letters,* 2:31.
99. O.R., vol. 27, part 1, 961.
100. Ibid.
101. Brooke-Rawle to his mother, June 12, 1863.
102. Mohr and Winslow, *Cormany Diaries,* 316.
103. Ibid.
104. Brooke-Rawle to his mother, June 12, 1863.
105. *New York Times,* June 16, 1863.
106. Williams to My Dear Anna, June 11, 1863.
107. McClellan, *Life and Campaigns of Major-General J. E. B. Stuart,* 284.
108. Warner, *Generals in Gray,* 40–41. For a good treatment of Butler's life and career that places him in his proper historic context, see Samuel J. Martin, *Southern Hero: Matthew Calbraith Butler—Confederate General, Hampton Red Shirt, and U.S. Senator* (Mechanicsburg, Pa.: Stackpole Books, 2001).
109. McClellan, *Life and Campaigns of Major-General J. E. B. Stuart,* 285.
110. Ibid., 286.
111. Wister, *Walter S. Newhall,* 104.
112. Williams to My Dear Anna, June 11, 1863.
113. Matthew C. Butler to O. G. Thompson, August 17, 1907, in *Butler and His Cavalry in the War of Secession, 1861–1865,* ed. U. R. Brooks (Columbia, S.C.: State, 1909), 152.
114. Ibid., 152–53.
115. Crowninshield, *History of the First Regiment,* 129.
116. Frost and Frost, *Picket Pins and Sabers,* 48–49.
117. McClellan, *Life and Campaigns of Major-General J. E. B. Stuart,* 287.
118. O.R., vol. 27, part 1, 961.
119. Crowninshield, *History of the First Regiment,* 133.
120. Butler to Thompson, *Butler and His Cavalry,* 153.
121. Stiles, *Fourth Virginia Cavalry,* 28.
122. Brooke-Rawle to his mother, June 12, 1863.

123. Stiles, *Fourth Virginia Cavalry,* 29.

124. O.R., vol. 27, part 1, 961.

125. Butler to Thompson, *Butler and His Cavalry,* 153. Wade Hampton blamed Williams C. Wickham for his brother's death, declaring, "But for the fact that the Fourth Virginia Cavalry, under the command of Colonel Wickham, broke and ran, my brother, Frank Hampton, would not have been killed that day." Brooks, *Butler and His Cavalry,* 169; Manly Wade Wellman, *Giant in Gray: A Biography of Wade Hampton of South Carolina* (New York: Charles Scribner's Sons, 1949), 109.

126. O.R., vol. 27, part 2, 744–45.

127. Brooks, *Butler and His Cavalry,* 154.

128. Ibid.

129. Ibid.

130. Robert J. Trout, *They Followed the Plume: The Story of J. E. B. Stuart and His Staff* (Mechanicsburg, Pa.: Stackpole Books, 1993), 112–13. Farley became delirious just before he died. His final words were, "To your post, men! To your post!" He died a few moments later. Stuart lamented the scout's passing almost as much as he mourned the loss of the gallant Pelham at Kelly's Ford three months earlier.

131. Brooks, *Butler and His Cavalry,* 160.

132. O.R., vol. 27, part 1, 962.

133. Wister, *Walter S. Newhall,* 104.

134. O.R., vol. 27, part 1, 975.

135. Brooke-Rawle to his mother, June 12, 1863.

136. Brooke-Rawle, *Third Pennsylvania Cavalry,* 247.

137. O.R., vol. 27, part 1, 962.

138. Frost and Frost, *Picket Pins and Sabers,* 49.

139. Mosby, *Stuart's Cavalry in the Gettysburg Campaign,* 12.

140. Williams to My Dear Anna, June 11, 1863.

141. Crowninshield, *History of the First Regiment,* 128.

142. Ford, *A Cycle of Adams Letters,* 32.

143. Mohr and Winslow, *Cormany Diaries,* 316.

144. Hopkins, *From Bull Run to Appomattox,* 92.

145. O.R., vol. 27, part 3, 876.

146. Von Borcke and Scheibert, *Great Cavalry Battle at Brandy Station,* 98.

147. Newhall, "Battle of Beverly Ford," 143.

148. Buford to Alexander, June 13, 1863.

149. Newhall, "The Battle of Beverly Ford," 144.

150. O.R., vol. 27, part 1, 1045.

151. Pleasonton to Hooker, June 9, 1863, Hooker Papers.

152. Norton, *Deeds of Daring,* 67.

153. O.R., vol. 27, part 1, 903–4.

154. Joseph I. Lambert, *One Hundred Years with the Second Cavalry* (Topeka, Kans.: Capper Printing Co., 1939), 70.

155. *New York Herald,* June 11, 1863.

156. H. A. Bull, "Brandy Station: Where the 8th N.Y. Cav. Had Its Full Share of Fighting," *National Tribune,* January 20, 1887.

157. Buford to Alexander, June 13, 1863.

158. Grimsley, *Battles in Culpeper County,* 12.

159. Moffatt, "Battle of Brandy Station," 75.

160. O.R., vol. 27, part 2, 682.

161. Ibid., part 1, 951.

162. Ibid., part 2, 683–84.

163. Ibid., 687.

164. Blackford, *War Years with Jeb Stuart,* 215.

165. Rosser, *Addresses,* 38.

166. Norton, *Deeds of Daring,* 66. It is interesting to note that another member of the same regiment said something similar. "It was talked by our boys that the Union cavalry would do the reviewing instead of Gen. Stuart." C. J. Phillips, "Stuart's Cavalry, and How It Was 'Reviewed' by the Union Troopers at Brandy Station," *National Tribune,* March 10, 1887.

167. John Gibbon to My Dearest Mama, June 11, 1863, Gibbon Papers.

168. William Penn Lloyd, Memoranda from May 13th, 1863, to May 31st, 1863, entry for June 9, 1863, William Penn Lloyd Papers, Southern Historical Collection, Wilson Historical Library, University of North Carolina, Chapel Hill.

169. McClellan, *Life and Campaigns of Major-General J. E. B. Stuart,* 234.

170. Merritt, "Recollections of the Civil War," 291.

171. Opie, *A Rebel Cavalryman,* 157.

172. *Morrison-Whiteside Journal,* June 25, 1863.

173. Glazier, *Three Years in the Federal Cavalry,* 223.

174. Preston, *History of the 10th Regiment of Cavalry,* 85.

175. Tobie, *History of the First Maine Cavalry,* 155.

176. O.R., vol. 27, part 3, 58.

177. Ibid., 45–46.

178. In fact, an infantryman of the 86th New York Infantry of the III Corps, part of Ames's select brigade of infantry, claimed, "I found General Lee's General Orders to his army. From them we learned that Hooker had been outwitted, that he was hopelessly in the rear, while Lee, unopposed, was marching northward. In the orders Lee enjoined perfect discipline, declaring that depredators would be severely punished." However, this account was written forty-one years after Brandy Station and cannot be corroborated. It supports Pleasonton's fictions and may have been based on his unsupported claims. Samuel G. Inram, "Beverly Ford: The Third Corps Helps the Cavalry Surprise Jeb Stuart and Give Him a Rough House," *National Tribune,* April 28, 1904.

179. Ford, *A Cycle of Adams Letters,* 2:32.

180. Emory N. Thomas, *Bold Dragoon: The Life of J. E. B. Stuart* (New York: Harper & Row, 1986), 227.

181. Peck, *Reminiscences,* 31 ("We were near enough to hear the firing but not near enough to engage in it. [Pleasonton] did not attempt to cross where we were, so we just stood guard all day").

182. Sutherland, *Seasons of War,* 256–57.

183. Jones, *A Rebel War Clerk's Diary,* 223.

184. Theophilus F. Rodenbough, "Cavalry War Lessons," *Journal of the U.S. Cavalry Association* 11, no. 5 (1889): 107.

185. *Richmond Sentinel,* June 12, 1863; *Richmond Daily Examiner,* June 12, 1863. Some historians have speculated that the harsh criticism of Stuart was the impetus behind his subsequent excursion around the Army of the Potomac in an effort to restore the luster to his tarnished reputation after the Battle of Brandy Station. This foray resulted in his absence from the Army of Northern Virginia during the first two days of the Battle of Gettysburg. For an interesting examination of this controversy, see Mark Nesbitt, *Saber and Scapegoat: J. E. B. Stuart and the Gettysburg Controversy* (Mechanicsburg, Pa.: Stackpole, 1994).

186. Mitchell, *Letters of Major General James E. B. Stuart,* 323–24.

Major changes lay ahead for the Cavalry Corps in the wake of the Battle of Brandy Station. One brigade commander ("Grimes" Davis) was dead, and another was badly wounded (Sir Percy Wyndham). A division commander had performed badly. Significant changes had to be made, and quickly. The Confederate army was moving north, headed toward its date with destiny in Pennsylvania less than a month later.

On June 11, Pleasonton reorganized his Cavalry Corps. He placed Buford in command of the First Division, which now consisted of three brigades. Col. William Gamble of the 8th Illinois Cavalry, who had been on extended recuperative leave from a severe wound suffered on the Peninsula in August 1862, assumed command of Davis's brigade, redesignated as the First Brigade. Devin continued to command the Second Brigade. The Reserve Brigade, now led by Maj. Samuel H. Starr of the 6th U.S., formally joined the First Division.[1]

The Second and Third Divisions merged, forming the Second Division. David Gregg commanded the reconstituted division, which now had three brigades. Although John B. McIntosh had commanded a brigade all winter, he learned that Col. J. Irvin Gregg of the 16th Pennsylvania was senior to him by a few days and that Gregg should have led the brigade all along. McIntosh briefly reverted to regimental command. By July 1, he commanded a different brigade.[2]

Duffié was more problematic. He performed quite poorly as a division commander. "Colonel Duffié . . . might be a good man," accurately observed Capt. Charles Francis Adams of the 1st Massachusetts Cavalry, "but he could not run a Division."[3] Although he no longer commanded a division as a result of the consolidation of the Second and Third Divisions, the Frenchman remained the senior colonel in his brigade, and was entitled to brigade command as a consequence.

Pleasonton's rabid xenophobia was well known. "I have no faith in foreigners saving our government," he wrote on June 23, 1863, in a letter to Congressman John F. Farnsworth of Illinois, a good friend of Abraham Lincoln's who served as the first commander of the 8th Illinois Cavalry. Pleasonton had a real gift for toadying, and he realized that a powerful ally like Farnsworth could advance his career. Pleasonton therefore did all he could to develop the relationship, including finding a spot on his staff for the congressman's nephew, Capt. Elon J. Farnsworth. His letter concluded, "I conscientiously believe that Americans only should rule in this matter & settle this rebellion—& that in every instance foreigners have injured our cause." In order to solve the Duffié problem, Pleasonton recommended that Judson Kilpatrick receive a promotion to brigadier general of volunteers. In the heady days following Stoneman's Raid, Kilpatrick's officers had written to Lincoln, requesting "Little Kil's" promotion. Pleasonton endorsed the request as a means of resolving the conundrum presented by the Frenchman, who was senior to Kilpatrick. When the promotion came through, Pleasonton placed Kilpatrick in command of the brigade, which meant that both Duffié and di Cesnola reverted to regimental command. Duffié returned to the 1st Rhode Island Cavalry. "I know that there was not the most cordial feeling between him and the controlling officers in the cavalry," recalled a Northern horseman. "I suspected that he was more or less a thorn in the side of the higher officers. He was not companionable with them; did not think as they did; had little in common, and, was perhaps inclined to be boastful."[5] However, Pleasonton was not finished with the Frenchman.

On June 17, 1863, Pleasonton dispatched Duffié and the 1st Rhode Island on a reconnaissance to Middleburg, in Virginia's lush Loudoun Valley. The vastly outnumbered Rhode Islanders were cut to pieces. They lost 6 killed, 9 wounded, and 210 missing and captured, leaving a fine regiment gutted. Pleasonton apparently sacrificed the 1st Rhode Island to rid himself of a hated foreigner.[6] John Singleton Mosby, the notorious Confederate partisan commander, offered his opinion of the Frenchman's leadership skills: "Duffié's folly is an illustration of the truth of what I have often said—that no man is fit to be an officer who has not the sense and courage to know when to disobey an order."[7]

Several weeks earlier, Hooker had endorsed a promotion for Duffié as a consequence of his good work at Kelly's Ford. A few days after the debacle at Middleburg, President Lincoln forwarded a letter to Secretary of War Stanton recommending that Duffié be promoted as a consequence of the Frenchman's good service at Kelly's Ford.[8] In spite of the mauling received by the Rhode Islanders, Duffié was promoted to brigadier general and was transferred out of the Army of the Potomac in a classic bump upstairs. He never commanded troops in the Army of the Potomac again. He ended up under Averell's command again, leading a brigade of cavalry in the Department of West Virginia. When the division commander was badly wounded, Duffié assumed command of the division, while Averell served as chief of cavalry in the Army of the Shenandoah. The two men came into conflict as a result of the clumsy command structure.

In September 1864, just after the important Union victories at Third Winchester and Fisher's Hill, Maj. Gen. Philip H. Sheridan, the new leader of the Army of the Shenandoah, relieved both Averell and Duffié from command. Sheridan directed Duffié to go to Hagerstown, Maryland, to await further orders.[9] On October 21, 1864, Duffié boarded an army ambulance to go see Sheridan about getting another command. Sheridan wanted Duffié to equip and retrain another cavalry force, duty for which the Gallic general was abundantly qualified.[10] After receiving his instructions from Sheridan, on October 24, as Duffié was headed back to Hagerstown to prepare for his new assignment, Mosby's guerrillas fell upon the Frenchman's wagon train. Mosby captured Duffié and quickly sent him back to Richmond as a prisoner of war. He sat out the rest of the war in a prisoner of war camp in Danville and was not exchanged until March 1865. After Duffié's capture, Sheridan put an exclamation point on the Frenchman's career in the U.S. Army. "I respectfully request his dismissal from the service," sniffed Sheridan in a letter to Maj. Gen. Henry W. Halleck, "I think him a trifling man and a poor soldier. He was captured by his own stupidity."[11] Duffié never served in the U.S. Army again, although he remained in public service for the rest of his life.[12]

Duffié was not the only target of Pleasonton's wrath. The Cavalry Corps commander also did not like Colonel di Cesnola, and the Italian count knew it. Di Cesnola was a loyal McClellan man, something that did not stand him well with either the administration or with the army's high command. In late May, a few days after Stoneman took medical leave, di Cesnola complained to a friend, "Here things go badly. I am the senior Colonel in Averill's Division, and since he left, other Colonels [Americans] were put in command when the law & any Regulations give me as by seniority of rank the command of it. Oh my heart is every day more sore! Nobody was more enthusiastic in fighting than I was. They succeeded now in making me cold like a stone." The frustrated officer concluded, "This & thousand other wrong things dishearten me that I shall not be able to stand great deal longer this life of humiliation, never revenged, and injustice."[13]

Incredibly, the proud count's humiliation grew. In the aftermath of Brandy Station, Pleasonton placed di Cesnola under arrest for moving some of his men through an infantry camp while on the way to the front. Subsequently, at the Battle of Aldie (fought while Duffié met his fate at Middleburg), di Cesnola led his men into battle without any weapons of his own and in spite of the fact that his arrest meant that he had no command authority. As a result of di Cesnola's valiant conduct, Kilpatrick asked Pleasonton to release the count from arrest, and Pleasonton agreed. Di Cesnola was awarded the Medal of Honor for his valor that day, something that undoubtedly rankled Pleasonton a great deal.[14] However, the count also suffered serious combat wounds and was captured and sent to Richmond's notorious Libby Prison, meaning that he, too, did not command troops in the Army of the Potomac for nearly a year.[15]

Thus, Wyndham, Duffié, and di Cesnola, the three high-ranking foreigners, passed from the Army of the Potomac's Cavalry Corps for the balance of the summer of 1863. Wyndham and Duffié were permanently banished. Di Cesnola eventually returned after being exchanged in the spring of 1864, but his regiment, the 4th New York Cavalry, carried a poor reputation as unreliable in combat. In the fall of 1863, while the Italian count languished in Libby Prison, the 4th New York drew John Buford's wrath for failing to meet his expectations in combat. Buford took away their regimental colors and unsuccessfully tried to have the regiment disbanded. This episode left a black stain on an already tarnished reputation that they would not redeem until the fall of 1864.[16]

One foreigner remained in Pleasonton's path. Maj. Gen. Julius Stahel commanded an independent division of cavalry assigned to the Washington defenses. Stahel was a Hungarian immigrant who had fought in the war for Hungarian independence. When the revolution failed, Stahel fled the country. He arrived in New York in 1859 and spent two years working for a German-language newspaper. With the coming of war, he helped organize the 8th New York Infantry (the German Rifles) and fought well at First Bull Run in 1861. He became colonel of the regiment in August 1861 and received a commission as brigadier general in November of that year. After serving competently in the infantry, he received a promotion to major general on March 17, 1863, and outranked every officer in the Cavalry Corps, including Pleasonton, a thought that rankled the xenophobic cavalryman.[17]

Having rid himself of Duffié, Wyndham, and di Cesnola, Pleasonton now turned his scheming toward getting promoted to major general, and to Stahel, whose troops he coveted for the Cavalry Corps. His efforts bore fruit on both counts. The Senate approved Pleasonton's promotion to major general of volunteers on June 22, 1863. Now he had to rid himself of Stahel.

The next day, Pleasonton penned a lengthy missive to John F. Farnsworth, complaining about Stahel's lack of good sense and energy, and again raising concerns about Stahel's foreign birth. "Our cavalry business is badly managed & will lead us into trouble unless speedily corrected," complained Pleasonton. "We have too many detachments independent of each other scattered over this country." Pleasonton informed the Congressman that he would resign if the Hungarian assumed command of the Cavalry Corps. "Stahel has not shown himself a cavalry-man," Pleasonton proclaimed. He implored that "the cavalry [be] consolidated and Stahel left out for God's sake do it."[18]

He then upped the ante. At Pleasonton's behest, Capt. Elon J. Farnsworth wrote to his uncle. Pleasonton forwarded the two letters to the Congressman together. "The Genl. speaks of recommending me for Brig[adier General]. I do not know that I ought to mention it for fear that you will call me an aspiring youth," wrote young Farnsworth. "I am satisfied to serve through this war in the line. But if I can do any good anywhere else of course 'small favors &c . . .' Now try and talk this into the President and you can do an immense good," he concluded.[19] That did the trick. Five days later, Stahel was removed from command of his division, which was incorporated into the Army of the Potomac's Cavalry Corps.[20]

Kilpatrick took command of the division, which was designated the Third Division of the Cavalry Corps. Col. John B. McIntosh took command of the Second Division brigade Kilpatrick had commanded at Brandy Station. McIntosh performed admirably in the Gettysburg Campaign, prompting Averell to pronounce McIntosh the inferior of no officer in command of a cavalry brigade in Federal service. While leading his brigade at the Third Battle of Winchester on September 19, 1864, McIntosh lost his right leg to a serious wound. He received a brevet to brigadier general in the Regular Army for his valor that day, and also received commissions as major general by brevet in both the volunteer service and the Regular Army. At the end of the war, he became lieutenant colonel of the 42d Infantry and retired a brigadier general in 1870. McIntosh was courageous and dependable, and deserved every accolade that he received. His star first rose during the spring of 1863.[21]

The newly absorbed Third Division was reorganized into two brigades, and Pleasonton immediately set about putting his own men in charge of them. On June 28, 1863, he arranged for promotions for Capts. Elon Farnsworth, Wesley Merritt, and George A. Custer to brigadier general.[22] Farnsworth's handling of the 8th Illinois Cavalry at Brandy Station, combined with his uncle's political patronage, destined the young staff officer for rapid advancement. Custer had captured Pleasonton's fancy at Brandy Station.[23] Although Custer was a mere staff officer, "he was always in the fight," recalled one of Pleasonton's orderlies, "no matter where it was."[24] Farnsworth and Custer took command of the two brigades that made up Kilpatrick's division, and Merritt took over the Reserve Brigade.

Custer, of course, had a spectacular and flamboyant career commanding horse soldiers in the Army of the Potomac, but he is best known for his 1876 defeat on the Little Big Horn. His legendary good luck propelled him to prominence at a precocious age. Farnsworth, on the other hand, only wore his general's star for five days. After leading a charge at Hanover, Pennsylvania on June 30, 1863, Farnsworth fell at the head of his troopers in the last attack at Gettysburg on July 3.[25] His death directly resulted from the unfettered ambitions of Judson Kilpatrick. However, victory salves many wounds, and Kilpatrick escaped sanction for his rash orders in sending Farnsworth to his death on the rocky slopes at Gettysburg.

Kilpatrick, whose perfidy knew no bounds, lamented that "the division lost many brave and gallant officers. Among the list will be found the name of Farnsworth; short but most glorious was his career—a general on June 29, on the 30th he baptized his star in blood, and on July 3, for the honor of his young brigade and the glory of his corps, he gave his life. At the head of his men, at the very muzzles of the enemy's guns, he fell, with many mortal wounds. We can say of him, in the language of another, 'Good soldier, faithful friend, great heart, hail and farewell.'"[26]

Merritt had one of the most remarkable careers in American military history. Very much John Buford's protégé, Merritt was quiet and very competent. Just a year removed from West Point in 1861 when the war began, Merritt became the commander of the Army of the Potomac's Cavalry Corps after earning that distinction in five long years of difficult battles. He soon became the most reliable commander of horsemen in the Union service. In 1864, he became Sheridan's commander of choice whenever the Cavalry Corps found itself in a tight situation, much as Buford was in 1863. He spent more than forty years in the Regular Army, serving as superintendent of West Point and capping his career as leader of the expedition that captured Manila during the Spanish-American War. He retired with a major general's commission in 1904 and was the army's second ranking officer at the time of his retirement. His talent and steady performance certainly justified Pleasonton's confidence in the young man.[27]

John Buford's star rose after the Battle of Brandy Station. His men fought hard during the advance into Pennsylvania, and he conducted a magnificent stand at Gettysburg on the morning of July 1, 1863. After hard fighting during the retreat from Gettysburg and in the fall of 1863, the Kentuckian was worn out. Perhaps his many years of brutal conflicts on the plains had finally caught up to him. The vicissitudes of service, combined with the loss of his beloved daughter in August, took an incalculable toll on the rugged horse soldier known as "Old Reliable."

Apparently, the Union high command believed Buford's tactics were the best hope of coping with the Confederate cavalry of Maj. Gen. Nathan Bedford Forrest. In late October 1863, Buford was assigned the command of the cavalry corps of the Army of the Cumberland.[28] This could have created an interesting confrontation, as by the late winter of 1863–64 Buford's first cousin Brig. Gen. Abraham Buford commanded a division of Forrest's cavalry. Unfortunately for John Buford, the fates were not kind to him, and he never got the opportunity to command the Army of the Cumberland's Cavalry Corps.

On November 19, a staff officer wrote, "We find the cavalry chief afflicted with rheumatism, which he bore with his usual philosophy."[29] However, the problem noted by Lyman was not rheumatism. The rigors of so many years of hard marching and fighting had taken their toll on Buford. He contracted typhoid fever "from fatigue and extreme hardship" after participating in the marches and fighting that on November 7–8, 1863, compelled Lee's Army of Northern Virginia to abandon the line on the Rappahannock and retire behind the Rapidan. Buford took a medical leave of absence and went to Washington, D.C., on November 20, 1863.[30]

There he was taken to the home of his good friend, General Stoneman. Buford's condition deteriorated quickly, and it soon became apparent that he would not survive. On December 16, 1863, President Lincoln sent a note to Secretary of War Stanton, who was said not to trust anyone with Southern antecedents and who disliked most of the officers associated with John Pope's Army of Virginia. Lincoln's note requested that the gravely ill Buford, whom Lincoln did not expect to survive the day, be promoted to major general. Although the promotion was well deserved and long overdue, Stanton permitted Buford's promotion only when it became certain that Buford was dying.[31]

The promotion was made retroactive to July 1, 1863, in tribute to Buford's service at Gettysburg.[32] Buford lapsed in and out of delirium, alternately scolding and apologizing to his black servant, who sat weeping by the general's bedside. Several old comrades, including his aide, Capt. Myles W. Keogh, and his host, George Stoneman, comforted him. When the major general's commission arrived, Buford had a few lucid moments, murmuring, "Too late. . . . Now I wish that I could live." Keogh helped him sign the necessary forms and signed as a witness, and Capt. Andrew J. Alexander wrote a letter to Stanton for Buford, accepting the promotion.[33] Ever the diligent cavalryman, Buford's last intelligible words were, "Put guards on all the roads, and don't let the men run back to the rear." He died in Keogh's arms on December 16, 1863, and was buried in the cemetery at West Point.[34]

Thus, the Army of the Potomac's Cavalry Corps lost its most able subordinate commander. "John Buford was the best cavalryman I ever saw," remembered his dear friend, Brig. Gen. John Gibbon. "I have always expressed the belief that had Buford lived he would have been placed in command of the cavalry of the Army of the Potomac, and once in that position he never would have been displaced."[35] "He had the respect and esteem of every man in the army, and the cavalry loved him as a father," noted an officer of the 1st U.S. Cavalry.[36] His death created an irreparable hole in the Cavalry Corps.

Col. Thomas C. Devin, who earned the flattering nickname of "Buford's Hard Hitter" for his role in the coming campaigns, toiled in unappreciated obscurity for far too long. Although he was the oldest brigade commander in the Army of the

Potomac's Cavalry Corps, and had certainly earned a promotion, that promotion did not come until the fall of 1864, when he finally received a brevet to brigadier general of volunteers. A long-overdue commission arrived in the spring of 1865. By the end of the war, he received a second brevet to major general of volunteers and commanded a division. "Uncle Tommy," as his men fondly called him, was steady and dependable, always in the thick of the fight. In recognition of his service, he received a commission as a lieutenant colonel in the Regular Army, a remarkable accomplishment for someone with no formal military training. He became colonel of the 3d Cavalry in 1877, but his health soon failed and he died of cancer in 1878.[37]

Capt. Ulric Dahlgren flashed across the horizon of the Civil War like a meteor—shining brightly and burning out quickly. Through his valor, Dahlgren made heroic contributions to the Union victory at Gettysburg, not the least of which was capturing dispatches intended for Robert E. Lee that indicated that Lee's army would receive no reinforcements from a Confederacy stretched too thin. His intelligence coup permitted the Army of the Potomac's high command to operate with the knowledge that Lee's army had to stand on its own. Then, during the retreat from Gettysburg at Hagerstown, Maryland, the impetuous youth was severely wounded while leading a mounted charge through the streets of the town. His leg had to be amputated, and most thought he would not survive. President Lincoln arranged for young Dahlgren to receive a promotion to colonel as a reward for his valor. He survived and resumed his duties at the end of January 1864 as a twenty-one-year-old full colonel.

In February 1864, Dahlgren's long-held and deeply desired dream of leading a cavalry raid on Richmond finally came to pass. Dahlgren led one column of the raid while Kilpatrick led the other. This raid, which resembled that proposed by Dahlgren in May 1863, was intended to liberate Union prisoners of war held on Belle Isle and at Libby Prison. President Lincoln endorsed Dahlgren's scheme and agreed that Kilpatrick should lead the expedition, in part because of his visit to Hungary Station in May 1863 during the Stoneman Raid. Prophetically, Dahlgren wrote to his father, "[T]here is a grand raid to be made, and I am to have a very important command. If successful, it will be the grandest thing on record; and if it fails, many of us will 'go up.' I may be captured, or I may be 'tumbled over'; but it is an undertaking that if I were not in, I should be ashamed to show my face again. . . . If we do not return, there is no better place 'to give up the ghost.'"[38]

Dahlgren commanded a column of about 500 men during this expedition, known as the Kilpatrick-Dahlgren Raid. The raid met none of its objectives, and Dahlgren lost his life in the process. When papers were found on his body suggesting that the raid's actual mission was the kidnapping or execution of Jefferson Davis, the Virginians grew enraged. One cut off his finger and stole a ring, and his mutilated body was buried in a shallow grave along the road. The body was taken to Richmond on March 4 and secreted outside Oakwood Cemetery on March 6. On April 5, ardent Unionists led by Elizabeth "Crazy Bet"Van Lew exhumed the body and hid it at Hungary Station. In April 1865, after the end of the war, Union officers recovered his body, which was taken home to Philadelphia and buried in the family plot at Laurel Hill Cemetery. A colonel at twenty-one, his promising young life was snuffed out before he turned twenty-two. What this young man might have accomplished will never be known for certain, but he demonstrated all of the signs of becoming a truly great horse soldier.

The firestorm of controversy surrounding Dahlgren's death ended Judson Kilpatrick's tenure with the Army of the Potomac. After Dahlgren died, a Detroit newspaper wrote, "[Kilpatrick] cares nothing about the lives of his men, sacrificing them with cool indifference, his only object being his own promotion and keeping his name before the public."[39] In the spring of 1863, Captain Adams, always a keen observer, correctly predicted, "Kilpatrick is a brave injudicious boy, much given to blowing and who will surely come to grief."[40] One of Meade's staff officers offered a similar assessment in the aftermath of the failure of the raid: "He is a frothy braggart without brains and not over-stocked with the desire to fall on the field. He gets all his reputation by newspapers and political influence."[41] Upon hearing that there was to be a new commander of the Army of the Potomac's Cavalry Corps in the aftermath of the failed raid, a Confederate officer sneered, "What a pity the Yanks would not entrust their cavalry to that fool Kilpatrick. Of all the Yankee humbugs he is the greatest."[42]

The disgraced horse soldier, who had lost the confidence of his men, was banished to Maj. Gen. William T. Sherman's Army of Tennessee. After a modicum of success during the 1864 Atlanta Campaign, Lt. Gen. Wade Hampton's Confederate cavalry caught Kilpatrick unawares and unprepared at Monroe's Crossroads, North Carolina, in March 1865. When Hampton's horsemen slashed their way into his camps, the terrified cavalryman fled, dressed only in his drawers.[43] Kilpatrick, who always had an eye out for his own self-aggrandizement, later admitted, "I had been working hard for promotion to a major generalship, but when I heard the Rebel yell . . . in my camp, I said 'Well, after all these years, all is lost.'"[44]

A few weeks later, as the war was winding down, Gen. Joseph E. Johnston sent a messenger under flag of truce carrying a message that indicated that Johnston wanted to enter into negotiations with Sherman to surrender his Army of Tennessee. The messenger, one of Hampton's staff officers, entered into a bantering dialogue with Kilpatrick, wherein Kilpatrick expressed the opinion that his command had not been treated to a fair fight at Monroe's Crossroads due to the surprise attack. "Well, General," said the messenger, "I will make you the following proposition, and I will pledge you that General Hampton will carry it out in every respect. You, with your staff, take fifteen hundred men, and General Hampton, with his staff, will meet you with a thousand men, all to be armed with the saber alone. The two parties will be drawn up mounted in regimental formations, opposite to each other, and at a signal to be agreed upon will charge. That will settle the question which are the best men." Kilpatrick declined the invitation, but the point festered—"Little Kil's" pride had already been wounded.[45]

A few days later, Kilpatrick and Hampton met during a truce. The two generals started rehashing their old campaigns and tempers flared. Finally provoked, the big South Carolinian rose from his seat. Hampton towered over the diminutive Kilpatrick. "Well," he said, "you never ran me out of Headquarters in my stocking feet!"

Kilpatrick retorted that Hampton had to leave faster than he came, and their words grew increasingly heated. Fortunately, Johnston and Sherman heard the commotion and adjourned their conference before things got out of hand. The cavalrymen suggested that the war should be left to the cavalrymen, who would fight it out to a conclusion.[46] Although "Little Kil" received a promotion to major general of volunteers, he never found the glory he sought. He died a painful and lonely death from Bright's disease while in the foreign service in Bolivia. In the meantime, good, brave men like Elon Farnsworth needlessly sacrificed their lives in furtherance of Judson Kilpatrick's relentless hunt for personal fame and glory.

Although he had opposed the Kilpatrick-Dahlgren Raid, Alfred Pleasonton also became a casualty of its failure. He was already unpopular with the men of the Cavalry Corps before the failed raid. "Pleasonton is a perfect humbug," declared Charles Francis Adams in December 1863, "and had and does unnecessarily, cost the Government 20,000 horses a year."[47] The men had taken to calling him by the decidedly unflattering nickname of "The Knight of Romance," because of Pleasonton's tendency to distort the truth in order to make himself look better at all costs. "I can't call any cavalry officer good who can't see the truth and tell the truth," observed Col. Charles Russell Lowell, the Harvard-educated commander of the 2d Massachusetts Cavalry. "With an infantry officer this is not so essential, but cavalry are the eyes and ears of the army and ought to see and hear and tell truly; and yet it is the universal opinion that P's own reputation and P's late promotions are bolstered by systematic lying."[48]

Pleasonton had proposed the formation of the Cavalry Corps, and when Stoneman was appointed to command it instead of him, the stage was set for Pleasonton to scheme and intrigue, particular talents of his. The Army of the Potomac had an especially vigorous rumor mill. That winter, a rumor surfaced that Pleasonton would supplant Maj. Gen. George G. Meade in command of the Army. That unhappy prospect left most of the Cavalry Corps's officer cadre "in a great stew." A captain of the 6th Pennsylvania Cavalry proclaimed the idea "absurd," announcing that Pleasonton was "not fit to command a regt in active service," let alone an army.[49]

In the wake of the failed raid on Richmond, blizzards of bad press whirled around the headquarters of the Army of the Potomac. "Although the service now possesses a considerable number of more than respectable leaders of horse, we have no one of such preeminent distinction . . . [as to be] the fit head of all the cavalry of so great an army as that of the Potomac," wrote the *New York Times*. "John Buford came the nearest to it," continued the editorial, "if he did not actually snatch the laurels." It concluded that Pleasonton lacked "the qualities, mental and physical, that go into the composition of a first class cavalry leader."[50] At the behest of general-in-chief Lt. Gen. Ulysses S. Grant, General Meade promptly relieved Pleasonton of command of the Cavalry Corps. Although Meade had long protected Pleasonton from his many critics, the cavalryman testified against Meade's conduct of the Battle of Gettysburg before the Committee on the Conduct of the War, enraging the ill-tempered Meade, who rightfully felt betrayed.[51]

One cavalry officer noted that "[e]ven [Pleasonton's] success and the proofs he had given of the value of the cavalry, when properly used and led, were not sufficient to overcome the force of traditions and customs, and among higher authorities the idea still prevailed that the mounted force was secondary to, and should be used for the protection, convenience and relief of the infantry." He continued, "Serious difference of opinion on these questions between Generals Meade and Pleasonton had from time to time occurred, and at last had gone so far that the latter . . . could no longer retain his command."[52] Sheridan took his place, inheriting a fine body of horse that had constantly improved since the formation of the Cavalry Corps. Pleasonton was exiled to Missouri under the command of Maj. Gen. William S. Rosecrans, where Pleasonton brought Gen. Sterling Price's 1864 Missouri Raid to bay. At the end of the war, he received a brevet to major general in the Regular Army in recognition of his service throughout the war, but his tendency to make enemies finally caught up to him.

Pleasonton reverted to major, his Regular Army rank, and declined the lieutenant colonelcy of a new infantry regiment, preferring to remain in the cavalry. When this choice left him subordinate to two officers who were his junior, Pleasonton resigned his commission in an angry huff. He occupied some minor bureaucratic positions in Washington, D.C., but he never received either the credit or the glory he so vigorously advocated for himself.[53] However, in spite of his mean-spirited nature and relentless campaigns of self-promotion, Pleasonton deserves a great deal of credit for competently running the Cavalry Corps and for finding and promoting aggressive young officers who led the blueclad horse soldiers to glory in the last twelve months of the Civil War.

David M. Gregg was the only member of the high command of the Army of the Potomac's Cavalry Corps still in place in the spring of 1864. His troopers had met Jeb Stuart's men on Fleetwood Hill at Brandy Station and fought them to a standstill. When they met again at Gettysburg a few weeks later, Gregg's men carried the day's fighting. Soon, the quiet Pennsylvanian became the steadiest of the Cavalry Corps' subordinate officers. Although his seniority entitled him to take command of the Cavalry Corps after Pleasonton's relief, the high command passed him over in favor of an outsider with little experience commanding saddle soldiers.

In 1864, Major General Sheridan, who had only ninety days' experience commanding cavalry when he assumed command of the Cavalry Corps, relied heavily on the quiet, modest, and competent Pennsylvanian. "He was the only division commander I had whose experience had been almost exclusively derived from the cavalry arm," correctly noted Sheridan.[54] In July 1864, after the long and grueling Trevilian Raid, where Gregg's division was nearly destroyed at the Battle of Samaria Church, Sheridan requested that the Pennsylvanian be promoted to major general, a request that fell upon deaf ears.[55] Gregg led the Second Division until February of 1865, when he suddenly and unexpectedly resigned his commission, citing a need to tend to personal business. The courtly Gregg never stated the true reasons for his resignation, which remain a mystery to this day.[56] Sheridan wrote, "[I]t is to be regretted that he felt obliged a few months later to quite the service."[57] However, Gregg received a brevet to major general of volunteers in recognition of his long and dedicated service in the Cavalry Corps. No officer commanded a division in the Cavalry Corps longer or better than he.

In 1866, with the ringing endorsements of Generals Grant, Sheridan, Meade, and Winfield S. Hancock, Gregg applied for the colonelcy of one of the U.S. Army's new cavalry regiments. In spite of these glowing endorsements, Gregg did not get the appointment, and he never served in the military again.[58] Gregg settled in his wife's hometown of Reading, Pennsylvania, where he became one of that city's leading citizens. He remained active in community affairs until his death in 1916, and was a much-sought-after speaker at veterans' reunions and other similar events.[59] The steady Pennsylvanian was always dependable, both in the field and on the march. His dramatic victory over a much larger force of Jeb Stuart's cavalry on East Cavalry Field at Gettysburg on July 3, 1863, remains one of the brightest moments in the history of the Army of the Potomac's Cavalry Corps.[60] David Gregg's quiet competence and modesty endeared him to his men and earned him the respect of his Confederate foes.

No two men cast a longer shadow over the Army of the Potomac's Cavalry Corps in the spring of 1863 than did George Stoneman and William Woods Averell. These two lifelong Democrats and protégés of George B. McClellan were the subjects of Hooker's disgraceful conduct in the wake of his crushing defeat at Chancellorsville. Neither has received the credit that they deserve for their contributions to making the Cavalry Corps a viable and respected force for the Confederates to reckon with. Without the significant contributions of these two men, the Army of the Potomac's Cavalry Corps could not have achieved the great deeds it accomplished, beginning with the fights in the Loudoun Valley of Virginia that June and during the advance into Pennsylvania just before the Battle of Gettysburg. The Federal horse soldiers shattered Stuart's lines at Upperville on June 21, 1863, scoring their first major battlefield victory over the vaunted Southern horse soldiers. The Army of the Potomac's Cavalry Corps honed its craft and had its first successes under the stewardship of these two forgotten figures, who deserve a great deal of credit for its later triumphs.

After taking medical leave on May 15, 1863, Stoneman underwent an unsuccessful surgical procedure in an effort to alleviate his suffering with hemorrhoids. As he convalesced in Washington, a new opportunity arose. In the wake of the Gettysburg Campaign, the Cavalry Corps required a great number of replacement mounts as a result of the spring and summer's hard campaigning. In response, the War Department formed a Cavalry Bureau to coordinate all purchases of equipment and horses. Depots were to be established for "the reception, organization, and discipline of cavalry recruits and new regiments, and for the collection, care, and training of cavalry horses."[61] Stoneman was the logical choice to head this new bureau, and received the appointment on July 28, 1863.

"The functions of the Bureau were to supervise the Cavalry Service of the entire Army," wrote Brig. Gen. James H. Wilson, who succeeded Stoneman in command of the Cavalry Bureau, "to furnish it with horses, equipment and arms, and to do all in its power to promote its discipline and efficiency."[62] While a wonderful idea, it did not work well in practice. Unfortunately, Stoneman's Cavalry Bureau was plagued by rumors of graft and corruption. By the fall of 1863, Stoneman had wearied of the administrative duties associated with his new post and longed for active service in the field. He craved an opportunity to redeem himself in light of the failed Chancellorsville Campaign. When his old friend Maj. Gen. John Schofield took command of the Department of Ohio, he assigned Stoneman to command the department's cavalry, with instructions to prepare it to take the field. His horse soldiers played a significant role in Sherman's ambitious campaign to capture Atlanta.

In the spring of 1864, as Sherman prepared to march, Stoneman proposed taking 1,500 selected horse soldiers on a raid to free Union prisoners of war held at Andersonville and Macon. "I would like to try it," proclaimed Stoneman, who was eager to redeem his battered reputation, "and am willing to run any risks."[63] Sherman approved the operation, writing, "If you can bring back to the army any or all those prisoners of war it will be an achievement that will entitle you and the men of your command to the love and admiration of the whole country."[64]

The raid was to be part of a three-pronged operation intended to ring Atlanta with Federal horse soldiers. The plan went awry when Stoneman's tired troopers encountered heavy resistance from the Georgia Home Guards and militia defending Macon.[65] The delay meant that Brig. Gen. Alfred Iverson's Confederate cavalry division caught up to the raiders. As Iverson's horsemen closed in on the weary Federals, Stoneman realized that he would either have to surrender his command or try to fight his way out. Although some men managed to cut their way to safety, the general's exhausted horse was killed. Along with 500 horse soldiers, Stoneman and his loyal aide, Captain Keogh, were captured, making Stoneman the highest-ranking Union officer to suffer that unhappy fate.[66] To make matters worse, Sherman accused Stoneman of disobeying his orders. Late in September 1864, Stoneman was exchanged for Brig. Gen. Daniel C. Govan. The New Yorker then grew even more resolute in his drive to redeem himself.

Stoneman led a successful raid into southwestern Virginia to destroy the saltworks near Wytheville in late 1864, and then conducted the Civil War's final cavalry raid in Virginia and North Carolina in March 1865, reaching as far as Salisbury. His men nearly captured the fleeing Jefferson Davis deep in North Carolina. While his two daring and successful raids redeemed his reputation, he remained Hooker's principal scapegoat for the defeat at Chancellorsville for the rest of his life.

Stoneman received a promotion to lieutenant colonel in 1864, as well as a brevet to major general in the Regular Army and was appointed colonel of the 21st Infantry in 1866. In 1869, Stoneman was assigned to the headquarters of the District of Arizona. He somehow managed to have his headquarters changed to Drum Barracks in Los Angeles, which was not in his district. As a result, the boundaries of the district had to be redrawn. He moved his headquarters to Prescott, Arizona, for a time in the spring of 1870 when ordered to do so by the War Department, but by that October, he had returned to Drum Barracks for good. While commanding the Department of Arizona, Stoneman demonstrated a marked tendency for saying the wrong thing at the wrong time, a trait that eventually cost him his command. He was relieved of his duties on May 2, 1871.[67]

Upon his relief, Stoneman took retirement by reason of disability. In recognition of his many years of service, Stoneman was retired as a major general. However, when President Grant learned that the disability was Stoneman's long-standing hemorrhoid problem and not war wounds, the President had the promotion revoked, and Stoneman retired a colonel. He settled on an estate near San Marino, California. Stoneman served as railroad commissioner of California, and became very popular along the West Coast. The lifelong Democrat was elected to a four-year term as governor of California in 1882, but was not nominated for reelection.[68] "His administration was as stormy as the weather at Chancellorsville had been in April 1863," noted a modern biographer.[69]

In 1887, he asked for restoration to the retired list as a major general. However, adverse responses, largely resulting from his status as a wealthy landowner, prevented his wish from being granted. George Stoneman died in Buffalo, New York, on September 5, 1894, and was buried near his hometown in upstate New York. All of his pallbearers were civilians. He never received the credit that he deserved for his critical role in molding the Army of the Potomac's Cavalry Corps.[70]

William Woods Averell suffered a worse fate. At the end of May 1863, the disappointed cavalrymen took command of the cavalry forces attached to the Department of West Virginia. He took a ragtag force, trained it, and made it an effective command. His men conducted three long raids, including a daring, successful, and perilous winter foray to Salem, Virginia, that helped break the Confederate siege of Knoxville.[71] Then, in August 1864, when Sheridan assumed command of the Middle Military Division, Averell, the senior cavalry officer associated with the newly formed Army of the Shenandoah, was entitled to command of Sheridan's Cavalry Corps.

Unfortunately, the taint of the 1863 raid's failure preceded Sheridan's arrival in the Shenandoah Valley. When he wrote his orders to Sheridan, Grant stated, "Do not hesitate to give commands to officers in whom you repose confidence, without regard to claims of others on account of rank. If you deem [Brig. Gen. Alfred T. A.] Torbert the best man to command the cavalry, place him in command and give Averell some other command, or relieve him from the expedition, and order him to report to General [David] Hunter." The lieutenant general concluded, "What we want is prompt and active movements after the enemy, in accordance with instructions you already have."[72] These orders created great problems as the campaign developed.

Sheridan chose Torbert. Years later, instead of admitting that he had selected Torbert himself, Sheridan blamed Grant, who was not alive to defend himself. "Little Phil" (as Sheridan was sometimes referred to) claimed, "When I was assigned to the command of the 'Middle Military Division' I had determined in my own mind to make General Averell my Chief of Cavalry. I knew him to be a thorough Soldier, and his success in the valley had won for him the position as the leading cavalry officer in the service, and with his knowledge of the country, he was in my judgment well qualified for this position." He continued, "In consulting with General Grant in relation to my new field, he specially requested me to assign General Torbert to that position." "Little Phil" claimed that he brought the question of Averell's seniority to Grant's attention, but that Grant insisted upon Torbert's appointment.[73] Sheridan's ex post facto rationalization of his conduct does not hold up under scrutiny, particularly because it directly contradicts the express language of Grant's orders.

In truth, Sheridan probably was prejudiced against Averell from the start. Sheridan's principal lieutenant, best friend, and West Point roommate, Maj. Gen. George Crook, did not like Averell and blamed the New Yorker for his defeat at Second Kernstown in July 1864. Crook said that Averell had been accused of getting drunk during the fight. "Our cavalry was of little or no assistance," claimed Crook. He blamed Averell's horse soldiers for stampeding, adding to the magnitude of the debacle.[74] Crook's opinions undoubtedly influenced Sheridan's handling of Averell's situation.[75]

"Major General Sheridan illegally assumed the prerogative of the President of the United States," complained Averell, "and ordered me to report to a junior officer on the 23d of August without any just cause."[76] On September 1, Grant responded to Sheridan: "The frequent reports of Averell falling back without much fighting or even skirmishing and afterwards being able to take his old position without opposition, presents a very bad appearance at this distance. You can judge better of his merits than I can, but it looks to me as if it was time to try some other officer in his place. If you think as I do in this matter, relieve him at once and name his successor."[77] Averell's constant protesting certainly did not endear him to "Little Phil," who began looking for reasons to relieve Averell of command. As the campaign developed, Sheridan grew increasingly unhappy with Averell's lack of aggression, even though Averell's troopers performed admirably at Third Winchester, where his men badly wounded Fitz Lee within sight of Averell.

Averell's horse soldiers participated in the successful assault on Fisher's Hill on September 22, 1864, coordinating and cooperating with Crook's crushing flank attack. They did not follow up on the successes of the attack with a vigorous pursuit because they really had nowhere to go. When Averell arrived at Sheridan's headquarters the next day, the army commander erupted. "We had some hot words," recounted Sheridan in his memoirs.[78] Sheridan demanded to know where Averell had been and asked why he had not pursued Rebel Lt. Gen. Jubal Early's beaten army during the night. Averell informed Sheridan that he had not received orders or information from headquarters. Sheridan exploded, declaring that he could not locate the horse soldier. Averell testily responded by asking whether Sheridan had even tried to find him. Livid, Sheridan described Early's army as "a perfect mob" which would disintegrate in the face of a vigorous pursuit. James Bowen, the chaplain of the 19th New York Cavalry, witnessed this exchange. "It can be stated from positive knowledge that while Averell maintained a calm and civil demeanor," recounted Bowen, "Sheridan manifested unreasonable anger, refusing to listen to any explanations."[79] "The tone, manner, and words of the major-general commanding indicated and implied dissatisfaction," complained

Averell in his report. "I did not entertain the opinion that the rebel army was a mob." Nevertheless, Sheridan instructed Averell to join Devin's brigade in pursuing the beaten Confederates.[80]

Just to make sure that he had driven the point home, Sheridan dispatched written instructions to Averell on September 23. "I do not want you to let the enemy bluff you or your command," warned Sheridan, "and I want you to distinctly understand this note. I do not advise recklessness, but I do desire resolution and actual fighting with necessary casualties, before you retire. There must now be no backing or filling by you without a superior force of the enemy engaging you."[81] Sheridan's warning could not have been more unambiguous.

With Early's entire army in front of him, Averell properly decided that the enemy position atop Rood's Hill was too strong to attack. Devin and Averell instead deployed their men along the Confederate front and watched Early's preparations for the day. Enraged, Sheridan exercised the discretion given him by Grant on September 1, and removed Averell from command two days later. "I have relieved Averell from his command," stormed Sheridan. "Instead of following the enemy when he was broken at Fisher's Hill (so there was not a cavalry organization left), he went into camp and let me pursue the enemy for a distance of fifteen miles with infantry, during the night."[82]

Sheridan claimed that Averell's "indifferent attack" was not worthy of "the excellent soldiers he commanded." Later, Sheridan wrote in his memoirs, "The removal of Averell was but the culmination of a series of events extending back to the time I assumed command of the Middle Military Division . . . I therefore thought that the interest of the service would be subserved by removing one whose growing indifference might render the best-laid plans inoperative."[83]

That night, Sheridan's assistant adjutant general delivered an order to Averell. "Bvt. Maj. Gen. W. W. Averell, commanding Second Cavalry Division, Department of West Virginia, is relieved from duty with that command and will at once proceed to Wheeling, W.Va.," Sheridan had written. Averell was "there to await orders from these headquarters or higher authority." Sheridan only permitted Averell to take his personal staff with him, and a colonel took command of his division.[84] The flabbergasted Averell rightly believed the removal to be unjustified.

Stunned and dismayed, Averell "called the officers together and addressed them, enjoining upon them to continue as energetic and attentive in the future as they had been in the past, and to yield the same obedience to his successor as they had to him." The men of his division were very fond of Averell, and his relief "caused a universal feeling of amazement in [the] army, and it is thought that some question of rank between General Averell and General Torbert is involved," reported a correspondent of the New York Herald. A member of the 14th Pennsylvania Cavalry recalled, "The release of General Averell was a great surprise to his command who loved him greatly. He was the very idol of the 14th [Pennsylvania] Cavalry whom he had led into nearly two-score battles, nearly one hundred skirmishes, and more than three-score charges."[85]

James E. Taylor, another newspaper correspondent, watched Averell's departure from Sheridan's camps. The "sight of a big blond general on horseback" caught Taylor's eye, and the correspondent watched Averell in "earnest conversation with a dismounted officer." Taylor had never seen Averell before, and the sight intrigued him. "It was with feelings of melancholy interest I observed him," commented the correspondent, "while speculating on the uncertainties of a military career, for his, up to a fortnight back, was full of promise. Now he clasps his friend's hand and rides away."[86] Sheridan exiled Averell to Wheeling to await further orders that never came. William Woods Averell never commanded troops in the field again.

When he wrote his report of the campaign, Averell was understandably bitter. He believed that Sheridan's order relieving him of command "tramped upon . . . [his] record and upon all military courtesy and justice." The unhappy general continued, "I have evidence that it was determined to relieve me in order to make Brigadier-General Torbert chief of cavalry before Major-General Sheridan assumed command of the Middle Military Division." He suggested that Sheridan had deliberately refused to acknowledge Averell's contributions to the Union victories at Third Winchester and Fisher's Hill.[87]

Averell could never forgive or forget the injustice done him by Sheridan, and he carried a grudge against "Little Phil" for ruining an otherwise distinguished military record. As a McClellan Democrat in the days just before the 1864 presidential election, Averell firmly believed that his relief was politically motivated. Five years after the end of the war, the two men had a chance encounter at a social event. Although social graces prevented Averell from showing his contempt in public, he nevertheless gave Sheridan a piece of his mind in a subsequent letter: "I was the victim of a grievous wrong or great mistake and I cannot permit you to entertain the impression from our exchange of civilities this morning that I am willing to resume friendly intercourse with you until some explanation from you of your actions on the occasion I have referred to has been received by me."[88]

The removal had devastated Averell and ended his military career. The New Yorker resigned his commission on March 18, 1865, claiming that his years of service had left him partially and permanently disabled from combat wounds, and that he chose to resign rather than remain "as an inefficient subaltern from the above noted disqualifying causes." Apparently regretting his decision later, Averell attempted, and failed, to obtain an appointment as colonel of one of the newly formed Regular cavalry regiments in 1866. When that effort foundered, he accepted an appointment as consul general to Montreal, a position he held from 1866 to 1869.[89]

In January 1879, in recognition of his dedicated service to the Union, Congress passed special legislation to give the President the power to place Averell on the Army's roll of retired brigadier generals. The Army successfully resisted the implementation of this legislation, however, and Averell was not placed on the roll—perhaps the final insult manipulated by a still-spiteful Sheridan.[90] Instead, in 1888, Congress enacted legislation that placed the New Yorker on the rolls as a retired captain, his Regular Army rank, which at least permitted him to draw a pension.[91]

Over the years, the general had accumulated a sizable interest in the Barber Asphalt Paving Co., which held a number of valuable patents necessary to the art of road building. Unfortunately, Averell had to sue to obtain his share of the profits, and the litigation dragged on until June 1898, when the former horse soldier was awarded the magnificent sum of $700,000. Averell only got to enjoy this bounty for a short time. He died on February 3, 1900, at his home in Bath, New York.[92]

"Sheridan's action shattered Averell in a way that physical damage incurred by bullets or fever during the war had not," claimed the editors of Averell's memoirs. "For the rest of his life he would try to refute this action and gather evidence to substantiate his belief that the removal was politically rather than militarily motivated."[93] The episode caused Averell so much pain that he could never address it when he wrote his memoirs long after the end of the Civil War. He spent years trying to get a satisfactory explanation but never succeeded. Nevertheless, Averell did get a modicum of satisfaction in the years after war. Several people reported to him that Sheridan regretted his actions in relieving Averell and that he had come to view them as a mistake.

Sheridan's justifications do not hold up under scrutiny. He claimed that the awkward command structure of having Averell report directly to him had created problems of command, control, and coordination: "I found it impossible to successfully direct the movements of my army without a Chief of Cavalry. I was compelled to relieve General Averell against my judgment, and personal preference." Astonishingly, Sheridan also boldly claimed, "I regarded Averell as a superior officer over Torbert. I have always regretted my action on General Averell's account and also for the reason that General Torbert failed to come up to the standard, and I was finally compelled to assign General Merritt to this position."[94] This postwar spin directly contradicts Sheridan's contemporary words and suggests that he was merely trying to mollify Averell, who remained deeply offended by the injustice of his removal from command. In fact, Sheridan never apologized to Averell, and he never did anything to right the wrong he perpetrated by relieving the New Yorker of command.

While Sheridan may not have appreciated Averell's skills, the government recognized and appreciated them, as well as his many contributions to the Union victory in the Civil War. Averell's principal attributes—discipline and caution—caused him to run afoul of Sheridan. The editors of Averell's memoirs noted, "William Averell was not a failure during the Civil War; he was a victim of change. He had been just what the army needed early in the conflict—disciplined, capable and cautious. He took untrained horsemen and molded them into a cavalry force of which any commander could be proud." Even though his career ended in disgrace like his mentor McClellan's, Averell, like McClellan, remained popular with the men who served under him. Those horsemen carried an abiding fondness for him for the rest of their lives.[95]

Averell's "greatest flaw might have been that he was an outsider, an officer not associated with the Cavalry Corps of the Army of the Potomac," observed historian Jeffry D. Wert in commenting upon the New Yorker's relief by Sheridan.[96] By contrast, Averell's West Point classmate Torbert, who was closely associated with the Army of the Potomac's Cavalry Corps, was guilty of the same sin that cost Averell his command. Torbert failed to make a vigorous pursuit of the beaten Confederates and had halted in front of New Market instead of assaulting a strong defensive position held by Col. Thomas T. Munford's Confederate cavalry brigade. When he wrote his report of the campaign in 1866, Sheridan publicly complained about Torbert's performance: "Had General Torbert driven this cavalry or turned the defile and reached New Market, I have no doubt but that we would have captured the entire rebel army. I feel certain that its rout from Fisher's Hill was such that there was scarcely a company organization held together."[97]

In his memoirs, Sheridan accused Torbert of making "only a feeble effort." While admitting that Munford held a formidable defensive position, Sheridan believed that "Torbert ought to have made a fight." In Sheridan's eyes, not even the strong Confederate defensive position excused his chief of cavalry's lack of aggressiveness. "To this day," he wrote years later, "I have been unable to account satisfactorily for Torbert's failure."[98] In spite of the same failures that he had punished Averell for, Sheridan did not censure his corps commander. Instead, Torbert remained in command of the Army of the Shenandoah's Cavalry Corps until the end of February of 1865.

Considering that Torbert's failure was worse, that Torbert received unequal treatment at Sheridan's hands, and that Averell's decision not to attack was a prudent and well-reasoned one, one must conclude that the harsh penalty meted out by Sheridan was unwarranted and unjust, at the high price of Averell's military career. It may also have brought about the resignation of David M. Gregg in February 1865. Fortunately, Averell had a successful career after the Civil War, and he became a very wealthy man, somewhat ameliorating the sting of Sheridan's actions. However, with his military career in ruins, Averell, in spite of his wealth, never fully recovered. Because of the ignominious endings to his two major cavalry commands, Averell never received the recognition or respect that he deserved. The Army of the Potomac's Cavalry Corps owed a great debt to the New Yorker, who merited a better fate than scapegoat and certainly deserved the respect of history.

As for the horse soldiers of the Army of the Potomac's Cavalry Corps, the spring of 1863 marked the true turning point for their fortunes. During the first two years of the Civil War, they had learned to be cavalrymen. They had mastered the traditional roles of the cavalry: reconnaissance, screening, covering the army's flanks and rear, attacking in shock charges against the enemy's infantry to rout them, supporting headquarters, and interdicting lines of supply and communication. Although the saddle soldiers of the Army of the Potomac learned to fight dismounted early in their training, the concept of massing cavalry and using it as an offensive striking force was a new approach.

Joseph Hooker's foresight in adopting Pleasonton's organizational plan—consolidating his cavalry into a single, cohesive command and putting it in the hands of veteran, capable officers—was the watershed event in the history of the Cavalry Corps. It marked the first time that Union horse soldiers were allowed to operate as an independent striking force. Beginning with Averell's foray across the Rappahannock River at Kelly's Ford in March 1863 and continuing with the tribulations of Stoneman's Raid, the blueclad horsemen slowly earned the grudging respect of their Southern counterparts. By Brandy Station, the myth of the invincibility of the Confederate cavalry had been shattered, and the Northern horse soldiers had learned to believe in themselves. At Upperville, on June 21, 1863, the Union horsemen scored their first true battlefield victory, breaking Stuart's lines and sending his troopers fleeing for safety under the protection of Lt. Gen. James Longstreet's infantry. But for some brilliant screening work by Jeb Stuart and his Rebel cavaliers, the Cavalry Corps might have detected the passage of the Army of Northern Virginia into Pennsylvania.

At Gettysburg, the Federal cavalrymen performed admirably. Buford's men made a stout stand on the first day of the battle, holding off a much larger force of enemy infantry long enough for reinforcements to arrive. Gregg's division did a marvelous job of protecting the Army of the Potomac's flank at Gettysburg, scoring a victory over Stuart's much larger force on East Cavalry Field on July 3, 1863, when they successfully repulsed Stuart's attempt to turn the Union flank.

During the retreat from Gettysburg, the Northern cavalry pursued the Army of Northern Virginia to the banks of the Potomac River. Their fine work continued throughout the rest of the summer and fall of 1863. Although the Cavalry Corps required a major reorganization in the spring of 1864, the Federal horsemen conducted five major raids and operated as an independent command for much of the summer's campaigning season. Unfortunately, history repeated itself in May 1864, when Grant sent the entire Cavalry Corps off on an extended raid on Richmond that left the Army of the Potomac without a cavalry screen. The lack of a cavalry force to gather intelligence caused the Union army to fight a protracted campaign of attrition. Grant had failed to learn a lesson from Hooker's debacle at Chancellorsville.

The Northern cavalrymen evolved into effective dragoons. They learned to fight and scout, and they believed in their ability to make an impact on the ultimate outcome of the war. By the end of the Civil War, the Federal cavalry was the largest and finest mounted force that the world had ever seen. In 1865, Maj. Gen. James H. Wilson took the field with a 15,000-man army made up entirely of cavalrymen, marking the first truly mobile strike force in history.[100] His horsemen fought equally well mounted or dismounted, and it did not matter whether they faced cavalry or infantry.

Wilson savored the success of his command, which resulted in the capture of Confederate President Jefferson Davis and in their being the only unit to defeat the vaunted mounted forces of Lt. Gen. Nathan Bedford Forrest. Wilson proudly proclaimed, "I regard this corps today as the model for modern cavalry in the organization, equipment, armament, and discipline, and hazard nothing in saying that it embodies more of the virtues of the three arms, without any sacrifice of those of cavalry, than any similar number of men in the world."[101] The Union cavalry of the Civil War became the prototype for the armored juggernauts of the modern era.

This evolution had begun with the formation of the Cavalry Corps in the winter of 1863, when the Federal mounted arm first mastered its trade under the command of such forgotten and unappreciated figures as George Stoneman and William Woods Averell, who had been there from the beginning of the war. The blueclad horsemen learned to believe in themselves and in their ability to make a significant contribution to the outcome of the war. Their service in the arduous campaigns of the spring of 1863 marked the turning point, and they met the challenge first with the seminal Battle of Kelly's Ford on March 17, 1863. They learned hard lessons that paid dividends for them on many fields for the balance of the war. Steely, competent officers emerged and assumed positions of authority and responsibility in the hierarchy of the Cavalry Corps as the cream rose to the top. They learned their trade under the guidance of men like Stoneman, Averell, Buford, Gregg, and Devin, and they employed those lessons to make a decisive impact on the ultimate Union victory in the Civil War.

Perhaps no Union trooper enunciated the bright prospects for the Army of the Potomac's Cavalry Corps in the spring of 1863 better than did the eloquent Capt. Charles Francis Adams, Jr. In the heady days following the Stoneman Raid, Adams correctly proclaimed, "As for the cavalry, its future is just opening and great names will be won in the cavalry from this day forward."[102] The brightest days for the Union mounted arm lay ahead.

NOTES

1. O.R., vol. 27, part 3, 64.

2. Ibid.; McIntosh to his wife, May 13, 1863, McIntosh Letters.

3. Ford, *A Cycle of Adams Letters,* 2:22.

4. Alfred Pleasonton to John F. Farnsworth, June 23, 1863, Alfred Pleasonton Papers, Manuscripts Division, Library of Congress, Washington, D.C.

5. George Bliss, *The First Rhode Island Cavalry at Middleburg* (Providence, R.I.: privately published, 1889), 48.

6. For a detailed examination, see O'Neill, *Cavalry Battles of Aldie, Middleburg and Upperville,* 66–76.

7. John S. Mosby, *Stuart's Cavalry in the Gettysburg Campaign* (New York: Moffatt, Yard, 1908), 71.

8. Abraham Lincoln to Edwin M. Stanton, June 22, 1863, Pearce Civil War Collection, Navarro College Archives, Corsicana, Tex.

9. O.R., vol. 37, part 2, 896–97.

10. *New York Times,* October 7, 1864.

11. O.R., vol. 43, part 2, 475.

12. In 1869, Grant appointed Duffié U.S. consul to Spain, and sent him to Cadiz, on the Iberian Peninsula's southwest seacoast. While he served in Spain, the Frenchman contracted tuberculosis, which claimed his life in 1880. Because of his conviction for desertion, Duffié never was able to return to his native France. His body was brought home and buried in his wife's family plot in Fountain Cemetery in Staten Island, N.Y. Unfortunately, the cemetery was abandoned long ago, and the grave is badly overgrown with vegetation. It is nearly impossible to find, and is as forgotten to history as the proud soldier that rests there. The veterans of the 1st Rhode Island Cavalry, who remained loyal to their former commander, raised money to erect a handsome monument to Duffié in the North Burying Ground in Providence. Capt. George Bliss, who commanded a squadron in the 1st Rhode Island, wrote a lengthy and eloquent tribute to Duffié that was published and distributed to the veterans of the regiment. See Bliss, "Duffié and the Monument to His Memory."

13. Di Cesnola to Hiram Hitchcock, May 24, 1863, di Cesnola Papers. A few days later, di Cesnola wrote of McClellan, "If he were tomorrow to come back he would be by all the regimental officers and men received as our father; he would electrify our hearts now cold more than ever and he would give a new life to the whole Army of the Potomac who does not want a better leader than their beloved McClellan. A general so young and who enjoys such formidable popularity cannot be but a good General and in my heart, in my conviction he is & will ever be far the best General that this Government may boast of." Di Cesnola to Hitchcock, May 28, 1863, di Cesnola Papers.

14. For more information on di Cesnola's Medal of Honor, see W. F. Beyer and O. F. Keydel, eds., *Deeds of Valor: How America's Heroes Won the Medal of Honor,* 2 vols. (Detroit, Mich.: Perrien-Keydel, 1903), 1:212.

15. O'Neill, *Cavalry Battles of Aldie, Middleburg and Upperville,* 45–56. For a sketch of the count's service in the Civil War, see Frank Alduino and David J. Coles, "Luigi Palma

di Cesnola: An Italian American in the Civil War," *Italian American Review* 7, no. 1 (winter/spring 2000): 1–26. Di Cesnola had a fascinating career after the Civil War. At the end of the war, he published an account of his time as a prisoner of war in Libby Prison. Luigi Palma di Cesnola, *Ten Months in Libby Prison* (n.p., 1865). In 1865, di Cesnola, now a naturalized American citizen, was appointed consul general to Lanarca, Cyprus, while the island was occupied by the Ottoman Empire. He remained there until 1876, illegally acquiring a large collection of antiquities taken from Cypriot tombs, which he removed to the United States. He wrote a well-regarded book about his excavations and archaeological studies of the island, and his vast collection of nearly 5,000 items is on display in Harvard University's Semitic Museum. He also wrote a lengthy description of the collection when it was placed on display. See Luigi Palma di Cesnola, *Cyprus: Its Ancient Cities, Tombs, and Temples* (New York: Harper & Brothers, 1878); and *A Descriptive Atlas of the Cesnola Collection of Cypriote Antiquities in the Metropolitan Museum of Art, New York,* 3 vols. (Boston: J. R. Osgood, 1885–1903). The count sold his collection to the new Metropolitan Museum in New York, and then became the museum's first director in 1879, a position that he held until his death on November 21, 1904, at the age of seventy-two. Di Cesnola's excavations remain an unhappy chapter in the history of Cyprus, which still views the collection as property of the State of Cyprus. The Italian count, almost 100 years after his death, is often viewed as a grave robber by Cypriots. There is one full-length biography of di Cesnola. See McFadden, *Glitter and the Gold.* For an interesting view of the development of the di Cesnola collection and catalogue of the collection from the Cypriot point of view, see Anna G. Marangou, *The Consul Luigi Palma Di Cesnola 1832–1904: Life and Deeds* (Nicosia, Cyprus: Cultural Centre of the Popular Bank, 2000).

16. John Buford to Alfred Pleasonton, September 16, 1863, Pearce Civil War Collection. Buford wrote, "I have just returned from my extreme front line and arranged it for the night. Just before sundown the Rebs made a dash after the squadron that had the extreme front at Raccoon Ford and captured the whole of it. The two squadrons in rear and under good cover and in easy support ran off and nearly returned to camp without firing a shot or being fired upon. This is the conduct of the 4th N.Y. Cav.— The Regt that came from Gen. Gregg—And the one that you have heard me say long ago I could not trust. It failed me awfully at Bull Run. As soon as I can get in a statement of the affair I will forward it and ask for the dismissal of all concerned. This mishap is owing entirely to the carelessness of the commanders of the Regt. Command." In fairness, when this incident occurred, di Cesnola was still a prisoner of war in Libby Prison.

17. Warner, *Generals in Blue,* 469.
18. Pleasonton to Farnsworth, June 23, 1863, Pleasonton Papers.
19. Elon J. Farnsworth to John F. Farnsworth, June 23, 1863, Pleasonton Papers.
20. O.R., vol. 27, part 3, 376. In spite of this shabby treatment, Stahel continued to render good service, commanding a division of cavalry assigned to Maj. Gen. David Hunter's Army of the Shenandoah. Stahel received a Medal of Honor for his valor at the June 5, 1864, Battle of Piedmont. His Medal of Honor citation reads, "Led his division into action until he was severely wounded." For more on the Battle of Piedmont, where

Confederate Gen. William E. "Grumble" Jones died while leading a mounted charge, see Scott C. Patchan, *The Forgotten Fury: The Battle of Piedmont, Virginia* (Fredericksburg, Va.: Sergeant Kirkland's Museum and Historical Society, 1996). In a remarkable stroke of irony, Alfred Duffié took Stahel's place in command of the division. Pleasonton had been exiled to Kansas by then, his place at the head of the Cavalry Corps taken by Maj. Gen. Philip H. Sheridan.

21. Warner, *Generals in Blue,* 300.

22. O.R., vol. 27, part 3, 373.

23. O'Neill, *Cavalry Battles of Aldie, Middleburg and Upperville,* 60.

24. Wert, *Custer,* 79.

25. For a detailed examination of Farnsworth's Charge and death, see Eric J. Wittenberg, *Gettysburg's Forgotten Cavalry Actions* (Gettysburg, Pa.: Thomas, 1998).

26. O.R., vol. 27, part 1, 993.

27. Warner, *Generals in Blue,* 321–22. The only full-length biography of Wesley Merritt is Don E. Alberts, *Brandy Station to Manila Bay: A Biography of General Wesley Merritt* (Austin, Tex.: Presidial Press, 1980).

28. O.R., vol. 30, part 4, 9; Cullum, *Officers and Graduates of the U.S. Military Academy,* 2:355. Maj. Gen. William S. Rosecrans, the commander of the Army of the Cumberland, specifically requested that Buford be transferred to the Western Theatre to take command of the Army of the Cumberland's Cavalry Corps.

29. George R. Agassiz, ed., *Meade's Headquarters 1863–1865: Letters of Colonel Theodore Lyman from the Wilderness to Appomattox* (Boston: Atlantic Monthly Press, 1922), 50.

30. Myles W. Keogh, "Etat de Service of Major Gen. John Buford," Special Collections, U.S. Military Academy, West Point, N.Y.

31. Abraham Lincoln to Edwin M. Stanton, December 16, 1863, Special Collections, U.S. Military Academy, West Point, N.Y.

32. See Buford's oath of office, dated December 16, 1863, Microfilm M1064, Letters received by the Commissions Branch of the Adjutant General's Office, 1863–1870, roll 9, file no. B1115, CB 1863, National Archives.

33. See letter to Edwin M. Stanton, December 16, 1863, written for Buford by Capt. A. J. Alexander, ibid.

34. Ibid.; see also Richard Kehoe letter to Tom Keogh, January 1, 1864, Brian C. Pohanka Collection, Alexandria, Va. The men of Buford's First Division all contributed at least one dollar, and a handsome monument was erected on their beloved commander's grave.

35. Gibbon, "The John Buford Memoir."

36. Hagemann, *Fighting Rebels and Redskins,* 215.

37. Warner, *Generals in Blue,* 124.

38. Ulric Dahlgren to his father, February 26, 1864, Dahlgren Papers.

39. *Detroit Free Press,* March 26, 1864.

40. Ford, *A Cycle of Adams Letters,* 2:44–45.

41. Agassiz, *Meade's Headquarters,* 79.

42. Joseph F. Waring diary, entry for April 12, 1864, Joseph F. Waring Papers, Southern Historical Collection, Wilson Historical Library, University of North Carolina, Chapel Hill.

43. Kilpatrick was apparently *in flagrante delicto* with a young woman who was not his wife at the time that the Confederate surprise attack fell upon his camps. For the most detailed examination of the war's final campaign, see Mark L. Bradley's fine book *Last Stand in the Carolinas: The Battle of Bentonville* (Campbell, Calif.: Savas-Woodbury, 1996).

44. Martin, *Kill-Cavalry,* 222.

45. Wellman, *Giant in Gray,* 181.

46. Mark L. Bradley, *This Astounding Close: The Road to Bennett Place* (Chapel Hill: University of North Carolina Press, 2000), 160–62.

47. Ford, *A Cycle of Adams Letters,* 2:111.

48. Edward W. Emerson, *The Life and Letters of Charles Russell Lowell* (Boston: Houghton-Mifflin, 1907), 279.

49. Charles B. Coxe to John Cadwalader, Jr., December 10, 1863, Charles P. Coxe Papers, Historical Society of Pennsylvania, Philadelphia.

50. *New York Times,* March 29, 1864.

51. "This evening an order has arrived relieving General Pleasonton, which, although I did not originate it, yet was, I presume, brought about by my telling the Secretary that the opposition that I had hitherto made to his removal I no longer should make," reported General Meade in a letter to his wife. "As the Secretary has been desirous of relieving him ever since I have had command, and I have been objecting, he has taken the first chance to remove him as soon as my objections were withdrawn." Meade, *Life and Letters,* 2:182–83.

52. Henry E. Davies, *General Sheridan* (New York: D. Appleton, 1895), 92–93. Lt. Gen. Ulysses S. Grant, the new commander in chief of the Union armies, went out of his way not to criticize Pleasonton in his memoirs. Speaking of Pleasonton's relief from command of the Cavalry Corps, Grant wrote, "It was not a reflection on that officer, however, for I did not know but that he had been as efficient as any other cavalry commander." Ulysses S. Grant, *Personal Memoirs* (New York: Library of America, 1990), 481.

53. Warner, *Generals in Blue,* 374.

54. Philip H. Sheridan, *Personal Memoirs of P. H. Sheridan,* 2 vols. (New York: Charles L. Webster, 1888), 1:352.

55. Philip H. Sheridan to Edwin M. Stanton, July 10, 1864, David M. Gregg Appointments, Commissions, and Pension (ACP) File, National Archives.

56. Gregg and William Woods Averell were West Point classmates and good friends. They had been friends for fifteen years in the fall of 1864 when Sheridan relieved Averell of command without justification. In February 1865, Gregg's division was with the Army of the Potomac in the siege lines at Petersburg when Grant learned that Sheridan and his two divisions of cavalry were going to return to the Army of the Potomac. The author believes that Gregg may have resigned in order to avoid having to serve under the man who had ruined the military career of his long-time friend, Averell. Gregg simply might have found the prospect of serving under Sheridan again so unpalatable that he may have felt that he had no choice but to resign from the army. This unfortunate decision meant that Gregg missed the end of the war and his moment of

appreciation at the Grand Review in Washington, D.C., where the victorious Army of the Potomac passed before a grateful nation for a last hurrah in May 1865. Unlike so many of his comrades, including his cousin Irvin Gregg, David Gregg never served in the military again. The issue of Averell's relief by Sheridan is addressed at length later in this chapter.

57. Sheridan, *Memoirs,* 1:435.

58. See various letters contained in the David M. Gregg ACP file, including Winfield S. Hancock to the Adjutant General, January 31, 1866, and George G. Meade to the Adjutant General, January 13, 1866.

59. Warner, *Generals in Blue,* 188.

60. For a detailed examination of Gregg's role at the Battle of Gettysburg, see Eric J. Wittenberg, *Protecting the Flank: The Battles for Brinkerhoff's Ridge and East Cavalry Field, Gettysburg, Pennsylvania* (Celina, Ohio: Ironclad, 2002).

61. O.R. series 3, vol. 3, 580. For additional information of the important role played by the Cavalry Bureau, see Keith Poulter, "The Cavalry Bureau," *North & South* 2 (January 1999): 70–71.

62. Wilson, *Andrew Jonathan Alexander,* 46.

63. O.R., vol. 28, part 5, 264.

64. Ibid., 265.

65. William T. Sherman, *Memoirs of General W. T. Sherman* (New York: Library of America, 1990), 571.

66. John P. Langellier, Kurt Hamilton Cox, and Brian C. Pohanka, eds., *Myles Keogh: The Life and Legend of an "Irish Dragoon" in the Seventh Cavalry* (El Segundo, Calif.: Upton and Sons, 1991), 81.

67. Constance Wynn Altshuler, *Cavalry Yellow & Infantry Blue: Army Officers in Arizona between 1851 and 1886* (Tucson, Ariz.: Arizona Historical Society, 1991), 321–22.

68. Ibid., 322.

69. Waugh, *Class of 1846,* 527.

70. Altshuler, *Cavalry Yellow & Infantry Blue,* 322; Warner, *Generals in Blue,* 481–82.

71. For a detailed analysis of Averell's Salem Raid, see Collins, *General William Averell's Salem Raid.*

72. O.R., vol. 43, part 1, 719.

73. W. Blakely to T. R. Kerr, March 18, 1889, Averell Papers.

74. Martin F. Schmitt, ed., *General George Crook: His Autobiography* (Norman: University of Oklahoma Press, 1960), 123.

75. When he penned his postwar memoirs, Crook used an interesting choice of words in describing Averell's subsequent removal from command: "Gen. Averell had been retired, and Col. W. H. Powell had his command." Ibid., 132.

76. O.R., vol. 43, part 1, 500–01.

77. Grant to Sheridan, September 1, 1864, Averell ACP file.

78. Sheridan, *Personal Memoirs,* 2:43.

79. James R. Bowen, *Regimental History of the First New York Dragoons* (Battle Creek, Mich.: privately published, 1900), 240.

80. O.R., vol. 43, part 1, 500.

81. Ibid., 505.

82. Ibid., part 2, 171.

83. Sheridan, *Personal Memoirs,* 2:44–45.

84. O.R., vol. 43, part 1, 505.

85. William Davis Slease, *The Fourteenth Pennsylvania Cavalry in the Civil War: A History of the Fourteenth Pennsylvania Volunteer Cavalry from Its Organization until the Close of the Civil War, 1961–1865* (Pittsburgh: Soldiers' and Sailors' Memorial Hall and Military Museum, 1999), 194.

86. Taylor, *Sketchbook,* 458.

87. O.R., vol. 43, part 1, 500–01.

88. Eckert and Amato, *Ten Years in the Saddle,* 400.

89. Altshuler, *Cavalry Yellow & Infantry Blue,* 13.

90. Averell ACP File, various entries, including copies of H.R. 5959 and S. 1623 of January 1879, the legislation authorizing placing Averell on the list of retired brigadier generals. The hierarchy of the Army resisted the appointment, claiming that the list was reserved for only those officers who retired due to age or term of service, and that those claiming disability had to have their applications approved by the President. Averell did not do so, so the Adjutant General's office prepared a lengthy report that objected: "There is no precedent for such a law, and it may not be considered that Gen. Averell has any greater claims for recognition in this way than other general officers of volunteers, who made distinguished records and were badly wounded in the war." See Report of the Adjutant General, January 22, 1879, Averell ACP File.

91. Averell ACP file.

92. Altshuler, *Cavalry Yellow & Infantry Blue,* 13.

93. Eckert and Amato, *Ten Years in the Saddle,* 401.

94. Blakely to Kerr, March 18, 1889. Several similar accounts also found their way back to Averell, but Sheridan never apologized to Averell for his actions.

95. Eckert and Amato, *Ten Years in the Saddle,* 403.

96. Jeffry D. Wert, *From Winchester to Cedar Creek: The Shenandoah Campaign of 1864* (Carlisle, Pa.: South Mountain Press, 1987), 133.

97. O.R., vol. 43, part 1, 48.

98. Sheridan, *Personal Memoirs,* 2:41–2.

99. Moses Harris, "The Union Cavalry," *War Papers* 1, Military Order of the Loyal Legion of the United States, Wisconsin Commandery (1891): 356.

100. For an interesting examination of the evolution of the Federal cavalry, see Laurence D. Schiller, *Of Sabres and Carbines: The Emergence of the Federal Dragoon* (Danville, Va.: Blue & Gray Education Society, 2001).

101. O.R., vol. 49, part 2, 663.

102. Ford, *A Cycle of Adams Letters,* 2:6–7.

The Army of the Potomac's Cavalry Forces under Command of Maj. Gen. Ambrose E. Burnside

ARMY OF THE POTOMAC
MAJ. GEN. AMBROSE E. BURNSIDE

RIGHT GRAND DIVISION
Maj. Gen. Edwin V. Sumner

CAVALRY DIVISION
Brig. Gen. Alfred Pleasonton

First Brigade
Brig. Gen. John F. Farnsworth

    8th Illinois Cavalry (Col. William Gamble)
    3d Indiana Cavalry (Maj. George H. Chapman)
    8th New York Cavalry (Col. Benjamin F. Davis)

Second Brigade
Col. David McMurtrie Gregg[1]

    6th New York Cavalry (Col. Thomas C. Devin)
    8th Pennsylvania Cavalry (Lt. Col. Amos E. Griffiths)
    6th U.S. Cavalry (Capt. George C. Cram)

Horse Artillery
    2d U.S., Battery M (Lt. Alexander C. M. Pennington, Jr.)

CENTER GRAND DIVISION
Maj. Gen. Joseph Hooker

Cavalry Brigade
Brig. Gen. William W. Averell

1st Massachusetts Cavalry (Col. Horace B. Sargent)
3d Pennsylvania Cavalry (Lt. Col. Edward S. Jones)
4th Pennsylvania Cavalry (Col. James K. Kerr)
5th U.S. Cavalry (Capt. James E. Harrison)

Horse Artillery
2d U.S., Batteries B and L (Capt. James M. Robertson)

LEFT GRAND DIVISION
Maj. Gen. William B. Franklin

Cavalry Brigade
Brig Gen. George D. Bayard[2]

District of Columbia, Independent Company (Lt. William H. Orton)
1st Maine Cavalry (Lt. Col. Calvin S. Doughty)
1st New Jersey Cavalry (Lt. Col. Joseph Kargé)
2d New York Cavalry (Maj. Henry E. Davies)
10th New York Cavalry (Lt. Col. William Irvine)
1st Pennsylvania Cavalry (Col. Owen Jones)

Horse Artillery
3d U.S., Battery C (Capt. Horatio G. Gibson)

NOTES
1. Assumed command of the Cavalry Brigade assigned to the Left Grand Division when Brig. Gen. George D. Bayard was mortally wounded at the Battle of Fredericksburg, December 13, 1862. Col. Thomas C. Devin assumed command of this brigade when Gregg assumed command of Bayard's brigade.
2. Col. David McMurtrie Gregg assumed command of this brigade after General Bayard was mortally wounded at the Battle of Fredericksburg, December 13, 1862.

ORDER OF BATTLE
THE BATTLE OF KELLY'S FORD
MARCH 17, 1863

ARMY OF THE POTOMAC
Cavalry Corps
Maj. Gen. George Stoneman

SECOND DIVISION
Brig. Gen. William W. Averell

First Brigade
Col. Alfred N. Duffie

    4th New York Cavalry (Col. Luigi P. di Cesnola)
    6th Ohio Cavalry (Lt. Col. William R. Steadman)
    1st Rhode Island Cavalry (Maj. Preston M. Farrington)

Second Brigade
Col. John B. McIntosh

    3d Pennsylvania Cavalry (Col. Edward S. Owen)
    4th Pennsylvania Cavalry (Lt. Col. William E. Doster)
    16th Pennsylvania Cavalry (Col. J. Irvin Gregg)

Reserve Brigade
Capt. Marcus A. Reno

1st U. S. Cavalry (Capt. Marcus A. Reno)
5th U. S. Cavalry (Lt. Robert Sweatman)
6th New York Independent Battery (Lt. George Browne, Jr.)
Total strength of Averell's command: 2,100 men[1]

ARMY OF NORTHERN VIRGINIA
Cavalry Division
Maj. Gen. J. E. B. Stuart

Fitz Lee's Brigade
Brig. Gen. Fitzhugh Lee

1st Virginia Cavalry (Col. James H. Drake)
2d Virginia Cavalry (Maj. Cary Breckinridge—captured; Capt. Edgar
  Whitehead)
3d Virginia Cavalry (Col. Thomas H. Owen)
4th Virginia Cavalry (Lt. Col. William H. Payne)
5th Virginia Cavalry (Col. Thomas L. Rosser)
Breathed's Battery of Horse Artillery (Capt. James Breathed)

Total strength of Fitzhugh Lee's brigade: 800 men

NOTE

1. Note that 900 men of Averell's Second Division, including the entire 1st Massachusetts Cavalry, were detached to guard Averell's flanks and the Orange & Alexandria
   Railroad. His actual strength should have been 3,000 men, not 2,100.

Order of Battle
Stoneman's Raid
April–May, 1863

ARMY OF THE POTOMAC
Cavalry Corps
Maj. Gen. George Stoneman

FIRST DIVISION
Brig. Gen. Alfred Pleasonton (Second Brigade detached and serving with Army of the Potomac at Chancellorsville)

First Brigade (temporarily attached to Averell's Second Division)
Col. Benjamin F. "Grimes" Davis

　　8th New York Cavalry (Maj. Edmund M. Pope)
　　9th New York Cavalry (Lt. Col. William Sackett)
　　8th Illinois Cavalry (Maj. John L. Beveridge)
　　3d Indiana Cavalry (Col. George H. Chapman)
　　1st Pennsylvania Cavalry (temporarily assigned to this division, but usually assigned to the 2d Brigade, Third Division)

SECOND DIVISION
Brig. Gen. William W. Averell

First Brigade
Col. Horace B. Sargent

1st Massachusetts Cavalry (Lt. Col. Greeley S. Curtis)
4th New York Cavalry (Col. Luigi P. di Cesnola)
6th Ohio Cavalry (Lt. Col. William R. Steadman)
1st Rhode Island Cavalry (Col. Alfred N. Duffié)

Second Brigade
Col. John B. McIntosh

3d Pennsylvania Cavalry (Col. Edward S. Owen)
4th Pennsylvania Cavalry (Lt. Col. William E. Doster)
16th Pennsylvania Cavalry (Col. J. Irvin Gregg)
Battery A, 2d U.S. Artillery (Capt. John C. Tidball)

THIRD DIVISION
Brig. Gen. David McMurtrie Gregg

First Brigade
Col. Hugh Judson Kilpatrick

1st Maine Cavalry (Col. Calvin S. Doughty)
2d New York Cavalry (Lt. Col. Henry E. Davies)
10th New York Cavalry (Lt. Col. William Irvine)

Second Brigade
Col. Sir Percy Wyndham

12th Illinois Cavalry (Lt. Col. Hasbrouck Davis)
1st Maryland Cavalry (Lt. Col. James M. Deems)
1st New Jersey Cavalry (Lt. Col. Virgil Brodrick)

Reserve Brigade (independent command, not assigned to any division)
Brig. Gen. John Buford

1st U.S. Cavalry (Capt. Richard S. Lord)
2d U.S. Cavalry (Capt. Wesley Merritt)
5th U.S. Cavalry (Maj. Charles J. Whiting)
6th U.S. Cavalry (Capt. George C. Cram)
6th Pennsylvania Cavalry (independent command, but attached to brigade)
    (Col. Richard H. Rush—left regiment due to illness; Maj. Robert Morris, Jr.)

Corps Horse Artillery (Capt. James M. Robertson)
  Batteries B and L (combined), 2d U.S. Artillery (Lt. Albert O. Vincent)
  Battery M, 2d U.S. Artillery (Capt. A. J. Clark)
  Battery E, 4th U.S. Artillery (Lt. Samuel K. Elder)

Total strength participating in Stoneman's Raid: 9,895 troopers supported by 22 guns and 427 horse artillerymen.

ORDER OF BATTLE
THE FIGHT IN ALSOP'S FIELD
APRIL 30, 1863

ARMY OF THE POTOMAC
Cavalry Corps
Maj. Gen. George Stoneman

FIRST CAVALRY DIVISION
Brig. Gen. Alfred Pleasonton

Second Brigade
Col. Thomas C. Devin

    6th New York Cavalry (Lt. Col. Duncan McVicar—killed in action[KIA];
       Capt. William Beardsley)

ARMY OF NORTHERN VIRGINIA
Cavalry Division
Maj. Gen. J. E. B. Stuart

Fitz Lee's Brigade
Brig. Gen. Fitzhugh Lee

    1st Virginia Cavalry (Col. James H. Drake)
    2d Virginia Cavalry (Col. Thomas T. Munford)
    3d Virginia Cavalry (Col. Thomas H. Owen)
    4th Virginia Cavalry (Lt. Col. William H. Payne)
    5th Virginia Cavalry (Col. Thomas L. Rosser)

Order of Battle
The Battle of Brandy Station
June 9, 1863

ARMY OF THE POTOMAC
Cavalry Corps
Brig. Gen. Alfred Pleasonton

RIGHT WING
Brig. Gen. John Buford

FIRST CAVALRY DIVISION
Brig. Gen. John Buford
Col. Thomas C. Devin

First Brigade
Col. Benjamin F. Davis (mortally wounded in action[MWIA]; Maj. William S. McClure)

8th New York Cavalry (Maj. Edmund M. Pope)
8th Illinois Cavalry (Capt. Alpheus Clark—MWIA; Capt. George A. Forsythe—wounded in action[WIA]; Capt. Elon J. Farnsworth)
3d Indiana Cavalry (Maj. William S. McClure; Maj. Charles Lemmon)
9th New York Cavalry (Five companies—Maj. William B. Martin—WIA)
3d (West) Virginia Cavalry (two companies—Capt. Seymour B. Conger)

Second Brigade
Col. Thomas C. Devin
Col. Josiah H. Kellogg

6th New York Cavalry (Maj. William E. Beardsley)
17th Pennsylvania Cavalry (Col. Josiah H. Kellogg; Lt. Col. J. Q. A. Anderson)

Reserve Brigade
Maj. Charles J. Whiting

1st U.S. Cavalry (Capt. Richard S. C. Lord)
2d U.S. Cavalry (Capt. Wesley Merritt)
5th U.S. Cavalry (Capt. James E. Harrison)
6th U.S. Cavalry (Capt. George C. Cram)
6th Pennsylvania Cavalry (Maj. Robert Morris, Jr.—taken prisoner, died in
    Libby Prison; Maj. Henry C. Whelan)
U.S. Horse Artillery (Capt. James M. Robertson)
1st U.S. Artillery, Battery K (Capt. William M. Graham)
2d U.S. Artillery, Batteries B and L (consolidated—Lt. Albert O. Vincent)
4th U.S. Artillery, Battery E (Lt. Samuel S. Elder)

Select Brigade of Infantry (1,500 officers and men)
Brig. Gen. Adelbert Ames

86th New York Infanrty (3d Corps—Maj. Jacob H. Lansing—east of Beverly
    Ford Road)
124th New York Infantry (3d Corps—Lt. Col. Francis M. Cummins)
33d Massachusetts Infantry (11th Corps—Col. Adin B. Underwood)
2d Massachusetts Infantry (12th Corps—Lt. Col. Charles R. Mudge)
3d Wisconsin Infantry (12th Corps—Lt. Col. Martin Flood)

LEFT WING
Brig. Gen. David McMurtrie Gregg

SECOND CAVALRY DIVISION
Col. Alfred N. Duffié

First Brigade
Col. Luigi P. di Cesnola

1st Massachusetts Cavalry (Lt. Col. Greely S. Curtis)
6th Ohio Cavalry (Maj. William Steadman)
1st Rhode Island Cavalry (Lt. Col. John L. Thompson)

Second Brigade
Col. J. Irvin Gregg

3d Pennsylvania Cavalry (Lt. Col. Edward S. Jones)
4th Pennsylvania Cavalry (Lt. Col. William E. Doster)
16th Pennsylvania Cavalry (Maj. William H. Fry—in reserve and dismounted)
2d U.S. Artillery, Battery M (Lt. Alexander C. M. Pennington)

THIRD CAVALRY DIVISION
Brig. Gen. David McMurtrie Gregg

First Brigade
Col. Hugh Judson Kilpatrick

2d New York Cavalry (Lt. Col. Henry E. Davies)
10th New York Cavalry (Lt. Col. William Irvine—captured; Maj. M. Henry Avery)
1st Maine Cavalry (Col. Calvin S. Doughty)
Orton's Independent Co. D.C. Vols. (Lt. William H. Orton—attached for the battle)

Second Brigade
Col. Sir Percy Wyndham—WIA; Col. John P. Taylor

1st New Jersey Cavalry (Lt. Col. Virgil Brodrick—KIA; Maj. John H. Shelmire—KIA; Maj. Myron H. Beaumont)
1st Pennsylvania Cavalry (Col. John P. Taylor; Lt. Col. David Gardner)
1st Maryland Cavalry (Lt. Col. James M. Deems)
New York Light Artillery, 6th Independent Battery (Capt. Joseph W. Martin)

Select Brigade of Infantry (1,500 officers and men)
Brig. Gen. David A. Russell

56th Pennsylvania Infantry (1st Corps—Col. J. William Hoffman)
7th Wisconsin Infantry & two companies from 2d Wisconsin Infantry (1st Corps—Col. William Robinson commanding both)
6th Maine Infantry (6th Corps—Col. Hiram Burnham)
119th Pennsylvania Infantry (6th Corps—Maj. Henry P. Truefitt, Jr.)
5th New Hampshire Infantry & 81st Pennsylvania Infantry (2d Corps—Col. Edward E. Cross, commanding both)
3d U.S. Artillery, Battery C (Lt. William D. Fuller)

ARMY OF NORTHERN VIRGINIA
Cavalry Division
Maj. Gen. J. E. B. Stuart

Jones's Brigade
Brig. Gen. William E. "Grumble" Jones

6th Virginia Cavalry (Maj. Cabell E. Fluornoy)
7th Virginia Cavalry (Lt. Col. Thomas C. Marshall)
11th Virginia Cavalry (Col. Lunsford L. Lomax)
12th Virginia Cavalry (Col. Asher W. Harman—WIA, remained in command)
35th Battalion Virginia Cavalry (Lt. Col. Elijah V. White—WIA, remained in command)

W. H. F. Lee's Brigade
Brig. Gen. William H. F. "Rooney" Lee—WIA; Col. James Lucius Davis; Col. John R. Chambliss, Jr.

2d North Carolina Cavalry (Col. Solomon Williams—KIA; Lt. Col. William H.F. Payne)
9th Virginia Cavalry (Col. Richard L.T. Beale)
10th Virginia Cavalry (Col. James Lucius Davis; Maj. Joseph Rosser)
13th Virginia Cavalry (Col. John R. Chambliss, Jr.)

Hampton's Brigade
Brig. Gen. Wade Hampton

Cobb's Legion Cavalry (Col. Pierce M. B. Young—WIA, remained in command)
1st South Carolina Cavalry (Col. John L. Black)
1st North Carolina Cavalry (Col. Laurence S. Baker)
Jeff Davis Legion Cavalry (Lt. Col. Joseph F. Waring)
2d South Carolina Cavalry (Col. Matthew C. Butler—WIA; Maj. Thomas J. Lipscomb—Regt. detached at Stevensburg)

Fitzhugh Lee's Brigade
Col. Thomas T. Munford

1st Virginia Cavalry (Col. James H. Drake)
2d Virginia Cavalry (Lt. Col. James W. Watts)
3d Virginia Cavalry (Col. Thomas H. Owen)
4th Virginia Cavalry (Col. Williams C. Wickham—Regt. detached at Stevensburg)

Robertson's Brigade
Brig. Gen. Beverly H. Robertson

4th North Carolina Cavalry (Col. Dennis C. Ferebee)
5th North Carolina Cavalry (Col. Peter G. Evans)

Stuart's Horse Artillery
Maj. Robert F. Beckham

Hart's Battery (Capt. James F. Hart)
Breathed's Battery (Capt. James Breathed)
Chew's Battery (Capt. Roger Preston Chew)
Moorman's Battery (Capt. Marcellus Moorman)
McGregor's Battery (Capt. William M. McGregor)

NOTE
The 15th Virginia Cavalry (Rooney Lee's brigade), Phillips Legion Cavalry (Hampton's brigade), and 5th Virginia Cavalry (Fitz Lee's brigade) were detached and serving picket duty at the time of battle and are therefore not included in this order of battle.

GLOSSARY

abatis	A defensive obstacle formed by felled trees with sharpened branches facing the enemy.
appui	Support (*d'appui:* of support).
beeve	A steer.
canister	Encased shot for close-range artillery fire.
enfilade	To rake or be in a position to rake with gunfire in a lengthwise direction.
guidon	A small flag borne by a military unit.
hors de combat	Out of combat, disabled.
limber	A two-wheeled vehicle to which a gun or caisson may be attached.
palm	A leaf of the palm as a symbol of victory.
parole	The promise of a prisoner of war to fulfill stated conditions in consideration of his release.
pioneer	A member of a military unit, usually of construction engineers.
vedette	A mounted sentinel stationed in advance of pickets.

PRIMARY SOURCES
Newspapers
Ashtabula Sentinel
Aurora Beacon
Bangor Daily Whig & Courier
Boston Transcript
Charleston Mercury
Detroit Free Press
Harper's Weekly
Indiana Reveille (Vevay, Ind.)
Litchfield Enquirer
Madison Daily Evening Courier
Morrison-Whiteside Journal
Mount Carroll Weekly Mirror
Naragansett Weekly
National Intelligencer
National Tribune
New York Daily Tribune
New York Herald
New York Times
Newark Daily Advertiser
Peoples Press
Philadelphia Inquirer
Philadelphia Press
Philadelphia Weekly Times
Providence Journal

Reading Eagle
Richmond Daily Dispatch
Richmond Daily Enquirer
Richmond Daily Examiner
Richmond Sentinel
Rochester Daily Union and Advertiser
Rochester Democrat
Rock Island Argus
San Francisco Chronicle
Savannah Republican
Washington Star

Manuscript Materials

Alderman Library, Special Collections, University of Virginia, Charlottesville, Va.
> Robert T. Hubard Memoir
> William H. Redman Letters
> Thomas L. Rosser Papers

Eleanor S. Brockenbrough Library, Museum of the Confederacy, Richmond, Va.

Brown University Library, Providence, R.I.
> John B. McIntosh Letters

Center for American History, University of Texas, Austin
> Alfred G. Sargent Letters
> Samuel H. Starr Papers

Civil War Museum and Library, Philadelphia, Pa.
> William Brooke-Rawle Papers
> George G. Meade Photographic Scrapbook Collection

Clements Library, University of Michigan, Ann Arbor
> Schoff Civil War Collection

Connecticut Historical Society, Hartford, Conn.
> Norman Ball Diary

David G. Douglas Collection, Ridley Park, Pa.
> Leonard Williams Letters

Olive Johnson Dunnett Collection, Hanover, Pa.
> John Wilder Johnson Letters

Arnold C. Franks Collection, Tucson, Ariz.
> J. Edward Carpenter, "The Charge of the 8th Pennsylvania Cavalry"
> Andrew B. Wells, "Charge of the 8th Pennsylvania Cavalry"

Fredericksburg and Spotsylvania National Military Park Archives, Fredericksburg, Va.
> Emmons D. Guild Letters
> Peter Keenan Papers
> Robert E. Lee letter of March 24, 1863
> Charles H. McKnight letter of May 6, 1863
> Phillip H. Powers letter of May 6, 1863
> Truman Reeves Memoir

John L. Smith letter of March 3, 1863
Edward W. Whitaker Letters
French Army Archives, Vincennes, France
Napoleon Alexandre Duffié Service Records
Blair Graybill Collection, Charlottesville, Va.
Virgil Brodrick Letters
Historical Society of Pennsylvania, Philadelphia
Cadwalader Family Collection
Louis Henry Carpenter Letters from the Field, 1861–1865
Charles P. Coxe Papers
John Gibbon Papers
W. M. Meredith Papers
Newhall Family Papers
Albert P. Huntington Library, San Marino, Calif.
Joseph Hooker Papers
George Stoneman Papers
Illinois Historical Library, Springfield, Ill.
Winthrop P. Allen Letters
Indiana State Archives, Indianapolis, Ind.
George Chapman Papers
Indiana Adjutant General's Office, Correspondence File, 3d Indiana Cavalry
Thomas F. Reid Diary for 1863
Library of Congress, Manuscripts Division, Washington, D.C.
Charles Francis Adams Letters
John Bigelow, Jr., Papers
Ulric Dahlgren Diary for 1863
Samuel J. B.V. Gilpin Diary
David M. Gregg Papers
William G. Hills Diary
Henry Jackson Hunt Papers
August V. Kautz Papers
Maud Wood Park Papers
Alfred Pleasonton Papers
Sue Martin Collection, Fairport, N.Y.
Frank T. Saunders Letters
Howard McManus Collection, Roanoke, Va.
Henry W. Owen Letters
Monroe County Library System, Monroe, Mich.
Lawrence Frost Collection of Custeriana
J. P. Morgan Library, New York, N.Y.
Gilder-Lehrman Collection
William Woods Averell Diary for 1863

National Archives, Washington, D.C.

Appointments, Commissions, and Pension file for William Woods Averell

Letters Received by the Commissions Branch of the Adjutant General's Office, Army of the Potomac, 1861–1865

Letters Received by the Appointment, Commission, and Personal Branch of the Adjutant General's Office, 1871–1894, Roll M1395

Letters Sent and Received, Quartermaster's Office, Army of the Potomac, 1861–1865

RG 94: Consolidated Military Service and Pension Files

William L. Heermance Medal of Honor file, 825 U.S. 1880, RG 94, Entry 496, Box 300

RG 393: Part 1, Army of the Potomac, 1861–1865, Entry 3976, Letters Received 1863, Box 10

Southern Claims Files

Navarro College Archives, Corsicana, Tex.

Pearce Civil War Collection

New York State Library and Archives, Albany

William Woods Averell Papers

Pennsylvania State Archives, Harrisburg

Samuel P. Bates Papers

Christian Geisel Letters

Samuel M. Potter Letters

Perkins Historical Library, Duke University, Durham, N.C.

Boeteler Family Papers

Click Family Papers

Lucius Haney Letters

Charles A. Legg Papers

Brian C. Pohanka Collection, Alexandria, Va.

Myles W. Keogh Letters

Paul Polizzi Collection, Rochester, N.Y.

Albert P. Morrow Letters

Rauner Special Collections Library, Dartmouth College, Hanover, N.H.

Luigi Palma di Cesnola Papers

Rhode Island Historical Society, Providence

George N. Bliss Letters

Rochester Public Library, Rochester, N.Y.

Daniel W. Pulis Letters

Rock Island Historical Society, Rock Island, Ill.

Rock Island Military Records

Records of Lt. Temple Buford

Rosenbach Library, Philadelphia, Pa.

Rush/Williams/Biddle Family Papers

Dona Sauerburger Collection, Gambrills, Md.

Thomas B. Lucas Letters

George F. Scott Collection, Mt. Carmel, Pa.
  John B. Coover Letters
Southern Historical Collection, Wilson Historical Library, University of North Carolina,
    Chapel Hill
  William B. Baker Papers
  George Stanley Dewey Papers
  Mary E. Grattan Papers
  William Penn Lloyd Papers
  Whitaker and Snipes Family Papers
  Charles Venable Papers
  Joseph F. Waring Papers
Staten Island Historical Society, New York, N.Y.
  Pelton-Duffié Family Papers
U.S. Army Military History Institute, Carlisle, Pa.
  William Bard/Arthur Martin Papers
  Peter Boyer Letters
  Civil War Miscellaneous Collection
  Civil War Times Illustrated Collection
  Thomas Covert Letters
  Harrisburg Civil War Roundtable Collection
  August V. Kautz Papers
  Lewis Leigh Collection
  Lloyd D. Miller Collection
  William Price Collection
  Michael Winey Collection
Special Collections, U.S. Military Academy Library, West Point, N.Y.
  George A. Custer Letters
  James E. Harrison Papers
  Myles W. Keogh, "Etat de Service of Major-General John Buford"
  Abraham Lincoln letter of December 16, 1863
Virginia Military Institute Archives, Lexington, Va.
  J. Kent Langhorne Papers
Western Reserve Historical Society, Cleveland, Ohio
  Wells A. Bushnell Diary
  Alcinus Ward Fenton Papers
  Carlos Lyman Letters
Eric J. Wittenberg Collection, Columbus, Ohio
  John Gibbon, "The John Buford Memoir"
  Miscellaneous correspondence
  Bernard Murrin Certificate of Disability

PUBLISHED SOURCES

Adams, Charles Francis. *Autobiography.* Boston: Houghton-Mifflin, 1916.

Agassiz, George R., ed. *Meade's Headquarters 1863–1865: Letters of Colonel Theodore Lyman from the Wilderness to Appomattox.* Boston: Atlantic Monthly Press, 1922.

Alexander, Peter Wellington. *Writing & Fighting the Confederate War: The Letters of Peter Wellington Alexander, Confederate War Correspondent,* edited by William B. Styple. Kearny, N.J.: Belle Grove, 2002.

Allen, Winthrop S. G. *Civil War Letters of Winthrop S. G. Allen,* edited by Harry E. Pratt. Springfield, Ill.: Phillips Brothers Printing, 1932.

"At Chancellorsville: The Spot Where 'Stonewall' Fell." *National Tribune,* August 27, 1882.

Averell, William Woods. "With the Cavalry on the Peninsula." In *Battles and Leaders of the Civil War,* edited by Robert U. Johnson and Clarence C. Buel, 429–33. 4 vols. New York: Century, 1880–1901.

Barton, Randolph. "A Cavalry Charge at Chancellorsville," *Confederate Veteran* 13 (1905): 452–53.

Baylor, George. *Bull Run to Bull Run; or, Four Years in the Army of Northern Virginia.* Richmond: B. F. Johnson Printing, 1900.

Beach, William H. *The First New York (Lincoln) Cavalry from April 19, 1861, to July 7, 1865.* New York: Lincoln Cavalry Assoc., 1902.

Beale, G. W. *A Lieutenant of Cavalry in Lee's Army.* Boston: 1918; reprint, Baltimore: Butternut & Blue, 1994.

————. "The Story of General Averell's Interview with a Confederate Prisoner Retold." *Richmond Times-Dispatch,* March 4, 1906.

Beale, Richard L. T. *History of the Ninth Virginia Cavalry in the War between the States.* Richmond, Va.: B. F. Johnson, 1899.

"The Beau Sabreur of Georgia." *Southern Historical Society Papers* 25 (1897): 146–151.

Beck, Elias W., M.D. "Letters of a Civil War Surgeon." *Indiana Magazine of History* (June 1931): 132–163.

Bentz, William H. "From One of Keenan's Men." *National Tribune,* October 22, 1881.

Blackford, Susan Leigh, comp. *Letters from Lee's Army, or Memoirs of Life In and Out of the Army in Virginia during the War between the States.* New York: Charles Scribner's Sons, 1947.

Blackford, William W. *War Years with Jeb Stuart.* New York: Charles Scribner's Sons, 1945.

Blaschek, Joseph. "The Story of Rush's Lancers." *National Tribune,* June 24, 1897.

Bliss, George N. "Duffié and the Monument to His Memory." In *Personal Narratives of Events in the War of the Rebellion, Being Papers Read before the Rhode Island Soldiers and Sailors Historical Society* VI, 316–376. Providence: Published by the Society, 1890.

————. *The First Rhode Island Cavalry at Middleburg.* Providence: privately published, 1889.

————. "Reminiscences of Service in the First Rhode Island Cavalry." In *Personal Narratives of Events in the War of the Rebellion* I. Providence: Rhode Island Soldiers and Sailors Historical Society, 1878.

Blue, John. *Hanging Rock Rebel: Lt. John Blue's War in West Virginia and the Shenandoah Valley,* edited by Dan Oates. Shippensburg, Pa.: Burd Street Press, 1994.

Bond, Frank A. "Fitz Lee in the Army of Northern Virginia." *Confederate Veteran* 6 (1898): 420–21.

Booth, George Wilson. *Personal Reminiscences of a Maryland Soldier in the War Between the States, 1861–1865.* Baltimore: privately published, 1898.

Borcke, Heros von. *Memoirs of the Confederate War for Independence.* Philadelphia: J. B. Lippincott, 1867.

Borcke, Heros von and Justus Scheibert. *The Great Cavalry Battle of Brandy Station,* translated by Stuart T. Wright and F. D. Bridgewater. 1893; reprint, Gaithersburg, Md., Olde Soldier Books, 1976.

Bowen, James R. *Regimental History of the First New York Dragoons.* Battle Creek, Mich.: privately published, 1900.

Brackett, Albert G. *History of the United States Cavalry, from the Formation of the Federal Government to the 1st of June, 1863.* New York: Harper & Brothers, 1865.

Brooke-Rawle, William. *History of the Third Pennsylvania Cavalry, Sixtieth Regiment Pennsylvania Volunteers, in the American Civil War 1861–1865.* Philadelphia: Franklin Printing, 1905.

Brooks, U. R., ed. *Butler and His Cavalry in the War of Secession, 1861–1865.* Columbia, S.C.: State, 1909.

Bull, H. A. "Brandy Station, Where the 8th N.Y. Cavalry Had Its Full Share of Fighting." *National Tribune,* January 20, 1887.

Burnett, Orlando. "The Sharp Fight of St. Patrick's Day, 1863." *National Tribune,* April 8, 1915.

Carter, William R. *Sabres, Saddles and Spurs,* edited by Walbrook D. Swank. Shippensburg, Pa.: Burd Street Press, 1998.

"Cavalryman." "Pistol and Saber: A Stoneman Raid and the Cavalry Fight at Aldie." *National Tribune,* September 13, 1900.

Cesnola, Luigi Palma di. *A Descriptive Atlas of the Cesnola Collection of Cypriote Antiquities in the Metropolitan Museum of Art, New York.* 3 vols. Boston: J. R. Osgood, 1885–1903.

———. *Cyprus: Its Ancient Cities, Tombs, and Temples.* New York: Harper & Brothers, 1878.

———. *Ten Months in Libby Prison.* N.p., 1865.

Chase, George H. "A Scrap of History: General Kilpatrick's Desperate Encounter with a Rebel Major." *National Tribune,* September 2, 1882.

Collins, John L. "When Stonewall Jackson Turned Our Right." In *Battles and Leaders of the Civil War,* edited by Robert U. Johnson and Clarence C. Buel, 3: 183–186. 4 vols. New York: Century, 1884–88.

Conway, William B. "The Battle of Kelly's Ford, Va." *Confederate Veteran* 27 (September 1919): 330.

Cooke, Jacob B. "The Battle of Kelly's Ford, March 17, 1863." In *Personal Narratives of Events in the War of the Rebellion, Being Papers Read Before the Rhode Island Soldiers and Sailors Historical Society* IV, 1–38. Providence: Published by the Society, 1887.

Cooke, John Esten. *Wearing of the Gray, Being Personal Portraits, Scenes & Adventures of the War.* New York: E. B. Treat, 1867.

Copeland, J. E. "The Fighting at Brandy Station." *Confederate Veteran* 30 (1922): 451–52.

Corson, William Clark. *My Dear Jennie: A Collection of Love Letters from a Confederate Soldier to His Fiancée during the Period 1861–1865,* edited by Blake W. Corson, Jr. Richmond, Va.: Dietz Press, 1982.

Couch, Darius N. "The Chancellorsville Campaign." In *Battles and Leaders of the Civil War,* edited by Robert U. Johnson and Clarence C. Buel, 3: 154–171. 4 vols. New York: Century, 1880–1901.

Crowninshield, Benjamin W. *A History of the First Regiment Massachusetts Cavalry Volunteers.* Boston: Houghton-Mifflin, 1891.

Davis, George B. "The Cavalry Combat at Brandy Station, Va. on June 9, 1863." *Journal of the U.S. Cavalry Association* 25 (1914): 190–98.

———. "The Cavalry Combat at Kelly's Ford in 1863." *Journal of the U.S. Cavalry Association* 25 (January 1915): 390–402.

———. "The Stoneman Raid." *Journal of the U.S. Cavalry Association* 24 (1917): 533–52.

Davis, Sidney Morris. *Common Soldier, Uncommon War: Life as a Cavalryman in the Civil War,* edited by Charles F. Cooney. Bethesda, Md.: SMD Group, 1994.

Dennison, Frederic. *Sabres and Spurs: The First Regiment Rhode Island Cavalry in the Civil War, 1861–1865.* Central Falls, R.I.: First Rhode Island Cavalry Veteran Assoc., 1876.

Dickerson, Frank W. "Letter from a Maine Cavalry Officer in Stoneman's Raid." *Bangor Daily Whig & Courier,* May 20, 1863.

Doster, William E. *A Brief History of the Fourth Pennsylvania Veteran Cavalry Embracing Organization, Reunions, Dedication of Monument at Gettysburg and Address, General W. E. Doster, Venango County Battalion, Reminiscences, etc.* Pittsburgh: Ewens & Eberle, 1891.

———. *Lincoln and Episodes of the Civil War.* New York: G. P. Putnam's Sons, 1915.

Doubleday, Abner. *Chancellorsville and Gettysburg.* New York: Charles Scribner's Sons, 1882.

Eckert, Edward K. and Nicholas J. Amato, eds. *Ten Years in the Saddle: The Memoir of William Woods Averell, 1851–1862.* San Rafael, Calif.: Presidio Press, 1978.

Emerson, Edward W. *The Life and Letters of Charles Russell Lowell.* Boston: Houghton-Mifflin, 1907.

Fifth Annual Reunion of the Veteran Association 6th New York Cavalry. New York: Russell Brothers, 1891.

Fitz Simmons, Charles. "Hunter's Raid." *Military Essays and Recollections: Papers Read before the Commandery of the State of Illinois Military Order of the Loyal Legion of the United States* 6 (Chicago, 1907): 395–96.

Ford, Charles W. "Charge of the First Maine Cavalry at Brandy Station." *War Paper: Read before the Commandery of the State of Maine, Military Order of the Loyal Legion of the United States* 2 (1902): 268–89.

Ford, Worthington C., ed. *A Cycle of Adams Letters, 1861–1865.* 2 vols. Boston: Houghton-Mifflin, 1920.

Foster, Alonzo. *Reminiscences and Record of the 6th New York Veteran Volunteer Cavalry.* Brooklyn, N.Y.: privately published, 1892.

Frost, Robert W., and Nancy D. Frost, eds. *Picket Pins and Sabers.* Privately published, 1971.

Gardner, Charles. *Three Years in the Cavalry: The Civil War Remembrances of Charles Gardner.* Tucson, Ariz.: A Plus Printing, 1998.

Garnett, Theodore Stanford. *Riding with Stuart: Reminiscences of an Aide-de-Camp,* edited by Robert J. Trout. Shippensburg, Pa.: White Mane, 1994.

German, Andrew W., ed. "Picketing along the Rappahannock." *Civil War Quarterly* 8 (March 1987): 32–38.

Gill, John. *Reminiscences of Four Years as a Private Soldier in the Confederate Army, 1861–1865.* Baltimore: Sun Printing Office, 1904.

Gilmor, Harry. *Four Years in the Saddle.* New York: Harper & Brothers, 1866.

Gilmore, David M. "Cavalry: Its Use and Value as Illustrated by Reference to the Engagements of Kelly's Ford and Gettysburg." In *Glimpses of the Nation's Struggle,* 2d series, 38–51. St. Paul, Minn.: St. Paul Book and Stationery, 1890.

Glazier, Willard. *Battles for the Union: Comprising Descriptions of Many of the Most Stubbornly Contested Battles in the War of the Great Rebellion, Together with Incidents and Reminiscences of the Camp, the March, and the Skirmish Line.* Hartford, Conn.: Gilman, 1878.

———. *Three Years in the Federal Cavalry.* New York: R. H. Ferguson, 1873.

Gracey, Samuel L. *Annals of the Sixth Pennsylvania Cavalry.* Philadelphia: E. H. Butler, 1868.

Grant, Ulysses S. *Personal Memoirs.* New York: Library of America, 1990.

Gregg, David M. "The Union Cavalry at Gettysburg." In *Annals of the War: Written by Leading Participants North & South,* 372–79. Reprint, Dayton, Ohio: Morningside, 1986.

Grimsley, Daniel A. *Battles in Culpeper County, Virginia, 1861–1865.* Culpeper, Va.: Raleigh Travers Green, 1900.

Gurowski, Adam. *Diary from November 18, 1862 to October 18, 1863.* 2 vols. New York: Burt Franklin, 1968.

Haden, Benjamin J. *Reminiscences of J. E. B. Stuart's Cavalry.* Charlottesville, Va.: Progress, 1912.

Hagemann, E. R., ed. *Fighting Rebels and Redskins: Experiences in Army Life of Colonel George B. Sanford, 1861–1892.* Norman: University of Oklahoma Press, 1968.

Hall, Hillman A., ed. *History of the Sixth New York Cavalry (Second Ira Harris Guards), Second Brigade-First Division-Cavalry Corps, Army of the Potomac 1861–1865.* Worcester, Mass.: Blanchard Press, 1908.

Hamlin, Augustus C. *The Attack of Stonewall Jackson at Chancellorsville* (Fredericksburg, Va.: Sergeant Kirkland's Museum and Historical Society, 1997).

———. *The Battle of Chancellorsville: The Attack of Stonewall Jackson and His Army upon the Right Flank of the Army of the Potomac at Chancellorsville, Virginia, on Saturday Afternoon, May 2, 1863.* Bangor, Maine: privately published, 1896.

Hard, Abner N. *History of the Eighth Cavalry Regiment Illinois Volunteers.* Aurora, Ill.: privately published, 1868.

Harris, Moses. "The Union Cavalry." *War Papers,* Military Order of the Loyal Legion of the United States, Wisconsin Commandery, 3 vols. Vol. 1(Milwaukee, Wis.: Burdick, Armitage & Allen, 1891–1903), 340–73.

Harris, Samuel. *The Personal Reminiscences of Samuel Harris.* Detroit: Robinson Press, 1897.

Harrison, William H. "Personal Experiences of a Cavalry Officer, 1861–66." *Military Essays and Recollections of the Pennsylvania Commandery of the Military Order of the Loyal Legion of the United States* 1 (February 6, 1895): 225–254.

Haskell, Peter Carl, ed. *To Let Them Know: The Civil War Diaries of Sumner Ansel Holway, Pvt., Company H, 1st Maine Cavalry.* Acadia, Maine: Acadia Lodge Press, 1990.

Heermance, William L. "The Cavalry at Chancellorsville, May 1863." *Journal of the United States Cavalry Association* 4, no. 13 (June 1891): 108–113.

Hess, Frank W. "The First Cavalry Battle at Kelly's Ford, Va." Part 1, *National Tribune,* May 29, 1890.

———. "The First Cavalry Battle at Kelly's Ford, Va." Part 2, *National Tribune,* June 5, 1890.

Hopkins, Luther W. *From Bull Run to Appomattox: A Boy's View.* Baltimore: Press of Fleet-McGinley, 1908.

Howard, Wiley C. *Sketch of Cobb Legion Cavalry and Some Scenes and Incidents Remembered.* Atlanta: Atlanta Camp 159, S.C.V., 1901.

Hubard, Robert T. "Operations of General J. E. B. Stuart before Chancellorsville." *Southern Historical Society Papers* 8 (1880): 249–54.

Hudgins, Garland C., and Richard B. Kleese, eds. *Recollections of an Old Dominion Dragoon: The Civil War Experiences of Sgt. Robert S. Hudgins II, Co. B, 3d Virginia Cavalry.* Orange, Va.: Publisher's Press, 1993.

Huey, Pennock. *A True History of the Charge of the Eighth Pennsylvania Cavalry at Chancellorsville.* Philadelphia: Porter & Coates, 1883.

Huntington, James F. "The Artillery at Hazel Grove." In *Battles and Leaders of the Civil War,* edited by Robert U. Johnson and Clarence C. Buel, 3: 188. 4 vols. New York: Century, 1880–1901.

Hyndman, William. *History of a Cavalry Company: A Complete History of Company A, Fourth Pennsylvania Cavalry.* Hightstown, N.J.: Longstreet House, 1997.

Inram, Samuel G. "Beverly Ford: The Third Corps Helps the Cavalry Surprise Jeb Stuart and Give Him a Rough House." *National Tribune,* April 28, 1904.

Instructions for Officers and Non-Commissioned Officers on Outpost and Patrol Duty, and Troops in Campaign. Washington, D.C.: U.S. Government Printing Office, 1863.

Jones, John B. *A Rebel War Clerk's Diary,* edited by Earl Schenck Miers. Baton Rouge: Louisiana State University Press, 1993.

Kesterson, Brian Stuart, ed. *The Last Survivor: The Memoirs of George William Watson.* Washington, W.V.: Night Hawk Press, 1993.

Kidd, James H. *Personal Recollections of a Cavalryman in Custer's Michigan Brigade.* Ionia, Mich.: Sentinel, 1908.

King, Matthew. *To Horse: With the Cavalry of the Army of the Potomac, 1861–1865.* Cheboygan, Mich.: privately published, 1926.

Lathrop, George Parsons. "Keenan's Charge." *National Tribune,* October 22, 1881.

Lee, Fitzhugh. "The Battle of Chancellorsville." *Southern Historical Society Papers* 7 (1879): 545–85.

Lee, Robert E. *The Wartime Papers of R. E. Lee,* edited by Clifford Dowdey and Louis H. Manarin. 2 vols. Boston: Little, Brown, 1961.

Lee, Capt. Robert E. *Recollections and Letters of Robert E. Lee.* Garden City, N.Y.: Garden City, 1924.

Lloyd, William P. *History of the First Reg't Pennsylvania Reserve Cavalry, from Its Organization, August 1861, to September 1864, with List of Names of All Officers and Enlisted Men.* Philadelphia: King & Baird, 1864.

Matthews, H. H. "Major John Pelham, Confederate Hero." *Southern Historical Society Papers* 38 (1910): 379–84.

McClellan, Henry B. "The Battle of Fleetwood." In *Annals of the War: Written by Leading Participants North & South,* 392–403. Reprint, Dayton, Ohio: Morningside, 1986.

———. *The Life and Campaigns of Major General J. E. B. Stuart.* Boston: Houghton-Mifflin, 1895.

McDonald, William N. *A History of the Laurel Brigade.* Baltimore, Md.: Sun Job Printing Office, 1907.

McKinney, Edward P. *Life in Tent and Field, 1861–1865.* Boston: Richard G. Badger, 1922.

McSwain, Eleanor D., ed. *Crumbling Defenses: Or Memoirs and Reminiscences of John Logan Black, C.S.A.* Macon, Ga.: privately published, 1960.

Meade, George Gordon. *The Life and Letters of George Gordon Meade,* edited by George Gordon Meade. 2 vols. New York, Charles Scribner's Sons, 1913.

Merington, Marguerite, ed. *The Custer Story: The Life and Letters of General George A. Custer and His Wife Elizabeth.* New York: Devin-Adair, 1950.

Merrill, Samuel H. *The Campaigns of the First Maine and First District of Columbia Cavalry.* Portland, Maine: Bailey & Noyes, 1866.

Merritt, Wesley. "Personal Recollections—Beverly's Ford to Mitchell's Station, 1863." In *From Everglade to Canon with the Second Dragoons,* edited by Theophilus F. Rodenbough. New York: D. Van Nostrand, 1875.

Meyer, Henry C. *Civil War Experiences under Bayard, Gregg, Kilpatrick, Custer, Raulston, and Newberry, 1862, 1863, 1864.* New York: Knickerbocker Press, 1911.

Mitchell, Adele H., ed. *The Letters of Major General James E. B. Stuart.* Richmond, Va.: Stuart-Mosby Historical Society, 1990.

Mitchell, Frederick W. "A Personal Episode of the First Stoneman Raid." *War Papers,* no. 85, Military Order of the Loyal Legion of the United States, Commandery of the District of Columbia, Read December 6, 1911.

Moffat, George H. "The Battle of Brandy Station." *Confederate Veteran* 14 (February 1906): 74–75.

Moore, Frank, ed. *The Rebellion Record: A Diary of American Events, with Documents, Narratives, Illustrative Incidents, Poetry, etc.* 11 vols. New York: D. Van Nostrand, 1864–68.

Moore, James, M.D. *Kilpatrick and Our Cavalry.* New York: W. J. Widdleton, 1865.

Morgan, C.H. "Narrative of the Operations of the Second Army Corps, from the time General Hancock assumed command, June 9, 1863, until the close of the Battle of Gettysburg." In Almira Hancock, *Reminiscences of General Hancock by His Wife.* New York, Charles L. Webster, 1887.

Mosby, John S. *Stuart's Cavalry in the Gettysburg Campaign.* New York: Moffatt, Yard, 1908.

Moyer, Henry P. *History of the Seventeenth Regiment, Pennsylvania Volunteer Cavalry.* Lebanon, Pa.: Sowers Printing, 1911.

Moyer, William F. "Brandy Station: A Stirring Account of the Famous Cavalry Engagement." *National Tribune,* March 28, 1884.

Myers, Frank M. *The Comanches: A History of White's Battalion, Virginia Cavalry.* Baltimore: Kelly, Piet, 1871.

Neese, George M. *Three Years in the Confederate Horse Artillery.* New York: Neale, 1911.

Newhall, Frederic C. "The Battle of Beverly Ford." In *The Annals of the War As Told by the Leading Participants.* Dayton, Ohio: Morningside, 1988: 134–146.

———. *With General Sheridan in Lee's Last Campaign.* Philadelphia: J. B. Lippincott, 1866.

Norton, Henry. *A Sketch of the 8th New York Cavalry: Unwritten History of the Rebellion.* Norwich, N.Y.: Chenango Telegraph Printing House, 1888.

———. *Deeds of Daring: or History of the Eighth New York Volunteer Cavalry.* Norwich, N.Y.: Chenango Telegraph Printing House, 1889.

Opie, John N. *A Rebel Cavalryman with Lee, Stuart, and Jackson.* Chicago: W. B. Conkey, 1899.

Peck, Daniel. *Dear Rachel: The Civil War Letters of Daniel Peck,* edited by Martha Gerber Stanford and Eleanor Erskin. Freeman, S.D.: Pine Hill Press, 1993.

Peck, Rufus H. *Reminiscences of a Confederate Soldier of Co. C, 2nd Va. Cavalry.* Fincastle, Va.: privately published, 1913.

Perry, Bliss, ed. *Life and Letters of Henry Lee Higginson.* Boston: Atlantic Monthly Press, 1921.

Phillips, C. J. "Stuart's Cavalry, and How It was 'Reviewed' by the Union Troops at Brandy Station." *National Tribune,* March 10, 1887.

Pickrell, William N. *History of the Third Indiana Cavalry.* Indianapolis: Aetna Printing, 1906.

Pleasonton, Alfred. "The Campaign of Gettysburg." In *Annals of the War: Written by Leading Participants North & South,* 447–459. Reprint, Dayton, Ohio: Morningside, 1986.

———. "The Successes and Failures of Chancellorsville." In *Battles and Leaders of the Civil War,* edited by Robert U. Johnson and Clarence C. Buel, 3: 172–82. 4 vols. New York: Century, 1884–1888.

Preston, Noble D. "Gregg's Cavalry: Its Participation in the Stoneman Raid of 1863." *National Tribune,* July 28, 1887.

———. *History of the Tenth Regiment of Cavalry, New York State Volunteers, August, 1861 to August, 1865.* New York: D. Appleton, 1892.

Pyne, Henry R. *The History of First New Jersey Cavalry.* Trenton, N.J.: J. A. Beecher, 1871.

Quaife, Milo S., ed. *From the Cannon's Mouth: The Civil War Letters of General Alpheus S. Williams.* Detroit: Wayne State University Press, 1959.

Reader, Francis Smith. *History of the Fifth West Virginia Cavalry, Formerly the Second Virginia, and Battery G First West Virginia Light Artillery.* New Brighton, Pa.: Daily News, 1890.

Reno, Marcus A. "Boots and Saddles: The Cavalry of the Army of the Potomac." *National Tribune,* April 29, 1886.

———. "Memoranda of Operations of Brig. Gen. W. H. F. Lee's Command during General Stoneman's Raid into Virginia." *Southern Historical Society Papers* 3 (1877): 181–82.

Reynolds, Milton. "The 8th N.Y. Cavalry at Beverly Ford." *National Tribune,* May 19, 1887.

Rhodes, Charles D. "Federal Raids and Expeditions in the East." In *Miller's Photographic History of the Civil War,* 4: 120–28. New York: Review of Reviews, 1911.

————. *History of the Cavalry of the Army of the Potomac, Including That of the Army of Virginia (Pope's), and also the History of the Operations of the Federal Cavalry in West Virginia during the War.* Kansas City, Mo.: Hudson-Kimberly, 1900.

Robertson, Mary D., ed. *Lucy Breckinridge of Grove Hill: The Diary of a Virginia Girl, 1862–1864.* Kent, Ohio: Kent State University Press, 1980.

Rodenbough, Theophilus F. "Cavalry War Lessons." *Journal of the U.S. Cavalry Association* 11, no. 5 (1889): 103–23.

————, ed. *From Everglade to Canon with the Second Dragoons: An Authentic Account of Service in Florida, Mexico, Virginia, and the Indian County, 1836–1875.* New York: D. Van Nostrand, 1875.

————. "Personal Recollections—The Stoneman Raid of '63." In *From Everglade to Canon with the Second Dragoons: An Authentic Account of Service in Florida, Mexico, Virginia, and the Indian Country, 1836–1875,* edited by Theophilus F. Rodenbough, 270–282. New York: D. Van Nostrand, 1875.

————. "Some Cavalry Leaders." In *Miller's Photographic History of the Civil War,* 4: 262–88. New York: Review of Reviews, 1911.

Rosser, Thomas L. *Addresses of Gen'l T. L. Rosser at the Seventh Annual Reunion of the Association of the Maryland Line.* New York: L. A. Williams Printing, 1889.

Royall, William L. *Some Reminiscences.* New York: Neale, 1909.

Scheibert, Justus. *Seven Months in the Rebel States during the North American War, 1863,* edited by William Stanley Hoole. Tuscaloosa, Ala.: Confederate, 1958.

Schmitt, Martin F., ed. *General George Crook: His Autobiography.* Norman: University of Oklahoma Press, 1960.

Sheridan, Philip H. *Personal Memoirs of P. H. Sheridan.* 2 vols. New York: Charles L. Webster, 1888.

Sherman, William T. *Memoirs of General W. T. Sherman.* New York: Library of America, 1990.

Shoemaker, John J. *Shoemaker's Battery, Stuart Horse Artillery, Pelham's Battalion, Army of Northern Virginia.* Memphis, Tenn.: privately published, n.d.

Slease, William Davis. *The Fourteenth Pennsylvania Cavalry in the Civil War: A History of the Fourteenth Pennsylvania Volunteer Cavalry from Its Organization until the Close of the Civil War, 1861–1865.* Pittsburgh: Soldiers' and Sailors' Memorial Hall and Military Museum, 1999.

Smith, B. F. "The Cavalry at Beverly Ford." *National Tribune,* August 7, 1913.

Souvenir: Fiftieth Annual Reunion of the Sixth Ohio Veteran Volunteer Cavalry Association. Warren, Ohio: Sixth Ohio Veteran Volunteer Cavalry Association, 1915.

Staudenraus, P. J., ed. *Mr. Lincoln's Washington: Selections from the Writings of Noah Brooks, Civil War Correspondent.* South Brunswick, N.J.: Thomas Yoseloff, 1976.

Stone, George C. "General Gregg's Narrow Escape." *National Tribune,* November 3, 1927.

"Stoneman's Raid in the Chancellorsville Campaign." In *Battles and Leaders of the Civil War,* edited by Robert U. Johnson and Clarence C. Buel. 3: 152–53. 4 vols. New York: Century, 1884–88.

Strang, Edgar B. *General Stoneman's Raid, Or, The Amusing Side of Army Life.* Philadelphia: privately published, 1911.

———. *Sunshine and Shadows of the Late Civil War.* Philadelphia: privately published, 1898.

Summers, Festus P., ed. *A Borderland Confederate.* Pittsburgh: University of Pittsburgh Press, 1962.

Supplement to the Official Records of the Union and Confederate Armies. 100 vols. Wilmington, N.C.: Broadfoot, 1995–99.

Taylor, Dr. Gray Nelson, ed. *Saddle and Saber: The Letters of Civil War Cavalryman Corporal Nelson Taylor.* Bowie, Md.: Heritage Books, 1993.

Taylor, James E. *The James E. Taylor Sketchbook.* Dayton, Ohio: Morningside, 1989.

"The Stoneman Raid." *National Tribune,* June 14, 1888.

The War of the Rebellion: A Compilation of the Official Records of the Union and Confederate Armies, 128 volumes in 3 series. Washington, D.C.: U.S. Government Printing Office, 1889.

Thomas, Hampton S. *Some Personal Reminiscences of Service in the Cavalry of the Army of the Potomac.* Philadelphia: L. R. Hamersly, 1889.

Tidball, John C. "Artillery Service in the War of the Rebellion." *Journal of the Military Science Institution* 13 (1892).

Tobie, Edward P. *History of the First Maine Cavalry 1861–1865.* Boston: Press of Emory & Hughes, 1887.

———. *Service in the Cavalry in the Army of the Potomac.* Providence, R.I.: privately published, 1882.

Tremain, Henry Edwin. *The Last Hours of Sheridan's Cavalry.* New York: Bonnell, Silver & Bowers, 1904.

Trobriand, Regis de. *Four Years with the Army of the Potomac.* Boston: Ticknor, 1889.

Trout, Robert J., ed. *In the Saddle with Stuart: The Story of Frank Smith Robertson of Jeb Stuart's Staff.* Gettysburg, Pa.: Thomas, 1998.

———. *With Pen and Saber: The Letters and Diaries of J. E. B. Stuart's Staff Officers.* Mechanicsburg, Pa.: Stackpole Books, 1995.

Vogtsberger, Margaret Ann, ed. *The Dulanys of Welbourne: A Family in Mosby's Confederacy.* Lexington, Va.: Rockbridge, 1995.

Wainwright, Charles S. *A Diary of Battle: The Personal Journals of Colonel Charles S. Wainwright, 1861–1865,* edited by Allan Nevins. New York: Harcourt, Brace & World, 1962.

Ware, W. H. *The Battle of Kelley's Ford, Fought March 17, 1863.* Newport News, Va.: Warwick Printing, n.d.

Waud, Alfred R. "The Cavalry Fight near Culpeper." *Harper's Weekly,* July 10, 1863.

Weaver, Augustus C. *Third Indiana Cavalry: A Brief Account of the Actions in Which They Took Part.* Greenwood, Ind.: privately published, 1919.

Weygant, Charles H. *History of the One Hundred and Twenty-Fourth Regiment, N.Y.S.V.* Newburgh, N.Y.: Journal Printing House, 1877.

Wickersham, Charles I. "Personal Recollections of the Cavalry at Chancellorsville." *War Papers,* Military Order of the Loyal Legion of the United States, Wisconsin Commandery. Vol. 3 (Milwaukee, Wis.: 1891), 453–62.

Wiles, C. W. "On Horseback: Leaves from the Record of the 10th N.Y. Cavalry." *National Tribune,* October 21, 1886.

Wilson, James Harrison. "The Cavalry of the Army of the Potomac." *Papers of the Military Historical Society of Massachusetts* 13 (1913): 33–88.

Winder, Robert L., ed., *Jacob Beidler's Book: A Diary Kept by Jacob Beidler from November 1857 through July 1863.* Mifflintown, Pa.: Juniata County Historical Society, 1994.

Wister, Sarah Butler. *Walter S. Newhall: A Memoir.* Philadelphia: Sanitary Commission, 1864.

Wittenberg, Eric J., ed. *"We Have It Damn Hard Out Here": The Civil War Letters of Sgt. Thomas W. Smith, Sixth Pennsylvania Cavalry.* Kent, Ohio: Kent State University Press, 1999.

Wyndham, Percy. "The Wyndham Question Settled." *New York Herald,* September 16, 1863.

Young, T. J. "The Battle of Brandy Station." *Confederate Veteran* 23 (April 1915): 171–72.

SECONDARY SOURCES
Periodical Articles

Alduino, Frank and David J. Coles. "Luigi Palma di Cesnola: An Italian American in the Civil War." *Italian American Review* 7, no. 1 (winter/spring 2000): 1–26.

Beck, R. Mc. "General JEB Stuart at Brandy Station, June 9, 1863." *Journal of the U.S. Cavalry Association* 44 (May/June 1935): 5–10.

Boehm, Robert B. "The Unfortunate Averell." *Civil War Times Illustrated* 5 (August 1966): 30–36.

Bowles, Richard, Jr. "Shannon Hill Encounter." *Goochland County Historical Society Magazine* 17 (1985): 36–49.

Bowmaster, Patrick A. "Beverly H. Robertson and the Battle of Brandy Station." *Blue & Gray* 14 (fall 1996): 20–22, 24–33.

Brennan, Patrick. "The Best Cavalry in the World." *North & South* 2 (January 1999): 10–29.

———. "Thunder of the Plains of Brandy." Part 1, *North & South* 5 (April 2002): 14–34.

———. "Thunder on the Plains of Brandy." Part 2, *North & South* 5 (June 2002): 32–51.

Carter, William Harding. "The Sixth Regiment of Cavalry." *Maine Bugle* 3 (October 1896): 295–306.

Gallagher, Gary W. "Brandy Station: The Civil War's Bloodiest Arena of Mounted Combat." *Blue & Gray* 7 (October 1990): 8–20, 22, 44–56.

Hall, Clark B. "The Battle of Brandy Station." *Civil War Times Illustrated* 29 (May–June 1990): 32–42, 45.

———. "Buford at Brandy Station." *Civil War* 8 (July–August 1990): 12–17, 66–67.

Hunt, Emmie Martin. "John Pelham of Alabama." *Confederate Veteran* 30 (September 1922): 329.

Longacre, Edward G. "Alfred Pleasonton, 'The Knight of Romance.'" *Civil War Times Illustrated* 13 (December 1974): 10–23.

———. "Judson Kilpatrick." *Civil War Times Illustrated* 10 (April 1971): 24–33.

———. "Sir Percy Wyndham." *Civil War Times Illustrated* 8 (December 1968): 12–19.

Meyers, Jerry. "Melee on St. Patrick's Day." *America's Civil War* (November 1991): 30–37.

———. "Shells and Saber Points." *Military History* (October 1992): 50–57, 88, 90, and 92.

Neilson, Jon M., ed. "The Prettiest Cavalry Fight You Ever Saw." *Civil War Times Illustrated* 17 (July 1978): 4–12 and 42.

Poulter, Keith. "The Cavalry Bureau." *North & South* 2 (January 1999): 70–71.

Sword, Wiley. "Cavalry on Trial at Kelly's Ford." *Civil War Times Illustrated* 13 (April 1974): 32–40.

Weigley, Russell F. "David McMurtrie Gregg: A Personality Profile." *Civil War Times Illustrated* 1 (November 1962): 11–13, 28–30.

———. "John Buford: A Personality Profile." *Civil War Times Illustrated* 5 (June 1966): 14–23.

Wittenberg, Eric J. "John Buford and the Gettysburg Campaign." *Gettysburg: Historical Articles of Lasting Interest* 11 (July 1994): 19–55.

———. "Learning the Hard Lessons of Logistics: Arming and Maintaining the Federal Cavalry." *North & South* 2 (January 1999): 62–75.

———. "The Nobleman Who Never Was: The Strange Case of Alfred Duffié." *North & South* 5 (April 2002): 26–7.

———. "Ulric Dahlgren in the Gettysburg Campaign." *Gettysburg: Historical Articles of Lasting Interest,* no. 22 (January 2000): 96–111.

Books

Ackinclose, Timothy R. *Sabres and Pistols: The Civil War Career of Colonel Harry Gilmor, C.S.A.* Gettysburg, Pa.: Stan Clark Military Books, 1997.

Alberts, Don E. *Brandy Station to Manila Bay: A Biography of General Wesley Merritt.* Austin, Tex.: Presidial Press, 1980.

Allardice, Bruce S. *More Generals in Gray.* Baton Rouge: Louisiana State University Press, 1995.

Altshuler, Constance Wynn. *Cavalry Yellow & Infantry Blue: Army Officers in Arizona between 1851 and 1886.* Tucson, Ariz.: Arizona Historical Society, 1991.

Armstrong, Richard L. *7th Virginia Cavalry.* Lynchburg, Va.: H. E. Howard, 1992.

———. *11th Virginia Cavalry.* Lynchburg, Va.: H. E. Howard, 1989.

Arnold, James R. *Jeff Davis's Own: Cavalry, Comanches, and the Battle for the Texas Frontier.* New York: Wiley, 2000.

Balfour, Daniel T. *13th Virginia Cavalry.* Lynchburg, Va.: H. E. Howard, 1986.

Bates, Samuel P. *The Battle of Chancellorsville.* Meadville, Pa.: Edward T. Bates, 1882.

———. *History of the Pennsylvania Volunteers, 1861–1865.* 5 vols. Harrisburg, Pa.: B. Slingerly, 1869.

———. *Martial Deeds of Pennsylvania.* Philadelphia: T. H. Davis, 1875.

Beyer, W. F. and O. F. Keydel, eds. *Deeds of Valor: How America's Heroes Won the Medal of Honor.* 2 vols. Detroit: Perrien-Keydel, 1903.

Bigelow, John B., Jr. *The Campaign of Chancellorsville.* New Haven: Yale University Press, 1910.

Blackwell, Samuel M., Jr. *In the First Line of Battle: The 12th Illinois Cavalry in the Civil War.* DeKalb: Northern Illinois University Press, 2002.

Boatner, Mark M., III. *Civil War Dictionary.* New York: David McKay, 1959.

Bowditch, Henry Ingersoll. *Memorial for Nathaniel Bowditch.* Boston: John Wilson & Son, 1865.

Boylston, Raymond P., Jr. *Butler's Brigade: That Fighting Civil War Cavalry Brigade from South Carolina.* Raleigh, N.C.: Jarnett Press, 2000.

Bradley, Mark L. *Last Stand in the Carolinas: The Battle of Bentonville.* Campbell, Calif.: Savas-Woodbury, 1996.

———. *This Astounding Close: The Road to Bennett Place.* Chapel Hill: University of North Carolina Press, 2000.

Burgess, Milton V. *David Gregg: Pennsylvania Cavalryman.* State College, Pa.: privately published, 1984.

Burnett, William G. *Better a Patriot Soldier's Grave: The History of the Sixth Ohio Volunteer Cavalry.* Privately published, 1982.

Bushong, Millard K. and Dean M. Bushong. *Fightin' Tom Rosser, C.S.A.* Shippensburg, Pa.: Beidel Printing House, 1983.

Carter, Samuel, III. *The Last Cavaliers: Confederate and Union Cavalry in the Civil War.* New York: St. Martin's Press, 1979.

Carter, William H. *From Yorktown to Santiago with the Sixth U.S. Cavalry.* 1900; reprint, Austin, Tex.: State House Press, 1989.

Catton, Bruce. *The American Heritage New History of the Civil War,* edited by James M. McPherson. New York: Metro Books, 2001.

Coddington, Edwin B. *The Gettysburg Campaign: A Study in Command.* New York: Charles Scribner's Sons, 1968.

Collins, Darrell L. *General William Averell's Salem Raid.* Shippensburg, Pa.: Burd Street Press, 1998.

Cullum, George Washington. *Biographical Register of the Officers and Graduates of the United States Military Academy at West Point, New York, from Its Establishment in 1802, to 1890, with the Early History of the United States Military Academy.* 3d ed. 3 vols. New York: Houghton-Mifflin, 1891.

Dahlgren, John. *Memoir of Ulric Dahlgren.* Philadelphia: J. B. Lippincott, 1872.

"David McMurtrie Gregg." Circular no. 6, Series of 1917, Military Order of the Loyal Legion of the United States, Commandery of Pennsylvania, May 3, 1917.

Davies, Henry E. *General Sheridan.* New York: D. Appleton, 1895.

Davis, Burke. *Jeb Stuart: The Last Cavalier.* New York: Rinehart, 1957.

Divine, John E. *35th Battalion Virginia Cavalry.* Lynchburg, Va.: H. E. Howard, 1985.

Dodge, Theodore Ayrault. *The Campaign of Chancellorsville.* Boston: Ticknor, 1881.

Downey, Fairfax. *Clash of Cavalry: The Battle of Brandy Station.* New York: David McKay, 1959.

Driver, Robert J., Jr. *1st Virginia Cavalry.* Lynchburg, Va.: H. E. Howard, 1991.

———. *5th Virginia Cavalry.* Lynchburg, Va.: H. E. Howard, 1997.

———. *10th Virginia Cavalry.* Lynchburg, Va.: H. E. Howard, 1992.

Driver, Robert J., Jr., and Harold E. Howard. *2nd Virginia Cavalry.* Lynchburg, Va.: H. E. Howard, 1995.

Evans, David. *Sherman's Horsemen: Union Cavalry Operations in the Atlanta Campaign.* Bloomington: Indiana University Press, 1996.

Fishel, Edwin C. *The Secret War for the Union: The Untold Story of Military Intelligence in the Civil War.* Boston: Houghton-Mifflin, 1996.

Fordney, Ben F. *Stoneman at Chancellorsville.* Shippensburg, Pa.: White Mane, 1998.

Freeman, Douglas Southall. *Lee's Lieutenants: A Study in Command.* 3 vols. New York: Charles Scribner's Sons, 1944.

Frye, Dennis E. *12th Virginia Cavalry.* 2d ed. Lynchburg, Va.: H. E. Howard, 1988.

Furgurson, Ernest B. *Chancellorsville 1863: The Souls of the Brave.* New York: Alfred A. Knopf, 1992.

Gallagher, Gary W., ed. *Chancellorsville: The Battle and Its Aftermath.* Chapel Hill: University of North Carolina Press, 1996.

Greene, A. Wilson. "Stoneman's Raid." In *Chancellorsville: The Battle and Its Aftermath,* edited by Gary W. Gallagher, 65–106. Chapel Hill: University of North Carolina Press, 1996.

Hackley, Woodford B. *The Little Fork Rangers: A Sketch of Company D Fourth Virginia Cavalry.* Richmond, Va.: Press of Dietz Printing, 1927.

Harrison, Noel G. *Chancellorsville Battle Sites.* Lynchburg, Va.: H. E. Howard, 1990.

Hartley, Chris J. *Stuart's Tarheels: James B. Gordon and His North Carolina Cavalry.* Baltimore: Butternut & Blue, 1996.

Hassler, William Woods. *Colonel John Pelham: Lee's Boy Artillerist.* Chapel Hill: University of North Carolina Press, 1960.

Hebert, Walter M. *Fighting Joe Hooker.* Indianapolis: Bobbs-Merrill, 1944.

Heitman, Francis E. *Historical Register and Dictionary of the U.S. Army.* 2 vols. Washington, D.C.: U.S. Government Printing Office, 1903.

Holmes, Torlief. *Horse Soldiers in Blue.* Gaithersburg, Md.: Butternut Press, 1985.

Hopkins, Donald A. *The Little Jeff: The Jeff Davis Legion, Cavalry, Army of Northern Virginia.* Shippensburg, Pa.: White Mane, 1999.

Hunt, Roger D. *Colonels in Blue: Union Army Colonels of the Civil War. The New England States: Connecticut, Maine, Massachusetts, New Hampshire, Rhode Island, Vermont.* Atglen, Pa.: Schiffer Military History, 2001.

Hunt, Roger D. and Jack R. Brown. *Brevet Brigadier Generals in Blue.* Gaithersburg, Md.: Olde Soldier Books, 1997.

Kelsey, Charles C. *To the Knife: The Biography of Major Peter Keenan, 8th Pennsylvania Cavalry.* Ann Arbor, Mich.: privately published, 1964.

Kester, Donald E. *Cavalryman in Blue: Colonel John Wood Kester of the First New Jersey Cavalry in the Civil War.* Hightstown, N.J.: Longstreet House, 1997.

Krick, Robert K. *Lee's Colonels: A Biographical Roster of the Field Officers of the Army of Northern Virginia.* 4th ed. Dayton, Ohio: Morningside, 1992.

———. *9th Virginia Cavalry.* Lynchburg, Va.: H. E. Howard, 1982.

Lambert, Joseph I. *One Hundred Years with the Second Cavalry.* Topeka, Kans.: Capper Printing Co., 1939.

Langellier, John P., Kurt Hamilton Cox, and Brian C. Pohanka, eds. *Myles Keogh: The Life and Legend of an "Irish Dragoon" in the Seventh Cavalry.* El Segundo, Calif.: Upton and Sons, 1991.

Longacre, Edward G. *General John Buford: A Military Biography.* Conshohocken, Pa.: Combined Books, 1995.

————. *The Cavalry at Gettysburg: A Tactical Study of Mounted Operations during the Civil War's Pivotal Campaign, 9 June–14 July 1863.* Rutherford, N.J.: Fairleigh-Dickinson University Press, 1986.

————. *Lee's Cavalrymen: A History of the Mounted Forces of the Army of Northern Virginia.* Mechanicsburg, Pa.: Stackpole, 2002.

————. *Lincoln's Cavalrymen: A History of the Mounted Forces of the Army of the Potomac.* Mechanicsburg, Pa.: Stackpole, 2000.

————. *Mounted Raids of the Civil War.* South Brunswick, N.J.: A. S. Barnes, 1975.

Luvaas, Jay, and Harold W. Nelson. *U.S. Army War College Guide to the Battles of Chancellorsville & Fredericksburg.* Lawrence, Kans.: University Press of Kansas, 1994.

Marangou, Ana G. *Life and Deeds: The Consul Luigi Palma di Cesnola, 1832–1904.* Nicosia, Cyprus: Cultural Centre of the Popular Bank Group, 2000.

Martin, Samuel J. *"Kill-Cavalry": Sherman's Merchant of Terror—The Life of Union General Hugh Judson Kilpatrick.* Madison, N.J.: Fairleigh-Dickinson University Press, 1996.

————. *Southern Hero: Matthew Calbraith Butler—Confederate Hero, Hampton Red Shirt, and U.S. Senator.* Mechanicsburg, Pa.: Stackpole, 2001.

Mathews, Byron H., Jr. *The McCook-Stoneman Raid.* Philadelphia: Dorrance, 1976.

McFadden, Elizabeth. *The Glitter and the Gold: A Spirited Account of the Metropolitan Museum of Art's First Director, the Audacious and High-Handed Luigi Palma di Cesnola.* New York: Dial Press, 1971.

Mercer, Philip. *The Gallant Pelham.* Macon, Ga.: J. W. Burke, 1958.

Milham, Charles G. *Gallant Pelham: American Extraordinary.* Washington, D.C.: Public Affairs Press, 1959.

Moore, Robert H., II. *Chew's Ashby, Shoemaker's Lynchburg and the Newtown Artillery.* Lynchburg, Va.: H. E. Howard, 1995.

————. *The 1st and 2nd Stuart Horse Artillery.* Lynchburg, Va.: H. E. Howard, 1985.

Morgan, James A., III. *Always Ready, Always Willing: A History of Battery M, Second United States Artillery from Its Organization Through the Civil War.* Gaithersburg, Md.: Olde Soldier Books, n.d.

Musick, Michael P. *6th Virginia Cavalry.* Lynchburg, Va.: H. E. Howard, 1990.

Nanzig, Thomas P. *3d Virginia Cavalry.* Lynchburg, Va.: H. E. Howard, 1989.

Nesbitt, Mark. *Saber and Scapegoat: J. E. B. Stuart and the Gettysburg Controversy.* Mechanicsburg, Pa.: Stackpole, 1994.

Nichols, James L. *General Fitzhugh Lee: A Biography.* Lynchburg, Va.: H. E. Howard, 1989.

Nichols, Ronald H. *In Custer's Shadow: Major Marcus Reno.* Fort Collins, Colo.: Old Army Press, 1999.

O'Neill, Robert F., Jr. *The Cavalry Battles of Aldie, Middleburg and Upperville: Small but Important Riots, June 10–27, 1863.* Lynchburg, Va.: H. E. Howard, 1993.

————. *"The Federal Cavalry on the Peninsula."* In *The Peninsula Campaign of 1862: Yorktown to the Seven Days,* edited by William J. Miller. Campbell, Calif.: Savas, 1997.

Patchan, Scott C. *The Forgotten Fury: The Battle of Piedmont, Virginia.* Fredericksburg, Va.: Sergeant Kirkland's Museum and Historical Society, 1996.

Pelton, Jeremiah M. *Genealogy of the Pelton Family in America*. Albany, N.Y.: Joel Munsell's Sons, 1892.

Pfisterer, Frederick. *New York in the War of the Rebellion 1861–1865*. 2 vols. Albany: J. B. Lyon, State Printers, 1912.

Price, George F. *Across the Continent with the Fifth Cavalry*. New York: D.Van Nostrand, 1883.

Reed, Thomas J. *A Profile of Brigadier General Alfred N. A. Duffié*. Manhattan, Kans.: MA/AH Pub., 1982.

Robertson, James I. *Stonewall Jackson: The Man, the Soldier, and the Legend*. New York: Macmillan, 1997.

Schiller, Laurence D. *Of Sabres and Carbines: The Emergence of the Federal Dragoon*. Danville, Va.: Blue & Gray Education Society, 2001.

Sears, Stephen W. *Chancellorsville*. Boston: Houghton-Mifflin, 1996.

Stackpole, Edward J. *Chancellorsville: Lee's Greatest Battle*. Harrisburg, Pa.: Stackpole, 1958.

Starr, Stephen Z. *The Union Cavalry in the Civil War*. 3 vols. Baton Rouge: Louisiana State University Press, 1976–1979.

Sutherland, Daniel E. *Fredericksburg and Chancellorsville: The Dare Mark Campaign*. Lincoln: University of Nebraska Press, 1998.

———. *Seasons of War: The Ordeal of a Confederate Community, 1861–1865*. New York: Free Press, 1995.

Swank, Walbrook D. *The War & Louisa County 1861–1865*. Charlottesville, Va.: Papercraft Printing & Design, 1986.

Thomas, Emory N. *Bold Dragoon: The Life of J. E. B. Stuart*. New York: Harper & Row, 1986.

Thomason, John W., Jr. *Jeb Stuart*. New York: Charles Scribner's Sons, 1929.

Thrapp, Dan L. *Encyclopedia of Frontier Biography*. 3 vols. Lincoln: University of Nebraska Press, 1991.

Tischler, Allan L. *The History of the Harpers Ferry Cavalry Expedition, September 14 & 15, 1862*. Winchester, Va.: Five Cedars Press, 1993.

Trout, Robert J. *They Followed the Plume: The Story of J. E. B. Stuart and His Staff*. Mechanicsburg, Pa.: Stackpole Books, 1993.

Urwin, Gregory J. W. *Custer Victorious: The Civil War Battles of General George Armstrong Custer*. East Brunswick, N.J.: Associated University Presses, 1983.

———. *The United States Cavalry: An Illustrated History*. Poole, Dorset: Blandford Press, 1983.

Walker, Paul D. *The Cavalry Battle That Saved the Union: Custer vs. Stuart at Gettysburg*. Gretna, La.: Pelican, 2002.

Warner, Ezra J. *Generals in Blue: The Lives of the Union Commanders*. Baton Rouge: Louisiana State University Press, 1964.

———. *Generals in Gray: The Lives of the Confederate Commanders*. Baton Rouge: Louisiana State University Press, 1959.

Waugh, John C. *The Class of 1846—From West Point to Appomattox: Stonewall Jackson, George McClellan and Their Brothers*. New York: Warner Books, 1994.

Wellman, Manly Wade. *Giant in Gray: A Biography of Wade Hampton of South Carolina*. New York: Charles Scribner's Sons, 1949.

————. *Gray Riders: Jeb Stuart and His Men.* New York: Aladdin/Macmillan, 1954.

Wert, Jeffry D. *Custer: The Controversial Life of George Armstrong Custer.* New York: Simon & Schuster, 1996.

————. *From Winchester to Cedar Creek: The Shenandoah Campaign of 1864.* Carlisle, Pa.: South Mountain Press, 1987.

Where 300 Gather. Hartwood, Va.: Hartwood Presbyterian Church, 1998.

Whittaker, Frederick. *A Complete Life of General George A. Custer.* New York: Sheldon, 1876.

Wilson, James Harrison. *The Life and Services of Brevet Brigadier-General Andrew Jonathan Alexander, United States Army.* New York: privately published, 1887.

Wise, Jennings Cropper. *The Long Arm of Lee: The History of the Artillery of the Army of Northern Virginia.* 2 vols. Lynchburg, Va.: J. P. Bell, 1915.

Wittenberg, Eric J. *Gettysburg's Forgotten Cavalry Actions.* Gettysburg, Pa.: Thomas, 1998.

————. *Glory Enough for All: Sheridan's Second Raid and the Battle of Trevilian Station.* Dulles, Va.: Brassey's, 2001.

————. *Protecting the Flank: The Battles for Brinkerhoff's Ridge and East Cavalry Field, Gettysburg, Pennsylvania.* Celina, Ohio: Ironclad, 2002.

Young, Bennett. *Confederate Wizards of the Saddle.* Boston: Chapple, 1914.

➳ ABOUT THE AUTHOR ⇐

Eric J. Wittenberg has spent much of his adult life studying Union cavalry operations in the Civil War. A practicing lawyer, Mr. Wittenberg is a graduate of Dickinson College and the University of Pittsburgh School of Law. He has authored several books on the Civil War, edited two, and contributed numerous articles to national Civil War magazines. Mr. Wittenberg is the winner of the Bachelder–Coddington Literary Award for 1998's best new work interpreting the Battle of Gettysburg. He and his wife Susan live in Columbus, Ohio.